art *to come*

TERRY SMITH

art *to come*

Histories of Contemporary Art

DUKE UNIVERSITY PRESS / *Durham and London* / 2019

Designed by Julienne Alexander
Typeset in Garamond Premier Pro by
Westchester Publishing Services

Library of Congress Cataloging-in-Publication Data
Names: Smith, Terry (Terry E.), author.
Title: Art to come : histories of contemporary art / Terry Smith.
Description: Durham : Duke University Press, 2019. | Includes
    bibliographical references and index.
Identifiers: LCCN 2018037351 (print)
LCCN 2018045064 (ebook)
ISBN 9781478003472 (ebook)
ISBN 9781478001942 (hardcover : alk. paper)
ISBN 9781478003052 (pbk. : alk. paper)
Subjects: LCSH: Art, Modern—21st century—Political aspects. |
    Art, Modern—21st century—Philosophy. | Art and globalization. |
    Decolonization in art. | Postcolonialism and the arts. |
    Art and society.
Classification: LCC N6497 (ebook) | LCC N6497 .S64 2019 (print) |
    DDC 709.05—dc23
LC record available at https://lccn.loc.gov/2018037351

Cover art: Josephine Meckseper, *The Complete History of
Postcontemporary Art*, 2005, mixed media in display window,
160 × 250 × 60 cm. © Josephine Meckseper. Image courtesy
Timothy Taylor, London / New York.

TO BAXTER, TALIA, HARVEY, AND RORY

contents

illustrations

acknowledgments

For ongoing discussions of the issues surrounding contemporary art during the past two decades, and for their contributions to these essays in particular, I thank the late Jacques Derrida, Fredric Jameson, Virginia Spate, W. J. T. Mitchell, Okwui Enwezor, Boris Groys, Anthony Vidler, Charles Green, Alexander Alberro, Blake Stimson, Nancy Condee, Gao Minglu, John Clark, Wu Hung, Cai Guo-Qiang, Ian McLean, Fred Myers, Henry Skerritt, Margo Neale, Margo Smith, Hans Belting, Andrea Buddensieg, Richard Leeman, Keith Moxey, Rex Butler, Saloni Mathur, Helen Hughes, Nicholas Croggon, Nikos Papastergiadis, Anthony Gardner, Huw Hallam, Alexander Dumbadze, Suzanne Hudson, Kate Fowle, Claire Bishop, Chika Okeke-Agulu, Robert Bailey, Peter Osborne, T. J. Demos, and Jacob Lund.

I am also grateful to my colleagues in the Department of the History of Art and Architecture at the University of Pittsburgh, led by Barbara McCloskey; dean of the School of Arts and Sciences N. John Cooper; and the librarians of the Frick Fine Arts Library. Students in my graduate seminars have worked over these ideas carefully and constructively, to my great benefit and that of my undergraduate courses on these topics.

Planning for this book began while I was a Clark Fellow at the Sterling and Francine Clark Art Institute, Williamstown, Massachusetts, in 2014. I thank Michael Ann Holly, Darby English, and David Breslin for their welcome, and my fellow Fellows for their support and stimulation.

For invaluable research assistance, I am grateful to Nicole Coffineau.

For enabling or assisting in the publication of earlier versions of parts of these essays, I thank Nicholas Toutas; Anna Rubbo, Glenn Hill, and Gevork Hartoonian; Hal Foster; James Elkins; Qigu Jiang, Cai Guo-Qiang, and Reiko Tomii; Tracey L. Alder; Richard J. Powell and Joe Hannan; and Reuben Keehan.

Chapter 1 is extracted from *What Is Contemporary Art? Contemporary Art, Contemporaneity and Art to Come*, Critical Issues Series 6 (Sydney: Artspace, 2001), with permission to reprint granted by Artspace, Sydney. Chapter 2 is republished from "A Questionnaire on 'The Contemporary': 32 Responses," *October*, no. 130 (Fall 2009): 46–54, copyright 2009 by October Magazine,

Ltd., and the Massachusetts Institute of Technology, reprinted by permission of the MIT Press. An earlier version of chapter 3 first appeared as "The Political Economy of Iconotypes and the Architecture of Destination," *Architecture Theory Review* 7, no. 2 (2002): 1–44, with permission to republish given by the *ATR* editor. Parts of chapter 7 appeared in "Placemaking/Displacement," in *A Sense of Place*, edited by Tracy L. Adler (Clinton, NY: Wellin Museum of Art, Hamilton College, 2013), who granted permission to republish. Chapter 9 first appeared in the *Art Bulletin*, 92, no. 4 (December 2010): 366–83.

For image permissions, I thank the artists, photographers, and the following institutions and organizations: Aboriginal Artists Agency; Acconci Studio; Adam Art Gallery, New Zealand; Alexander Gray Associates, New York; Andrea Rosen Gallery, New York; Anna Schwartz Gallery, Melbourne; ARC ONE Gallery, Melbourne; Art Gallery of New South Wales, Sydney; Art Resource; Artists Rights Society; Assemble Studio; Asymptote; Bett Gallery, North Hobart; the Broad Art Foundation; Buku-Larrnggay Mulka Centre; Cass Sculpture Foundation; CNAC/MNAM/Dist. RMN-Grand Palais; DACS, London; DBOX/Little, Brown, and Company; David Zwirner, New York; dOCUMENTA; Diller Scofidio + Renfro; Donald Young Gallery, Chicago; estate of Gordon Bennett; Estudio Palma; Estudio Teddy Cruz and Fonna Forman; Frith Street Gallery, London; Gagosian Gallery, New York; Galerie Buchholz, Cologne; Galerie Isabella Bortolozzi, Berlin; Galerie Max Hetzler; Galerie Thomas Schulte; Galleria Continua; Gladstone Gallery, New York and Brussels; Grand Space Gallery, China; Hauser & Wirth; Hosfelt Gallery, San Francisco; Inexhibit; J&Z Gallery, Shenzhen; *Leap Magazine*; Kurimanzutto Gallery, Mexico City; Lorcan O'Neill, Rome; Luhring Augustine, New York; Lyon Housemuseum, Melbourne; Magician Space, Beijing; Marian Goodman Gallery, New York; Max Hetzler, Berlin; Mike Kelley Foundation for the Arts; Milani Gallery; MoMA; Monika Sprueth Galerie; Museum of Contemporary Art, Australia; Museum of Contemporary Art, Los Angeles; Museum of Fine Arts, Boston; National Gallery of Australia; Office of Metropolitan Architecture (OMA); Pace Gallery, New York; Project Row Houses, Houston; Redux; Regen Projects, Los Angeles; Roslyn Oxley9 Gallery, Sydney; Royal Academy of the Arts, London; Ruth Benzacar, Buenos Aires: Sadie Coles, London; Salon 94, New York; San Francisco Museum of Modern Art; ShanghArt Gallery, Shanghai and Beijing; SITE; Sperone Westwater, New York; Sprueth Magers, Berlin; Steven Holl Architects; Sullivan and Strumpf, Sydney; Tate Images; Tanya Bonakdar Gallery, New York; Timothy Taylor, London / New York; Tolarno Gallery, Melbourne; Urban-Think Tank—ETH

Zurich U-TT; VAGA; VG Bild-Kunst, Bonn; Victoria Miro, London; Viscopy, Sydney; White Rabbit Collection, Sydney.

At Duke University Press, I thank Ken Wissoker for his continuing support, Elizabeth Ault, Olivia Polk, Joshua Tranen, and especially the two anonymous readers of the manuscript, whose comments prompted me to lift my gaze.

Introduction

anticipation and historicity

What does it mean to say, in the same breath, that contemporary art is an art to come and is also subject to—indeed, calls out for—historical interrogation? The title and subtitle of this book plunge us into the workings of a three-part dynamic that drives contemporary art today. Contemporary art is, pervasively, an art to come; it is—in various senses, and increasingly, perhaps infinitely— anticipatory (of a future, however, that is becoming ever more unpredictable). At the same time, it harbors, often to the point of saturation, unbidden memories and historical longings—resonances, residuals, recursions, repetitions, and reconstructions that revive times past as well as earlier art (both of which are growing in quantity, complexity, and interest, as researchers reveal more and more about them). Contemporary art also manifests a volatile ambivalence about what, on the face of it, is its main temporal location: the time when it is being made and the time that makes it. Moreover, these three temporalities do not coexist as roughly equal, parallel congeries. Rather, multiple futures, many pasts, and a plethora of presents subsist simultaneously, all moving in many different directions at once. The sense that time marches forward—from the past, through the present, to the future—seems old-fashioned. Faced with this constant temporal conundrum, artists, critics, curators, gallerists, and collectors—even some theorists and historians—range wildly from a fulsome embrace of its dazzling disarray to a wary, total rejection of everything happening now, of all art that presents itself as being of this multilayered present.

Seeming contradictions abound, as do unseemly paradoxes. Let us confront them directly, starting with my opening question, the puzzle of why an art to come should be viewed through a historical lens. When those who would be historians of contemporary art search for its origins, when they look for signs of modern art becoming significantly contemporary, the more cautious favor decades as temporal markers: the early 2000s, say, or the 1990s, the 1980s, the 1960s and 1970s, or perhaps the 1950s. Bolder minds fix on specific dates: 2000, 1989, and 1968 (or, more inclusively, 1965). Each of these back projections is an attempt to understand the source of what counts most in art practice now. In 2000, for example, the congruence of several recent developments— among them, the market rebound of the 1980s, the eruption of groups such as the Young British Artists, exhibitions such as *Magiciens de la terre*, the proliferation of biennials during the 1990s, the pervasiveness of postmodern theories, and the spread of globalization—made 1989 seem a turning point in art as much as it was in world affairs. Late in the second decade of the twenty-first century, however, as the international order established in the postwar years so spectacularly unravels, 1945 looms as an important marker of the prehistory of the present, and the concerns of those years seem to many commentators to prefigure the challenges that preoccupy contemporary artists, as they do people everywhere.

The sheer scale, the overwhelming quantity, and the global propinquity of contemporary art—as well as, increasingly, its market prominence—has meant that historical approaches to understanding it have been rare, especially when compared to records of first reactions, attempts at neutral description, and promotional hype. In the last few years, however, some considered interpretations of the nature and development of contemporary art—covering between two to five decades of the past up until now and encompassing more and more of the globe—have been advanced. This sudden surge requires historical mapping, and each interpretation needs to be assessed as to its value as a historical hypothesis. Writing histories of contemporary art has itself become a subject for art-historiographical inquiry and reflection.

The chapters in the first part of this book are examples of how I have, since 2000, been consciously writing histories of contemporary art as it was happening and is happening now. Architecture and design are very much included as major visual arts. Close studies of how the three-part temporal dynamic plays out within contemporary Chinese art and in Australian Aboriginal art are followed by examinations of crucial spatial thematics: placemaking, world picturing, and connectivity. The chapters in the second part are systematic proposals about how writing contemporary art's histories might—indeed, should—be done, including close assessments of how others (curators, critics, philosophers, artists, and art historians) are attempting to do so. All essays were written preparatory to, alongside, and after books such as *The Architecture of Aftermath* (2006), *What Is Contemporary Art?* (2009), *Contemporary Art: World Currents* (2011), *Thinking Contemporary Curating* (2012), and *Talking Contemporary Curating* (2015). Only two chapters (2 and 9) are reprints, five are extensively revised and expanded from earlier essays or lectures, and four were written specifically for this volume. Together, they profile how I have canvassed and continuously revisited a set of ideas about contemporary art, attempting to track its abrupt yet protracted birthing from within modern art; its fraught, uneven yet pervasive globality; and its complex, multiplicitous contemporaneity. Gathering these texts in this volume has enabled me to demonstrate this tracking as a work-in-progress, to reflect further on why and how I went about the work, and to suggest something about what will always remain to be done.

OUR CONTEMPORARY CONTEMPORANEITY

Today, everyone involved in the visual arts registers the intense presence of global forces within local situations, and many of us, in our travels, actively valorize signifiers of locality, working with and against the grain of both globalization and parochialism. We are inside what it means to be contemporary, where art is the art of our contemporary condition. I have argued for some years now that an expansive concept of *contemporaneity* is crucial to grasping what it is to live in the world today, and to make art within this world. Of course, most of today's conditions were shaped in earlier times: modern times, ancient ones, and those outside Western historical parameters. But some conditions are new in ways different from earlier differentiations. Yes, our present contemporaneity shares much with the self-evident facts of what it has always been like to be contemporary: immediacy (it is happening now), simultaneity (at the same time as something else), and coincidence (to more than one person, thing, situation). Emphasis on "the contemporary" in current art and theoretical discourse is, I argue, an acknowledgment of presentism—the prioritization of the present—as the contemporary lure. Use of this vague marker as the biggest idea defining contemporary art and life, however, usually means falling into its self-deluding trap. In contrast, an acute understanding of our contemporary contemporaneity begins by recognizing that, unlike every earlier period, today no larger framework, no inevitable world-historical orientation, and no commanding narrative remains strong enough in its actual unfolding in the world to save us from having to find, with increasing urgency, our futures entirely within the resources available to us now. Our time, to which we necessarily belong, and which we share like it or not, is no longer a time *for* us. Naked to the present, we are obliged to understand our situation without illusion: "Contemporaneity consists precisely in the acceleration, ubiquity, and constancy of radical disjunctures of perception, of mismatching ways of seeing and valuing the same world, in the actual coincidence of asynchronous temporalities, in the jostling contingency of various cultural and social multiplicities, all thrown together in ways that highlight the fast-growing inequalities within and between them."[1] This description was italicized in my introduction to the 2008 volume *Antinomies of Art and Culture: Modernity, Postmodernity, Contemporaneity*, in which several thinkers, using various perspectives, began to take on the daunting task of understanding how forces such as these were shaping contemporary life and art, and, indeed, had been doing so, throughout the world, since at least the 1980s.

The notion of contemporaneity, understood in this expansive sense, pinpoints the dynamic at work *between* the many factors usually adduced as predominant explanations of what shapes the contemporary world: modernity, globalization, neoliberalism, decolonization, fundamentalism, terrorism, network culture, and global warming, among many others less prominent but just as profound, such as indigenization. Each of these terms cluster a particular set of world-changing forces into a configuration that, its discursive chorus claims, encompasses the others—in fact, in principle, or in the future. Yet none has succeeded in doing so, nor seems likely to succeed. Nor can any of these factors, singly or together, account for every aspect of contemporary life as it is experienced today. Nevertheless, their contention creates the divisive differentiations that define our contemporaneity—precisely those qualities of multeity, adventitiousness, and inequity that I list in the description just quoted—but it also generates counterresponses, the most important of which are an insistence on the value of place, the search for constructive world pictures, and the reach for coeval connectivity in all dimensions of our relationships with one another. All these are ongoing processes, feeding a historical condition that is in constant, contentious, unpredictable evolution. The *work* of contemporary art in these circumstances, therefore, is not only to picture these divisive differences but also to counter their destructive effects by helping to build coeval connectivity. Tracking how artists are taking on the paradoxical challenges of our shared but divided contemporaneity is the work of the historian of contemporary art, and it is what I attempt throughout these essays.[2]

THE WORK OF CONTEMPORARY ART HISTORY

Many contemporary artists continue to believe, or at least hope, that they can make a constructive difference in these unpromising circumstances, and many attract the support of curators who share their optimism. Yet few commentators on the arts, and even fewer art critics and historians, see much evidence for such a positive outlook. Listen to their skeptical voices: You feel obliged to plot the history of contemporary art, as it is happening—that is your goal? You cannot be serious! *Histories*, perhaps, as a set of provisional, potentially historical prospects, but that, too, seems premature and a mistaken notion of what historical inquiry ought to be. How will you go about the research without being misled by proximity to your sources? What counts as an archive? Art being made today is just too unformed to be clearly understood, too unpredictable as to how it might turn out, too soon to tell. Give the art, and its interpretive apparatus, time to evolve; allow them their own unfolding; and let them work out their mutual accountability in due course.[3]

The skeptical voices continue to wail. Surely, they say, this enterprise should be discipline-wide; in fact, it would need to be an interdisciplinary effort, given that the leading art history institutes, and nearly all professional art historians, see themselves in embattled retreat from potential invasion by a younger generation dazzled by the art of their own times. Stop interfering; stay with writing art criticism—that, at least, might enable a few artists to see their trajectories a little more clearly and help your readers appreciate what those artists are trying to do. Who are you, anyway, to take on such a task? What gives you the right, in conscience, to speak on these matters, as a white male academic based in institutions in the United States, Australia, and Europe—in states, economies, and regimes whose developments have been based on exploiting the resources of their own Indigenous peoples and those of the rest of the world?

An implicated participant and a contrarian stranger in several art worlds, I constantly ask myself these kinds of questions. I answer them in two basic ways. First, I counter that to defer to such doubts means conceding the ground as is, leaving the prevailing art-world fictions in place, along with the iniquitous, countercreative, and world-endangering social, economic, and political structures that currently sustain them. Retreat from responsibility by those of us who wish to work toward a better world permits the vast nonsense of promotional art babble to fill the available discursive space, which leads directly to my second answer: yes, one should honor the realism underlying these doubts, acknowledge the justified anxieties, absorb the obstacles, then just do it. Make the art. Say what needs to be said. Write the essays and books. Mount the exhibitions. Engage in the debates. Deliver the lectures. Teach the courses. Always and everywhere, face up to the test of critical accountability, which is to make a manifest, constructive difference in how the world is seen, and in how it might be occupied.

SEEING HISTORICALLY IN THE PRESENT

Historical understanding is necessary for achieving critical distance. It is the essential precondition—not sufficient, but absolutely necessary—during every stage of the process, from the doubts that pose the problems to the point when inquiry turns, as it must, into active agency. So, I have striven to maintain, always, at each instant and continuously, the necessity of taking a *historical* perspective on the present, as it is happening. Insisting on the historicity of the immediate slows down its durational mass, catches visible traces of its multiple movements, freeze-frames some of its specters, evaporates its most attractive mystifications, and points to aspects of its possible futurity. There is, as well, a welcome reverse effect. Seeing the present historically is disjunctive: it is freed from determination's concrete channeling, from the rolling thunder of inevitability, and from the subtler straitjacket of probability. It is aflame with the formative force of contingency, alive to the many temporalities that flow through each given present, one of which—or, more likely, a combination of some—will mold the moment. Our present contemporaneity demands this and eclipses all other frames, while including their persistence. As well, and as a consequence, historical perspectives on times past have changed accordingly: they have shifted from seeking out stories of, or lessons from, "the past" toward an engaged picturing of cotemporalities in particular places at specific times prior to the present. Everything, including all art made in the past, was once contemporary. Everything, including all art made in the past, is doubly so now.

Dichotomy, antinomy, and paradox animate all our relations today, not least in the discursive worlds in which contemporary art is produced and circulated: in art practice, of course, but also in art theory, architecture, art criticism, general art history, art historiography, as well as in curating, museum work, marketing and collecting art, teaching it, and administering the arts and culture. Over the past few decades, without conscious planning, I have written books and essays seeking to map, occupy, and change orientations in one after another of these worlds, exploring the discursive strategies operative within each one, asking always how its self-descriptions appear when compared to those prevalent in nearby and distant worlds. I have taken special note of how each has negotiated the confused but epochal shift from modern self-conceptions to more contemporary ones; from modernity as the master narrative of how these worlds connect, through postmodernity as modernity's internal counternarrative; toward the current situation in which contemporaneities of difference prevail, proliferating multiplicity as the basis of constructive being. Meanwhile, earlier modes of world picturing vigorously push back, insisting on their universality, their fundamentalism, or, at least, their relevance.

These changes are taking place because contemporaneous differences abound in all the institutional and social settings in which each of these worlds is embedded, continuously challenging the habitus that incessantly seeks to structure them as worlds. Differencing and repetition: the dynamic interaction between these two deep impulses is what constantly constitutes our contemporaneity. It calls us to articulate it, most seductively in its own, relatively easy terms. Instead, I believe, we must acknowledge the salience of these terms for those who use them, but then rub them hard, against their grain, however variegated and elusive that might seem.

For these reasons, all the essays in this book—while being focused on accounting for the art under examination, and on mapping the contexts of its making—are art historiographical; that is, they are studies of aspects of contemporary art and architecture that explicitly highlight pertinent questions of art-historical method. Each particular inquiry is set directly and overtly in relation to relevant debates within the discipline—or, at least, the discipline as I imagine it to be, as it gradually, reluctantly, includes contemporary art within its purview. At the same time, in these essays I constantly question the standard assumptions of art history as a discourse, alert to its entanglement with the other discourses that surround the making, disseminating, and interpreting of art. I also strive to be alive to how art enters and leaves and reenters the many other ways of world making, placemaking, and connecting that constitute our contemporary condition.

The chapters are arranged in two parts, each organized chronologically. The first tracks key steps in my journey since 2000 toward a theory of contemporary art within the conditions of contemporaneity, as I sketched its vital elements through public lectures, panel papers, journal articles, and occasional essays. In the opening chapter, I present the occasion in early 2001 when my core views on these topics first came together in a systematic way. The next chapter is one of the many summaries of my views that I wrote during the subsequent decade; it condenses the accounts offered in the books mentioned earlier. In chapters 3 and 4, I ask whether contemporary architecture and design are evolving in parallel to the currents within contemporary art, and what concurrences exist between these visual arts today. The next chapters present, in turn, my views on contemporary Chinese and Australian Indigenous art, while the final chapters of part I explore the key themes that, I claim, are being addressed by contemporary artists everywhere: placemaking, world picturing, connectivity, and planetarity. Part II begins with an essay written in 2010 about the challenges of thinking contemporary art in historical terms. I discuss the awkward emergence of contemporary art history as a field of study, then comment on the ideas about contemporary art offered by some philosophers whose theories have been taken up within art discourse, and on the approaches of the few art historians and the even fewer artists who have suggestions about how contemporary art might be approached historically. Aimed primarily at professional readers, these essays are more explicitly art historiographic than those in the first part.

Transmediality in contemporary art practice, and interdisciplinarity in the interpretive discourses around it, both gathering pace since the 1960s, have, I believe, opened up the prospect of a genuinely contemporary art–historical profession. This would be a discipline that approaches art from everywhere, and from all times, with the presumption that the starting point is to discern— sensitively, accurately, and on the evidence—the contemporaneity of that art. The field's subject would be the various temporalities present within each work of art, the materialities employed during its making, the symbolic orders the art deploys, and its actual effects within the worlds where it first appeared and circulated. As well, a fully contemporary art–historical inquiry into past art would not hesitate to find ways to demonstrate when and how that artwork, or that kind of art, has achieved contemporaneity since then—at later times, and in other places, including, but not privileging, right here and right now. Once we see these interests driving art-historical inquiry into past art, we also see that taking an art-historiographical approach to the art being made today is the other side of this same methodological coin. We may be a long way from achieving a kind of art history that is contemporary in all these senses, but that fact only increases the urgency of bringing it into being.

Chapter 1, "Contemporary Art, Contemporaneity, and Art to Come," is the first public statement of what I had come to see as the outlines of an overall idea—not yet a set of historical hypotheses, much less a theory—about the nature of contemporary art. For a host of reasons, including those voiced by the hypothetical skeptics above, the question "What is contemporary art?" seemed, to many people, a strange one to pose in May 2001, when I used it as the title of a lecture "Contemporary Art, Contemporaneity, and Art to Come." The occasion was my farewell lecture as the Power Professor of Contemporary Art at the University of Sydney, before taking up my position at the University of Pittsburgh. I had held the title for five years and had been teaching courses in modern and contemporary art for decades. Yet, like my academic colleagues all over the world who did the same, I would regularly resile from offering overviews of what was, then, unacknowledged as a period within the history of art and, thus, was institutionally impossible as a field within the discipline of art history. My reluctance went beyond caution in the face of the pragmatics, prematurity, confusions, uncertainties, and challenges of sorting the actual from the dazzle within the booming market for contemporary art, as well as the implications of the explosion of art from everywhere, a profusion that seemed, during the last decades of the twentieth century, to be expanding faster than could ever be knowable and diversifying in unprecedented, quite unpredictable ways.

For decades, scholars committed to critical practice in art making, writing, curating, and theoretical work agitated against the use of generalized descriptors to perpetuate established power and hierarchical values—against, that is, the master narratives of great art, by great men, at great centers of great civilizations. Since the 1980s, we had also contended against the rapacious commercial greed of the burgeoning art markets, promoted largely through a language that appropriated art-historical scholarship mixed with excited, uplifting, but profoundly conservative fables about aesthetic feeling. Our critiques created within art history as a discipline a tendency often labeled "the new art history," but what I call "radical revisionism," an approach subjecting the insights of the discipline's founders to those arising from New Left politics, feminism, poststructuralism, and postcolonialism, each of which constantly revises itself and its adjacent critiques.[4] This array of critical theories became prominent in universities, art publications, some museums, and many contemporary art spaces. Focused on the heroic story of dissident avant-gardists and the rise of modernism during the nineteenth and twentieth centuries in certain cities in Europe and North America, radical revisionism was mostly blind to modern art created elsewhere in the world. And it tended to regard contemporary art as the current phase of a debased modern art, basically complicit with capitalism and thus in inevitable decline, an art most suited to its moment—one dominated by the requirements of a rampant, globalizing neoliberalism.

During the 1990s, however, it became increasingly obvious to some of us that none of the approaches under the umbrella of radical revisionism was capable of providing an adequate account of the new kinds of art being made throughout the world, and that these approaches were starting to fall short as pathways toward completely understanding the art of the past. By 2000, I was fed up. Faced with the odd task of having to give a farewell lecture without having given an inaugural one, I cast around for models, starting with that of my predecessor, Bernard Smith, first director of the Power Institute, who, in 1969, outlined his vision for the teaching department and the collection of contemporary art then being formed. Strikingly, he profiled John Power, doctor, painter, and philanthropist, as "an unconventional, restless, alienated spirit," and the institute therefore as "a kind of institutionalization of restlessness, the gift of an alienated man, a gift for the promotion of change."[5] I was equally fond of Michel Foucault's scintillating mapping out of how he would tackle "The Order of Discourse" at the Collège de France in 1970. It was the prolegomenon to a new interdiscipline: discourse studies.[6] I found a pathway between them in George Steiner's "What Is Comparative Literature?," an inaugural lecture of 1994 which, it seemed to me, both defined his field in fresh terms—"Comparative literature listens and reads after Babel"—and boldly insisted that it be pursued in a completely contemporary way: "Comparative literature is an art of understanding centered in the eventuality and the defeats of translation."[7] Each of these men offered a unique answer to the same question: How might an essentially deinstitutionalizing practice be taught within one of the oldest, most flexible yet insistently self-sustaining human institutions, the university?

In the 1939 will that founded the Power Institute, its donor specified that it "make available to the people of Australia the latest ideas and theories in plastic arts by means of lectures and teaching and by the purchase of the most recent contemporary art of the world." During my directorship, the mission expanded beyond this much-needed but nonetheless one-way exchange. It became "to develop the latest ideas and theories concerning visual art and culture—past, present, and future—and to communicate them, both nationally and internationally."[8] The first chapter in this volume is one attempt among many during those years to do just that: reverse this flow. By 2000, it was obvious that many Australian artists and some curators were contributing to the burgeoning circulation of international art, that original thinking by Australians was enriching critical theory in multiple languages, and, less obviously but insistently, that Indigenous artists had been making unique kinds of contemporary art for decades (perhaps millennia). These factors shaped my experience and my thinking, as did years of effort, following John Power and the instincts of my generation, to assist in the internationalization of Australian art.

Like everyone else, I was responding to the eruption of contemporary art into museum and market prominence during the 1990s, and to its growing role within the spectacle economy of late capitalist modernity. I sought first to understand this art in its own stated or implicit terms; these had to be at least part of what would become, in time, an art-historical understanding. Yet I was impatient with its frequent refusal, in the name of an "anything goes" postmodernism, to exercise critical judgment, its ironic yet feeble embrace of this economy of excitement and distraction. Instead, I identified a particular "constellation of problems and possibilities," detailed in chapter 1, which, I argued, artists of the day must embrace as their problematic or otherwise fail to be contemporary artists. I also drew on conversations with Jacques Derrida, as we tested the idea of contemporaneity evoking the internal multiplicity of contemporaneous immediacy, and puzzled over whether, in such situations, awareness could take form and art could be made—or would all art, from now on, be anticipatory, each work an instance of one among many kinds of "art to come"?[9] For explanations of the overall world (dis)order, including the cultural logic that it engendered, I continued to rely on the critical theories of postmodernity, especially those of David Harvey and Fredric Jameson.[10]

Critical postmodernity, deconstruction in its most engaged and encompassing forms, the most spectacular but also the most self-searching and socially conscious contemporary art—these were the most advanced, subtle, and searching forms of geopolitics, philosophy, and art. In chapter 1, I discuss examples of all of them. They should, I initially thought, add up to the best explanation of the current state of play between each of these worlds. But they did not, which raised some questions. Do we need improved versions of each of these, or a different mix of politics, theory, and art practice? Or has the time of total ideologies, overarching explanations, and dominant period styles passed?

CONTEMPORARY ART AND CONTEMPORANEITY

In our daily lives, as we strive to reconstitute normalcies and adapt to unpredict-able circumstances, we confront a present in which many distinct and mutually incompatible pictures of future worlds compete, none of them carrying the con-viction once won by the now-discredited master narratives of the world's uneven but inevitable modernization. The possibility arises that no overarching world picture will ever again achieve anything approximating the kind or degree of consent once won by modernity. Okwui Enwezor, Nancy Condee, and I, along with many outstanding thinkers, first examined this sense of contemporaneity in detail at a 2004 conference exploring the implications of a loaded question: *In the aftermath of modernity, and the passing of the postmodern, how do we know and show what it is to live in the conditions of contemporaneity?*[11]

I have devoted much of the first decade of this century and since to devel-oping answers to this question, especially to showing how it was shaping the practice of contemporary artists all over the world. These answers appear in po-lemical form in my book *What Is Contemporary Art?* (2009), which traces the struggles of major European and North American museums, mostly dedicated to modernism, as they face the challenges of contemporary art and of mass spectatorship; the effects of burgeoning high-end markets on contemporary art practice and discourse; the rise to prominence of art from third and fourth worlds, especially through the second wave of biennial exhibitions, such as the Bienal de la Habana, peaking in Documenta 11 (2002); and the emergence of a generation of artists exploring the nature of time, place, mediation, and mood in what they are experiencing as a world undergoing unprecedented, largely incomprehensible change.[12] Written as an introduction to the topic for a general readership, *Contemporary Art: World Currents* (2011) highlights the contemporary elements in mid-twentieth-century late modern art in Europe and North America; the postmodern return to figuration in the 1980s; the contemporary art boom in subsequent decades; the transitions from na-tional modern arts to contemporary art in Russia and (east of) Europe, South and Central America, the Caribbean, China and East Asia, India, South and Southeast Asia, Oceania, the Middle East, and Africa; and the ways in which artists all over the world are working on world picturing, making art political on issues such as climate change, and navigating the complexities of multiple temporalities and social mediation.[13]

Chapter 2, "In a Nutshell: Art within Contemporary Conditions," is a sum-mary of the main arguments of these books. It responds specifically to *October* editor Hal Foster's concern, expressed in a 2009 questionnaire, that "much present practice seems to float free of historical determination, conceptual definition, and critical judgment," and that "such paradigms as 'the neo-avant-garde' and 'postmodernism,' which once oriented some art and theory, have run into the sand, and, arguably, no models of much explanatory reach or intellectual force have risen in their stead." He went on to ask, "What are some of its salient consequences for artists, critics, curators, and historians—for their formation and their practice alike?"[14]

Reacting to these questions, I set out, succinctly, the core elements of my argument about how contemporary art arises in the conditions of contemporaneity as I define them. After profiling the limits of art-world discourse on these questions, I suggest that three broad currents may be discerned in art today, each quite different in character, scale, and scope. They are, I argue, the manifestations in art practice and discourse of the major currents in global geopolitics, cultural exchange, human thinking, and geophysical change. They have taken distinctive forms in the many art-producing centers throughout the world since the 1950s, thus patterning the shift from modern to contemporary art that, in my view, is the defining art-historical fact of the recent past and the present. The first current prevails in the metropolitan centers of modernity in Europe and the United States (as well as in societies and subcultures closely related to them) and is a continuation of styles in the history of art, particularly modernist ones, in the form of various remodernisms. The second current arose from movements toward political, economic, and cultural independence that occurred in the former colonies of Europe, and on the edges of Europe, and then spread everywhere. Characterized above all by clashing ideologies and experiences, this "transitional transnationalism" leads artists to prioritize the imaging of both local and global issues as the urgent content of their work. Meanwhile, increasing numbers of artists working within the third current explore concerns—about self-fashioning, immediation, precarity, futurity, and climate change—that they feel personally yet share with others, particularly of their generation, throughout an increasingly networked world. Taken together, I suggest, these currents constituted the contemporary art of the late twentieth century, and their unpredictable unfolding and volatile interaction continue to shape art in the early twenty-first.

The novelty of these ideas as an art-historical hypothesis deserves, perhaps, some remark. They stand in sharp contrast, for example, to the promotional pluralism that still pervades markets, museums, and public art writing in the major art centers, and to the binary oppositionality or recalcitrant parochialism that constrains even critical regionalism elsewhere. They contrast, too, with other understandings of the main thrusts and broad developments of contemporary art, such as the de facto position of not yet taking a position embodied in the editorial program of the journal *October*. Founded in 1975, *October*'s brilliant coterie of editors made it the leading US journal for detailed, empirical histories and innovative, theoretical explorations of modern art, mainly the early twentieth-century European and US avant-garde and their neo-avant-garde successors of the 1960s and 1970s. Art from elsewhere was rarely examined in *October*, unless it bore a direct relation to that of the Western centers. Nor was art from any other time, including the present, examined in the journal, with occasional exceptions for studies of artists' work deemed to have continued to confront the issues tackled by the neo-avant-garde. Not until 2009 did the editors of *October* directly invite commentary on a set of broad-scale questions about contemporary art, a step that has been rarely followed up (Foster being an exception to this rule). In the first edition of their textbook, *Art since 1900*, the *October* editors embraced the idea of treating past art in terms of its contemporaneity in their historical perspective on modern art. Rather than offer an integrated historical narrative, each editor introduced a partial perspective, a method for reading aspects of modern art—psychoanalytic, structuralist, poststructuralist, and sociological—with the implication, but not the claim, that they added up to a sufficient whole. In the main body of the book, the contributors vividly discussed each artwork, exhibition, event, or publication in the context of its year of origination, but they made or suggested few links. The authors held back from anything more than provisional sketches of contemporary art.[15] The updates in the second and third editions, mainly written by David Joselit, continued this almanac format but also floated some suggestions about the nature of broader global flows.[16] I discuss the *October* approach in more detail, along with several others, in the art-historiographical studies that constitute the second part of this book, particularly in chapter 11.

CONTEMPORARY DIFFERENCE

The dawning realization that our contemporaneous differences not only were defining our present but would also, most likely, fill all imaginable futures was confirmed, dramatically, on September 11, 2001. For some time before then, my thinking about contemporary art had extended to architecture, because the convergences evident between the various visual arts required explanation, as did the striking role spectacular buildings were playing within the larger economy. In those days, buildings such as Frank Gehry's Guggenheim Museum, Bilbao, were routinely referred to as "iconic." The word was overused, as if anything could become iconic if it attracted enough attention and pushed everything else that was anything like it into invisibility. But that was part of the illusion. A long-term process was at work: a logic of repetition, absorption, and exclusion elevated one structure to symbolize an entire category, a period, a regime, a country, a continent, an idea, or a value. During tourist promotions for the Sydney Olympics, for example, the Opera House replaced the Harbour Bridge in symbolizing Australia in general, while Uluru (Ayer's Rock) evoked Aboriginal Australia: come to the city, visit the outback. Gehry's museum, at the time, stood for architecture itself, or at least architecture's contemporary possibilities, fully realized at Bilbao in what seemed an unmatchable way. The ubiquity of standard images of these few structures and places secured their status, kept competitors at bay, and sustained their preeminence. I thought of this circulation of images as an economy of images, an "iconomy," and wondered if this idea opened up a way to contribute to the emerging work on visual cultural studies by augmenting Guy Debord's famous theory of "the society of the spectacle," which was central to the field.[17]

Osama bin Laden was way ahead of me and most everybody else. He knew that images were not simply symbols but were also targets; that icons were invested with enormous inherent power, so that obliterating them—even wounding them—exposed the fragility of the worldviews of those who believed in them. Iconic structures seemed permanent, but they could be damaged; the violence inherent in architectural expressions of power could be made visible by a contra-violence, by destroying the structures that embodied that power. An ancient logic of violence renewed itself on 9/11, revealing its global reach. It erased, in an instant, the post-1989 American autumn, the nation's brief reign as an unchallenged hyperpower. To many in the West, the events of 9/11 seemed to abruptly, and radically, realign the distribution of difference in the world, but in fact, that difference was making itself known in unmistakable terms to those who would deny it. The specter of mutual destruction shadowed what we shared as a species. The closeness of our contemporaneous differences suddenly became the most important fact about our existence.

My response to this realization was the book *The Architecture of Aftermath* (2006).[18] Its first half, "Dispacing Time," considered architecture before September 11, 2001, in chapters devoted to Gehry's museum at Bilbao; its chief precedent, the Sydney Opera House (compared and contrasted to Uluru); the museum's competitor, Richard Meier's Getty Center, Los Angeles; and Daniel

Libeskind's Jewish Museum, Berlin, a museum of an earlier and still resonant aftermath. In the second part of the book, "Targets and Opportunities," I explored the displacements in which the World Trade Center was grounded and out of which it was conceived and built; argued that the unconscious of architecture was revealed in the discursive responses to the attacks; and traced the mixture of shock, defiance, hope, and denial in the designs for the destroyed site. Chapter 3 in this volume, "Contemporary Architecture: Spectacle, Crisis, Aftermath," introduces the analyses and arguments I advanced in that book, situates them in relation to debates within architectural theory and history about whether and how modern architecture has become contemporary, and pursues the responses of architects in many parts of the world to the symbolic and social centrality of their profession during those years. As I show, architects were deeply affected by the larger lessons of 9/11 but struggled to find forms appropriate to its complex aftermath. Chapter 4, "Concurrence: Art, Design, Architecture," focuses on another aspect of contemporary architecture's contemporaneity: its close relationships, intense often to the point of saturation, with contemporary art's imagery, styles, ideas, and practices.

NO END TO HISTORY

Being shocked into acknowledging one's contemporaneity with otherness is the enduring legacy of 9/11. We can regain a sense of its full impact on sensibilities widely held in the West if we return to a moment before the attacks. In a landmark 1989 article, political scientist Francis Fukuyama argued that "a remarkable consensus concerning the legitimacy of liberal democracy as a system of government had emerged throughout the world over the past few years, as it conquered rival ideologies like hereditary monarchy, fascism, and most recently communism," and that "liberal democracy may constitute the 'end point of mankind's ideological evolution' and the 'final form of human government,' and as such constituted the 'end of history.'"[19] In his 1992 book, *The End of History and the Last Man*, he argued that liberal democracy—by which he meant representative government combined with a free market economy—however imperfect its current instantiations may be, could not be improved on as an ideal and was, for that reason, being adopted "throughout the world," suggesting that "it makes sense for us once again to speak of a coherent and directional History of mankind that will eventually lead the greater part of humanity to liberal democracy."[20] Although Fukuyama would retreat from these views as the world rapidly became a very different place, they typify hardcore Western self-centeredness in its late twentieth-century forms: the presumption that the kind of social organization that had developed in Europe and then the United States in recent centuries was natural to all proper human association, that actually existing societies had caught up with its historical inevitability, and that it would become universal, from now until forever. In these senses, neoliberal democracy was the outcome of a world-historical victory over all opponents as well as transcending history by precluding change in any other direction. History had reached its own goal or was on its way to doing so; life need only go forward in the ways that it would; historical consciousness was no longer necessary.

A similarly blinkered perspective appeared within art discourse in the major museum and market centers during the postwar years. It retreated during the 1960s and 1970s—the years of decolonization in much of the world and of crises of legitimacy in the main centers—but roared back in the 1980s, claimed confirmation in the events of 1989, and was buttressed by the neoliberalization of most economies until the global financial crisis of 2008. Since then, the high end of the art world has become a rare bastion of the .01 percent, perpetuating the unthinking acceptance of whatever appears in top-end galleries and auction houses as viable contemporary art, there being no point to thinking critically and historically about this art. No accident, then, that during this period, those of us committed to securing global recognition for the art being produced outside these centers framed our presentations in historical and political, rather than purely aesthetic or only art-historical, terms. Curator Okwui Enwezor, for example, positioned art created in Africa and by members of the African diaspora as a powerful force within contemporary art through exhibitions, such as *A Short Century: Independence and Liberation Movements in Africa, 1945–1994* (2001–2), that instructed audiences in Europe and the United States about the dynamics of claiming historical agency on the African continent, and by exhibitions in Africa itself, notably *Trade Routes: History and Geography*, the Second Johannesburg Biennale (1997), that emphasized the necessities of international connectedness for art made everywhere. Even more ambitiously, he sought, through the five "platforms" that made up his Documenta 11 (2002), to apply this postcolonial critique of what he calls "Westist" globalization to the entire international art world. Such efforts have earned much admiration and attracted considerable criticism, both attesting to their efficacy. Exhibitions of this kind have profoundly influenced how traveling shows, biennials, and even museum-based survey exhibitions are conceived today. In a complex dance of complicity and resistance, as neoliberal globalization spread through many parts of the world, such exhibitions became the major vehicles through which the contemporaneous differences within the world's art could show themselves to one another, could switch and bait their local imperatives, renovate their traditions, and subject themselves to necessary change.[21]

Chapter 5, "Background Story, Global Foreground: Chinese Contemporary Art," plots these transformational energies as they have played out in China since the late 1970s. Chinese contemporary art is a recent phenomenon, which exists alongside artistic practices in China that are conducted by many more practitioners, within massively larger support structures, and with much greater official and popular approval. These traditional practices include ink painting, modern figurative painting and sculpture, calligraphy, and many crafts, all of which continue to evolve, as artists renovate their traditions. In contrast, contemporary artists, critics, and curators were initially inspired by intense desires to break from the historical weight of these practices and to catch up with what were perceived as the greater innovative energies of artists elsewhere, from the early twentieth-century European avant-gardists to the then-contemporary British retro-sensationalists. I discuss the phases through which art in China has passed since the end of the Cultural Revolution in 1978, noting highlights such as the *China Avant-Garde* exhibition (1989), curated by a team led by Gao Minglu. We can review these developments in such a structured way because each exhibition, action, and event was accompanied by not only manifesto-like statements and vigorous publicity, but also careful record keeping and exhaustive historical accounting. Artists, as much as curators and historians, are committed contributors to this process of incessant self-documentation, taking it to be an international norm (which, indeed, it has become). As a result, contemporary Chinese art may be the most historicized of all recent art movements. In my chapter, I read the various historical framings offered by Chinese critics, curators, and art historians alongside and against the model of changes in contemporary art on a worldwide scale that I have been mapping.

The movement known as contemporary Aboriginal art is an art-historical development even more unpredictable from Eurocentric perspectives than the emergence of distinctive kinds of contemporary art in China. Artistic exchange was an element in many of the contacts between Indigenous Australians and white settlers, beginning soon after British colonization of the continent in 1788. Although sporadic, such contacts increased in frequency and intensity until, in the decades since 1970, they have come to constitute a density of aesthetic exchange between Indigenous and non-Indigenous peoples that is not matched elsewhere in the world.[22] In chapter 6, "Country, Indigeneity, Sovereignty: Aboriginal Australian Art," I analyze this phenomenon by rhetorically posing the question of whether art by Indigenous Australians can be categorized as (neo)traditional, modern(ist), or contemporary. I argue, instead, that many Indigenous artists, working in remote communities and in the urban centers where most Australians live, have succeeded in creating kinds of art that, like innovative art made anywhere, deserve understanding on their own terms—specifically, the art is concerned above all with country, indigeneity, and sovereignty. I show this to be the case in the work of artists such as Emily Kame Kngwarreye, Turkey Tolson Tjupurrula, Gordon Bennett, and Warlimpirrnga Tjapaltjarri, among others. Considering the circumstances in which most Indigenous Australians are obliged to live, and the racist screen through which they are mostly viewed, this level of achievement has been hard won and sustained against great odds. I explain these odds in some detail and track the evolving understanding of this art by multiple commentators, critics, anthropologists, and, recently, art historians. The art and the commentary on it are transcultural phenomena: the art reaches out from inside Indigenous knowledge to both defend secret, sacred knowledge and invite access to nonsecret aspects of this knowledge, while the writing about this art, mainly by non-Indigenous authors, marks pathways toward it while warning of the harmful effects of misplaced expectations, greed, and bad faith.

I have frequently claimed that placemaking, world picturing, and connectivity are the distinctive concerns of contemporary art because they are the definitive challenges facing those of us living in the world today. Chapter 7, "Placemaking, Displacement, Worlds-within-Worlds," examines how various artists are showing how they, or peoples they represent, seek to establish a sense of place in world conditions that increasingly tend toward disruption and dislocation. Artists imagine other ways of living in these conditions, ranging from warnings that they could become worse to constructive, sustainable alternatives. Thinking about place includes traditional settings, such as those provided by family structures and social organizations (e.g., cities and governments), as well as the opposite, dislocation, which is being experienced by record numbers of people throughout the world, especially in regions experiencing long-running civil wars, such as Syria, continuing colonization, such as Palestine, and famine and corruption, such as many central African states.

Chapter 8, "Picturing Planetarity: Arts of the Multiverse," charts some of the ways in which artists are closely observing the earth's processes to learn more about our place on this planet and in the universes of which it is part. These explorations are tentative, glimpses of elemental movement and differential temporalities that usually remain invisible. Such interests indicate the emergence of a consciousness that might become, at last, truly worldly and fully contemporary.

INSTITUTIONAL ART HISTORY: ADVANCE AND RETREAT

The second part of this book begins from the question, Why have professional art historians offered so few historical overviews of contemporary art until very recently? One core reason is institutional reluctance. The "schism" between art-historical research, teaching, and publication devoted to the art of the past and that concerned with contemporary art is one of the most readily observable facts about the state of the profession today, in institutional terms. Fifteen years ago, in many university departments, graduate schools, research institutes, professional representative organizations, and most publications claiming a discipline-wide scope, contemporary art was treated as an afterthought—gestured at in the concluding lecture in a modern art survey, accorded one session via a visiting critic in a graduate seminar, allotted some low-key slots on the annual conference schedule, and given a review or two at the back end of the peak professional journals.

Since then, however, in most parts of the world, universities and colleges that offer art-historical studies are seeing increasing numbers of graduate applications to study contemporary art. Today, these match those wanting to work on modern art, the two fields outshining all other periods and areas of study.[23] Undergraduate student interest also intensified, until these areas commanded a majority of new appointments in university art history departments, colleges, and art schools. Specialist contemporary art journals proliferate; markets have ambiguous but undeniable influence; stories about contemporary art and artists abound in newspapers and in fashion and lifestyle magazines, in print and online; while museumgoers flock to exhibitions of contemporary art in new or expanded museums. Curators have been active in the field for decades, museums regularly publish art-historical reflections on recent and current art in their catalogs, textbooks have expanded to cover the new developments, and academic publishers have reoriented their lists. Attention is shifting, and resources are following, with seeming inevitability. Yet these changes have been met with considerable resistance—some active, mostly passive—by research, teaching, and representative institutions, especially in leading world centers, where they are most densely concentrated.

Chapter 9, "The State of Art History: Contemporary Art," was commissioned by editor Richard J. Powell for the *Art Bulletin*, the field's leading professional journal in the US, and was published in that journal in December 2010.[24] Part of a long-running occasional series surveying subfields in the discipline, the December 2010 issue was the first to treat contemporary art as such. I open the essay by highlighting the excitement among younger art historians; then point out the license suggested by the art-historiographic interests of certain prominent artists, such as Jeff Wall, Tacita Dean, Josiah McElheny, and Josephine Meckseper; and chart how, in art-world nomenclature, the quantitative incidence of the word "contemporary" has come to almost entirely eclipse that of "modern" when referring to art of recent decades and the present. Under the heading "The Prehistory of the Contemporary," I trace the various meanings of the terms "modern," "contemporary," and "contemporaneity" as used in artists' statements, museum and artist organization missions, art-critical writings, and curatorial discourse, from the French realists to contemporary Chinese artists. Postmodernism, I argue, was a symptom of the arrival of contemporaneity, not a period in itself nor an entirely adequate theory of late capitalist modernity. A brief survey of how regularly updated undergraduate textbooks deal with the art of recent decades reveals a profile in cautious confusion. Newly minted textbooks fare little better. In contrast, since the mid- to late 1980s, certain curators have led the way in struggling to grasp the larger flows shaping contemporary art, especially those operating regionally and worldwide. A few historians, such as Alexander Alberro, and maverick philosophers, such as Peter Osborne, offer tentative but promising suggestions.

I remain reluctant to regard contemporary art as a period within the history of art precisely because contemporaneity, as I understand it, doubts modern assumptions that history unfolds through successions via rupture, and, more specifically, doubts that art will continue to develop in epochal stages, one art movement succeeding another, each originating at a center of economic, cultural, and political power, then disseminating outward. I also wonder how long the already dispersive diversity of both contemporary art and contemporary life will permit us to read it as having a predominant, or core, character—even one as close to the bone as its "post-conceptuality."

Several unresolved issues, like anxious interrogators, continue to attend my ongoing efforts. The first set focuses on questions of method. Is art-historical methodology, no matter how radically and subtly revised, adequate to the task of tracing the extraordinarily complex shifts from modern to contemporary art, and from modern to contemporary regimes of visuality, that have occurred in recent decades—changes that are not only worldwide and culturally specific, but also ongoing and unpredictable? If contemporary art today is arguably more atomistic, elusive, and dispersed than in any prior period, are art criticism, curating, art theory, and visual culture studies more appropriate than art history as interpretive disciplines? Contemporary art and visual culture are changing so quickly and so profoundly that even these disciplines require radical revision to cope with the interpretative challenges being thrown at them. Perhaps even they are being found wanting. New discursive forms must be created.

What are the chances that art history as a discipline might embrace a truly radical approach to writing histories of contemporary art and take up the challenge of reinterpreting the art of the past (including modern art) in terms that acknowledge its inherent contemporaneity, that of its originary moment and that which pertains to now? In a 2015 survey of institutes for art-historical research in the United States, most of which were founded by private philanthropy during the 1980s and 1990s, Elizabeth C. Mansfield argues that they have evolved from offering havens to art historians during the "culture wars" toward watching with some dismay what she characterizes as the "civil war" between art historians concerned with "traditional" subject areas and those committed to the study of contemporary art.[25] She begins from the premise that "as privately-financed organizations with explicit or implicit mandates to promote advanced research on canonical Western art history, these institutions have contributed to a scholarly economy in the United States that has, until recently, turned on monographic and collections-based studies in areas deemed culturally important by America's Gilded Age collectors and philanthropists," a situation in which "the exclusion of contemporary art from the original research programs of the Getty, CASVA and the Yale Center for British Art helped to create a disciplinary rift that would have major repercussions for art history in the early twenty-first century."[26] After a useful portrait of the far-reaching, and mostly positive, effects of the Getty Research Institute, the Center for Advanced Studies in the Visual Arts (CASVA), the Yale Center for British Art, and the Clark Art Institute on art-historical research, publication, career development, and teaching (in the United States especially, but also elsewhere), she concludes by noting that—led by the Clark, then the Getty most ambitiously, and CASVA tardily—all now facilitate some programs supporting scholarship in contemporary art. Within the discipline, however, she believes that a "mutual sense of alienation threatens to harden into antagonism" and suggests that the institutes actively bring "historical and contemporary scholars together for residencies, symposia, and other programs," thus functioning as "a kind of academic Switzerland," which would, she hopes, help prevent "a fatal disciplinary secession."[27] Bringing scholars together, however, is exactly what these institutes have always done, choosing them, as far as possible from among those who apply, to echo the entire history of art in each cohort. Even when a theme is announced, wide scope and agnostic pluralism are usually preferred to anything as programmatic and metadiscursive as rethinking divisions within the discipline. Many, if not most, traditional art historians remain unconvinced that contemporary art is a viable subject for art-historical research, and to them it remains outside the proper purview of the discipline. Recently, their resistance has been lowered, less by a convincing picture of how art history could include contemporary and past art, and more by the influence on their students of external factors—market buzz, museum attendance, and wide public interest—as well as, more deeply, their students' search for a profession relevant to their lives.

The overall picture, however, is that historical approaches to contemporary art—which, after all, has been with us for at least forty years, some would say sixty—remain rare. There are many reasons for this rarity, not least the realization that modern modes of historical knowledge are no longer appropriate to these times. Modernity is now our past, but it is not our antiquity; reviving it will not lead to a contemporary renaissance. A new kind of historical thinking is needed to track the traces of contingent connectivity, parallel differencing, and lateral networking that together create the seemingly infinite complexity of our relations—a watchful inquiry into history as it is actually happening, while remaining always open to its unpredictable yet constrained futurity.

In 2010, when I wrote the article that begins the second part of this volume, only a tiny minority of historians offered perspectives of this kind. I was hopeful that more of my peers would attempt to do so, not only because the art called on us to interpret it to its various audiences, but also for the sake of providing guidelines and acting as targets for the flock of younger scholars enthusiastically entering the field. Some scholars have since taken up the challenge. In chapters 10 and 11, I consider the contributions of several key philosophers, theorists, artists, critics, and historians to the understanding of contemporary art today. I critique placeholder concepts such as "the contemporary," and half-formed gestures toward "the postcontemporary," an as-yet-empty signifier. Some steps are being taken toward detailed empirical work on contemporary art and artists, and on the histories of the multiple platforms that together constitute the contemporary visual arts exhibitionary complex.[28] I welcome them. Their work does not threaten anything like the presentist takeover that established art-historical institutions seem to fear. Yet disciplinary anxieties and institutional politics of these kinds are fleeting phenomena. The important goal before us is to account for contemporary art within the conditions of contemporaneity more fully, more fairly, more accurately, and in radically rethought critical and historical terms. This task awaits those to come whose minds bend toward thinking historically, synthetically, and critically about *their* art, that is, about art to come—as it is now, as it was, and as it might be.

thinking
contemporary art

contemporary art,
contemporaneity,
and art to come

WHAT IS CONTEMPORARY ART?

The word "contemporary" has come to replace the words "modern" and "post-modern" to describe the consequential art of our time, even though the meaning of "contemporary" is at once obvious and opaque. What are we to make of this situation?

Another way of putting this would be to ask, What is contemporary art? or perhaps, What has it come to mean these days? The point is not, of course, to seek an essence, or even a set of qualities, that would characterize art for inclusion in some long-term definition, nor even limited criteria that would certify art as contemporary nowadays. To do either would imply a position outside and above a discursive and practical world in which I, like all others concerned with such questions, am thoroughly implicated. Rather, the point of asking about usages past and present, to distinguish between them, is to grasp the meaning and purpose of what is thought and done in the name of the two terms "contemporary" and "art" when they are brought into relation. In other words, the issue arises because a set of social and aesthetic values with the name "contemporary art" attached to them is emergent, yet the nature of these values is unclear—they are much contested and surrounded by ambiguity, despite their evident cultural energy.

So I posit the question provisionally, using it as a hermeneutic bomb, that is, in the expectation of only "as if" kinds of answers. Yet I believe my suggestions to have purchase, to have explanatory and exemplary power. I approach them in three quite distinct, but connected, ways.

The first is the most obvious: contemporary art is the institutionalized network through which the art of today presents itself to itself and to its interested audiences all over the world. It is an intense, expansionist, proliferating, global subculture with its own values and discourse, communicative networks, heroes, renegades, professional organizations, events, meetings, monuments, markets, museums, and distinctive structures of stasis and change.

Contemporary art galleries, biennials, art fairs, auctions, magazines, television programs, and websites, along with whole ranges of associated products, are burgeoning in both old and new economies. They have carved out a constantly changing, but probably permanent, niche in the ongoing structures of the visual arts and in the broader cultural industries of most countries. As well, they are a significant, growing presence in the international economy, being closely connected with high culture industries, such as fashion; mass culture industries, such as those related to tourism; and, to a lesser but still important degree, specific sectors of reform and change in education, media, and politics. If you doubt any of this, go to the vernissage of the Venice Biennale, open the pages of *Artforum*, check out the list of cultural institutions in tourist guides to any significant city in the world, or peruse local and national newspapers to see the up-front treatment of events at contemporary art museums, such as the Museum of Contemporary Art (MCA), Sydney, or its equivalents in other cities. This is a culture that matters, to itself—its own subculture, local cultural formations, and the complex exchanges between cultures—and as a force within the culture of internationality, currently in globalizing mode.

The second approach is, to me, more fundamental, the kind of answer a philosopher might give to the question "What is contemporary art?" The response is difficult to explicate, although easy to state in a definition-like form: contemporary art is art infused with the multiple modes of contemporaneity and the open-ended energies of art to come. I am identifying here the driving spirit of the contemporary, not its overt, institutional, well-shaped forms. A certain spirit of contemporaneity is present in the most significant art of our time, and only some of it is found—along with much art with merely a superficial relation to the deeply contemporary—in the institutions of contemporary art.

The third way of putting the matter is even more particular, with resonance mainly within contemporary art practice and theory. It is about the internalities of style: the approach, therefore, of an art historian. It requires that I introduce special meanings to several terms, meanings that will become clear as I explore examples of current and recent art. The reasoning goes like this.

To give compelling communicative form to the spirit of contemporaneity, artists these days must, I believe, work through a particular set of representational problems. They cannot overlook the fact that they make art within cultures of modernity and postmodernity that are predominantly visual, that are driven by image, spectacle, attraction, and celebrity, on a scale far beyond what their predecessors faced. Furthermore, artists are embroiled willy-nilly in the shaping and reshaping of these cultures by constant warring between the visceral urgencies of "innervation," on the one hand, and the debilitating drift toward "enervation" on the other. In artists' efforts to find figure within form, to win it from formlessness, they cannot avoid using practices of surfacing and screening that, along with the rise of the photogenic and the impulse to the conceptual provisionalization of art itself, are the great technical and aesthetic legacies of the nineteenth and twentieth centuries. Artists who turn their backs on this constellation of problems and possibilities cease to be contemporary artists.[1]

I explore in this chapter the implications of all three ideas about contemporaneity in art, but I begin with the theme just introduced: the implications of the popularity of contemporary art.

ART AND POWER

Outside the Power Institute, the words "power" and "art" rarely occur in the same sentence. Yet they did so when the Tate Modern opened in May 2000, partly because the gallery is located in what was the Bankside power station in London. Indeed, Channel 4 made a television series about the project and produced a book to commemorate the event, titled *Power into Art*. Maybe this was what British performance-artist duo Gilbert and George had in mind when they announced, gleefully, during the opening celebrations that the Tate Modern demonstrated that "Art is power!" Knowing them, however, I am sure that they were pointing to the massive conjunctions of private and public patronage behind the £134 million raised to convert the building, as well as to the political maneuvering that would be required to maintain it from there on out. Given their Thatcherite political outlook, perhaps they were permitting themselves the frisson of contemplating (abstractly, of course) the casualties that such focusing of public wealth would occasion. Being erudite avant-gardists, they would have been punning on the famous slogan of Joseph Beuys, "Kapital = Kunst" (to be found, not so incidentally, scrawled by him on a preserved blackboard in the museum's Beuys Room; echoed in Imants Tillers's fund-raising mural in the foyer of the MCA; and parodied by Jeff Koons's self-parody, in his photo-poster titled *Artforum*, 1988–89, as his generation's reincarnation of Andy Warhol.

In some ways, Britain has come rather late to the institutionalization of contemporary art—at least compared to Europe, where, on average, two new museums of modern or contemporary art have been built each year since the mid-1980s. In the United States, new or expanded public galleries of modern and contemporary art have been a regular occurrence every few years, recently in such major cities as Chicago and San Francisco. Sydney has had the Power Gallery of Contemporary Art since 1968 and the MCA since 1991.

Until the opening of Tate Modern, those Londoners interested in contemporary art would regularly visit the Institute of Contemporary Art, the Whitechapel Gallery, the Serpentine Gallery, and a host of smaller, scattered venues around London and the provinces. The Young British Artists (yBa) phenomenon was sustained and displayed by private capital, notably that of the Saatchi brothers, advertising moguls closely associated with the Conservative Party during its years of ascendancy. The late 1980s and early 1990s was a time when, in the words of critic Adrian Lewis, "Art aspired to the condition of advertising."[2] Unfortunately, a lot of highly celebrated art achieved this goal.

It fell subject to the glitzy superficialities of media hook, the empty noise of advertising repetition, the attenuated vacuity of the hyperreal—in other words, it succumbed to the disco drift into enervation, one of the two great forces shaping visual imagery in our times. Examples from the later 1980s include Damien Hirst's various split sheep in formaldehyde sculptures. Australian artist Dale Frank preceded these British shockers by a few years with his "bad paintings." As with Koons, contemporary art surrenders its critical impulse and becomes itself just another hot item in the shop window of current visual culture.

These trends certainly helped contemporary art become hip. Attendance at Tate Modern began at double the level anticipated and has grown to tens of thousands per day, approaching Metropolitan Museum of Art numbers. Specifically, the Tate had 2.7 million visitors in the first five months, 118 percent over target, and 5.25 million in its first year of operation.[3] Crowds came from Europe, Asia, and the Americas, ranging in age from early twenties to late sixties, mostly female but not overwhelmingly so—demographics shared by museums of modern art everywhere, now spread to those with an emphasis on the contemporary.

What were the crowds surging to see? A display that began, on each of its four floors, with rooms in which important works by the modern masters quickly gave way, often in the same room, to works by artists who had recently come into prominence: Monet *Water Lilies* eclipsed by a Richard Long floor piece and mud wall; Matisse's wonderful sequence of *Jeannette* backs facing off in gentle struggle with South African artist Marlene Dumas's watercolors, meditating, in a way possible only after feminism, on the exigencies of being in a woman's body. In the Turbine Hall, visitors lined up for over an hour to climb and descend the three thirty-meter-high towers making up Louise Bourgeois's exploration of her psychic chambers (*Untitled*), and to walk beneath the spider legs of her giant *Maman* (1994). A whole floor was given over to installations commissioned for the occasion, exploring the dialogue, in video artist Gary Hill's words, as inscribed over the entrance, "Between cinema and a hard place."[4]

Crowds lined up and surged at the Royal Academy of Arts, too, which was showing *Apocalypse: Beauty and Horror in Contemporary Art*.[5] Visitors entered the exhibition through a small hole that brought them to the space beneath the stairs of Gregor Schneider's *Haus ur* in Rhedyt, Germany, and then through the claustrophobic labyrinth he had created there. Soon after, they were shocked to see that a meteorite had burst through the roof and felled a life-sized trompe l'oeil sculpture of the pope—Maurizio Cattelan's *La Nona Ora* (*The Ninth Hour*). New Age escape was possible if visitors immersed themselves in Mariko Mori's lotus bubble; and a romanticism of rubbish was to be found in Tim Noble and Sue Webster's installation *The Undesirables*.

Horror was more in evidence than beauty. The strongest works used one quality to evoke the other: British artist Darren Almond's *Bus Stop (2 Bus Shelters)*, 1999, fixated viewers with the clean precision of German industrial design, until they realized that the two bus shelters in his icy cold room had been transported from outside Auschwitz (figure 1.1). In the second-to-last room, Jake and Dinos Chapman presented eight museum display cases, each containing hundreds of intricate, toy-sized quasi-humanoids committing unspeakable atrocities on one another, acting out the worst nightmares of Nazi concentration camps. It was titled, appropriately, *Hell*, and it was hell to take in

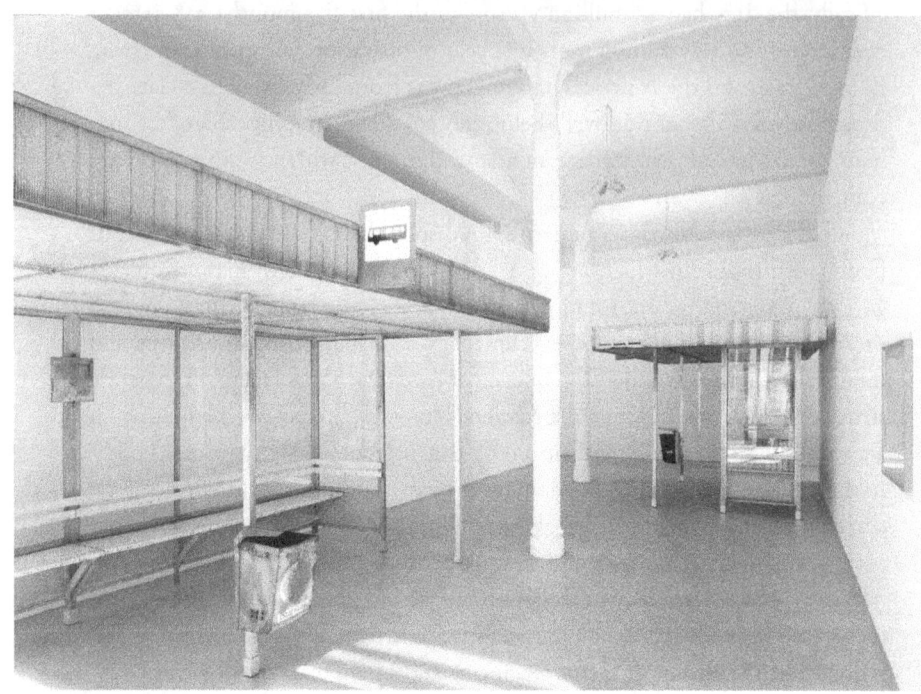

Figure 1.1

Darren Almond, *Bus Stop (2 Bus Shelters)*, 1999, aluminum and glass, 603 × 303 × 270 cm. Image courtesy of the artist; the Royal Academy of Arts, London; and Galerie Max Hetzler, Berlin/ Paris. Photo by Jörg von Bruchhausen.

(figure 1.2). In the final room, three huge, brightly colored, happy jingle paintings by Jeff Koons surrounded his sculpture *Balloon Dog (Blue)*, 1994–2000 (figure 1.3).

My first thought as I exited the exhibition was that the organizers were giving us a soft landing after so much horror. Halfway down the stairs, it struck me that perhaps the last room could have been titled *Hell* as well. What kind of world is it when we celebrate our manipulation as consumers of yet another commodity, as amusing ironist Jeff Koons encourages us to swallow, with a knowing smile? At moments I think that Koons's imaginary world is a symptom of our contemporary trauma, that he is the interior decorator from hell.[6]

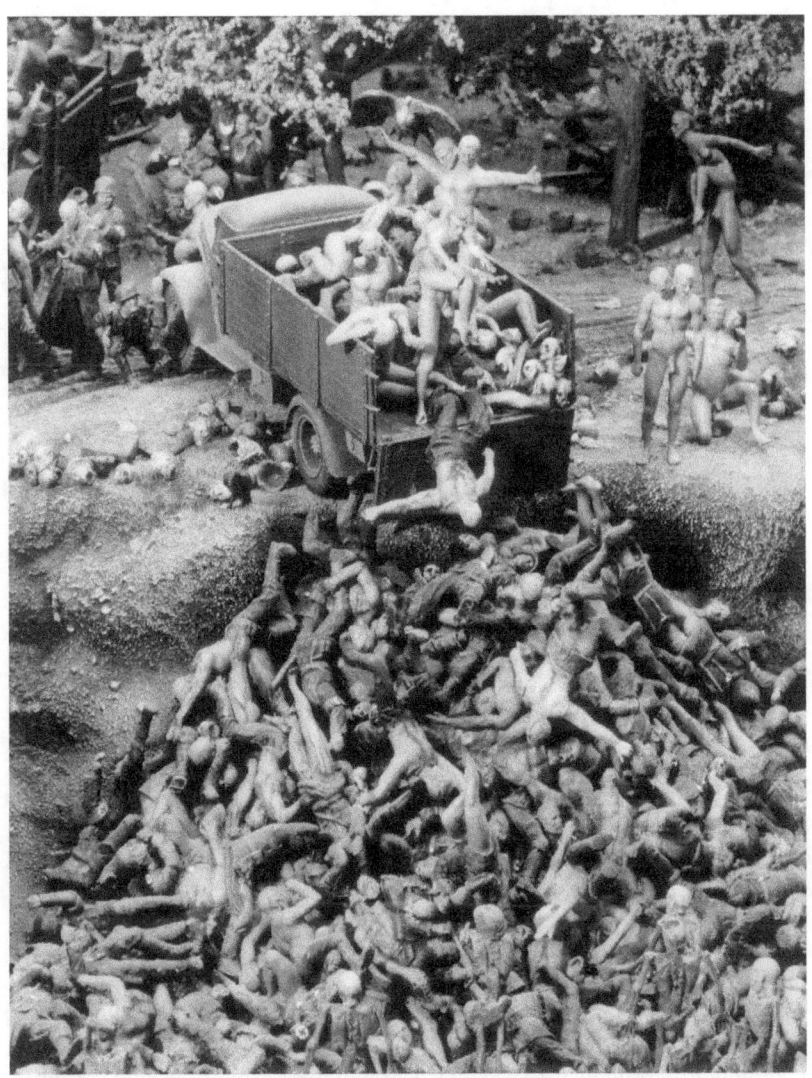

Figure 1.2

Jake Chapman and Dinos Chapman, *Hell* (detail), 1999–2000,
wood paint, glass fiber, plastic, and mixed media in eight parts,
each 215.0 × 128.7 × 249.8 cm. Images courtesy of the artists.
© Jake and Dinos Chapman. All rights reserved, DACS/Artimage
2018. Photo by Jake and Dinos Chapman Studio.

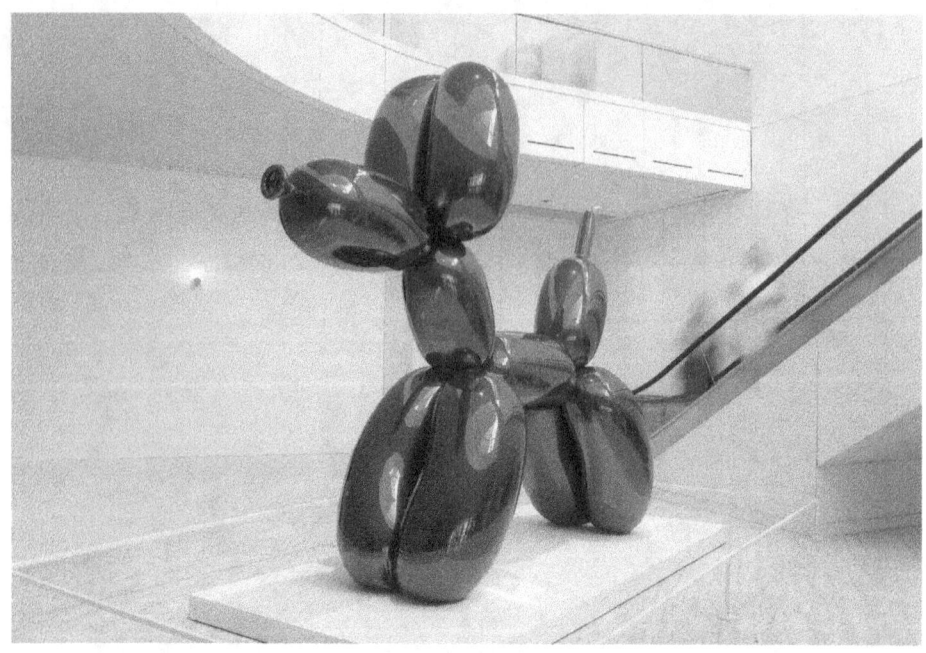

Figure 1.3

Jeff Koons, *Balloon Dog (Blue)*, 1994–2000, mirror-polished
stainless steel with transparent color coating, 307.3 × 363.2 ×
114.3 cm. © Jeff Koons, image courtesy of the Broad Art
Foundation, Museum of Fine Arts, Boston, and the artist.

The point of these recollections of exhibitions recently seen is that they prod
us to pinpoint reasons for the popularity of often quite challenging current art.
Certainly, expert publicity is assembled around these exhibitions, and yes, much
of this art has achieved the condition of not just advertising but fashion, so the
works can be quick to digest and easy to like. Concentrations of power, cultural
and otherwise, attract interest like magnets, sometimes for adventitious reasons,
such as then-mayor of New York Rudolph Giuliani deciding, during a 1999 election campaign, to attack the exhibition *Sensation: Young British Artists from the
Saatchi Collection* when it traveled to the Brooklyn Museum.[7]

Mayor Giuliani's response itself precipitated a media sensation. The mass
media feeds off stories structured around conflict between classes, races, cultures,

and individuals. In Sydney, contemporary art hits the front pages when it coincides with our city's obsession with clashes between powerful personalities and the battle over property, especially waterfront real estate, most notably at Circular Quay. Yet contemporary art as art becomes news, mostly when artists create works that seem to come from another cultural planet than that on which most readers of a given newspaper or watchers of a given television channel live.

George Pell, archbishop of Melbourne, objected to the display of Andre Serrano's photograph *Piss Christ* at the National Gallery of Victoria, and like Pell, Mayor Giuliani found Chris Ofili's painting *The Holy Virgin Mary* "blasphemous" and "disgusting" because he saw a willful, arbitrary, and probably atheistic defilement of a sacred icon (figure 1.4). Yet anyone who gave these works the contemplation that all artworks, as all icons, deserve, would come to see them as, in fact, efforts to situate transcendent (and perhaps even religious) experience in settings that create a new, contemporary kind of beauty. Ofili combines elements of Zimbabwean, glam-rock, and gangsta rap aesthetics; Serrano's draw to spirituality is evident in most of his work, such as *White Christ* (1989).

The Council of the National Gallery of Australia retreated from these values when it cancelled the *Sensation* exhibition.[8] National Gallery of Victoria director Timothy Potts took a similar path when he withdrew the Serrano work from exhibition on the grounds that violent objection to the work by crazed members of the public endangered the safety of museum attendants. The mistake being made here, by all concerned, is that of reading works of visual art as literal statements, as offering up their meanings at first glance or not at all.

All those who made censorious decisions in these cases failed to allow the communicative time that is due even to the most media savvy works of contemporary art. Indeed, each of these would-be and actual censors succumbed to reading the artworks as media events. By assessing art based on how they imagine it would play with the people, as mediated by the media at its worst, these leaders became subject to "spectacularization," that is, to the values of immediacy, superficiality, and commodity that they would, in other fora, sententiously condemn.

But the people are not that stupid. Politicians, fear-ridden arts bureaucrats, and sensation-seeking media have got it wrong: the main reason contemporary art exhibitions continue to be popular is that they are answering public needs. That is, at least some of the art is engaging with the most important issues of our time, and it is doing so in full-blooded ways, as Damien Hirst's work does. His *The Physical Impossibility of Death in the Mind of Someone Living*, a shark suspended in fluid flight, is, to me, a visual embodiment of unconscious fear, of

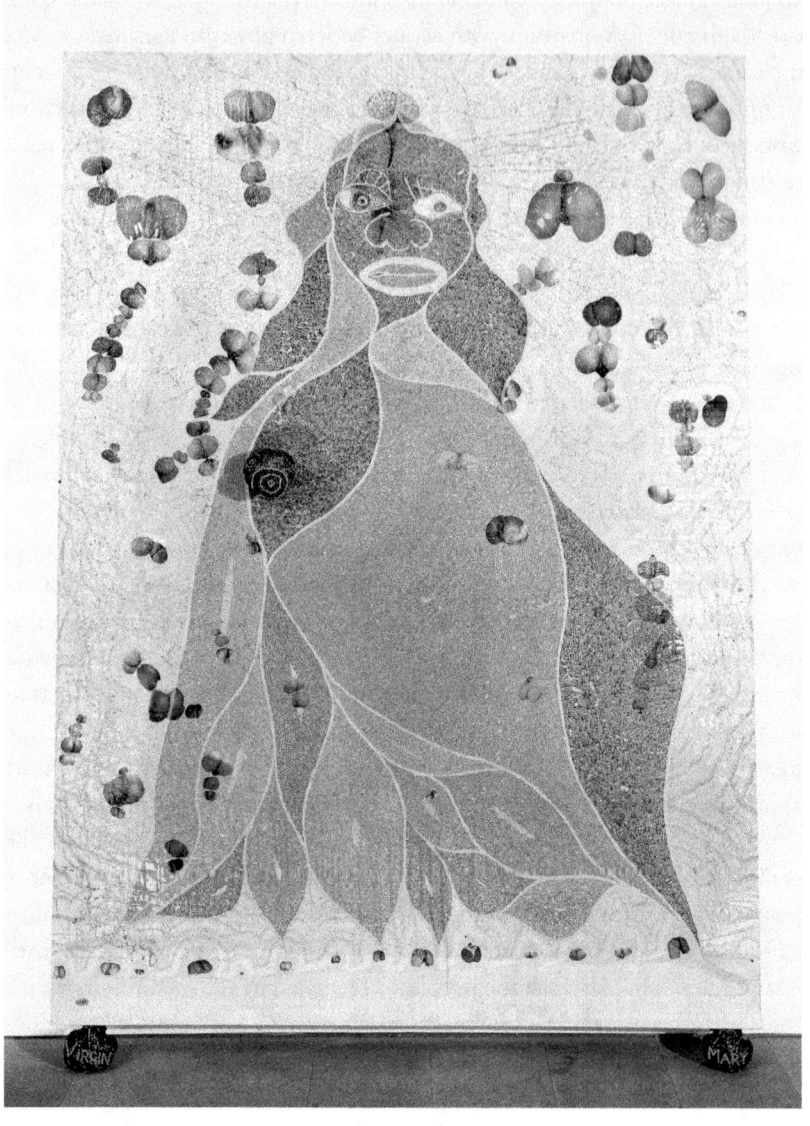

Figure 1.4

Chris Ofili, *The Holy Virgin Mary*, 1996, acrylic, paper collage, oil paint, glitter, polyester resin, map pins, and elephant dung on linen, 243.8 × 182.9 cm. © Chris Ofili. Courtesy Victoria Miro, London/Venice and David Zwirner, New York/London/Hong Kong.

the emotional state ubiquitous in our time, and the trauma that is the overwhelming psychosocial legacy of the twentieth century. This interpretation is not, of course, the only one, but the art is powerful enough to work as a landscape of the unconscious for most of us.[9] The piece contains many counterdrives and other movements. The naked, clean energy of the shark's trajectory may be read as embodying another force, one outside human history as it has been written into most of us for some centuries, a logic perhaps of indifference to that history. Still, other imagery must be found if one wishes to contemplate the joy of freedom that can arise from within awful, often deadly, constraint. Does this complicated joy not appear, for example, in the video installations of Shirin Neshat and Chris Cunningham? In the photography of Tracey Moffatt and others? These works do not convey universal values; rather, they are quite particular to present experience; they are contemporary in that they have—like all trauma and much joy—concrete yet unspecifiable causes and ambiguous yet tangible effects. They are ripe, indeed, for the terrain of subtlety—the shifting, floating de-territories of art.

THE TERMS

I now turn to the terms of debate, particularly the interplay between "modern" and "contemporary." Both words evoke not only a set of contra-concepts ("the past," "the old," etc.) but also a plethora of allied concepts, such as "avant-garde," "art of today," "work by living artists," "rising artists," "up-and-coming," "new wave," "new art," "modernism," "modernist formalism," "modern-contemporary," "formalesque," "ultramodern," even, recently, "neomodernism," among others (including, of course, "postmodern"). Yet all these arguably fall within (even as they often press against) the scope of the two terms "modern" and "contemporary." Indeed, these all may be part of one, not necessarily always happy, family of terms, tied together around a directional device, a pivoting between present, future, and past (in that order, probably) in art. If so, the question then becomes, Does this passageway itself have a history? Or better, What would be its histories at particular times and places?

An example: During the protracted planning for the Museum of Contemporary Art, Sydney, we had some difference of opinion about whether we should retain the name Power Gallery of Contemporary Art, shift to a more Contemporary Art Centre concept, or come up with something else. Bernice Murphy and Leon Paroissien argued, successfully, that you could make a museum out of the contemporary, that the past/future divide was itself passé, that you could build the past and future into the present as it was being created—a classic 1980s postmodern idea. *This* is how you resolve the evident contradiction of a museum and contemporary art, of museumizing the new: embrace the contradiction as an enabling one. Bernice is articulate about this in the opening chapter of her book *Museum of Contemporary Art: Vision and Context*.[10]

So we can say that the MCA, when it opened in 1991, was the first postmodern art museum in the world. It also exemplified another worldwide tendency, wherein the term "postmodern" all but disappeared, to be replaced by the term "contemporary"—acting, as it has done so often these past few hundred years, as a default term between new period styles. The Museum of Sydney, which opened on the site of the first Government House in Sydney in 1995, was the next postmodern museum, and it has arguably been even more successful than similar institutions in conveying a sense of the city's atomized history, of fragmented memory, much to the chagrin of some audiences.

The MCA opened in the early nineties, so it was actually the first museum of the art of that decade. The moment that contemporary art, in its postmodern form, was just finishing, it turned into a museum. Experiencing the early exhibitions—from *Opening Transformations*, the Contemporary Art Archive exhibitions, *TV Times*, and *Headlands: Thinking through New Zealand Art* to *Tyerabarrbowaryaou (I Will Never Become a White Man)*—was like entering a collector's cabinet of the present.

These were the best art museum ideas of their time—from perspectives affirmative of the potential of museums to educate constructively, even radically. They paralleled the work that many artists, such as Fred Wilson and Joseph Kosuth in the United States, were doing inside museums, installations that operated as internalized institutional critique.[11]

My overall point is that contemporary art has, on the level of official culture, replaced modernism and postmodernism as the general category for the art of the present and the recent past. On this level, it is the new modern art. Next, I explore this idea historically.

THE TWO HALVES OF ART

Despite the self-proclaimed ahistoricism of the postmodern moment, everything has its discoverable and still effective history, including the concepts "modern" and "contemporary." The French poet and critic Charles Baudelaire, in his 1863 essay "The Painter of Modern Life," pinpointed the central value at the heart of artistic modernism. He spoke of "the quality you must permit me to call *modernité*, by which I mean the ephemeral, the fugitive, the contingent, the half of art whose other half is the eternal and the immutable."[12] He ruminated on fashion plates and the newspaper illustrations of Constantin Guys, but Édouard Manet is the outstanding example. Manet's *Luncheon on the Grass* (1863) gained instant notoriety for its subject matter and technique, yet, as every art history student knows, it replays a well-known etching of a meeting of the gods, made by Marcantonio Raimondi in about 1517.

Baudelaire's emphasis was on the kind of art that embodies in subject matter and technique the novel experiences of social modernity: accelerated yet increasingly measured time, transience of relationships, chance contacts, and impermanent institutions. Modernity was understood as a cluster of circumstances that appeared to be valuable in and of itself but actually stood in contrasting connection to the slower, long-term, permanent values of classicism, history, and heritage. The desire to "be modern" was tempered by a profound awareness of the persistence of the past.

Soon this desire would include a trenchant critique of the excesses and inequities of modernity itself, and an anxious questioning of art's nature and role in this context. Avant-garde art became an art of disjunction, highly critical of the dominant aesthetic and social values of its time.

The story of contemporary art—and of much modern life—may be one of forgetting these critical connections. When separated from its disjunctiveness, contemporary art progresses along like a combine harvester, leaving deposits of modern art in its wake. The term "contemporary" was in widespread use during the 1920s and 1930s, throughout Europe, the United States, and their economic and cultural colonies. It worked, mostly, as a default term for modern art, as a pointer to art that was slightly less threatening than that of the ultramodernists but still comfortably up-to-date. A gradual acceptance of the contemporary at face value triumphed in the 1960s, when modernist abstraction became an official art. Then, in the crisis of the 1970s, all such generalities evaporated, and their institutions imploded. With the recent commoditization of contemporary art, institutions are reappearing, rebuilding. By 2000, it had become commonplace to merge the terms "modern" and "contemporary," or to drop modernism into the past. The same happened, around 1990, to postmodernism.

THE CONTEMPORARY NOW

Shifts in perspective on contemporary art are evident in some recent widespread usages of the word "contemporary"—in museums, book titles, and course names, for example—as a period-style term. Using it in this way engenders a methodological puzzle: it attempts to pinpoint the art of a time not, as has become conventional, by listing its features as indicative of its structures, but by finding features elusive of definition as well as structurelessness to be typical of it.

For many, contemporary art is visual art produced in the wake of the pop-minimal-conceptual, or postmodern, moment, especially art that rehearses or replays that moment. Key examples include postconceptual painters such as German artist Gerhard Richter; artists who pursue their concerns across media, as does Mike Parr; and conceptual photographers such as Canadian Jeff Wall, Australian Bill Henson, and American Cindy Sherman. This was the kind of art that the late Peter Fuller attacked as biennale international club class art.[13]

Another way that the art world has responded to the postminimal, conceptual moment effectively transforms the ordinary senses of the word "contemporary" into its opposite. Since around 1970, no tendency has achieved such prominence that would make it a candidate for becoming the dominant style of the period. Much effort went into promoting the "return to painting" in the early 1980s, and installation and large-scale video modes have been ubiquitous in recent years. But nothing has succeeded minimalism and conceptualism as art styles, nor does the de facto minimal-conceptual aesthetic that pervades much practice seem to amount to a style. Sometime in the late 1980s, it began to dawn on art-world opinion makers that perhaps we would always live in the aftermath of this "crisis"—that this would be our "history"—to be suspended in a continuous shifting that would never bring another paradigm into place. "Contemporary," therefore, may well mean periodlessness, being perpetually out of time, or at least not subject to historical unfolding. Will there ever be another predominant style in art, another period in social cultures, or a new epoch in human thought? In this sense, the word "contemporary" comes to mean out of time, suspended in a state after or beyond history, a condition of being always and only in the present. Do you find this liberating, debilitating, or horrific?

Hans Belting presaged this usage regarding art history in general, as did Arthur Danto in relation to art practice. The latter's influential idea of "art after the end of art" is a direct application of Hegelian philosophy to the history of art, with Andy Warhol as the linchpin. In the introduction to Danto's 1995 Mellon Lecture at the National Gallery of Art, Washington, DC, he said, "So just as 'modern' has come to denote a style and even a period, and not just *recent* art, 'contemporary' has come to designate something more than simply the art of the present moment. In my view, moreover, it designates less a period than what happens after there are no more periods in some master narrative of art, and less a style of making art than a style of using styles."[14] Contemporary art, to him, has this quality of being about history—in the case of one of his favorite examples, LA artist David Reed—while also being "posthistorical." In the etymological sense, the word "contemporary" is so "with it" that it can be with any time, replaying any past time and any imagined future in any combination. Art is contemporary in that it has as its core concern states of being indistinguishable from time (in Reed's case, a past "present" and the present moment). This is the replicant world of *Blade Runner*, and it echoes the urges, during the mannerist and rococo periods, to avoid the consequences of historical change through immersion in emphatic fashionability.

A softer, more colloquial usage of contemporary art as a style term is rapidly gaining ground. Any art that clearly echoes something of twentieth-century avant-gardism and is connected somehow to new technologies and the experiences of globalized internationalism is instantly, easily seen as contemporary, especially when set in contrast to art that uses inherited subject matter presented in traditional mediums. Examples often include art that employs digital media, such as that of Patricia Piccinini of Melbourne; but if we followed the progress of her work, we would see how it moved from irony about computer-game-type manipulation to uncanny evocations of how digitality is transforming contemporary and perhaps future life. Her photograph *Waiting for Jennifer* (2000), from the series *SO2 (Series 1)*, pictures a cybermorphic creature sharing the everyday life of a young man as if it were at once a child and a pet (figure 1.5). The nature of Piccinini's practice is also changing in ways indicative of fresh contexts for visual creativity: she works with a new technologies specialist, Peter Hennessey, in developing and realizing her ideas, and recent projects have been marketed commercially as art and design products via their company Drome.

It is now art-world orthodoxy to attack not just Koons for his seduction by the spectacle but also artists such as Andreas Gursky for being official visualizers of globalization. Closer analysis reveals a more interesting ambivalence at work in Gursky's photographs, such as his *Chicago, Board of Trade III* (1999), in the color blurs and repeats, and in the color and light excesses in his *Times Square, New York* (1995). His *Rhine II* (1999), with its coolly manic, relentlessly machinic framing of the river, evokes by contrast a paradigmatic image of Romantic individualism, Caspar David Friedrich's famous painting *Monk by the Sea* (1809).

Some writers, including me, search for and value the critical and redemptive drives within current art, art that is about survival within, and transformation of, the present social structures, art that is against art that merely reflects these

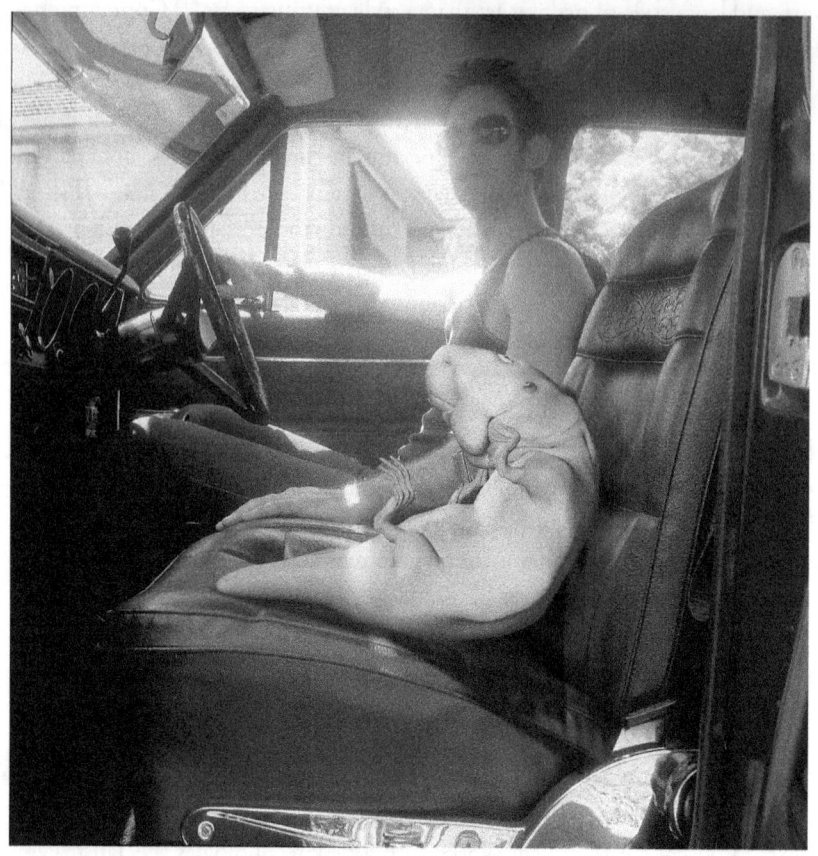

Figure 1.5

Patricia Piccinini, *Waiting for Jennifer*, from *SO2 (Series 1)*,
2000, digital C-type photograph, series of three images, each
80 × 80 cm. Courtesy of the artist; Tolarno Gallery, Melbourne;
Roslyn Oxley9 Gallery, Sydney; and Hosfelt Gallery,
San Francisco.

structures. Yet it is simplistic and misleading, nowadays, to line up artists and theorists on either side of a critical versus complicit divide. A different disposition of values is coming into being, and they are closely tied to the complexities of contemporaneity itself.

THE CHALLENGES OF CONTEMPORANEITY

Any good dictionary will provide a diverse etymology around the concept of "contemporary." A review of the term's linguistic history reveals some philosophical implications worth exploring.

In the banal sense of mere currency, the contemporary is that which is in circulation now, and thus the term can be affixed to any art that happens to be made at this time, no matter how reactionary or anachronistic its impetus. Appeals to this usage can be dismissed as the bleating of those who do not wish to think on anything too difficult. It is slightly more interesting to set "contemporary"—in the sense of "signs of the times"—against qualities in works of art that have lasted, that are of relevance today, that may challenge us in the future. These types of comparisons arise more and more often in museums of modern art. In New York, for example, in front of Picasso's *Woman with a Zither (Ma Jolie)*, a viewer might say, "Yes, the title *Ma Jolie* echoes one of the period's popular songs, but that is a case of period bric a brac, a dapper wink intended to signal 'contemporaneity,' not an indication of where the painting's real work is being done."[15] This kind of disjunction between social contemporaneousness and artistic modernism has been largely enabling for the latter. It set modernism the task of creating its own critical terms. In this sense, it is the twentieth-century turn of Baudelaire's essentially nineteenth-century doublet.

Perhaps, then, a useful definition of "contemporary art" requires turning away from the "ephemeral, the fugitive, the contingent" half of the modern doublet, the sense of "contemporary" as with-it-ness. Contemporary art theorists could treat this connotation of the term as having lost its purchase when set against the great achievement of modern art, itself looking more and more immutable (at least in its museums). But we cannot. This up-to-date-ness, this way-out-ness, continually returns to the incessantly burgeoning fashion industry, and given the economic and cultural contingency of fashion and art, to say nothing of the likely persistence of the connection, these qualities in contemporary art will be back. Etymologically, the term has an interesting prehistory relevant to this sense of "with-it-ness": during the seventeenth and eighteenth centuries, the word "cotemporary" all but displaced "contemporary," foregrounding the sense of "temporary" (a sense that the *Oxford English Dictionary* tries to expel by fiat). Yet living with the temporary, whatever it happens to be, but above all because it has the excitement of suddenness and transitoriness, is precisely what fashion, and the most fashionable art, prizes above all.

The OED online acknowledges all this in its cluster of meanings around the special usages that "contemporary" attracts in relation to art: "4.a. Modern; of or characteristic of the present period; *esp.* up-to-date, ultra-modern; *spec.* designating art of a markedly avant-garde quality, or furniture, building, decoration, etc., having modern characteristics (opp. *period n.* 10)." The subsequent list of examples are excerpted from a range of sources, from an 1866 issue of the *Contemporary Review* to Len Deighton's 1962 novel *The Ipcress File*, in which he describes an ambience as "a 'tasteful' piece of contemporary: natural wood-finish doors, stainless steel windows and venetian blinds everywhere." Dictionary entries really are stage directions for usage: you have your choice of options, as in a thesaurus. Yet, this entry does no work toward distinguishing "modern" from "contemporary." On the contrary, it reminds us that there was a contemporary style—in England, especially, just after the Second World War, a usage that echoes in Deighton's novel—and that this style still appears in furniture and interior design catalogs.[16] The dilemma is this: if the contemporary has already had its time as a style of art, architecture, and design, how could it—given the rule of novelty that apparently operates in style naming—have that time again? If it does become a style term, as it shows many indications of doing, would it not have to do so with a doubly new set of referents, markers, and values? What would these be?

Earlier, I called for a sustained study of the various inflections of the term "contemporary" in art contexts past and present, and of a long list of allied concepts beginning with "modern art" and ending with "postmodern."[17] These terms may turn out to mark, as they also mask, a persistent procedure for transforming not only the contemporary into the modern but also the modern into the traditional. This result is inevitable if the orthodox history of the modern art world is the starting point and the finishing framework. But if contemporary art is considered among the various meanings carried within contemporaneity itself, a much richer picture emerges.

More significant meanings cluster around the "with the times" or "of one's time" elements of the contemporary. A multiplicity of relationships is at work here, ranging from overt interventions in the major public sphere, through taking on broad political issues (the art of the times), to subtle resonances between the normal activity of world making and the artist's task of world picturing. Of most interest is the precise quality of what it might mean for a set of ideas or values, a practice, an institution, or a relationship—indeed, a period, a "time"—to be *ours*.

Another central meaning of contemporary is "at the same time," that is, co-eval, contemporaneous, and simultaneous. This can amount to nothing more than simple, inconsequential coexistence or the distanced coupling of happening to be someone's contemporary. Yet here in Australia, we are experiencing an extraordinary example of art being produced simultaneously in closely connected cultures that nevertheless have different time conceptions. Distinct kinds of contemporary art are being produced within Indigenous and non-Indigenous cultures, hybrids are emerging between them, and many noncontemporary art practices are continuing within and alongside them. Distinguishing these pathways and theorizing their import are important tasks at present. The efforts of many European artists, exemplified by the 1989 exhibition *Magiciens de la terre*, to merge their yearnings for "spirituality" with the quite other, and quite specific, belief systems and artistic practices of Indigenous peoples goes in the wrong direction. I do recognize, however, that this urge, too, is a contemporary one.

All art making in Australia occurs at oblique angles to more traditional practices—although much contemporary Aboriginal art includes traditional surrogate practice, and much contemporary non-Indigenous art promulgates modernist traditions. Communication across these divides occurs quite frequently, but so, too, does miscommunication. We see this at work in the exchanges between, for example, Imants Tillers and Gordon Bennett in the exhibition *Commitments* (Institute of Modern Art, Brisbane, 1993; and Artspace, Sydney, 1994).

Contemporary Aboriginal art is a movement with multiple aspects and a complex history (see chapter 6). The direct inspiration of ceremonial stories is still evident in works by elders from remote communities: the *Papunya Tula: Genesis and Genius* exhibition at the Art Gallery of New South Wales in 2000 was a powerful testimony to the depth of these forces.[18] The continuing power of self-replenishment in contemporary Aboriginal art is obvious in the extraordinary work being done by artists in communities across the country.

Outstanding work of this kind is, to me, a contemporary art, not because of its use of acrylics, or its smart gallery settings and marketing, but because it is about one of the most pressing personal, social, and political needs of our time: the need to communicate, plainly, constructively, and gracefully, yet with an eye to the complexities, across the divides between cultures. Its contemporaneity is in being forged in the double time—that is, the fissures of temporal difference—between two, at base, incommensurable cultures. Aboriginal contemporary art is alert to the warring between the reconcilable and the unreconciled that roils Australian polity and affects the everyday life of all Australians. In such a contested field, Indigenous art offers long and deep pathways for negotiation.

In terms of my third, technical, meaning of "contemporary," this art has given new depths of meaning to the surface as a communicative field in art. For the significant tribal Aboriginal artists, painted surfaces work as surrogates for bodies marked for ceremony, and rocks painted as sacred sites, particularly but not exclusively in bark painting, and for land seen ceremonially, especially in desert acrylics, but, again, not exclusively. Politically, these often-resplendent surfaces act as double-sided screens, at once revealing glimpses of but also concealing secret, sacred content. Hiding in the *rarrk*, or dazzle.

The photographic work of Tracey Moffatt is traced by similar yearnings. Using the language of international contemporary art, she has for many years explored the details of racial tension and guilt, including their explosive, if temporary, resolutions. From her films *Night Cries* and *Bedevil*, through such photo sequences as *Scarred for Life* to the dream memories in *Up in the Sky*, the theme of the iniquitous coupling of crippling trauma and exultant freedom keeps returning (figure 1.6).[19] Parallel issues occur in specific forms in the Pacific, and in Northeast and Southeast Asia, for example, in the delicious parodies of Yasumasa Morimura and in the uncanny, disturbing installations of Do-Hu Suh.

In his 1984 essay "Philosophy and Painting in the Age of Their Experimentation: Contribution to an Idea of Postmodernity," Jean-François Lyotard makes two moves that prefigure some of those that I am proposing. The first is this:

> One must account for the fact that certain descriptions from the 1767 *Salon*, despite the genre's obsolescence, are more current than certain axioms from Kandinsky's *Point, Line, Plane*, dated 1926; certain aspects of Duchamp's *Bride*, which has already passed fifty, are fresher than the latest Balthus. According to my timepiece, at least. By this I mean, without wanting to impose my own time, that examples of parachrony such as these are possible and are possible for everyone. Thus we must admit a multiplicity of current times, which necessarily gives rise to paradox.[20]

He goes on to point out that for the philosopher Alexandre Kojève to celebrate Kandinsky in Hegelian terms shows that both philosopher and artist lack contemporaneity, even though the celebration is "of today and aims at extolling what is currently most-up-to-date." There is a warning for Arthur Danto here.

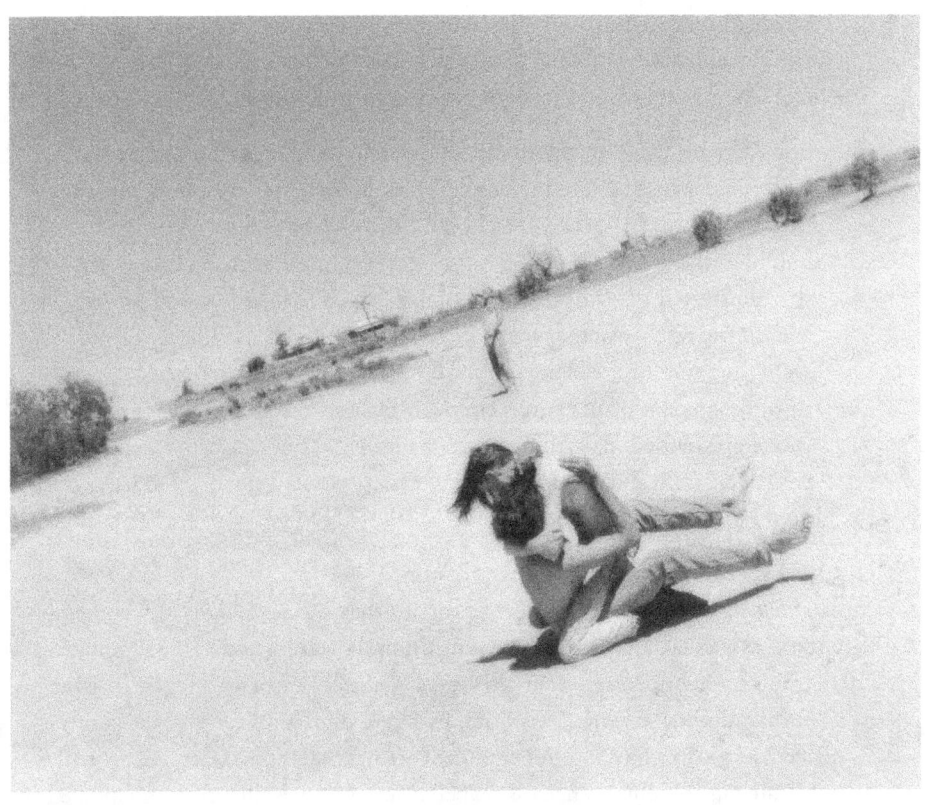

Figure 1.6

Tracey Moffatt, *Up in the Sky 17*, 1997, from the series of
twenty-five toned photolithographs, each image: 61 × 76 cm.
Art Gallery of New South Wales, Sydney. Purchased with funds
provided by the Art Gallery Society of New South Wales Contemporary Group 1997. Photo by AGNSW. © Tracey Moffatt.
Courtesy of Roslyn Oxley9 Gallery, Sydney.

Lyotard's second move is to illustrate that contemporaneity can be broached within the equivalent of what I call the institutions of contemporary art. He evokes Documenta 5 (1972), suggesting that the works on display there formed

> both a satire through the immense diversity of the genres, and at the same time a field where the whole point is always to try out whether that situation, that event, that hole in the ground, that wrapping of a building, those pebbles placed on the ground, that cut made on a body, that illustrated diary of a schizophrenic, those *trompe l'oeil* sculptures, and all the rest—whether that too says something to us. The powers of seeing and sensing are being probed on the limits of what is possible, and thus the domain of the perceptible-sensing and the speakable-speaking is being extended. Experiments are made. This is our post-modernity's entire vocation, and commentary has infinite possibilities open to it.[21]

Although postmodernism's time has come and gone, postmodernity in the sense Lyotard is defining it here is still "ours."

Lyotard's approach leads me to propose that the etymology of "contemporary," as well as the artist examples I mention above, tells us that the simultaneity (the "con-temporality," we might say) of all these ways of working in, of, with, against, and outside time (its fixities, passages, diurnality, surprises, transcendences) is at once the condition and the core of contemporaneity. An art truly imbricated in contemporaneity is shaped from its deepest impulses and marked across its surfaces by the interplay between all these usages, from the most fashionable through the most forward looking to the most paradoxical, from the firm to the irresolute, from trenchant dichotomies to random particularities.

ART TO COME

My emphasis on the qualia of contemporaneity in art that is truly contemporary raises the question, How do we think about the art of the future? My answer is unequivocal. We cannot think about the art of the future in any specific, predictive sense except as a projection of present practice. (This accords with the reality of our general experience: we cannot plausibly predict the specific future, no matter how hard we might try.) Yet we can and, I argue, must embrace wholeheartedly the most salient characteristic of art to come as a practice within a condition or context: its unknowability in particulars, yet its inevitability as a generality, the unavoidable fact that what we cannot now know will nevertheless come into being, will come to pass, will come into us and, at the same time, pass us by.

I have adapted this idea from Jacques Derrida's concept of "democracy to come," as introduced in his book *Specters of Marx*. The manifestations in art are of this same impulse he identifies in the post-fall-of-the-wall world as the counterweight to multinational globalization. I clarify the complexities and the energies of his concept—as well as, I hope, its relevance—in the exposition that follows.

In a recent conversation with him about these matters, he responded positively to my outline of the ideas I have been advancing, and then made an important speculative comment. In his view, pure contemporaneity would never be possible, because being absolutely *with* time would permit no future, no past, and thus no present. It would amount to the identity of being and time—an impossibility. Yet, he continued, if it is impossible to be completely contemporary, entirely *with* time, then it must also be possible to be so totally *out of* time that time becomes of no consideration. Are there not moments when time seems not to exist, if only briefly? When you experience the other— the otherness of the other, and your own otherness—so much that you both lose contact with the present, indeed, with any sense of time? Is this not, perhaps, the core experience of love, of writing, of thought? Of art, certainly. This is the "to come" in its purest sense, it is pure *différance*, a kind of grace.[22]

Typically, Derrida takes the two poles implied by the range of "contemporary" definitions I have canvassed—and which the dictionary entries set out—and turns them, like a glove being folded inside-out, a gesture in perpetual motion between these two states, but with a disposition toward openness. I take this as a further unfolding of what I have been seeking to identify as contemporaneity.

Given that the idea of the avant-garde has lost its axiomatic force, why do we—indeed, why *should* we—commit to contemporary art to come? I suggest three types of answer.

1. Because of the ways in which art—engaged, twistingly, with its times—has been contemporary to date, art will likely open out contemporaneity in times to come in further, albeit unknown, ways. This answer is based on the general fact of human continuity in the face of risk and self-destruction. It is, to me, a weak argument from tradition of the kind of bland pessimism that characterized Clement Greenberg's 1968 Power Lecture, "Avant-Garde Attitudes."[23]

2. Because current art, as I have shown, is anticipatory it is constantly on the verge of self-transformation, of proliferation, rather than recursion and sameness. This may be a residue of the avant-garde axiom, or a kind of improbable nostalgia for the future, but I think that it points to a situation much more open, unpredictable, and diversifying than the single or relatively few (but

nearly always exclusionist) kinds of avant-gardism that prevailed in the twentieth century.

3. Because the world is becoming even more complex than it was during the time of modernity, Baudelaire's *modernité* dialectic (contingency working on eternality leads to modernity) continues to have force, but only the fading, institutionalized force of convention and habit. Contemporaneity in art constantly pushes this now 150-year-long tradition of modern art into a condition of mere continuity. Yet social contemporaneity is increasingly complex, both in its relationships to art within continuing cultures and in the emergent relationships between cultures.

Therefore, contemporaneity within art is becoming at once more complex and more central to practice. Contemporaneity is an opening, constantly redefining set of forces and operations. In philosophical terms, it would be a "deconstructive" par excellence in Derrida's early sense, which has by now become at the same time an "undeconstructible" in his more recent sense.[24]

So, if I were pressed to match the question "What is contemporary art?" with a shorthand response, it would be art that is marked by art to come—by contemporaneity as I have (re)defined it. A slightly longer way of putting this would be to say that contemporary art today is art driven by the multiple energies of contemporaneity, the art that figures forth those energies so that we can glimpse them in operation, the art that works to transform those energies in ways that keep our futures open, an art that draws us into commitment to what is to come. This is, of course, to return the question to the realm of further questioning, but to a specified set of questions and a framework of interrogation as outlined in this chapter.

If I were to answer the lesser question, "What is contemporary art now?," I would say that, yes, within the institutions of art these days—the international museum and exhibition circuit, and all of us who dance attendance on it—"contemporary" is functioning as a default term for persistent modernisms and residual postmodernism. The forces of spectacularization have indeed led to an evident dulling, even homogenization, of the modern/contemporary art doublet. It has become official culture, not unlike the dead end reached by high modernism in the 1960s. That impasse released the still unrealized possibilities of pop, minimalism, and conceptualism. So now, the option of official postmodernism is not the banal populism advocated by the mediocrities of the ugly Right, their dream of an art that goes forward pleasantly, as if modernism, let alone postmodernism, never happened. Rather, it is the significant and increasing body of practice that releases the differentiating energies inherent not so much in modernity or postmodernity, but in the multiple internalities of contemporaneity itself.

I have been giving examples of this kind of art throughout these remarks. It is relevant that most works I reference take the form of large-format backlit photographs or video installations. These are the currently most favored technical solutions to the demand that effective art function as surface and screen simultaneously, and that it does so conceptually and photogenically. This bring me to my third approach to the question "What is contemporary art?"

Brazilian artist Adriana Varego makes past colonization of her country viscerally present in her works, in which intestines pour out from cracks in the veneer of upper-class culture and design. British artist Gillian Wearing video records testimonies about harrowing experiences, such as domestic violence or sexual abuse, that often receive public recognition only when those involved appear in the courts, but that constitute the substance of everyday life for many. In her most recent work, *Trauma*, people who responded to an advertisement in *Time Out*, the London events guide, tell their "worst" story from behind a mask (figure 1.7). Sydney artist Dennis del Favero also concentrates on the impact of trauma on memory, sense of self, and the tactility of bodies. His photo installations have been exploring this subject, often in central European settings, for years. Christopher Cunningham is best known for his MTV promos for Bjørk (for example, the superb *All Is Full of Love*), Madonna, and others, as well as for creating the models in *Alien 3* and for Playstation video games. In the *Apocalypse* exhibition, he showed in an art gallery for the first time his film *Flex*, in which he staged an extraordinarily intense interplay between aggression and tenderness, an elemental warring and marrying of the sexes.

When I presented these ideas during a lecture in Sydney in 2001, I illustrated the artworks through projected slides but also screened a netcam of Australian artist Mike Parr presenting his performance *Water from the Mouth* (figure 1.8). At the time of the lecture, Parr had been locked into a room at Artspace, a contemporary art center not far from the university, for 157 hours. He had 133 more hours of self-imposed isolation to come. During that period, water was his only sustenance, and his wife and his doctor the only visitors.[25] I concluded the lecture with these remarks:

The empty white room in which Parr persists is a parody of the famous "white cube" of modernist art museology. He is in there alone, for the sake of his art, of his career-long *Self-Portrait* project, and in the name of all those restricted, detained, or imprisoned, in any and every way

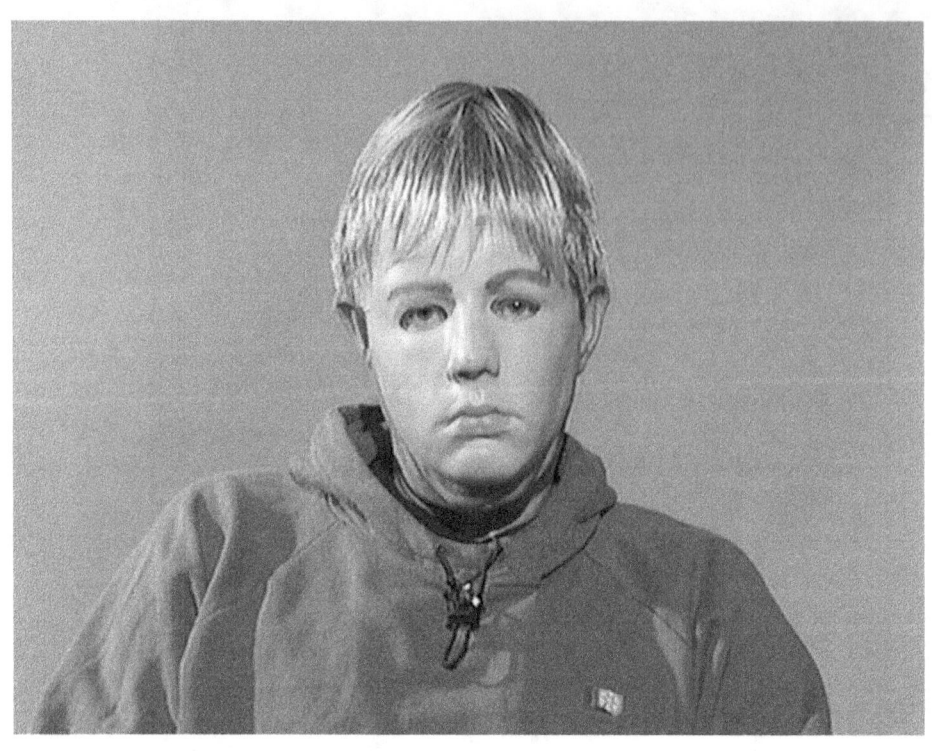

Figure 1.7

Gillian Wearing, *Trauma* (still), 2000, color video with sound.
Image courtesy of Gillian Wearing and Tanya Bonakdar Gallery,
New York.

whatsoever (including refugees, such as "the boat people," desperate to
reach Australia, and usually confined in offshore detention before they
get here). On the monitors, we can see a person with no obviously artistic
materials to hand, someone enacting no evidently artistic protocols. Yet
his effort is to create an ongoing visual image of duration itself, projected
via video link, to spectators at Artspace outside the room, and to those
watching monitors elsewhere, including us there, then, in that lecture
hall. If I were to interpret Parr's performance in the terms advanced in
my lecture, I might say that the enervation he was experiencing physi-
cally, and perhaps psychically, produced, paradoxically, an affect of in-

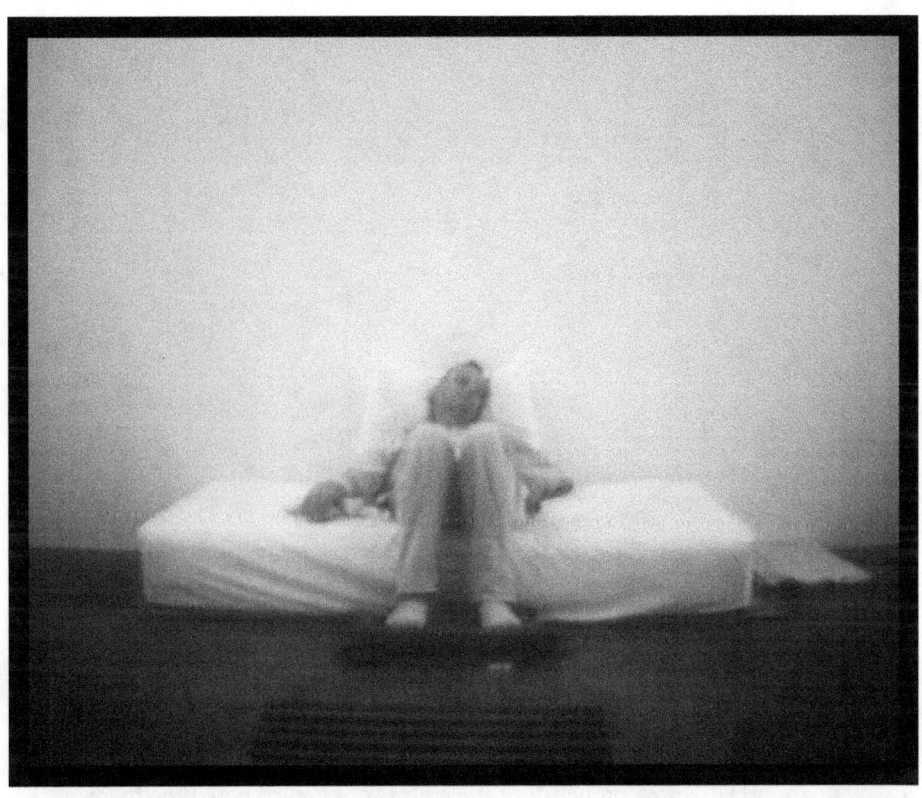

nervation in us, its observers. What were we seeing? Only the artist (as a
person), only the image (as a screened surface), only the spectator (as we
considered, alongside others, the implications of that degree of dedica-
tion). This was an art that prefigured its own obliteration, as well as his
and ours; an art pure in spirit, yet deeply tainted by the world (as all purity
must be); an art against which labels faded into insignificance. The question to be asked about commitment such as this is not "Is it contemporary
art?" It is, rather, "Why does work such as this matter to us today?"

in a nutshell

Art within Contemporary Conditions

In 2009 Hal Foster, on behalf of the editors of *October*, posed the following question:

> The category of "contemporary art" is not a new one. What is new is the sense that, in its very heterogeneity, much present practice seems to float free of historical determination, conceptual definition, and critical judgment. Such paradigms as "the neo-avant-garde" and "postmodernism," which once oriented some art and theory, have run into the sand, and, arguably, no models of much explanatory reach or intellectual force have risen in their stead. At the same time, perhaps paradoxically, "contemporary art" has become an institutional object in its own right: in the academic world there are professorships and programs, and in the museum world departments and institutions, all devoted to the subject, and most tend to treat it as apart not only from prewar practice, but from most postwar practice as well. Is this floating-free real or imagined? A merely local perception? A simple effect of the end-of-grand-narratives? If it is real, how can we specify some of its principal causes, that is, beyond

general reference to "the market" and "globalization"? Or, is it indeed a direct outcome of a neoliberal economy, one that, moreover, is now in crisis? What are some of its salient consequences for artists, critics, curators, and historians—for their formation and their practice alike? Are there collateral effects in other fields of art history? Are there instructive analogies to be drawn from the situation in other arts and disciplines? Finally, are there benefits to this apparent lightness of being?[1]

My response to these questions follows, my core argument—the nutshell version—about how contemporary art is being made within current conditions.

In recent decades, the most pervasive idea about contemporary art has been that one cannot—indeed, should not—have any idea about it. So it is not surprising that contemporary art's current bout of self-questioning has occurred so tardily: over half a century since the first stirrings of a distinctively contemporary art became evident (as retreats, voids, and absences) in the work of artists such as John Cage, Robert Rauschenberg, Yves Klein, Lucio Fontana, and members of the Gutai group; more than forty years since its immediacy insisted itself in the work of artists such as Andy Warhol, Allan Kaprow, Lygia Clark and Hélio Oiticica, Robert Smithson, Joseph Beuys, and performance artists and conceptualists everywhere; and at least thirty years after its demands were interpreted as symptoms of our shift to the postmodern, yet we nevertheless found ourselves standing, unblinking, in spectacularity's spotlight. The market bubble built so assiduously during the 1980s has recently burst: its contribution to conceiving the contemporary as a state of witless presentism cannot be underestimated.

Yet other voices did contribute to the clamor. If we can say that during the 1950s and the early 1960s, artists led the way in responding to the contemporary, and in defining it, critically, for the rest of us, it is becoming a cliché to note that in each successive decade since then, agenda setting was done, in turn, by critics, theorists, arts administrators, gallerists, curators, and collectors—accompanied, of course, by much excitable role swapping. Yet the continued rise of a vacuous pluralism seemed unstoppable, especially in northern hemispheres. By the 1990s, every new art institution, and each new department of existing ones, was busy naming or renaming itself "contemporary." Few had any firm idea of what this meant: mostly, the word served as a placeholder for what had recently occurred, was going on right then, or might happen next.

Despite the wistful nostalgia for bearable lightness expressed in the metaphor with which the *October* questionnaire concludes, those days are gone—indeed, the undertow has been felt since the 1980s. How do we unpack decades of disinformation about contemporary art? How do we inject critical consciousness into the morass of upbeat mindlessness that has come to pass for art discourse? How do we avoid the twin dangers of, on the one hand, inflating some explanation of a part (postmodern irony, poststructuralist informalism, melancholy Marxism, relational aesthetics, altermodernism, etc.) into an account of the whole and, on the other, running for shelter behind the minutiae of particularism?

One obstacle is the self-interest and inflexibility of the art institutions: the flailing about so evident at the Museum of Modern Art, for example, as it struggles to absorb the contemporary into its core commitments to historical modernism and to medium-based bureaucracy. A deeper challenge to historians of the contemporary is that we cannot escape finding ourselves in the position of the central figure in Kafka's parable "He." Pressed from behind by past forces—insistently nagging, unbeaten, still vital, seeking advantage—and from in front by the future's infinite expectations, we struggle to grasp our present, to find even a temporary place in it. All three temporalities need one another to be themselves, yet, Kafka notes, *we* have a secret dream, that "some time in an unguarded moment—and this would require a night darker than any night has ever been—he will jump out of the fighting line and be promoted, on account of his experience in fighting, to the position of umpire over his antagonists in their fight with each other."[2]

I cannot, here, gloss this glaring insight—and could not, in any case, come close to matching Hannah Arendt's brilliant commentary on Kafka's aphorism in her *Between Past and Future*, a collection of essays full of pointers on how the present might be thought.[3] Suffice it to say that in contemporary conditions, no one is going to elevate us to some time-space outside the struggle. Indeed, we are hard pressed nowadays to imagine the future having the kind of presence in the present that it had for Kafka in 1920, Arendt in 1961, or for many of us until 1989, or 2001. Utopian thinking has all but disappeared, and confidence in the inevitability of progress has evaporated. Today, reactionary pasts insist most strongly on their right to occupy the times to come. Meanwhile, old—that is to say, modern—remedies remain in place, even as they fall conspicuously short of securing their own perpetuation. This situation was as evident in worldwide efforts to cope with the recent financial crisis as it is in many more specific domains, including those of art.

Considerations such as these, along with a refusal to settle for them, have shaped the kind of explanation I have been exploring for some time: a historical hypothesis about the nature of art in contemporary conditions. We might begin by asking: what does contemporaneity mean in these circumstances?

How has the current world picture changed since the post–World War II aftermath led to the reconstruction of an idea of Europe; since decolonization opened up Africa and Asia, with China and India emerging to superpower status but others cycling downward; since the era of revolution versus dictatorship in South America led first to the imposition of neoliberal economic regimes and then to a continent-wide swing toward populist socialism? As the system built on divisions among the first, second, third, and fourth worlds imploded, what new arrangements of power came into being? Now that the post-1989 juggernaut of one hyperpower, unchecked neoliberalism, historical self-realization, and the global distribution of ever-expanding production and consumption tips over the precipice, what lies in the abyss it has created? Above all, how do we, in these circumstances, connect the dots between world picturing and placemaking, the two essential parameters of our being?

My suggestion is that we start by taking seriously, and then carefully scrutinizing, our instinctual reach for the contemporary. The concept of the "contemporary," far from being singular and simple—a neutral substitute for "modern"—signifies multiple ways of being with, in, and out of time, separately and at once, with others and without them.[4] These modes have of course always been there. The difference nowadays is that the multiplicities of contemporary being predominate over the kinds of generative and destructive powers named by any other comparable terms (for example, "the modern" and its derivatives). After the era of grand narratives, they may be all that there is. What we take to be contemporary is the primary indicator of what matters most to us about the world right now, and what matters most to artists.

In these circumstances, would-be historians of contemporary art face some methodological challenges. Only by working together do we have a chance of rising to them. Track the occurrence—intermittent, occasional, gradually insistent, then suddenly ubiquitous—of ideas of the contemporary within modern art discourse.[5] Examine when, how, and why art became modern in each distinct yet related cultural region of the world, in each city where this change occurred. Then show how each of these accommodations with modernity underwent, or is still undergoing, its unique yet connected transition to contemporaneity.[6] Finally, look around you: What does the present look like when seen from these historical perspectives? In the space available, I can offer only the most schematic, assertive outline of a response to this last question.[7] It comes in two parts: a claim about the present itself, and a claim about how art is being made within it.

Contemporaneity is the most evident attribute of the current world picture, encompassing its most distinctive qualities, from the interactions between humans and the geosphere, through the multeity of cultures and the ideoscape of global politics, to the interiority of individual being. This picture can no longer be adequately characterized by terms such as "modernity" and "post-modernity," not least because it is shaped by friction between antinomies so intense that it resists universal generalization—indeed, it resists even generalization about that resistance. It is, nonetheless, far from shapeless. Within contemporaneity, it seems to me, at least three sets of forces contend, turning one another incessantly. The first is globalization itself, above all its thirsts for hegemony in the face of increasing cultural differentiation (the multeity that was released by decolonization), for control of time in the face of the proliferation of asynchronous temporalities, and for continuing exploitation of natural and (to a degree not yet imagined) virtual resources against the increasing evidence of the inability of those resources to sustain this exploitation. Second, the inequity between peoples, classes, and individuals is now so accelerated that it threatens both the desires for domination entertained by states, ideologies, and religions and the persistent dreams of liberation that continue to inspire individuals and peoples. Third, we are all willy-nilly immersed in an infoscape—or, better, a spectacle, an image economy, a regime of representation—capable of the instant and thoroughly mediated communication of all information and any image anywhere. This iconomy—indeed, the entire global communication system—is, at the same time, fissured by the uneasy coexistence of highly specialized, closed knowledge communities; open, volatile subjects; and rampant popular fundamentalisms. Globalization has proved incapable of keeping these contradictions in productive tension. We see now that it was modernity's last roll of the dice (which does not mean that it will desist from playing to win).

How is art being made in this situation? Recent books on contemporary art tend to be pictorial compilations accompanied by minimal information and brief artists' statements (the Taschen model); anthologies of interpretive essays by theorists, critics, and curators (the Blackwell model); or surveys showing how certain artists are tackling one or another theme in long lists of current concerns.[8] Meanwhile, art-critical discourse finds itself in an oddly suspended state between promotional chat and melancholy, anxious historicism. *Artforum* editor Tim Griffin asks, "What, then, happens when the overturning that defined modernism is itself overturned, with the result that past moments are never done away with, their residues instead seeming to accrue? When, to put it another way, the critical models of previous eras do not, and cannot be asked to, function as they once did?"[9] Contrast this picture to what many outside observers see in at least some contemporary art. For example, philosopher and sinologist François Jullien: "For hasn't art always been ahead of philosophy? (And is it not alone in the contemporary period in having attempted, through its practice, to uproot itself?) Art today demonstrates how a practice can explore diverse cultures in order to purge its atavisms and reinvent itself."[10] If these observers are looking at the same thing, they are doing so with their backs to each other.

Can the fundamental forces shaping contemporary art be discerned, and can the shaping effects be described—plausibly, accurately, critically? A polemical proposition: like contemporaneity itself, art today is made in relation to the unfolding of three major currents, each of which has distinctive features while being tied to the others—its contemporaries—and is in contestation with them. Each is changing before our eyes yet has its own historical destiny; each will transmute, and each will pass.

The first current amounts to an aesthetic of globalization, serving it through both a relentless remodernizing and a sporadic contemporizing of art. It has two discernible aspects, each of which is perhaps a style in the traditional sense of being a marked change in the continuing practice of art in some significant place that emerges, takes a shape that attracts others to work within its terms and to elaborate them, prevails for a time, and comes to an end. One aspect is the embrace of the rewards and downsides of neoliberal economics, globalizing capital, and neoconservative politics, pursued during the 1980s and since through repeats of twentieth-century avant-garde strategies, yet lacking their political utopianism and theoretic radicalism, above all by artists such as Damien Hirst and the yBa, but also by, for example, Julian Schnabel, Jeff Koons, and many others in the US, as well as by Takashi Murakami and his followers in Japan. In honor of the 1997 exhibition at which this tendency, in its British form, surfaced to predictable consternation among conservatives but also to mainstream acceptance, we might call it "retro-sensationalism." This current has burgeoned alongside the constant efforts of institutions of modern art (now usually designated contemporary art) to rein in the effects of contemporaneity on art, to revive earlier initiatives, to cleave new art to the old modernist impulses and imperatives, and to renovate them. The work of Richard Serra, Gerhard Richter, and Jeff Wall exemplifies different versions of this tendency, which might be called "remodernism." In the work of certain artists, such as Matthew Barney and Cai Guo-Qiang, both aspects come together in a conspicuous consummation, generating an aesthetic of excess that might be tagged (acknowledging its embodiment of what Guy Debord theorized as "the society of the spectacle") the art of the spectacle, or "spectacularism." In contemporary architecture, similar impulses shape the buildings, especially those for the culture industry, designed by Frank Gehry, Santiago Calatrava, and Daniel Libeskind, among others. Mercifully, the work is usually better looking, and more meaningful, than this binge of ugly style terms would imply.

How does art of this kind appear when we pose the question "What is contemporary art now?" To me, this first current comes across as a late modern art that, half-aware of being too easily in tune with the times, continues to pursue the key drivers of modernist art: reflexivity and avant-garde experimentality. In this sense, it is the latest phase in the universal history of art as such. Its bet is that art emergent within the other currents I identify will fade into oblivion, and that it alone will persist as the art remembered by the future. (Each of the currents—like the central figure in Kafka's parable—harbors this assumption about the others.) Yet these hopes are tempered by the realization that today, such values are being held against the grain of the present, with little hope that the times will change favorably, or that art can do much to effect desirable change. This contrasts greatly with the attitudes of many artists in the early twentieth-century avant-gardes, whose critiques of the abuses of capitalism or of the iron cage of modernity were based on what seemed then to be possible, even plausible, utopias. Nostalgia for this failed project is widespread, spurring recurrent interest (not least among contemporary art historians) in moments when it seemed still viable. Transitions toward the contemporary have become of great interest to artists: thus, for example, the heartfelt recycling of Warhol's critical imagery of the early 1960s in the work of artists such as Christian Marclay, and Warhol's later work by Tracey Moffatt.

The second current emerges from the processes of decolonization within what were the fourth, third, and second worlds, including decolonization's effects in what was the first world. This current has not coalesced into an overall art movement, or into two or three broad ones. Rather, the transnational turn has generated a plethora of art shaped by local, national, anticolonial, independent values (diversity, identity, critique). It has enormous international currency through travelers, expatriates, and new markets, but especially biennales. Local and internationalist values are in constant dialogue in this current—at times they are enabling, at others disabling, but always they are ubiquitous. With this situation as raw material, artists such as William Kentridge, Jean-Michel Bruyère, Shirin Neshat, Isaac Julien, Georges Adéagbo, John Mawurndjul, and many others produce work that matches the strongest art of the first current. Postcolonial critique, along with a rejection of spectacle capitalism, also informs the work of several artists based in metropolitan cultural centers. Mark Lombardi, Allan Sekula, Thomas Hirschhorn, Zoe Leonard, Steve McQueen, Aernout

Mik, and Emily Jacir, among many others, have developed practices that critically trace and strikingly display the global movements of the new world disorder between the advanced economies and those connected in multiple ways with them. Other artists base their practices around exploring sustainable relationships with specific environments, both social and natural, within the framework of ecological values. Still others work with electronic, communicative media, examining its conceptual, social, and material structures: in the context of struggles between free, constrained, and commercial access to this media, and its massive colonization by the entertainment industry, artists' responses have developed from expanded cinema and net.art toward immersive environments and explorations of avatar-viuser (visual information user) interactivity.

What kind of answer do we get when we pose the question of the contemporary to the art of this current? To artists who participated in the early phases of decolonization, that is, those being asked for an art that would help forge an independent culture during the nation-building days of the 1960s, a first move was to revive local, traditional imagery and seek to make it contemporary by representing it through formats and styles that were current in Western modern art. Elsewhere, in less severe conditions, for artists seeking to break the binds of cultural provincialism or of centralist ideologies, becoming contemporary meant making art that was as experimental as that emanating from the metropolitan centers. Geopolitical changes in the years around 1989 opened up a degree of access between societies that had been closed for one, and sometimes two, generations. The work of unknown contemporaries became visible, and the vanquished art of earlier avant-gardes became suddenly pertinent to current practice. Frenzied knowledge exchange ensued, and hybrids of all kinds appeared. The desire soon arose to create and disseminate a contemporary art that, toughened by the experiences of postcoloniality, would, as Cuban critic Geraldo Mosquera puts it, remake Western culture, and thus resonate throughout the entire world.[11] The transnational turn during the 1990s and the first decade of the twenty-first century—a shift into transitionality, especially regarding concepts of the nation—has led to the art of the second current becoming predominant on international art circuits, in the proliferating biennales, with profound yet protracted effects at the modern metropolitan centers. It is a paradigm shift in slow motion that matches the world's changing geopolitical and economic orders. From this perspective, contemporary art today is the art of the global South.

The third current I discern is different in kind yet again, being the outcome, largely, of a generational change and the sheer quantity of people attracted to active participation in the image economy. As art, it usually takes the form of quite personal, small-scale, and modest offerings, in marked contrast to the generality of statement and monumentality of scale that has increasingly come to characterize remodernizing, sensationalist, and spectacular art, as well as to the conflicted witnessing that continues to be the goal of most art consequent on the transnational turn. Younger artists certainly draw on elements of the first two tendencies, but with less and less regard for their fading power structures and styles of struggle, and more concern for the interactive potentialities of various material media, virtual communicative networks, and open-ended modes of tangible connectivity. Working collectively, in small groups, in loose associations or individually, these artists seek to arrest the immediate, to grasp the changing nature of time, place, media, and mood today. They make visible our sense that these fundamental, familiar constituents of being are becoming, each day, steadily stranger. They raise questions about the nature of temporality these days, the possibilities of placemaking vis-à-vis dislocation, the meaning of immersion in mediated interactivity, and the fraught exchanges between affect and effect. Within the world's turnings and life's frictions, these artists seek sustainable flows of survival, cooperation, and growth. Attitudes range from the dystopian scenarios favored by Blast Theory and the International Necronautical Society, through the countersurveillance activity of the Center for Land Use Interpretation, to Daniel Joseph Martinez's fervent protests, Paul Chan's symbolic shadow profiles, and the insouciant receptivity of Francis Alÿs to Rivane Neuenschwander's wide-eyed optimism.

The mindset and modes of practice of this generation of artists make clear that they share no single answer to the question of what contemporary art is. Indeed, their radar of operations—that is, their politics—is mostly lower and more lateral, yet also more networked, than the global perspectives that exercise transnational artists. The third current of artists is also indifferent to the generalizations about art itself that remain important for the remodernists. Most of this generation abhors the superficialities of the spectacle, however much they acknowledge that it has permeated all our lives. These artists begin from their experiences of living in the present, so the question for them is less about what *is* contemporary art, and more about which kinds of art might be made now and how might they be made with other kinds close at hand.

Each of the three currents disseminates itself (not entirely, but predominantly) through appropriate—indeed, matching—institutional formats. Remodernist, retro-sensationalist, and spectacularist art are usually found in major public or dedicated private museums, prominent commercial galleries, the auction rooms of the "great houses," and the celebrity collections, largely in or near the centers of economic power that drove modernity. Biennales, along with traveling exhibitions promoting the art of a country or region, have been an ideal venue for postcolonial critique. These have led to the emergence of a string of new, area-specific markets. The widespread art of contemporaneity appears rarely in such venues—although some of it doubtless will, as the institutions adapt for survival, and certain artists make their accommodations—preferring alternative spaces, public temporary displays, the net, zines, and other do-it-yourself-with-friends networks. There is, of course, no exclusive matching of tendency and disseminative format. Just as crossovers between what I am discerning here as currents are frequent at the level of art practice, connections between the formats abound, and artists have come to use them as gateways, more or less according to each format's potential and convenience. The museum, many artists will say today, is just one event site among the many that are now possible. But this mobility is recent and has been hard won. While convergence certainly occurs, temporary alliance—the confluence of differences—is more common.[12]

The same is true of the three currents I have outlined: they are tied to one another, as sibling differences and their friction sparks contemporary art's repetitions as well as its diversity. These are, in a word, antinomies—like all other relationships characteristic of these times. The questionnaire is acute in highlighting the necessarily interrogatory character of contemporary art making, and of interpretative responses to it. Yet the questioning is occurring in modes that, however much they share, have some distinctive qualities. Remodernists, by presenting their works as propositions—bold, singular assertions about what art *should* look like now—remain within the modern project. Trying it on, seeing what you can get away with, what average people will accept being flung in their faces, is the retro in sensationalism. Asking about identity, nationality, selfhood, and otherness, as each of these whirls through volatile transition, is an urgent necessity—at times liberating, at others debilitating—for artists activated by the transnational turn. Doubt-filled gestures, equivocal objects, bemused paradoxes, tentative projections, diffident proposals, or wishful anticipations: this is the tone struck by most younger artists today. What makes all these approaches distinct from the contemporary preoccupations of previous art is that they are addressed—explicitly, although more often implicitly—by each work of art to itself and to its contemporaries, and that, definitively, they are interrogations into the ontology of the present, asking, What does it mean to exist in the conditions of contemporaneity?

contemporary architecture

Spectacle, Crisis, Aftermath

Did architecture—in the myriad forms through which it makes places—become contemporary in the same or similar ways, at around the same times, and in the same places as the other visual arts? This question has yet to receive a clear answer from critics, theorists, and historians of architecture, and architects themselves have reached no consensus. Even the more internal query—when, where, and how did modern architecture become contemporary?—is usually dismissed as misleading, a distraction from the real, concrete challenges at hand. Of course, such questions mean little if answers to them are sought only at the level of style, or within a history of architecture conceived as an autonomous unfolding. Instead, their value is that they can provoke us toward closer, more uncomfortable, but ultimately more illuminating insights into how architects and planners actually respond to the living contexts in which buildings are conceived, built, inhabited, adapted, and, if necessary, demolished.

The authors of the major textbooks on recent architecture routinely omit consideration of these kinds of question, a reluctance they share with some but not all those writing surveys of modern and contemporary art (as I show in the second part of this book). The most comprehensive, carefully planned textbook, *A Global History of Architecture*, by Francis D. K. Ching, Mark Jarzombeck, and Vikramaditya Prakash, moves from essays about built environments in early civilizations, through profiles of the main cities of significant civilizations and definitions of prominent styles, to close studies of key sites, monuments, and buildings, with the time scale shortening, and the number of entries increasing, as the book comes closer to the present. The globality of their approach lies in the unprecedented scope of what they survey, and the aligning of architectures wherever in the world they were made according to simultaneity ("time cuts"). This global approach appears, too, in their effort to be "faithful to the specificities of each individual building while acknowledging that every specific architectural project is embedded in a larger world that affects it directly or indirectly," and to interpret local architectures both on their own terms but also more comparatively than the "post-19th century penchant to see history through the lens of the nation-state."[1] The second edition, published in 2011, culminated in chapters on postmodernism; postmodern museums; the preservation movement; the postmodern non-Western world; and Glen Murcutt's Magney House (1982–84, Bingie Bingie, NSW, Australia). These were followed by a short essay titled "Globalization Takes Command," which notes the effects on architecture of multiple globalizing forces, including high design solutions within the global economy; new urbanism; requests by nongovernmental organizations for shelter for the needy; amateur ready-made structures; and environmental sustainability. The third edition, which came out in 2017, deals with the present in an even more compact way by bringing the postmodern material together, retaining the Magney House as the most recent monument, and concluding with a slightly revised, short chapter on "Globalization Today." In both editions, contemporaneity appears mostly in its ordinary senses, as in the citation of Rem Koolhaas's goal for his Office of Metropolitan Architecture (OMA), to blend "contemporary architecture, urbanism, and cultural analysis," which is glossed with the comment that OMA tries to "address the problems associated with globalization with truly innovative and radical solutions."[2] This book is no doubt the best introduction yet to the broad scope of architecture and built environments all over the world since the beginning of time. Yet even this volume struggles as it approaches the present. In contrast to other visual artists and their interpreters, the history of architecture and the massive accumulation of still-extant buildings, cautious clients, and practical constraints seem to act on architects and their interpreters alike as a logjam, pressurizing the present, overloading it with a still commanding—indeed, an ever-expanding and mostly modern—pastness.

Surprisingly, a logjam is also evident in the work of scholars engaged in debating these issues, including those who adopt consciously critical postures. In the most recent attempt to survey the field from a critical perspective, Elie G. Haddad and David Rifkind's anthology *A Critical History of Contemporary Architecture, 1960–2010*, the first chapter's opening sentence puts my question in these unadorned terms: "When did 'modern' architecture become 'contemporary' architecture?"[3] The title of Peter L. Laurence's chapter points to an equivocal answer: "Modern (or Contemporary) Architecture circa 1959." He rightly discounts as too limited Charles Jencks's famous dating of "the death of modern architecture" to the demolition of Minoru Yamasaki's Pruitt-Igoe housing estate projects on July 15, 1972.[4] As do I, Laurence finds unpersuasive the widely shared default position exemplified by chroniclers such as historian William Curtis, who insists that the ephemerality of postmodernism demonstrates that "the core ideas of modern architecture" continue to be "re-examined but in a new way."[5] Instead, Laurence pinpoints CIAM '59, the 1959 meeting in Otterlo, the Netherlands, at which a younger generation of European and Latin American architects, including Robert and Alison Smithson, John Voeckler, Jacob Bakema, Aldo van Eyck, and Blanche Lemco, disbanded the Congrès Internationaux d'Architecture Moderne (International Congresses of Modern Architecture) or CIAM. CIAM was the event and meetings organization established by Le Corbusier, Siegfried Gideon, and others in 1928, and which included many major international modernists, such as Walter Gropius, Hannes Meyer, and Josep Lluís Sert, as active members. In van Eyck's presentation to the 1959 meeting, he urged his fellow architects and urban planners to abandon their rationalist "Euclidian groove," engage directly with the world's urgent needs, and thus discover "a new architecture—real contemporary architecture."[6]

None of the participants at CIAM '59 envisaged a whole-scale shift to a new paradigm of the same dynamic yet coherent kind as the now-deceased modern movement had been, with its shared functionalist principles, formal styles, preferences for materials, and favored technologies. On the contrary, the architects were recognizing that no such movement existed now, or was likely to in the future. Instead, smaller-scale emphases, such as regionalism (by definition, specific and differential) were sought, as were careful experiments in blending elements of two or more approaches. Thus Ernesto Rogers, defending his and BBPR's mix of Lombardian fortress forms and international modernist design and construction in their concrete structure Torre Velesca, a residential and commercial high rise built in Milan in 1950–57, explained, "To be modern means simply to sense contemporary history within the order of all of history and thus to feel the responsibility of one's own acts not from within the closed barricade of an egoistic manifestation, but as a collaboration that, through one's contribution, augments and enriches the perennial contemporaneity of the possible formal combinations of universal relationship."[7] Heterogeneity within an overall, yet increasingly embattled—indeed, crisis-ridden—modernity was the rule during this period, as Jean-Luis Cohen has persuasively suggested.[8] In Cohen's most recent retrospective, he argues that crisis has prevailed in architectural thinking and practice since 1950, producing logjams everywhere:

> Thus, by the mid-1950s, the worldwide triumph of modernism was nearly total, and most conservative circles within the profession had been forced to adapt to the new situation and adopt the tropes of a language they had previously rejected. Paradoxically, it was the victors who became assailed by doubts about the universality of the principles guiding their actions, about their relationship with history and with the city. The unfolding of architectural ideas and projects, far from resembling the course of a long quiet river, came to evoke instead a stream disturbed everywhere by logjams. Crisis followed crisis, undermining professional institutions and schools, and leading to an increasingly rapid succession of opposing discursive constructions. Rather than an exception, crisis would become the permanent condition of architectural culture and practice in the decades to follow.[9]

The subtlety of discourse that emerged from this situation is explored in fascinating detail by Anthony Vidler, who writes of four men—Emil Kaufmann, Colin Rowe, Reyner Banham, and Manfredo Tafuri—who, in distinct but convergent ways, set out to shape a coherent historical narrative about the history and currency of modernism, explicitly to provide accounts that contemporary architects could use in their practice.[10] Their ideas continued to resonate during the rise of architectural theory in the 1970s and 1980s.

Taking the broadest view of architectural discourse since then, however, reveals that heterogeneity within modernity has continued as the default big picture of how architecture subsists in its worlds. This has not encouraged depth of insight or subtlety of thought. Haddad and Rifkind title their introduction to *A Critical History of Contemporary Architecture* "Modernism and Beyond: The Pluralism of Contemporary Architectures." They begin with this observation: "The second half of the twentieth century witnessed an unprecedented pluralism in architecture, following the spread of modern architecture around the world, in various interpretations, and the subsequent wave of movements that came in its wake. No previous period had seen an equivalent diversity of architectural production, nor a comparable volume of building construction on such a wide scale."[11] Their brief scan of architectural discourse during this period finds that this spread remains tied to modernism:

> The attraction of the new characterizes much of what has been produced under the label of "contemporary" architecture, which in Jamesonian terms may be nothing more than the revival of the "modern" under new guises. This re-emergence of a new "Post-Modern" Modernism, consciously markets itself through the techniques of "shock," making it possible for emerging economic centers to instantly place themselves as equal partners on the global map of the new capitalist order. Yet in our view, this remains a modified or hybrid version of Modernism, stripped of any social or political objectives.[12]

While chapters in their volume profile developments in postwar architecture in eastern Europe, Finland, Africa, Iran, West Asia, Southeast Asia, India, China, Japan, New Zealand, and Australia, Haddad and Rifkind nonetheless remain unapologetic for their emphasis on European developments, claiming that it is justified

> by the variety of approaches and problematics that architects in Europe have explored in our times, which manifests itself particularly in the growth of three important "traditions" within the European context: the Dutch, the Spanish–Portuguese and the Swiss; which have exerted a significant influence on architecture around the world. The impact of these three traditions has led to a variety of approaches in contemporary architecture, ranging from a concern with local traditions, to a continuing faith in a technological utopia, which has become more feasible through the dissemination of digital tools of production.[13]

While this is doubtless true as far as it goes, it does not go far when what we need is a robustly contemporary, global, and critical historical accounting. The editors of *ARCH+* are more vigorous in introducing the articles in their fiftieth anniversary edition:

Architectural discourse in recent decades becomes visible in a sequence of crisis after crisis, optimistic restart after optimistic restart. We touch on the failure of functionalism, which triggered a return to vernacular and historical built forms; the oil shock, which brought a sudden end to the utopias of the 1960s; the crisis of the modern city, which stirred the populace into action and put questions of participation onto the agenda; postmodernism, which ended by toothlessly playing with architectural citation; deconstructivism, which demoted architecture to a mere linguistic game; globalization, which led to the sprouting of megacities in boom economies around the world; and finally, digitalization, currently in the process of stripping architects of authorship.[14]

The difference from Haddad and Rifkind, however, is mostly in rhetorical tone and remains superficial. If only Anthony Vidler would continue the narrative of architectural thinkers that he began for the postwar period in *Histories of the Immediate Present*! Whose work would we expect to see examined in such a history? Among the most obvious names that come to mind: Fredric Jameson on postmodernity; Kenneth Frampton on critical regionalism; Robert Venturi on complexity and contradiction; Jencks on postmodern architecture; Vidler on warped space; Peter Eisenman on conceptual architecture; Rem Koolhaas on junkspace and the generic city; Teddy Cruz on borders and crossings; Mike Davis on slums; Giuliana Bruno on intersections with artistic practices.[15] That most of these ideas were prompted by the situation in the 1980s and 1990s is remarkable. Where are the voices of a younger generation? We will hear from some of them later in this chapter, and in the next.

The one feature common to the critical accounts we have just surveyed is a sense that architectural practice and thought have been in crisis for decades, not least because they are, necessarily, responses to social crises that have, it seems to all concerned, increased in number and intensity during that time to such an extent that they have come to dominate perceptions of the present. One crisis that receives rather less attention than seems warranted in discussions of what makes architecture contemporary is that embodied in, and precipitated by, the events of September 11, 2001. These events had architectural structures at their literal and symbolic center. Were they a flashpoint that accelerated certain processes through which architecture was already becoming contemporary, while acting as a brake on others? Let us freeze-frame that moment, and then slowly unspool its fallout, so that we might form a better picture of how architectural practice has been thought since then, and how that thinking takes place today.

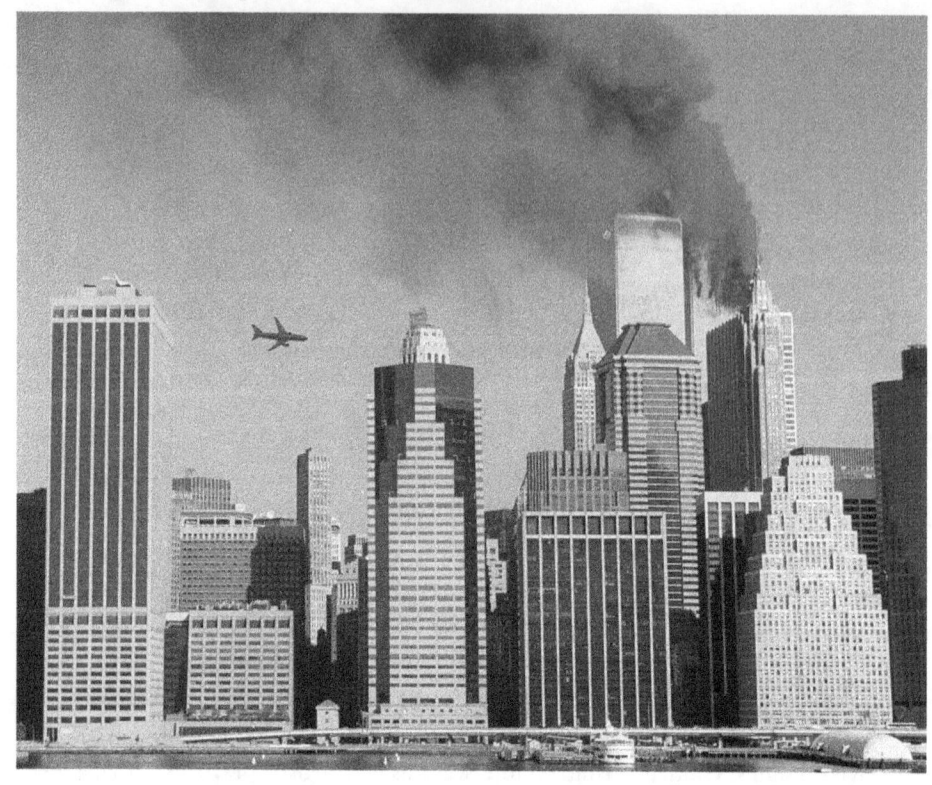

Figure 3.1

Kelly Guenther, *September 11*, 2001, photograph, *New York Times*, September 12, 2001. © Kelly Guenther/The New York Times/Redux.

WORLDS COLLIDE

The opening words of my book *The Architecture of Aftermath* zoom in on the moments the planes hit the Twin Towers on 9/11:

> If one were to slow down a videotape of the first plane approaching then hitting the north tower of World Trade Center, New York, at 8:46 AM on September 11, 2001, and then zoom in to the instants of impact, one would see the word "American" slide, letter by letter, into oblivion. In

Kelly Guenther's *New York Times* photograph of the second plane as it hurtled through the skyscrapers of the Financial District towards the south tower, the blue and gray colours made it, unmistakably, a United Airlines flight. As images that draw us to imagine the deaths of actual human beings, these pictures were, and remain, deeply affecting. They record, among much else, an act of spectacular terrorism—an action of one group of humans against another within a war that is conducted at both symbolic and literal levels—a raid that was, and remains, profoundly disturbing. The profundity it disturbed was expressed, through perversely exact metaphor, in the violent obliteration of the word "UNITED."[16]

The main message sent by that attack was that the disposition of power in the world had just changed, perhaps irredeemably and forever, from Western-style modernity setting the global agenda to no one formation, no matter how powerful, capable of setting agendas that would be widely followed.[17] Yet this should not have been the surprise that it was. For several years there had been indications of profound realignments between the great formations of modernity in all spheres, and of the emergence of distinctively contemporary currents. The 9/11 moment was a flashpoint of both civilizational and region-to-region conflict, and governments of all kinds soon used it as a justification to declare open-ended states of emergency and as an umbrella for imposing repressive agendas in many countries, not least the United States under the dystopian slogan "war on terror." Intractable, irresolvable "events" of this kind have come to seem almost normal in the state of aftermath: the wars in Afghanistan, Iraq, and Syria; the arrival then retreat of a US imperium; the uncertainty of European polity, internally and externally; the implosive fallout of the second world and the reemergence of authoritarianism and kleptocracy within it; on the ex-Soviet peripheries, the suddenness of unreal states; continuing conflicts in the Middle East, central Europe, Africa, and the Pacific; the deadly inadequacy of both tribalism and modernization as models for decolonization in Africa; the crisis of post–World War II international institutions as political and economic mediators (UN, IMF, World Bank); the revival and subsequent corruption of leftist governments in South America; the accelerating concentration of wealth in few countries, and within those countries, further concentration in the hands of very few; the forced coexistence of multiple economies and cultures within singular state formations, notably the combination of rampant capitalism and state authoritarianism in China; ecological time bombs everywhere, and the looming threat of societal collapse; the ubiquity and diversification of specular culture; the concentration and narrowing of media, in contrast to the spread of internet; contradictions within and between regulated and coercive economies and deregulated and criminal ones; the proliferation of protest movements and alternative networks; the retreat toward bunker architecture at the centers of swelling cosmopolises matched by a proliferation of ingenious, adaptive architecture in their border zones; and the emergence of distinctively different models of appropriate artistic practice, as manifested in recurrent mega-exhibitions, such as Documenta and the Venice Biennale, which switch like a metronome between direct engagement with contemporary challenges and feel-good aesthetics.

How might we make sense of this multilayered complexity? To what extent does it complicate and, perhaps, exceed the internal contradictions that drove modernity in all its aspects? What are the implications for architecture, design, and planning practiced in modernity's aftermath?

FROM BEIRUT TO MANHATTAN

The 9/11 attacks were directed, Osama bin Laden revealed in an interview published in the *Guardian Weekly*, November 12–15, 2001, toward "America's Icons of Military and Economic Power." In his October 29, 2004, videotape intervention into the US presidential election, he detailed his source of inspiration:

> The events that made a direct impression on me were during and after 1982, when America allowed the Israelis to invade Lebanon with the help of its third fleet. They started bombing, killing, and wounding many, while others fled in terror. I still remember those distressing scenes: blood, torn limbs, women and children massacred. All over the place, homes were being destroyed and tower blocks were collapsing, while bombs rained down mercilessly on their homes. . . . As I looked on those destroyed towers in Lebanon, it occurred to me to punish the oppressor in kind by destroying towers in America, so that it would have taste of its own medicine and would be prevented from killing our women and children. On that day I became sure that oppression and intentional murder of innocent women and children is a deliberate American policy. It seemed then that "freedom" and "democracy" are actually just terror, just as resistance is labelled "terrorism" and "reaction."

He went on to mention the impact of US sanctions against Iraq imposed by "Bush Sr.," and the vast bombing campaign "Bush Jr." launched, as he put it, "to remove a former collaborator, and install a new one who will help steal Iraq's oil, as well as commit other atrocities."[18] There is no denying the facts here, however different might be our conclusions about how to act in their light, nor the power and impact of bin Laden's rhetoric, timing, and media savvy regarding his intended audiences. In the months after September 11, 2001, and for many years subsequently, it matched in its effectiveness that which the Bush administration—massively more resource rich—mustered in defense of its own policies and actions. Thus, *Time* magazine, on May 26, 2003, devoted its cover to an image of serried ranks of people in Middle Eastern dress holding bin Laden masks before their faces. The caption: "Why the War on Terror Will Never End." US Secretary of Defense Donald Rumsfeld, in a February 17, 2006, speech to the Council on Foreign Relations, whined: "Our federal government is really only beginning to adapt its operations to the twenty-first century. Today we're engaged in the first war in history—unconventional and irregular as it may be—in an era of e-mails, blogs, cell phones, BlackBerrys, Instant Messaging, digital cameras, a global Internet with no inhibitions, handheld video cameras, talk radio, 24-hour news broadcasts, satellite television. There's never been a war in this environment before."[19]

The fallout from these actions continued: in July 2006, Israel responded to a Hezbollah rocket attack with a full-scale invasion of Lebanon. Among the many anticipations of the resultant destruction is the work of New York–based Lebanese artist Walid Raad, who since 1999 has exposed the insanities of political violence in his home country through a series of projects undertaken by a fictive artists' cooperative, the Atlas Group—for example, the video "We Can Make Rain But No One Came to Ask" (2005).[20]

ARCHITECTURE IN THE IMAGE WARS

As an event, that which occurred on September 11, 2001, has been much inflated, its repercussions exaggerated, its real effects smothered in hyperbole. But the deeper shifts, of which it is indeed one of many morbid symptoms, cannot be denied. Responding in 2006 to questions from Hal Foster of *October*, the San Francisco–based group Retort gave an acute formulation of the general issues at stake:

> Everything about the basic furnishing of human oppression and misery has remained unchanged in the last 150 years—except that the machinery has been speeded up, and various ameliorations painted in on top. . . .

Nevertheless we do think that there is something distinctive about the Old New of the past four years. *Afflicted Powers* is an attempt to describe it. Very roughly, what seems to us unprecedented is the starkness—the extremity—of the confrontation between New Oldness and Old Newness. No one, surely, came close to anticipating that the opening of the twenty-first century would be structured around a battle between two such virulently reactionary forms of world power (or will to world power), and that both sides would see so clearly that the battle is now to be fought by *both* bombs (crude attempts at recolonization, old-time resistance struggles, crowds waving the latest version of the Little Red Book) and images.[21]

To this list of what constitutes bombs, we can add airplanes, explosives wrapped around a suicide bomber, videotapes of all sorts, online postings, and so on, a list of denotations that will soon merge into visual images of many sorts, as they call up settings in which images of the work of bombs—instantly and globally disseminated—become vital to their effectiveness.

Retort remobilizes Guy Debord's famous analysis of spectacle society, his condemnation of capital's commodification of all relations, its colonization of everyday life through saturation with the imagery of unfulfillable desire.[22] Retort is rightly skeptical of generalization and imprecision, but we might ask, Does Debord's conception of the spectacle encompass everything we need to know about the image in the present situation? Might not those of us with some sense of how visual images work find ways to add something to what Retort rightly poses as "the political question of the years to come." Against the fundamentalists, against the supine compromise all around, they ask, "What *other* imagery, what other rhetoric, what other set of descriptions might be possible—ones that find form for the horror and emptiness of the modern, but *hold out no promise of Going Back?*"[23]

Many artworks being made now, many actions undertaken, and a few structures being conceived do propose such *other* imagery. I want to suggest that, in architecture, iconic spectacle and its specters might have reached their historical apogee. Certainly, structures of this type continue to be built: versions of the New York skyline dot financial hubs around the world (London, Hong Kong, Shenzen, Pudong, Abu Dhabi, Dubai, Doha, Kuwait City, Mysore, etc.). Yet these structures are also becoming shining, heavy, instantly sterile monuments to an oil- and finance-based age that is passing even as it asserts its purchase on the future. They are signposts, perhaps, along the road of an endless aftermath. In contrast, a different architecture—a diverse architecture of difference—struggles into being. How is this dialectic playing out? Let us look first at the architectural face of what seemed an infinitely expansionist, unstoppable globalizing regime, and then at the kinds of architecture that have arisen from an equally, if not more powerful set of worldwide forces, those of decolonization.

REMODERNISTS, OR THE LAST OF THE LATE MODERNS

The icons attacked on 9/11 happened to be buildings. A fatal convergence of architecture and terrorism occurred on that day. All buildings, built and unbuilt, suddenly attracted a shadow play of darting forces, a chimera of the possibility that they could come under attack, could become target architecture. Yet the buildings attacked on September 11, 2001, were well entrenched within the economy of images, which I call the "iconomy." Having become key symbols within the later, twentieth-century society of the spectacle—icons with the capacity to stand for crucial values—they were actively traded within it. Each of them iconized entire sectors of US society, great formations of US nationality. But they were more than symbols, and the attacks were not (as some commentators rushed to say) a spectacular confirmation of popular postmodern analyses of our times in which appearances had triumphed over reality. Rather, the actual buildings were central, tangible embodiments of the complex functions they housed, the most visible point of concentration of the complex array of powers associated with them. They were literal and figurative portals—gateways to, in turn, the US economy, the US military, and US governance. The degree to which symbol and reality are embedded in each other is evident in the seismographic impact of the attacks on each of these sectors, and in the differences of register between these impacts— differences that seem related to the degree of effectiveness of each attack. From this point of view, the special—indeed, spectacular, but also specular—role of architecture in the iconomy of later modernity becomes plain to see.[24]

Architecture is also of relevance here because the conjunction of architecture and symbolism had become, during the 1990s, indicative of both the flashiest surfaces and some of the deepest currents of contemporaneity as a global condition. Of all the arts, architecture was the most socially prominent, the best looking, a hot story in the media—in a word, the buzz. Frank Gehry's Guggenheim Museum, Bilbao (1997), was the apogee of this quality: a building defined above all by its striking and infinitely repeated image as an iconotype of high culture (figure 3.2). The final ascendency of the image in architecture

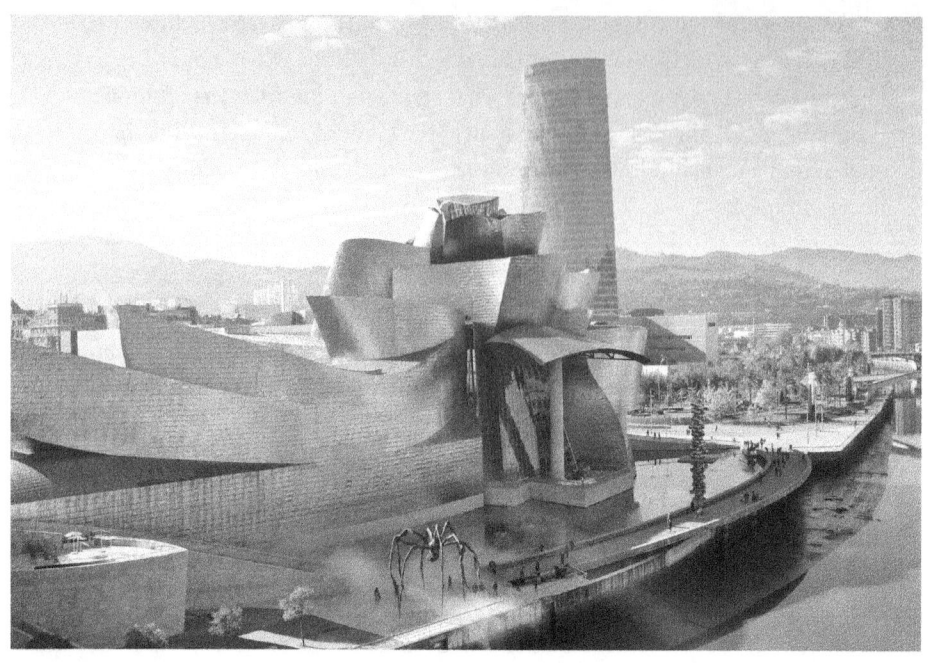

Figure 3.2

Frank Gehry, Guggenheim Museum, Bilbao, 1997. Photo by
Naotake Murayama, CC BY 2.0.

can be understood as a deep reversal of the early modernist premise, as the prioritizing of form over function. Exciting clusters of shapes, seemingly arbitrary conjunctions, a vast variety of materials, hidden structures, wild plans, multiple historical allusions, manifest technological symbolism—all this amounted to a much more complex array of form, but it was form nonetheless.

I distinguish five other tendencies within this current. All of them prioritized form—in the complex sense just indicated—over function. True to the "post" in the sense of "after" in postmodernism, all are inheritances from one aspect or another of the two most prominent European modernisms of the early twentieth century—Bauhaus functionalism and expressionism—inheritances that they transform, not least by combining elements from both. These contemporary tendencies are, in this sense, equivalent to what I understand to be the remodernist and spectacularist tendencies that constitute the first current in contemporary art. Gehry's Bilbao drew both Bauhaus functionalism and expressionism into a spectacular concoction. Richard Meier's "Past-Modernism"—at, for example, the Getty Center, Los Angeles (1997)—was more inclined toward evoking the appearance of constructivist rationality but was equally the servant of globalizing spectacularity. Another tendency within this current, the technological featurism practiced most dramatically by Santiago Calatrava—in structures such as the Quadracci Entrance Pavilion to the Milwaukee Art Museum (1997–2001) and the Tenerife Auditorium, Santa Cruz, Canary Islands (1997–2003)—is a reprise of the achievement of the early twentieth-century engineer architects, and, like Gehry at Bilbao and in Los Angeles, of the quasi-organic imagery and symbolic flourishes of the 1950s (the outstanding instance being the Sydney Opera House). This third approach makes a structure's engineering into the primary point of the spectacle. A more subtle variant on this tendency is what Sarah Deyong calls "high tech," which continues the modern ideals of being true to materials, honoring the construction method, and valuing technological innovation for the social good, but in updated and more subtle ways, against the grain of postmodern exposés of "the fiction of function." She has in mind the Centre Pompidou (1971–77), by Richard Rogers and Renzo Piano; the work of the Renzo Piano Building Workshop on the De Menil Museum, Houston (1981–86); Foster and Partners at the Renault Distribution Centre, Swindon (1980–82); and Foster and Associates' Hong Kong and Shanghai Bank (1979–86).[25] Paralleling these four tendencies were the "tiger towers" in Kuala Lumpur, Shenzhen, Pudong, Taipei, Dubai, and elsewhere. Structures such as Cesar Pelli's Petronas Towers, Kuala Lumpur, are inflections of the Western skyscraper with local filigrees, produced by both Western and local architects, that serve as the command centers of "Asian values" capitalism.

These, then, were the primary, and most highly resolved, resources available to contemporary architects active in the corporate centers of neoliberal capitalism when faced with the irruption of contemporaneity on September 11, 2001. There was, however, one other viable tendency: the possibilities represented by Libeskind's Jewish Museum, Berlin (1989–99), outstanding among those few efforts by contemporary architects to cope with modernity's deepest contradictions—in this case, the fact that the city of Berlin was able, in 1942, to imagine itself without its Jews.[26] Modernism's ghost, a kind of antimodernism, one that haunts its utopianism, is the specter of those whose brutal elimination was the cost of fulfilling its dreams. A similar depth of critique is rare in recent architecture: it may be found in the symbolic war architectures of Lebbeus Woods, for example, in his Berlin Free Zone Project (1990), Zagreb Free Zone (1991), and Terrain Project (1998–2000).[27] This depth may also be found in such uncanny prefigurations as *Exodus, or the Voluntary Prisoners of Architecture* (figure 3.3). Devised by Rem Koolhaas, Elia Zenghelis, Madelon Vriesendorp, and Zoe Zenghelis in 1972, the work was an extraordinary fantasy of modernity gone seductively dystopic. In the piece, the architects imagine north-central London slashed by a zone of architectural forms so beguiling that the city's inhabitants clamor to enter it, leaving the old city a distant spectacle, lapsing slowly into ruination, while inside the zone, creative architectural forms are generated daily. Within the zone is an area of respite, one that looks uncannily like the garden-style plots that some Londoners (among others) still maintain. The brilliant text that accompanies each frame ends as follows: "Time has been suppressed. Nothing ever happens here, yet the air is heavy with exhilaration."[28]

SPECTERS

The reaction of architects to September 11, 2001, was the same as that of most others: shock, horror, mourning, then slowly rebuilding. But "rebuilding" does not capture the depth of the challenges that the event made visible. These went to the question of building at all, to the unconscious of architecture, to the nether regions of any kind of construction, to some strange, spectral shadows, well away from the glare of spectacle. The degree of destruction at the site, the necessity to clear away most of it before building could commence, made literal the sense of having to begin again, but from a deep division: between replicating what was lost and inventing another kind of structure to meet the now hugely complex and conflicted calls on the space. The design needed to perpetuate what had been lost at the site—the lives, feelings, hierarchies, powers, and interests of those who had worked there (and their surviving relatives), those who owned it, had visited, or had used it as a landmark. At the same time, the design needed to encompass in a real way the new world that had, on that day, become unmistakable: a world in which otherness was now and would forever be always and already present, a condition in which the contemporaneity of difference had become fundamental.

On December 18, 2002, the Lower Manhattan Development Authority unveiled the "land use designs" of the groups of architects, planners, artists, and so forth that it had chosen to rethink Ground Zero.[29] Among the outstanding firms active in corporate architecture at the time, their efforts were a profile of both impact and possibility for their subfield. The five tendencies of late modern

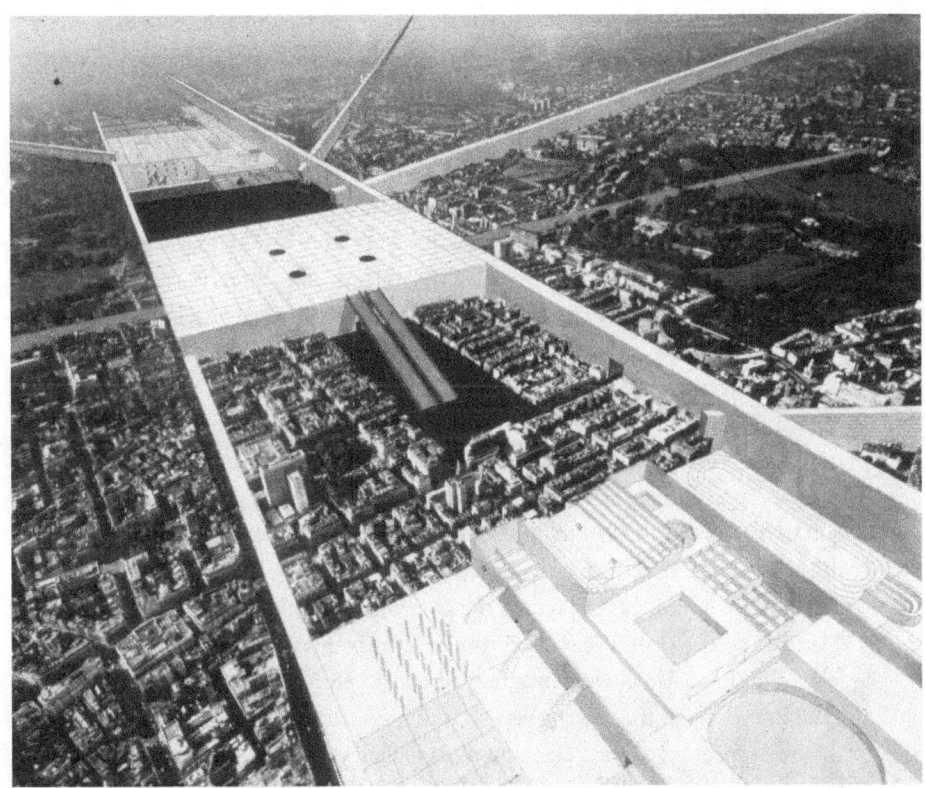

Figure 3.3

Rem Koolhaas, Elia Zenghelis, Madelon Vriesendorp, and Zoe
Zenghelis, *Exodus, or the Voluntary Prisoners of Architecture*,
1972, cut-and-pasted paper, watercolor, ink, gouache, colored
pencil, on silver gelatin print, 40.6 × 50.5 cm. Collection
Museum of Modern Art, New York. Gift of Patricia Phelps de
Cisneros, Takeo Ohbayashi Purchase Fund, and Susan de Menial
Purchase Fund. © OMA (Office of Modern Architecture).

spectacle architecture identified above were very much in evidence. Extraordinary technology dominated most submissions. Without exception, each design attempted to generate an instant iconotype. The Twin Towers appeared in most of the proposals, as specters. Yet several recent innovations and speculations as to how to live differently in dense conurbations were also advanced, albeit figuratively—sky cities, interstitial parks, roaming ecologies, free-form communities. All these are key ideas for the building of future dwellings, although they have mostly found expression in places well outside the centers of capitalism.

Gehry-style complexity infused the United Architects proposal (perhaps attributable to the input of the Greg Lynn FORM firm), and it pervaded the organic, staged "vertical city" of the group led by modernist firm Skidmore, Owings, and Merrill. The assertive geometry of the Meier group's design would have imposed on New York a past-modernism more implacable than it had ever absorbed. The thought of its gridded gates marching through the rest of Manhattan is a neo-Corbusian nightmare. Recycling the past was even more specific in Peterson/Littenberg's Garden for New York, a quiet place of recreation surrounded by buildings that repeat the comforting ordinariness of deco period Manhattan. Foster and Associates' project was two crisscrossed "kissing" paralleloids, the lost Twin Towers imagined as benign, gently related forms, as extruded glass Brâncuşis, as the towers were so fondly misremembered by so many after their disappearance. Yet their economic efficiency was well disguised with ecological inclusions. Small wonder that this design received, by far, the most votes in public polling. Yet the computer graphic of the building pasted in to the existing skyline shows it, instantly, to be a ghost of the original WTC, albeit crystal prismed for the New Age, and to be as out of place as its predecessor had been.

Among the three ideas advanced by Think was a pair of open steel-frame towers, with various functions strung within them, such as a world cultural center, a performing arts space, a conference center, and a 9/11 museum. The last took the form of a white shape twisted against itself. Inserted into the towers, and strung between them, was what looked like the wreckage of an airplane: indeed, it was positioned in the skeletons at the points and angles of impact of the attacking planes. The net result was a curious picturing of September 11, 2001, partway through its cinematic unfolding, as if the event were freeze-framed at a moment when the antimodernist attackers could be seen to have dashed themselves fruitlessly against the might of modernist structure and flexibility, that impossible moment—so deeply desired ever since by the attacked—before time resumed its rush and drew the towers down into the self-destruction that now seems natural to them.

Another proposal, by Libeskind Studio, building on the Jewish Museum experience, began from a set of antispectacular premises (the slurry wall inspiration) and yet did not avoid spectacle in its proposed design, however much it dispersed and diverted its elements. Libeskind worked against iconotypy for most of his design, but he succumbed to the pull of Manhattanist literalism by inserting a "vertical world garden" that would jut from the skyline up 1,776 feet, a sword-like echo of the Statue of Liberty. For a time, still shaken by the attacks, the Development Authority was sufficiently moved by these designs to appoint Libeskind the master planner of the site. His role was soon eroded by the interests of the dominant real estate developer, Larry Silverstein, and by the narrower architectural imagination of David Childs of Skidmore Owings, and Merrill.

An interrogatory spirit appeared among the first design responses to September 11, 2001, for example, in the proposal that the abandoned New York Stock Exchange building be transformed into a set of spaces for information gathering and public discussion, devoted, above all, to arriving at recognition of the root causes of such events, and of equitable ways of addressing them.[30] For a few years, this spirit continued to inform plans for a cultural center on the Ground Zero site, as it did the programming of the Drawing Center, a contemporary art museum located there. After relatives of the victims and others expressed concern that such places might countenance viewpoints other than outright condemnation of terrorism, and as the influence of Libeskind waned, Governor George Pataki pulled the cultural center, and the director of the Drawing Center resigned.

In September 2006, just before the fifth anniversary of the attacks, designs were released for three further tower blocks on the edges of the site. Norman Foster, Richard Rogers, and Fumihiko Maki each produced variations on a conventional theme. In contrast to the challenges taken up by many of the 2002 designs, they were, in the view of *New York Times* critic Nicolai Ouroussoff, about "forgetting." He elaborated: "Conservative and coolly corporate, they could be imagined in just about any Western capital, paralleling the effacement of history in the remade, blatantly commercial Potsdamer Platz in Berlin or La Défense, the incongruous office-tower district just outside Paris."[31] In retrospect, we can see that the capitalist fantasia of the "tiger towers," already nostalgic, continues to reverberate in the centers of Western commerce, not least in the skyscrapers of the Ground Zero minicity, above all in the dull, compromised Freedom Tower by David Childs. Armor plated on its lower floors, a slab of Yamasaki's WTC quoted just above, then a rectangle rising floor after floor, shaved at its sides ("torqued," in the PR parlance), it is capped with a stripped-down monument to nothing in particular. Libeskind's highly connotative imagery

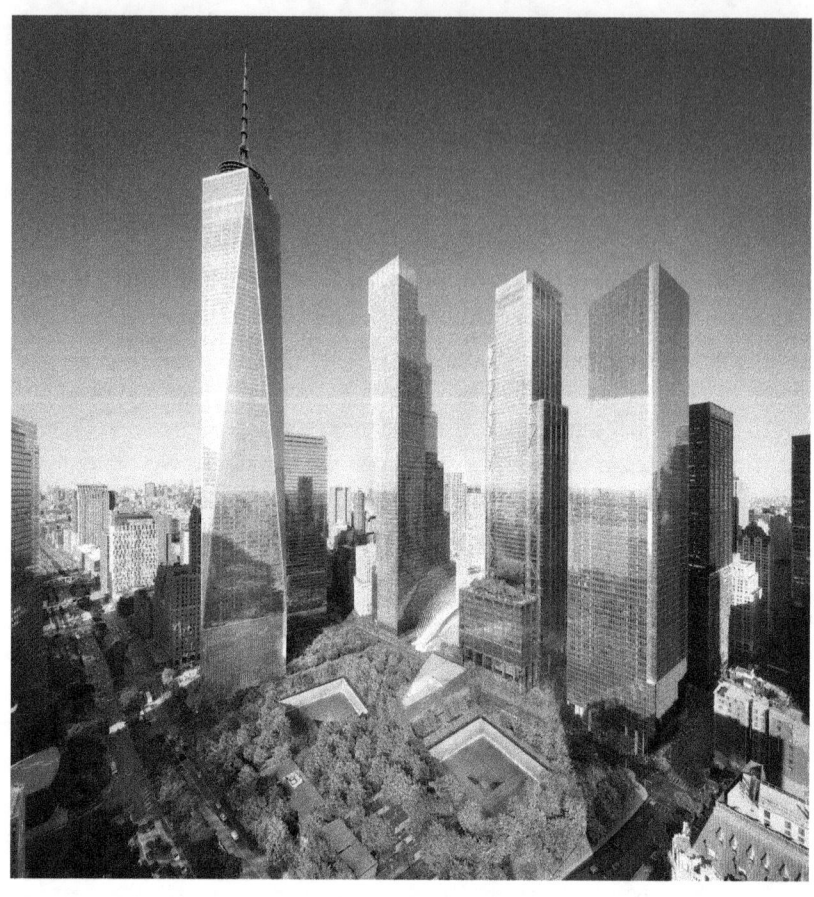

Figure 3.4

World Trade Center, general view, 2017. © DBOX. Image courtesy of DBOX/Little, Brown, and Company.

has entirely evaporated. Meanwhile, Calatrava's transport hub, completed in
2016, squats like an albino hedgehog at the feet of these mild-mannered, glassy,
wall-eyed monsters (figure 3.4).[32]

Despite these bets on the longevity of spectacle, bunker architecture has
become another norm throughout the main citadels of the West and the
East, although a great—yet too often specious—effort is being made to make

many of these structures into "green towers."[33] At least some ecological principles are pursued in, for example, the proposal by UN Studios for a library for
New Orleans following the disastrous flood caused by hurricane Katrina in
April 2005. The absurd heights to which this clash of values led is, perhaps, nowhere more evident than in a $145 million private residential tower on the hills
outside Mumbai, India (figure 3.5), designed in 2004 by Sculpture in the Environment (SITE). A palatial residence—four thousand square meters, including a helipad—is located atop a huge column that also supports six subsidiary
levels, each of which is devoted to a distinct compound (hangar, film studio,
forest, amphitheater, acropolis, temple). All are, the architects claim, "ecologi-
cally sound." Bollywood meets the Hanging Gardens of Babylon. Intended for
"a well-known personality," the entire structure is isolated, guarded, protected,
and solid enough at its base to "withstand possible bombs."[34] This is a parody
of the gated community, stacked up into a tower, maximizing its views, and
exposed for all to see its magnificence—a more blatant example of hubris
parading itself as a target is difficult to imagine.

DWELLING WITHIN DIFFERENCE

Against the continuing insistence on late modernist, corporatist, and consumerist values in institutional and domestic architecture in the headquarters of
global economies, other kinds of architecture are emergent throughout the
world. They are grounded in both critique and hope, because their architectural outcomes usually evolve from a detailed process of contextual questioning. They differ mostly in scale, in their lesser reliance on iconic language, in
their distance from the demands of neoliberalism, and in being more directly
responsive to contemporary necessities, such as environmental sustainability,
the creation of habitat, the problems of swelling cities, and the special needs of
Indigenous peoples and the displaced multitudes. If much of the architecture
I have discussed to this point parallels the first current in the contemporary
visual arts, do the projects and practices I consider next amount to the architectural equivalent of the second current, that of transnational transitionality?
Do they also contain seeds of a third current, that of a fully contemporaneous,
worldly architecture that is beginning to respond to the needs of worldly, virtual, and planetary habitation?

    As I suggest in chapter 2, the second current in contemporary art is driven,
at its base, by the constellation of energies known as decolonization, the rejection of all aspects of colonialism by peoples who have been subject to its

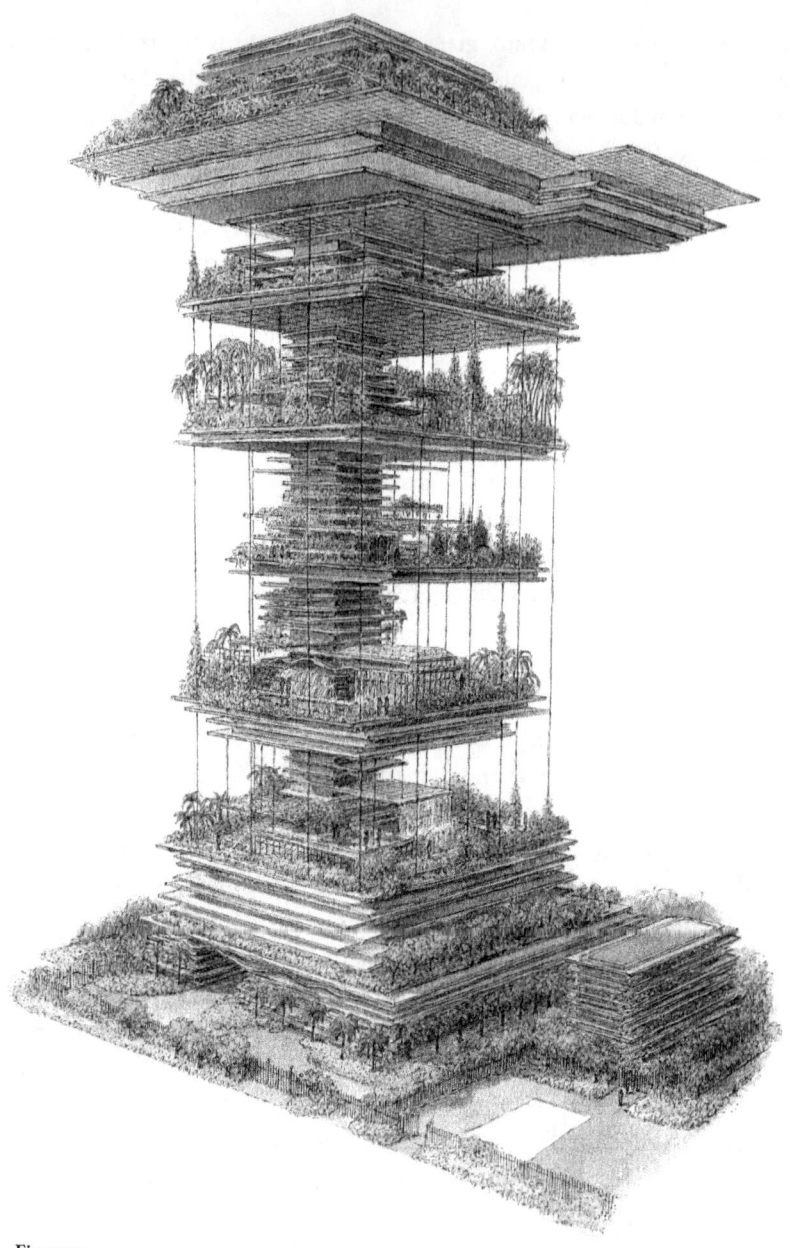

Figure 3.5

SITE, Antilia "Vertiscape" private residential tower—vertical public park spaces and private residence, Mumbai, India, 2003. Tower drawing by J. Wines showing the multilayered Hindu gardens and cable support system. Image courtesy of SITE.

rule, and the envisioning of local autonomy in a postcolonial world. While this became an irresistible historical force throughout the world from the 1960s onward, relative independence from colonial rule had been achieved in many parts of Latin America during the nineteenth century, where modernization was led by local elites who were closely connected with European economies, knowledge, and cultures, including architectural practice and discourse. During the twentieth century, the contribution of Latin American architects to the modern movement was considerable, as is obvious in the work of Oscar Niemeyer, Roberto Burle Marx, Juan O'Gorman, Luis Barragán, up to and including Lina Bo Bardi and Paulo Mendes da Rocha. CIAM '59 may well have been a moment when the French and German architects who dominated the first generation realized that the next would be led, or at least enlivened, by architects from elsewhere in Europe and from the rest of the world. This may have been a small step toward a genuinely contemporary architecture, but it remained steeped in the power structures of Western discourse and called out for postcolonial critique. Esra Arcan has cogently spelled out the necessity, but also the limits, of such a critique in our contemporary situation:

Globalization has shifted architects' attention to the world at large. Even though many architects have worked outside their home countries (or adopted lands) in the past, transnational practice has become a common routine in the architectural office today, due to the new legal arrangements, international trade agreements and advanced communication technologies. Architectural services are now designated by the World Trade Organization as globally tradable commodities. Yet, more often than not, architects find themselves unprepared for such a task due to the relative lack of theoretical sophistication and historical knowledge about architecture beyond European and North American countries. Moreover, as common as the words globalization, multinational and cross-cultural might be, the future remains unclear, since the forces of history are acting in contrary directions about opening and closing borders. Postcolonial theories aspire for an architecture better equipped for a global future, so that globalization does not unfold as a new form of imperial imagination.[35]

While we can say, now, that globalization is in retreat as a world economic order, the disarray it is leaving in its wake, and the persistence of many kinds of shock doctrine capitalism throughout the world, mean that postcolonial critique is even more urgent as a component of contemporary critical theory. Arcan recalls path-finding studies such as Edward Said's exposure of Orientalist attitudes toward the "non-Western Other," and Gayatri Chakravorty Spivak's exploration of the limits on subaltern speech. Arcan correctly identifies poststructuralist approaches as key to postcolonial theory worthy of the name, and usefully distinguishes between two perspectives within it toward the systemically inequitable operations of power in play, even as decolonization takes place. The first draws on Jacques Derrida's argument that, in such situations, pluralistic notions of diversity are traps favoring the status quo, and that incommensurable difference (radical, untranslatable alterity) must therefore be insisted on as a response to keep open future possibilities for the less powerful. This leaves both parties locked in a state of constantly marking their differentiation. Clear architectural expressions of this tensioned negativity are found in Jean Nouvel's Arab World Institute, Paris (1981–87), and Charles Correa's Jawahar Kala Kendra, Jaipur (1986–91). Recognizing that this fast becomes debilitating, Arcan suggests a "humanist postcolonialism," recognizing that, "in a globalizing world, the viable alternative is to improve the notion of universality from below and construct a new non-Eurocentric humanism, without skipping the poststructuralist challenge."[36]

The sheer volume of population growth, and the disorder engendered by economic inequality, bad governance, warfare, and natural disaster, are obliging architects to overcome historical hierarchies. For example, connecting peoples who live in neighborhoods segregated by class or culture to general public services such as transport systems has become crucial in the world's ever-growing cosmopolises. In Latin America, several innovative projects unify divided cities via cable car access, with architects then building civic facilities, such as public parks and libraries, at pivotal points along such networks. Among these projects are the Favela-Barrio project, by Jorge Mario Jauregui and collaborators (Rio de Janeiro); Metro Cable (Medellín); TransMilenio (Bogotá); the Ligeirinho (Curitiba); and Metro Cable by Urban-Think Tank (San Agustín, Caracas; figure 3.6).[37] Housing the increasing populations of such cities is also a worldwide need. Vicente Guallart proposes a Sharing Tower for Valencia, within a sociopolis, a campus of 2,500 residential units on an eleven-acre area at the edge of the city. The key principle is that by sharing a range of resources between two to eight people, greater useful surface area is released for private use, achieving ratios of 45 square meters of individual space to 75 shared, thus enabling the enjoyment of 120 for each person.[38] Another interesting tendency is the proposal of add-on structures, small-scale additions to large buildings, and transportable

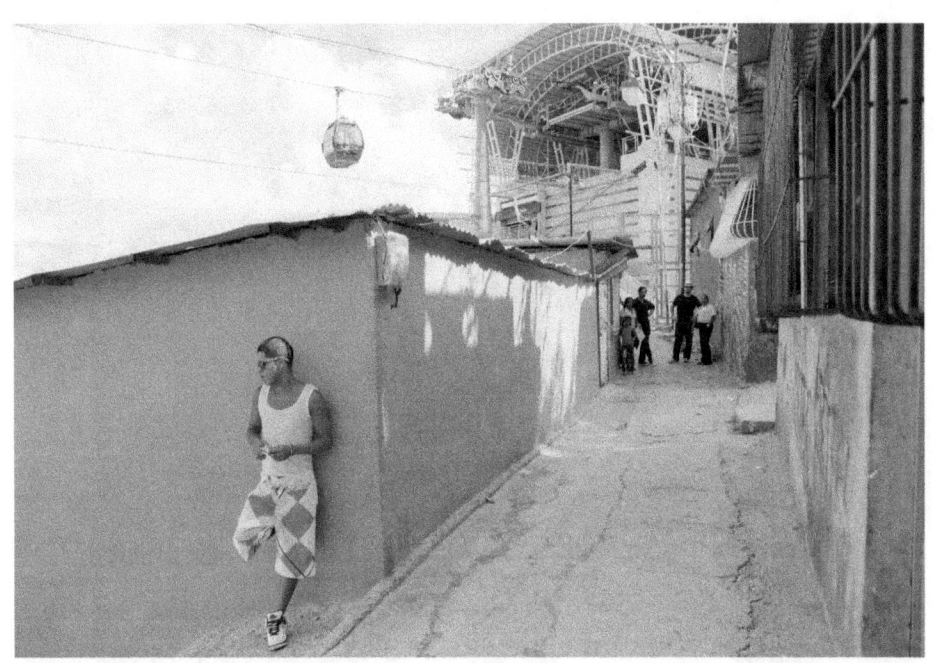

Figure 3.6

Urban-Think Tank, Metro Cable, San Agustín, Caracas, 2013.
© ETH Zurich U-TT and Daniel Schwartz.

attachments. Examples include Werner Asslinger's Loftcube, Berlin (2003), and Stefan Eberstadt's Rucksack House, Leipzig and Cologne (2004–5).[39] Related to these are such temporary structures as Shigeru Ban's Nomadic Museum, erected on a Hudson River pier for four months in 2005. A massive edifice, 205 meters long, its columns were large paper tubes, and its walls were shipping containers stacked four stories high in alternating solids and voids. Stretched membranes were used for roofing, and the whole was coated with waterproof sealant. Commissioned to display a set of egregious photographs unlikely to be shown in a conventional museum, and tied to the exhibition's traveling display, the museum was less valuable in itself than for its suggestiveness as to similar structures for various purposes relevant to shifting populations.[40]

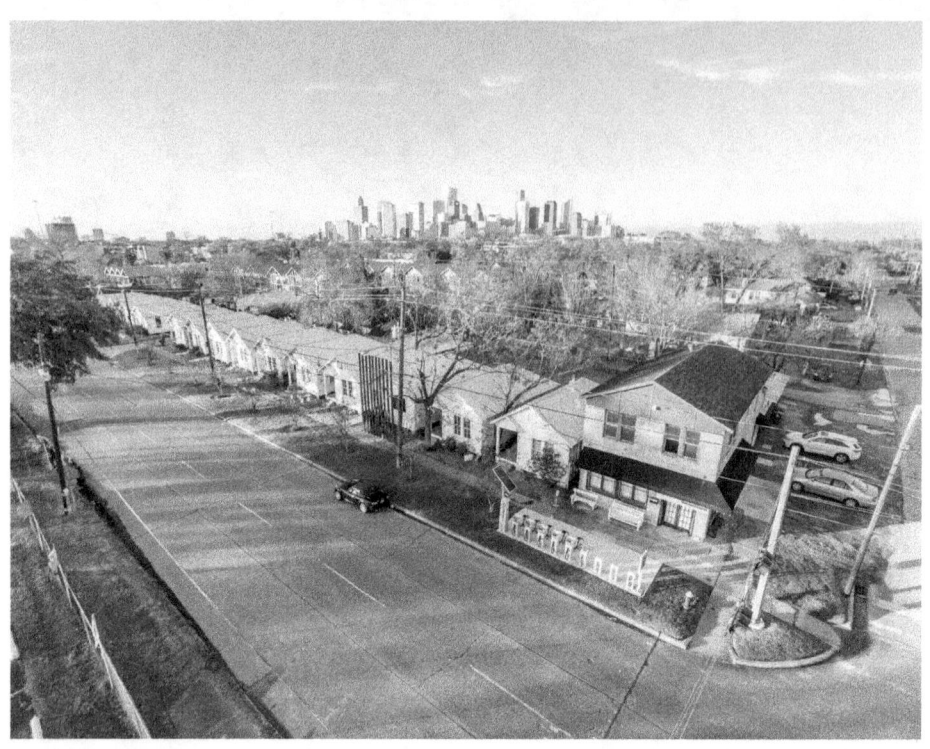

Figure 3.7

Rick Lowe, Project Row Houses, Houston, since 1993. Aerial
view of Project Row Houses during Round 41, curated by Ryan
N. Dennis. Image courtesy of Project Row Houses. Photo by
Peter Molick.

Since 1993, Project Row Houses has been bringing together artists in residencies and members of the African American community of Houston's Third
Ward to renovate the low-income "shotgun" houses in the area (figure 3.7). A
public art initiative led by Rick Lowe, the project has been a major factor in
transforming the neighborhood and, the artist believes, in modeling a mode of
urban renewal applicable to elsewhere in the city.[41] Inspired by Lowe, Theaster
Gates—potter, artist, and, in his own words, hustler—has been developing the
Dorchester Projects since 2008 in the South Side neighborhood of Chicago

where he lives. Gates's own artworks usually deploy materials from the demolitions of buildings he has bought, shaping them into hybrid sculptures/furniture or wall hangings/installations. Interlaced with these are performances by the Chicago jazz group the Black Monks of Mississippi. His *Twelve Ballads for Huguenot House* concentrated these elements on a historical structure in downtown Kassel during dOCUMENTA (13), creating an intense, deeply integrative installation.[42] A disparate set of renovated houses, apartment blocks, and businesses (including an ex-bank), the Dorchester Projects is home to large collections of books, LP records, and a café; it offers classes in crafts, stages performances and concerts, and hosts meetings and parties—in sum, it operates as a cultural center for the poor and crime-ridden African American neighborhood.[43]

Innovatory thinking in third and fourth world contexts about adaptation to degraded environments has not escaped those with responsibility for designing solutions to areas left fallow by the globalization of industrial production within developed countries. A striking example is the High Line, a 2.5-kilometer abandoned railway line elevated above the streets of Manhattan's Lower West Side, converted by architects Diller Scofidio + Renfro and landscape architect James Corner Field Operations into a public park. Opened in 2009, it links a popular restaurant area to the Chelsea art district and subsequently was extended to reach the Hudson Yards. It has become a well-known recreation space for New Yorkers, and a prime tourist attraction.[44] Less positive outcomes have been the displacement of local residents and recreations (it was a well-known gay beat), and accelerated gentrification of the areas through which it passes. Art hotels and iconic buildings by "starchitects" dot its length, capped by the move of the Whitney Museum of American Art from its midtown location to a new building, by Renzo Piano, which opened in 2015 right next to the High Line's southern entrance.[45]

PRACTICAL REASONING

Increasingly, architects seek to respond to the chaos of contemporaneous differencing by offering practical remedies to the poor, the marginalized, the migrant, the refugee, the endlessly mobile itinerant worker, and the homeless. Elemental, founded by architect Alejandro Aravenna and engineer Andres Iacobelli to address issues of social housing in Chile, devised an ingenious solution to the inadequate financing of public housing for the poor. At the Quinta Monroy project, in Iquique, Elemental built "half a good house" for the cost allocated to each family, providing essentials such as kitchens, bathrooms, and a basic frame

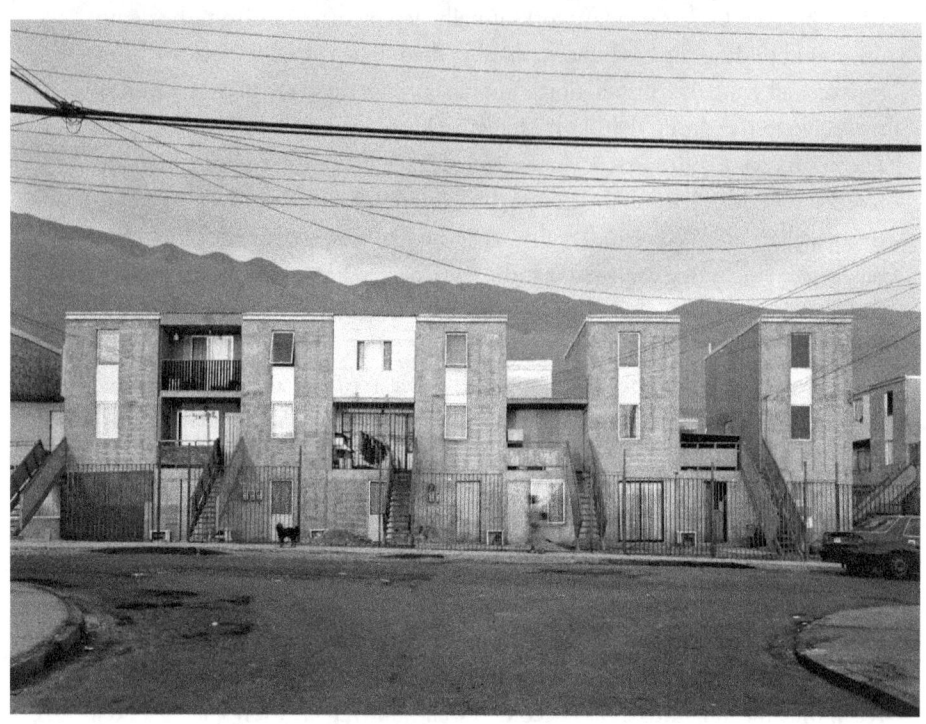

Figure 3.8

Elemental (Alejandro Aravenna and Andres Iacobelli), Quinta
Monroy project, Iquique, Chile, 2003–4. Image courtesy of
Estudio Palma.

while leaving the rest of the forty-square-meter structure open for residents to
complete with whatever materials they could find, according to their own taste,
and using their own savings (figure 3.8). In 2016, as curator of the Venice Architecture Biennale, Aravenna invited participating architects to "Report from the
Front," that is, present a project that successfully investigated challenges such as
housing shortage, migration, urban slums, waste, or natural disasters.[46]

"Incremental housing" for the world's poor and displaced has been a challenge to architects for centuries. The numbers of people in these situations
are increasing and, despite overall improvements, will remain in the billions
for the foreseeable future. After the 1995 earthquake in Kobe, Japan, Shigeru

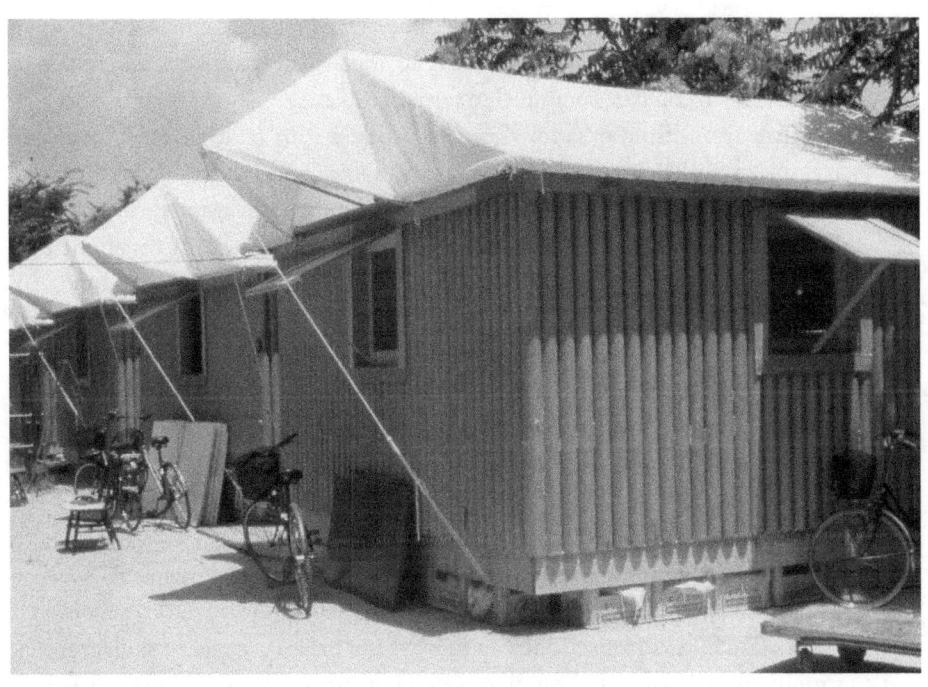

Figure 3.9

Shigeru Ban, Paper Log House, Kobe, Japan, 1995. Image
© Takanobu Sakuma.

Ban offered ingenious designs for temporary houses and a community center
using cardboard tubes. His Paper Log House design was adapted successfully
in Turkey and India after earthquakes struck those countries in 1999 and 2001,
respectively (figure 3.9). Images of Rwandan refugees struggling to survive with
little more than plastic sheeting inspired him to devise a framework of cardboard tubes to turn sheeting into tents, which the United Nations High Commissioner for Refugees (UNHCR) supplied to the refugees. Ban continued as
a consultant to the UNHCR until 1999. Parallel efforts occur throughout the
world. Designed in 2000 as a prototype for use in the Australian outback by
Aboriginal people, Peter Myers's Knockabout Walkabout house is transportable on a truck anywhere, can be entirely assembled with a power drill, and
is livable on or off the grid.[47] A similar spirit is evident in the Portable House

proposed by the Los Angeles–based Office of Mobile Design in 2003, an "eco-sensitive and economic" alternative to available housing stock and trailer homes, which could be combined to form Ecovilles.[48]

Since 2001, Estudio Teddy Cruz has worked with multiple local organizations in San Diego and Tijuana to create frameworks that enable local residents to create living places, often by occupying public spaces and by recycling building materials from overprovisioned sectors (figure 3.10). Cross-border art and architecture are important ways of registering place in the new conditions of transience, exclusion, and surveillance.[49] Since 1992, Nader Khalili, founder of the Cal-Earth Institute in Hesperia, California, has developed several sandbag shelter prototypes. Stability is secured by layers of sandbags stacked in various circular or elliptical shapes, with barbed wire in between to prevent movement. Prototypes have been built in Iran, Mexico, Thailand, Siberia, and Chile, and they have been used by the UNHCR since 1995 for temporary shelters.[50]

Of parallel importance is the work of globally networked people's organizations such as Shack/Slumdwellers International.[51] Global Studio, an affiliation of architects from Sydney and elsewhere, brings a range of skills from various distant sources to bear on specific, extreme problems of housing.[52] For similar reasons, Shigeru Ban established the Voluntary Architects' Network, a nongovernmental organization focused on shelter needs in poor countries. Architects without Frontiers, based in Melbourne, is devoted to offering direct assistance with shelter and planning needs in crisis situations.[53] The needs of peoples subject to the disorders of contemporary life are great. One particular area crying out for commitment is that of indigeneity: architecture by and for Indigenous peoples may be the exchange that brings out architecture's latent indigeneity, one that reaches back to the first dwellings. *In Gunyah, Goondie and the Wurley: The Aboriginal Architecture of Australia*, Paul Memmott traces what he calls "ethno-architecture" in the dwelling practices of Indigenous Australians, including those who today wish to continue traditional lifestyles. He notes that in the provision of housing to Indigenous Australians by federal, state, and local governments, three emphases have been prominent: cultural design built around continuing domiciliary practices, design to encourage environmental health (in the work of Paul Pholeros, for example), and housing as a process of community building and sustenance.[54] While few architectural firms are fully Indigenous in personnel and ethos—the Merrima (Bright Star) Aboriginal Design Unit in the New South Wales Department of Public Works, and Melbourne-based Greenaway Architects among the rare exceptions—a

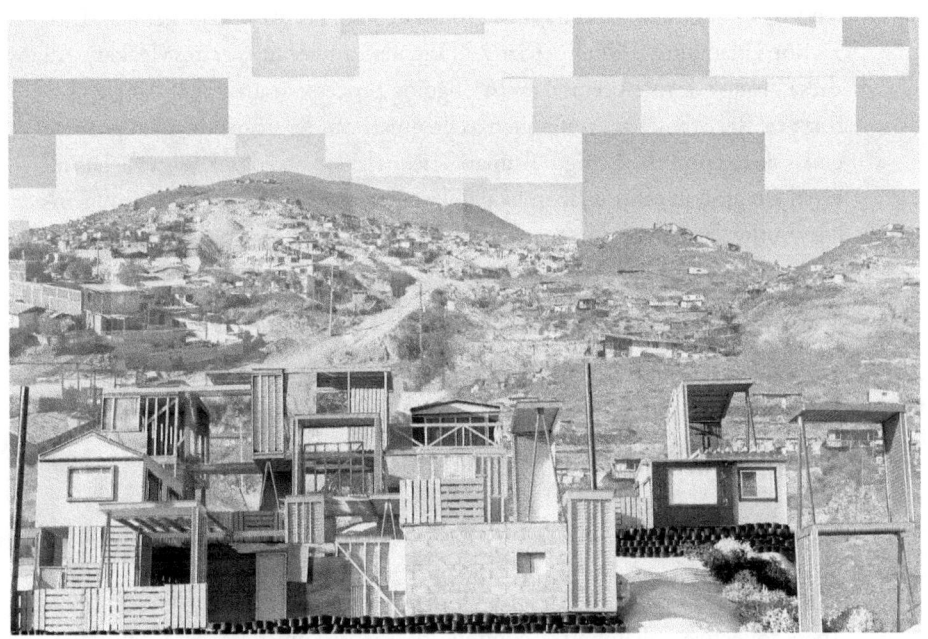

Figure 3.10

Estudio Teddy Cruz and Fonna Forman, Manufactured Sites, San
Diego/Tijuana, 2006. © Estudio Teddy Cruz + Fonna Forman.

small but growing number of Indigenous graduates from Australian universities are establishing individual practices.

Green architecture is a requirement in a world seemingly destined for ecological crisis and collapse if current practices continue. Again, a range of solutions is currently on offer, as well as many precedents, at least on the symbolic
level, not least the Houses of Parliament, Canberra (1984–88) and the Fu-
kuoka Prefectural International Hall (1990). At one end of the spectrum might
be Greg Lynn FORM's 2003 design for the Ark of the World Museum, San
Jose, Costa Rica, a storage, research, exhibition, and education facility for the
world's biodiversity. The literalism with which its structure embodies an image
of its content has generated an effect bordering on the bizarre.[55] More concrete
responses require artists to work directly with communities, from the poor
ones served by artists such as Navjot Altaf (Central India) and René Francisco

Rodriguez (Havana), and by such groups as Ala Plástica (Buenos Aires), Park Fiction (Hamburg), WochenKlausur (Vienna), and Huit Facettes (Dakar). All these groups devote themselves to ongoing processes rather than single prototypes. Recurrent art events such as biennials can be shaped to such positive ends: since 2000 the Echigo-Tsumari Triennale, led by Fram Kitagawa, has revived a region in central Japan by regularly inviting artists to work with members of the community on sustainable ecological projects. A different strategy is for artists to form temporary groups to address critical issues, for example, the Agua-Wasser project, Mexico City (2005). Another is for architects, poets, sculptors, and students to work together to create experimental dwellings in one area over a long period, as resources become available and the inspiration strikes. Thus the structures constituting the Cuidad Abierta, which names itself "Utopia in Progress," built since 1970 by the Cooperativa Amereida on a 270-hectare seaside park near Valparaiso, Chile.[56]

NETWORK CULTURES

These collective, collaborative, community-oriented practices share many qualities with visual artists active in the third, and most recently emergent, current in contemporary art. Indeed, as I show in the next chapter, these practices not only overlap but also share a close identity with the work of certain artists and groups of artists. What of the network culture shared by most active third current artists? This, too, has become pervasive within architectural practice, first as a means to more traditional ends, as in the use of Computer Aided Three dimensional Interactive Application (CATIA) by architects such as Frank Gehry during the 1990s, and then, increasingly, as the basis for the entire process, its outcomes, and its ongoing use.

Since the early 1990s, NOX/Lars Spuybroek has explored computer-generated architectural imagery and interactive electronic artworks, bringing them together in projects such as the *Son-O-House* (figure 3.11), at Son en Breugel, the Netherlands (2000–2003). Its forms are derived from the movements of bodies through space that are rendered by cut strips (in the manner of the aleatory elements in Marcel Duchamp's *The Large Glass* [1923]); the structure is then wired such that the sounds it produces are modified by its users moving through it.[57] Using Xfrog software, which consists of "botanic, L-system algorithms" to compute biological simulations to grow plants and landscapes for laboratory tests, Dennis Dollens designed a digitally grown tower on the Lower East Side of Manhattan.[58] Marcos Novak has developed a series of structures, commissioned by a Spanish

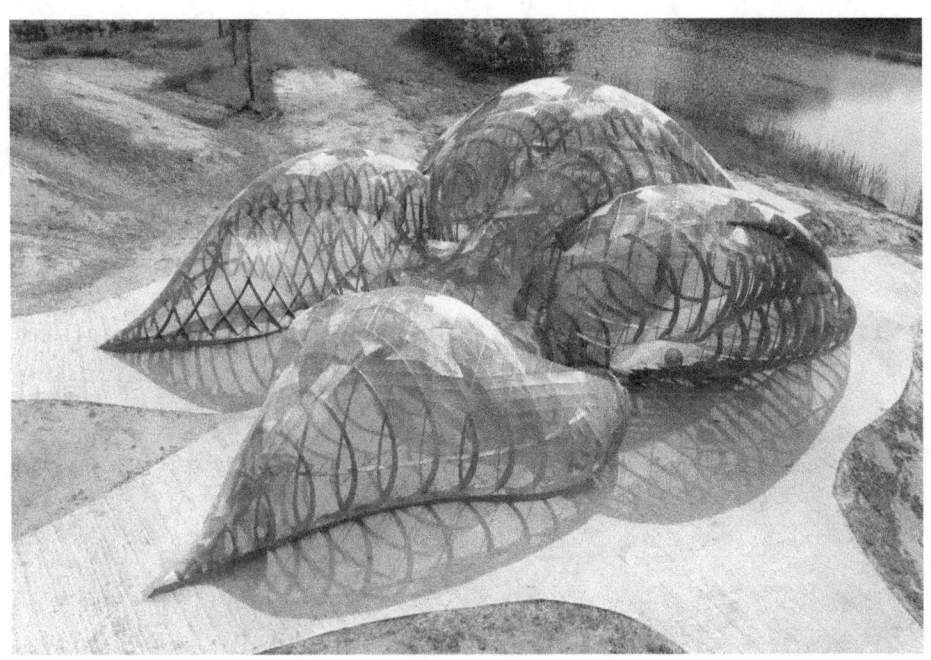

Figure 3.11

NOX/Lars Spuybroek, *Son-O-House*, 2000–2003. Image
courtesy of Lars Spuybroek.

hotel group, derived from scans of his own brain, titled AlloCortex/AlloNeuro.[59]
Topological design might be seen as a variant of this current. French architects
Jakob and MacFarlane designed the H House in Propriano, Corsica, in 2003,
by deriving its forms from the hilly topography of its site. An interlocked set
of cellular rooms flow and spread down a series of stepped levels, generating a
variegated exterior of walls, windows, and entrances.[60] François Roche evolved
the Green Gorgon design for a proposed museum of modern art in Lausanne
by deriving the essential flow of forms, and an extraordinary vegetal cladding,
from the water and vegetation at the lakeside site.[61]

In a globalized era, digital technologies are most intensely concentrated in
financial markets, so architects following the money is no surprise. In 1999 Asymptote designed a Virtual New York Stock Exchange for the NYSE that was

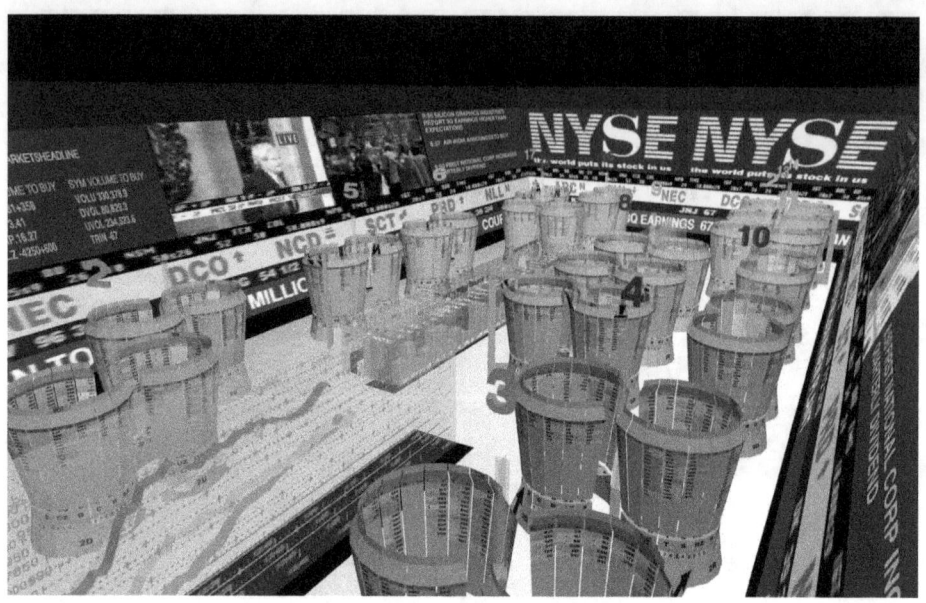

Figure 3.12

Asymptote, Virtual New York Stock Exchange, NYSE, 1999.
Image courtesy of Asymptote.

implemented in just after the turn of this century as a three-dimensional virtual trading floor used via interfaces and monitors on the actual trading floor (figure 3.12). At the same time, the company designed a Guggenheim Virtual Museum for the Solomon R. Guggenheim Museum, intended to complement the actual Guggenheim museums at sites around the world. In 2015 Asymptote developed a conceptual design for a Museum of the Present Future for the State Hermitage Museum, St. Petersburg, Russia, to be known as the Hermitage Modern Contemporary Museum. In Hani Rashid's essay on these projects, he argues,

> Architecture ultimately needs to evolve away from what we have traditionally thought of as pristine galleries and agnostic spaces for "display." The process of rethinking "museum" architecture today must take into consideration the impact of all different types of new and on-the-horizon

technologies where VR and AR are but two of many profound ways of thinking and seeing the world that are already affecting the production and experience of art. Add to these voice control, visual and sensory response systems, artificial intelligence, robotics, and machine learning, and the changes become ever more nuanced and complex, with the potential to radically shift museum culture itself. Our notions of what is thought of and experienced as "real" increasingly results [*sic*] from a profound shift in the interface between technology and space. The architecture of the hyperreal meets these radical shifts in technology, perception, and experience head on.[62]

As these remarks suggest, technological innovation in architecture is a fast-growing tendency, although it is still focused on posing useful questions and in no position to announce confident, integrated solutions. In fact, the editors of *Fabricate 2017*—Achim Menges, Bob Sheil, Ruairi Glynn, and Marilena Skavara—argue that "the multifaceted cultures of computational design and digital fabrication can no longer be generalized as 'digital architecture,'" because their boundaries are "being questioned by cyber-physical productions systems and challenged by new forms of man-machine interaction."[63] A May 2017 conference on "Post-Internet Cities" at the Museum of Art, Architecture and Technology in Lisbon asked for reflection on this emergent situation:

In a scenario of constant hybridisation and connectivity, physical distances have shortened, giving rise to ubiquitous and parallel cities, mapped by interactive and collaborative systems. This process explains how the main political protest movements of the last decade appeared online first and then only afterwards occupied the symbolic places of our cities. But are these new socio-cultural dynamics calling into question the role of the built public environment? To what extent should the city be understood as an overlapping between the material reality and a collective imagination that has been reinvented on the social media?[64]

The conference led to the posting of a series of essays on the e-flux Architecture website and an editorial on "Digital Realism," which ended with this call:

All over the world, cities have been, are, and will continue to be modernizing themselves with digital infrastructures, as much as they are able, willing, and feel the need to. Yet digital infrastructures have been, are, and will continue to be modernizing the city itself, as much as they can, on their terms. The temples of commodity that Benjamin identified in the Parisian arcades have long-since moved out of the city and onto the internet, leaving something like a void in the capital of cities that has been quick to be filled in and fought over by start-up ventures. Solutions are the commodity of today, and we know the ones we have to be insufficient in addressing the challenges we face. What is needed is a different way of seeing; a different language for questioning.[65]

Marisa Olsen, coiner of the term "post-internet art" (by which she meant artworks made in any available medium created after having spent hours on the internet, or while being online), gives an acute profile of the challenging conditions within which she and her colleagues are trying to arrive at this different way of seeing, to imagine "post-internet architecture":

> If there is any reason at all to have a word like "postinternet" (and at this point, it really could be any word), it is to have a placeholder to discuss the situation of network conditions. Feeling unable to unplug (due to the forces of capital, the infrastructural reach of the grid, family expectations, FOMO, etc.) is but one of many symptoms of network culture, which may also include the perversion of the notion of "transparency" in the slippage between surveillance and software lingo; the dismissal of failure and the abject along with a conflation of "disruption" and experimentation; a naiveté as to the physicality of infrastructures and the spatial logic of the net; the ongoing veiling of physical, intellectual, and affective labor involved in the production and maintenance of network culture and its participants; an outdated assumption that technological determinism is somehow teleological; and finally two that relate most to our purposes here: an overarching internet centrism, a la Jaron Lanier's "cybernetic totalism" that casts an anthropomorphic lens on the net privileging a singularity in which nature and technology are fusing in a misguided assumption that technology and the net will solve all of our emotional problems; and lastly a kind of eschatological cynicism of the doomedness of the network (and hence human cultures) that has led to the misnomer (and subsequent criticism) that 'post-internet' refers to the death of the internet, a fallacious techno-apocalypse.[66]

These words take us back to the beginning of this chapter, to the sense of crisis pervasive in the thinking of architectural theorists, and in the accounts of architectural historians. The events of 9/11, itself an epochal crisis, embroiled the upper reaches of the architectural profession, to which they responded, mostly, by reaffirming—indeed, elaborating—the corporate spectacularism that preceded and in some ways induced the attacks. Another, major current of contemporary practice has devoted itself to the urgent task of finding specific, local, workable architectural solutions to the crises of housing, amenity, planning, and circulation occurring on a massive scale throughout the world: an architecture for the 90 percent. Against enormous odds, and with few utopian illusions, this remains nevertheless an optimistic enterprise. The remarks of the architects, planners, designers, theorists, artists, and activists cited in this chapter signal the emergence of a third current consciousness, which gets that crisis and aftermath will continue to predominate in contemporary conditions—in the real world, in virtual realities, and in the imaginative worlds that operate within and between them.

It is precisely in this conjunction that Forensic Architecture (FA) works. Led by Eyal Weizman, and based at Goldsmiths, University of London, FA is a collective "research agency" consisting of architects, artists, filmmakers and theorists that, since 2010, has undertaken "advanced architectural and media research on behalf of international prosecutors, human rights organizations and political and environmental justice groups."[67] Recognizing that contemporary conflict increasingly takes place in urban areas, and that the ubiquitous surveillance of cities has made them "media-rich environments," FA uses such data, as well as orthodox and innovative architectural modeling techniques to create virtual models of secret sites, such as those used for torture by various governments, and of events denied or suppressed by governments and military agencies, such as the huge quantity of drone strikes carried out in recent decades by the United States in Pakistan. FA also knows that the presentation of "fake news" and manipulated versions of such materials on the internet, in broadcast media and in courts has led to doubts about the veracity of this now ubiquitous media landscape itself, and is careful to present its findings with a full reveal of how it arrived at them and why the presentation is taking the specific form that it does. In the drone strikes investigation, for example, analysis of massive amounts of digital data was grounded in "the unassuming work of building surveyors—the careful and systematic analysis of the structural and infrastructural conditions of a building."[68] A striking example is "The Architecture of Hellfire Romeo: Drone Strike in Miranshah, Pakistan, 2012." This project was requested by the UN Special Rapporteur for Counter Terrorism and Human Rights, and was done in concert with the Bureau for Investigative Journalism and Situ Research.[69]

An early intervention involved tracking the responses of the military sea and aircraft off the coast of Libya in the early months of 2011, as a NATO coalition enforced an arms embargo, and, FA showed, left a boatload of refugees to die on the open waters.[70] Other investigations are inherently cooperative, for example, FA has an open invitation to those with video and other information about the fire that consumed Grenfell Tower in London on June 14, 2017 to submit materials to their site, where it is collated to create a detailed visual and audio timeline of what occurred outside and inside the building on that day, when sub-standard external cladding spread a fire throughout the structure, causing many deaths.[71] FA's approach is unapologetically partisan and activist. As Weizman puts it, "Seen from the perspective of forensic architecture, investigating this material geology of contemporary conflict still requires a building surveyor, but a building surveyor of a new kind: the survey can no longer be immediate and haptic; the trained surveyor's eye and the notepads on which his/her observations are recorded are replaced by remote-sensing technologies that augment the aesthetic sensibility of material formations: images of localized forms of damage that have occurred are extended by mathematical algorithms to model the damage that might occur in the future."[72]

In this complex, shifting and often dangerous contemporaneity, architects and those in related fields find their shifting sense of place. Whichever current is mainly ours, the others are always present. For all of us, crisis and aftermath are our constant companions. All three currents in contemporary architecture owe much to their intersection with the currents of contemporary art. It is to this intersection that I turn in the next chapter.

4

concurrence

Art, Design, Architecture

Whether the three currents hypothesis will be as useful in mapping broad-scale developments in contemporary architecture as it is in contemporary art, time will tell. But there can be no doubt about the density, variety, and intensity of the convergences between architecture and the other visual arts in recent decades. Of course, connections between them go back to the origins of human dwelling, the first stirrings of human imagining and of social communication. Their integration was a fundamental ideal of the modern movement, famously at the Bauhaus, but also in the daily creativity of masters such as Le Corbusier. Interactions between art, design, and architecture have inflected all aspects of their contemporaneity, from the simplest of coincidences between these arts to their most definitive products. These have not, however, been random occurrences. Some recurrent, persistent patterns can be distinguished. In this chapter, I map four of these: architecture that incorporates aspects of contemporary art into its design aesthetic; art that becomes architecture or architectural design; architectural practices that borrow strategies from contemporary art as well as art that uses architectural motifs; and art that acts as architectural theory, or as speculation about the history of architecture.

The most obvious point of convergence occurs in the building type devoted to art, to its storage, interpretation, and display—that is, the museum of art.[1] While the exteriors of early modern palace museums signaled their history, and the history of much of their contents, as having previously been in the homes and possession of the aristocracy, the modernist museum pursued the principle that the visible forms of a structure should follow directly from the efficient fulfillment of its internal functions, that is, the unimpeded display of modernist art that was committed to the same kind of transparent materiality. The postmodern museum, in contrast, collapsed both types into an image: a container immediately readable as being the same kind of thing as its content—the museum building as itself a work of art. In the famous metaphor of Robert Venturi, Denise Scott-Brown, and Stephen Izenour, it was a duck, not a decorated shed.[2] Frank Gehry's art museums, from the Guggenheim Museum at Bilbao (figure 3.2) to the Luis Vuitton Museum, Paris, and the yet-to-be-built Guggenheim at Abu Dhabi, have become the iconic examples of this architecture/art convergence. Although Gehry himself routinely denies seeing himself as an artist, others, including many artists, have no hesitation in characterizing his buildings as works of art, and paradigmatically contemporary ones at that.[3] Hal Foster is skeptical: "Is this designer of metallic museums and curvy concert halls, luxury homes and flashy corporate headquarters truly Our Greatest Living Artist?"[4] He argues that Gehry, in his art museums and in works such as his *Fish Sculpture*, Barcelona (1989–92), devised a mode that collapses the duck into a decorated shed, with the result that his buildings cannot be read as truly sculptural: their viewing breaks up into seemingly disconnected fronts and backs; interiors cannot be read from exteriors, and vice versa.[5] Foster is applying modernist criteria to a postmodern, or more accurately, a remodernist architect. Throughout Gehry's career, he has drawn on compositional modes, specific forms, and attitudinal connotations in the works of artists of preceding generations, such as Alexander Calder, and from his artist contemporaries, such as the sculptors Mark de Suvero and Claes Oldenburg, who play with the constraints of modernist sculpture. Foster goes on to argue that "like many other new museums, [Gehry's] colossal spaces are designed to accommodate the expanded field of postwar art—of Andre, Serra, Oldenburg and assorted descendants. But actually these museums trump this art: they use its great scale, which was first posed to challenge the modern museum, as a pretext to inflate the contemporary museum into a gigantic spectacle-space that can swallow any art, let alone any viewer, whole."[6]

While I agree that this is a fair assessment of the hubris effect one often experiences in Gehry's museums when taken as a whole, each of them also offers many more specifically architectural pleasures if read on small scales and in more mobile modes. When Gehry attempts to define the nature of his inspiration, he often has recourse to statements such as this: "The fleeting trapped within the immutable creates a sense of displacement so necessary for an architecture embodying sculptural or pictorial, emotive relationships."[7] Despite the inflated banality of this language, it is evident that, like many of his contemporaries and a majority of younger architects, he genuinely seeks to instantiate a paradox: built form that, while necessarily still and occupying a concrete place, embodies and suggests multiple variable movements in and through that space, even as it serves, and hopefully enhances, the commissioned purposes.[8] These affective affiliations in the work of a range of contemporary architects, artists, and filmmakers are most thoroughly explored by Giuliana Bruno in her path-finding books *Atlas of Emotion* and *Public Intimacy*.[9]

Whether we accept that Gehry's art museums—and those of his fellow starchitects, such as Tadao Ando, Norman Foster, Daniel Libeskind, Zahar Hadid, Jean Nouvel, Santiago Calatrava, Rem Koolhaas, SAANA, Peter Zumthor, Herzog and De Meuron, Diller Scofidio + Renfro, among others—are striking examples of contemporary art as much as of contemporary architecture, the visual imaginations and the modes of practice of these architects are undoubtedly grounded in strategies, forms, concepts, and tastes shared with many contemporary artists. Indeed, many of them spent much of their early years making paintings, drawings, and conceptual designs before attracting commissions that would enable them to continue to pursue key artistic ideas in their built structures. At the heights of their careers, their work is reverentially displayed in major art museum exhibitions throughout the world. They, along with younger compeers such as David Adyade, regularly collaborate on the design of exhibitions inside these museums. At these levels, sharing between the arts is so densely woven as to seem total.

In *The Art-Architecture Complex*, Foster argues that hybrids between the two arts, generated most visibly by the architects just listed, have come to dominate globalized image economies, and that their work is symptomatic of the repressions on which those economies are structured.[10] At the same time, as my comments on Gehry's design aesthetic indicate, however complete the immersion in art might seem, the applied art of architectural space continues to be shaped by the purposes specified in the program, albeit in an attenuated manner. This differentiation may be consequential for architecture that serves the public good, or it may, as Foster fears, be deceiving us. For the remodern-ist, spectacularist current that he discusses, this is indeed the case. In Sylvia Lavin's *Kissing Architecture*, she explores the connection in the work of these and other architects, as well as collaborations in which artists, such as Pipiloti Rist and Doug Aitken, project videos onto exteriors of buildings, or work with architects to shape interiors, a conjunction that Lavin likens to the kiss, "a cen-trifugal force of attraction between two exquisitely similar but yet distinctive things" that generates an affective interface she calls "superarchitecture."[11]

ART AS ARCHITECTURE

What of the other side of this relationship, when art making becomes a form of architecture or architectural design? Already in the 1970s, this implicit poten-tial took form in ways ranging from Dan Graham's glass and mirrored pavilions to key earthworks, most of which were, or became, architectural—for example, as a contra-space in Michael Heizer's *Double Negative* (1969), across two edges of Mormon Mesa, Nevada, or as a kind of supra-architecture, as in his project *City*, in a remote part of Nevada, begun in 1972. During the 1980s, conceptual artist Vito Acconci—known for works such as *Following Piece* (1969), in which he followed people he randomly encountered on the streets of New York at a slight distance until they entered a private destination, and *Seedbed* (1972), in which he hid beneath the inclined floor of the Sonnabend Gallery, masturbat-ing and talking into a microphone, for the duration of the exhibition—moved toward making sculptures that referenced architecture and furniture. In the late 1980s, he set up Acconci Studio, a design collective that focuses on public art and architecture, and has produced a substantial body of work that responds to the requirements of specific sites in imaginative ways. Best known, perhaps, is *Mur Island* (2003), a steel and glass structure floating in a fixed position in the Mur River, Graz, close to the Kunsthaus Graz (itself an extraordinary design by Peter Cook and Colin Fournier), and accessible via bridges from either bank (figure 4.1). Shaped to morph between a bowl and a dome, it serves many func-tions: theater, café, plaza, resting place, and playground, among others.[12] In a parallel shifting between mediums, photographer Hiroshi Sugimoto has often pictured architectural settings, such as movie house interiors, museum diora-mas, and modernist icons, highlighting through blurring the slowing down or

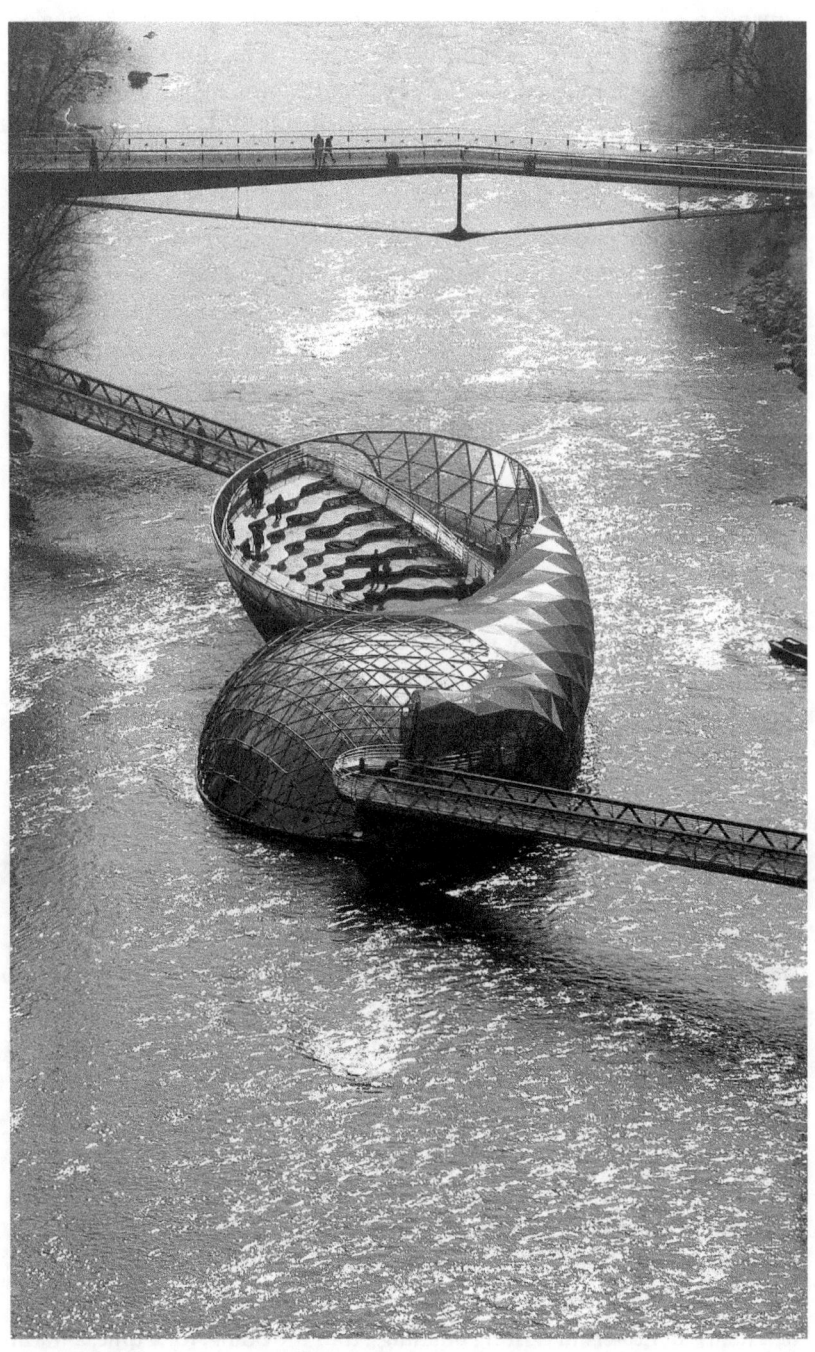

Figure 4.1

Acconci Studio, *Mur Island*, Mur River, Graz, Austria, 2003.
Image courtesy of Maria Acconci.

suspension of time that can occur in experiencing such places, or reflecting on images of them. Recently, working with architect Tomoyuki Sakakida as the firm New Material Research Laboratory, Sugimoto has applied insights from his photographic seeing to the design of actual buildings, such as the Observatory at Enoura, outside Tokyo, which houses his Odawara Art Foundation.[13]

A quite specific art/design/architecture interface occurs in the stream of public memorials inspired by minimalist sculpture's address to its spectators. Maya Lin's *Vietnam Veterans Memorial* (1982) took cues from Richard Serra's steel insertions into landscape settings (notably, his *Shift* [1970–72]) for its cut into the Washington Mall, creating a space of profound reflection for those commemorating American deaths during that war. Its affect is blunted by the subsequent insertion of figurative sculptural groups representing suffering soldiers near its entrances and exits. Of all the structures erected on and around the 9/11 site, Michael Arad and Peter Walker's *National September 11 Memorial* stands out for its subtle blend of careful commemoration—in the names around the rims of the two fountains—and uncompromising recognition of the finality of death, of those killed on the day and of the Twin Towers, in the reversal of water flow downward, into unfathomable depths (figure 4.2). The 9/11 Museum consists of, above ground, a modest entrance structure designed by Snøhetta, while below, its exhibition rooms are overloaded with objects of grief and not helped by the mediocre quality of the commissioned artworks. But the experience is saved by Davis Brody Bond's design of the pacing through the large spaces that take visitors into the vault beneath, to the slurry wall that girds the genius loci of the place.

In contrast to an architecture that incorporates art in its effort to address the ages, increasing numbers of artists have been experimenting with more flexible, temporary, provisional forms, that is, with models for alternative, nomad, and survival architecture. This, too, has a short contemporary history. In 1988–89 Krzysztof Wodiczko and David Laurie addressed threats to homeless people on the streets of New York by proposing several prototype Homeless Vehicles, ingeniously designed carts that provided shelter, storage, and relative protection while asleep.[14] In 2000 Ilona Németh designed a fixed structure that, when located near bus depots in Budapest, allowed homeless people to sleep in safe and clean circumstances.[15] Since 1988, Michael Rakowitz has custom-made multiple paraSITE shelters for individual homeless people living in various cities in the United States. His vinyl and nylon structures are inflatable through the exhaust of heaters in existing buildings, thus providing, for a time, a warm and portable sleeping environment.[16] London-based designer Lucy Orta has

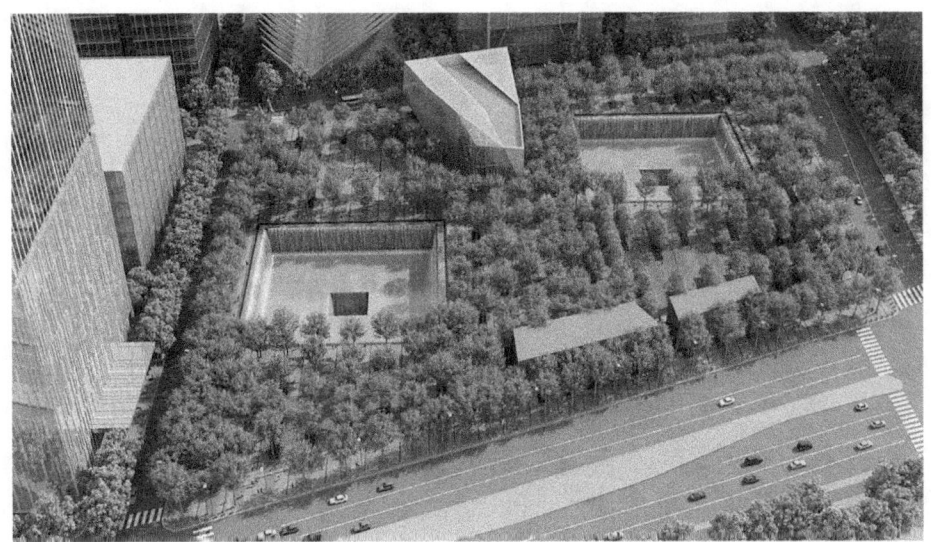

Figure 4.2

Michael Arad and Peter Walker, *National September 11 Memo-*
rial, 2011, image originally published in Ted Loos, "Architect
and 9/11 Memorial Both Evolve over the Years," *New York*
Times, September 1, 2011. © Michael Arad/Squared Design
Lab/The New York Times/Redux.

been creating what she calls "refuge wear," or wearable architecture for urban
refugees, since 1992.[17] In perhaps the most comprehensive and sustained commitment of this kind by a visual artist, Andrea Zittel has, since the early 1990s,
taken her experiences of living near Joshua Tree, California, as the subject of a
series of experiments in redesigning living spaces, clothing, furniture, fittings,
and the like (figure 4.3). Her A–Z Enterprise is "an institute of investigative
living," which "encompasses all aspects of every day living," in that "home, furniture, clothing, food all become sites of investigation in an ongoing effort to
better understand human nature and the social construction of needs."[18]

Another obvious concurrence of this kind is the focus on placemaking, and
place changing, by those artists whose vision as painters, sculptors, collagists,
or conceptualists spreads from their studios to their houses, neighborhoods,
and sometimes entire precincts of cities: for example, Hundertwasser in a

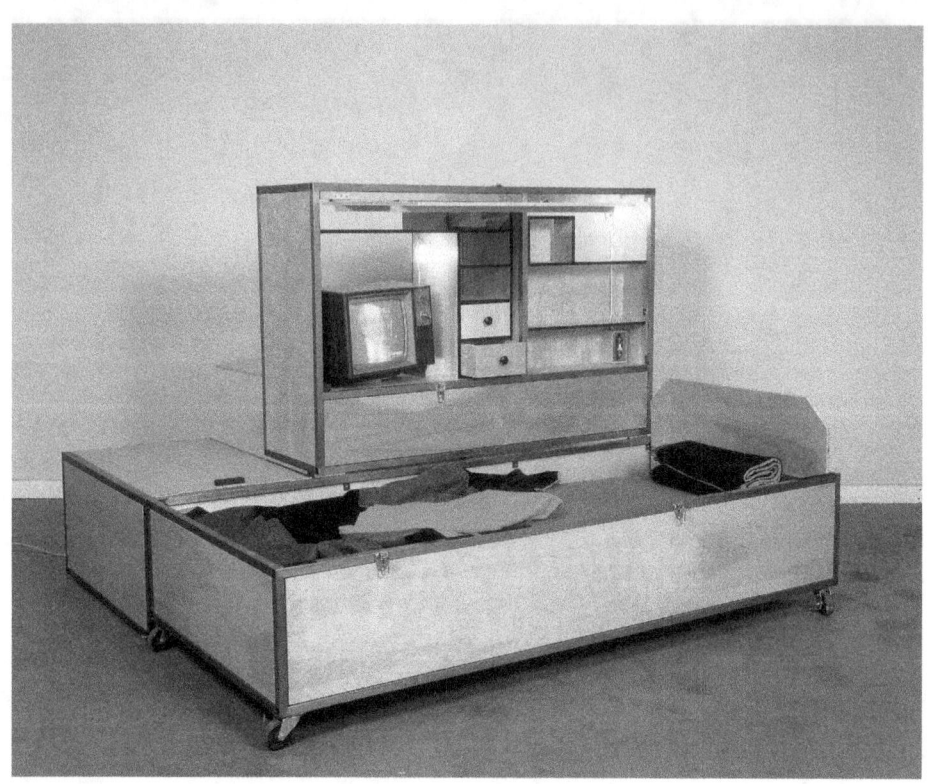

Figure 4.3

Andrea Zittel, *A to Z Living Unit Customized for the Jadermann Collection*, 1994, steel, wood, paint, mattress, glass, mirror, lighting fixture, upholstery, 93.3 × 213.4 × 96.5 cm (closed), 149.9 × 213.4 × 208.3 cm (open). © Andrea Zittel. Image courtesy of the artist and Sadie Coles HQ, London; Regen Projects, Los Angeles; and Andrea Rosen Gallery, New York.

suburb of Vienna; Tyree Guyton in Detroit; Gordon Matta-Clark's "anarchitecture"; Donald Judd at Marfa, Texas; Rick Lowe in Houston; Theaster Gates in Chicago; and Design 99, the Detroit Unreal Estate Agency. Their enterprise has been taken up at a larger scale by artist-mayor Edi Rama, whose ongoing transformation of Tirana, Albania, involves splashing great swaths of color across the façades of its public housing. Another public official alert to the transformative potential of the arts is Antanas Mockus, a mathematician and philosopher who was mayor of Bogotá for two terms, during which he tackled social problems through demonstrative, absurd, unexpectedly humorous performances, including dressing in a Supercitizen costume and employing 420 mimes to act as traffic police.[19]

INTERMEDIAL STRATEGIES

While Mockus is an unusual politician, who borrowed strategies from contemporary performance art to advance the public good, architects have been doing likewise in recent decades, albeit at a slower rate than the more direct borrowings and repurposing noted earlier. Aspects of the work of important installation artists echo in much recent architecture, not least high-style hotels that seek to brand themselves by association with spectacular architecture and design: Ian Schrader's hotels in the US, and some of the Silken Group's in Spain, for example, the Hotel Puerta América, Madrid (2002–5), which features the ingenuity of Various Architects.[20] Few architects, however, have matched the challenges coming from the most radical installation artists, although some of the former will doubtless find ways to incorporate their aesthetics into their interior designs. Swiss artist Thomas Hirschhorn makes installations such as *Cavemanman* (2003), *Utopia, Utopia = One World, One War, One Army, One Dress* (2005), *Crystal of Resistance* (2011), and *Concordia, Concordia* (2012), which show globalization as a kind of war machine bent on creating nightmare scenarios, caves of banality and standardization, as well as revelations of what the world would look like if the desires precipitated by globalization were actually realized. In another stream of his work, he draws attention to the revolutionary potential of the thinking of certain philosophers and political theorists by establishing temporary memorials to them in the streets of poor neighborhoods, all of which take architectural form: community centers, cafés, temporary libraries, reading rooms, and internet access sites. A controversial example of these inhabitable, usable antimonuments was his *Bataille Monument (Bar)*, situated in a Turkish guest-workers neighborhood in Kassel, Germany, during Documenta II, in 2002 (figure 4.4).[21]

ARCHITECTURAL THEORY ACTUATED

Art that acts as a form of architectural theory, or as a kind of historical record of architecture or speculation about the history of architecture, may seem esoteric in contrast to the socially engaged practices I have been reviewing, but

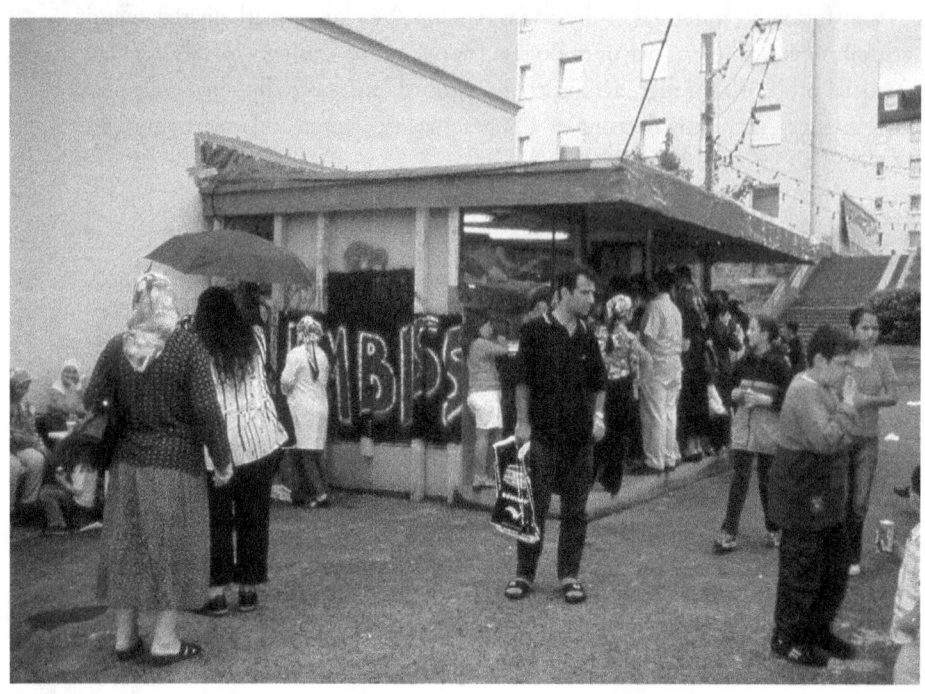

Figure 4.4

Thomas Hirschhorn, *Bataille Monument (Bar)*, 2002, Documenta 11, Kassel, Germany. © Thomas Hirschhorn. Image courtesy of the artist and Gladstone Gallery, New York and Brussels. Photo by Werner Maschmann.

it is highly relevant to the concerns of this book. Isabelle Loring Wallace and Nora Wendt, in the introduction to their anthology *Contemporary Art and Architecture: A Strange Utility*, make a strong case for it as an important theme in contemporary art. They begin with an evocation of Iñigo Manglano-Ovalle's *Le baiser/The Kiss* (1999–2000), a video installation that shows on one side of the screen, a worker cleaning the external windows of Mies van der Rohe's Farnsworth House, a structure famous for its glass walls, while on the other side of the screen, a young woman, entirely immersed in the world of her headphones, is shown inside the house. The viewpoint toward the worker (in fact, the artist) is from inside the house, while that showing the self-involved

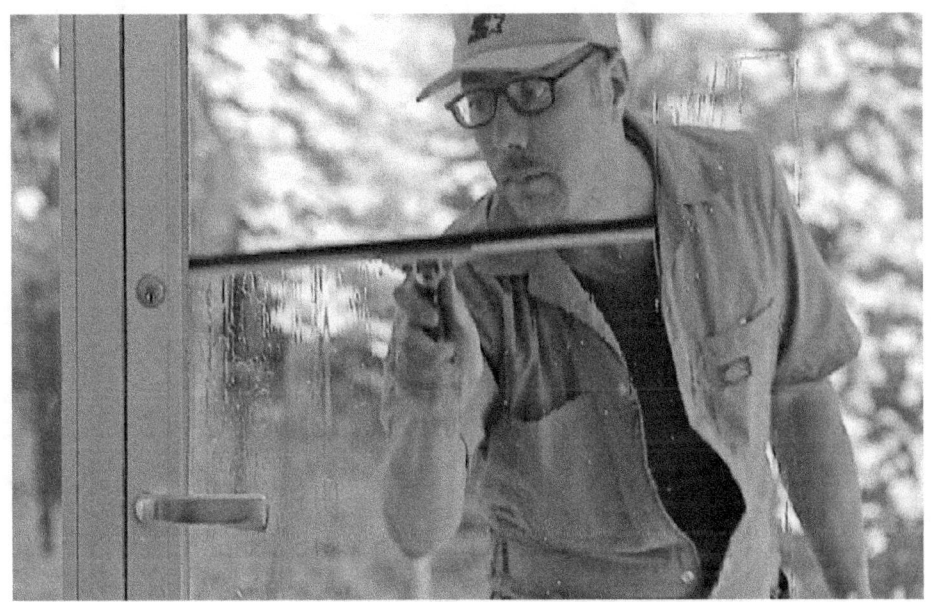

Figure 4.5

Iñigo Manglano-Ovalle, *Le baiser/The Kiss*, 1999–2000, video installation, still of artist cleaning window. Image courtesy of the artist and Galerie Thomas Schulte, Berlin.

woman is from outside (figure 4.5). In art such as this, Wallace and Wendt note, "architecture is useful not toward the usual ends—shelter, monumentality, empire-building—but toward other ends that reveal architecture's utility as medium" for art.[22]

Of Rachel Whiteread's work, Wallace and Wendt rightly say, "though it clearly uses architecture, it is also obviously about architecture, and thereby functions as a silent form of architectural history, critique and analysis."[23] Whiteread's well-known public sculpture *House* (1993–94), the interior of a Victorian home cast in concrete, stood for some weeks as a tangible reminder of an entire terrace of such houses that had been torn down for redevelopment of the neighborhood (figure 4.6). In photographs ever since, it echoes as a more general symbol of such destruction and embodies the important concept of "places of memory."[24] To Wallace and Wendt, Whiteread's work

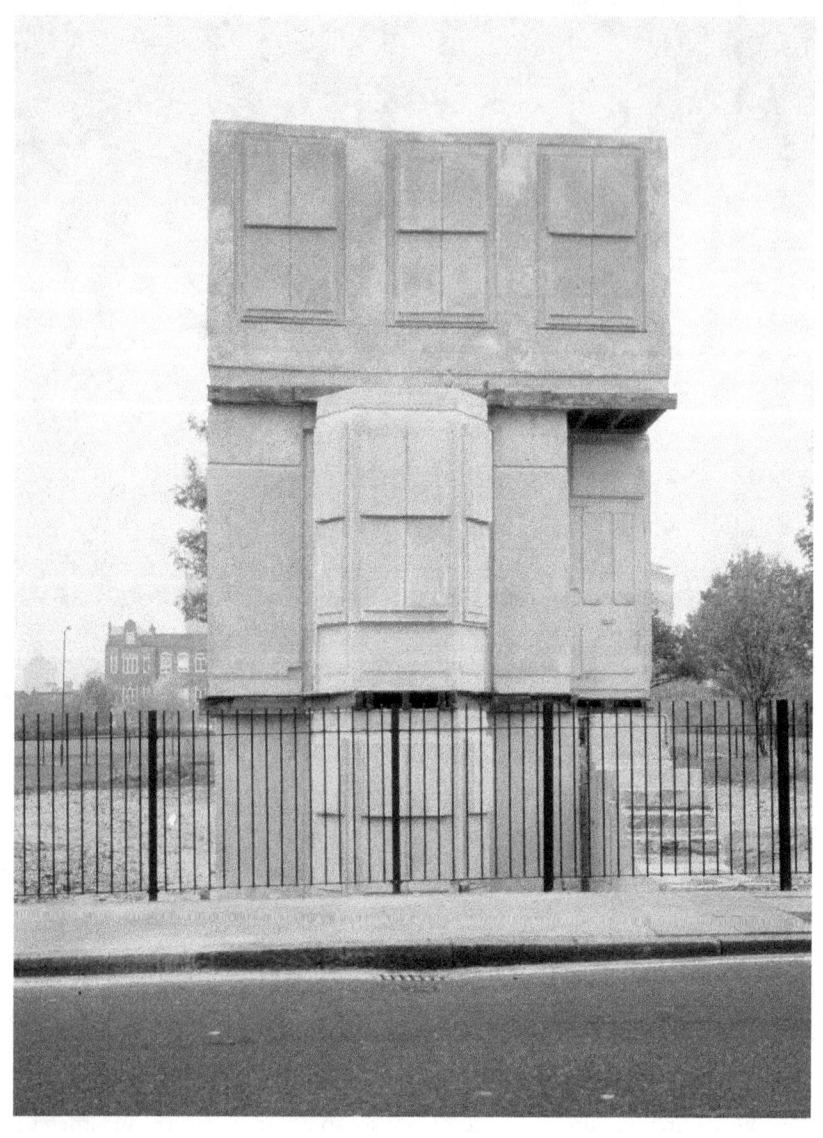

Figure 4.6

Rachel Whiteread, *House*, 1993–94. © Rachel Whiteread.
Courtesy of the artist; Luhring Augustine, New York; Lorcan
O'Neill, Rome; and Gagosian Gallery, New York.

is emblematic of "a decidedly contemporary trend in which *art is itself a site* where architecture is analysed, engaged, laid bare—often through an appropriation of architecture's own materials and strategies."[25] For Hans Haacke's installation *Germania* in the German Pavilion at the Venice Biennale in 1993, he applied the architectural practice of demolition to the stone floor of the pavilion, which had been remodeled by Third Reich architects in the 1930s; thus, the work recalls that earlier history and illustrates the fact that architecture is subject to temporal transformation, of many kinds, and for many purposes.

A number of artists have asked whether the icons of modernist architecture, and the city plans of modernist architects, have fulfilled the utopian vision that inspired their creators. Wallace and Wendt cite Damián Ortega's *Skin* (2006–7), in which floor plans of famous buildings from Warsaw, Mexico City, and Berlin are printed on leather hides and hung from the ceiling on meat hooks. Manglano-Ovalle's abstract speculations on seeing out and seeing in are located in more concrete social relationships in Lorna Simpson's two-screen video *Corridor* (2003). It follows the daily lives of two women of color: a household servant from the 1860s in a house similar to Monticello, and a single woman of the 1960s in a modernist house. Both are trapped, albeit in different ways. Australian artist Callum Morton's sculpture *International Style* (1999) makes this relationship explicit. Drawing on research into Edith Farnsworth's displeasure at being constantly exposed within the house that Mies built for her, Morton creates a 1:10 scale model of the house, inserts interior curtains, and includes a tape of a woman's voice screaming, "Don't you dare touch me!" followed by five gunshots. His installation *International Style Compound* (2000) consists of four scale-model Farnsworth Houses facing one another in closed community, while interior projections and sounds suggest that a party is occurring in one, a burglary is in progress in another, and a horror movie is being watched on television in a third. The fourth remains silent, as befits an architectural model (figure 4.7).[26]

Photography was pivotal to the dissemination of modern architecture, not only to a wider public, but also as a source of inspiration among architects themselves.[27] The photographic imagery of twentieth-century modernism, however, has settled into what seems to be a relatively limited, carefully managed repertoire. Some outstanding contemporary photographers have been drawn to challenge this iconology. The entire career of Bernd and Hilla Becher was devoted to underscoring the inherent beauty of various kinds of vernacular architecture and anonymous industrial structures. A side effect of their relentlessly

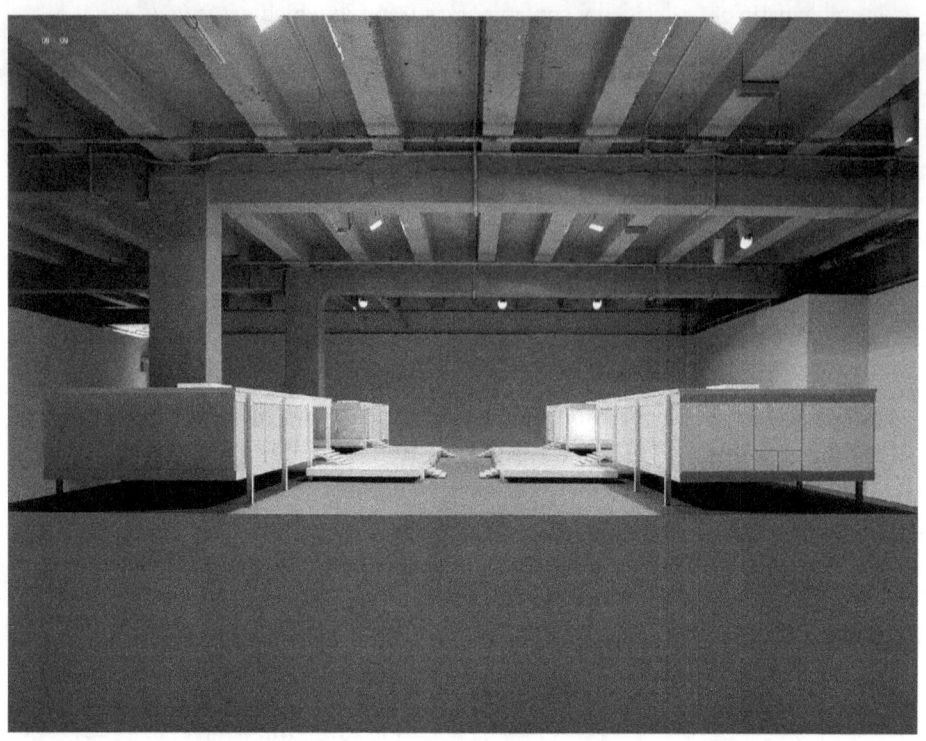

Figure 4.7

Callum Morton, *International Style Compound*, 2000, acrylic,
automotive print, vinyl, lights, sound, 674 × 405 × 180 cm.
Image courtesy of the artist and Lyon Housemuseum,
Melbourne.

systematic approach, one that seems to match in photography the utilitarian
commitment and the engineering aesthetic of their subjects, is that the celebration of these structures by the modern masters comes to seem tokenistic in
comparison. Inspired by the Bechers, a generation of German photographers
has turned its gaze on modern and older architecture, paying careful attention
to resonances between the two arts. These photographers include Thomas
Ruff, Candida Höfer, Thomas Struth, Andreas Gursky, and Günther Förge.
Outside Germany, Luisa Lambri photographs modern interiors in ways that

reveal the nuanced beauties of their aging, and James Casabere shows the dark depths of their false promises or the too bright banalities in the spruikings of real estate agents. (I touch on Jeff Wall's work relevant to this in chapter 9). The profound relationships between the close, searching perspectives that seeing photographically encourages, and the critical interrogations necessary in revising architectural history, are highly developed by Mark Lewis, notably in his 35mm films, usually silent, that search out the uncanny in modern architectural settings, such as housing estates, views from skyscrapers, and pedestrian passageways. He is interested in how these settings, and his use of predigital film, answer the question "Is Modernity Our Antiquity?"[28] Lewis's concerns parallel those pursued in equally subtle ways in the installations of Jane and Louise Wilson.

The return to narrative—however wildly discontinuous—in the work of some contemporary artists has included speculative rewriting of well-known stories from architecture's past. Matthew Barney's five-part series of installations, performances, films, sculptures, and exhibitions, the *Cremaster Cycle* (1994–2003), has at its heart an elaborate allegory of architectural apprenticeship in analogy to the succession of reputation in the visual arts. Using Masonic symbolism and a fiction about the construction of the Chrysler Building, New York, Barney enacts the role of the Entered Apprentice who betrays Hiram Abiff, presumed architect of the Temple of Solomon, played by Richard Serra.[29] In a similarly speculative vein, Le Corbusier's struggles to design the Carpenter Center for the Visual Arts at Harvard University are the subject of Pierre Huyghe's video *This Is Not a Time for Dreaming* (2004), a work commissioned for the building's fortieth anniversary (figures 4.8–4.11). Huyghe manipulates small puppets of the architect, elements of the building, himself, and other figures, such as a gigantic insect, in a meditative fantasy on the history of the building, Le Corbusier's life, and the creative process in both architecture and the visual arts.

ARCHITECTURAL MOTIFS

A slightly separate, perhaps fifth kind of concurrence can be found in the work of contemporary artists who use architectural elements as crucial parts of the language of forms, through which they tackle the main concerns of their work. For these artists, the theory and history of architecture is of less interest than, say, the experience of city life, or the nature of structures. As examples of this perspective, Wallace and Wendt cite the work of Julie Mehretu, Sarah Sze, Toba

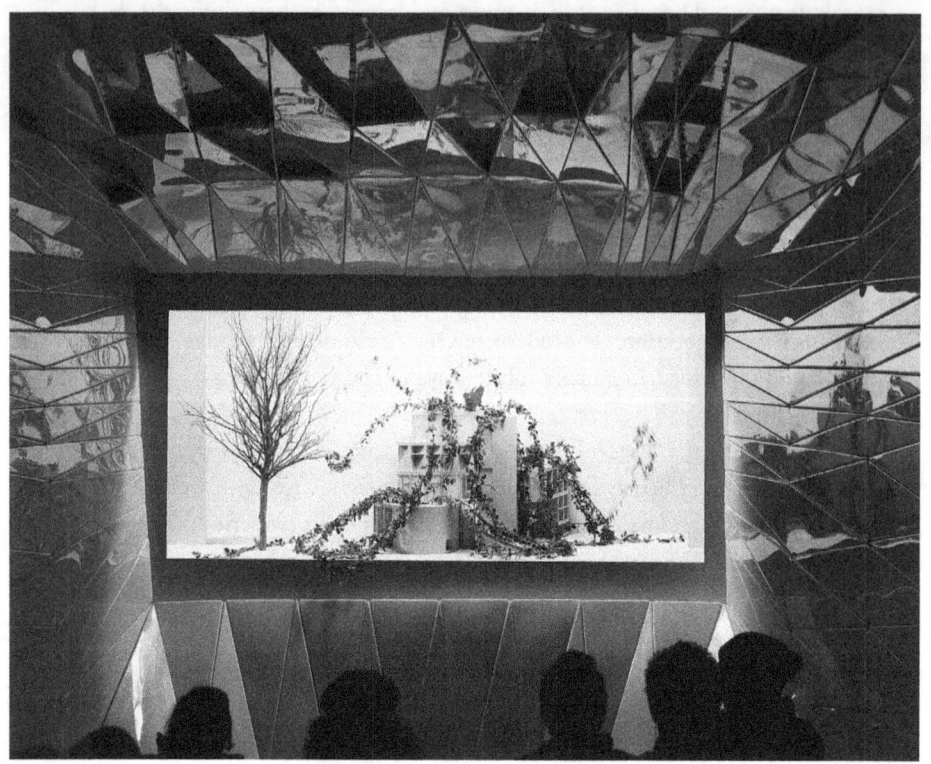

Khedoori, Los Carpinteros, Ernesto Neto, and Janet Cardiff. Many more could
be added—Liam Gillick and Mark Bradford, for starters. Similarly, artists such
as Gregor Schneider, in his *Totes Haus Ur* series (begun 1985), create environments in which the psychological experience of particular spaces and places—
in this case, Schneider's own, rendered uncomfortably small—is paramount.
Certain of Mike Kelley's works, such as his *Educational Complex* (1995), a scale
model of his high school that manifests its programmatic character, and especially his *Mobile Homestead* (2008–2012), discussed in chapter 7, share this
concern with demonstrating the strangeness of what seems to be totally ordinary. Swiss artist Christoph Büchel, throughout his career, has consistently
explored the nature and limits of mis-fitting in architectural terms. This has
led to his exhibitions being severely constrained and sometimes closed down.
Invited to present the Icelandic Pavilion at the Venice Biennale in 2015, Büchel
worked with local Muslims to transform Santa Maria della Misericordia, which

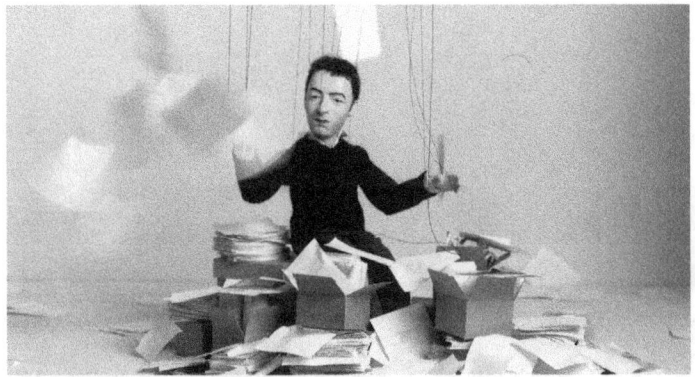

Figures 4.8–4.11

(HERE AND OPPOSITE) Pierre Huyghe, *This Is Not a Time for Dreaming* (production stills), 2004, *Art 21* (PBS). Images courtesy of the artist and Hauser & Wirth, New York.

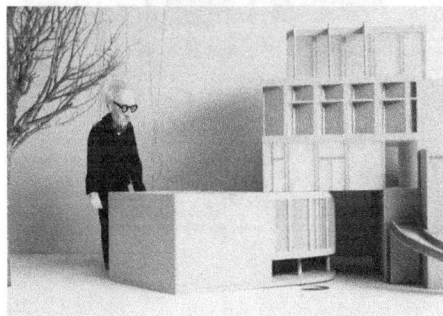
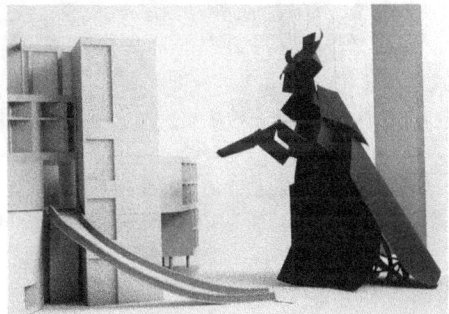

had not functioned as a church for forty years, into a mosque, the first ever in the city of Venice. It stayed open for two weeks. (I examine more works of this kind in chapter 7, which explores placemaking in contexts of dislocation.)

Architectural settings are prevalent in the work of artists interested in addressing important moments of historical change. German photographer Thomas Demand builds life-size simulations of such places in paper and cardboard, photographs them and then destroys them. His subjects have included the podium from which Serbian dictator Slobodan Milošević gave an inflammatory speech; the security checkpoint at Logan Airport, Boston, through which the 9/11 attackers passed; the tally room of the Florida Electoral Office, where disputed votes cast in the 2000 US presidential elections were counted; the kitchen of the house where Saddam Hussein was captured; and the control room of the Fukushima nuclear plant during its 2011 meltdown (figure 4.12). He has also made films that, for example, track through a model based on the tunnel in which

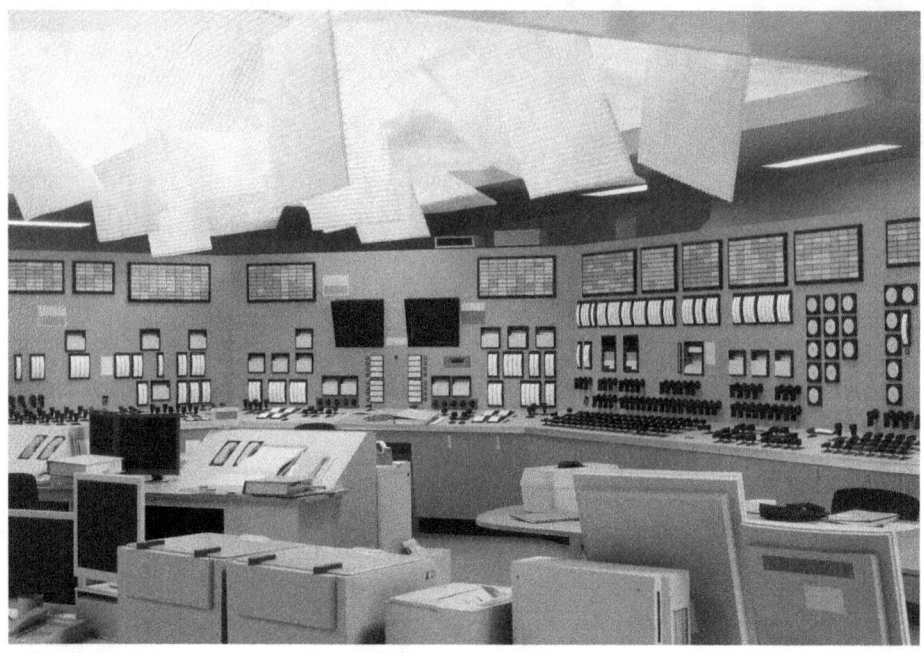

Figure 4.12

Thomas Demand, *Control Room*, 2011, C-print/diasec,
200 × 300 cm. © Thomas Demand, VG Bild-Kunst, Bonn/ARS,
New York. Image courtesy of Sprueth Magers, Berlin.

Princess Diana had her fatal accident, and through a painstaking re-creation of an online video recorded from the interior of a cruise ship caught in a Pacific Ocean storm. The disjunction between Demand's low-key presentation of these settings, and the historical significance of what happened in them, is crucial to the affective impact of his works. His 2006 installation *Grotto*, however, is an elaborate re-creation of events and places of no particular historical consequence.[30] In a similar way, Deimantas Narkevicius traces resonances of the Soviet occupation of his region in films such as *The Dud Effect* (2008), shot on abandoned missile bases in his native Lithuania. In this film, a former officer goes through the routines of preparing to launch a missile, while the camera focuses on details of the bases and their natural settings, creating a powerful sense of both the absurdity of such places and the dread of deadly consequences to their (thankfully) unrealized purpose.[31]

These examples suggest that less obvious concurrences between the visual arts would also be worth pursuing to assess their contemporary resonances. For example, the influence of the cinematic on all visual arts, not just on video art and big-scale photography, is strikingly evident (in the work of Andreas Gursky and David Claerbout, for example), but cinema also plays a role in some architectural thinking, literally in Diller Scofidio + Renfro's *Slow House*, a 1991 design for a vacation house that brilliantly juxtaposes automobile windshield, picture window, and video screen. Michael Jantzen's 2002 *Malibu Video Beach House* takes the idea of occupying a filmic existence even more literally.[32] Less directly, cinematic imagining of lifestyle echoes in the work of the Italian collective Stalker—named after Andrei Tarkowsky's famous film—as the group's artists seek out tangential, interstitial, noninvasive ways of experiencing cities so that they can enable as many people as possible to experience the psychogeographies celebrated by situationist Guy Debord.[33] Few architectural firms have been as willing as Diller Scofidio + Renfro to experiment with the concerns for intermediality and conceptual interrogations that typify contemporary art. An outstanding example is their Blur Building, a media pavilion for Swiss EXPO 2002 that conveyed information about the local climate. Erected on the shoreline at Yverdon-les-Bains, a pier projected out into Lake Neuchatel, at the end of which was a pavilion whose main structure was an artificial cloud, created by mixing expelled water with local mist (figure 4.13). A brilliant conception, it had many precedents in the expanded cinema of the 1960s and 1970s, such as that of the Eventstructure Research Group (Jeffrey Shaw and Theo Botschuijver), and in the installations of contemporary artists such as Olafur Eliasson.

Artists from all over the world are highlighting the terrors and the delights of life in cities undergoing constant deformation in the fallout from decolonization and globalization. In Africa, for example, these circumstances have inspired works in a variety of media, from photography, animation, and sculpture to installation, performance, and digital projection, by several outstanding artists, such as David Goldblatt, William Kentridge, Bodys Isek Kingelez, Georges Adéagbo, Antonio Ole, Allan de Souza, and Jean-Michel Bruyère.[34]

Comprehensive exhibitions about these relationships between architecture and art are surprisingly rare. Germano Celant's *Art and Architecture*, a gargantuan

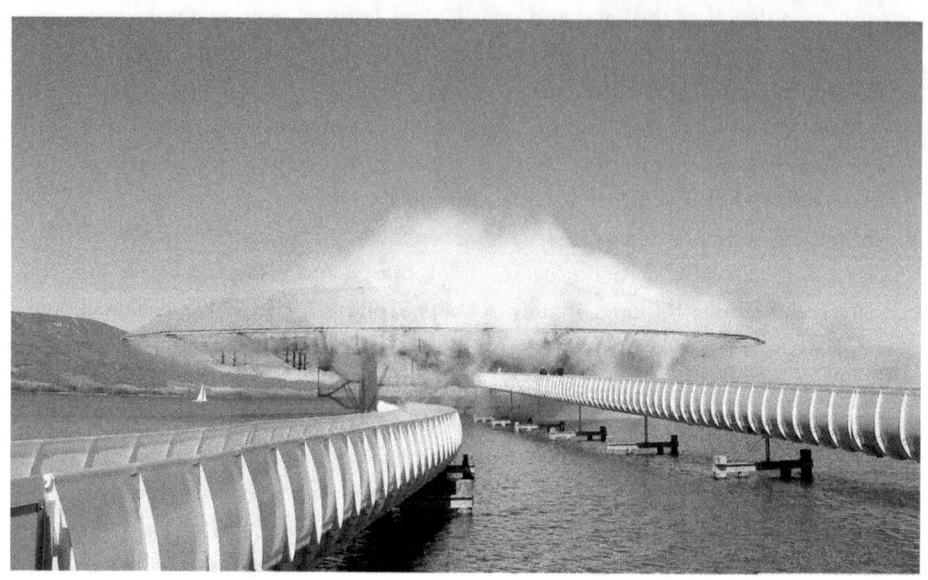

Figure 4.13

Diller Scofidio + Renfro, Blur Building, a media pavilion for
Swiss EXPO, 2002, Yverdon-les-Bains, Lake Neuchatel,
approach from shore. Photo by Beat Widmer.

survey at the Palazzo Ducale, Genoa, in 2004, is a striking exception.[35] One of
the first exhibitions at the Tate Modern, London, was a wide-scale exploration
of the changing nature of world cities, titled *Century City: Art and Culture in
the Modern Metropolis*.[36] In 2006, the Bienal de la Habana devoted itself to
this theme from a third world perspective, attracting hundreds of artists and
cultural collectives from all over the global South whose work is committed
not only to drawing attention to the complexities of living in the burgeoning
cosmopolises, but also to quite specific applications of art practices to create
place and community.[37] Other relevant exhibitions include *Psycho Buildings:
Artists Take on Architecture*, Hayward Gallery, London, 2008, and *Automatic
Cities: The Architectural Imaginary in Contemporary Art*, Museum of Contemporary Art, San Diego, 2009.[38] Ongoing museological projects that offer
a platform for exploring these relationships are also important: among these,

the annual commissions for a pavilion at the Serpentine Gallery, London, have been outstanding.[39]

TOP DOWN MEETS BOTTOM UP

I conclude this chapter by comparing two approaches to creating contemporary architecture, each deeply shaped by immersion in contemporary art practice, theory, and historical thinking, and each an interesting token of its type. The first assumes a top-down attitude, from general idea to particular instance, while the second is resolutely bottom up. Which raises the question, Is there a middle ground on which they might meet?

The art-historical idea that, broadly speaking, three contemporaneous currents course through contemporary art inspired Steven Holl's design for the Institute for Contemporary Art at Virginia Commonwealth University, Richmond (figure 4.14). The site is a corner block at an intersection where the university most directly abuts the surrounding community. Holl visualized a welcoming foyer that would offer viewers entering it a "plane of the present," that is, an array of options for moving through what he labels "forking time." The array is a set of entrances into parallel galleries on two floors, each containing a different kind of contemporary art. In his 2012 Windmueller Artist Lecture at the university, Holl describes the design as meeting the change in art from the dominance of the "master narratives" to the current state of open-ended possibility, within which artists could now work in different mediums for different purposes, and do so simultaneously. Each direction is "fine" as to its inherent value and its potentiality. As examples for each of the three kinds of art, he cites Spanish sculptor Eduardo Chillida and Richard Serra; Brice Marden (Holl's comment: "Now, no one says painting is dead"); and video installation artist Doug Aitken. Holl's design also contains a fourth gallery upstairs, for usages and for artworks as yet unimaginable, a dimension of art that he labels "scalelessness." Finally, and as an extension of this open-endedness, visitors may leave the building and enter a garden, which Holl calls a "thinking field," that permits views of videos projected onto gallery surfaces (as Doug Aitken so brilliantly does) and links directly to the university's Monroe Park campus (figure 4.15).[40] Holl's strict focus on mediums is not exactly my way of thinking about the three currents, their differentiations and their convergences, but it is close, as close as architectural design has come to recognizing these currents as structuring contemporary artistic practice.

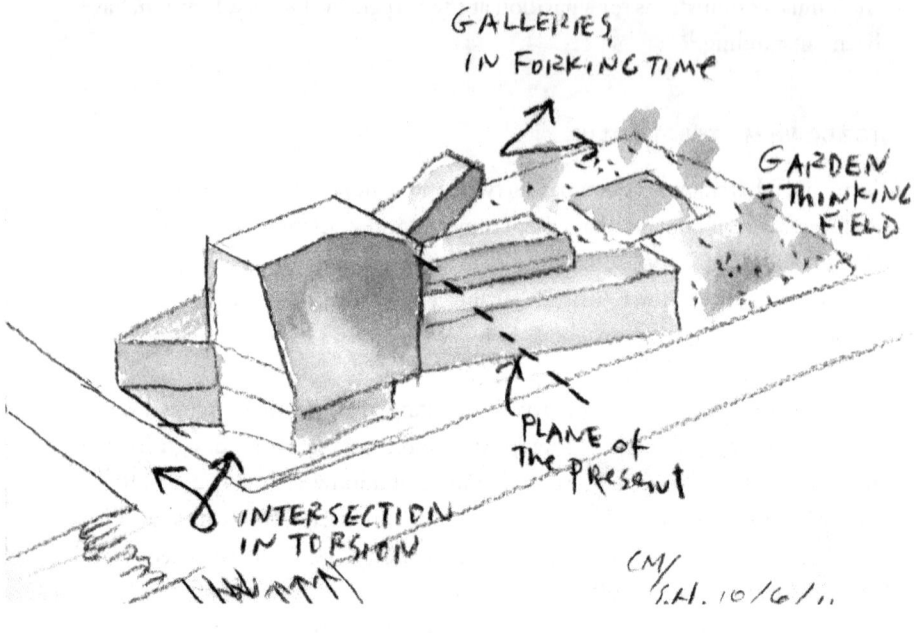

Figure 4.14

Steven Holl, Institute for Contemporary Art conceptual drawing, 2011, Virginia Commonwealth University, Richmond.
Image courtesy of Steven Holl Architects.

Begun in 2011, the museum opened in April 2018 with an exhibition titled
Declaration. The curatorial rationale reads as a summary of the concerns of contemporary artists that I explore in this book:

"Declaration" will assert contemporary art's vital role in society through
works that raise urgent questions about the state of the world and how
artists and other citizens choose to respond to our times. The exhibition
will explore questions of speech and silence, conflict and connection, the
interrelation between the many and the one, and between institutions and
the communities they serve. It will demonstrate how artists participate
in civic conversations, activate diverse creative communities and catalyze
reflection and renewal. Featuring a cross-generational mix of artists who
offer a range of perspectives and approaches, the exhibition will embody

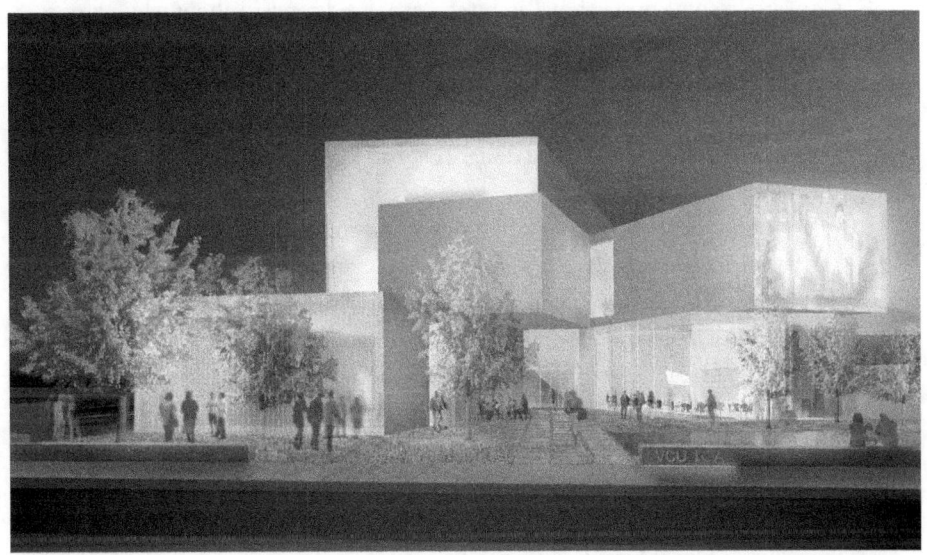

Figure 4.15

Steven Holl, Institute for Contemporary Art model, view of "thinking field" garden, 2012, Virginia Commonwealth University, Richmond. Image courtesy of Steven Holl Architects. Building opened April 2018.

the range of formal, thematic and emotional decisions artists make in their work. The ICA's open circulation will allow works to be experienced from multiple sightlines, reinforcing the importance of choice and agency and illustrating the wide-ranging responses art can foster.[41]

If Holl's program calls for a building that will contain (in the sense of "pause the flow of") the currents that course through contemporary art, the work of Assemble, a London-based art, architecture, and design collective, typifies the opposite: the infusion within contemporary architectural practice of the values, procedures, and outcomes of contemporary installation, performance, and social-practice art.

When Assemble was awarded the Turner Prize in 2015, there was some public interest in why a group of architects were awarded a prize usually given to painters, sculptors, photographers, and performance or installation artists.

Conversely, some professional architects expressed concern about why a group of artists, none of whom are registered architects, should be regarded as such.[42] But among members of art worlds, few were surprised, as the groups' work is so obviously a response to many of the challenges facing the current generation of artists, activists, architects, and designers of all kinds, in all fields, and in those constantly emergent.

Assemble aims to "address the typical disconnection between the public and the process by which places are made" by championing "a working practice that is interdependent and collaborative, seeking to actively involve the public as both participant and collaborator in the on-going realisation of the work."[43] Beginning in 2010, their first projects were pop-up entertainment venues, ingeniously transforming derelict or interstitial urban spaces into temporary cinemas and meeting places. Working with a team of three hundred volunteers, Assemble's first work, *The Cineroleum*, converted an abandoned service station (one of an estimated forty thousand throughout Britain) on a busy London street into a film theater by suspending curtain walls, hand sewn from roofing membrane, from the station's canopy, and by inserting tiers of seats constructed from scaffolding boards. *Folly for a Flyover* attracted thousands of local residents to a space beneath a motorway and alongside a canal in Hackney, which became, for nine weeks, an arts venue (figure 4.16). Deploying the conceit that a long-term resident had refused to leave, volunteers joined Assemble in building a "construction kit" style house that served as a café, next to a cinema under the concrete motorway. Subsequently, London Legacy Development Corporation funded infrastructure to enable the site to be used as a public space.

Reshaping such spaces in close consultations with their user communities has become another thread within Assemble's work, including the main street of suburban New Addington, in the Limborough Gardens housing estate, and elsewhere. The group created shared workspaces for small-scale manufacturing and crafts in projects such as Blackhorse Workshop, Yard House, and Sugarhouse Studios. Rethinking theatrical performance as occurring both inside and outside closed halls is another thread apparent in Assemble projects, such as *Theatre on the Fly* and the *School of Narrative Dance*. Perhaps the most inventive projects are those dedicated to reconceiving the nature of play. These range from meta-architectural reflection in conferences and in projects such as *The Brutalist Playground* (working with Simon Terrill, the group reconstructed to scale, but in foam, play structures, originally in concrete and steel, from three famous Brutalist buildings); to new ideas for equipment, such as *The Big Slide* (shared by up to a dozen kids at once), and public playgrounds constructed

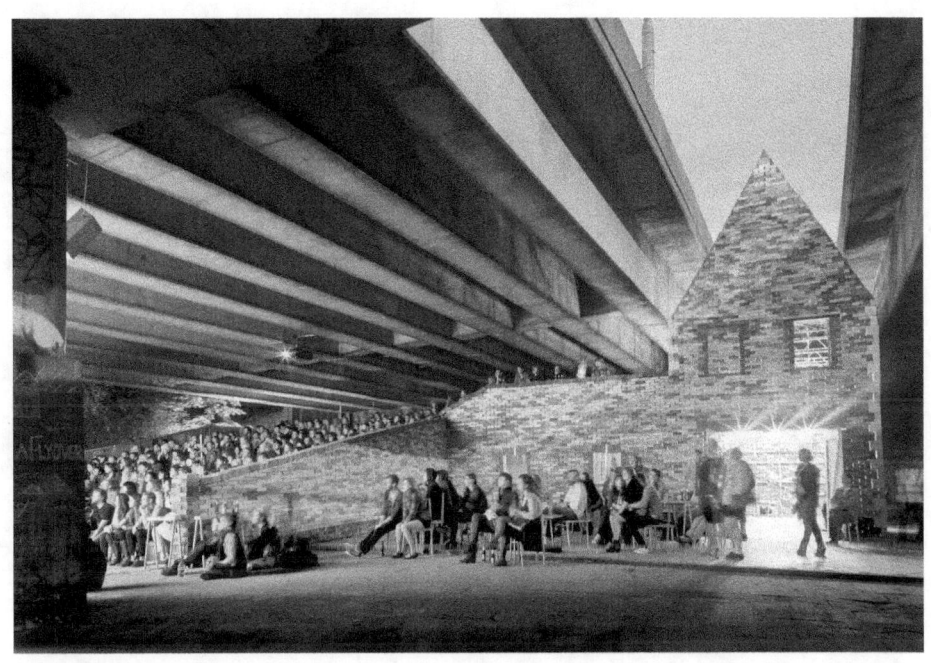

Figure 4.16

Assemble, *Folly for a Flyover*, 2010, Hackney Wick, London.
Image courtesy of Assemble Studio.

around children-driven play (*Baltic Street Adventure Playground*, Glasgow, and *Spirit of Play*, Leigh Wood, Bristol). Assemble won the Turner Prize for the group's work with a local community land trust to convert the mainly derelict Victorian houses along four streets in suburban Granbury, Liverpool, into sustainable living spaces, and for initiating the Granbury Workshops, in which residents are trained in creating handmade products for home, using materials from, and drawing on the aesthetic of, their immediate surrounds.

Although winning the Turner Prize might seem to be an occasion when designing from the bottom up meets with total approval from those at the top, stepping back and viewing the patterns of connection and differentiation among the architecture, art, and design surveyed in this chapter reveals that within the overall contemporary situation, this is no more, but also no less, than what it seems to be: a moment of concurrence within a world of differences.

background story, global foreground

Chinese Contemporary Art

Chinese contemporary art is a phenomenon that, during the past few decades, has come to seem familiar to interested art audiences inside China and out. Its bold mix of styles, impressive major figures, and signature contents all took distinctive shape in the 1990s and, despite some setbacks, seem to have burgeoned since then. Where else can this art go but up and out, ever expanding in scope and ambition, attracting ever higher prices, and increasingly influencing international art? After all, it is the most resplendent driver in the symbolic engine room, the "soft power" center, of the fastest-growing economy in the world—one of few that seemed recession proof, until 2015. Yet clichés such as these hide a more interesting background story about how art in China got to be where it is now, and they occlude a clear understanding of how the various tendencies in Chinese art relate to the currents that constitute contemporary art in the world today. Simplified stereotypes also prevent recognition of what is, in fact, an increasingly challenging situation for artists and critics working in China, one that is having marked effects on their art. The following remarks, the perceptions and perspective of a non-Chinese-speaking but deeply interested visitor, work toward a profile of that situation, one that sets out its accomplishments, pitfalls, and potentials as I see them.

INSIDE CHINA, LOOKING OUT

How are these issues addressed within Chinese contexts? Let us take one instance, from a moment when contemporary Chinese art seemed, to many observers, to be fulfilling all the expectations of its most ardent champions, and to be the vehicle of even greater future achievement. In late May 2009, China held its first China Contemporary Art Forum (CCAF), the *Beijing International Conference on Art Theory and Criticism*. The statement of intent in the official conference booklet was unequivocal:

> Against the background of an ever-changing international economic and cultural landscape, this forum works to facilitate high-level exchanges and cooperation between Chinese and western scholars and institutions on cultural studies, with the hope of exploring modes of communication in the 21st century between Chinese and western art circles, which are on different tracks of development. These efforts are expected to enhance mutual recognition and understanding between China and the outside world in terms of art and culture at large, promote the development of contemporary Chinese art, raise the voice of Chinese art in the international area, build up the soft power of contemporary Chinese art, increase its importance in the new order of world art, strengthen its coordinating role in this new order and export China's cultural values.[1]

Obviously, this is written in the rhetoric of international trade discourse, not in any recognizable art language. Yet it advances beyond official policy formulations of "learning from the West" and "taking the best from the West" that were prominent in the post-Mao era. It also casts aside assumptions that modernization necessarily means following Western models as thoroughly as possible. It frankly asserts that "Chinese and western art circles" are on "different tracks of development." It does not specify the character of either, but it does list a set of domains of cultural practice and exchange, treating them as processes in need of intensification and improvement—in China, at least (diplomacy would prevent any such comment about the West). Doing so will, the CCAF hopes, place Chinese art in a leading role worldwide and enable the "export" of "China's cultural values." These formulations are still within a China-versus-the-West framework, but they locate China in a more advanced position than would have been plausible to claim during the 1980s and 1990s. They presume that the competition will be won when China overtakes the West, and "China's cultural values" become universal. Or, more modestly, they suggest a desirable future in which Chinese art and society matches Western achievement and Chinese values are in unfettered circulation, openly available for others who may be interested in them.

We can, however, view this situation from less of an either/or perspective. China's long history, the ancientness of its discourse on art, and the paramodern nature of its experiments with modernity since the fifteenth century suggest that, in contemporary conditions, thinking about art in China today might usefully acknowledge its location within in a third discursive space, that of postcolonial and transnational art theory and criticism. This kind of *decolonial* thinking—originating in South America, South Asia, Africa, and elsewhere, and refined in the mobility of intellectuals and artists from those regions, as well as in their impact on certain thinkers in metropolitan centers— has dislodged Euro-American discourses from the worldwide dominance they enjoyed within modernity.[2] I am not suggesting that Western conceptions of modernity no longer have an influence in China or elsewhere outside Europe and the United States. Nor am I claiming that Chinese thought has become indebted to postcolonial theory (which does not, strictly speaking, fit the situation in China), or that purely "Chinese" thinking has replaced all comers in Chinese debates. What I am saying is that conceptions of transnationality are at the heart of thinking about the experience of living in China today, as they are everywhere else. "Transnationality" is not simply about trafficking between nations, each conceived as a relatively stable unit. Rather, it conceives each "nation" (an always combustible combination of "imagined community," state power, economic interaction, and cultural self-interrogation) as *a nation in transition in the context of all other nations also in transition*, and thus presumes that these transitions will occur in distinctive yet related ways—not as variant instances of a greater whole, but as independent *and* interdependent elements, whose internal dynamics and volatile interaction constitute the geopolitical world's always incomplete becoming.

In *Globalization and Cultural Trends in China* (2004), Liu Kang argues, "Since China has abandoned its revolutionary legacy and is recovering its traditional values, a new cultural formation is emerging as the nation further integrates itself into the world-system of capitalism. This new cultural formation cannot be simply defined as socialist, capitalist, modern, or postmodern.

Instead, it should be understood as a hybrid postrevolutionary culture that embodies the fundamental tensions and contradictions of globalization."[3] In China, with an intensity accelerating since 1992, this hybrid has been widely adopted under many names, including "Deng Xiaoping thought" and "reform and opening up" (*gaige kaifang*). From the late 1970s, these policy positions encouraged unfettered economic developmentalism (increasing engagement with the forces of globalizing capital on their own terms, with the goal of matching them at their own game), allied with principles of no or little change in Chinese political, social, and cultural spheres. This, Liu Kang argues, is an essentially empty ideology that has "failed spectacularly to reconstruct a new cultural and ideological counterhegemony."[4] Its predecessor, Maoist modernity, which prevailed from 1949 to the late 1970s, was conceived as an alternative to Western modernization in that it privileged "cultural revolution" over economic development of productive forces. Although originally internationalist in spirit (as part of what was anticipated to be a worldwide communist revolution), this utopian vision of China continues to resonate in contemporary life throughout the country, as a set of values, memories, images, a "cultural Maoism" that represents above all the possibility of *collective and mutually beneficial* social transformation, as distinct from changes that benefit individuals, families, or classes. To theorists like Liu Kang, China today is a disjunctive, improvisatory standoff between two failed, yet persistent and still powerful, constructs: Maoist utopianism and Dengist developmentalism. This leaves Liu wondering whether China's polity has advanced beyond that pictured in a controversial book of 1994, *Di san zhi yanjin kan Zhongguo* (Viewing China through a third eye).[5]

In a similar vein, Shanghai-based cultural theorist Wang Xiaoming noted in 2003, "Almost every generalization about China—that it is a communist-led society as before, that at its core it is a society of traditionally centralized power, that it has virtually become capitalist, that it is a fully fledged consumer society, or even that it is already postmodern—can be supported with examples, as can its opposite." He claims that "the social system established in the fifties and sixties is collapsing," that "new classes" are emerging (super-rich, white-collar strata, the unemployed, the rural migrant worker), and that confidence in the ability of government to hold society together is crumbling as China seems "caught in the whirlpool of globalization." How might this situation be interpreted? "When set in sharp relief against this complex reality, the extraordinary persistence of intellectuals in thinking in terms of such dichotomies as traditional/modern, closed/open, conservative/reformer, market/planned, socialism/capitalism, communist/anticommunist, seems simple-minded." The result? "It seems impossible to define contemporary China. In almost every respect she fails to fit existing theoretical models, whether familiar or novel. She seems to be an unwieldy behemoth, the most difficult and unprecedented case of social change in twentieth-century history." His alternative is a more precisely calibrated and independently critical study of contemporary popular culture, particularly the spread within it of "new thought," which he sees as a pervasive yet essentially toxic mix of Deng thought, state power, and the interests of the new rich, "a mainstream ideology that simultaneously poses as a bold heterodoxy."[6] It shares these characteristics with neoliberal economic, political, and cultural policies (a.k.a. globalization) that have dominated the international arena since the 1980s, only recently reaching their limits. While there is clear awareness and use of postmodern concepts and techniques in China, they are deployed in the service of an unabashedly modernizing project. The embrace of globalizing, late capitalist postmodernity by "new thought" includes a subsidiary move to inscribe itself as *Chinese* new thought: a reversal through time to capture the style and spirit but not the politics or ideology of the immediately preceding modernity—that is, of Maoist revolutionary idealism.

In light of subtle interpretations such as these, our understanding of both modern and contemporary art in China might benefit from a more complex theorization of the concepts of "modern" and "contemporary," and of their resonance in social policy and everyday life. The concept of "postmodern" captures, perhaps, some of the strategies and something about the style of these changes, but not their deeper character. I suggest, instead, that what these theorists are describing is precisely China's arrival at its particular condition of contemporaneity. The crisis that erupted in the years around 1990 suddenly shifted a vast national discourse and social praxis from a modernizing, indeed utopian, teleology into one that, while pronouncing its allegiance to an apparently updated and globally resonant modernity, was in fact grappling with a bewildering diversity of proliferating, antinomic cotemporalities. And despite China's extraordinary economic growth and international prominence since then, this condition has remained fundamental. It became starkly evident at the end of 2008, as the global economic crisis began to strip away the illusions of perpetual expansion for most societies—with the striking exception of China. Not until 2015 did China's record-breaking growth suddenly begin to slow, with Premier Xi Jinping moving to promote nationalist sentiment and crack down on dissent.

Arguing against the adequacy of the term "globalization" to encompass the complexities of the current world situation, Fredric Jameson contends, "We

therefore need a global or geographical term for the ways in which chronological nonsynchronicity manifests itself in a spatial or even national form."[7] The
account of postmodernity Jameson and David Harvey developed is a highly
flexible reconceptualization of Marxist base and superstructure theory.[8] Yet it
struggles to match the intense, unsystematic admixture of stasis and dispersion
that characterizes the present. Liu Kang notes that "the explanatory power of
such concepts as 'uneven development' or 'nonsychronicity' is limited in delin-
eating China's historical conjuncture, insofar as the globalizing theorization is
premised on a Eurocentric and teleological narrative of modernity (and postmodernity), which may ultimately exclude possibilities of historical alternatives
and/or alternative histories."[9] I argue that an expanded conception of contemporaneity is necessary, not only to meet Jameson's call for an adequate term, but
also to recognize the actual contemporaneity of historical alternatives and alternative histories—on a global scale, within regions, and within national formations.[10] This leads precisely to a layered picture of how "chronological nonsynchronicity" has manifested itself in Chinese society and art since the late 1970s.

CHINA MODERN

Many scholars argue that modernizing tendencies are evident in China from
the fifteenth to the nineteenth centuries, reminding us that "in the seventeenth-
century world the encounter between Chinese and Euro-American modernities was an encounter of equals, developmentally speaking."[11] Subsequently,
while Europe's industrial revolution in the mid-eighteenth century accelerated
growth and precipitated large-scale cultural transformation, China's technological development was slower in comparison. Yet its social and cultural formations did not cease to modernize, arguably not even when Euro-American
influence in the late nineteenth century led many Chinese intellectuals to
argue that everything Oriental was static and tradition bound, and that innovation originated only in Europe or the US. Updating this outlook in 1949, the
communist state announced the emergence of a new, tradition-destroying, revolutionary modernity. The revolution connected China to the world, this time
within the framework of world revolution and solidarity with international
workers' movements and the governments based on them. Yet this modernization, too, was shaped according to circumstances on the ground, most notably
in its concentration on the peasantry and city workers as "revolutionary classes,"
rather than the industrial proletariat. For artists, Mao Zedong's *Talks at the
Yan'an Forum on Literature and Art*, a collection of speeches originally delivered

in May 1942, became a set of guidelines that continue to resonate, if somewhat faintly, within the vast echo chamber that is official Chinese thought today.

Painter and historian Pan Gongkai, for many years director of the Central Academy of Fine Arts, applies a picture of successive, multilayered modernizations to the development of art in China during the twentieth century. He describes it as having unfolded along four major lines, each modernizing in its own ways and in its own time.

CURRENTS OF MODERN CHINESE ART (*ZHONGGUO XIANDAI YISHU*)

1. Western-style painting (*xiyanghua, xihu,* or *yanghua*) from 1904 onward.
2. National painting (*guohua*), a medieval tradition revived during the 1920s.
3. Chinese socialist realism (*shè huì zhǔ yì xiě shí huà*), from the 1930s, but especially from 1949, up to and including the Cultural Revolution.
4. Popular art (*mínjiān yishu*), including peasant painting as well as crafts throughout the twentieth century.[12]

Elements of each current continue within contemporary art, which most commentators view as beginning to take on its distinctive shapes in the 1970s, and as becoming prominent in the 1990s.

FROM MODERN TO CONTEMPORARY

Most scholars no longer dispute that a shift from modern to contemporary art occurred throughout the world during the late twentieth century. We recognize that this shift did not originate from one or two major metropolitan centers spreading their influence outward, but that it arose independently from within communities all over the globe, that it was a worldwide revolt of the peripheries, the regions, and the decentered centers themselves. Most of us even agree that this differential development accounts for much of the evident diversity of contemporary art. I argue in chapter 2 that we can discern three strong currents within the extraordinary quantity and seemingly limitless diversity of art made since 1989, and in chapter 3 I describe similar tendencies (with distinct internal variations, and different rates of development) in contemporary architecture and design. A brief summary of these arguments might be useful, as a reminder.

Remodernist, retro-sensationalist, and spectacularist tendencies fuse into one current, which continues to predominate in Euro-American and other modernizing art worlds and markets, with widespread effects both inside and outside those constituencies. Against these tendencies emerges art created under nationalist, identitarian, and critical priorities, especially in previously colonized cultures, an art that came into prominence on international circuits, such as in biennials and traveling temporary exhibitions: this is the art of "transnational transitionality." For many artists, curators, and commentators in this second current, art evolves through at least three discernible phases: a reactive, anti-imperialist search for national and localist imagery; then a rejection of simplistic identitarianism and corrupted nationalism in favor of a naïve internationalism; followed by a broader search for an integrated cosmopolitanism, or worldliness, in the context of the permanent transition of all things and relations. The third current cannot be named as a style, a period, or a tendency. It proliferates below the radar of generalization, resulting from the great increase in visual artists worldwide and the opportunities offered by new informational and communicative technologies to millions of users. These changes have led to the viral spread of small-scale, interactive, do-it-yourself art (and art-like output) that is concerned less with high art style or confrontational politics and more with tentative explorations of temporality, place, affiliation, and affect—the ever-more-uncertain conditions of living within our differentiated, divided contemporaneity on an increasingly fragile planet.[13]

How did these global changes manifest in China? First, around 1980, they appeared as local developments within the second current, that of transnational transitionality, as artists responded, in various ways, to the dramatic changes in their nation's conception of itself, changes that seem to have propelled the nation into a state of incessant, accelerated transition. More recently, signs of Chinese artists participating in the third current began to appear, as I show later in this chapter.

The changes that occurred in art around 1980 showed up in exhibitions, such as *China Avant-Garde* (1989), and were quickly historicized by observers at home and abroad. Scholars writing in English, led by Wu Hung and Gao Minglu (both art history professors in the United States and in China), express considerable agreement on the main outlines of developments since the mid-1970s, although they differ on details of emphasis and specifics of interpretation.[14] Most who study Chinese contemporary art distinguish four phases in its development.

PHASES OF CHINESE CONTEMPORARY ART (*ZHONGGUO DANGDAI YISHU*), OR EXPERIMENTAL ART (*SHIYAN MEISHU*)

1. 1976 to 1984: the post–Cultural Revolution period, marked by uncertainty and historical reflection.
2. 1985 to 1989: the new wave (*xinchao*), or avant-garde (*xianfeng*, or *quanwei*), moment.
3. 1989 to the mid-1990s: a time of repression, exile, and protest through performance.
4. Late 1990s to 2008: the rise of internationalist attitudes, the staging of large-scale, survey exhibitions overseas and in China, a burgeoning art market, and a renewed search for "Chinese characteristics."

From summaries available in English, I have noticed that many authors writing in Chinese use similar frameworks when outlining developments that occur during the same period.[15] As narratives, these accounts are structured as if describing a succession of changes within the same kind of art made in China during the modern period. Is this impression of sequential historical development accurate? Is Chinese contemporary art just the latest phase of modern Chinese art, itself a period in the general history of Chinese art? Or is at least some contemporary art made in China markedly different in kind from previous Chinese art?

Wu Hung has offered a careful exploration of the specific contemporaneity (*dangdaixing*) of Chinese contemporary art. In his 2008 essay, "A Case of Being 'Contemporary': Conditions, Spheres and Narratives of Contemporary Chinese Art," he suggests, "Instead of assuming that this type of contemporary art is linked with Modern (and Postmodern) art in a linear, temporal fashion and within a self sustaining cultural system," we should instead pay attention to the "heterogeneity and multiplicity in art production, as well as the creativity of a new kind of artist, who creates contemporary art through simultaneously constructing his or her local identity and serving a global audience." He notes a symptomatic shift from the 1980s to the 1990s in the language used by Chinese artists and critics to characterize their art in general terms: a change from *xiandai yishu* to *dangdai yishu*. Throughout the 1980s, he observes, "Chinese avant-garde artists and art critics envisioned themselves as participants in a delayed modernization movement, which aimed to reintroduce humanism and the ideal of social progress into the nation's political consciousness." These values, they believed, had been derailed during the Mao era, so they attempted to fast-track Western-style modernist development, with a disregard for chronological determinism that paralleled postmodern strategies elsewhere: "It was as if a century-long development of Modern art was simultaneously restaged in China."[16] Their utopian efforts to reinstate and build on these values, however, were set back by the official government reaction to the Tian'anmen uprising, which created another "sharp historical gap," and by the subsequent embrace of globalization under the aegis of Deng Xiaoping thought.[17]

During the 1990s, Wu shows, much leading Chinese art became contemporary in three senses. Many artists turned away from traditional mediums toward installation, performance, and site-specific art that focused on the direct, contemporaneous experience of the participant. Often, in a paradox typical of contemporary art around the world, participants were invited to imagine a suspension of everyday life, a temporal black hole, as in performances staged in city ruins or renovation sites. Second, many Chinese artists learned to create works within the international art language that was emerging within the biennial circuit. This language, in another typical paradox, deploys local and national imagery, but as a highly mobile set of signifiers of nationalities in transformation. In reaction, some Chinese artists emphasized local problems and situations, the Chinese side of this double equation, their art making most sense as a contrast to work they regarded as too concerned with presenting "Chinese symbols" for external consumption. In sum, "This art not only responds to China's startling transformation over the past ten to fifteen years, but further enhances the feeling of speed, anxiety, and theatricality inherent in this external transformation through artistic representation." Wu concludes with an important reflection: the intensity of China's extraordinary economic surge and its burgeoning contemporary art will both, in time, diminish. Contemporaneity, he correctly observes, "inevitably involves the condensation of time."[18]

Wu seems to see the modern art of the 1980s as continuous with modern Chinese art of the twentieth century, however externally inspired its avant-gardism might have been (indeed, its eclectic adoption of multiple Western modes is treated as itself typically modernist). Contemporary art of the 1990s and since, however, he seems to see as a different kind of art, a real rupture in the history of Chinese art and a genuine contribution to the history of world art. This work has been successfully if contentiously created by a strong, innovative, and celebrated cluster of contemporary artists, who continue to work in China as well as abroad. In a sense, they are obliging their cultural milieu to accept their work—however unprecedented, paradoxical, and internationalist in character—as Chinese.

To Gao Minglu, Chinese art has always been concerned with contemporaneity in the general sense that Chinese artists have always been alert to how art might relate to the time in which it is being made. In a 2008 essay, he argues that the concept of modernity in China during the twentieth century was spatial and political rather than temporal, because it emphasized the construction of a new kind of nation, rather than the need to conform to a more global or Western idea of the modern as an epoch in general human development. In this context, contemporaneity understood as a "permanent condition" of continuous, differential transformation has become "a fundamental characteristic" of Chinese modernity. Yet while modernity in the West is understood to proceed by dialectical struggle between absolutes, in China it seeks a more pragmatic, yet nonetheless totalizing (even, arguably, Confucian) path, following, in the words of Hu Shi, a leading figure in the early twentieth-century new cultural movement, "not absolute principle and reason, but rather particular time, specific space, my truth."[19]

Later modern and contemporary Chinese art is created in contexts substantially different from those within which Euro-American artists work. Gao notes that "both socialist and capitalist forces are influential" simultaneously, and have, since 1990, been expected to work together. Nevertheless, "there remain in Chinese society clear markers of cultural and political boundaries." Thus, when Chinese artists during the 1980s created some extremely violent works, they "did so not to attack the public, but rather to resist authority while trying to stimulate thought among the populace."[20] Artists also use actions at historical sites to provoke reflection on official ideologies, performances at new constructions or demolished areas to question the uncritical acceptance of globalization, and exaggerated representations to critique consumerism.[21] Undaunted, the Central Committee in 2006 made "social harmony" a major policy goal (through its Building a Harmonious Socialist Society resolution), and Premier Xi has made it a core of his China Dream ideology.

Close commentaries of the type offered by Wu and Gao suggest that some finer distinctions need to be made within the story presented by the "Phases of Chinese Contemporary Art," that, indeed, it should be split into two sets of developments, each beginning in its own decade, but then continuing to unfold contemporaneously. The first set of phenomena is, in my view, distinctive to the 1980s, and it delineates late modern Chinese art.

LATE MODERN TENDENCIES (1980S)
Western-style painting continues, mostly by overseas Chinese, but within China, it takes the form Gao labels "Maximalism."[22]
National painting (including minorities art) continues, becoming naturalistic scene and portrait painting.

Romantic revolutionary idealism ceases, except as propaganda and a
source of recyclable imagery.

Peasant painting reverts to folk art; crafts continue their traditions.

Avant-garde artists are inspired by both the Western "historical" avant-
garde *and* by late modern Western neo-avant-garde practices (political pop, cynical realists).

Exiled Chinese internationalists (Huang Yong Ping, Xu Bing, Gu Wenda, Cai
Guo-Qiang, Guan Wei) remain important as cosmopolitan translators.

Some of these tendencies are, indeed, continuations of those that constituted modern Chinese art during the main part of the twentieth century. Artists working within each of them were conscious of the others and often incorporated techniques, artistic ideas, or aesthetic strategies from another tendency.
Traditional and national painting continued to be important elements within
Chinese art, although they ceased to dominate it. What I call "Romantic revolutionary idealism" (usually known as Chinese socialist realism) declined in
importance during the 1980s, although thousands of artists throughout the
country continued to produce art for official purposes and events.[23] Avant-
garde art emerges to become a strong current, and Chinese artists in exile make
important contributions to international contemporary art. Each of these currents is an artistic response to aspects of social modernization during the twentieth century. Each builds on precedents in modernized traditional Chinese
art, modernized European academic art, or Euro-American avant-garde art.
Artists remain active within these currents into the twenty-first century, but in
many cases, their work is tending toward repetition and entrenchment rather
than the expansive transformations demanded by our contemporary situation.

Looking at the art produced in China starting in the 1990s in the same
synchronic/diachronic way reveals a further set of developments bursting into
prominence. These are, I believe, the bases of contemporary art in China today.

CONTEMPORARY ART, CONTINUING TENDENCIES (1990S-2000S)

Contemporary artists inspired by Western retro-sensationalists (Zhu
Yu, He Yunchang).

Postrevolutionary critical realism (Zhang Dali, Song Dong, Zhou Xian-
hou, Wang Youshen, Ai Weiwei, Wang Bing).

Postcommunist critical Romanticism (Yang Fudong, Long March Project, *The Revolution Continues!* exhibition).

Internationalist spectacular art (Cai Guo-Qiang, Zhan Wang, Sun
Yuan, and Peng Yu)

Cosmopolitan translators come home but also keep traveling (Xu Bing).

Olympics 2008: overt Chinese nationalist imagery; globalized and renovated traditionalisms.

Chinese art produced by artists of the diaspora, sometimes second and third generation, not national but civilizational in orientation.

Worldly contemporary art, without specifically Chinese characteristics, global in its orientations.

This chart offers a provisional mapping of how contemporary Chinese artists are responding to the world's complexities today. I seek to build on the standard art-historical profile of the main tendencies in contemporary Chinese art since 1980 by describing some of them in a different way, and by highlighting tendencies that are noted in China but not widely discussed there. The artists named exemplify the tendencies within which they have made important, definitive works; many other names could, of course, be cited. Unsurprisingly, a similar variety and contradictory diversity may be found in the contemporary art of all major art-producing countries in the world today.

BOOMING MARKETS, FRAGILE INFRASTRUCTURE

Since 2000, developments inside Chinese art practice have been eclipsed by spectacular changes in the exhibitionary and market infrastructure for art in general and contemporary art in particular. The commercial gallery system in Beijing, Shanghai, and other cities grew at a rapid rate, as did an auction market for Chinese art and antiquities, sustained initially by European and overseas Chinese collectors, not least in Hong Kong, who were soon joined by newly rich, local Chinese buyers. Although ancient art attracts astronomical bids from these collectors, the works of late modern artists also command stellar prices at sales inside China and overseas. Not long after the turn of this century, Chinese artists outnumbered artists of all other nationalities in the top ten highest earners globally. In October 2007, for example, Sotheby's sold Yue Minjun's *Execution* (1995) in London for $6 million, then a record for a living Chinese artist (figure 5.1). In 2010, China overtook the United States as the world's largest market for art and antiquities, although the accuracy of reported data and the completion of contracts are in doubt. In 2013, Artprice.com, a leading monitor of global art markets, joined with Artron,

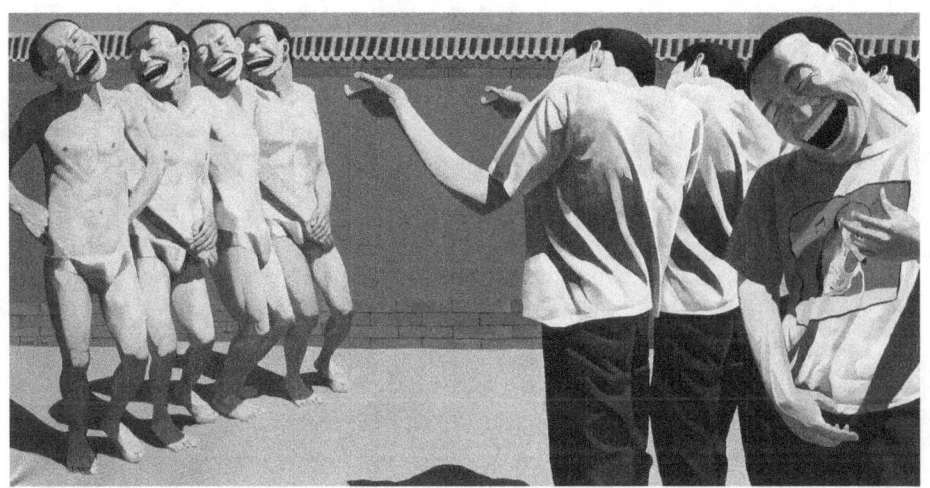

Figure 5.1

Yue Minjun, *Execution*, 1995, oil on canvas, 150 × 300 cm.
Image © 2018 Yue Minjun, courtesy of Pace Gallery, New York.

a Chinese monitor, to report on what they dubbed a "bi-polar" market for art, one split between China and the traditional Western centers, such as London, Paris, and New York, yet with sales of fine art in China amounting to $5.1 billion in 2012, or 41.3 percent of world sales, a clear lead over the US, at 27 percent.[24]

The spate of museum building throughout China is no coincidence, with 451 new museums built in 2012 alone, many of them privately funded art galleries tied to real estate projects but lacking adequate services, expert management, and sustained programming.[25] These developments proceeded on the assumption that boom conditions would continue unabated. But the 2015 crisis in the Chinese share market raised doubts about the future of projects that depend on fallout from the activities of the super rich and the princelings.[26] By 2016, Artprice.com reports of auction sales showed the US leading world markets with 29.5 percent, followed by the UK with 24 percent and China with 18 percent. These figures are more in line with the overall curve since 2000 and reflect a relative slowing of the Chinese economy. Nevertheless, auction sales in China accounted for 90 percent of such sales within Asia, while the region as a whole accounted for 40.5 percent of world volume, followed by Europe at 31 percent, and the Americas at 27.5 percent.[27] If dealer figures are included, overall market share of the world total of US$56.6 billion for sales of art and antiquities is estimated at 40 percent for the US, 21 percent for the UK, and 20 percent for China.[28]

In Euro-American and Latin American art worlds since the 1960s, artist-run collectives and nonprofit contemporary art spaces have offset the commercialization of art by providing young artists with supportive and challenging settings in which to find their ways toward a sustainable career. These environments are still rare in China. Without them, the recent growth in artistic achievement will not be sustainable. Exceptions such as the Ullens Center in the 798 Art District also fill another absence in most if not all major Chinese cities: not-for-profit *museums* of contemporary art. The Today Art Museum, for example, does not fit this bill, as it is a space for hire and is associated with an adjacent private venture. The privatization of contemporary art infrastructure is a striking feature of Chinese developments, reflecting the fact that art galleries, museums, and art districts were conceived in the 1980s and went live in the 1990s, when neoliberalist economics, conservative politics, and spectacularist values dominated public spheres throughout the world, as visual arts fell under the spell of a burgeoning market for contemporary art. Many artist's studios have a commercial gallery orientation (with their own shop-front galleries, and a factory-cum-studio at back); single-artist museums are being built in cities throughout the country as potential tourist sites; and small to quite large exhibition venues are usually run for profit, even when sponsored by a governmental agency (e.g., a school, a district, a suburb, a city, a state, the nation). Some not-for-profit institutions, such as BizArt in Shanghai and the Long March Project in Beijing, are obliged to run businesses to sustain themselves. For similar reasons, philanthropy is difficult in this setting.[29]

Nevertheless, the lineaments of not-for-profit infrastructure can be seen in the major cities and in some provincial settings, although its existence is fragile. Since 1994, Guangzhou painter Chen Tong has sold his work to support the activities of his French-language bookshop and art space, Liberia Borges Institut d'Art Contemporain. Shanghai artists Yu Ji and Deng Yeming founded am Art Space in 2008 as a locus to support young curators by offering them a residency, workshops, and spaces to stage exhibitions and performances. They, too, prefer to fund the space through sales of their work, rather than seeking the patronage of the state, foundations, companies, or private individuals.

About twenty not-for-profit spaces are active in Beijing. For some years, artists divided their work between those institutions that saw themselves as critical supplements to art-world institutions, such as Arrow Factory and Telescope, and those more oriented toward the perceived interests of their *hutong*, or village neighborhoods, such as HomeShop (active 2007–14). Within the regime of the property market, certain developers support art galleries as lifestyle attractors, with some, such as the New Century Art Foundation, even offering support to alternative art spaces, such as LAB47. Alternative art spaces are few, with exceptions such as Radical Space, led by artist Shi Qing. Individuals like philosopher Lu Xing Hua, working with artists such as Made In (Xu Zhen), pour energy into spreading the word about contemporary French theory to artists and others. For example, Lu worked with the Raqs Media Collective to stage *Theory Opera: An Excellent Excuse* at the 2016 Shanghai biennial. Among the few other not-for-profit spaces in Shanghai is the Dinghaiqiao Mutual-Aid Society. It is not oriented toward the art world, but it is located in a distant working-class and migrant suburb, where it focuses, as its name implies, on socially engaged practices. Similarly, Chongqing has a growing art scene based on mixed-purpose alternative spaces, such as Organhaus, which offers self-funded international artists residencies, workshops, participatory projects (such as *Red Line*, on curatorial projects in developing cities), and exhibition opportunities. Experimental art pursued through unusual art spaces is not confined to the cities. For example, ON Space and Blackbridge OFF Space are developing programs far outside the Beijing city center.[30]

Infrastructural support for the education, training, encouragement, and recognition of independent art-critical writers has been conspicuously absent throughout the boom years and remains rare. Some prizes have been offered, but much more needs to be done by educational institutions, government departments, and private individuals if the essentials of "intellectual infrastructure" are to take root. Without the challenge coming from fully resourced, independent criticism and curating, Chinese contemporary art will struggle to move beyond its present stage. While the market itself has clearly been a major factor in the contemporary art boom, the recent downturn will expose the fact that markets are, after all, not in themselves creative generators but instead merely distribution systems, essentially dependent on the creativity and productivity of artists, the ideas and interpretations supplied by critics, the exhibitions organized by curators, the informed audiences trained by educators, and the goodwill of those who can see beyond the narrow perspective of their own immediate interests.

How have these art-historical and infrastructural developments played out where it really counts, that is, inside the practice of artists? In the decades of confused aftermath following the Cultural Revolution, the opening up of Chinese culture to the rest of the world meant that artists became aware, simultaneously, of the three enormously powerful but mutually contradictory models of how to pursue a relevant art practice. The stunning array of artistic achievement throughout the world during the twentieth century, especially that of Euro-American avant-gardism; the postmodern presumption that all past art was available to the present, singly or in any imaginable combination, and without the need to work through art's own historical development; and the rewards offered by the international market to those artists, such as Jeff Koons and Damien Hirst, who followed the Andy Warhol model of holding up to their cultures easily understandable mirror images of their own consumerist distraction. This third option, which I have named "retro-sensationalism," became so prominent in the 1990s that it seemed at the time to constitute the leading edge of contemporary art. Its signature stylistic features, such as shocking imagery, single concept, unusual medium, and exaggerated size, were adopted by many Chinese artists, and adapted to the late modern styles that they had already developed.

Other artists pursued postmodern repeats of late modernism, notably pop art, presenting them as interrogations of Chinese modernity (Maoist style). At the time, these artists were called "cynical realists." In my view, this was inaccurate: "cynical" mistranslates the *ironic* orientation of these artists. And if "realism" refers to their use of figurative rather than abstract styles, then it, too, is inadequate. Yet the title does suggest something about the artists' underlying intention: like the Sots Artists and Moscow Conceptualists in Russia during the last years of the Soviet Union, the cynical realist artists presented ironic restatements of official imagery, obliquely displaying its hollow duplicity. This was, in the circumstances, a realist approach. Collectors in Hong Kong, overseas Chinese, Euro-American collectors, and the new Chinese bourgeoisie have warmly welcomed this art. Since then, however, the work of leading artists such as Fan Lijun, Wang Guangyi, Zhang Xiaogang, and Yue Minjun has become locked into increasingly inflated repetition. By staying with their signature styles, and repeating them at an ever-larger scale, these artists cement their location within late modernism but risk becoming less and less contemporary as time goes on.

Given the strength and pervasiveness of Deng Xiaoping thought, as well as China's evident commitment to rapid internal modernization and embrace of globalizing capitalism while maintaining static conceptions of state power, I am obliged to characterize the period since 1979 as "postrevolutionary." Nevertheless, many artists remain committed to a resistant realism. In my view, this is the most important tendency in contemporary Chinese art, the one with the inner strength to secure its future as art. It can be pursued in any style or medium, from the most traditional to the newest. Ai Weiwei is the outstanding representative of this orientation. Essentially a sculptor working in the post-Duchampian vein of assisted readymades, he accumulates found objects and molds them into silent yet resonant condemnations of official corruption, hypocrisy, and repression. His dogged persistence against state persecution, and his brilliance at revealing its squalid details through social media, has made his quest for freedom of expression the main topic in global understandings of contemporary Chinese art.[31]

In the hands of other artists, critique may take the form of a resigned nostalgia for Maoist modernity. Wang Youshen, well known for covering of a section of the Great Wall in newspaper advertisements in 1993, exemplifies this response in his subsequent work. His *1991–2006 Announcement Board* series of installations (2006) were based on photographs of popular exhortations chalked up on blackboards in hutong neighborhoods during the Mao years (figure 5.2). Typically, three tomb-like white plaster monuments show, in turn, a mounted photograph from the Cultural Revolution, the same image occluded by clouds of forgetting, and finally the image now entirely devoid of color, a barely visible set of lines on the pale surface of the slab. Subsequently, he presented images of Beijing's massive modernization program in emblematic architecture but paired each photograph of a new building with one that had been subject to immersion in water or erosion by exposure to the elements, as if anticipating the future ruination of these structures. Another kind of implied critique was apparent in his mural-sized display of more than one hundred Polaroid photographs that record details of the response to the SARS epidemic of 2003. In images of individuals and local organizations actively responding, in contrast to the slow official reaction, we can see the embattled seeds of civil society struggling to take root.

Many contemporary artists revisit traditional artistic modes but treat them as a medium through which to make a statement of current relevance, creating attractive yet artificial screens through which a hidden truth about the present might be revealed. For example, Sha Yeya often uses what looks like a meticulous literati style to paint what seem to be traditional hanging-scroll landscapes, yet the brush marks record the text of important contemporary statements, using illegible characters. A striking example is his 2002 work *Powell Denies the Possibility*

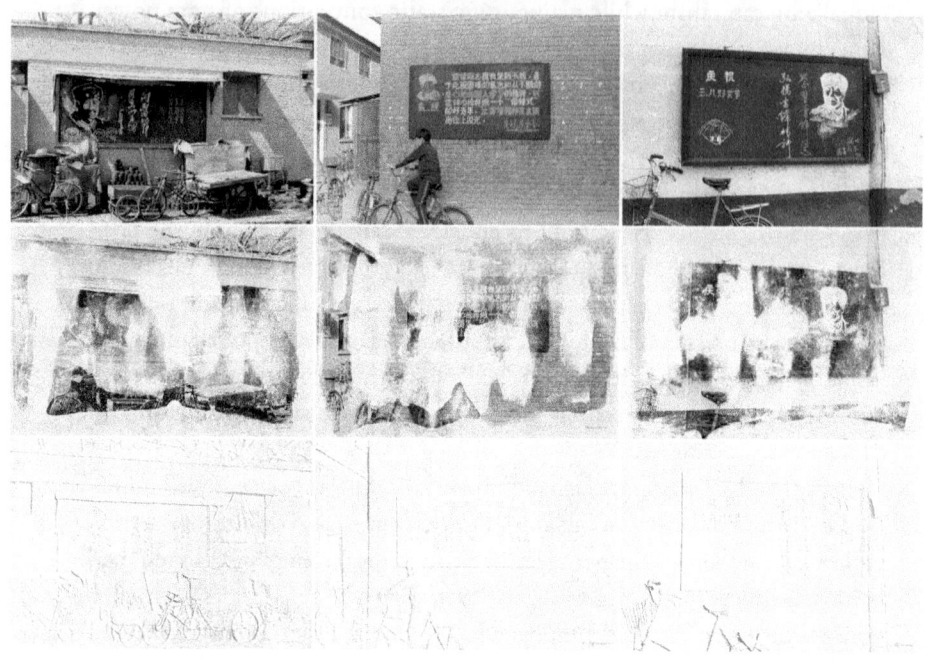

Figure 5.2

Wang Youshen, *1991–2006 Announcement Board*, 2006, photographs and fiberglass (in three pieces). © Wang Youshen and ShanghArt Gallery, Shanghai and Beijing.

of War Declaration on Iraq, Saying That America Will Not Take Action without Consulting Its Allies, in which the artist captures a now notorious instance of official misinformation. Along with Gu Wenda, Xu Bing is a longtime master of using such techniques to suggest the deceptive nature of official discourse. His *A Book from the Sky* (1988) is the most famous example, later matched by his gigantic work *Phoenix*. Commissioned in 2009 to create a large public sculpture for the foyer of a major Beijing office and hotel building, he chose two phoenixes—traditional symbols of spiritual growth through the conjunction of the sexes (and the logo of the commissioning company)—as resplendent, suspended forms. But he insisted on composing them entirely from leftover materials at the building site and highlighted the tools of the farm workers who had migrated to the city to serve as laborers in the building of the Chinese "economic miracle." When

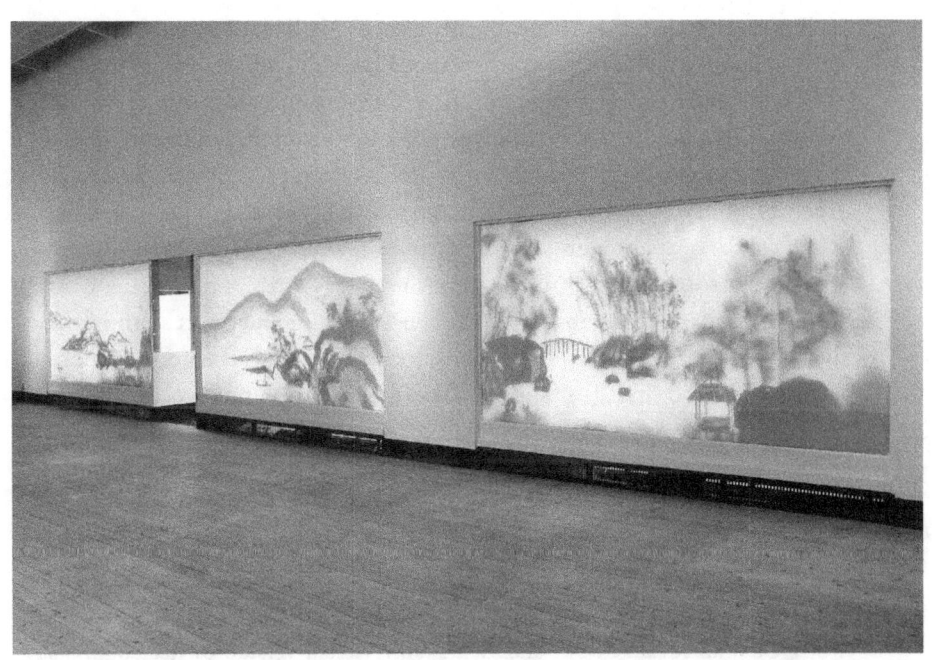

Figure 5.3

Xu Bing, *Background Story*, 2004, mixed media. Installation
view at Museum für Ostasiatische Kunst, Berlin, 2004.
© Xu Bing Studio, Beijing and Brooklyn, NY.

I saw the phoenixes in his studio in 2009, the huge, colorful assemblages were
covered with the fine, chalky dust that settles on everything at every building site
in Beijing, often spreading throughout the city. The dust is essential to the realism
of this work, as it was to his 2004 installation *Where Does the Dust Itself Collect?*
a poignant memorial to the victims of the September 11 terrorist attacks, victims
who, in the broadest sense, had come to include all of us. Xu Bing's *Background
Story* series, begun in 2004, comprises installations in which he re-creates, across
a large backlit screen, the illusion of famous ancient scroll paintings, using actual
plant material, plus natural and industrial refuse, such as straw and newspapers
(figure 5.3). While the tradition of Chinese ink painting is respectfully evoked, it
is also shown to be a construction, something viewers may discover by looking
behind the screen, as they are invited to do.[32]

The reverse trajectory occurs in the work of Hu Zhijun, a peasant potter who for many years has directed his considerable craft skills toward chronicling the developments in contemporary Chinese art, creating an in-between world of fantasy figurines, based on images in well-known paintings and sculptures by his famous professional contemporaries. In his hands, these images cease to be trophies signifying wealth. They leave the realms of the rich to join the visual worlds of the people, to dwell among their souvenirs.

Among artists active within the third current, the work of new media artist Cao Fei stands out. Her 2006 video *Whose Utopia* is a three-part study of the Siemens Company OSRAM lightbulb factory in Foshan, Guangdong province (figure 5.4). In the first, the camera follows the manufacturing processes in the spirit of Fernand Léger's famous film of 1926, *Ballet mécanique*; in the second, certain factory workers enact their fantasy lives as an angel, a rock guitarist, and, in the case of a middle-aged supervisor, a Michael Jackson–style break dancer; while in the third, several workers pose for the camera in their work-places while the musical voice-over suggests that utopia is not for them, whatever their dreams. From 2007 to 2012 Cao Fei created, on the site Second Life, RMB City, an idealized but crazily unstable virtual version of her country's hyperdeveloped reality, which she visits as her avatar China Tracy. Recently, she has moved to a darker, more dystopic vision of the world's future. Her film *Haze and Fog* (2013) immerses us in the polluted environments too common in turbo-capitalist cities, while in her long film, *La Town* (2014), the camera eye relentlessly pans over settings suggestive of a postapocalyptic future in a place that could be anywhere on the planet.[33] Currently she is rebuilding a cinema in Hongxia, originally erected in 1959 in the Soviet-inspired Jiuxianqiao factory district to commemorate the fabrication of China's first computer, and devoted to showing films that would entertain and encourage local workers. Based on extensive interviews with residents, the artist aims to document this past utopian space, and to re-present it as genuinely nostalgic: a utopic dream of a socialist way of life now lost in the past as a general ambition for the whole of society, but available in this one space for the few who wish to visit.[34]

Other new media artists of Cai Fei's generation and younger, such as Jenova Chen and Lu Yang, prefer to use video game settings and pictorial logics, creating immersive environments that, in contrast to the violent rites of passage common in most Western video games, tend toward providing rather vapid fantasies of escape from the pressures of the present.

For many years, personal experience appeared as the core subject mostly in the work of women artists, such as Lin Tianmao, Cui Xiuwen, Bingyi, and Chen

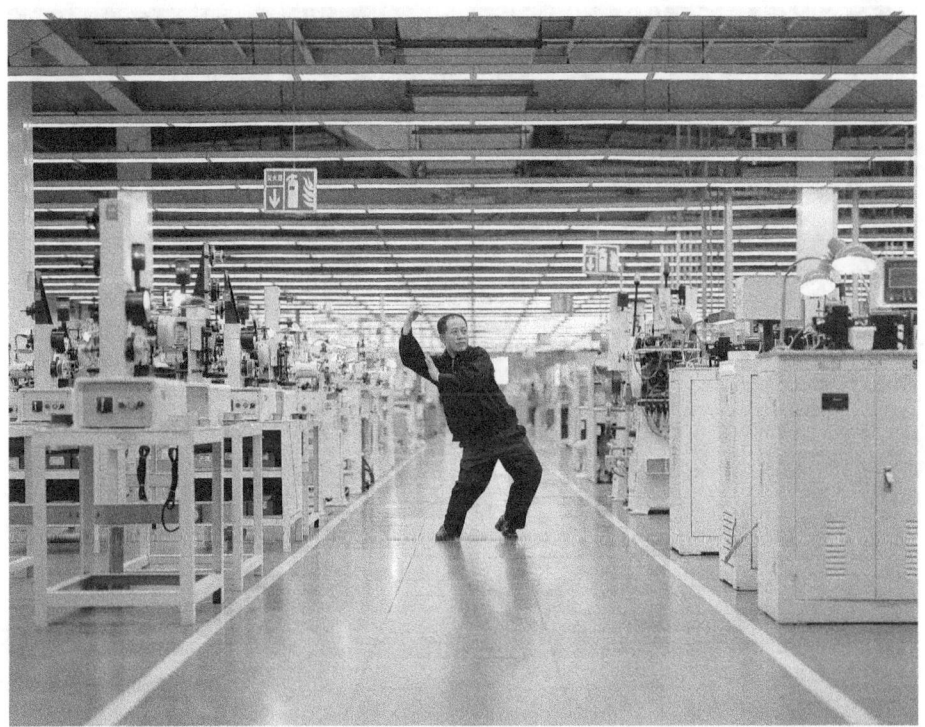

Figure 5.4

Cao Fei, *Whose Utopia*, 2006, video, projection, color, and
sound, twenty minutes, Tate Collection, London. © Cao Fei
and Tate Images.

Lingyang. Each is concerned in different ways with the fragility of selfhood in
worlds dominated by political ideologies, commercial brands, and patriarchal
power. These concerns animate the thousands of "postinternet" artists active in
China today. Many seem content to reproduce virtual imagery or follow its protocols in a relatively unquestioning way. Others, such as Cheng Ran, pay attention to how its seemingly infinite capacity to mash mediums can fragment a person's sense of self. In Jing Yuan Huang's 2013 series *I Am Your Agency*, she scours
the internet to find photographs posted by ordinary people of the banal objects
and scenes from everyday life that are meaningful to them (figure 5.5). She then

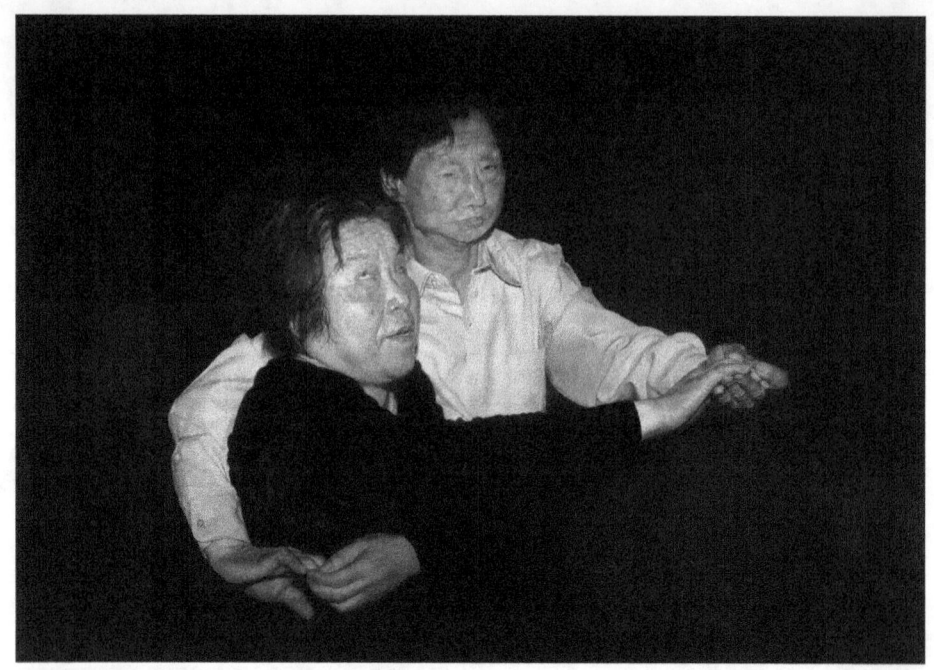

Figure 5.5

Jing Yuan Huang, *I Am Your Agency 22*, 2013, oil on canvas,
73.0 × 107.5 cm. © Jing Yuan Huang and White Rabbit Gallery,
Sydney. Image courtesy of White Rabbit Collection, Sydney.

paints them with painstaking attention and respectful care, creating a frisson between her highly skillful artistry and these poorly made, socially awkward, and frankly ugly subjects. In so doing, she exposes traces of something almost impossible to represent: the ways in which the pictorial logics of the globalized image world are affecting the private unconscious and the public consciousness of the world's peoples.[35]

Questions such as this interest the current generation of increasingly mobile artists, who are becoming accustomed to working all over the world. Like many Chinese artists of her generation, Jing Yuan Huang was trained overseas (at the Art Institute of Chicago), has lived overseas for long periods (in her case, Canada), and, while based in Beijing, travels and exhibits abroad. Responding to this situation, a few exhibitions have been devoted to the work of over-seas Chinese artists, some including work by artists of other ethnicities, rais-ing the question, What is a Chinese artist?[36] While museums for showing all forms of art, but mostly modern and contemporary art, are being built all over China at an astonishing pace, significant collections have been formed by overseas collectors, such as Uli Sigg (although that is returning to China, to Hong Kong's M+), Guy Ullens (although its future location remains un-certain), and Judith Neilson (her White Rabbit Gallery in Sydney is build-ing a major extension for its collection of "21st century Chinese art"). A 2015 article in the *Art Newspaper* made the point that "much of the most interest-ing art produced in China today is no longer easily identifiable as Chinese."[37] The authors highlight the fact that, while the ideas and situations that trigger younger artists' work remain quite specifically local, the forms through which they express these contents are overtly international, even universalizing. Li Jinghu's *White Clouds* (2009) is a Dan Flavin–type installation of suspended neon tubes, except that in this work, they hover over the space to evoke the glare of fluorescent lighting in the mass production factories of the artist's home city, Dongguan, where work goes on day and night to meet the needs of global markets for products made by cheap labor (figure 5.6). Sculptor Wang Yugang's *Identity* (2015) is a six-meter-high tower of overlapping layers of wood, stone, and brass, the dimensions of which were established by com-puter modeling of pages from an edition of Karl Marx's classic text *Capital: A Critique of Political Economy*, published in 1867 and still relevant, even con-temporary, today (figure 5.7).

In a hyperconnected world, it has even become possible for non-Chinese artists to create works about China's mythical and actual connectedness to the world's economic and symbolic currents that match those created by Chinese artists. British artist Isaac Julien's *Ten Thousand Waves* (2010) is a profoundly moving, seductively beautiful nine-screen cinematic installation shot in China during the preceding four years (figure 5.8). There is no coherent narrative; rather, fragments from various events, stories, memories, and other films are projected in overlapping time sequences on nine screens that hang at oblique angles in the installation space. Grainy black-and-white footage shot from a he-licopter records attempts to rescue a group of Chinese cockle pickers stranded by incoming tides in Morecambe Bay, Cumbria, in northwest England. Unable to communicate, twenty-one of the male and female illegal immigrants from Fujian province drowned; only one survived. Visiting the site afterward, Julien learned of a sixteenth-century tale of a goddess who led fishermen lost at sea to

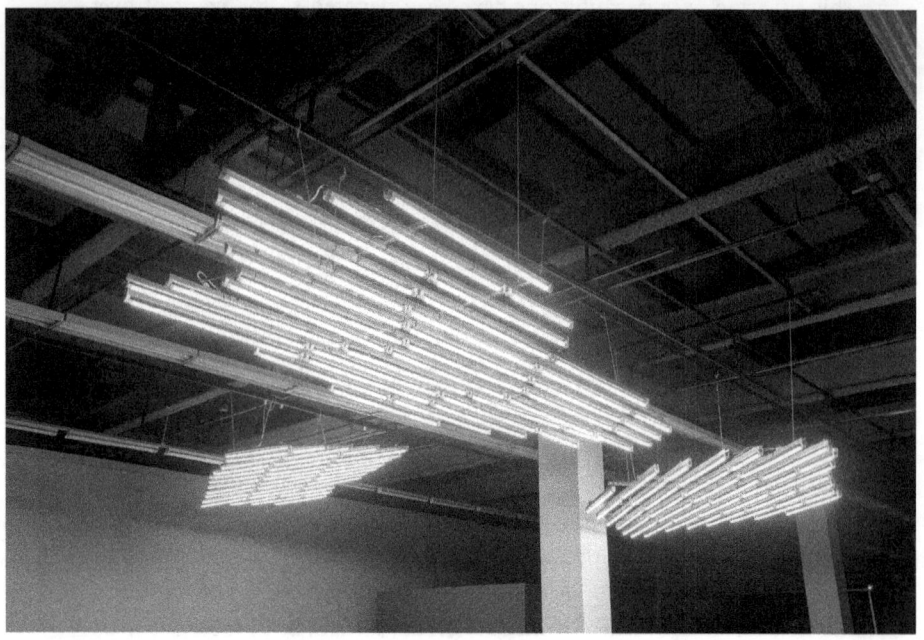

Figure 5.6

Li Jinghu, *White Clouds*, 2009–16, LED lighting, metal frame,
dimensions variable. Image courtesy of the artist and Magician
Space, Beijing. Photo by Doyun Kim. © Leap Magazine,
Li Jinghu, and J&Z Gallery, Shenzhen.

safety. Well-known actress Maggie Cheung plays this goddess in the film, while
a ghostly protagonist, played by rising star Zhao Tao, leads us to the famous
Shanghai Film Studio, via a restaging of the 1934 classic *The Goddess*. In other
sequences, we hear a poem, "The Waves," by Wang Ping, which is also rendered
using ink on glass in masterful calligraphy by Gong Fagen, which is then wiped
away by young men in contemporary dress. Viewers are invited to sit for a time
as one scene unfolds, to walk between screens, seeking associations, making
connections, imagining narratives, or acknowledging those moments when the
world's chaos just is what it is. In this case, the nine double-sided screens seem
essential to creating a sense of the terrible dangers but also the fragile beauties
of global connectedness.

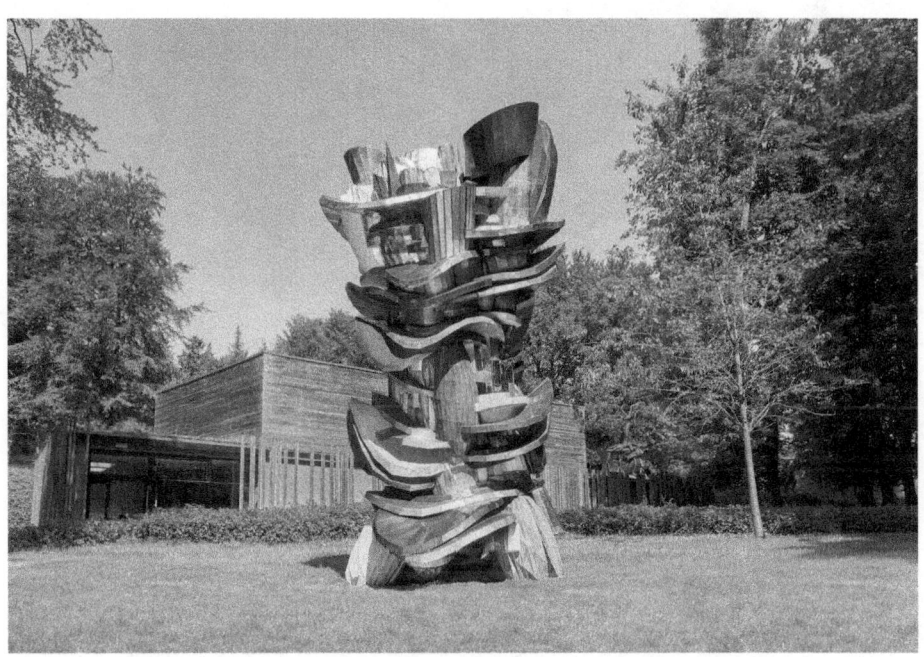

Figure 5.7

Wang Yugang, *Identity*, 2015, wood, stone, and brass, Cass
Sculpture Foundation, West Essex. © 2017 Cass Sculpture
Foundation. Photo by Barney Hindle.

DOES THE REVOLUTION CONTINUE?

Many unresolved questions remain. One stems from the idea that, however dramatic the changes constituting contemporary Chinese art may seem, they may simply be minor variations in the centuries-long evolution of "Chinese art"—a diverse yet essentially coherent output of fine art and craft that is distinctively Chinese in character. "China," here, is understood less as a nation than as a civilization. One version of this is the concept of "Cultural China" theorized by Tu Wei-ming in the 1980s and early 1990s.[38] If this perspective is combined (against its grain) with extreme nationalism, such that only certain Chinese—those with the correct understanding of the essence of "Chineseness"—can determine which art shares this quality, then the diametrically opposite view is also

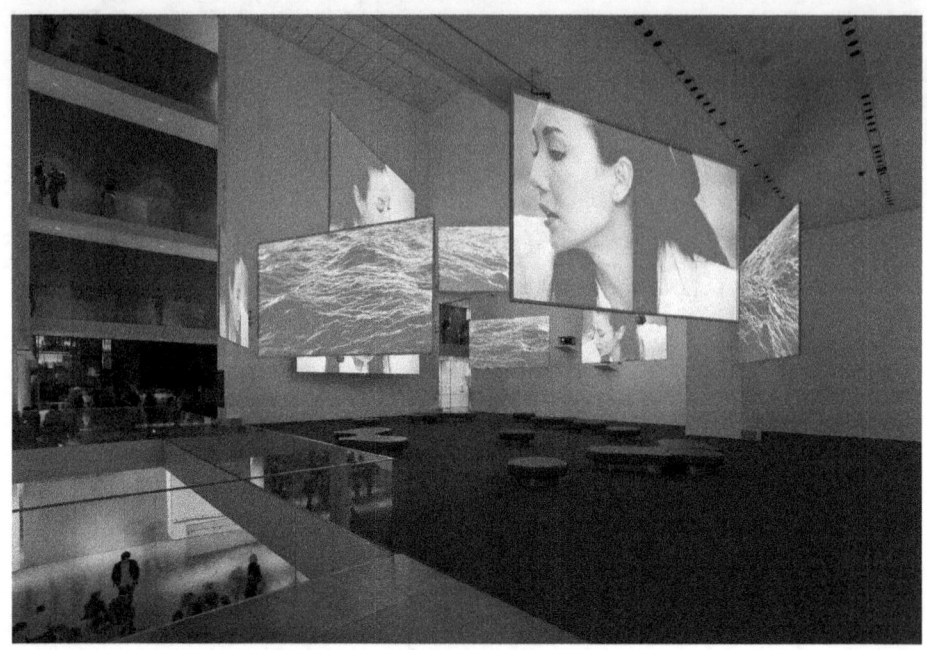

Figure 5.8

Isaac Julien, *Ten Thousand Waves*, 2010, nine-channel video,
fifty-five minutes. Installation view, Museum of Modern Art,
New York, 2013–14. Photo by Johnathan Muzikar. © The
Museum of Modern Art/Licensed by SCALA/Art Resource, NY.

possible: "contemporary art" is a foreign, anti-Chinese imposition that should be
rejected with the same vigor that finally threw out the opium importers.[39]

In recent years, the tendency known during the twentieth century as "national painting" is reappearing. It does not picture the bland, brand-name
imagery that typifies globalization but is precisely a brand-oriented rework-
ing of traditional styles, techniques, and mediums. A notable example is the
ink paintings of Xu Longsen. Entirely and painstakingly brushed by the artist
and assistants, their distinctive feature is their massive size (figure 5.9). They
are of the spectacular scale of Richard Serra's museum-filling sculptures or Jeff
Koons's public art. The effect is uncanny: gestures that we are used to seeing
at the human scale of a handheld brush loom over the spectator like huge bill-

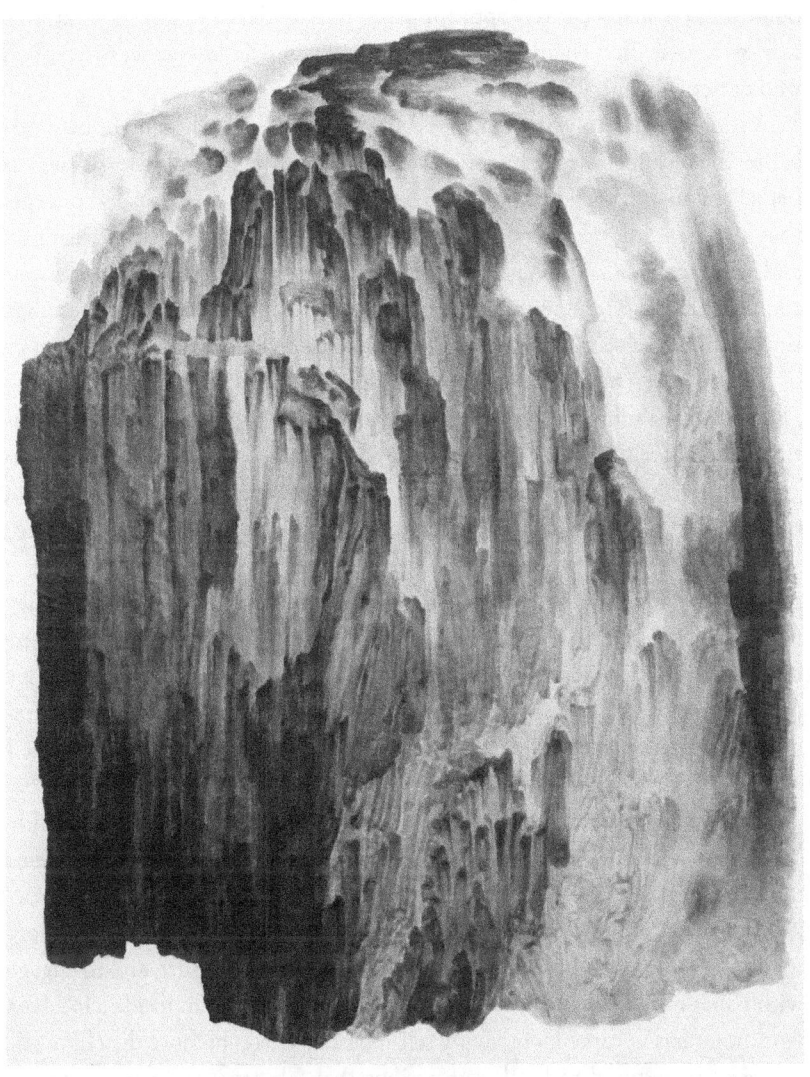

Figure 5.9

Xu Longsen, *A Mountain Is None the Worse for Being High No. 2*,
2015, ink on rice paper, Grand Space Gallery, China. Image
courtesy of the artist.

boards. Their size is entirely appropriate to the façades of buildings or motorway overpasses. In such gigantism, are we witnessing the emergence of a globalized national imagery?

A more subtle, universalizing appeal to "national thought" might be motivating the recent efforts of historians such as Gao Minglu and theorists such as Peng Feng to draw on ideas proposed by their predecessors, especially concepts that seek a middle way between Chinese and Western aesthetics, art theories, and art practices. Gao advances a theory that presents *yi pai* as such a pathway, claiming that Western aesthetic theories are fatally limited by their presumption that art is always a representational practice, whereas the conjunction of *li*, *shi*, and *xing* (principle, concept, and likeness) identified during the Tang Dynasty in the ninth century, offers a historical and pluralistic conceptualization of art more suited to the present.[40] Peng has suggested a return to the concept of *xiang*, the state of becoming into being between the thought (*dao*) and the thing (*qi*), as most suited to the sense of presence in contemporary art.[41] Whatever their merits or shortcomings, these ideas may be seen as gestures toward the nationalism often required of intellectuals in "rising China," or they may be a strategy to "save" innovative and critical contemporary art from its neotraditionalist, Mao modernizing, and Deng postmodernizing critics. They may, of course, also be a buffer against the limitations of external interpretations of contemporary Chinese art, however well intentioned, such as those I offer in this essay.

Taken all together, as an ensemble of actually diverse but also constantly convergent practices, Chinese contemporary art, wherever it is made, seems tenacious and likely to outlast the inevitable decline in its hyperinflated market, signs of which have been evident in recent years. Many of the artists whose work I have discussed continue to react to changes in world art, and to engage with issues raised by global contemporaneity, although from inside a local art world that has become increasingly self-focused. This is because they have felt the need to respond to local expectations that Chinese artists contribute in some way—supportively, critically, or from positions in between—to the national project, itself a highly contested domain, as is obvious to all observers, both inside and outside the country. The wild overstatements that have stocked the Chinese Pavilion at Venice Biennales in recent decades attest to this impossible expectation.

At the 2009 forum, curator Jiang Jiehong gave voice to many of the tensions, contradictions, and confusions, as well as to the hopes and inspirations, which I review in this chapter.

"Contemporary art" ought not to be interpreted in a chronological way in the first place, since each era has its own art full of its own contemporaneity. "Contemporaneity" and "critique" of visual arts should be the top, essential, and pertinent issues for intellectuals engaged in the practice of contemporary art. Without such consideration as a foundation, one may still be an artist, but not a "contemporary" artist in any sense. If the practice of "contemporaneity" could be said as the vocation of contemporary artists, the so-called Chineseness that probably exists can be regarded as an instinct of rising to the occasion, an inherent quality, and a kind of wisdom to achieve success one way or another, for better or worse. . . . When silence goes beyond the limits of being bearable, it begins to change and rebellion ensues. In the context of contemporary Chinese art, it is this hidden spirit of rebellion that prompted challenging changes in visual practices.[42]

Since then, art making in China has, paradoxically, become more open to interaction with artists, critics, curators, and collectors in the rest of the world yet also more internalized and isolated in spirit. This reflects a larger paradox in China's relationships to the wider world, and in its struggles to manage the nature and pace of internal change. This paradox is, of course, a problem not confined to China. For artists, critics, curators, and everyone involved in creative practices, everywhere in the world, the main challenge is not to decide whether to be "contemporary," "modern," or "traditional" in one's practice and values. Whatever one's orientation, the real challenge is to work outward from where one is located, and to work toward a situation in which, together, we might forge a critical, coeval, and constructive engagement with the world's accelerating complexity.

country, indigeneity, sovereignty

Aboriginal Australian Art

For the past forty years, Indigenous artists in Australia, most of whom are Aboriginal and Torres Strait Islanders, have overcome one difficulty after another to create a diverse yet coherent, locally grounded yet nationwide art movement, remarkable in itself, and exceptional in its capacity to generate surges of self-replenishment. While being very much of its present time, this art is also founded on beliefs, procedures, and imagery that, despite countless vicissitudes, have been adaptable enough to maintain definitive continuities for at least fifty thousand years. Such a conjunction of radically different temporalities is characteristic of our contemporaneity and provokes many questions, each with far-reaching implications. Those wishing to enter this labyrinth by asking how this art might be best understood in general terms soon strike the conundrum of whether it is traditional or neotraditional, modern or contemporary. Like many matters attending the lives of Indigenous peoples in Australia, especially those involving their relationships with non-Indigenous Australians, this question seems urgently in need of an accurate and enabling answer, yet at the same time, the question is so complex in its connotations as to admit only quasi-resolutions that, however well intentioned on all sides, would seem fated to cause harm. Imposing an external "solution" in such situations is a guarantee of failure, as the recent (and still current) Intervention into Aboriginal communities in the Northern Territory demonstrated—indeed, it joined an unending succession of failed governmental policy.[1] In the face of such challenges, the impulse to treat Indigenous art, especially that issuing from remote communities, as sui generis, a phenomenon unique in itself, maybe as a miracle, is understandable.[2] This view leaves us gaping in awed admiration, then eventually turning away, toward boredom, because we have assigned this art to the categories of eighteenth-century European aesthetics—to a sublime-every-time—and when that is exhausted, as it soon must be, we will have reduced our response to a watered-down, aestheticized version of Kantian disinterest. These are acts of pure externalization that strive to push everything back into its prior artistic, cultural, social, and political place, but, in fact, in contemporary circumstances, they debilitate all that they touch.

The conventional art-historical equivalent of such responses is to subsume this art within *one* of the categories listed above—traditional, neotraditional, modern, or contemporary—as if the category itself somehow preceded the art and, moreover, fundamentally governed its making, distribution, meaning, and affect. Both of these moves—aestheticization and applying conventionalized art history—ignore key agents in this game: the artists themselves as producers of their own communicative meaningfulness, as well as the enabling efforts of those committed to assisting its circulation to the world, and those interpreters of their art dedicated to explicating precisely this quality within it. Both approaches also militate against what is arguably the greatest value of this art, its significance as a gesture that, for a considerable period, went beyond art worlds and art history to achieve a politico-ethical dimension, indeed, to create a field of conciliation between cultures, one of which has, for over two centuries, been determined to eradicate or, at best, assimilate the other. We are then obliged to pursue the opening question, and to quickly recast it so that it yields realistic yet generative answers, historically accurate and of value to all concerned.

EMPTY UNIVERSALISM

We might begin by locating the question within the longest possible historical trajectory, that of humankind on the planet. David Christian's *This Fleeting World: A Short History of Humanity*, a handbook for teachers of "big history" in the secondary schools of the US and elsewhere, includes a one-page chart headed "Three Major Eras in World History."[3] Of course, any such condensation of information must trade in massive oversimplification. Accompanying texts are then full of qualifications.[4] Yet such generalized mapping tends to recast the core question along these lines: How can we regard as modern or contemporary the art of a foraging people, whose way of life has been displaced for centuries, and whose near extinction by the forces of ever-accelerating population growth, urbanization, and industrial consumption of the world's resources is one of the defining features of the modern world? The implied answer is obvious: they exist in the "contemporary era," but they are anachronisms; their way of life will, sadly, disappear from the forward march of history; their art and their culture will survive only in museums. This attitude toward others in their midst is not peculiarly Eurocentric, as it is, regrettably, shared by many people in cultures elsewhere in the world, but it is Occidentalist—a prime example of what Okwui Enwezor labels "Westism."[5]

Within art-world discourse, where anachronism is widely prized—for example, the core experience of being in an art museum presumes it—such issues are usually treated more specifically, yet no less narrowly. Consider two quite common ways of registering the contemporaneity of Indigenous Australian art.

The output of certain Aboriginal artists from remote communities since 1970 has been widely heralded as the most accomplished art produced in Australia, and among the best abstract painting being made anywhere during the period. It achieves attention in the local and international markets for contemporary art as a specific category. The implication is clear: this art is contemporary because the critics, the markets, the collectors, and the museums say so. In actuality, even though marketing does label Indigenous Aboriginal art of all kinds as "contemporary," the auction houses have, until recently, tended to sell it in specialist sales, usually separate from those featuring the work of non-Indigenous Australian artists or "international" old master or modern art. Incremental change is, however, occurring, for reasons I discuss in the latter sections of this chapter.

A second response is to note that the art of city-based artists with Indigenous heritage, such as the late Gordon Bennett, is prominent among art that deals powerfully with the contradictions of contemporary life. Tracey Moffatt's photographic and video allegories of our thoroughly mediated condition are highly, and rightly, esteemed in international contemporary art circles. The implication of observations such as these is equally clear: this art is contemporary because its content, techniques, and meanings are consonant with those prevailing in these circles. It is, therefore, at home in the commercial galleries specializing in contemporary art, in the biennials that feature it, and in the museums that show it.

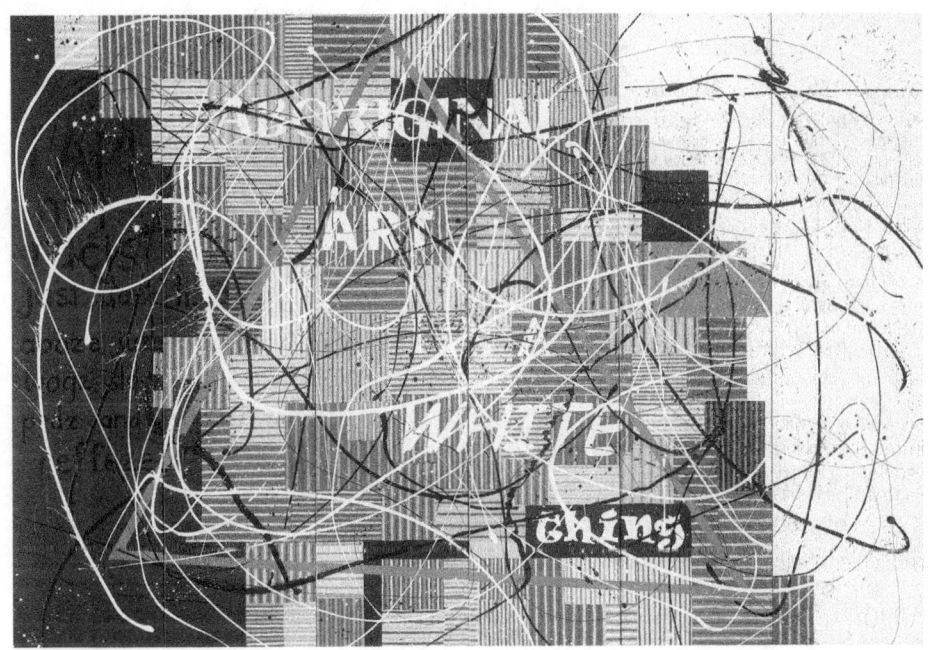

Figure 6.1

Richard Bell, *Bell's Theorem: Aboriginal Art—It's a White Thing*,
2002–3, acrylic on canvas, 240 × 540 cm. Image courtesy of the
artist and Milani Gallery, Brisbane.

Do these judgments assimilate Indigenous Australian artists to incompatible, Western aesthetic criteria? They certainly accept that the Euro-American art world and its institutions most powerfully define what contemporary is. From this perspective, if Indigenous art fits within the prevailing criteria, or can be made to fit them with some artful adjustments, then it is contemporary, but if not, too bad. Such gatekeeping, and its inevitable statement of cultural power, is parodied in Murri artist Richard Bell's "theorem": *Aboriginal Art—It's a White Thing* (figure 6.1).[6]

Once we begin to consider these questions from the perspective of artists from remote communities, however, it becomes immediately apparent that their main goal has never been to deposit their output into an imagined, universal, art-historical canon—to line up for assessment as contributors to phases labeled with terms like "traditional," "modern," "postmodern," or "contemporary." Rather, their art making is first the product of existential necessity, as it is for most artists anywhere, but in this case, it is one of the few available strategies for surviving the conditions of colonization and for finding a sustainable mode of reconciliation with the colonizing other. These conditions have changed in major ways since British settlement in 1788, but they remain colonial in structure. This does not mean that Indigenous peoples have accepted these conditions lying down. Aboriginal art, as an industry, might be a "white thing," as Richard Bell states, but the whole "white art thing" can be Aboriginalized, as he is also fond of saying. This is clearly the case for city-based Indigenous artists. That it is also true for those working in remote communities is less obvious, but I show it to be so, albeit differently, in the course of this chapter. Indigenous Australian art is, therefore, a *contemporary* creation of cultural value: it presents carefully and conscientiously wrought manifestations of a multimillennial temporality *as it makes it way through the present*.[7] Aboriginal art also draws on lessons learned from two hundred years of adapting to the modernizing forces brought to the continent by the invaders, whose overwhelming presence sought to establish Western modernity as the prevailing normality, only to find that this, too, is passing into a world shaped by a multiplicity of different temporalities that compete for space, and a multiplicity of kinds of art that compete for visibility. As I have been arguing, this has created another arrangement of temporalities, a contemporaneity of difference, which plays out on a world stage that is at once more closely connected than ever before but also more disparate, open-ended, and unstable. Alongside the rest of us, Indigenous Australians are now making their way through this new disposition of time zones.

A CULTURAL COLONIALISM

To grasp the full complexity of the cultural exchanges in play requires some basic information. Migrating to the island continent between fifty thousand and sixty thousand years ago, Aboriginal peoples subsequently lived in relative isolation from external contact, except for Macassan traders in the North and rare visits from European explorers, until the British possession of 1770, followed by settlement, commencing in 1788. The roughly 750,000 Indigenous people then living on the continent are understood to have spoken languages that linguists divide into around six hundred groups. Their narratives of generation and continuity, known as "Dreaming stories," vary from place to place while sharing many structural features in common. All are accounts of origin and descent, in which the Originary Beings are understood to be alive in the present, in the specific aspects of the world that they created and in the living beings descended from them. To evoke this presence, these narratives are ritually repeated in ceremonial song cycles and dance performances, as well as indicated through formal compositions of visual signs that are painted on bodies, carved into rocks or tree trunks, painted on rocks or bark cut from trees, or marked out in the desert sands using natural minerals or other colored materials. In remote communities, and in many towns and cities, these practices are taught to every-body, through graduated initiation, as the essential means to understand "coun-try" and to respect "the law." The authority to represent sacred knowledge, and to share secular versions of it, remains with the relevant elder who is responsible, through inheritance, for the particular "story." Artistic competences are wide-spread within each community, but they are also pursued in a sustained way by those with the authority, talent, and commitment to emerge as artists.[8]

Extensive "galleries" of sacred images, many more than survive in Africa, Asia, Europe, or the Americas, have been painted using natural ochres on rock formations throughout northern Australia, with intense concentrations on the Mitchell Plateau, the Kakadu region, and Quinkan country. Major rock engrav-ing sites are found in the Sydney and Illawara regions, and in the Pilbara region of Western Australia. Developed traditions of carved and painted burial poles are also prominent in the North, notably those of the Tiwi people on Bathurst and Melville Islands and of the Yolngu of North East Arnhem Land. The same sacred imagery painted on bark thrives throughout this region, with notable centers at Maningrida, Ramingining, and Yirrkala. In the desert areas, ceremo-nial grounds for the ritual retelling of Dreaming stories are marked out in the sand. Secret sacred imagery is inscribed using handful-sized deposits of colored minerals and crushed vegetative matter. Since the early 1970s at Papunya, and then at communities throughout the Central and Western Deserts such as Yuen-dumu and Balgo, sacred and secular versions of this imagery have been painted on boards, then linen, canvas, and paper, for widespread circulation to markets in the outback and coastal cities. Art centers in these communities operate as places to come to paint, share knowledge, and obtain resources and income. Now numbering around one hundred, they are the primary points of distribu-tion of Indigenous artworks from remote communities to the wider world, and the main gateway through which they enter Western aesthetic and marketing frameworks, that is, become a fine art.[9] Work by city-based artists reaches the markets more directly, and both kinds now appear in sponsored festivals, such as the annual National Aboriginal and Torres Strait Islander Art Award.

The impact of fine art created by Australian Aborigines and Torres Strait Islanders is extraordinary given that they compose a relatively small portion of the national population, at 649,171 among a total of 23,401,892 people, as measured in the 2016 census, the most recent. This is a considerable increase on the relative numbers for the censuses of 1976 (160,915 of 14.03 million) and 1981 (159,897 of 14.93 million), that is, the period of the emergence of Aboriginal art making as a movement.[10] The increase is higher than standard demographic factors, such as the relativities of births and deaths, would predict and reflects a strong growth in individuals and families identifying as Indigenous. Nonetheless, proportionally, the Indigenous population remains at 2.8 percent, although expected improvements in living conditions have lead the Australian Bureau of Statistics to project Indigenous populations of over 900,000 by 2026. Approximately 35 percent of Australian Aborigines live in major cities, 45 percent in towns in the regions around these cities, while 13.7 percent, that is 91,600 people, live in very remote communities.[11]

Indigenous artists are active in the cities and the country towns, although their numbers are difficult to quantify. Up until recently, Indigenous Australian contemporary art was dominated by the output of artists from remote communities. Between 2003 and 2012, approximately thirteen thousand artists worked in remote centers, almost all producing paintings, while some made "sculptural" works, such as painted burial poles, figurines of various kinds, and variants of ceremonial objects, while others crafted fabrics and works on paper. In those years, $99.3 million was achieved in sales of 222,437 products, while around 60,000 remained unsold. Most of the items produced and sold were valued at under $1,000 each. Around 3,500 works valued higher than $5,000 were sold for a total of $21.35 million. The most productive artists, whose larger paintings achieve the higher prices, are those over fifty-five years of age.[12] This picture contrasts with the sharp contraction within the auction-house market for Indigenous art from these communities, which in 2015 was two-thirds down from its peak in 2007, a level widely regarded, at the time, as a "bubble."[13] Overall, however, the annual figures for local sales of Indigenous and non-Indigenous art are comparable. For both, the total figures are a tiny fraction of the global market for art, which was estimated for 2016 at between $45 billion and $56.6 billion.[14] They pale in comparison with the multimillion-dollar sales at the top end of the market for contemporary art, where the total for two decades in Australia is regularly eclipsed in one night in New York or London.[15]

More important than these statistics and the generalities they suggest is the evolution of a structure that has encouraged the making and enabled the distribution of Indigenous fine art. In accounting for its persistence within remote communities where breakdowns in social relationships are constant, attention is rightly drawn to the constructive roles of *balanda* and *kardiya* (to use the Yolngu and Warlpiri words for "whitefellas") art center advisers, local teachers, and welfare officers; certain area station owners; key policymakers; administrators in funding bodies; some politicians at all levels; a few art dealers in Alice Springs and Darwin; and even fewer based in the major capital cities of the continent, as well as a small number of committed collectors.[16] For the first three decades, the hard graft, foresight, and good faith of these supporters outweighed the double-dealing, self-serving bad faith and outright exploitation practiced by carpetbaggers, traders, tricksters, and other misfits who find themselves at home in the outback. By 2006, however, the underside had surfaced to stain the whole. In journalist Nicolas Rothwell's article "Scams in the Desert," he pulled no punches: "It is at once the finest artistic movement in today's Australian culture and the nation's most unstable, most spectacular investment market. It was born in a triumphant renaissance that brought Aboriginal traditions alive in a wider world, but a growing cancer of exploitation is gnawing at its heart."[17] He went on to detail sharp practices, especially the inducements to well-known Indigenous artists to sign works made by others, or only nominally by them. He challenged dealers in the capitals who knowingly distributed such works, and those who knowingly purchased them with the aim of quickly selling them on.[18]

Despite the destructive and self-destructive practices noted by Rothwell, the pervasive greed within the system, and the inevitable market corrections after 2008, the artists themselves have gradually turned the situation around. With the assistance of many in the industry who have spurned corruption and continued in their constructively mediating roles, they have slowly pushed back against these seemingly intractable circumstances. Major artists in long-running centers, such as Nyapanyapa Yunupingu at Yirrkala, continue to innovate (although many are reaching the end of their productive lives); elders in other areas continue to take up the challenge of painting (in recent years, notably, the late Mirdidingkingathi Juwarnda Sally Gabori), as do some from the middle generations, who throughout have been slow to do so (not only because of the attractions and debilitations of modernity, but because it takes time and commitment to acquire the requisite authority, Yukultji Napangardi being a striking case in point). Meanwhile, some younger people also are becoming more engaged, especially through their use of new media, for example, Ishmael Marika of Yirrkala. Since the global financial crisis of 2008, remote art centers have seen a modest increase in output and sales. As well, quite unexpected kinds of art have appeared, for example, the tourist art/fine art hybrids of the Hermannsburg potters and the Tjanpi Desert weavers.[19] Finally, a steadily increasing number of Indigenous artists, professionally trained and based in capital cities, have taken their places alongside non-Indigenous artists as creators of significant contemporary art. Artists such as Trevor Nickolls, Lin Onus, Bronwyn Bancroft, Fiona Foley, Destiny Deacon, Judy Watson, Michael Riley, and Brenda Croft led this change during the 1990s, and most remain active. A younger generation of artists, including Brook Andrew, Daniel Boyd, Jonathan Jones, Christian Thompson, Michael Cook, Richard Bell, Vernon Ah Kee, Tony Albert, Julie Gough, and Reko Rennie, continue to engage with issues of race, inequity, and identity, taking the cosmopolitan artistic language of international contemporary art as given, and forging their own distinctive modes of address within it.

ABORIGINAL MODERNISM?

How do these considerations bear on my initial question concerning whether Indigenous art should be understood as being traditional, neotraditional, modern, or contemporary? The leading art-historical interpreter of Indigenous Australian art, Ian McLean, has argued that, from the moment of first contact in 1770 to the present, Indigenous peoples on the Australian continent have made continuous adjustments and accommodations to European/settler-imposed modernity, and have done so, largely, according to their own values, and often in their own terms. Their art, therefore, has been throughout, and remains, *modernist*.[20] In contrast, the leading anthropological interpreter, Howard Morphy, believes that we should consider this interaction more concretely, and within shorter time frames. Of the Yolngu artists with whom he has worked for decades, he states,

> From the perspective of contemporary Arnhem Land artists, the third or fo[u]rth generation, they have never known a time when making a living as an artist was not a possible occupation. They have grown up as artists in the context of capitalism. But they have equally continued as artists in their own society, using art for the diversity of purposes it has in their religious and social life. They are contemporary Yolngu artists articulating

with the world outside, and inevitably entangling with the contemporary art market with its percepts of a still influential modernist concept of what art is. But they are not Indigenous modernists.[21]

He is concerned that "accepting Aboriginal art as Indigenous modernism under the constraints of the modernist definition of art is likely to set the art concerned on a particular trajectory that accepts the modernist conditions for the definition of works of art." He has in mind "individual creativity, innovation, formalist aesthetics, the intention to produce art for sale," qualities that Indigenous art, he believes, is able to challenge rather than be absorbed by. Further, he recommends that interpreters acknowledge the reality that "the history of art compromises a multiplicity of relatively autonomous trajectories, each occupying its own relatively autonomous space-time," that of Western fine art being one, and that of the various Indigenous arts another, with the two intersecting at specific historical points and in specific places.[22] The precise nature of the intersection remains to be explicated, in general and comparative terms, as the protocols concerning the degree to which sacred knowledge may be shared change over time within tribes, and vary between them. Furthermore, contradiction and contention occur on both sides of this divide: the history of twentieth-century avant-garde art shows that the major tendencies listed by Morphy were subject to as much challenge as acceptance by Western artists. In fact, in contemporary circumstances, worldwide, these tendencies are in disarray and no longer constitute a system.

On a general level, however, Indigenous artistic adjustment to the imposition of an external culture can certainly be considered one response among the many that non-Europeans have been obliged to make since the sixteenth century, as European countries expanded their imperial reach and established colonies throughout the world. The art created in those colonies by settlers, especially those who eventually fought for and achieved independence, has for some decades been regarded as less dependent, imitative, and provincial than previously thought; indeed, it is now everywhere evaluated for its contributions—both celebratory and contrarian—to emergent national arts. Being a vital part of modernizing social, economic, and cultural developments, these tendencies are understood by art historians to be part of a worldwide set of "multiple modernities," within which the modernist art made in the metropolitan centers of Europe and, later, the United States is being accorded a less central place. The connections between these modernities—which were many and varied—may be understood as a "cosmopolitan modernism" in the sense defined by Kobena

Mercer: as an intra- and cross-cultural complex, within which the various tendencies are seen as artistic expressions of specific cultural chronotopes within a multiplicitous modernity.[23] Even in this context, care needs to be taken to avoid Indigenous art being seen as a kind of third cousin: modern in its own way, but less modern than the modernism of the settler colonialists, whose own art was itself a minor modernism compared to the modernisms originated and most strongly developed in the Western metropolitan centers.

Can we subsume all these developments under the term "modern*ism*," not only during the modern era, but also within the present contemporary condition? The "modernisms" that McLean tracks so closely in his "Aboriginal Modernism" essay are not the same thing as the "Dreaming modernity" with which he concludes his essay in the *Remembering Forward* catalog.[24] Of course, in general and in the specifics, we are talking about essentially the same developments, and doing so in essentially the same way, but with two important differences of emphasis. For me, artistic modernism is a fundamentally autonomous, deeply reflexive, subtle, and resilient art-historical tendency inextricably tied to the double-sided (welcoming and rejective) response to modernity of Euro-American artists (including those from its cultural colonies) from the mid-nineteenth century to the 1960s.[25] When artists culturally outside these Western centers responded to how the forces of technical, social, and cultural modernization affected their regions and localities, they did so, I believe, in distinctively different ways from those of artists working in the centers where many of these forces originated (not least because many of these artists, and nearly all of the most innovative ones, came to these centers from outside them, from the provinces). Therefore, at least a three-way dynamic operates in even the simplest hierarchy of metropolitan/provincial, or center/periphery, relationships. All the art made within this dynamic, no matter who made it, where it was made, and what it looks like, was undoubtedly modern art. But not all of it, not even most of it, was modern*ist*. This applies, also, no matter who made it, where it was made, and what it looks like.

What, then, counts in making this distinction? The brutal core of artistic modernism's exclusivist and exclusionary logic, its hierarchical power plays, should be acknowledged as historical fact in European and US centers, as well as generators of the provincialist bind throughout their empires, and in their cultural colonies. The complex matrix in operation at any given time within the multiple modernities as they emerged around the world *includes* these Western cultural logics and power plays—first as the external agenda setter, then, gradually and mostly recently, as another, adjacent modernity within a multiplicitous global picture. In contemporary art, Euro-American modernisms echo as re-modernisms of various kinds. But the multiple modernities resonate more and more powerfully, because they were the seedbed of contemporary art's second current, the transnational transitionality that I identify in earlier chapters.[26]

Unless we make these kinds of distinction, contemporary Indigenous art movements, emerging as they did at the twilight time for modernism in the West during the 1960s and 1970s, risk being positioned as anachronistic, a be-lated outcrop of that benighted, now belated tendency, a living casualty of its slow decline. Indeed, the early reception of Indigenous Australian art was laced with evidence of nostalgia for the modernism that was slipping away in the West, but which, it seemed, was being unexpectedly, magically, prolonged by these (supposedly) artistic innocents from the deserts of Australia. This was a replay of the "myth of isolation," the apparent ignorance of the renaissance tra-dition that made Sidney Nolan, Arthur Boyd, Albert Tucker, and others seem like "natural painters" to art writers in London in the early 1960s.[27] On the contrary, a broad view of developments in art since the 1960s reveals that In-digenous Australian art is one among many conflicted modernizing/contem-porary art tendencies that have appeared throughout the world, notably since the 1980s. Their appearance, and persistence, is changing the temporal logic of modern art history, replacing its story of large-scale periods, and successive styles within them, with a picture of many, various, yet parallel developments that unfold unevenly, in their own times, and according to their own purposes.

Indigenous creators rarely labeled their art "modern," as they put little stock in general labels, especially kardiya or balanda ones. Nor was "modern" used much by its distributors, perhaps because, during the period of modernity's dominance, Euro-Americans could not conceive of Indigenous peoples as being modern in any sense beyond freakish exceptions—in Australia, most notably, in the case of Albert Namatjira.[28] Instead, in art-market sales, auction-house categories, museum exhibitions, and in the titles of both scholarly and popular publications, Indigenous artistic output from Africa, Oceania, and Australia was divided (roughly, but structurally) into "traditional" and "contemporary," with the latter meaning art made by Indigenous peoples using modern and current materials and techniques. These crude markers remain in place within most of these discourses, except for a slowly increasing number of anthropolo-gists, curators, art historians, and theorists who have begun to identify more precisely the ways in which this art became contemporary.

A clear view of contemporary conditions is hard to make out, mostly because of the cacophony of competing complexities within everyday life, as well as the persistent obscurities caused by myths of religious deliverance, natural development, and shared progress. Nevertheless, aspects of its actual character can be glimpsed precisely within this cultural complexity. We can see some of the ways in which the world's cultures internally differentiate as they negotiate their own relays between the conservation and renovation of tradition, at the same time negotiating their relationships of divergence from and convergence with similar processes in other cultures. Australians are aware of a kind of contemporaneity that goes to the heart of what being Australian means: that Indigenous and non-Indigenous peoples have profoundly different senses of what time is, of how it unfolds, of what it is for a body to be in time and for memory to do its work. White people clearly do not have the same shared sense of time, while all Indigenous people have another, shared sense of time—that is obviously nonsense. Both cultural spheres include multiple ways of being in time, and multiple ways of existing in time appear *between* those spheres, precisely because they are contemporaneous with each other, as they are with people from other cultural backgrounds: the 33 percent born elsewhere, and the children of earlier generations of migrants. Understanding the nature of this transculturality is the challenge facing contemporary criticism.

Immersed in this complexity, and emergent from it, all genuinely contemporary art is about the multiplicity of ways of being in time, including those of the living past, the recent past, and the distant past, as they are experienced right now. In this sense, we cannot say that Australian Aboriginal art is "traditional" or "modern" or "postmodern" or "contemporary." It is, however, tempting to see it as each and all of these, at once, contemporaneously. For example, Christine Nicholls tells us that Kame Kngwarreye's art, in paintings such as *Untitled (Alhalker)*, 1992, "permits a kind of 'double vision': it is not only deeply meaningful to other Aboriginal people as religious art, but it can also be read equally as abstract, expressionist, impressionist, minimalist, or postmodern" (figure 6.2).[29] Imprecision abounds: leaving aside "double vision" as simply unfortunate, "other Aboriginal people" does not distinguish between the artist's own people and other Australian Aboriginal peoples; "equally" implies an evaluative equilibrium available to some godlike observer; while the list of largely incompatible art styles is a loose throwing around of labels in the hope that one will stick long enough to act as bridge for an imaginary non-

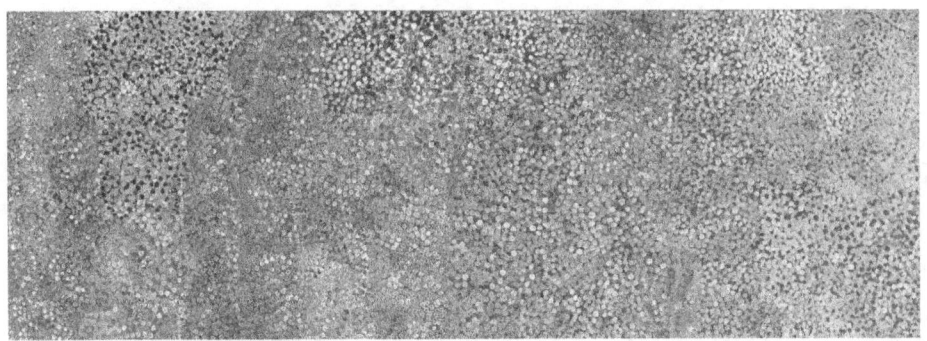

Figure 6.2

Emily Kame Kngwarreye, *Untitled (Alhalker)*, 1992, synthetic
polymer paint on canvas, 165 × 480 × 4 cm. Molly Gowing
Acquisition Fund for Contemporary Aboriginal Art, Art Gal-
lery of New South Wales, Sydney. © Emily Kame Kngwarreye
/ Copyright Agency, licensed by Artists Rights Society (ARS),
New York, 2018. Image © Emily Kam Ngwarray, licensed by
Viscopy, Sydney, 229.1992. Photo by Christopher Snee, AGNSW.

Indigenous viewer. In the remark's listing of late modern art styles, with conceptualism the most obvious omission, it also exemplifies the reception of this
art as a late modern art, in this instance as late modern art on steroids. Indeed,
the author goes on to credit Kngwarreye with generating "the newly-created
hybrid category the 'Global Indigenous.'"

A more exact broadscale picture needs to be drawn. We humans on the
planet earth have moved, I believe, beyond what were previously considered
periods, epochs, and eras, including those named "modernity" and "postmodernity." The current coexistence of profoundly different ways of being in
the world reveals so many degrees and kinds of incommensurability that, while
none are unprecedented in any given aspect, their totality has become newly
unfathomable. We may have brought ourselves to a global condition, or a state of
being, that does not have the overall shape and form of previous eras of human
history. It would follow that we are not necessarily moving forward in time in
a way that, taken as a whole, is continuous with past time. In earlier chapters I
identify three broad currents within what seems the endlessly multiplicitous,

eye-popping heterogeneity of the art of the present. How might we see the work of Indigenous Australian artists in relation to them?

Damien Hirst is an artist who works with visual images to create shock and intense sensations. He is, as well, a sensational promoter of his work. Artists such as Jeff Koons and Takashi Murakami create instant visual sensations that embody, as easy-to-read reflections, the values and tastes of the high end of the market. Their tactics echo avant-garde practice throughout the twentieth century. I call it retro-sensationalism. Parallel to this is a tendency devoted to reshaping and renovating modernist art practices, to renewing modernist values and traditions. Artists such as Richard Serra, Gerhard Richter, and Sean Scully are what I call remodernists. These two tendencies together form the current of spectacular art, which, today, attracts most public attention, propels the upper reaches of the market, and fills the museums and galleries of the main metropolitan cultural centers, as well as their satellite institutions, around the world. Few Indigenous artists participate in this current, although some, such as Tracey Moffatt, use some of its modes.

Second current: For the past thirty or forty years, largely as a result of decolonization, vastly different ways of making art, thinking about visual images, relating to mediums, and communicating values have appeared. Initially, these artists were concerned above all with creating senses of identity, often nationalist ones, against the colonial regimes, for example, in Africa: the archival installations of Georges Adéagbo, from Benin, and those of Nkosinathi Khanyile, *Wathint' Abafazi Wathint' Imbokodo* (1994–2004), a monument to the need for *ubuntu* (I exist because you exist). The reach for reconciliation has nowhere been better expressed than in *The Aboriginal Memorial* (1987–88; figure 6.3). Forty-three elders from the Ramingining community painted two hundred hollow logs with clan designs specific to their lands around the Glyde River in north-central Arnhem Land, and then arranged them into a configuration that evoked that area, inviting viewers to walk through them. Based on the burial poles used in the region, they were made expressly for the 1988 celebration of the British settlement of the continent but intended as a countermemorial commemorating the thousands of Indigenous people who have perished since the European invasion of the country.[30]

A key element within reconciliation is the struggle for land rights, social recognition, and acknowledgment of past wrongs. Thus, Ngurrara artists, in the absence of written legal documents, used the evidence provided by their paintings to demonstrate the depth of their ownership of their ancestral lands in the Great Sandy Desert of Western Australia. Their decade-long struggle fi-

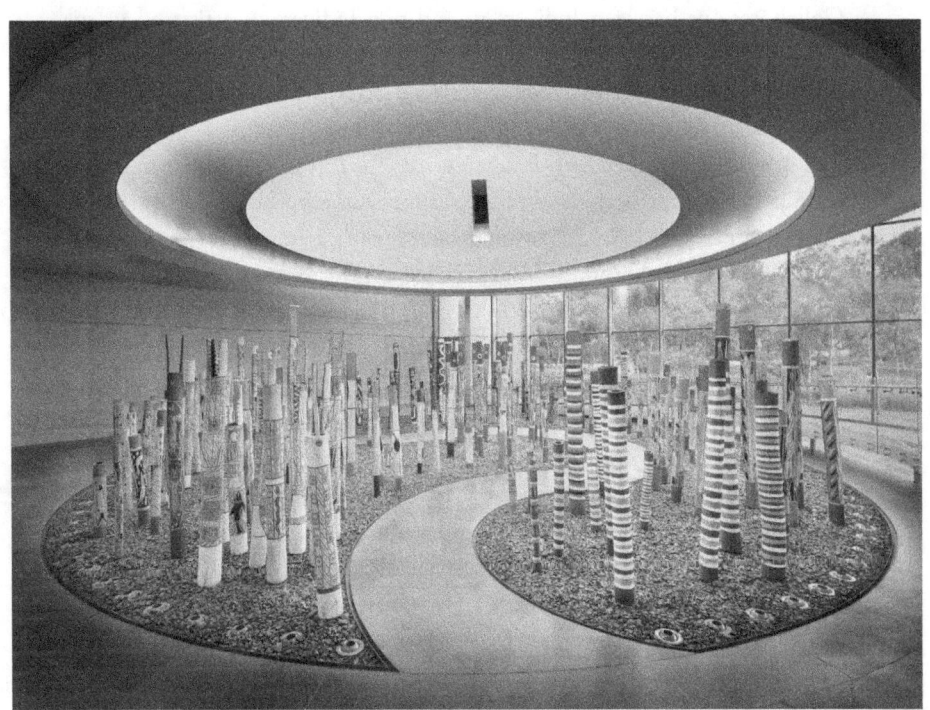

Figure 6.3

Ramingining artists, *The Aboriginal Memorial*, 1987–88, installation, natural ochres on two hundred hollow logs, dimensions
variable. National Gallery of Art, Canberra. © National Gallery
of Australia.

nally achieved success in 2007, at a meeting of the Land Rights Commission at
Pirnini, at which they laid out a large painting of their country, collectively produced.[31] The constant battle to arrive at some equilibrium in relations between
the races has activated some moving responses by a few white artists, that of
Rod Moss, from Alice Springs, being exemplary. He demonstrates, from a non-
Indigenous perspective, what the artists from the North, and from the deserts,
as well as those from the cities, have been proposing all along: that art can be the
affective ground of imagined and actual reconciliation. He is explicit about this
being a hard, quixotic, and—given incommensurability—unending process.[32]

Collaborations between Indigenous and non-Indigenous artists occur spasmodically but become important when they explore a set of shared concerns in depth, as in the painterly dialogue between Peter Adsett and Gija artist Rusty Peters that, over a two-week period in 2000, led to the series of fourteen paintings in seven pairs titled *Two Laws: One Big Spirit* (figure 6.4); when they are sustained over long periods, through distinct times in each artist's career, as is the case for Michael Nelson Jagamara and Imants Tillers; or when several artists of different backgrounds from various parts of the country work together on a collective project, such as *Two Worlds*, a major confluence of Indigenous and non-Indigenous world picturing, created over a two-year period, 1995–97, by artists and gallerist Michael Eather and his circle of no fewer than thirteen "friends." This work was a centerpiece of *Black, White and Restive: Cross-Cultural Initiatives in Contemporary Australian Art*, a path-finding exhibition curated by Una Rey at the Newcastle Art Gallery in 2016.[33]

Modern art historians deployed the idea of art *movements* as a key tool in their efforts to trace the historical origins and development of national cultures. Contemporary Australian Indigenous art is "national" in the limited sense that many city-based artists have attempted to create some connections to artists in remote communities. This is, however, the exception rather than the rule. Similarly, when confronting governments, business interests, and pervasive racism, Indigenous activists and policymakers have emphasized an Aboriginal spirit shared among all Indigenous Australians. Otherwise, the idea that Indigenous art in Australia is a national art has more to do with tourism and souvenir marketing. Such modern senses of what an imagined community might be are qualified by a deeper, nonmodern sense of tribal or clan communality: for each people, from relatively large populations to small groups with only a few language speakers, their sovereignty is regarded as paramount (however parlous its execution in the material world may seem to be). Certainly, icons of Aboriginal Australia, including, more and more prominently, Aboriginal art, have been taken over by governmental and advertising agencies and absorbed into official state imagery, becoming a vital part of the nation's regional and international "brand." But Emily Kame Kngwarreye's art, for example, like that of every Indigenous artist working in remote settings, is rooted in local cultural formations—in fact, it enacts the re-creation of the world that the artist's ancestors are continuously undertaking. Indigenous art, therefore, is grounded in an originary contemporaneity. The demonstration of this possibility through Indigenous art is one of the ways in which the South is remaking the North, a process that is perhaps the most important social change occurring in the world today.

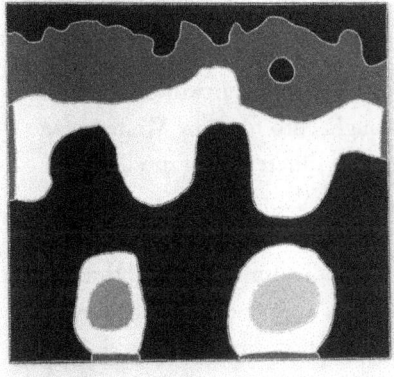

Figure 6.4

Left: Rusty Peters, *Father and Grandfather Teaching Place for Me*, 2000, natural ochres on linen, 122 × 135 cm.

Right: Peter Adsett, *Painting Number 6*, 2000, acrylic on linen, 122 × 135 cm.

Rusty Peters and Peter Adsett, *Two Laws: One Big Spirit*, painting collaboration, 2000, Adam Art Gallery, New Zealand. Images courtesy of Peter Adsett.

The third broad-scale current of contemporary art is the work mostly of a younger generation than those who are driving the first two. These artists are more concerned with specific questions of time, place, mediation, and mood. They work in a wide variety of mediums, in a much lower key, and usually more cooperatively. They produce works of art that try to seek a way beyond the dialectical conflict that is in effect embodied in the first two tendencies. Most Indigenous artists work within the second current, but increasing numbers are helping shape the emergent practices of the third: Vernon Ah Kee, Tony Albert, Reko Rennie, Warwick Thorton, Yhonnie Scarce, and Ishmael Marika, among others.

Ian McLean has identified the moment when art by Indigenous Australians was acknowledged as contemporary in the strongest sense: as the most vital and inventive art of the day, a kind of art that, more than any other art being made anywhere in the world, revealed most about what it was to be alive in the present moment, and did so in a flash. In an essay in his important anthology *How Aborigines Invented the Idea of Contemporary Art*, he concludes with these remarks:

In the 1980s Papunya Tula painting revealed to the artworld something about itself that had not yet been brought into focus by Western contemporary art. Because the constitutional differences of modernity no longer mattered, Aborigines initiated in tribal lore could also make contemporary art. This lesson, that difference was the opportunity for something more, is also the first prerequisite of globalism. In a straightforward historical sense then, Australian Aborigines were among the first to show an artworld, raised in the ethnocentric and historicist blinkers of European modernism, what contemporary art after modernism felt like. In doing this, they played a decisive role in the artworld's globalisation at the end of the twentieth century.[34]

This advent dawned within the Australian art world first, when outstanding works were included in pivotal surveys of contemporary art at state museums, notably the Biennale of Sydney in 1979, curated by Nicholas Waterlow, and *Australian Perspecta* in 1981, curated by Bernice Murphy. With major exhibitions and extensive collection displays in the state and national galleries as its landmarks, it has reshaped art in Australia more fundamentally than in comparable settler colonies, such as Canada and New Zealand, despite the powerful presence of Indigenous art in those countries.[35] Even though several important overseas exhibitions have been staged, beginning with *Dreamings: The Art of Aboriginal Australia* in New York in 1989, the message has been slow to penetrate the major centers of world art. Nevertheless, significant collections of Indigenous Australian art have been formed overseas, notably in the United States.[36] The global spread of Indigenous ways of creating contemporaneity will, it seems, take its own time.

WORLD PICTURING: CONTEMPORARY CONTENT

These considerations lead us to the broader, global idea of contemporaneity as the setting in which, I believe, we should see this work operating: the worldwide coexistence of major cultural differences, our accelerated awareness of these differences, along with an emerging sense that we all need to work much harder at creating a mutuality in which coevality rather than divisive difference or abstract unity becomes the basis of our world community. Is the work of Indigenous artists from remote communities and from the cities relevant to such a quest?

In a work such as *Two Sites* (2000)—a concentrated image of two sacred sites—we enter some strange territory with respect to time (figure 6.5). The work is one of Turkey Tolson Tjupurrula's mono-prints, which I purchased just as it was done. I took it with me to the United States, to Los Angeles, where I arrived on September 10, 2001. Next morning, I watched the television images, the striated buildings imploding, the people jumping, falling past them. As I looked at them, I held Turkey's image, thinking, *What is going on here?* Deeply shaken by the events of that day, it took me some hours to realize that I already had the gift of his answer, which was the need to insist on the possibilities of peace even inside such threatening circumstances. This spirit kept me going during the writing of *The Architecture of Aftermath*, which was my way of working through the trauma of that long, and still lingering, moment. I concluded that book with the suggestion that the priority architectural purpose at the rebuilt Ground Zero should be the erection of a mosque.[38] Fittingly, despite considerable opposition, a mosque and community exchange center was eventually built on a street near the site.

Turkey Tolson also painted a series of important works during the 1990s and up to his death in 2001 on the theme of "straightening the spears" (figure 6.6). He made many great paintings based on the Dreaming story of the first awareness that one group of men, gathered at a clay pan named Ilyingaungau, formed of another group of men gathering elsewhere in the Central Desert. A sense of an imminent conflict was shared by both groups. The matter was resolved by the elders focusing for so long and so carefully on the straightening of the spears that the urge to fight slowly dissipated. The first conflict, therefore, did not take place—until, some time later, it did. The moral essence of the story, however, is about becoming aware of potentially deadly difference, of the prospect of war and massive destruction, but at the same time seeing it as an opportunity to build community and coexistence. These are paintings about peace, about how to generate a calm accord with the country that you are in, while recognizing the destructiveness that is also innate to it. Turkey Tolson tackled this through his practice of carefully, steadily painting dots, lining them up in rows, and taking lots of time, until he arrived at a mesmerized state. Each color evokes one or more of the players within the narrative: the bodies of people, the sand, the sun, fire, land, the ashes as well as the actual spears. Painterly practice and subject matter are deeply integrated; one comes out of the other. As it happens, this is the key test in assessing the quality of a modernist painting: the deepest content of the work should be expressed above all through the forms deployed, the process through which the work was produced.[37] Here lies the ethics internal to modernism in

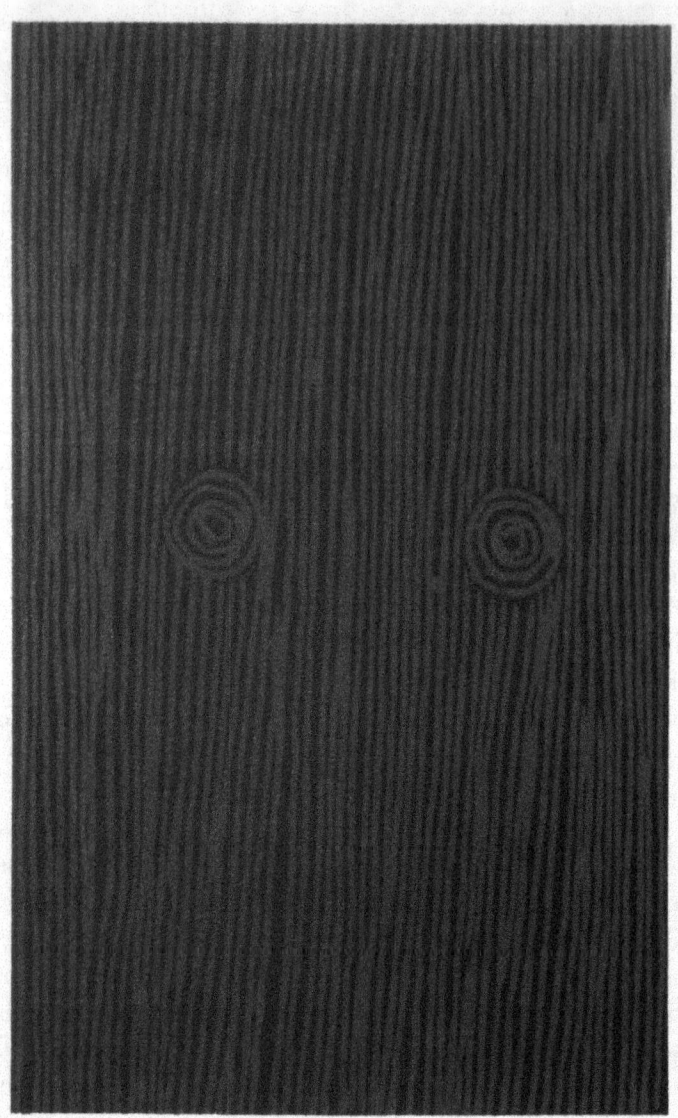

Figure 6.5

Turkey Tolson Tjupurrula, *Two Sites*, 2000, woodcut, 30 × 23 cm.
Private collection, Sydney, Australia. © Estate of Turkey Tolson
Tjupurrula. Licensed by Aboriginal Artists Agency, Sydney.

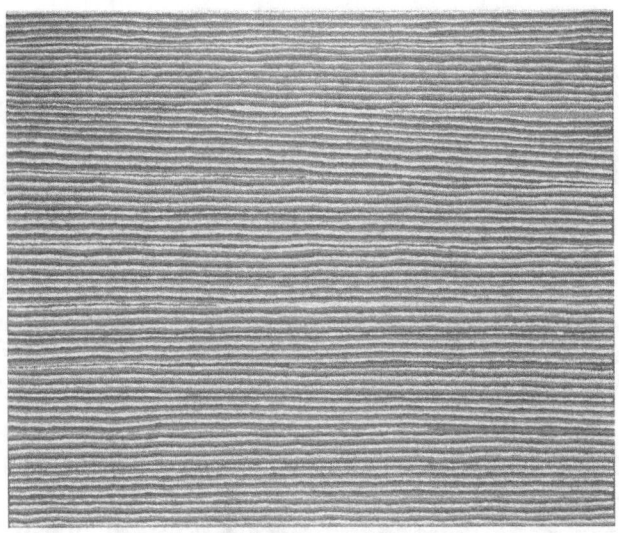

Figure 6.6

Turkey Tolson Tjupurrula, *Straightening the Spears*, 1999,
synthetic polymer paint on canvas, 149.6 × 182.5 cm. Molly
Gowing Acquisition Fund for Contemporary Aboriginal Art,
Art Gallery of New South Wales, Sydney. Photo by Brenton
McGeachie, AGNSW. © Estate of Turkey Tolson Tjupurrula.
Licensed by Aboriginal Artists Agency, Sydney.

art. Such criteria are no doubt important among the range of measures—from
the psychological to the social—that making art during the modern era invites.

Other artists responded to the post-9/11 situation very differently. Gordon
Bennett was already in dialogue with the Lower East Side artist Jean-Michel
Basquiat, who was of course dead by then, but the spirit of Basquiat was one of
Gordon's alter egos. Part of Gordon's response was to be shocked back to some
of his early works. *Notes to Basquiat (The Coming of the Light)*, 2001, references
one of his own first paintings: the convict chain, or chain of death, is connected
to the Statue of Liberty, as indicating Indigenous peoples' loss of freedom (figure 6.7). The attacks on the towers he shows as an impact on bodies—he clearly
sees the buildings as bodies. Near the center of this painting, he lists a series of
words he regards as cant. It is a salutary reminder to us that they include "modern," "contemporary," "current," "fashionable," and so on.[39]

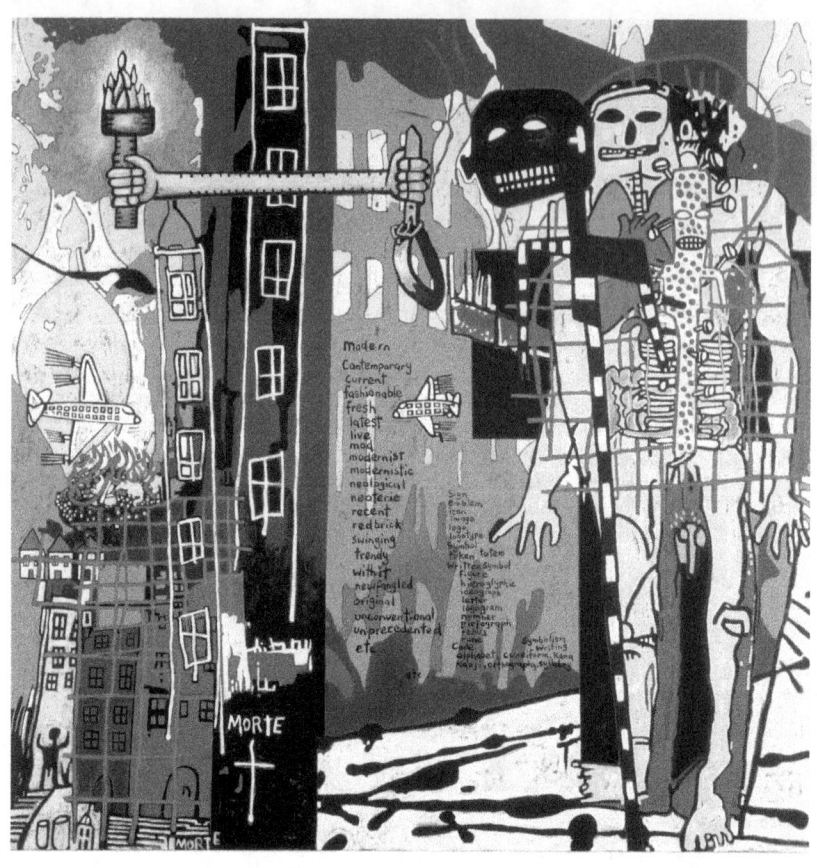

Figure 6.7

Gordon Bennett, *Notes to Basquiat (The Coming of the Light)*,
2001, acrylic on linen, 152 × 152 cm. © The Estate of Gordon
Bennett. Image courtesy of the Estate of Gordon Bennett.
Photo by Richard Stringer.

During this period, in *The Light* series (2005–7), Paul Chan achieved some
of the most acute and moving responses by a New York–based artist (Robert
Gober being one of the few others able to develop some response, however
tentative). *The Light* series were installations of projected shadows that showed
things in the world rising slowly up out of Manhattan, as if they were being
resurrected, or as if the Rapture was happening.[40] Turkey Tolson, Bennett, and

Chan are three among many contemporary artists today trying to understand the presence of the spiritual within the secular, to understand the secularization of the spiritual, seeing the process as two way, with relays ranging from the most subtle to the most extremely violent.

Several younger generation Indigenous artists are attempting to address these questions, although, as befits their generation, on a less epic scale than that of Emily Kame Kngwarreye, Turkey Tolson Tjupurrula, or Rover Thomas. The 2014 National Aboriginal and Torres Strait Islander Art Award was given to Brisbane-based Tony Albert for his work *We Can Be Heroes*, about racial profiling of Indigenous youth by white policemen (figure 6.8). Nicolas Rothwell reads the prize as a "statement about the present position and future trajectory of indigenous art" by the curators and administrators now dominant in the industry, a statement that "what speaks most strongly is new work that builds on traditional culture and memory, rather than work seeking to entrench culture in aspic."[41] Albert is one of many younger Indigenous artists who are seeking to explore whether his concerns connect with similar issues occurring elsewhere; racial profiling by law enforcement is a widespread problem, not least in the United States, where the situation for many young African Americans seems to be sliding backward into unemployment, criminality, and imprisonment.

THE CONTEMPORARY REORIENTATION

Obviously, an issue of power is at stake in these debates. The temporal process at the core of colonization, everywhere in the world, is that the colonizers regard the colonized, particularly if they are Indigenous peoples, as survivors from an earlier era in human evolutionary development, as living anachronisms, as noncontemporaneous contemporaries. Against this, the singular focus of Indigenous peoples is to outlive the colonizer's modernity and the rest of the world's contemporaneity by becoming, to a degree, first modern then contemporary, on their own terms. To do this successfully under conditions of relative powerlessness, simply demanding the right to do so, or working out how to live a divided life, is not enough. It becomes necessary to try to change the terms of the equation, to persuade the more powerful to reimagine their world as a world in which people who live differently are also genuine contemporaries—other people who *belong* to the same time as you. This was Turkey Tolson's fundamental, and universal, message.

In Australia in particular during the 1990s and into the subsequent decade, this thirst for a coeval contemporaneity was at the heart of national polity. Despite this, the conservative government that held office from 1996 to 2007

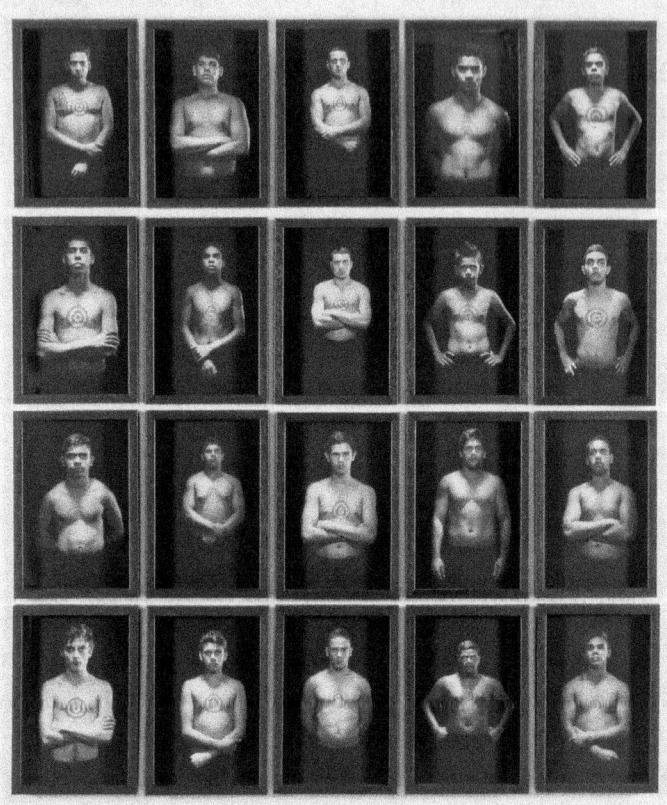

Figure 6.8

Tony Albert, *We Can Be Heroes*, 2014, pigment on paper,
124 × 115 cm. Image courtesy of the artist and Sullivan and
Strumpf, Sydney.

refused to apologize to Indigenous peoples for past wrongs, slowed down recognition of land rights, imposed greater state regulation on remote communities, and stalled the process of reconciliation. It did so within a broader set of policies that promoted a fortress-Australia mindset and encouraged racist attitudes toward immigrants and refugees. This was the context in which the sustained creation and wide dissemination of a complex, subtle, profound, and beautiful aesthetic became a powerful counterdemonstration, showing that Indigenous Australians were not the Stone Age survivors that many had imagined them to be but were many-sided, multiskilled people who loved their lands and were capable of managing their own lives. In Bill Hayden's 1996 Australia Day address, the outgoing governor general of Australia avowed, "Aboriginal creativity has taken its place as a major influence on our national consciousness."[42] Commenting on the broader implications of the issues raised in the address, Nicolas Rothwell noted, "But the purest instance of the shifting image of the Aborigine remains the most obvious one: the startling, unprecedented creation, out of next to nothing, of a whole school of art, with its own visual language, multi-million-dollar dealing networks and showcase galleries. . . . Aboriginal Australia has done something that resonates worldwide, and knows it, and we know it."[43] As we have seen, much has changed since the later 1970s and early 1980s, when the art of Indigenous Australians began to circulate on a scale, with an inner variety, and at a level of accomplishment that changed not only the look of art in Australia but also, as the remarks just cited attest, the racist disposition of the national polity. Since then, and despite many setbacks, this art has continued to replenish itself, in waves emerging from one remote center after another and in the determined, resistant work of many city-based artists.

There are hints, too, that the messages sent by this art are reaching audiences beyond Australia, attracting a scattered but also slowly and steadily expanding interest. Certain curators of international biennials are beginning to include work by Indigenous artists, valuing it not only for what it shows about their indigeneity but also for what it has to say about the larger questions explored as the exhibition's theme. In Carolyn Christov-Bakargiev's dOCUMENTA (13), in Kassel, Germany, 2012, which examined artists' responses to world conflict, she dedicated a room in the main pavilion to recent works by Doreen Reid Nakamarra and Warlimpirrnga Tjapaltjarri, which were shown directly and without contextual setting as powerful pieces of abstract painting (figure 6.9). Yet she also devoted a room in the Neue Gallerie to the parallelism between the response to "native art" by Canadian painter Emily Carr and Australian artist Margaret Preston during the 1930s and 1940s, relating this rich historical parallel to its reflective

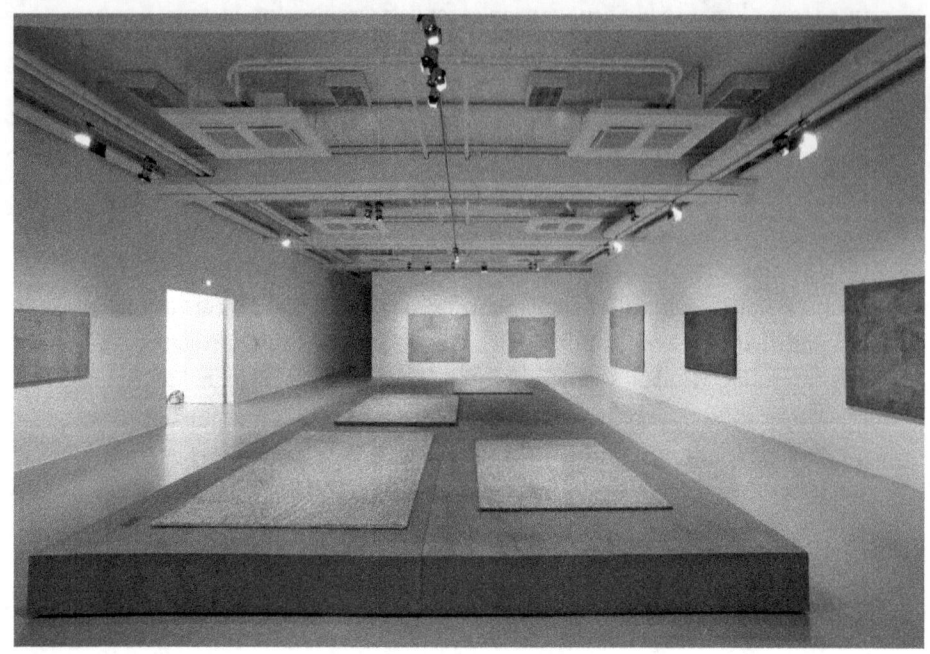

Figure 6.9

dOCUMENTA (13), 2012, Kunsthalle Fridericianum, Kassel:
installation of works by Doreen Reid Nakamarra (floor) and
Warlimpirrnga Tjapaltjarri (walls).

reversal in the work of Gordon Bennett some fifty years later (figure 6.10). She
further ratcheted up the implicit tensions by locating, in the center of the space,
an anger-management workshop conducted by Perth artist Stuart Ringholt.

In the Fifty-Sixth Venice Biennale, within the theme *All the World's Futures*,
artistic director Okwui Enwezor juxtaposed recent paintings by Daniel Boyd
based on the Marshall Islands navigation chart with earthworks by US land
and environmental artist Robert Smithson. He also curated a room that centered on devastated humanoid forms by Pakistani sculptor Huma Bhabha, contrasting them with a lyrical suite of paintings by Ellen Gallagher that evoked a
mythical undersea city inhabited by African slaves. Both were framed by a major
painting by Emily Kame Kngwarreye, her 1994 *Earth's Creation* (figure 6.11).
When asked about the content of this and similar paintings, Kngwarreye re-

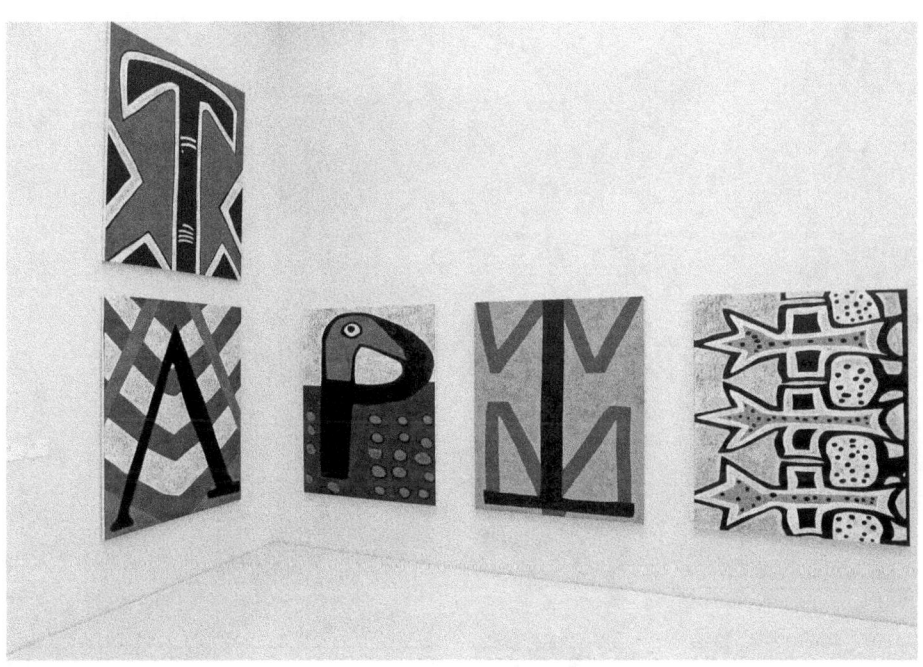

Figure 6.10

dOCUMENTA (13), 2012, Neue Gallerie, Kassel: installation
of works by Gordon Bennett from his *Home Décor* series, 2010,
acrylic on canvas, each 185.5 × 152 cm. © The Estate of Gordon
Bennett. Image courtesy of the Estate of Gordon Bennett.

plied that they represented "'Whole lot, that's all, whole lot, awelye, arlatyeye, ankerrthe, ntange, dingo, ankerre, intekwe, anthwerle and kame. That's what I paint: whole lot.' (. . . Whole lot, my dreaming, pencil yam, mountain devil lizard, grass seed, dingo, emu, small plant emu food, green bean and yam seed.)"[44] She pictures her own, most immediate environment as a site of incessant self-replenishment, one that is also big enough, in principle and potential, to suggest that the destructive and recuperative powers of all the other worlds of the world, the worlds envisaged in the many other works on show in the biennale, may indeed amount to "All the World's Futures."[45]

When it comes to modes of curating these questions in museum exhibitions, to grasping the pitfalls and the potentialities of the exchanges between Indigenous

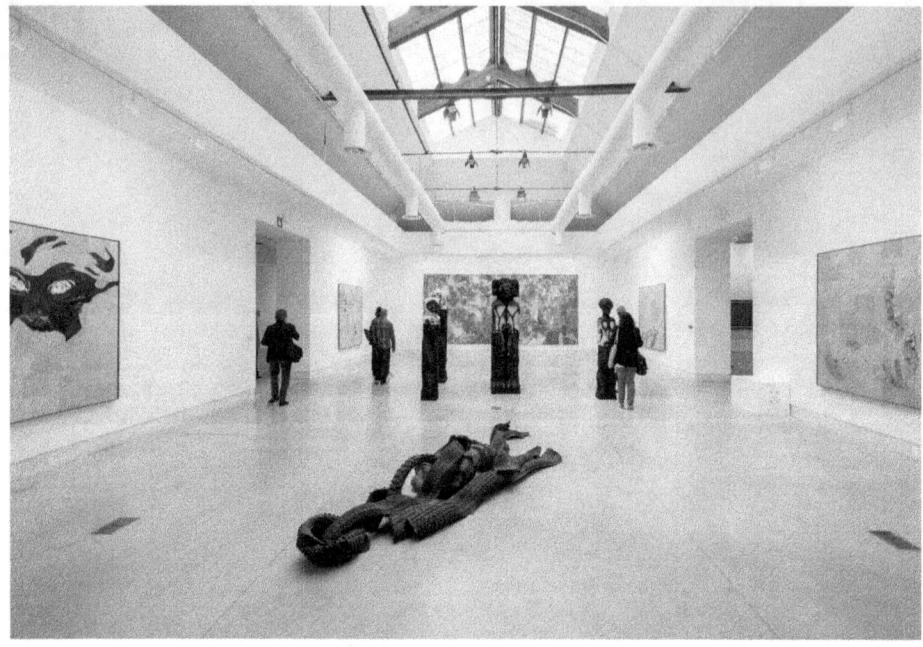

Figure 6.11

Fifty-Sixth Venice Biennale, 2015: installation of works by Ellen Gallagher, *Dew Breaker* (2015), on side walls; Huma Bhabha, *Atlas* (2015), center room; and Emily Kame Kngwarreye, *Earth's Creation* (1994), in background. © Inexhibit, 2015. Image by Riccardo Bianchini/Alamy Stock Photo.

art and contemporary art, one image recurs as emblematic: a photograph of part of the exhibition *Magiciens de la terre*, at La Villette, Paris, in 1989, curated by Jean-Hubert Martin. In the background looms a huge circular shape titled *Red Earth Circle*, made for the occasion, with splattered river mud, by the English land artist Richard Long, on the wall at the end of the great gallery, while on the floor in front lies a ground painting consisting of sacred symbols evoking the *Yam Dreaming*, made with imported sand and other natural materials by a group of Warlpiri elders from Yuendumu, a remote settlement in the Central Desert of Australia (figure 6.12). In the exhibition, works by Western artists, mainly European, known for their interest in spirituality were matched with ritual cre-

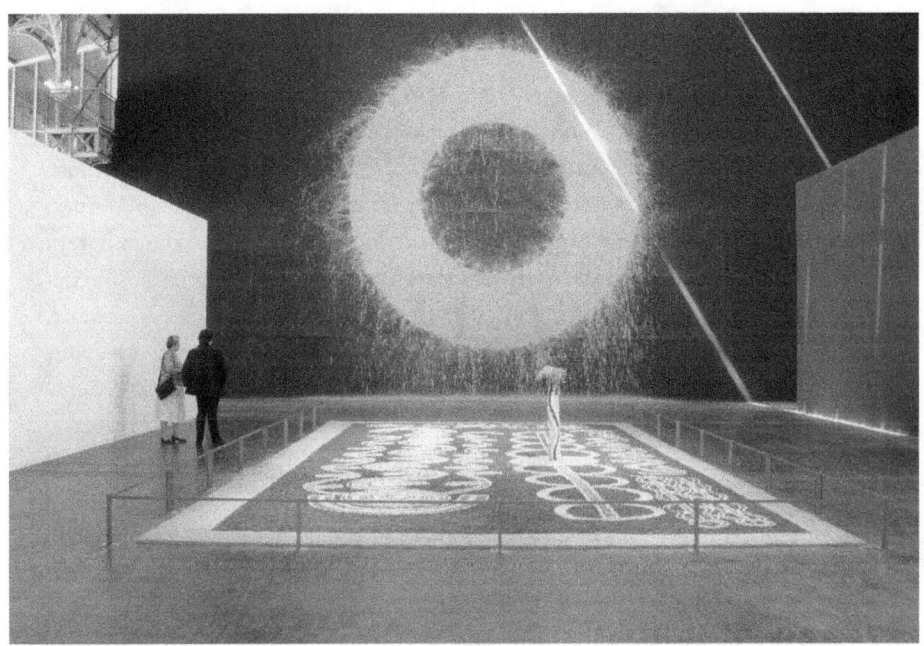

Figure 6.12

Magiciens de la terre, 1989, Grande Halle de la Villette, Paris:
installation of works by Richard Long, *Red Earth Circle*, on
wall; Yuendumu artists, *Yam Dreaming*, ground painting. Photo
by Konstantinos Ignatiadis. Musée National d'Art Moderne.
© Deidi von Schaewen. © CNAC/MNAM/Dist. RMN–Grand
Palais/Art Resource, New York.

ations by shamans, priests, folk artists, village decorators, and other craftsmen
and women chosen from non-Western cultures throughout the world. A 50/50
split, the intention was to counter the condescension toward non-Western artists in the infamous exhibition *Primitivism: Affinities of the Tribal and Modern*,
shown at the Museum of Modern Art, New York, in 1983. *Magiciens* curator
Jean-Hubert Martin received criticism for treating the Western artists as individuals while presenting the others as representative of their cultures in general.[46]
Positive side effects were that the exhibition introduced multiple non-Western
artists to European and international audiences, that it provided a springboard

for some of them to develop substantial international careers, and that it inspired many curators to offer more nuanced displays of the complex questions that it raised.[47] The pairing of the Yuendumu elders and Richard Long at La Villette was such a succinct condensation of these issues that it has gradually become, in art-historical and museological memory, the visual icon of the exhibition as a whole.

In September and October 2015, a coincidence of exhibitions in New York, both in the hot gallery district around the New Museum of Contemporary Art on the Bowery, enables us to take one measure of how this relationship has changed and, as it happens, not changed, since 1989. At Sperone Westwater, the most prominent piece in Richard Long's exhibition *Crescent to Cross*, his fifteenth with the gallery since 1978, was a "large-scale mud work" that recapitulated his work in *Magiciens de la terre*, something he has been doing regularly ever since (figure 6.13). One block farther down the Bowery, Salon 94 showed seven acrylic paintings by Warlimpirrnga Tjapaltjarri, a Pintupi man from the Central Desert, his first solo exhibition in the United States (figure 6.14). The paintings encapsulate the most recent stage of his style as it has evolved since 1984, when he, in his mid-twenties, "came in" from the remote desert to live in Indigenous settlements such as Papunya.[48] With a riveting yet constantly flickering precision, the intricate dotted lines suggest sheaths of space and oblique movements through time, evoking aspects of the experience of his major Dreaming site, Marawara, a clay pan in Lake Mackay.

This is not a curated conjunction. It is a coincidence that typifies the contemporaneity of differences that define our present situation. Yet our contemporaneities have their histories: they accumulate an actual, consequential history of differences. Compared to 1989, in 2015 the Aboriginal artist's work displays the most striking, unexpected, and seemingly infinite generative power, whereas the British artist seems locked into a time warp, ever more elegantly repeating a moment that is long past. The temporal terms of colonization are, suddenly, reversed.

Oblivious to such changes in the world, the Sperone Westwater press release describes the Long wall piece as follows: "A large-scale mud work will dominate the main gallery's double-height wall, on which the artist will apply red clay mud directly by hand. The work is an index of the intensely physical act of its making. While it possesses an archaic quality, the work's site-specific installation in the gallery underscores its spontaneous creation, calling attention to the artist's human scale and the passage of time."[49] Of course, this is typical art-world promotional babble, a swarm of buzzwords aimed at mystifying the obvious, inflating it into something that would be sublime. In his own statement, the artist is more modest yet no less ambitious in his reach for the most

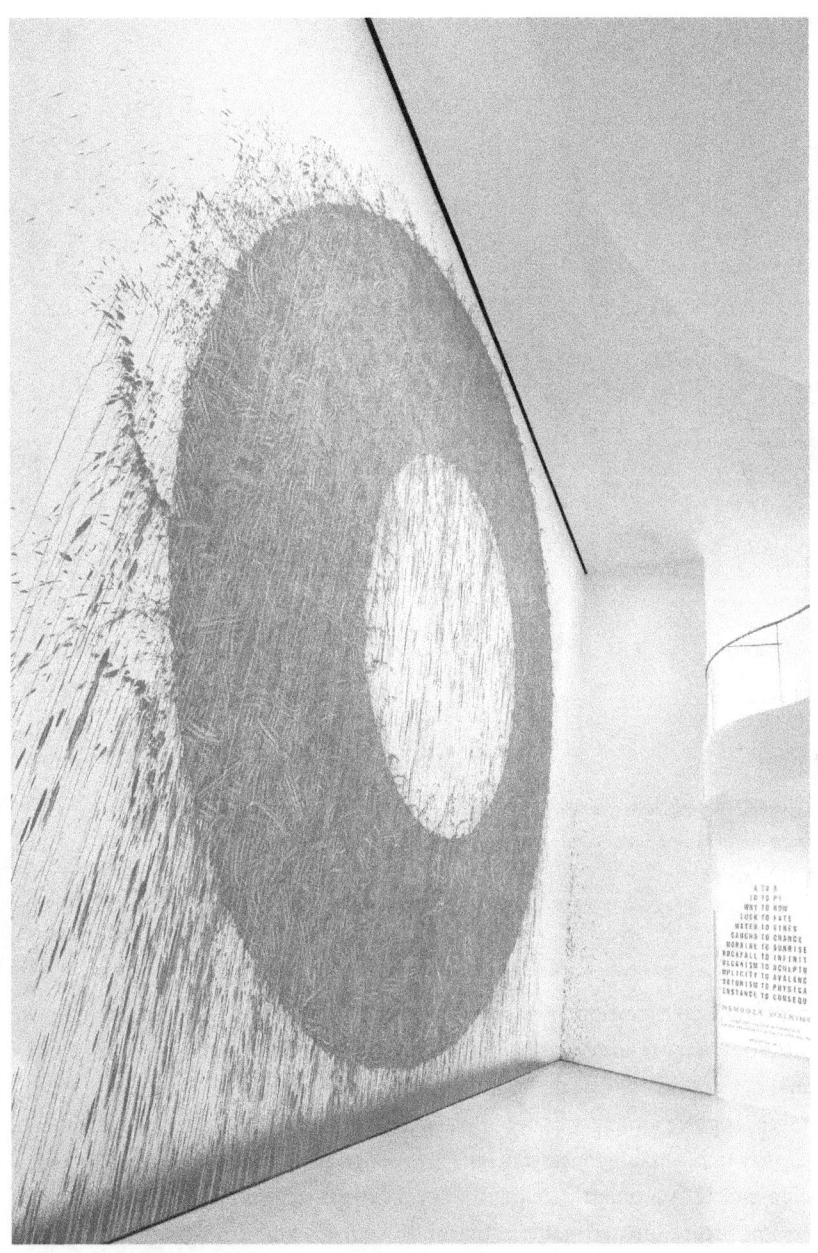

Figure 6.13

Richard Long, *Red Gravity*, 2015, red clay, 391 × 1,143 cm. Installation at *Crescent to Cross* exhibition, Sperone Westwater Gallery, New York, 2015. Image courtesy of the artist and Sperone Westwater Gallery. Photo by Robert Vinas Jr. © 2018 Richard Long. All rights reserved, DACS, London/ARS, New York.

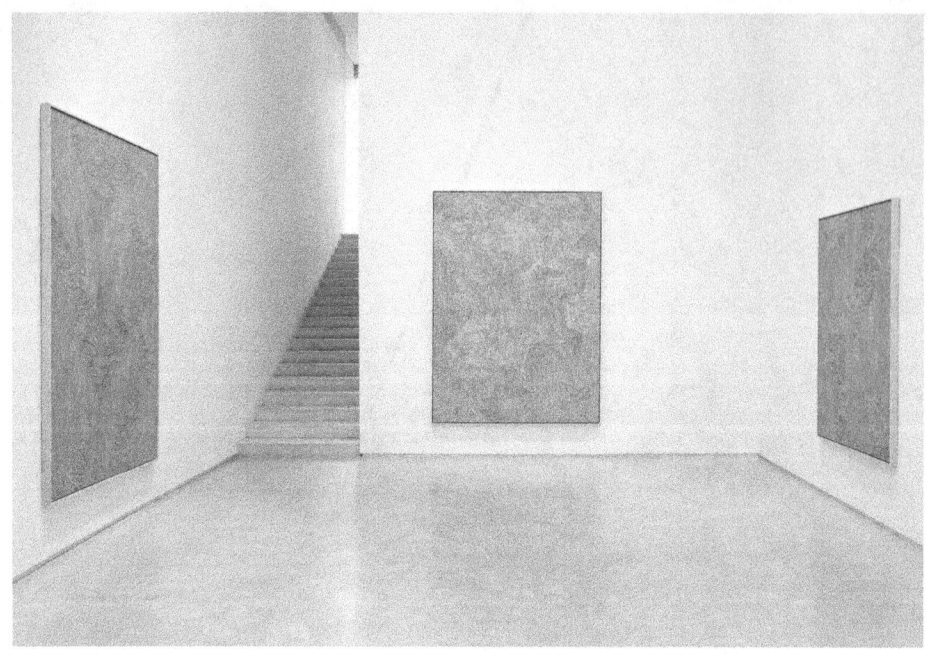

Figure 6.14

Warlimpirrnga Tjapaltjarri, *Maparntjarra*. Installation view,
Salon 94, New York, 2015. Image courtesy of the artist and
Salon 94, New York.

profound connotation possible: "Early on, I realized the world outside the
studio was more interesting than what was going on inside. People have been
making impressions in the earth for thousands of years—in general my work
takes its place amongst many other man-made marks."[50] Long's work consists
mostly in his making interventions into actual landscape by rearranging found
elements into geometric shapes that evoke the structures of prehistoric peoples
or importing into art galleries natural materials and arranging them within
geometric confines. The "archaic quality" is actually a subdued primitivism, a
generalizing evocation of the unknowable practices, beliefs, and values of long-
extinct peoples. Long has refined this generalization since he first began to take

it up in the years around 1970, deepening its metaphorical subtlety but also, inevitably, increasing its distance from its "sources."

When the art of actually existing *anciens* is juxtaposed with such evocations, the effect can be quite powerful. At its base, for the colonizer, it is the shock of confronting in real time, now, those who had been presumed dead, a people who were thought to be extinct. The conjunction, in effect, removes the "source" from the modernist artist's work, takes away from the non-Indigenous artist the presumed "right" to use this imagery, thus evacuating what is, after all, the secret source of its real value, its authenticity as art, its claim to be closest to timeless noncontemporaneity. Instead, the prehistoric world is shown to be alive, to have survived, adapted to all subsequent changes, and quite ready to represent itself, thank you very much, drawing on the assistance of Western mediators when it is needed. Furthermore, these living dead are, evidently, busy making art that keeps renewing itself; they are constantly setting out on new trajectories rather than staying still, remaining unchanged, staying in their expected place. What can modern primitivists like Richard Long do? Their work cannot match these changes because it does not originate them. It is obliged to surrender the connection, and thus a key element of its core logic as art. On a worldwide scale, this is the challenge that contemporary art by Indigenous peoples has been mounting against the modernist presumptions that still prevail at the traditional art centers, those not so coincidentally of the colonial powers.

For the continuing Euro-American modernists, those I name remodernists, the only option in such circumstances is to keep repeating the originary moment when the idea of making this allusive connection first occurred. This is Richard Long's route. By repeating the mud wall, and the assemblages of found materials, in various materials, at different locations, and at site-specific scales, his art settles into the stasis once ascribed to the art of "primitive man": it aspires to be unchanging, timeless, eternal. In fact, the reverse is occurring. Precisely because of the revivification of Indigenous cultures through the resistance, revival, and, despite everything, at times flourishing of Indigenous peoples, and because of their constant renovation of their own art, art such as Long's becomes anachronistic. His "solution" becomes yet another instance of late modernism endlessly rehearsing its breakthrough moment, ever more beautifully, at larger and larger scales, in even more expensive and exotic materials, and at greater prices. This is what the leading galleries and museums in New York and London constantly celebrate. It is the bedrock of their economic growth, the driver of their instinctive real estate expansionism: Gagosian and Zwirner meet the Modern and the

Whitney, via Dia. The most contemporary aspect of this art scene is its incessant recursion to its late modern glory days.

A measure of the impact of Warlimpirrnga Tjapaltjarri's painting on art-world insiders in New York is this brief notice in the *New Yorker* for October 5, 2015, one of ten aimed at informing readers of the week's most interesting art shows.

> The paintings of this outstanding Australian artist, who lived nomadically until 1984, when he was in his mid-twenties, are marvels. Against soft backgrounds of gray or coral, Warlimpirrnga paints lambent circuits of white dots whose irregular contours seem to tremble and to oscillate. In the clean white cube of the gallery, these pulsating paintings might, at first, seem consistent with nonobjective art as we know it (based on description alone, the Op Art of Bridget Riley may come to mind, or Yayoi Kusama's "Infinity Nets"). But these works aren't abstract. They are ardent, knowledgeable depictions of specific sites in the bush, irrefutable evidence that modernity and the sacred are not mutually exclusive.[51]

Another measure is the response of *New York Times* senior critic Roberta Smith, who began her review with "It's always thrilling when examples of a given art form makes you think this is the best (fill in the blank) I've ever seen." She goes on to offer some acute formal descriptions and ends by inviting the viewer to expand on them "through looking, a ritual unto itself."[52]

The confused acknowledgment that normal categories do not apply here should not surprise us, nor should the genuine response to an art that stakes its own claim to attention. Indigenous Australian art comes from quite other places, from a quite distinct temporality, and has established its own grounds of validity by negotiating with those that prevail within colonizing cultures—cultures that have, recently, been obliged to undergo a reluctant, painful decolonization.

PRECARITY FOR THE WORLD

In the last week of August 2015, then–prime minister Tony Abbott and members of his cabinet visited the Torres Strait, the Northern Territory, and northern Queensland. Echoing the optimistic projections of the national statisticians cited earlier, he said in an interview, "I think people need to know that a lot of good things are happening in Indigenous Australia. It's not just that Indigenous artists making good or Indigenous sport people making good . . .

but enough lives are in the process of being transformed for us to be more confident about the future for Indigenous people than at any time in the last couple of hundred years."[53] This is politicians' bromide for a dilemma that this politician actually took seriously, but never as a priority that would override his commitment to broader economic and political interests inimical to the welfare of Indigenous people. Indigenous artists know this, and some do not resile from pointing it out. Vernon Ah Kee's four-channel video *The Tall Man* (2010) uses footage shot during the riots on Palm Island protesting the death in police custody of a local man (figures 6.15 and 6.16). The artist celebrates the role of local resident Lex Wotton, convicted of instigating the riots, and the on-going protests against the injustice of police brutality.[54] Artworks such as these remind us that, despite the gains I have been outlining, the overall situation for Indigenous people, including their artists, remains precarious, as it has been not only for the past two centuries, but also, perhaps, for millennia.

Returning, then, to our original question, we can see that for most of the twentieth century, Indigenous Australian art remained based in traditional practices, which it continued to renovate, according to the circumstances, as it had always done. In other words, it became modern in its specific engagements with the world in which its creators were obliged to live. These show up in the use of new materials as mediums, in the occasional registration of current content, and in the use of stereotypical symbols to achieve legibility for non-Indigenous audiences. By the 1980s, however, these adjustments had gathered a momentum powerful enough to challenge the categories and the art-historical timetables employed by categorizers and agenda setters within Western art discourse. This occurred in Australia first, flowering during the 1980s and early 1990s within a framework of public support provided by social democratic governments, and actually revving up as a kind of aesthetic resistance during the dark years of conservative governance. Subsequently, it has persisted through the enforced corrections to markets that have been occurring since the global financial crisis. Economic necessity is a bottom line, but another one goes deeper still. This art is motivated, in its depths, by the fundamental drive to secure Indigenous cultural continuity and sovereignty, a key aspect of which requires reaching out across racial, social, and cultural divides to construct and sustain a shared national culture. We are also seeing more than a few hints that this reach has spread beyond the continent to appear with some regularity in international art exhibitions and to establish beachheads in the art centers of the old West.

We can conclude, then, that Australian Aboriginal art is contemporary not merely in the weak sense of art these artists happen to have made during

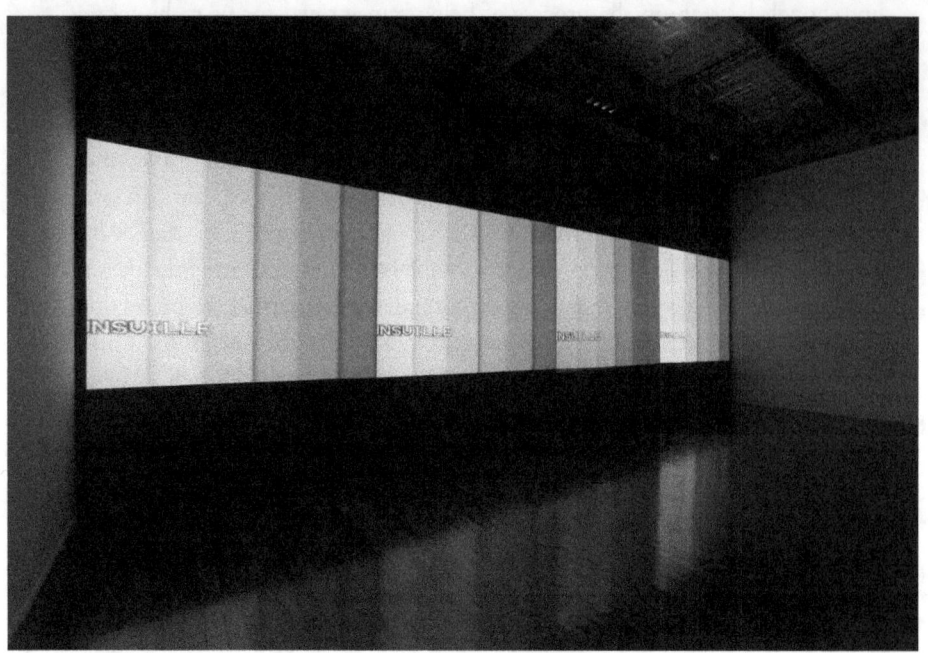

recent decades and are making today in the circumstances in which they find themselves, but in several much stronger senses. Far from imitating the styles and practices of contemporary artists from the dominant cultures, Indigenous artists have adapted inherited imagery and modes of composition to the potentials inherent in new materials, refigured ways of picturing the contemporary situations in which they live, and oriented the affect of their work toward the publics required for effective reconciliation. Far from being absorbed by modernism or succumbing to the poison of unprincipled market greed, they have, despite many setbacks and casualties, negotiated with both and developed sustainable ways of distributing their work. The result has been an art movement that, instead of following the pattern of birth-maturity-decline that has typified modern movements in art (no matter how brief some of them were), continues to revive and refresh itself through the inventive energies of artists coming together to work at remote centers or to create new ones, and through the increasing sophistication of Indigenous artists working in the cities. Above and beyond these artistic achievements, however, is the fact that some key members of what were once regarded as the most noncontemporaneous peoples still surviving in the world today have devised subtle ways of revealing to the rest

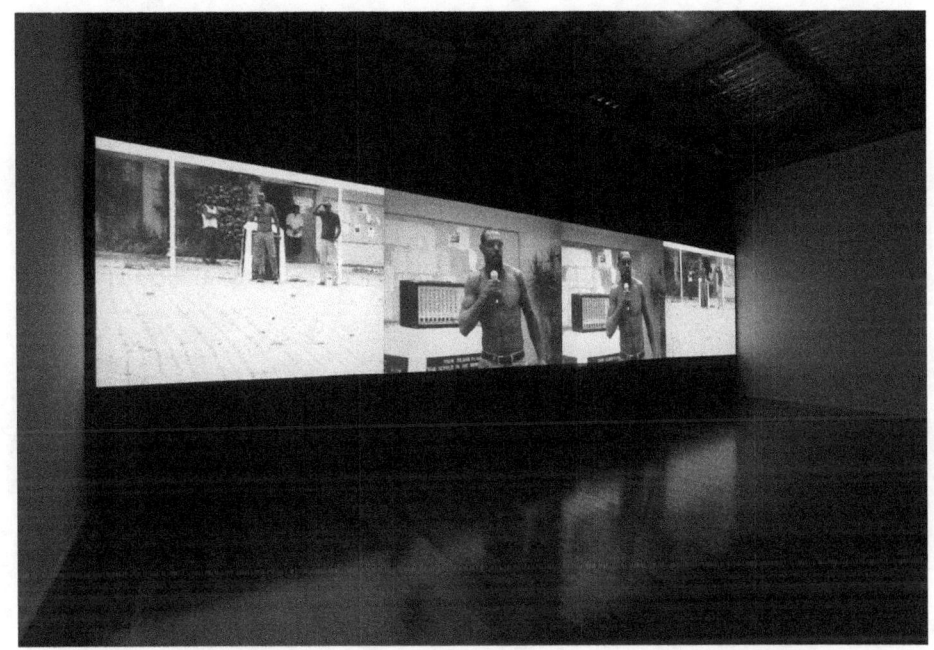

Figures 6.15 and 6.16

(ABOVE AND OPPOSITE) Vernon Ah Kee, *The Tall Man*,
2010, four-channel video installation, charcoal, crayon, synthetic
polymer paint on canvas, National Gallery of Australia,
Canberra. © Vernon Ah Kee and Milani Gallery, Brisbane.

of us the deeper dimensions of the contemporaneity that we all confront, and
of pointing us toward how we might best live together within its complex currents, in their and our "country," on this, our earth.

FROM THE ORIGINS, IN THE PRESENT

Connectivity to place may be understood less as a state of being connected in
some fixed array, and more as an ongoing process of seeking out the lineaments
of connection, catching glimpses of them, allowing them to resonate, change,
and inevitably loosen, only to seek them again. Something of this spirit informs
the 2006 collaboration between Pura-lia Meenamatta, a poet from the Ben

Lomond clan of the Cape Portland nation of Northeast Tasmania who is also named Jim Everett, and Jonathan Kimberley, a painter who lives and works between Hobart and Kununurra, Western Australia. Their *Meenamatta lena narla puellakanny—Meenamatta Water Country Discussion* took the form of an exchange between thirteen of Pura-lia Meenamatta's poetic/prosodic reflections and ten of Kimberley's paintings, along with associated drawings. Pura-lia Meenamatta's poems range from evocative observations of creeks, rivers, and rainwater at places in his country to speculations on water's centrality in global politics. "Some call me water" begins:

> some call me water
> nearly all need me
> i touch nearly everything
> connecting the inanimate
> with living things
> whereas "Europa" consists entirely of these lines
> colonies established post-colonialism
> which became neo-colonialism in the
> new nation of people exclusively
> under the controlling marketplace
> until all-life dies and neo-colonialism
> reaches its final regression
> in broken water dead.[55]

A student in Melbourne during the late 1980s, Jonathan Kimberley is of a generation of painters for whom the contemporary Aboriginal art movement was no longer a fascinating from-the-deserts phenomenon, its future filled with as much uncertainty as hopefulness. Yet it had not quite achieved the diversity of output and continentwide spread and depth of market that have made it, since 2000, a structural force at least as definitive of Australian art as the work of non-Indigenous artists. Interaction between the two kinds of "Australian" art has waxed and waned, often becoming intense, even volatile—especially when artists on both "sides" use appropriative strategies.

Kimberley and Pura-lia Meenamatta have inherited this history. Their approach, however, is postappropriative. After graduating, Kimberley elected to live and work in remote communities and was the founding manager of the Warmun Art Center at Turkey Creek (1998–2000). In his paintings are echoes of some major Aboriginal artists (Michael Nelson's wild brushstrokes, Emily

Kame Kngwarreye's lines), as well as of others (Jackson Pollock's thrown networks, Colin McCahon's textual admonitions), but these are faint. And these echoes are much less important than his tipping and tilting of the canvas to let lines of poured paint run in rivulets, randomly, all over the linen, or his picking out the shapes of natural growth, or his writing across the resultant surfaces the words that should be sung over them.

The core figure—the "diagram"—in the left panel of the diptych *Beyond the Colonial Construct: Meenamatta lena narla walantanalinany (Meenamatta Map of Unlandscape)*, 2006, suggests at once a bush, a brain, and a fish trap (figure 6.17). It is a freestanding shape but also a watery stain across a surface, one that leaves dissolving charcoal in its wake. It bursts up within a forest of trees. It hovers above four flowing rivers. Or it runs, shadowlike, beneath them. These are markings of a projective imagination. They are tokens of Kimberley's efforts to think, visually, like a plangermairreener person—something Pura-lia Meenamatta has invited him to do. They are his best shot at trying to see the world—in large, in small, and in between—from a plangermairreener perspective. They are as close as he can get to their picturing of watery presence in their country, to showing how they might "map" what is, to them, not a landscape. Kimberley pursues this goal in all the paintings in the series: some come close to landscapes; others are conjunctions or overlays of entirely abstract forms. When joined to its companion painting, *Meenamatta Water Country*, it becomes a diptych. It also becomes the summa of the series. The words inscribed across the surface, "meenamatta walantanalinany," mean "meenamatta country all round."

Pura-lia Meenamatta writes prose poems that seek to grasp the same subject in his own language, but also in English. These are written out in neat longhand on paper and then cut into shapes that are pasted to the painting. The shapes float, as if they are floating on water, like leaves, but also in water, like continents. Reading around *Beyond the Colonial Construct: Meenamatta Map of Unlandscape* from top left to top right, down to the bottom left, then across to the lower right quadrant, these are the titles of each text: "some call me water," "this place is outside the bible," "water," "blue tears in manalargenna country," "water spirits," "in the time of living origin," "birthing water," "tubuna," "antipodes," "planegarrtoothenar," "asia," "africa," and "europa." They range in imaginative scope from precise locations in the poet's country to the evocations of movements outside locative space and measurable time. Reversing Kimberley's approach but matching it, they use English in ways that attempt to show plangermairreener perceptions about being in the world to Western presumptions

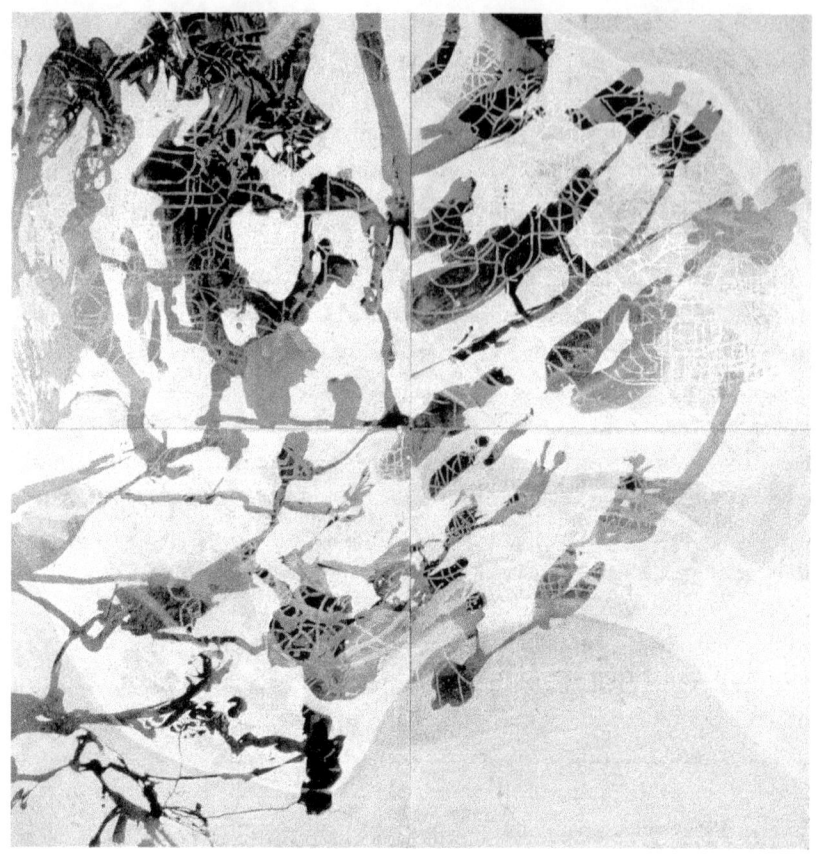

Figure 6.17

Pura-lia Meenamatta (Jim Everett) and Jonathan Kimberley, *Beyond the Colonial Construct: Meenamatta lena narla walantanalinany (Meenamatta Map of Unlandscape)*, 2006, synthetic polymer, charcoal, and handwritten text on linen, diptych, eight panels in total, each 244 × 244 cm. Images courtesy of the artists and Bett Gallery, North Hobart.

about space and time. They are Pura-lia Meenamatta's best shot at locating his worldviews within those of the other.

For both artists, the point is to arrive at a state of connectivity between their separate ways of seeing what they take to be a shared world, one that is fully, but inadequately, described by the other's ways of world picturing. Each perspective is inadequate because, for it to be complete, it would necessarily exclude the other. Neither wishes for this outcome. Nor is such an outcome generalizable any longer. Is there a larger perspective that can encompass both? If there is, it is not what is in front of us. *Beyond the Colonial Construct: Meenamatta Map of Unlandscape* may have gotten beyond the colonial construct, but it has only arrived as far as showing us a Meenamatta mode of mapping the nether space in which water moves, the nexus of actual terrain and mythic time-space for which the two artists use the word "unlandscape." Theirs is a deconstructive gesture, not as yet a constructive action. Perhaps this is why both the painted and the textual surfaces read so flatly, why their evident thirst for depth and movement seems so stilled. Nevertheless, to get this far is no inconsiderable achievement. Given the divided differentiation that pervades our contemporaneity, this may be as far as we can get at making place together. For now . . .

placemaking, displacement, worlds-within-worlds

Placemaking, world picturing, and connecting are among the most prominent of the processes we use to make sense of our daily lives and to understand what it is to be contemporary. No doubt, they are also among the core processes that have shaped being in the world since sentience became possible. But experience today is marked by certain striking features—its accelerated complexity, ubiquitous connectedness, deepening differences, intense proximities, layered multiplicity, pervasive transitionality, and vast violence—which suggests that these processes are unfolding and interacting in unprecedented, difficult, and often dangerous ways. Contemporary artists have, for some time now, been responding to the changes wrought by the current interactions between these and related processes: by aggregating appearances, exposing negativity while sustaining necessary opacities, and, at the same time, searching, always searching, for constructive capacity. Artists show us world pictures in operation and imagine other ones. They highlight connective threads, or breakages, and point out pathways forward. And they celebrate locality, or demonstrate dislocation, often as a loss, but also, in some situations, as an opportunity. In pursuing these processes, artists, like the rest of us, manifest the desire for a sense of ourselves as being *in place*, in *a* place that has a clear connection to other places, close and distant. We do so in a world everywhere defined by the contradiction between the ever-present contemporaneity of difference and the need to forge a shared future on an increasingly fragile planet.

The instinct toward placemaking is important to each of us because our standing in relation to temporality and locality, and to affect and effect, is at the core of every kind of identity formation. The configuration of these elements at the conjunctions between broadscale world picturing and particular, local world making shifts constantly—sometimes incrementally, at other times taking on patterns sharply visible and widely influential. Certain key thinkers and some artists have been especially alert to these changes. In 1951 the German philosopher Martin Heidegger reached for the image of a farmhouse in the Black Forest not, he cautioned, to exemplify the ideal solution to the post–World War II housing shortage (a topic that frames his essay "Building, Dwelling, Thinking") but rather to illustrate "the essence of dwelling," the core aims of which he defined—in terms as shamanistic as they were philosophical—as follows: "To preserve the fourfold: to save the earth, to receive the sky, to await the divinities, to initiate mortals."[1]

If we think, even at this level of abstraction, about how the processes of placemaking, world picturing, and connecting relate to one another, we quickly see that the first step toward making a place is to picture a particular world, and then work toward building it, usually around oneself and one's family, friends, neighbors, and colleagues—that is, from the connections close to hand. Of course, we never begin ab initio; we are always seeking to modify a given world, to make a place for ourselves *within* it, by striving to shift its connective skein toward how we have pictured it, or how it might appear as picture after having been made over. Moreover, we are always doing this *with others*, however much we might seek "a room of one's own." These early steps modify existing connection with proximate worlds by establishing boundaries, marking *this* world off from similar settings, rendering them adjacent, nearby, elsewhere. We also recognize that still other places are located at certain farther distances, and we imagine them as other worlds, like ours but with discernible differences. Eventually, the distances between worlds seem to increase until disconnection occurs: the kind of world that other worlds might be becomes hazy, generalized, and eventually unimaginable. Differences, too, increase in kind while declining in relevance. Nevertheless, at sufficient furtherance in space and time, certain settings—if they have been, or are, expansive enough or powerful enough—reappear at the outer limits of the placemaker's conscious world picture, in muted forms, as distant worlds. They are imagined, mostly, in the terms that they have projected outward—through their actions, their interactions, and their images of their own sense of place.

WORLD-PICTURING HYPERICONS

When it comes to picturing these settings through a gestalt, a single visual image, it is striking that only three metapictures, or, in W. J. T. Mitchell's term, *hypericons*, have been pervasive during recent decades: the projective map of continents and oceans, the image of the globe, and the communicative network conceived as a rhizome.[2] Just how difficult it is to move from this limited repertoire of models can be seen from recent surveys of modes of massive data visualization.[3] Yet if we are to develop a contemporary conception of worlds-within-the-world that gets us from placemaking through connectivity to world picturing and back, we must come up with something more suggestive than these necessarily reductive, static models.

The map of continents is a metageographic presumption that has historically become saturated with the ages of European expansion, as we see if we contrast the ubiquitous image of the Mercator projection with maps made outside Europe—such as those that locate the warring kingdoms we now know as China at the center of the known and imagined world.[4] Just how ideologically loaded seemingly universal presumptions can be is striking when we consider the world picturing underlying Samuel P. Huntington's conception of the "Clash of Civilizations," so central to the warlike foreign policy of the George W. Bush administration and to the revived isolationism of Donald J. Trump.[5] A more balanced, and simpler, mapping of the realities of continental difference are found in "A Heuristic World Regionalization Scheme," proposed by geographers Martin W. Lewis and Kären E. Wigen.[6]

Among artists interested in these matters, Alfredo Jaar's *Weltanshauung* (1998) offers us a simple demonstration of the ideological work these projections may do if they are taken as neutral totalizations: it consists of a simple juxtaposition of the "Political Map of the World" from the 1994 edition of the *Times Atlas of the World* (of course, a Mercator projection) with the continents and oceans arrayed according to the projection of Swedish geographer Arno Peters. Whereas the former lowers the equator significantly to show more detail about countries located in northern hemispheres, thus shrinking those in the South, the latter displays the actual areas of the earth's curved surface taken up by each continent and ocean. The South is enlarged to truly global pro-

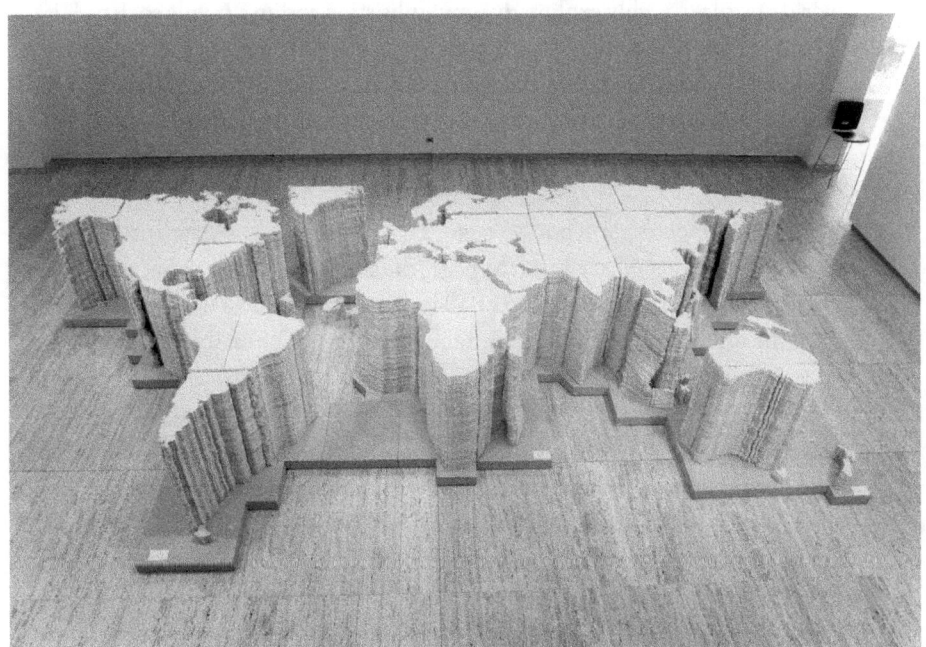

Figure 7.1

Ai Weiwei, *World Map*, 2006–9, cotton, wooden base,
1 × 8 × 6 m. Installation at Fifteenth Biennale of Sydney, 2006,
Art Gallery of New South Wales, Sydney. Image courtesy of
the artist.

portions, and North America, Europe, and Russia are squeezed into the upper quartile of the map.

Given the ideological weight of such representations, it might be puzzling, at first, that the Chinese sculptor and activist Ai Weiwei used the Mercator projection as the basis for his work *World Map* (2006–9; figure 7.1). The continents are made up from layers of raw cloth of the kind used in cotton factories in China—two thousand layers, in fact, making it not only labor intensive to install, but also self-evidently nonutilitarian, conspicuous labor for little apparent purpose. Ai Weiwei's subliminal political points are that this is a Western-oriented industry (China manufactures and exports over one-quarter of the world's textiles), highly exploitative, and subsisting within a fragile society. His artistic strategy to convey these implications is to add on layer after layer of cloth, up to about one meter in height, until the continents become as literally unstable as the political conflicts within them and between them.

The Globe

In Ursula K. Heise's 2008 book *Sense of Place, Sense of Planet*, she critically reviewed environmentalist efforts to image "the global."[7] She noted that the "Blue Planet" image has become a potent allegory of environmental connectedness since the 1960s, the most famous instance being the "blue marble" photograph taken by the Apollo 17 mission on December 7, 1972. Heise cites *Our Common Future*, the 1987 report of the World Commission on Environment and Development, known as the Bruntland Report, which claimed that "this vision has a greater impact on thought than did the Copernican Revolution.... From space, we see a small and fragile ball dominated not by human activity and edifice but by a pattern of clouds, oceans, greenery, and soils. Humanity's inability to fit its doings into the pattern is changing planetary systems, fundamentally."[8] She notes that the image serves all sides of the debates: the product of the most advanced technology, it is often enlisted in a crusade for ecological unity that is, largely, antitechnological:

> From McLuhan's "global village," Fuller's "Spaceship earth," and Lovelock's "Gaia" to visual portrayals of Planet Earth as a precious, marble-like jewel exposed in its fragility and limits against the undefined blackness of outer space, these representations relied on summarizing the abstract complexity of global systems in relatively simple and concrete images that foregrounded synthesis, holism, and connectedness. The efficacy of these tropes depended not only on their neglect of political and cultural heterogeneity ... but also on a conception of global ecology as harmonious, balanced, and self-regenerating.[9]

This conception, however, no longer secures consensus among biologists, who now favor explanations of biological development along more dynamic lines (as do many physicists).[10] Certain artists have been aware of global disequilibrium for some time: since 1998, Ingo Gunter and his Worldspace Corporation have been feeding information about changes to all aspects of the world's climate into their installation *Worldprocessor*. True to his outlook, the artist lives on a boat, which he sails from place to place, gathering information to tie the various presentations of this installation to its locality.[11]

Similarly, Helen and Newton Harrison have been working on these issues, and finding local solutions to them, since the early 1970s. Their procedure is to respond to a local invitation to help deal with an ecological problem by engaging in intense discussion until a visual image with local resonance emerges. The actual built solution takes that form: in their *Peninsula Europe as a Centre of a World* project (2001), a lynx unites the waterways of western Europe.[12]

Networked World
In recent years, the Blue Planet image has been transformed into an icon of technological connectedness, by being quite literally subject to digital photography that has created a network topology. Since 2004, Blue Planet has become Google Earth. There were some precedents, however, such as Earthviewer, developed by the CIA to scan Iraq during the US war and occupation of that country. It was later bought by Google and fed into the development of Google Earth. The company ART+COM, inventor of Terravision in 1995, has lodged an IP suit against Google. Google Earth and companies with similar technoplanetary perspectives are committed to essentializing technological exchange as the all-pervasive mode of contemporary connectivity. Becoming the platform for *all* human communication and identity formation is clearly the goal of Alphabet (Google's parent company). It is also the ambition of Facebook, as CEO Mark Zuckerberg made clear in his 2017 post "Building Global Community." After a decade devoted to connecting friends and family, Facebook now wants to lead in "developing the social infrastructure for community—for supporting us, for keeping us safe, for informing us, for civic engagement, and for inclusion of all."[13] The idea that these enterprises "do no evil" is delusory. However well-intentioned their origins and current self-belief, their near-monopoly of most forms of communication and their ever more skillful shaping of these forms to require us to use them, and use them constantly if we wish to communicate, all in the interests of building their vast revenues from advertising, blatantly contradict their pronouncements about being simply open mediums to link individuals and to "build community."

Can networked worlds be imagined in ways that go beyond the limits of the technoglobal? Web artist John Klima is an example of an imagineer of the technoglobal, as evident in his 2001 internet game project *Stand-Alone Earth*.[14] Artists such as Seth Price, especially through his essay *Dispersion*, written in 1998, and under revision since 2002, and painter Julie Mehretu evince a slightly more critical consciousness of the dispersive effects of globalization, as in her painting *Dispersion* (2002).[15] In Harm van den Dorpel's collage poster *Assemblage*

(*Everything vs. Anything*), he uses internet imagery printed onto a Mobius strip to capture the ubiquity yet evasiveness of net imagery, its subtitle summarizing the dilemma: it is a matter of *everything versus anything*. With no generals capable of capturing all relevant particulars, the situation has become, as the title of Peter Osborne's book on the "philosophy of contemporary art" indicates, a matter of *Anywhere or Not at All.*[16] It is no coincidence that the organizers of a conference on *Art Post-Internet*, at the Ullens Center, Beijing, 2013, used van den Dorpel's design as their poster image.[17]

So with a limited repertoire, and a consistent failure to corral the world's particulars into a generalization that remains true to their disposition, it seems that contemporary artists interested in these issues are struggling to come up with a hypericon that would be adequate to the complexities of our contemporary condition. We might, then, wonder whether the searching for an all-encompassing image—one that offers itself convincingly as *the* container for all the lesser images pressing toward visibility—is not a fruitless enterprise. Instead, smaller steps are gradually generating pictures that are becoming useful and richly suggestive, especially when matched with the imagery of place-making, and that of connecting.

THE WORLD INSIDE ONE'S HEAD

"How does one bring [about] the entire representation of the world inside one's head?" With this question, South African artist William Kentridge expressed his anguished recognition of the existential challenge that his art, and his world, demanded of him.[18] He had in mind the multiplicity of forces that bore down to shape his experience and that of those around him. How might an artist make these forces visible? How else but as effects on that which is observable? We might characterize Kentridge's individual approach as one of incessant collage: The world's force field is registered as it happens to him, as it delivers effects on those around him, and as he imagines its effects on those distant from him. It constantly changes shape, even in its equally constant repetitions. Kentridge's art, in its modes as much as in its details, suggests that because the world in all its complexity is too much for human vision to grasp, the actions of any one of its particular inhabitants, or even more, any group of them, is manifestly incomprehensible, often to the point of absurdity. Yet this is our world, and we are entirely within it.

A favorite Kentridge image is that of a globe unsteadily staggering on tripod-like legs across a blasted, desultory landscape. Sometimes the place is recognizable: the hinterlands of Johannesburg, the environs of Elephant River—to the artist a featureless interzone between the city and the tribal lands beyond, as well as the domain of Soho Eckstein's bewildered wandering, and the terrain of the people's uprising. Processional figures have been foundational to Kentridge's art from his early days as a set designer, notably in *Ubu and the Truth Commission* (1997). In Kentridge's hands the unsteady walker suggests the overweening ambition of those who strive to imagine the world but succeed only in creating increasingly absurd scenarios of their falling short. In one version, *Drawing for Il Sole 24 Ore (World Walking)* (2007), the Italian business daily newspaper referenced in the title—the sun, twenty-four hours—is shown as a symbol of globalization itself, pierced by struts like a wounded matador, signs of its connectedness trailing like unearthed electrical wiring (figure 7.2). Blinded by self-absorption, its absurd bowtie signifies that this worldview is all dressed up but has nowhere to go. Instead, it wobbles through the widespread devastation that its policies have created.[19]

Suggested here is a larger picture, that of the world as a whole, with many worlds nested within it, and many connections among them; yet, each world is a place in itself, with, in turn, many places within it. Connections among these worlds are dynamic and can take varied forms, all the way from mutual sustenance to apocalypse. The subtlety of Kentridge's visual thinking alerts us to the fact that, in contemporary conditions, each of the three processes—placemaking, world picturing, and connecting—has a double nature. Each tends to define itself against the others, seeking its distinctive characteristics and its core in its fundamental difference from the others. At the same or other times, and in the same or other places, each seeks to integrate itself into the others, to expunge difference, or, more realistically, to accommodate it. These antinomic tendencies have uneven effects; they are not the outcome of natural laws, a divine plan, or a historically determined dialectic. They tend neither toward equilibrium, nor toward entropy. At a level beyond our capacity to world picture, they may be shaped by both equilibrium and entropy, and thus amount to a kind of self-managed chaos. But if so, human agency—in the form of organized societies, international governance, organized belief systems, structures of thought, or customary ties—does not effectively set the human agenda. In fact, nothing more or less than the interaction among the processes themselves shape our understanding of contemporary being.

To me, Kentridge's image signals a central fact about the world today: that globalization is failing in its efforts to create a systematic world order. This is not the last stage of capitalist development; "late capital" makes no sense as a

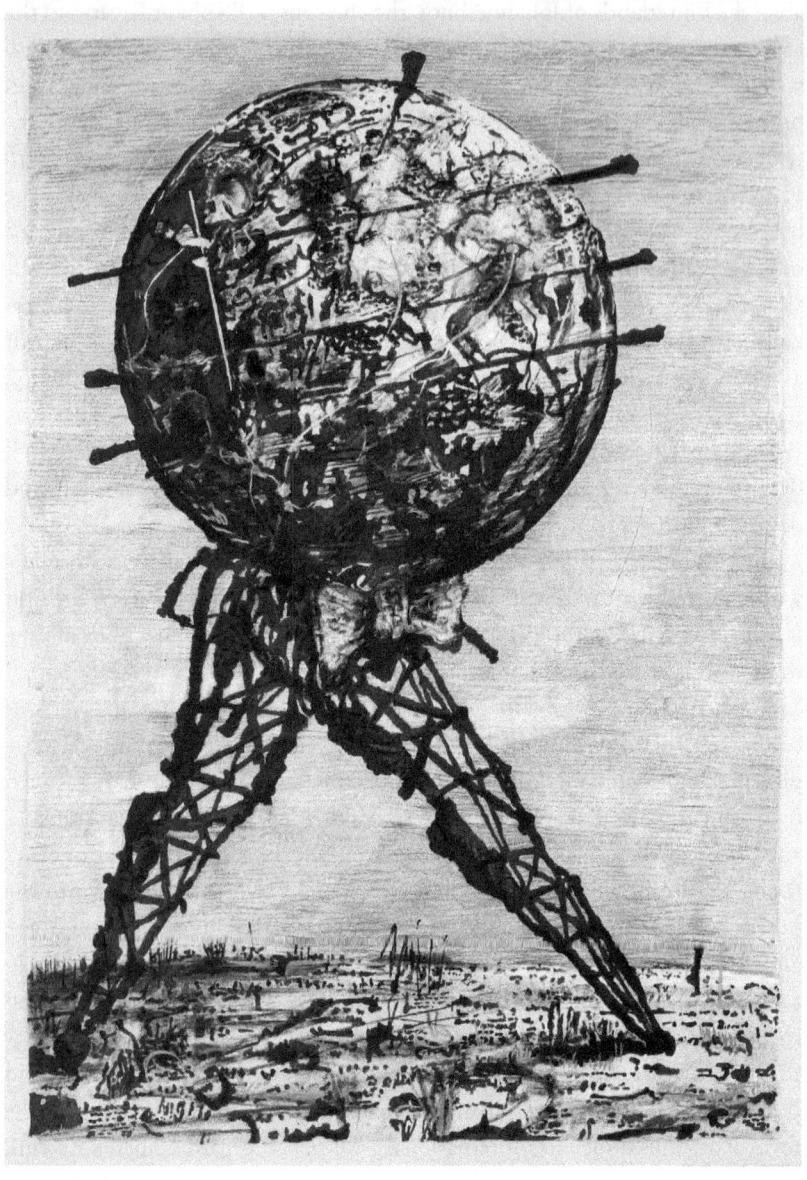

Figure 7.2

William Kentridge, *Drawing for Il Sole 24 Ore (World Walking)*, 2007, charcoal, gouache, pastel, and colored pencil on paper, 213.5 × 150.0 cm. The Doris and Donald Fisher Collection at the San Francisco Museum of Modern Art. © William Kentridge. Image courtesy of the artist and Marian Goodman Gallery. Photo by Ellen Page Wilson.

term—it is wishful thinking. Neoliberal globalization was the most recent phase of the uncontrollable destructiveness that has always driven capital, a destructiveness that precipitates pushback, which always limits its thirst for totality, its self-contradictory efforts to become systemic. There will be other forms of capitalism in the future. The good news is that they will be less than global. Because of contemporary pushback, globalized capitalism is shrinking as it spreads.

Pushback often takes the form of digging into locality. These days, however, location is possible only within the surround of potential dislocation. Some artists know this. Those who remain rooted see constant movement all around them. *Building Stories*, a 2012 graphic novel by American cartoonist Chris Ware, which took a decade to complete, is made up of fourteen printed works—clothbound books, newspapers, broadsheets, and flip books—packaged in a boxed set. The intricate, multilayered stories pivot around an unnamed female protagonist with a missing leg. They mainly focus on her time in a three-story brownstone apartment building in Chicago, but follow her later in her life as a mother. The stories can be read in any order. Ware spatializes the idea of "worlds-within-the-world."[20]

The last major piece made by Los Angeles artist Mike Kelley was *Mobile Homestead*, on which he worked from 2008 to 2012 (figure 7.3). It is, at once, a collection of installation rooms, spaces for private or small group creativity, a public art project, and a functioning social welfare center. The container for all these purposes is a full-scale replica of the 1950s ranch-style home in which the artist was raised in a suburb of Detroit. From 2010 it has been traveling the devastated, and now officially bankrupt, city, dispensing needed social services. In a reversal of the "white flight" that has plagued the city center, it was installed there in May 2013, on the parking lot adjacent to the Museum of Contemporary Art Detroit. Kelley is explicit about the contradictions and bad faith that this work embodies: "*Mobile Homestead* covertly makes a distinction between public art and private art, between the notions that art functions for the social good, and that art addresses personal desires and pleasure. *Mobile Homestead* does both; it is simultaneously geared toward community service and anti-social private sub-cultural activities. It has a public side, and a secret side."[21] Works such as *Mobile Homestead* demonstrate that place counts for us in many different ways, and on many different and difficult levels, usually simultaneously: the personal, private sense of home, as one place within a nest of varied yet roughly similar ones, as one world within a constellation of other worlds that circulate along parallel trajectories, with waxing and waning awareness of one another. Yet further senses of place have become important in

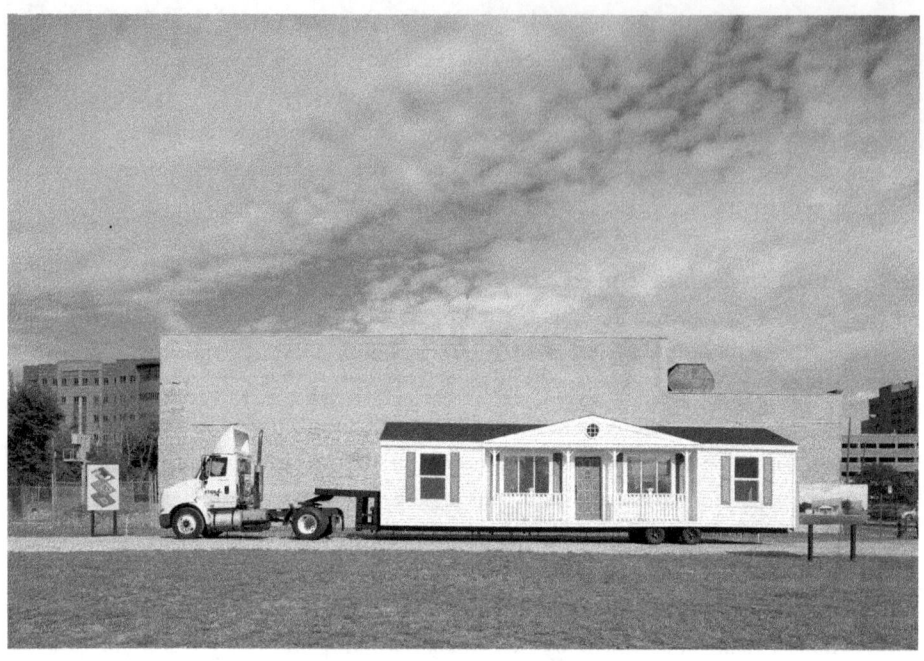

Figure 7.3

Mike Kelley, *Mobile Homestead*, 2008–12. Museum of Contemporary Art Detroit. © Mike Kelley Foundation for the Arts.

contemporary circumstances: official precincts, nonplaces, holding places for the displaced, and the transitional, between-worlds places woven by those who have become mobile by choice, happenstance, or coercion. Artists everywhere also contribute to the imagining, the making, the understanding, and the valuing of each of these senses of place.

THE SQUARE

During a visit to Brasília in 1960 as part of a US delegation, designer Frederick Kiesler escaped the opening ceremonies to visit the shantytown created by the workers who were building the capital city. There, he found himself drawn into the shack of one family, sensing an extraordinarily powerful conception of what it meant to make a place for oneself and one's intimate others. Despite being improvised, temporary, and deliberately underresourced by an irresponsible government, the shack and its surrounds stood in stark contrast to the elaborately planned, brilliantly designed, but ultimately hollow homage to European modernism and Brazilian modernization that was the new capital. This experience enabled Kiesler to finalize the design of his *Endless House* project, itself a striking effort to imagine the essence of dwelling.[22] Since then, Cidade Livre and other satellites outside Brasília have dramatically outgrown the official city and now constitute one of the largest conurbations in the region.

As an official precinct, the Plaza de la Revolución and its surrounding buildings is the Cuban equivalent of the governmental precinct at Brasília. These two join many other public domains throughout the world—including the Washington Mall, Red Square, the grounds outside Buckingham Palace, Tian'anmen Square, Zócalo, Plaza de Mayo, Tahrir Square, Maidan Nezalezhosti—as places created to enable the members of a state's population to constitute themselves as citizens of that state, places where the imagined bonds between oneself and one's nation can be experienced as an action in physical reality, an act of being there and doing what everyone else is doing, an act of fealty, of democratic association, or of revolutionary insurrection performed in plain view of the authorities and, above all, one's fellow citizens. On smaller scales, places like these serve similar purposes in neighborhoods, towns, cities, and villages all over the world. On every scale, they are sites of connectivity among those who are there, those who watch broadcasts or stream imagery of official or unofficial events that take place there, and those who visit at other times and imagine such events. These sites are regularly, and often ritually, connected with one another as well, through the people's participation in national holidays, irregularly in nationwide rallies demanding political or social change, or, less contentiously, in worldwide celebrations of the new year.

Placemaking by a belief community takes the form, usually, of a centralized location designed for large-scale meeting or for worship, in which those attending are regularly reminded that the real home of belief is their own hearts and minds. However inclusive the elements of the belief system may be, intense focus on one set of beliefs in one location—even when it is echoed by similar congregations elsewhere—inevitably operates to exclude other ideas, other individuals, and other peoples. Literally, spatially, and conceptually, these others are put to the side, or put at a distance. If the central place accumulates sufficient power, it becomes—over time, and at a certain degree of high visibility—iconic. Official images of it enter a local, and perhaps eventually global, economy within which a competitive exchange of imagery is constantly taking place. Repeated images of a place that is pivotal to a national imaginary, or is a center of economic power or a node of international tourism, engage in a kind of territorial warfare to seize and maintain maximum visibility and prime position within communicative media. This "iconomy" works mostly to secure for its major players political or economic advantage, or both, and to reinforce the disadvantage of the rest.[23]

Yet this economy is also a distributor of imagery and meanings that concern "universal" values, those understood to be of importance to humanity at large. The World Heritage List is a registry of "sites of outstanding universal value" that signatories of the relevant United Nations (UN) convention—most of its member nations—acknowledge "need to be preserved as part of the world heritage of mankind as a whole."[24] To be considered for the list, the site or building must meet at least one of ten selection criteria, six cultural, and four natural. These criteria include "to represent a masterpiece of human creative genius"; "to exhibit an important interchange of human values, over a span of time or within a cultural area of the world, on developments in architecture or technology, monumental arts, town-planning or landscape design"; "to bear a unique or at least exceptional testimony to a cultural tradition or to a civilization which is living or which has disappeared"; "to be an outstanding example of a type of building, architectural or technological ensemble or landscape which illustrates (a) significant stage(s) in human history"; and "to be an outstanding example of a traditional human settlement, land-use, or sea-use which is representative of a culture (or cultures), or human interaction with the environment especially when it has become vulnerable under the impact of irreversible change."[25] Since 1992, the UN Educational, Scientific, and Cultural Organization (UNESCO) has augmented its prioritizing of exceptional artworks and outstanding architectural settings by listing certain significant interactions between people and the natural environment as what it dubs "cultural landscapes."[26] A Heritage listing declares that *this* particular civic site, building, or environment has a value that includes but also transcends those attributed to it by those who live in or around it, and by those responsible for its governance. Its value as itself, in its place, is acknowledged as valid for all humans, from now onward. This is placemaking at its most ambitious.

In the image economy, official images are constantly supplemented by unofficial ones: those taken and circulated by advertising agencies and by visitors, usually in modes of celebration or documentation. Supplementary imagery adds other tonalities: irony, or criticality, for example. Which is where art comes into the picture. The Plaza de la Revolución is not a World Heritage site,

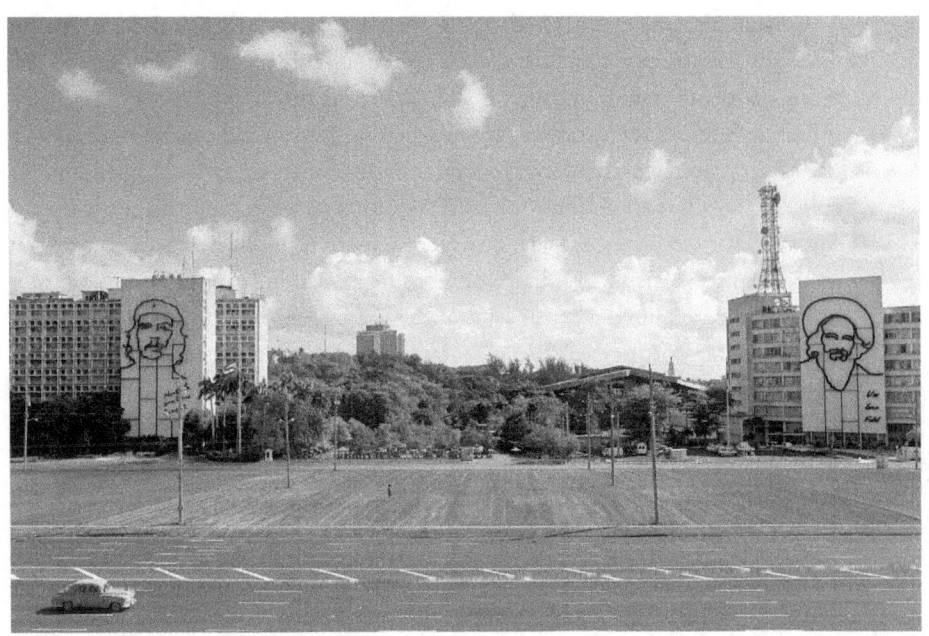

Figure 7.4

Coco Fusco, *The Empty Plaza/La plaza vacia I*, 2012, digital
chromogenic print, 66.36 × 100.33 cm. © 2017 Coco Fusco/
Artists Rights Society (ARS), New York. Image courtesy of
Alexander Gray Associates, New York.

but it is crucial to the government of Cuba, and it is an iconic site for its people
as well as for visitors to the country. Coco Fusco's video *The Empty Plaza/La
plaza vacia* (2012) takes viewers by taxi to the site, and while we watch a Stea-
dicam shot of the mostly empty plaza, a voice-over tells the story of the place
in the style of a documentary narrative, with accompanying film clips of rallies
there since the 1959 revolution (figure 7.4). As we observe a young woman in a
red dress walking into the distance and back, we learn that the plaza is policed
against everything except tourist snaps and short visits, that nothing occurs
there unless people are summoned for an officially sanctioned event, and that
the nearby neighborhood is a place of natural vitality. The contrast with the
sites of the Arab Spring is marked and, for the commentator, a portent.

Official placemaking has had a great past, but it may have a limited future. The main contemporary value of such symbolic centers is that they offer enticing opportunities for occupation. Undergirding the Occupy movement are initiatives such as radical cartography, which is burgeoning among artists, in the United States particularly. Individual artists such as Trevor Paglen and collectives such as the Center for Land Use Interpretation point to the widespread existence of secret places, sequestered from public access by certain government agencies, the military, and businesses serving these purposes. Our sense of place is shifted when artist groups publicize maps locating the surveillance cameras dotting Manhattan, infiltration routes across the US-Mexico border, the global connectivity of water distribution in Los Angeles, or the economic and social reliance of states such as California on their vast prison systems.[27]

DISPLACEMENT

Under contemporary conditions, placemaking as a contained process of picturing and providing a world-within-the-worlds-of-the-world has become increasingly tenuous and embattled. If the public squares of the old national states are becoming the sites and occasions of occupation by those demanding and resisting change, this is at least in part because the possibility of making a place for oneself in the world is shrinking fast for entire generations of young people. On a global scale, the world has been put into continuous motion by the unprecedented flows of people who have chosen or been obliged to move away from their homes. The International Organization for Migration (IOM) estimates that in 2012, 200 million legal migrants worked outside their countries of origin, two and a half times the number in 1965. Most come from Asia, hoping to work in the cities of Europe or the US.[28] In 2013, the UN estimated this number at 233 million, up from 154 million in 1990, with the migrant stock in the global North doubling that of the global South.[29] By 2015, the number had grown to 244 million. The numbers of illegal immigrants cannot, by definition and in practice, be accurately tabulated, although many countries keep statistics on those who come to official notice, as their presence is a volatile political issue.[30] The UN High Commissioner for Refugees (UNHCR) reports that, as of the end of 2017, more than 68.5 million people, or one every two seconds, had been displaced against their will, usually by war, with over 85 percent of them moving within the borders of developing countries, or from one developing country to another, mainly in the Middle East and Africa. The total includes 25.4 million refugees, over half under the age of eighteen, and 10 million stateless people. On each day of 2017, 44,000 people were forced to flee their homes because of conflict or persecution, yet only 102,800 in total were resettled during that year. These are the highest levels of displacement on record.[31] The world population is estimated to reach 8 billion in about a decade, and 9.8 billion by 2050. The contest for the food, water, land, and energy that is essential to mere survival is ratcheting up. Flourishing becomes more and more the preserve of the few. Meanwhile, global warming shrinks the earth's capacity to provide the essentials for life.

A few artists, such as Allan Sekula, in his decades-long *Geography Lessons* project, and Alfredo Jaar, in his works about Rwanda and in installations such as *The Sound of Silence* (2006), have been at the forefront in exposing the deleterious effects of these tendencies on both those involved and those who ignore them.[32] From 2001 to 2005, Dierk Schmidt devoted a series of paintings, *SIEV-X—On a Case of Intensified Refugee Politics*, to the Australian government's hardline policy toward refugees (mostly from Afghanistan and Iran) seeking asylum on the island continent by sailing to it from nearby countries. The government actively promoted xenophobia against the "boat people," despite their relatively low number and the fact that most were found, when processed, to be genuine refugees. Schmidt created an installation consisting of large paintings, wall hangings, and watercolors. In the large paintings, such as *Xenophobe—Shipwreck Scene, Dedicated to the 353 drowned asylum seekers that died in the Indian Ocean on the morning of October 19, 2001*, he jumbles fragments of images from newspapers and television broadcasts to produce a kind of contemporary history painting (figure 7.5). Another work in the series evokes the gallery in the Louvre where Eugène Delacroix's *Liberty Leading the People*, a supreme statement of sacrifice in the name of freedom, is hung near Théodore Géricault's *The Raft of the Medusa*, a coruscating exposé of the moral cowardice of the then–recently restored monarchy, whose incompetence was, at the time, taken to be highlighted by the incident depicted in the painting. By juxtaposing present-day viewers with an imagined scene of the painting's first showing in the 1819 Salon, Schmidt ruminates on the extent and the limits of art's ability to address the complexity of these issues, suggesting that we tend to do so as if they were problems for art itself. Smaller paintings in the series sketch newspaper photographs of the Australian politicians who developed these egregious policies. Several Australian artists have also taken up this issue—among them, performance artist Mike Parr, photographer Rosemary Laing, and artist-theorists Lyndell Brown and Charles Green.[33]

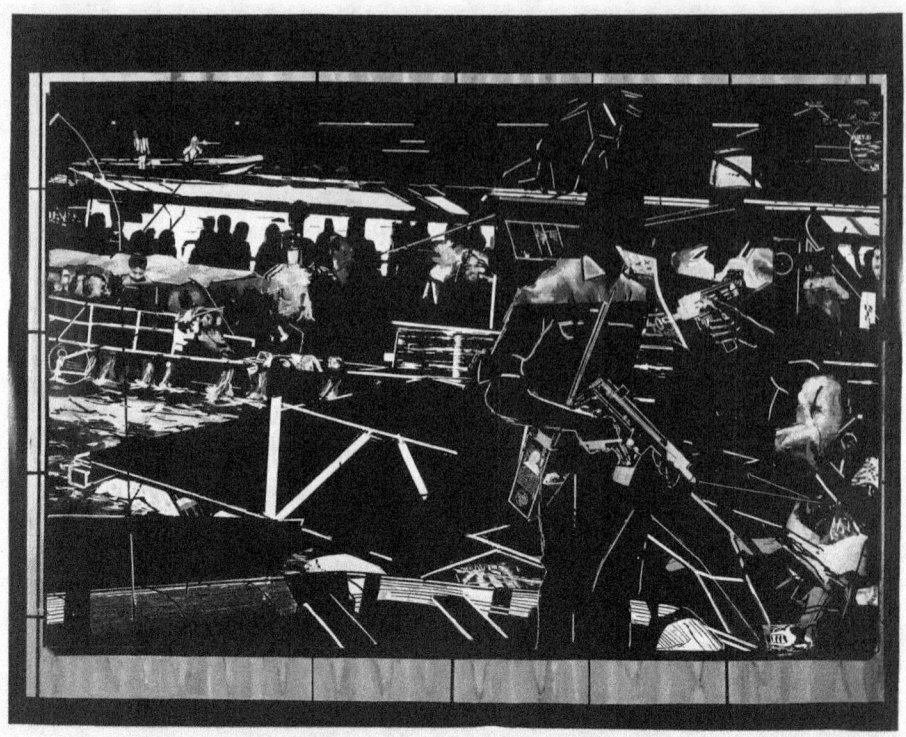

Figure 7.5

Dierk Schmidt, *Xenophobe—Shipwreck Scene, Dedicated to the*
353 drowned asylum seekers that died in the Indian Ocean on
the morning of October 19, 2001, 2001–2, oil and acrylic on foil,
177.0 × 229.6 cm. Städel Museum, Eigentum des Städelschen
Museums–Verein e.V. © VG Bild-Kunst, Bonn 2015. Image ©
Städel Museum—Artothek.

The multilayered complexities of such situations have pushed the documentary approaches to these issues, which served for much of the nineteenth and
twentieth centuries, beyond the breaking point. *The Migrant Image,* by T. J.
Demos, is the subtlest exploration to date of this issue in contemporary art,
especially in photography and video.[34] Demos examines the efforts of multiple
artists working in the Middle East, North Africa, Europe, and the US to rep-

resent the experiences of refugees, migrants, the politically dispossessed, and the stateless. Artists such as Steve McQueen, the Otolith Group, Hito Steyerl, Walid Raad (the Atlas Group), Emily Jacir, and Ahlam Shibli have felt obliged to reinvent the documentary modes that previously served to highlight the plight of victims of inequality, disaster, or war. Artists now tend to be up front about their own involvement in the documentation process and frank about their limits as observers. They refuse to ignore contradiction; they expose misinformation and parade obfuscation for what it is. They highlight the role of the imagined, the desired, and the fantastical in everyday life. They seek to empower their "subjects," by sharing skills, equipment, and insights.

Community-oriented, participatory art practices are coming to the fore as being more immediately useful and potentially longer-lasting responses to current conditions than representations of crisis that have the art world as their first and last audience. Artists such as Thomas Hirschhorn create installations—including his *Bataille Monument* (2002), at Documenta 11, and his *Musée Précaire Albinet* (2004) in Landy, a distant suburb of Paris—that operate as both artworks and "temporary autonomous zones" for residents of working-class and immigrant neighborhoods.[35] Other artists and groups—notably Pablo Helguera, Navjot Altaf, Carole Condé and Karl Beveridge, Ala Plástica, Huit Facettes-Interaction, WochenKlausur, Park Fiction, Oda Projesi, the Critical Art Ensemble, and the Yes Men, among many others—work in response to the needs of threatened communities and show evidence of these interactions in art-world and other contexts to raise awareness of the specific issues involved and to provide information for those who might be drawn to such activism.[36] Displacement is, as the UN Human Rights Council (UNHRC) tells us, *the* challenge of the twenty-first century.[37]

MIGRATION

Bangkok-born, Sydney-based installation artist Phaptawan Suwannakudt is the daughter of the famous Thai traditional mural painter Paiboon Suwannakudt (a.k.a. Tan Kudt). As a young woman, she worked in her father's studio and at mural sites in temples, hotels, and public buildings, eventually becoming, after her father's death, the first woman to lead a team of muralists in the Thai capital. She moved to Sydney in 1996, where she found herself navigating cultures:

> The art practice I used was not a common normal practice and therefore no longer fitted with the expectations of the local audience. However,

the surrounding society, I observed, was not at odds with me. I did not have to look far but around my neighborhood in the Marrickville area of Sydney there was always someone who came from elsewhere, who was different from the others. They were individuals with views and expectations not necessarily shared with me, but they may not have shared them with anyone else in the same locality either.[38]

Phaptawan did not waver in her understanding that it was the role of the artist to picture the worlds, material and spiritual, in which she and her fellow beings lived, but she now confronted increased layers of complexity as an artist working within two cultures: one ancient, hierarchical, and familiar, the other relatively new, egalitarian, and unfamiliar. She continues, "Rather than borrowing the use of another expression unfamiliar to me, I went on using the process of Thai mural painting to approach my new home environment."[39]

She continued to use tempera on silk as her main medium, and to depict an intersection of visual imagery and texts from both Thailand and Australia, using extracts from novels by Thai immigrants and phrases from the Trai Phum Phra Ruang (The Three Worlds according to King Ruang), a fourteenth-century Thai Buddhist cosmology that divides the world into three realms: *Kāma bhūmi* (the senses, desire), *Rūpa bhūmi* (form, materiality), and *Arūpa bhūmi* (the immaterial). This three-worlds typology gave an open-weave structure to a series of works, including *Un(for)seen* (2010), an installation consisting of eight scrolls in which she applied ink and dye paint to silk, fabric, and draft paper (figure 7.6). Phaptawan comments on her intent in this work:

> I began weaving semi transparent fabric, which has come to resemble the cast-off layers of the skin of a snake. It is a concrete way to think about the abstract layers of culture, of memory and my own history and life in Australia. This body of work intersects with the Thai mural painting I had developed in Thailand before leaving for Sydney. I will always be a stranger and relate to Sydney from the perspective of a third person, but this is the same way I was in Thailand.[40]

We can hear here, in the artistic life of one individual, resonances of Simon Njami's lucid characterization of the shifting senses of selfhood experienced by African artists during the massive social upheavals that have convulsed Africa since the 1960s:

> There are many reasons for leaving beyond the obvious political and economic ones: no longer being able to share, in the case of contemporary

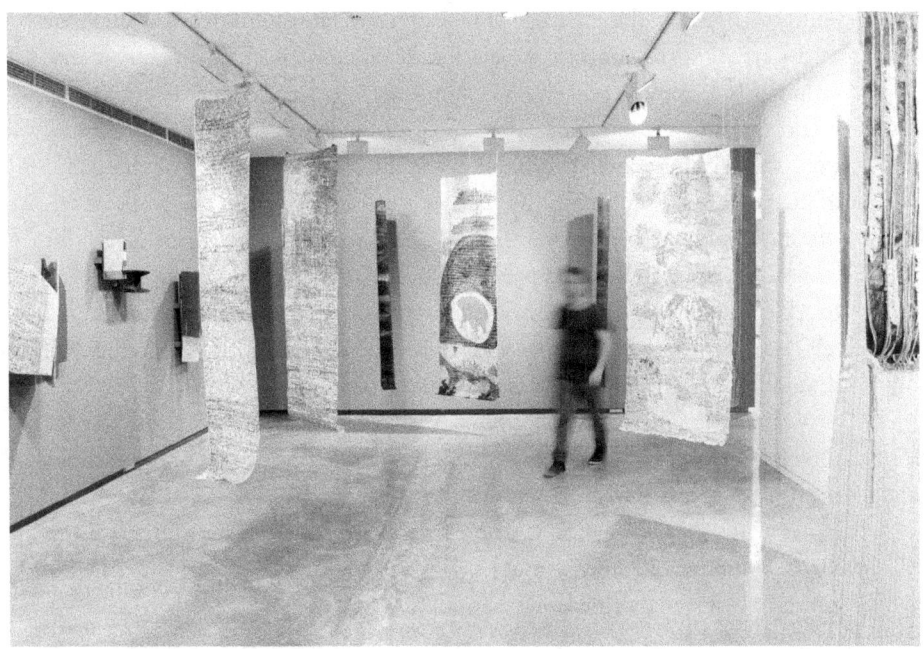

Figure 7.6

Phaptawan Suwannakudt, *Un(for)seen*, 2010, scrolls, ink and
dye paper on silk, fabric and draft paper, dimensions variable.
Left wall: *Not for Sure*, 2012, drafting paper, paper with vegetal
fibers, ink, bitumen, gold leaf, dye, and pigment, dimensions
variable. Installation view, Eighteenth Biennale of Sydney,
Museum of Contemporary Art. Image courtesy of the artist.

artists, for example, your inner language with the people around you. Re-
alising that you will have to go elsewhere to find a silence that corresponds
to you. This is no doubt what being contemporary is all about. Artists
share the same quality of silence, expressed according to different accents
and sensibilities, and through these silences their background and vision
of the world appear.[41]

Based in Lausanne, Switzerland, and with Cameroon roots, Njami is the
editor of *Revue Noire*. His comments evoke the essential isolation of artists

amid their people, the exchange of rejection and obligation that is at the heart of the artist's social contract, no matter the circumstances. Artists forced into immigration, or those who choose it (and every shade in between), seek a social world that will accommodate their inner distance from it. Since decolonization, and within globalization, this is the life trajectory of tens of thousands of artists all over the world. We can see this playing out in the work of artists such as Georges Adéagbo, Jean-Michel Bruyère, and Kendell Geers, for whom African experience is paramount. The metaphor of silence goes back to Albert Camus, to his sense of the paradoxical, contrary nature of existential self-realization and social obligation in the context of the world's absurdity. We should not be surprised at its recurrence.

Visual artists may, however, overcome silenced speech, or the unsayable, by showing it in operation, as it resonates in the mind, the psyche, and, for some, the soul. Phaptawan is one of countless artists these days who seek to do this, as in her 2012 series *Not For Sure*, where a set of shapes—disparate off-cuts from some unfathomable process, mute objects covered with unreadable texts—are arranged in a straight line along the wall (left wall of figure 7.6).

Here [in Sydney], people asked about my origin: "Tell me where you come from, so I can understand you." If I went back [to Bangkok], they stated: "You don't understand us. Since you no longer live here." The dialogue presented in the group of works *Not For Sure* (2012) starts here. It explores how humans connect by the process of writing text into fabric paper made from Thai plants and herbs. . . . It creates layers that make the context illegible. Writing performs a counter-conversation in a space where human stereotypes are inadmissible. Shapes and forms are no longer barriers for information to cross. . . . This allows room for individuals to indicate their presence and that they exist.[42]

IN-BETWEENNESS, UNREAL STATES

The changing nature of place that becomes apparent to those who move between worlds is the theme that Do Ho Suh pursues in his installations. Some symbolize official control of public spaces: As we walk across his *Floor* (1997–2001), we become aware that the thick glass is supported by thousands of tiny figurines, male and female, in quasi-uniforms, colored like mottled grass or camouflage. Their arms are raised as if in praise of a leader (me, you, us? no) and in a desperate effort to resist their crushing confinement. Other works track his own migrations

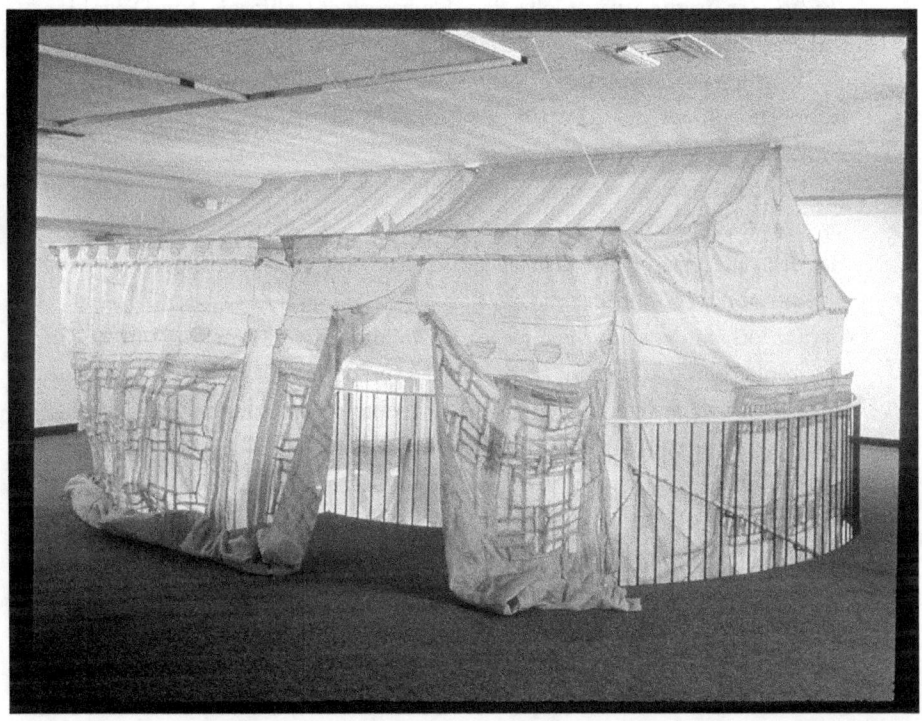

Figure 7.7

Do Ho Suh, *Seoul Home/L.A. Home/New York Home/Baltimore Home/London Home/Seattle Home/L.A. Home*, 1999, silk and metal armatures, 378.5 × 609.6 × 609.6 cm. The Museum of Contemporary Art, Los Angeles, purchased with funds provided by an anonymous donor and a gift of the artist. Image courtesy of the Museum of Contemporary Art, Los Angeles.

between Seoul, New York, and elsewhere: sculptures such as *Seoul Home/L.A. Home/New York Home/Baltimore Home/London Home/Seattle Home/L.A. Home* (1999) are scaled evocations of the spaces in which he has lived—rooms, stairwells, apartments, or entire houses or blocks—using delicately colored, suspended silk, ghostly wisps of remembered places (figure 7.7). Suh's more recent works address the cultural clashes that occur as worlds collide and distinct conceptions of what counts as a place are obliged to occupy the same space. The 2012

Fallen Star (in the Stuart Collection, University of California, San Diego) is a modest clapboard bungalow installed precariously on the edge of an upper-floor balcony of a postmodern apartment building, as if it had dropped from the sky after being uprooted by a tornado.

Paris-based US artist Eric Baudelaire explores these themes in works such as *Site Displacement* (2007), which consists of forty-four C-prints arranged as diptychs. Commissioned by the French city of Clermont-Ferrand to create a work reflecting on the delocalization that affected the previously thriving industrial city, Baudelaire took twenty-two photographs of buildings, parks, vacant lots, gardens, nearby forests and mountains, some interiors, and one of a school group visiting a lookout. He then hired New Delhi–based photographer Anay Mann to shoot scenes in his country "after" those that Baudelaire had taken. The pairings are, at first, striking in their similarities, as both photographers avoid stereotypical imagery, focus on everyday subjects, adopt incidental points of view, and deploy a low-key informational style. Within these seemingly loose parameters, Mann evidently took considerable pains to match Baudelaire's images as exactly as possible, generating an apparent but tension-filled sameness. Apartment houses arising from empty fields, for example, are indistinguishable in both places. Slowly, however, differences emerge, especially in the details. While a well-equipped French school group visit a lookout, the Indian group consists of schoolboys playing in a desultory fashion in a sandy yard. The street outside a rundown restaurant in the French village has less external electrical wiring than the similar-looking house in an Indian town.[43]

On a broader geopolitical register, Baudelaire's thinking about belonging to a place is manifest in his ongoing work *The Secessions Sessions*. This grew from the artist's email then personal relationship with Maxim Gvinjia, for a time the de facto foreign minister of Abkhazia, an "unreal state" that seceded from Georgia during the 1992–93 civil war. It has specified territorial borders, a working government, a distinct language, and a national flag, but it is recognized by no other state, nor by the UN. Learning this, in 2012 Baudelaire wrote to Gvinjia, and from their exchange evolved a series of exhibitions, publications, and online postings, most notably installations in Paris, Bergen, Doha, and elsewhere known as *The Anembassy of Abkhazia*, in which Gvinjia conducted consular business and shared information about his country with visitors (figure 7.8). Baudelaire comments:

> To many observers, Abkhazia is simply a pawn in the Great Game Russia and the West have always played in the Caucasus. "The Secession Sessions" acknowledges these competing narratives and does not seek to

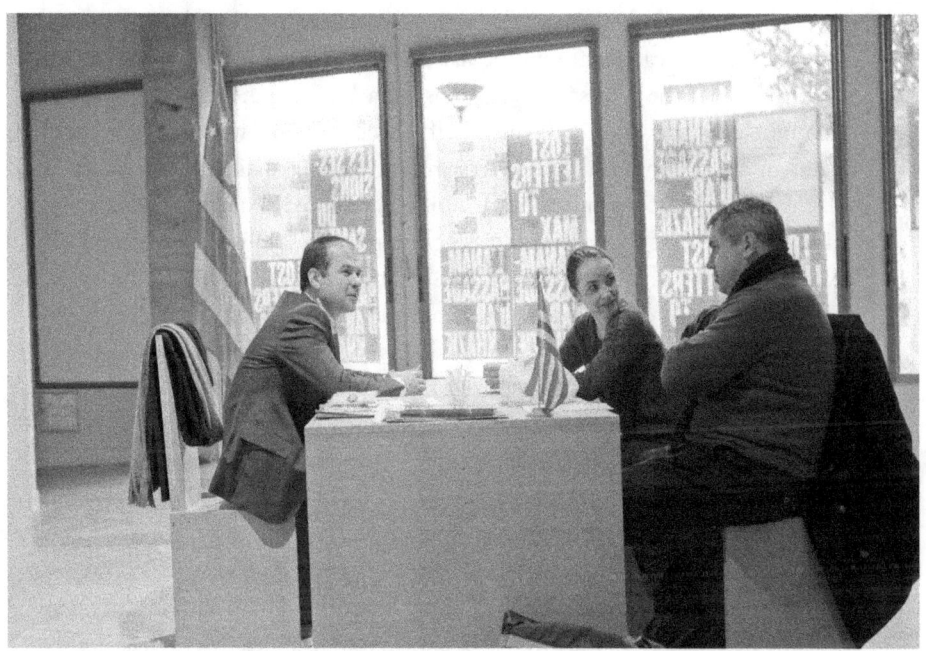

Figure 7.8

Eric Baudelaire (with Maxim Gvinjia), *The Anembassy of Ab-khazia*, within the exhibition *The Secession Sessions*. Installation view, Bétonsalon—Centre d'art et de recherche, Paris, 2014. © 2018 Artists Rights Society (ARS), New York/ADAGP, Paris. Image courtesy of the artist.

write an impossible objective historiography. It does not parse, verify or document any competing claims to a land. The project starts with this observation: Abkhazia has had a territorial and human existence for twenty years, and yet it will in all likelihood remain in limbo for the foreseeable future, which makes the self-construction of its narrative something worth exploring. If Abkhazia is a laboratory case for the birth of a nation, then its Garibaldis and George Washingtons are still alive and active. Maxim Gvinjia is one of them.[44]

The Secession Sessions has a major precedent in the project *State in Time*, launched by the Neue Slowenische Kunst (NSK) collective in 1992. Responding to the breakup of Yugoslavia's "self-managed socialism" and its relapse into various versions of reactionary ethnic nationalism, these artists—among whom Group Irwin is the consistent core—posited a "state" in the form of a utopian communality that would constitute itself as such when and wherever it met, and as an always-present ideal. While its symbolic paraphernalia parodied those of institutionalized social and political entities, it claimed no territory. Among its absurdist actions is the request for recognition from established states, none of which has given it. Nevertheless, the NSK state offers citizenship freely and issues passports. As of July 1, 2017, its membership numbered 15,500. Occasional meetings, temporary embassies, or pavilions in the form of art installations, convene as places to reimagine citizenship, belonging, statehood, nationality, transnationality, and cosmopolitanism in the then-prevailing circumstances. A pavilion at the 2017 Venice Biennale collected opinions on global disorder as it relates to Europe and developed *Beyond Borders*, "a transnational model for the reception of asylum seekers."[45]

The work of artists such as NSK, Do Ho Suh, and Eric Baudelaire epitomize the distinct but interwoven senses of world being that I have been exploring in this chapter: place shadowed by displacement, coeval connectivity versus hostile adjacency, and a planetary grasp of worldliness compared to a fear of arbitrary acts by external forces. Much more could, of course, be said—about, for example, the picturing of new kinds of places and nonplaces that have been introduced into the world by the workings of economic globalization (such as the zones of scaled-up production captured in the panoramas of Andreas Gursky), the devastation of nonrenewable natural resources that has driven industrial capitalism (the perverse beauty of which is pictured too elegantly in the oilfield and refinery imagery of Edward Burtynsky), and the atmosphere of accelerated decay that envelops places abruptly rendered anachronistic (as portrayed in the videos of Deimantas Narkevicius or Almagul Menlibayeva, for two among many examples). Other artists expose the repressed paradoxes entailed by systems of surveillance and of distant destruction, which involve detailed and precise envisioning of the living places of others and, at the same time, a presumption that those others are less than human, or simply targets, so that they and their place of abode may be obliterated (thus Omer Fast's 2011 video "5,000 Feet Is the Best," based on an interview between the artist and a Predator drone operator). As I discuss in chapter 4, the concurrence with architecture that is prominent in some contemporary art (such as that of Andrea Zittel and Lucy Orta) is a quite literal searching for materials useful to placemaking. Similarly, the ubiquity of installation as *the* contemporary format is arguably founded in the need for a concentrated, located intensity of experience, however temporary, within an exhibitionary domain that announces itself as entirely symbolic, in contrast to the instability and uncertainty that have come to rule the "real world" outside.

UTOPIAS, OLD AND NEW

Conversely, we might wonder whether the fond wish of many contemporary artists, curators, and viewers to escape the present, and the past-present-future triad, is actually a deep desire to find another temporal inhabitation, a kind of placelessness. A fascination with imagined places, and imaginary ones, or with projected utopias and dystopias, animates many artists today. Two works at the 2016 Singapore Biennale—the theme of which was *An Atlas of Mirrors*—may help us see this, by their contrast. In the central space of the National Museum hung a huge globe-shaped installation, six hundred centimeters in diameter, by Subodh Gupta, titled *Cooking the World* (figure 7.9). Composed of thousands of used aluminum and steel cooking utensils from all over the world, varying considerably in their origins and cost, it attests to our subsumption to consumerism, but also to the basic necessity of preparing food to eat. In the state that we see them, however, they are mostly unusable, exhausted by constant usage. As an image of the globe, suspended by thin plastic lines, this pictures a world that seems bent on self-destruction—less through the cataclysm of, say, nuclear war (something he evokes in his 2008 work *Line of Control*) than through the fact that conditions of massive inequality constrain millions, as part of their everyday existence, to repeat simple acts that hasten the entropy of things.

In another room within the biennale, Qiu Zhijie presented his installation *One Has to Wander through All the Outer Worlds to Reach the Innermost Shrine at the End* (2016). Across two long walls hung scrolls painted with ink, showing islands and seas that recall the maps of maritime explorers who were active in the Indian Ocean and elsewhere both before and after the invention of the mariner's compass in the eleventh century. Qiu's murals are conceptual cartographies, however, maps of the thinking about the unknown world by famous navigators, notably Zheng He, who is reputed to have reached East Africa well before the seventeenth century, the great age of European exploration. A Sea of the Old World fills much of the central space of one wall and is populated with sailing ships. One large island is, indeed, named Pre-Columbian Transoceanic Contact Theories. Nearby, a Sea of Nautical Science is divided from the Sea of Sinbad by treacherous currents. In the top right corner, the limits are reached in the Sea of Human Outpost. Aware that these early explorers, in search of

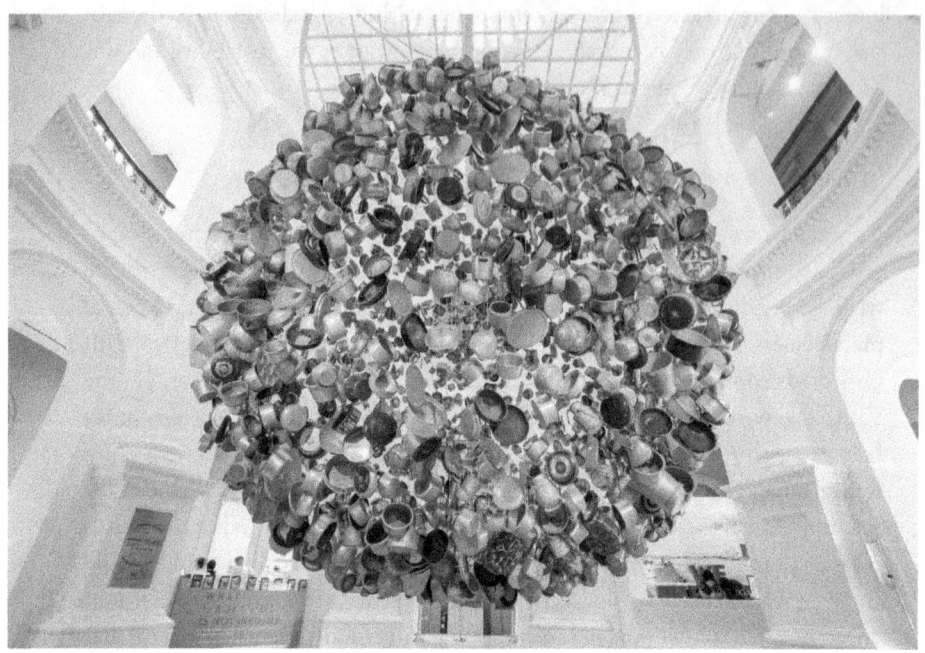

Figure 7.9

Subodh Gupta, *Cooking the World*, 2016, found aluminum utensils, monofilament line, and steel, 600 cm (diameter). Installation view in Singapore Biennale—An Atlas of Mirrors, at the National Museum of Singapore, October 27, 2016–February 26, 2017. Collection of the artist. Image courtesy of Singapore Art Museum.

places that could become the utopias that their homes were not, also believed that they would encounter monsters in these unknown lands, Qiu Zhijie sets out on the floor several rough rocks and mounts on many of them a glass bestiary of fantastical creatures based on drawings from the period.

We are entering the domains of meta–world picturing. In 2015 Qiu Zhijie began his *Mapping the World Project*, recognizing an emergent theme in his art. A series of large ink paintings on scrolls has resulted. They range from the grotesque humanoid shape taken by the central island in *People Who Claim to Be Messiah Crowding History* to *Map of the Third World*, both drawn in 2015. In the latter, a River of the Third World flows through a mountainous landscape, fed by tributaries such as Nonaligned Movement, which enter it from the Plateau of Colonialism, the Mount of Monotheism, the Lake of the Leaders, Mt. Geopolitics, and a mountain carved like Mount Rushmore labeled "American Dream." A Wetland of Political Islam faces Mt. Globalization, which has War on Terror and Islamophobia written on its flanks. The river flows through flatlands, such as the Eurasian Chessboard, into an estuary, with muddy islands appearing, one labeled BRICS.

In 2017, as part of his *Maps* series, Qiu drew *Map of Utopia*, in which the ideal no-place appears as a small island off the shore of a large landmass shaped like Ubu Roi, the absurd king in Alfred Jarry's play of that name (figure 7.10). Its awkward bulbous shape is made up of regions each named for failed utopian projects, such as Plato's Republic, the Jungle of Hobbes, the Land of the Golden Age, Marxism, the Gulf of Anarchist, and the most recent fantasy, the current Chinese government's vision of New Harmony. Above its absent head, in the Sea of Heaven, an archipelago includes the Islamic Firdaus, the Christian Kingdom of Heaven, the Buddhist Nirvana and Pure Land, the Moksha of Hinduism, the Chinese Sky (mainly Tao), and Atlantis. Below, in the Sea of the Future, floats an island named the Utopia of Technological Revolution. It lies between the dancing feet of the main landmass, one labeled "The Cape of the End of History" and the other "The Cape of Uninterrupted Revolution." Within these regions is another, more local and specifically historical layer. Train stations on the Cape of Uninterrupted Revolution are named for Lenin, Trotsky, Mao, and Che Guevara. The heels of the capes are, respectively, the bylands of globalization and of world revolution, and within them are ports for historical events such as Occupy Wall Street and Cominform 1947. The small, circular island Utopia (of Thomas More) is populated by the ports of Open to Foreigners, Common Ownership, Political Equality, and Free Education, and villages with names like Meditation in Free Time, Prison for Deadbeats, and Golden Toilet.

In these works, Qiu Zhijie has vividly reimagined the hypericon of continents and oceans. He knows that mountains turn streams into rivers that flow into seas and suggests that human history and thought change through time in analogous ways. This is a generalizing metaphor, but the process of drawing across an unbounded paper surface concretizes it into a template for ongoing exploration, despite the prevalence of obstacles. Certainly, the actual, conceptual, and imagined journeys of the past accumulate as the slow-settling sediments of failed aspirations. Yet the evident fact that there have been so many such attempts tells us, at a glance, that there will be many more. And that many will persist, even grow, despite their inevitable sedimentation. Some, he seems to suggest, may be very long lasting—indeed, they may be cosmic processes.

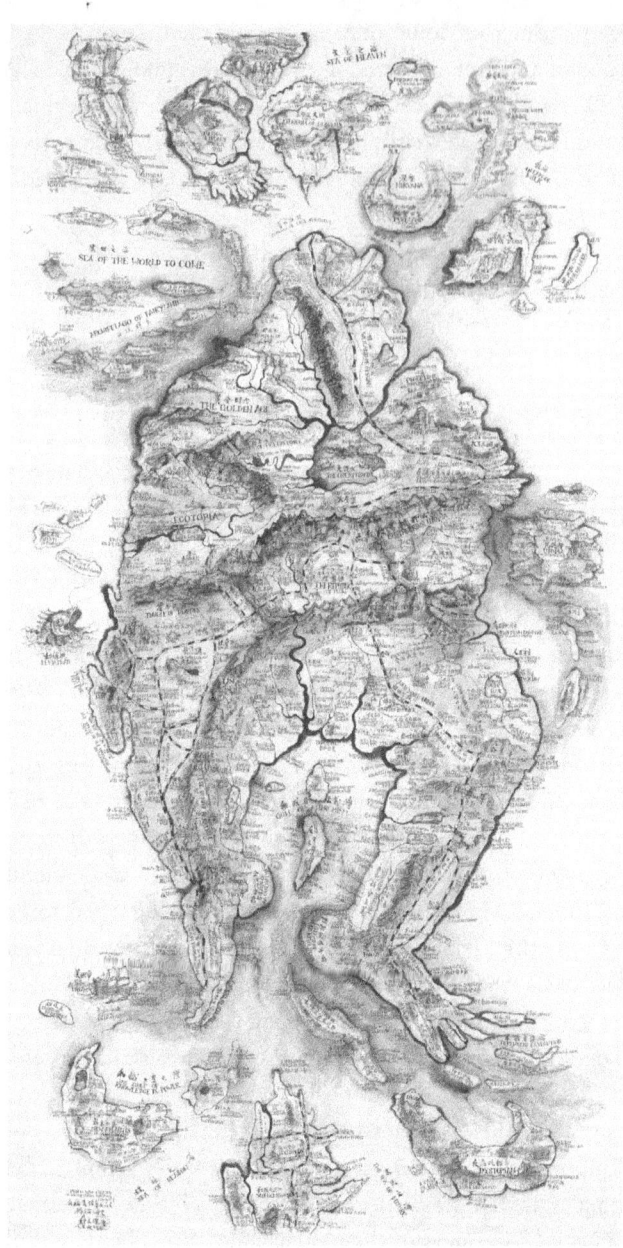

Figure 7.10

Qiu Zhijie, *Map of Utopia*, 2017, ink and graphite on paper,
245 × 126 cm. Image courtesy of the artist and ARNDT Fine Art,
Singapore.

This brings us to the mode of world picturing that seems most urgent today, a mode precipitated by the many complexities of our contemporaneity but above all the present and prospective consequences of global warming. The greatest challenge facing us: to imagine our being in the world from the perspective of inhabiting the planet earth within our solar system, and then within the vast knowable universe, and, perhaps, within as yet unknowable multiverses. The response by artists to this challenge is the focus of the next chapter.

8

picturing planetarity

Arts of the Multiverse

Indigenous peoples were the first placemakers and have suffered from displacement for longer than any others. They were also the first to imagine the origins of their worlds, to picture the patterns of recurrence and variation within them, and to establish relationships between peoples who possess other world pictures.[1] Since the 1960s, as part of a worldwide exertion of agency toward sovereignty, Indigenous peoples in many parts of the world have turned to art making based on the representation of their deep and abiding relationship to the lands of their ancestors. On all continents but most notably in Australia, Indigenous artists have renovated traditional practices and developed distinct forms of modern and contemporary art.[2] As I discuss in chapter 6, theirs is the most remarkable testimony that art can offer of the necessity, longevity, and continuing centrality for what it is to be a living being, to have a sense of place that is, at the same time and in the same space, worldly.

Like other Indigenous peoples, the Yolngu of North Australia understand the sky to be continuous with the earth. Recently deceased elder Gulumbu Yunupingu explained it this way:

Now we are painting these designs for non-Indigenous people to tell them our story. My story is of the universe. . . . I found the story of the constellations from the sacred songs my father used to sing. We grew up listening to him sing about them. Every day at dawn he would sing until the sun came up. When he saw the first light glow before dawn he would start to sing the Djulpan constellation [Orion and the Pleiades]. He would sing those stars. That is the story that came from him.[3]

Her painting *Garak, the Universe* (2009), made with natural ochres on bark, pictures each of those stars as a cross form with a white dot at its center (figure 8.1). To her, each dot represents a visible star, and each cross form the convergence of energy that made it so. In their convergence, the star forms constitute the constellations of the visible universe. The small dots that float on the black ground beneath are the scarcely visible stars of the further constellations. This is a picturing of our planetary interconnectedness that does not rely on the model of the planetary system as material objects rotating in space offered by Western science.

Without the benefit of this kind of spiritual embedment in the world's self-making, but profoundly affected by it, non-Indigenous artists all over the world are searching for imagery of planetarity, and of ways of orchestrating an experience of it. Since 2003, Murray Fredericks has made over twenty visits to Lake Eyre (Kati Thanda), a vast salt lake in South Australia, walking across it and living within it for days on end. Taking digital photographs as he walks, he combines them into panoramic studies built around the infinite distance inherent in the horizon line, the compaction of light at dusk, and its release of the night sky, the resonance between land and sky enabled by the reflective surface of the low-lying lake, and the seemingly endless repetition of the diurnal cycle. *Salt 406*, made in 2015, is part of a series (figure 8.2). The work has striking parallels but also clear contrasts with Yunupingu's *Garak, the Universe*, although *Salt 406* is ostensibly of a closely similar subject. Fredericks shows us the entirety of the constellation that non-Indigenes know as the Milky Way, and viewers understand that they are within it, even though its seems a long way away. At right, the evening star rises twice, and above the last burst of the setting sun are glimpses of two further constellations. Seeing in this image conjures awe and a sense that these phenomena would consume viewers were they able to experience them directly. Frederick speaks of his search for "pure space," for "a landscape without landscape," that is, to find a place untouched by the

Figure 8.1

Gulumbu Yunupingu, *Garak, the Universe*, 2009, natural ochres on
bark, 107 × 40 cm. Image courtesy of the estate of the artist, Buku-
Larrnggay Mulka Centre, Yirrkala, North East Arnhem Land, and Art
Gallery of New South Wales, Sydney. Photo by Mim Stirling, AGNSW.

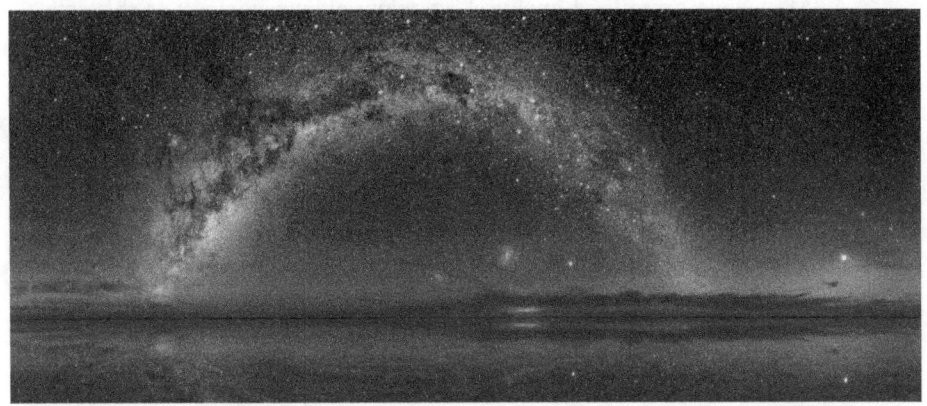

Figure 8.2

Murray Fredericks, *Salt 406*, 2015, digital pigment print,
105 × 250 cm. Image courtesy of the artist and ARC ONE
Gallery, Melbourne.

signs of human presence. Yet, while the processes he pictures would, and will, unfold without any need of human presence, we viewers can hardly forget that we are actually looking at a highly sophisticated digitized image.[4]

Fredericks has also photographed and filmed extraordinary natural phenomena in Greenland and Iceland, notably glaciers. The impact of climate change on glaciers preoccupies James Balog, whose 2012 film *Chasing Ice* tracks the slow calving of the Illulissat Glacier in Western Greenland during 2008, at one point superimposing an image of Lower Manhattan on it, so that no one can miss the point about the scale of the destruction. This video is drawn from the Extreme Ice Survey, founded by Balog in 2007, which coordinates images taken by forty-three Nikon cameras set up at sites in Antarctica, Greenland, Iceland, Alaska, Canada, Austria, and the Rocky Mountains. The survey documents the transformations being caused by global warming and other human activity.[5] Greg Stimac's video loop *Old Faithful Inversion* (2012) takes from the internet a tourist posting of the Yosemite geyser erupting and turns its white water and gas into a black cloud connoting oil.[6] Photographer Justin Brice Guariglia has developed an app After Ice that allows selfie takers to see what their surrounds will look like when predicted sea level rises occur.[7]

Meanwhile, generalized, apolitical evocations of human impact on the earth abound in the spaces (caverns) currently opening up between actual political action and what is required to mitigate the effects of climate change. Aestheticizing the observable impacts is becoming common, especially in Euro-America. In Frank White's 1987 book *The Overview Effect*, he named the cognitive shift that occurs in astronaut's perception when contemplating the whole of the earth from outer space.[8] In 2013, photographer Benjamin Grant turned this idea into an Instagram project, posting each day an image, taken by Digital Globe, a satellite circling the planet, of a section of the earth's surface changed in some significant way by human intervention. Each is organized as a flat surface, densely colored, and patterned in ways that echo the grid and variation format of high modernist abstraction. The project mission statement concludes with these words: "The mesmerizing flatness seen from this vantage point, the surprising comfort of systematic organization on a massive scale, or the vibrant colors that we capture will hopefully turn your head. However, once we have that attention, we hope you will go beyond the aesthetics, contemplate just exactly what it is that you're seeing, and consider what that means for our planet."[9] No other indicators are given to orient viewers, except that one link on the website, "Juxtapose," enables us to overlay before and after shots of the same place taken at two different times. While images of the fallow fields for Dutch tulips at Lisse, Holland, compared to the scorching colors released at harvest time are an instant hit, and those of the populated then cleaned-up site of the Burning Man Festival are amusing, we pause, shocked, at the images of the site of what became, in July 2012, the Zaatari Refugee Camp, Mafraq, Jordan. The first was taken on August 2011, the second on June 2014, when its population had grown to approximately 800,000 people fleeing the conflict in Syria. This is a compelling graphic of the points made earlier about the sheer magnitude of enforced migration. It freeze-frames, in a bird's-eye view, an instant in one of the great flows occurring across the planet at this time. It illustrates how the flow is also obliged to ground itself, locking these hundreds of thousands of forcibly dislocated people into barely livable conditions, in an inhospitable place and for an indeterminate amount of time.

PLACE AND PLANET

The impulse that has for decades driven the great engineering projects known rather banally as "land art"—such as Charles Ross's *Star Axis*, James Turrell's *Roden Crater*, or Michael Heizer's *City*—is the desire to provide a physical space in which feelings such as those conjured by Frederick's photographs can be experienced quite directly, without the need of a representational image carried in a medium. These massive earthworks are, nonetheless, heavily mediated experiences, which deliberately include the process of journeying to the site, providing limited, somewhat privileged access. A parallel trajectory within the art of the period tracked human journeying across the world, with locations linked by more conceptual markers. Canadian artist Bill Vazan's *Worldline* project (1969–71) entailed setting down black tape markers in twenty-five locations in eighteen countries that joined the latitudinal and longitudinal positions of each place to the others by means of the imaginary lines between them. Like many conceptualist projects at the time, this work highlighted the shortfall between the banality of such measuring and the social, cultural, and political actuality of each location as well as that of the vast "worlds" between them. Subsequently, Vazan has made several earthworks and engraved rock sculptures, echoing the world picturing of premodern peoples, that he regards as "cosmological shadows."[10]

William Lamson made *A Line Describing the Sun* in a dry lakebed in the Mojave Desert over a twelve-hour period one day in 2010. A Fresnel lens, mounted on a wheeled contraption (figure 8.3), concentrated the sunlight to such a degree that it melted a thin line across the lake bed (figure 8.4). Videos of the performance show the surface melting under the intense heat, turning into a black, glassy substance. An arc, of considerable length, appears on the surface of the earth, echoing its trajectory during those hours in relation to the sun. Lamson has devised a way to enable the sun to inscribe the earth, or, perhaps more accurately, for the earth to tattoo a trace of its own exposure to the sun on itself.[11]

Argentinian artist Tomás Saraceno is as fascinated by the web building of spiders as he is by the currents that are shaping the world's solar systems. His *How to Entangle the Universe in a Spider Web* at the Museo de Arte Moderno, Buenos Aires, in 2016–17 consisted of two closely related immersive installations. In *The Cosmic Dust Spider Web Orchestra*, a beam of light made filaments of cosmic dust visible, while their movements were tracked by sensors and transformed into sounds determined by their position in space and the speed that they traveled through it. In *Quasi-Social Musical Instrument IC 342 Built by 7,000 Parawixia bistriata—Six Months*, thousands of spiders of an Argentinian species that regularly cooperates to build its webs did so for the duration of the exhibition, filling the space with delicate structures that were also lit and

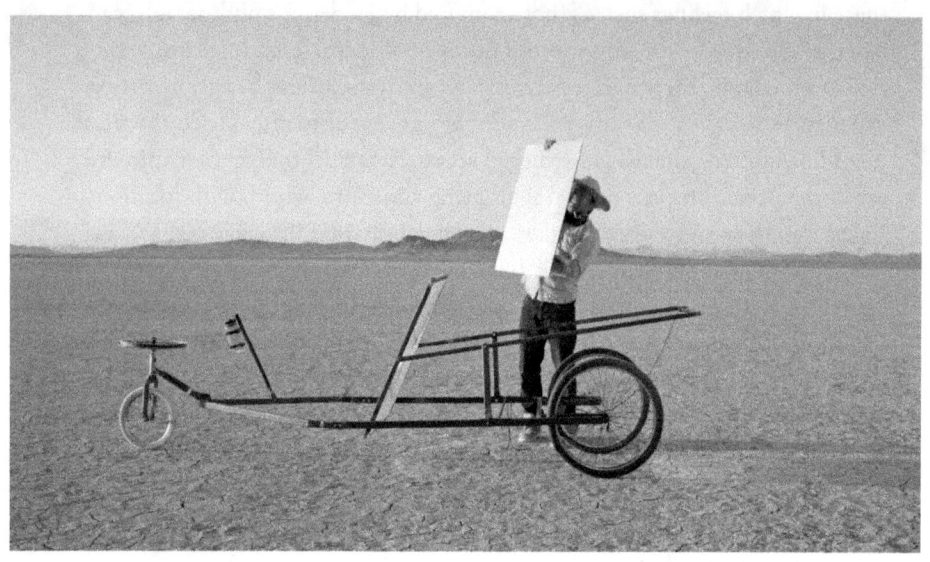

Figures 8.3–8.4

William Lamson, *A Line Describing the Sun*, 2010, Fresnel lens
on mobile contraption (ABOVE), melted salt (OPPOSITE).
Double-screen video. Images courtesy of the artist.

tracked to generate amplified sounds (figure 8.5).[12] In 2016 Saraceno launched
Aerocene, "an open-sourced community project for artistic and scientific exploration," which takes the form of a backpack that "becomes buoyant only by the
heat of the Sun and infrared radiation from the surface of the Earth."[13]

These works are part of another trajectory in art since midcentury that links
a sense of place to a sense of planet, best exemplified during the years around
1970 in the work of Robert Smithson, Mary Miss, Nancy Holt, and Richard
Long. It was subsequently refined in the ephemeral installations, using found
materials in natural settings, of artists like Andy Goldsworthy. More recently,
the installations of artists such as Olafur Eliasson evoke immersed experience
of natural phenomena but without disguising the machinery necessary to produce such effects. The contradiction between these two orders acknowledges
the fact of our relatively recent awareness that we have entered what is becoming widely, and controversially, known as the Anthropocene.

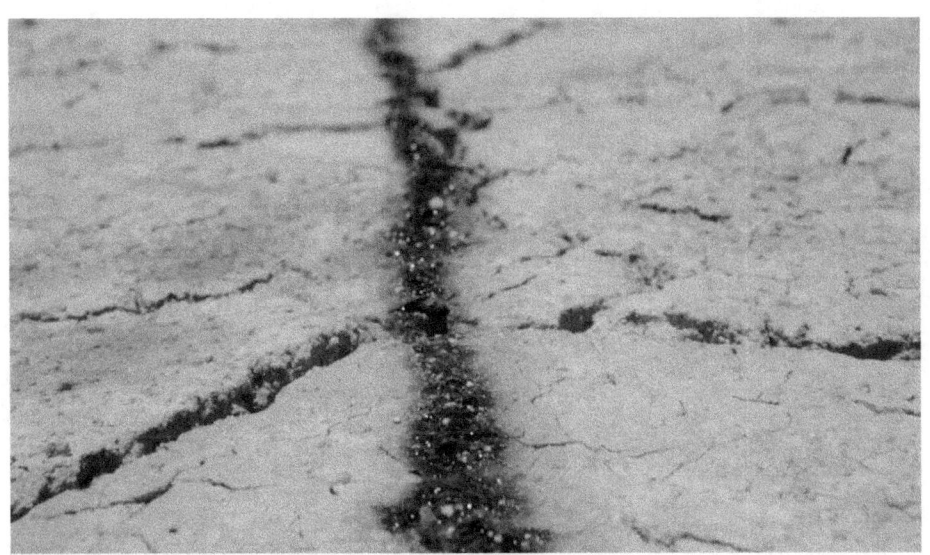

Art of this kind prioritizes the appeal of geometric form alongside that arising from the structures of natural phenomena, and it finds its aesthetic in the perceived resonances, tending hopefully toward equilibrium, between them. This is the dream of utter connectedness at the core of ecological fantasies such as the Gaia hypothesis. While this dream no longer convinces as a picture of a possible future for humans on the planet, artworks such as those I have been discussing do fix our attention on the actual things that the earth, as a planet, one among millions of others, actually does, all the time, as it constantly constitutes itself. Indeed, increasing numbers of artists are asking themselves what might we humans learn from close observation of these processes, and how can we connect ourselves to them in ways that share in their spirit rather than exploit them for our perceived needs? We have also seen that their answers remain tentative and share much with the sense of urgency about the future of life on planet earth that inspired almost all the world's nations to sign the 2016 Paris Agreement on climate change. For a moment, in an unprecedented way, the world spoke with one voice. Despite all the backtracking since, and despite the recursion to rampant shock doctrine capitalism by the Donald Trump Administration, there remains good reason to hope that, on this most urgent of issues, the world will continue on its path toward understanding itself as a planet.[14]

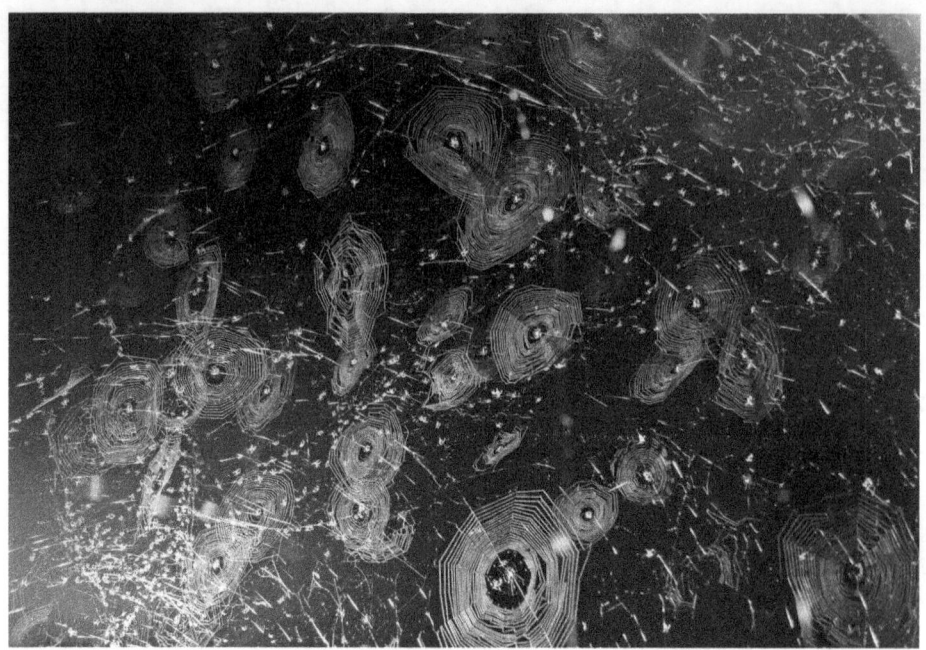

Figure 8.5

Tomás Saraceno, *Quasi-Social Musical Instrument IC 342 Built by 7,000* Parawixia bistriata—*Six Months*, 2017. Installation view, *Tomás Saraceno: How to Entangle the Universe in a Spider Web* at Museo de Arte Moderno de Buenos Aires, curated by Victoria Noorthoorn. © 2017 Studio Tomás Saraceno. Image courtesy of the artist; Ruth Benzacar, Buenos Aires; Esther Schipper, Berlin; Tanya Bonakdar Gallery, New York; Andersen's Contemporary, Copenhagen; Pinksummer Contemporary Art, Genoa.

HARNESSING THE TECHNOGLOBAL

The seductions of the technoglobal, mentioned in the chapter 7 discussion of hypericons, haunted the early iterations of *Exit*, an installation by New York–based architects Diller Scofidio + Renfro, such as the 2008 single-screen DVD version, which used public data to visualize multiple measurable exchanges—for example, armed conflicts, relative energy consumption, and remittances by migrants—as they occur around the world. Inspiration came from these re-marks by Paul Virilio: "It's almost as though the sky, and the clouds in it and the pollution of it, were making their entry into history. Not the history of the seasons, summer, autumn, winter, but of population flows, of zones now uninhabitable for reasons that aren't just to do with desertification, but with disappearance, with submersion of land. This is the future."[15]

By 2015, working with other architects, artists, and scientists, including Laura Kurgan, Mark Hansen, Ben Rubin, Robert Gerard Pietrusko, and Stew-art Smith, Diller Scofidio + Renfro developed an immersive video installa-tion that was presented at the Palais de Tokyo, Paris, during the UN Climate Change Conference (figure 8.6).[16] Focusing on the root economic, environ-mental, and political causes of the recent massive waves of migration, the data were collected under six categories: population shifts from country areas to cit-ies; migrant remittances; forced migration, political refugees; the impact of rising seas on cities; the occurrence of natural disasters; deforestation; and the extinction of languages. Worldwide changes between 2000 and 2015 in each of these categories are displayed, one after the other, on a digital screen that wraps around the walls of a darkened, circular room. The artists have combined the three-world picturing hypericons and set them in motion to tell a story of how planetary degradation and human conflict has precipitated migration since the turn of the century. A Blue Planet, three meters in diameter, is the major signifier, and it rolls around the space, visualizing each data set as if the world were writing, or posting, its own information about itself. It becomes a brown, yellowed, more diffused, and unstable figure as the work unfolds. Each spread shows one of the six categories. As the globe rotates, it lays out a hori-zontal scroll of the continents and oceans, a kind of wraparound world map of statistics. The changing data numbers become moving points of light, each rep-resenting, say, ten people on the move, or amounts of money, or places where named disasters occurred, or deforestation spreading. The growing quantities, and the accelerating intensities, of each factor causing migration are graphi-cally evident in this networked world. So, too, by evident implication, are the impacts of climate change, disaster capitalism, bad governance, human greed, and existential desperation.

Exit is a striking visualization of these facts. But data flows are one thing; their actuality, as a felt bodily effect, is another. In *The Contemporary Composition*, I remark that it is no surprise to find artists reaching for metaphors of flowing currents, of rivers and seas, of continents and oceans to frame their explorations of the tides and storms of historical change in which we are embroiled today. I

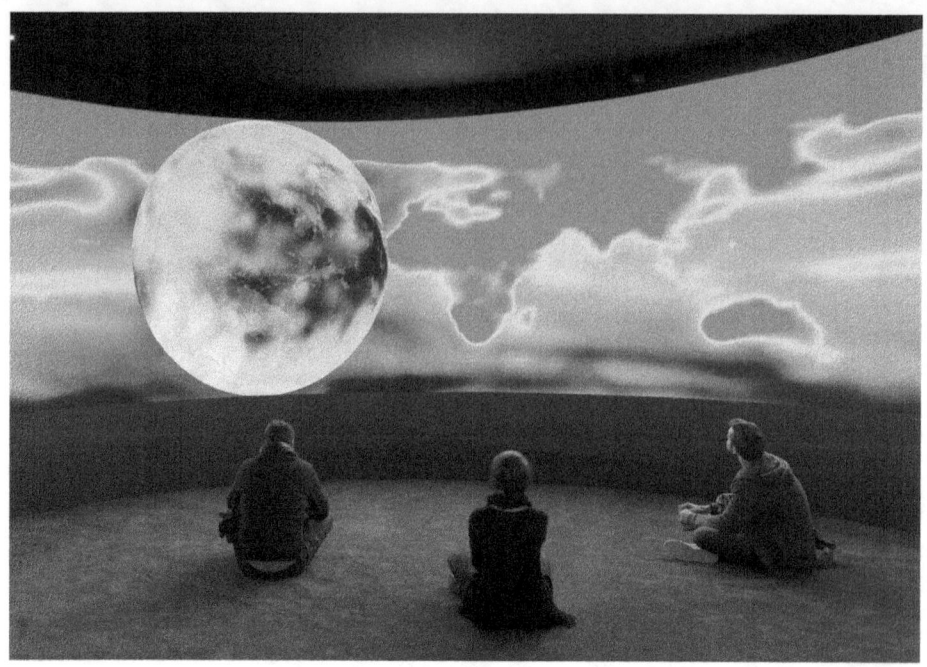

Figure 8.6

Diller Scofidio + Renfro, *Exit*, 2015, immersive video installation, Palais de Tokyo, Paris, during the UN Climate Change Conference, December 2015. Image courtesy of Diller Scofidio + Renfro, New York. Photo by Luc Boegly.

describe in some detail Richard Misrach and Kate Orff's *Petrochemical America* project, carried out since 1998, presented as photographic panels charting industries polluting the Mississippi River; Allan Sekula's moving filmic exploration of the seas as a global working environment, *The Forgotten Space* (2010); the confronting video close-ups of industrial-scale fishing in *Leviathan* (2012), by the Harvard-based Sensory Ethnography Lab; and John Akomfrah's *Vertigo Sea* (2014), a three-panel video that juxtaposes imagery of desperate immigrants, thousands drowning as they try to cross the Mediterranean, with breathtaking underwater shots of surging seas and fish life, and archival film of seal hunting, whale catching, and slave transportation.[17] In chapter 5 of this volume, I discuss Isaac Julien's seven-screen installation *Ten Thousand Waves* (2010) as a meditation on ancient, modern, and contemporary aspects of "Chineseness" as they are imagined differently yet connectedly in various parts of the world. Like the works just mentioned, and like Julien's earlier explorations of the contemporary resonances of the black Atlantic slave trade, such as *WESTERN UNION: Small Boats* (2007), these works share the ambition, scope, and compelling visuality of the most advanced contemporary art. But they are distinguished by the historical vision of their creators, by their highly developed sense of how the conflicts and contradictions of past relationships between natural forces and human desires continue to play out through the present—in ways, however, only partly predictable. We can add to this short but ever-growing list of art that truly grasps our contemporaneity the decolonizing archives of Kader Attia and Renee Gabri, and the acute probing of the gaps between intention and effect when ideologies meet reality in the work of Eve Sussman, Laura Poitras, and Julian Rosefeld (especially the Rosefeld's multiscreen installation *Manifesto* [2015], more so than the 2017 film). While highly political in the sense that they are eloquent appeals to the necessity of seeing clearly the complexities of still-resonant pasts, and to the need to act constructively in the present, these works are also, and most compellingly, dreamscapes—portraits of the unconscious dynamics at work in the natural world, in human societies, and in the interactions between them. In this deep sense, they show the world *worlding*.

ONLY CONNECT!

Placemaking, world picturing, connectivity: these are the themes that preoccupy contemporary artists. Damián Ortega's public sculpture *Cosmogonía doméstica* (2013–14), installed in the courtyard of the Museo Jumex in Mexico City, is a vivid condensation of the urgency of their mutuality (figure 8.7). It is based on a simple yet profound idea. What would happen if I fixed the things that constitute *my* place in the most immediate sense—say, the objects that I use every day in my own apartment—to the large-scale movements of the knowable universe? Ortega's answer: arrange these homely items as the significant features of a kind of astrolabe, laid out on horizontal axes, the parts of which move according to different kinds of time: that of the hours, the days, the planets, the stars.[18]

Cosmogonía doméstica is a clear visualization of the idea of worlds-within-the-world. In Ortega's diagram for this work, he evidently sees the relationships

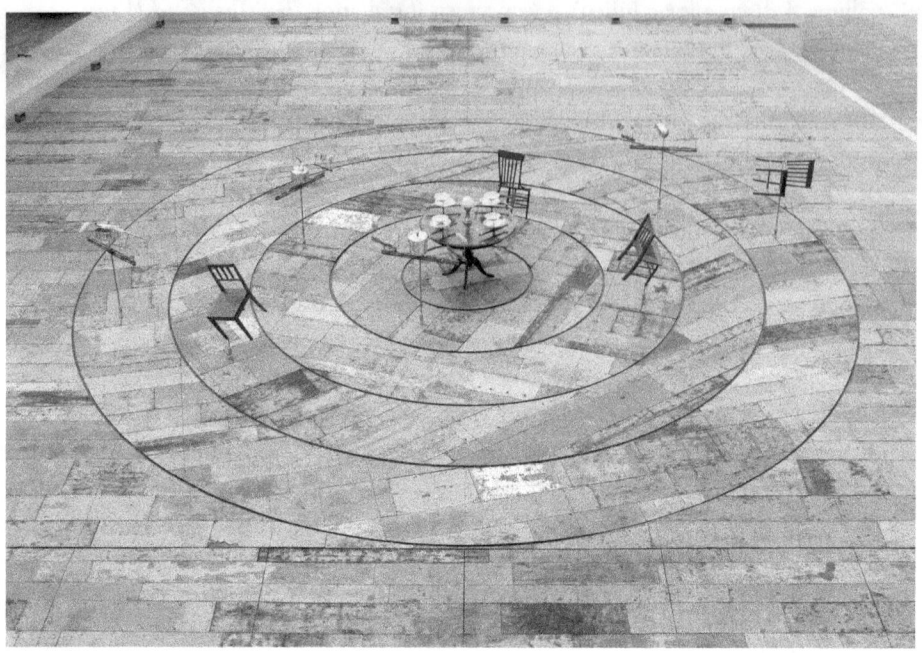

Figure 8.7

Damián Ortega, *Cosmogonía doméstica*, 2013–14, public
sculpture, iron, wood, plywood, brass, aluminum, polyurethane
foam, leather, four wooden chairs, ceramic dishes, cutlery,
glass lamp, light bulb, circular table, 175 × 1,060 × 1,060 cm.
Courryard, Museo Jumex, Mexico City. © Damián Ortega.
Image courtesy of the artist and Museum Jumex, Mexico City;
Gladstone Gallery, New York; and kurimanzutto, Mexico City.

between space and time through the metaphor of things on wheels, and he
has flipped the poetic sense of these objects' independent movement into their
being moved by flat plates, themselves on wheels. It is an oddly anachronistic,
eighteenth-century way of showing metaphor engulfed by metonymy. Seen
more broadly, Ortega has taken the spatial idea of simultaneous worlds and
married it to the idea of these worlds sharing temporal contemporaneousness
to envisage the structure of *scale* in the world as we experience it. Without the
constraints of having to actually build a model that would be the same size

as the world, a more layered metapicture of scaling up and down becomes imaginable.[19]

Cosmogonía doméstica is an awkward but also eloquent reminder that nothing less than the visual imaging of world-being as it needs to be now is what is at stake for contemporary artists, as it is for all of us. Throughout this book I ask whether, how, and to what extent contemporary artists are meeting this challenge. As a proximate generalization, it could be said that most contemporary art has—in recent decades, and perhaps for the first time—become unmistakably an art *of* the world, in that most art manifests one or another aspect of the contemporary world's multiplicity. Further, the proliferation of biennials, traveling exhibitions, international exchanges, residencies, mobile artists, curators, and collectors—to say nothing of the spread of exchange media, most obviously the internet (although access is by no means universal)—attest that art now comes *from* much of the world. More specifically, it comes from a growing number of art-producing localities that no longer depend primarily on the approval of a metropolitan center and are, to an unprecedented degree, connected to one another in a multiplicity of ways. Locality, regionality, and globality are being constantly, expansively redefined. Geopolitical change has shifted the world picture from presumptions about the inevitability of modernization and the universality of Euro-American values toward the shared recognition that the coexistence of multicultural difference, of disjunctive diversity, inside societies and between them, is now a defining characteristic of our contemporary condition. Contemporary life draws increasing numbers of artists to imagine the world—here understood as comprising several contemporaneous "natures," the natural world (encompassing the universe), built environments (second nature), virtual space (third nature), and lived interiority (human nature)—as at once highly differentiated and thoroughly connected, a hugely complex entity that, for these very reasons, does not amount to a whole yet whose diverse elements have to work together for their own survival. In this new, definitively contemporary sense, looking from what we can begin to call a planetary perspective, we must ask, Is contemporary art becoming an art *for* the world—for the world as it is now, and as it might be?

The short answer to this question is that, while the most visible, celebrated, expensive, and notorious contemporary art is little more than a noisy distraction, a growing amount of the art created outside such contexts does indeed take up the challenge of showing the multiplicity of worlds-within-the-world today as they are and, where necessary (which is, now, everywhere), of imagining them differently.

In the chapters so far, I have shown how understandings of contemporary art have been changing constantly since the 1980s, as new, unexpected kinds of art keep appearing, with increasing rapidity. These innovations have been accompanied by recursions of many kinds, which continue to assert themselves with a matching, sometimes overwhelming tenacity. Artists have been challenged by the constant, random shocks to the economic, social, and political conditions within which this art is made; by major transformations in the modes of its dissemination; and by the proliferation and splintering of its public reception. Similar challenges face those of us drawn to seek overviews of such complex phenomena.

Looking back over the past thirty years, I can see that my efforts to comprehend this multiplicity have moved through three phases, broadly conceived. First, I attempted to understand the distinctiveness of contemporary art in general, relative to the modern and postmodern practices that preceded it, which were led by innovators in the Euro-American art centers within a world being systematically globalized through economic control exercised from those centers. Second, I had the counterrecognition that contemporary art practice was in fact deeply divided and was becoming equally if not more energetically driven by artists and curators working from experiences outside these centers, from the imperatives of a fast decolonizing world. Third, I realized that three key factors—the spread of technological interconnectivity, combined with the increasingly apparent failure of neoliberal globalization as an economic, cultural, and political system, along with the accelerating impacts of global warming—compel all of us, artists included, to imagine our being in the world in qualitatively new ways, beyond the West/East, North/South geopolitical divisions and the binaries dividing cultures, races, and sexualities. The methodologies I deployed to address each of these phenomena were, in turn, a Marxist critique of capitalism; a feminist critique of the patriarchy; a postcolonial critique of imperialism, colonization, and decolonization; and a deconstructive interrogation of our contemporaneity. While my awareness of these sets of changes and my use of relevant critical methodologies may have occurred in this sequence, one after the other, obviously—in the real world, including contemporary art practice, and in all the disseminative and interpretive apparatus around it—these changes, and these interpretive strategies, have been, and continue to be, contemporaneous with one another. In the chapters that follow, I reflect on this journey, showing it to be a quest for an engaged, interpretative methodology, a quest also undertaken by some others, whose efforts I review.

art historiography

Conjectures and Refutations

the state of art history

Contemporary Art

What are we to make of the recent signs that contemporary art has become—to the surprise of many, including many of those most directly involved—a field within the discipline of art history? An initial reaction is that this has been a long time coming. Throughout the twentieth century, in places of concentrated visual arts production across the globe, the word "contemporary" appeared—intermittently but then with increasing frequency—in the names of art societies, artists' organizations, private galleries, public art centers, and alternative art spaces, until during the 1990s it reached its institutional culmination in the names of museums and auction-house departments. Throughout this period, the public interpretation of current art remained mostly the province of art critics, art theorists, and curators. Contemporary art has long been the primary focus in art schools, as the end point of practical instruction and the hot topic of informal discourse, but rarely has it been framed in historical terms. In university departments of art history until the 1990s, contemporary art appeared—if at all—during the closing days of courses covering longer trajectories, such as "Introduction to Art," "Modern Art," "Art of the Twentieth Century," "Postwar Art," or "Art since 1945," or as examples in courses on the art of a country or a region. With few exceptions, textbook coverage reflected this situation. The Library of Congress system maintained the subject heading "Modern Art—20th century" until 2000, when it added "Modern Art—21st century." "Contemporary art" appears as a variant but is not regarded as a subject field in itself.

Out there in the world of art, however, wide-scale shifts toward the contemporary have occurred at accelerating rates, affecting all these arrangements. Recent art, the work of artists in midcareer, issues in contemporary theory, and transformations in museum, market, and gallery practices now pepper lists of dissertation topics. A clear majority of applicants to graduate schools of art history intend to make contemporary art their major research field and their teaching or professional specialization. They expect art history departments to serve this need. Already shaken by decades of critique and the option of subsuming art history within the emerging visual culture discipline, departments debate cutoff dates that would place the modern as an earlier, separate period and worry if the contemporary, too, will demand a different kind of art history—indeed, if it favors historical consciousness at all. Despite these concerns, academic opportunities are increasingly opening up. While "contemporary art" has appeared in the titles of chairs for some time, "contemporary art *history*" remains rare—the first such title dating from 2001.

At the College Art Association Annual Conference in Los Angeles in 2009, the recently formed Society of Contemporary Art Historians held its first public panel before a huge crowd. Excited speculation abounded: Can we *do* history *of* contemporary art? Should we do history that is *like* the art it studies? Are we *really* doing criticism, or perhaps theory (note to self: it may already be out of fashion)? Whatever happened to critical distance, scholarly objectivity, disinterested judgment? What counts as an archive? How do I claim a topic before all the others? What if "my artist" suddenly refuses to cooperate? How do I relate my topic to "the field" when no one seems to have any idea of its overall shape and direction? What do I do when my artist changes her work before I finish my dissertation?[1] Meanwhile, the journal *October* circulated a "Questionnaire on 'The Contemporary,'" which asked for reflection on the strange conjunction between the fact that "'contemporary art' has become an institutional object in its own right" and the "new ... sense" that "in its very heterogeneity, much present practice seems to float free of historical determination, conceptual definition, and critical judgment."[2]

Four years earlier, in the buzz that followed the 2005 publication of *Art since 1900*, a nascent concept of contemporary art history surfaced, haltingly and somewhat shamefaced—a mood caught in Pamela M. Lee's apt characterization of the phrase as "a useful catachresis."[3] To me, this awkwardness was a sure sign of its timeliness, its challenge, and its potential—in short, its contemporaneity. The questions filling the air in Los Angeles were precipitous and, inevitably, flushed out premature answers in their rush. Presentism is only the most obvious danger that lies in taking the contemporary on its own terms. Compliant parroting is, for art scholars, just one of the traps in taking contemporary art at its own word. Because contemporary art history is, however belatedly, just coming into being, a report on the state of research would be premature.[4] Nevertheless, considerable work is in progress. In what follows, I set out a prolegomenon to contemporary art conceived as a field of critical, theoretical, historical, and, above all, art-historical inquiry.[5]

CONTEMPORARY ARTISTS DO ART HISTORY AS ART

Direct participation by artists in art-historical debate is not new. In the early and mid-1970s, some members of Art & Language, a group of conceptual artists, contributed, in their published writings and their exhibited work, to intense rethinking about the conflicted nature of the origins of modernism, then a hot topic within the discipline.[6] These debates motivated Jeff Wall's first major works, and the issues raised then continue to resonate: indeed, his own writings and his actual works count as key contributions. Michael Fried correctly calls attention to the presence—in Wall's history-painting-sized, digitally manipulated, but seemingly everyday backlit photographs—of his interpretations of the absorption/theatricality dialectic in modern French painting.[7] In *Morning Cleaning, Mies van der Rohe Foundation, Barcelona* (1999), this appears in, among many other elements, the posing of the cleaner as concentrating on adjusting his equipment, oblivious to the shaft of sunlight raking across the foreground of the picture (figure 9.1). Yet this emphasis on a workingman displaced within a building that was, and remains, a temple to the most expensive and refined aesthetic (one symbol of which, a sculpture titled *Dawn*, he obscures with his sudsy fluid) is equally important to this work's affect. T. J. Clark, then, might reasonably feel that his narrative of modernism's embedded sociality has also had an influence. And, in fact, the initially distinctive but increasingly convergent approaches of both scholars (and, of course, many others) have been thematized in Wall's work since 1978. This kind of engagement with art's history, and with historians' struggles with that history, has nothing to do with postmodernist pastiche, quotation, appropriation, or historicism. It takes art-historical

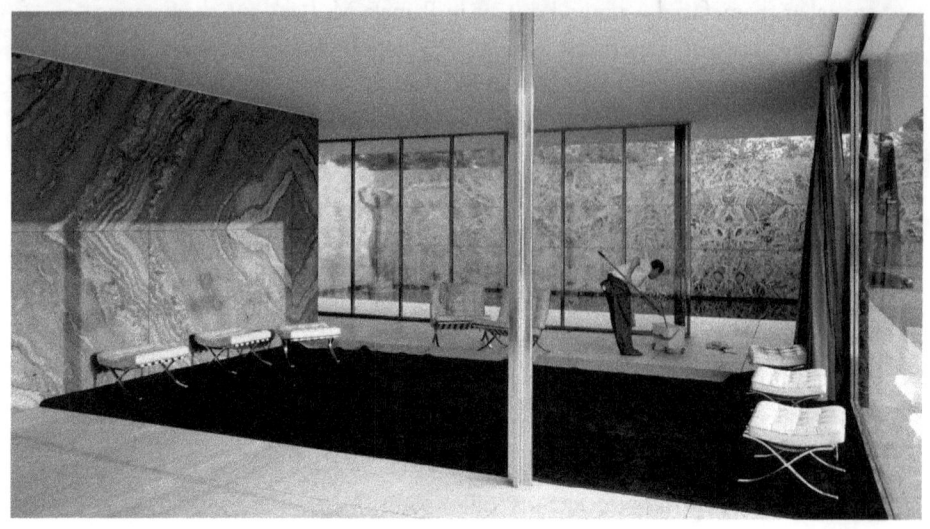

Figure 9.1

Jeff Wall, *Morning Cleaning, Mies van der Rohe Foundation, Barcelona*, 1999, transparency on lightbox. © Jeff Wall. Image courtesy of Jeff Wall Studio and Tate Images.

definition of what is, and has been, at stake in modernist art to be an important component within what is most at stake in making art now.

Other kinds of art-historical rumination are woven into the work of several younger contemporary artists, and they go just as deep. How are we to interpret a work made in 2005 by an artist who lives between Berlin and New York, and exhibited at the 2006 Whitney Biennial, titled *The Complete History of Postcontemporary Art* (figure 9.2)? Josephine Meckseper creates installations similar to those pioneered by artists ranging from Mike Kelley to Isa Genzken and now ubiquitous among her generation: objects selected from the delirious output of commercial culture and the detritus of urban waste, then gathered into awkward, flashy allegories of the contradictions of contemporary life. Presented in a darkened room, Meckseper's *The Complete History of Postcontemporary Art* suggests, at first, a shop-window-style display of easily recognizable everyday commodities. At the same time, we are invited to see them as if we are looking from the future, an increasingly common experience these days. Spe-

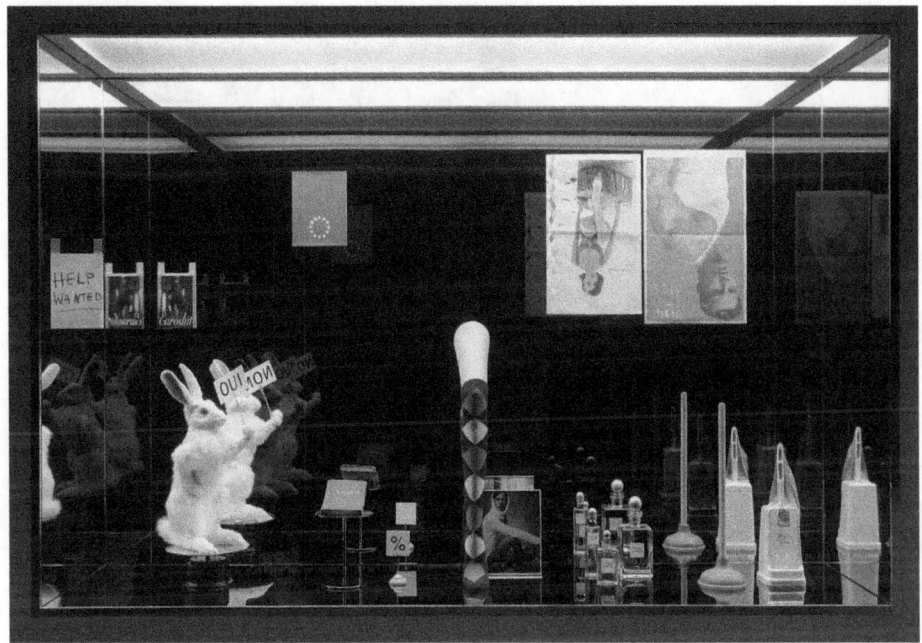

Figure 9.2

Josephine Meckseper, *The Complete History of Postcontemporary Art*, 2005, mixed media in display window, 160 × 250 × 60 cm. © Josephine Meckseper. Image courtesy of Timothy Taylor, London/New York.

cifically, this display recalls those shops in East Germany exposed, after 1989, as repositories of modernity's wastes, symbols of a system that had become, suddenly, a temporal cul-de-sac. Pockets from various pasts exist everywhere and will do so more frequently as inequalities of income increase in all societies. Meckseper symbolizes the confusion over the 2005 vote against the European Union constitution by including a toy rabbit that holds a flag with "Oui" and "Non" on either face, and which spins on its base. Each of the objects wittily references a famous work of contemporary art; her implication is that the reputations and the relevance of artists such as Joseph Beuys and Jeff Koons will fade just as quickly: late modern contestatory art and the art of high capitalism

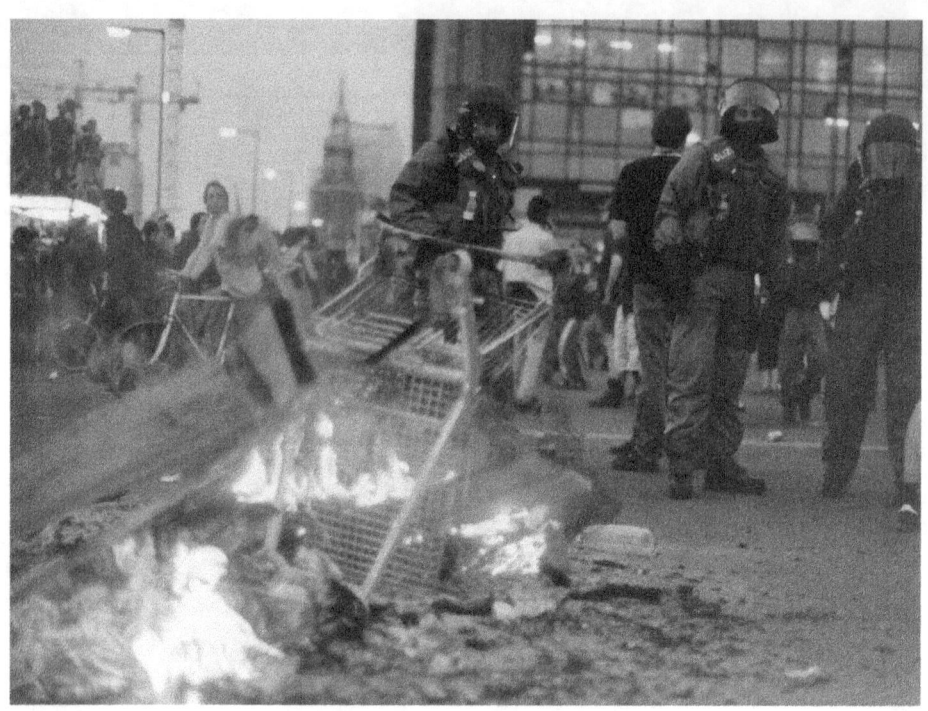

Figure 9.3

Josephine Meckseper, *Untitled (Berlin Demonstration, Fire, Cops)*, 2002, C-print, diasec mounted, 76 × 101 cm. © Josephine Meckseper. Image courtesy of Timothy Taylor, London/ New York/Paris.

triumphant are alike subject to entropy. Thus, the ironic title of her installation appears inside the display, inscribed in gold on the cover of a leather-bound volume: the book itself is clearly over a century old. It sits behind glass, in a shop that is closed, making it impossible to read. Nonetheless, its title taunts us with the thought that even postcontemporary art is, already, ancient history.

Meckseper's larger argument is even stronger than what this array of failed allegories implies. She often shows her vitrines alongside sets of her photographs or videos of antiglobalization demonstrations in Berlin, Washington, and elsewhere (figure 9.3). She clearly favors the protestors' perspective but recognizes (as Beuys arguably foresaw) that its current imagery—and art that simply serves it—is also losing its power, its purchase on a critical contemporaneity. Both leftism, locked into dialectical historicism, and globalizing capitalism, distracted by its own delusory paradise of commodities, are projects that are past their peaks—indeed, are in decline. A different politics, a different ethics, and a different imagery are needed. Meckseper's work projects an archaeology of the future to draw our attention to the urgent need to develop an ontology of the present.[8]

Many artists today, unsurprisingly, are deeply interested in the nature of time, in temporalities of all kinds—social, personal, bodily, geologic, world historical, scientific, eternal—and in the intersections between them. Many artists are fascinated by how temporality was treated by their predecessors, from which they draw inspiration in their efforts to deal with present concerns. For some, this becomes a way of approaching art's internal history, that is, the densely textured interplay between artists, those who know one another as well as those connected by imaginative sympathy. Its raw materials are example and influence, suggestion and orientation, trial and error, ideas incompletely realized, trails laid for one's successors, and so forth—in other words, the connectivity between objects, ideas, people, and institutions that is the core subject of the art historian's attention. In the hands of artists as different as Tacita Dean (figure 9.4) and Josiah McElheny (figure 9.5), this interplay becomes a primary material for their art.[9]

Despite their differing perspectives, many artists today use art-historical reflection to tackle pressing issues about what it is to live in the present. Art historians might be emboldened to follow suit, beginning with the reality that many have assiduously avoided for decades, until it became so obvious as to no longer seem remarkable: the worldwide move—nascent during the 1950s, emergent in the 1960s, contested during the 1970s, but unmistakable since the 1980s—from modern to contemporary art. How might this phenomenon be conceptualized? Is it a question of style, of change within the history of art taken as a relatively autonomous entity? Or is it a (contestatory, unpredictable, and incomplete) confluence of what took shape initially as distinct developments in the visual arts in various regions of the world, taking place at the separate nodes of artistic production, but then filling the transnational yet multidirectional connections between them? In either case, has this change in art occurred independently of all other transformations in the world, or is it part of a more complex, multifaceted shift from one set of conditions to another? I suspect that the latter answer to each of these pairs of questions is closer to the truth of the situation, indicated by some aspects of how contemporary art came to be made within the world's shift from modernity to contemporaneity. Certain lines of inquiry, taken together, might

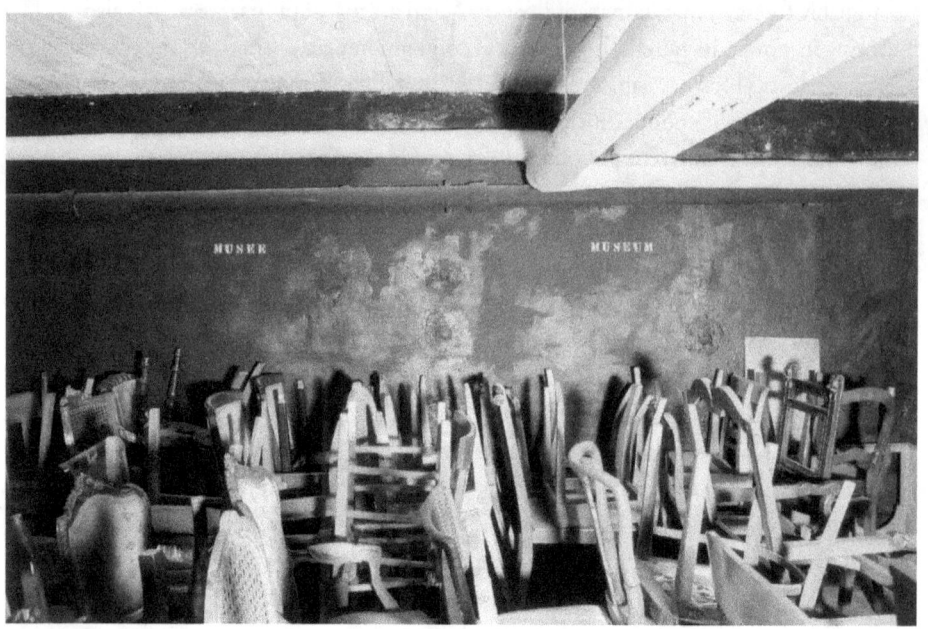

Figure 9.4

Tacita Dean, *Section Cinema*, *Homage to Marcel Broodthaers*
(still), 2002, 16 mm film, optical sound, thirteen minutes. Image
courtesy of the artist; Frith Street Gallery, London; and Marian
Goodman Gallery, New York.

help us to approach contemporary art from perspectives that are, at once, theoretically acute, historically accurate, and open toward art to come.

BECOMING CONTEMPORARY

How might the emergence of the contemporary within the modern be traced
in language use in general, and art discourse in particular? Confining ourselves
to English, we may note that the word "modern" is given a long list of meanings in the online *Oxford English Dictionary*. First, the root, adjectival definition: "Of or pertaining to the present or recent times, as distinguished from
the remote past; pertaining to or originating in the current age or period." The

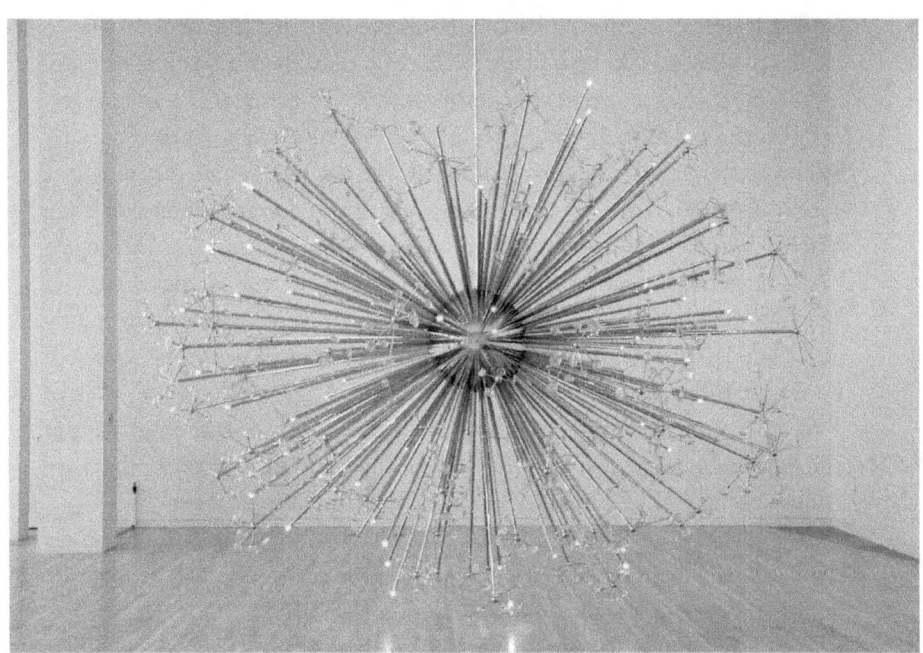

Figure 9.5

Josiah McElheny, *An End to Modernity*, 2005, aluminum,
electric lights, hand-blown glass, steel. Wexner Center for the
Arts of Ohio State University. © Josiah McElheny. Courtesy of
Donald Young Gallery, Chicago; and Andrea Rosen Gallery,
New York.

second meaning is an applied one: "Of a movement in art and architecture, or
the works produced by such a movement: characterized by a departure from
or a repudiation of accepted or traditional styles and values."[10] Contrastive
periodization is, clearly, essential to the core modern meaning of "modern":
that which is modern is, first and foremost, no longer of a time, age, or period
that is past. This is itself a modernization: the sixth-century CE Latin usage de-
rives from *modo*, "just now," and becomes *modernus*, "modern," on analogy to
hodiernus, "of today." The *Oxford English Dictionary* recognizes this movement
of meaning by listing "Being at this time; now existing," as its first definition,
while acknowledging it to be obsolete, rare.

The word "contemporary" is commonly used in most languages to refer to the passing present. Its etymology is as rich as that which Hans Robert Jauss, among others, has shown to exist for "modern."[11] It is capable of calibrating several distinct but related ways of being *in* or *with* time, even of being, at once, *in* and *apart from* time. Current editions of the *Oxford English Dictionary* give four major meanings. They are all relational, turning on prepositions, on being placed "to," "from," "at," or "during" time. There is the strong sense of "belonging *to* the same time, age, or period"; the coincidental but also entangled sense of "having existed or lived *from* the same date, equal in age, coeval"; and the mostly adventitious "occurring *at* the same moment of time, or *during* the same period; occupying the same definite period, contemporaneous, simultaneous." Each of these three meanings comprehends a distinctive sense of presentness, of being in the present, of beings that are present to one another and to the time that they happen to be in while also being aware that they can be in no other.

The *Oxford English Dictionary*'s fourth definition of "contemporary" brings these radically diverse conjunctions of persons, things, ideas, and time together and heads them in one direction: "Modern; of or characteristic of the present period; especially up-to-date, ultra-modern; specifically designating art of a markedly avant-garde quality, or furniture, building, decoration, etc. having modern characteristics." Why does this strike us now as odd, even anachronistic, as a definition of the word "contemporary"? After all, the definition lists those elements of contemporary life and art that are most modern, that exceed modernity as we know it, and that are thus most likely to lead, define, and eventually constitute the modernity to come. When we pair the two sets of definitions, however, another interpretation insinuates itself: the contemporary has not only reached parity with the modern, it has eclipsed it. The two concepts have finally exchanged their core meaning: the contemporary has overtaken the modern as the fundamental condition of *this* "time, age, or period." Both of these usages have been prevalent in recent decades, in art worlds as in wider spheres, with the weight overwhelmingly on the side of the modern being a strand within the contemporary, not vice versa. But this changeover has not been a simple transfer, or translation, from one state (modernity) to another, similar one (contemporaneity). The state of what it is to be a state, the conditions as to what counts as a condition have changed. We might anticipate, then, that whatever we might identify as characteristic of the contemporary, it will not be singular but rather multiple in nature.

Some art historians have made it a point to track when, how, and why writers on art have noted contemporaneous elements in their descriptions of art:

traces within the work under examination of any occurrence that coincides with its moment of creation, or of attention paid by an artist to events or qualities that happen at the same time as others. Some art historians tend to regard contemporaneous elements in a work of art as distractions that, they believe, will recede in importance—even disappear from sight—once a more measured historical gaze recognizes the true nature of the work's achievement. This clearing away of the afterbirth has been applied even to the most innovative moments in the history of modern art. In chapter 1, I cited Lawrence Rainey's comments on a key 1911–12 painting by Pablo Picasso, "Yes, the title *Ma Jolie* echoes one of the period's popular songs, but that is a case of period bric a brac, a dapper wink intended to signal 'contemporaneity,' not an indication of where the painting's real work is being done."[12] He has conventionalized Baudelaire's great insight, that *modernité* requires us to find the eternal and immutable within the ephemeral and the contingent.

When tracking the usage of the term "contemporary" as a general descriptor of current art in contemporaneous texts written in major European languages in the writers' home countries and their colonies from the 1870s until now, along with its deployment in the naming of visual arts museums, galleries, and departments of museums and auction houses, a clear picture quickly emerges. "Contemporary" appeared rarely and randomly for much of the period, there being a plethora of alternative terms for new, current, emergent art ("modern" was usually just one of these, and "modernism" did not become prominent until the 1960s). Usage increased noticeably during the 1920s and 1930s, followed by a substantial upsurge in the 1960s, and from then on, it almost doubled in each decade. By the 1990s, "contemporary" had come to be the predominant descriptor of both current and recent art, and of all its associated modes of presentation, distribution, and interpretation, almost entirely banishing other labels, including those associated with "modern."[13] Quantity, of course, has its own kinds of weight. But the main interest for art history lies in the actual meanings and the critical purchase of these usages in their specific situations of utterance.

THE PREHISTORY OF THE CONTEMPORARY

That increasing numbers of French realist painters and sculptors during the 1850s and 1860s rejected imaginary, timeless, and historical themes in favor of depictions of contemporary life has long been regarded as foundational to the creation of a truly modern art. Among English-language art historians, Linda Nochlin most effectively drew attention to the centrality of contemporaneity to this moment. In her now classic study *Realism*, she showed that the realist artists chose to paint concrete, tangible objects, as opposed to imagined ones, and to do so in the most direct manner possible, as distinct from academic illusionism; moreover, they selected subjects from the everyday life around them rather than from the allegorical, symbolic, or historical themes favored in the Académie Royale des Beaux-Arts. This is to use the term "contemporaneity" in its ordinary "of today" meaning, the sense that it had at the beginning of the modern period in art.[14]

Intimations of the contemporary as a distinct value had begun to appear earlier. Indeed, they are present whenever art institutions are inclined to favor the work of currently practicing artists as opposed to their deceased—or already institutionalized—predecessors. During the seventeenth century, openness to art as it was freshly made played a part in the replacement of guilds by academies and other professional organizations of artists, albeit a small one, given artists' guiding aspirations to join the ranks of the great artists of the past. Yet specific circumstances could surprise the contemporary into prominence. In Prague in 1796 the Society of Patriotic Friends of the Arts set up their Picture Gallery of living artists, open to the public. These Patriotic Friends were Bohemian noblemen whose high cultural aspirations had been suddenly isolated by Emperor Joseph II's centralization of imperial administration in Vienna.[15] Under the aegis of Louis XVIII, the Musée des Artistes Vivants was established in the Luxembourg Palace, Paris, in 1818. In contrast to the other public collections in Paris, each devoted to old masters—at the Palais Royal (open since 1784), other rooms of the Luxembourg itself (since 1750), and, above all, the Louvre (since 1793)—it was conceived as a *musée de passage*, a site of display and judgment that would pass on to the Louvre, ten years after an artist's death, those artworks deemed worthy of permanent protection. Lesser works were destined for provincial museums or storage in attics. This multimuseum cooperative system subsequently appeared in all spheres of European cultural influence, soon proving itself flexible enough not only to negotiate between generations of artists but also to serve national patrimony and international exchange.[16] On a less lofty but equally pragmatic level, pioneer social Darwinist Andrew Carnegie, in Pittsburgh in 1896, conceived "the Chronological Exhibition"—the best paintings produced in the world each year, from which the best would be awarded a prize, purchased for the Carnegie Museum, and hung in annual sequence to create a self-replenishing display.[17] In each of these historical cases, a different kind of distinction was drawn between art's past, present, and anticipated manifestations, but in each instance there was a strong sense that the chosen works of art would, despite their necessary time boundedness, coexist productively for overlapping periods, thus contributing to the historical continuity of art itself.

Explicit institutional naming occurred mostly during the twentieth century. In 1910, patrons, writers, and collectors associated with the Bloomsbury group set up the Contemporary Art Society in London to acquire works "not more than twenty years old" for national collections.[18] In British colonies throughout the 1930s, contemporary art societies were formed, mostly as artists' exhibiting organizations, in opposition to local academies. The charter of the Contemporary Art Society founded in Melbourne in 1938 is typical: "By the expression 'contemporary art' is meant all contemporary painting, sculpture, drawing and other visual art forms which is or are original and creative or which strive to give expression to contemporary thought and life as opposed to work which is reactionary and retrogressive, including work which has no other aim than representation."[19] In contrast, most French institutions had, by the 1930s, come to see "contemporary art" more broadly, as the latest phase in the development of a self-enriching tradition of modern art, especially "modern painting [*peinture moderne*]," dating back at least to Paul Cézanne, if not all the way to Édouard Manet.[20] Now, in official usage, *l'art contemporain* encompasses the entirety of art since 1798, that is, since the French Revolution.

A similar switching between rhetorical uses of the words "contemporary" and "modern" is evident in the conception of the Museum of Modern Art, New York. Regarding collecting policy, director Alfred H. Barr Jr. noted in a 1931 address to the trustees:

> The historical museum, such as the Metropolitan, acquires what is believed to be certainly and permanently valuable. *It cannot afford to run the risk of error.* But the opposite is true of museums of modern art such as the Luxembourg Gallery in Paris, the Tate Gallery in London, or the Stedelijk Museum in Amsterdam. It is the proper part of their program to *take chances on the acquisition of contemporary painting and sculpture*, a policy which would be unwise on the part of their conservative counterparts, the Louvre, the National Gallery or the Rijksmuseum.[21]

Angelica Zander Rudenstine comments, "To this extent, the original conception of the museum equated the notion of the modern with that of 'contemporary,' and it offered an interesting solution to the dilemma of institutionalizing the modern."[22] But when, two years earlier, in the museum's foundational document, Barr sought to isolate the values at the core of modern art itself, he insisted on "the progressive, original and challenging rather than the safe and academic which would naturally be included in the supine neutrality of the term 'contemporary.'"[23] The Museum of Modern Art quickly succeeded in defining the modern in its preferred terms, at least for audiences in the United States—so much so that, in 1948, when its Boston branch wished to break away from what it regarded as the narrow, Francophile focus on abstraction of its parent organization and to give space to German expressionist, American scene, and other kinds of figurative art, it renamed itself the Institute of Contemporary Art.[24]

It should not surprise us that around this time—a period of extraordinary economic and political turmoil—certain art historians began to notice "the uncontemporary nature of the contemporary" (Wilhelm Pinder) and "the contemporary existence of older and younger" (Arnold Hauser).[25] Nor should it surprise us that, in reaction to this chaos, a "contemporary style" appeared, especially in Britain during its efforts at economic and social reconstruction following World War II, largely in household design ware (where it remains a category to this day).[26]

The important point about all these examples is that each represents a quite different, utterly specific conjunction of artistic tendencies, one of which took the name "contemporary"—for that time, in that circumstance. Taken together, however, the examples hint at the richness and complexity of the prehistory of the contemporary within the modern. They suggest, too, the interest that may lie—for the "alternative modernities" project—in tracking these largely forgotten pathways.[27]

SETTING THE CONTEMPORARY AGENDA

In the long aftermath of World War II, visual memory was haunted by specters of recent trauma: photographs from the death camps, and the human silhouette burned into the pavement by the atomic flash. This spirit informs Lucio Fontana's 1946 "Manifesto Blanco," written in Buenos Aires, as well the Gutai artists' 1954 determination to "create what has never been done before" through concrete embodiment (*gutai*), using everyday objects and simple actions. Meanwhile, Yves Klein sought the void, and Guy Debord fixed the cinematic limits of mechanical reproduction with his antifilm *Hurlements en faveur de Sade* of June 1952, with its random alternation of white screen and mix of mediated quotation and voice-over comment with varying lengths of blank black screen. Robert Rauschenberg's surfaces, covered with black or white house paint during 1951 and 1952, were mere receivers of light, shadows, and the passage of time. In the latter year, John Cage used these works in his *Concerted Action* (later renamed *Theatre Piece No. 1*) at Black Mountain College, North Carolina. Cage's famous *4' 33"*, first performed by David Tudor on August 29, 1952, in a concert of contemporary music, is less a stretch of silence, as it is often described, and more a staged interruption of the flow of measured time, so that temporality itself can be experienced as taking place, right there and then. Andy Warhol's contemporaneity, in his *Death in America* series, derived not simply from the use of up-to-date images (many, in fact, were up to a decade old, and he constantly recycled his imagery), but rather from his evocation of the rising tide of the spectacle society's image flow, through his ability to *arrest* each image—by stamping it out, pinning it down, through singularity, repetition, and variation. Warhol applied his entire strategic ensemble to the depiction of the most pressing issues of the day, not least the seemingly endless assassinations of leading political figures, including those offering hope. Common to all these works is a retreat from historical time, from socially managed timekeeping, and an openness to adventitious occurrence, to the common incipience of things, to the coming into being of a subjectivity that displays itself to other becoming subjects. These qualities appeared in art throughout the world: for example, in the shift from concretism to neoconcretism in the work of Lygia Clark, Hélio Oiticica, and many others in Brazil during the 1960s.

If artists took the lead in facing the demands of the contemporary in the 1950s and 1960s, can we say that critics were most prominent in both obstructing (the formalists) and facilitating (everyone else) openness to these values during the latter decade, to be followed by theorists in the 1970s? That the market returned to reclaim the agenda during the 1980s, whereas curators dominated art-world self-definition during the 1990s? And that since the turn of the century, collectors, followed quickly by auction houses and art fairs, have led in highlighting what counts as current art? Generalizations of this type are themselves evidence of the "branding" priorities that prevailed within communications media during the later twentieth century and early years of the twenty-first. They were, however, often heard in "art talk," so let us take them as indicators and ask how ideas of contemporaneity surfaced within and between them. "It is this continuous and entire presentness, amounting, as it were, to the perpetual creation of itself, that one experiences as a kind of *instantaneousness*, as though if only one were infinitely more acute, a single infinitely brief instant would be long enough to see everything, to experience the work in all its depth and fullness, to be forever convinced by it."[28] These words, the culmination of Michael Fried's

1967 essay "Art and Objecthood," would seem to define contemporaneity as the portal to transcendence. But his goal—in concert with that of his mentor, Clement Greenberg (for whom the term "contemporary" had no special meaning)—was to identify what was essentially modernist in modernist art, and to do so by denying its contemporaneity as incidental to it. To Fried, this art did not in any important way participate in modern times, modernity, *modernité*, or the like; however much it might be a product of these times, it did not figure them, represent them, or least of all, picture them. Nor was it, in its most profound register, contemporary to its viewer. Minimal art's insistence that the viewer take a specific kind of actual, material time to apprehend the work, Fried saw as a crude, even theatrical literalism. The truly modernist work of art, in contrast, achieved a degree of autonomy so great that it became, in effect, its own time zone. It was so absorbed in itself that, in the strictest sense, it required no viewer. Nor could any viewer rise to its occasion. At most, the above quotation makes clear, one might glimpse the possibility of doing so. This is apprehension of art as a kind of supplication before its messianic presence. Small wonder that Fried concludes with the words of eighteenth-century preacher Jonathan Edwards: "Presentness is grace."

If Fried had in mind the highly attuned individual art critic trembling on the cusp of aesthetic election, Leo Steinberg was more concerned with "Contemporary Art and the Plight of Its Public." In this 1960 lecture, he defined "plight" as "simply the shock of discomfort, or the bewilderment or the anger or the boredom which some people always feel, and all people sometimes feel, when confronted with an unfamiliar new style."[29] More important, he offered a useful understanding of what it meant (and, perhaps, still means) to be a member of the "public" for contemporary art. Membership happens at those moments when viewers pass through the initial shock to recognize that they are being asked *by this work of art* to throw out the framework for responding to works of art that had served hitherto, and to accept—without fully knowing why—the new world of seeing that this work requires for an adequate response to it. This is what is "contemporary" about such art: it invites the viewer into a new temporality and insists that the time for just this new kind of art has arrived. The contemporary, then, is first a matter of direct experience, and then it is one that claims further significance because it may be epochal. It combines instanteity—total immersion in the present—with a demand that an unknowable future be instantly accepted. This double experience, Steinberg suggests, makes one a member of contemporary art's public.[30]

The broader relevance of these examples is that they point to the widespread tendency to isolate one quality of, in this case, the experience of a work of art as the key to art's contemporaneity in a more general sense. We have already seen examples where certain qualities of the artwork, or aspects of its dissemination, or certain ideas or attitudes held by the artist are assumed to be similarly definitive. In contrast, I am suggesting not only that these "definitions" are in fact emphases that are quite specific to time and place, but also that they gradually become—at least with regard to the intentional outlook of those holding them—more and more encompassing of variety in the present and open to the future.

In many parts of the world, especially in local art worlds that saw themselves as in some way tied into the example of one of the metropolitan culture centers, contemporaneity had the quite specific meaning of identifying the inequitable, conflicted state in which artists felt themselves to be working. They sought acknowledgment that at least some local artists were producing art of the same kind and quality as that issuing from the center, and that they were doing so at the same time ("contemporaneously"). In contrast, other local artists might consciously reject such an ambition. Their priorities were local, provincial, or national—contemporaneous in their avowed difference. These kinds of value distinctions had long since marked avant-garde art practice in many South American countries, notably Brazil, Argentina, and Uruguay.[31] They accelerated during the 1960s, following the increasing ease of international travel and the greater distribution of publicity about contemporary art. Such finely tuned relationships could change quickly, as Andrea Giunta has demonstrated by tracking how Argentine artists, critics, curators, and cultural officials understood the idea of "internationalization":

> Whereas in 1956 internationalization meant, above all, breaking out of isolation, in 1958 it implied joining an international artistic front; in 1960 it meant elevating Argentine art to a level of quality that would enable it to challenge international spaces; in 1962 attracting European and North American artists to Argentine competitions; in 1964 it brought the "new Argentine art" to international centers; in 1965 it brandished the "worldwide" success of Argentine art before the local public; and, finally, after 1966, internationalism became increasingly synonymous with "imperialism" and "dependence," upsetting its previous positivity.[32]

In Australia, similar relationships were articulated in terms of a concept of provincialism, seen not only as a bind for ambitious art produced in the settler colonies, but also as pervading the entire art system, then centered in New York.[33] Reiko Tomii has explored the emergence in Japan in the 1960s and 1970s of a sense that truly contemporary art (*gendai bijutsu*) should be part of an international contemporaneity (*kokusaiteki dojisei*). Local critics had Euro-American art in mind as their model of the latter, as well as a set of distinctions between earlier kinds of modern and avant-garde art in Japan and the West.[34] Olu Oguibe, Sidney Kasfir, and Simon Njami, among others, have drawn attention to the trafficking back and forth between art centers in Africa and those in Europe, as countries actively struggling for their independence called on their artists to participate in freedom fights and then nation building, while the artists were also discovering the enticements and challenges of presenting their work to international audiences.[35] Since 1989, much curatorial, critical, and historical attention has been paid to developments at the peripheries of the Soviet Union, as that structure contracted toward its center, precipitating a renewed attention to cultural change at the borders of Europe, as they hesitatingly expanded.[36]

Concepts of modern and contemporary art have had a complex, layered history in Chinese art history, as I showed in chapter 5. Maoist revolutionary idealism was the dominant framework for late modern art in China from 1949 until the end of the Cultural Revolution in 1978. During the 1980s, a resurgence of critical consciousness allied with interest in early and mid-twentieth-century Western models, and concurrent postmodernism led to avant-garde experimentation. Taking up the Japanese term for contemporary art (gendai bijutsu), this was labeled *xiandai yishu* and translated as "modern art." During the 1990s, when Chinese artists reacted against a newly censorious state regime, and at the same time became more aware of international contemporary art, the term *dangdai yishu* (today's art) came to represent what was clearly a contemporary art movement. Dangdai yishu is now the standard translation of "contemporary art." External interest in such art opened up patronage and markets. Subsequently, as a result of China's relentless pursuit of the "four modernizations," some of the conditions that led to realism and then high modernism in European art in the middle and late nineteenth century have been experienced in Beijing, Shanghai, and elsewhere. Could they be turning art practice in a modernizing direction? While some sharp contrasts in medium, subject matter, and style still separate traditional, modern, and contemporary aesthetic tendencies, all of which persist, China's determined commitment to modern nation building within a globalized context is evidently encouraging many artists to seek consonances between these tendencies.[37]

Discerning what is distinct and what is shared in these shifts from the modern to the contemporary (or, in some cases, the reverse) in different parts of the world is, I submit, the greatest challenge facing those who would write histories of recent and current art. The diversity of these changes guarantees that there will be no single story (and thus no style change in art as such) but rather many parallel, contingent, but identifiably specific histories.

THE POSTMODERN MOMENT

"What is postmodernism?" was a key question of the 1970s that persisted into the 1980s, but it lost much of its punch when it became a taste throughout the culture. While it was a style in architecture for a time (signifying little more than pastiche historicism, despite—and perhaps partly because of—Charles Jencks's manic efforts to make it a catchall), it did not add up to a period style in any other of the visual arts. Indeed, these arts were rapidly diversifying beyond the limits of each medium and delighting in the unpredictable potentialities of exchanges between mediums (intermediality, not medium specificity, was the new direction). These changes occurred while artists saw themselves and their culture becoming increasingly immersed in mass media. The label "postmodern" is too narrow to capture the purport of such brief but important moments as that of the "pictures generation" in New York and Los Angeles, and of the continuing work of artists such as Cindy Sherman, Marlene Dumas, and Candice Breitz.

In the short retrospect available to us, it seems obvious that the postmodernism debate was a symptom of one of its own premises: that progress was no longer inevitable, that no one big story was going to dominate any sphere of human activity, including the arts and the history of thought, in the foreseeable future. This sense of the plurality of the present reached its apogee during the 1970s and 1980s. While the attack on universalizing theories—whether secular "master narratives," such as presumptions about human progress and historical succession, religious ones about predestination, or specialist discourses, such as the unfolding history of art—launched by, among others, Jean-François Lyotard, was influential in the art world, the interpretation of postmodernity as the current state of "late capitalism," offered by theorists such as David Harvey and Fredric Jameson, was more powerful and has been longer lasting. The latter maintained that the work of artists such as Andy Warhol displayed "the cultural logic of late capitalism."[38] Art-world discourse varied between an "anything goes" inclusiveness of whatever was presented as art, or whatever, and efforts to give responsible and grounded accounts of the "de-definition" of contemporary art as itself (of course, paradoxically) definitive of contemporaneity. Australian curator Bernice Murphy, realizing in 1993 that "contemporary art, although it has for a long time belonged within the sphere of modernity, is increasingly adopting other frameworks of value and meaning that break beyond the classical period of modern art's development," was led to the following: "Defining 'contemporary' art: a moving framework of time and concerns."[39] American curators Dan Cameron and Anna Palmquist, sensing in 1989 that current art was increasing in quantity and diversifying in scope so rapidly that it was ceasing to be subject to the (generally benign and enabling) control of art-world institutions and personnel, noted, "This grip on contemporary art's code of values has loosened in recent years, and much of the more interesting art being produced today seems to be a result of this significant change, wherein values are both more up in the air and more hotly debated than at practically any single point in the recent past."[40] Precisely in possessing these qualities, they imply, certain current art has become specifically, totally, and *only* contemporary.

Few art historians responded to these discussions of "de-definition" going on among artists and curators. Hans Belting and philosopher–art critic Arthur Danto were among the exceptions. Belting recognized that changes in art practice and in broadscale social formations had pushed the profession of art history into its second major crisis: the dramatic struggle, during the twentieth century, between iconography, iconology, and *Kulturgeschichte* on the one hand, and modernist historicism on the other, was now played out. No new paradigm had come into view as a replacement, nor was one likely if it were to be confined to the traditional, studio, and craft-based arts. Art history had reached its "end," fulfilled its self-designated academic purpose.[41] In a parallel vein, as I noted in chapter 1, Danto succinctly summarized the effect of changes in art since the 1980s: "So just as 'modern' has come to denote a style and even a period, and not just *recent* art, 'contemporary' has come to designate something more than simply the art of the present moment. In my view, however, it designates less a period than what happens after there are no more periods in some master narrative of art, and less a style of making art than a style of using styles."[42] To Danto, the gulf between modern and contemporary art had opened up because the great historical role given to art within modernity (above all by Georg Wilhelm Friedrich Hegel) had been fulfilled in late modern art. Art had achieved its "end," served its historical purpose. Warhol's *Brillo*

Boxes, conceptualism, and other "philosophical" tendencies signified that the most advanced human thought had changed its nature. Art had, in effect, become philosophy. It could not, therefore, transmute into a new style of art: that story was over. In the aftermath of this achievement, it is no surprise that subsequent art would seem "posthistorical." The sense of aftermath becomes a rich vein in the works by Wall and Meckseper discussed above. In the later 1980s and early 1990s, however—before the institutionalization of contemporary art, the global impact of the transnational turn, and the emergence of the diversifying art of contemporaneity—the "posthistorical" amounted to a rather comfortable pluralism. Others identify a *dis*comforting pluralism, for example, Amelia Jones: "Perhaps most profoundly, art since 1945 has insistently, in ways varying as widely as the kinds of people making it, explored the *contingency* of the visual arts (like any form of expression)—the way in which works of art (including performances, live events, etc.) exist and come to mean within circuits of meaning, economic and social value, and personal and collective desire that are far more complex than we can ever fully understand."[43]

THE TEXTBOOKS CHALLENGED

How have art historians dealt with this challenge, this sense of the *impossibility* of the contemporary? Let us begin at the most conventional end of the spectrum. Since the 1960s, English-language visual art dictionaries, encyclopedias, companions, glossaries, and collections of art terms have consistently devoted entries to terms such as "modern art," the "modern movement" in architecture, and "modernista," among other local design styles. Some include an entry on "modernism," although it is often conflated with modern art in general and the avant-garde in particular.[44] Although entries on organizations that include "contemporary" in their titles appear, the term "contemporary art" is rarely granted an entry of its own, and, if so, it receives either derogatory comment as to its impossibility as a concept or is blandly sketched.[45] Online definitions register the ongoing confusion. In March 2009, *Wikipedia* led with "Contemporary art can be defined variously as art produced at this present point in time or art produced since World War II. The definition of the word contemporary would support the first view, but museums of contemporary art commonly define their collections as consisting of art produced since World War II."[46]

A similar picture of neglecting the obvious emerges from a survey of the major English-language textbooks published during the past thirty or so that include accounts of the art of those years. Many have appeared in multiple editions; some are updated every two to five years in response to their continued use, in massive quantities, in school, college, and university art and art history courses. As of 2008, only one book had used "Contemporary Art" as a chapter heading and meant by it art since World War II, from abstract expressionism to "Neo-Expressionism, Photography and the 1980s."[47] The phrase "contemporary art" is used in passing in the 1999 edition of Marilyn Stokstad's *Art History*, the only time it is indexed as a category in all the volumes surveyed.[48] Alert to the languages of the moment and to the need to keep the mammoth tomes up to date, all the canonical survey text editors plumped, during the 1980s and 1990s, for "postmodern" as their preferred term.

Overall, academics and publishers have lagged a long way behind the rest of the art world in adopting "contemporary" as the name for its current and recent activity. Even in the subspecialist field of books on the art of recent decades, surveys by authors—mainly British—alert to the variety of contemporary art and the convolutions of its discourse, are undertaken beneath such titles as *Art since 1960* or the more combative *After Modern Art*.[49] Open-ended compilation books favor titles such as *Art Now* or *Art in the Twenty-First Century*.[50] Others carry into print some of the flavor of the art they favor; thus, English artist-critic and television presenter Mathew Collings—in a typical, against-the-grain yet market-savvy move—labeled his irreverent, yBa-promoting, all-over-the-shop, paintball-style celebration of post-1960s art *This Is Modern Art*.[51]

Recent books on contemporary art are divided between pictorial compilations accompanied by minimal text and brief artists' statements (the Taschen model); anthologies of interpretative essays by theorists, critics, and curators (the Blackwell model); or provisional attempts at showing how certain artists are tackling themes—such as time, place, identity, the body, language, or spirituality—deemed to be of current concern.[52] One uses the rubric "Art and . . ." then devotes chapters to art and, in turn, popular culture, the quotidian object, abstraction, representation, narrative, time, nature and technology, deformation, the body, identity, spirituality, globalism, architecture, politics, and audience.[53] A few textbooks have been attempted, with more sure to come. The first of this crop was Brandon Taylor's *The Art of Today* (1995), revised and retitled *Contemporary Art* (2004), and *Contemporary Art: Art since 1970* (2005).[54] Like other English authors, such as Julian Stallabrass, who have experienced firsthand the excesses of the yBa, Taylor begins from a critical premise: "Willful obscurity in the artwork, then, combined with a massive expansion in the infrastructure for contemporary art—this may be taken as the defining contradiction that has animated and in some cases helped to generate much of the art of our time."[55] This has been true since the late 1960s but reached its peak, perhaps, in the 1990s. Through a series of acute, engaged descriptions, Taylor narrates the unfolding of various tendencies in international art, including a wider range than is usual in such surveys. Also unusual is that he includes, in the later chapters, work by artists recently prominent in biennials whose formative experiences took place outside Euro-America. More typical is that the cultural contexts from which these artists emerged receive scant attention.

Pragmatic, wait-and-see open-endedness typifies the closing chapters of most omnibus textbooks. An interesting recent exception is *Art since 1900*, produced by four authors, all outstanding historians of modernist art and active critics of contemporary art, especially through their association with the journal *October*. Instead of presenting an account organized around styles, mediums, or themes, the book is divided into short chapters, each of which treats one work, exhibition, publication, or event according to the year of its occurrence. The paradoxical result is a fascinating display of the contemporaneity of modern art, rather than of its unfolding history. This is, in itself, an effect of contemporaneity's prioritizing of the contemporary: in making their collective decision as to how to organize the book, the authors applied the process that they had evolved as editors of *October*, that is, they acted first as critics and only by implication as historians. Nevertheless, because of the differing perspectives of each author (engagingly set out in long introductory essays), a set of parallel histories is implied, although never spelled out. For two of the authors, Rosalind E. Krauss and Yve-Alain Bois, this amounts to what we might call double modernism—formal vis-à-vis informal, sourced in cubism and surrealism, respectively—that continues into the present. For Benjamin H. D. Buchloh, a revolutionary avant-gardism, sourced in Dada and Russian *faktura*, has echoed since the 1960s as a heroic but ultimately futile struggle by certain neo-avant-garde artists against the seductions and the degradations of the "culture industry." The fourth author, Hal Foster, emphasizes the psychoanalytic aspects of art making within these trajectories.[56] Taken together (itself a breathtaking historical hypothesis), these views amount to the closest thing to orthodoxy about the development of modern art that exists among scholars—in the United States, especially.

Art since 1900 includes many entries devoted to artists active since the 1960s, but it leaves ambiguous the question of whether anything fundamental has changed. The implication is that it has not, that contemporary art remains a late modernism, or, more accurately, an *after*modernism, condemned in conscience to mourn, as elegantly and trenchantly as possible, its own anachronism. In the roundtable discussion with which the book concludes, the authors acknowledge that art has indeed changed in ways that exceed the frameworks used in the book. Foster asks, "Are there plausible ways to narrate the now myriad practices of contemporary art over the past twenty years?" He describes the two "primary models" they have used during this period—"on the one hand, the model of a medium-specific modernism challenged by an interdisciplinary postmodernism, and, on the other, the model of a historical avant-garde . . . and a neo-avant-garde"—as having become "dysfunctional." Buchloh is equally candid, noting that "the bourgeois public sphere" to which both previous avant-gardes were related, albeit critically, has "irretrievably disappeared," to be replaced by "social and institutional formations for which we not only do not have any concepts and terms yet, but whose modus operandi remains profoundly opaque and incomprehensible to most of us."[57] The only option left to contemporary artists, it seems, is to bear exacting witness to the present (and future) impossibility of the cold optimism that drove the modernist avant-garde.[58]

The impasse here may be that of criticism, not art. Peter Osborne has recently put a sharp edge to this possibility. Citing the deeply reflexive work of the Art & Language group during the 1980s and 1990s, he argues,

> It is the historical movement of conceptual art from the idea of an absolute antiaesthetic to the recognition of its own inevitable pictorialism that makes it a privileged mediating form; that makes it, in fact, the art in relation to which contestation over the meanings and possibilities of contemporary art is to be fought out. . . . In this respect, "post-conceptual art" is not the name for a particular type of art, so much as the historical-ontological condition for the production of contemporary art in general.

"Postconceptual art" understood in this broader sense, he goes on, determines the contemporaneity of all contemporary art, and that requires art criticism and art history to articulate "the qualitative historical novelty of the present," from which the past may be "made legible."[59] This strikes me as an acute perception in its recognition of the force of postconceptualism as the most trenchant critique of late modern art, especially that created within Euro-American frameworks and spheres of influence. And it correctly recognizes that art criticism, in contemporary circumstances, must be historical in its orientation, albeit paradoxically so.[60] But his prescription remains, as he acknowledges, essentially modernist as art, art criticism, and art history. It does not, I believe, fully meet what contemporaneity now requires of art and its articulators: demands that are broader in geopolitical scope, more lateral in their experiential character, and deeper in their theoretical challenge than modernism of whatever stamp can allow.

To grasp this, we need to acknowledge that since the 1990s, there have been in circulation certain other, quite substantial, and wide-ranging ideas, advanced most effectively by curators, who made their arguments through what became known as "mega-exhibitions." The contention between them came to a head in the years around 2000, and they resonate still.

CURATORS IN CONTENTION

From 1984, the curatorial team at the Centro Wifredo Lam in Havana dedicated itself to building networks between artists in the "nonaligned" countries constituting the third world and to showcasing the results in the Bienal de la Habana, most successfully in the 1989 exhibition. In the same year in Paris, at the exhibition *Magiciens de la terre*, contemporary art from "the Global South" entered the mental landscape of the Euro-American art world. The power of this work, rather than the relatively simplistic curatorial program, signaled the possibility of a genuine internationalism. This global movement culminated in Documenta 11 in 2002, an exhibition in which work by artists whose origins and inspirations were transnational stood out. In between these dates, certain curators, artists, and critics undertook a major educational mission: a series of historically oriented exhibitions drawing worldwide attention to the importance of the visual arts during decolonization struggles, particularly in Africa.[61] Okwui Enwezor, a leader of this effort, summarized the overall outcome as the manifestation in art of the world having arrived at a state best described as a "postcolonial constellation."

> Contemporary art today is refracted, not just from the specific site of culture and history but also—and in a more critical sense—from the standpoint of a complex geopolitical configuration that defines all systems of production and relations of exchange as a consequence of globalization after imperialism.... The current artistic context is constellated around the norms of the postcolonial, those based on discontinuous, aleatory forms, on creolization, hybridization, and so forth, all of these tendencies operating with a specific cosmopolitan accent.... Any critical interest in the exhibition systems of Modern or contemporary art requires us to refer to the foundational base of modern art history: its roots in imperial discourse, on the one hand, and, on the other, the pressure that postcolonial discourse exerts on its narratives today.[62]

In sharp contrast to such views, many believe that the significant art of today remains modernist at its core. In 2000, Museum of Modern Art chief curator Kirk Varnedoe firmly locked the museum's collections of recent art into modernity's unstoppable project:

> There is an argument to be made that the revolutions that originally produced modern art, in the late nineteenth and early twentieth centuries, have not been concluded or superseded—and thus that contemporary art today can be understood as the ongoing extension and revision of those founding innovations and debates. The collection of the Museum of Modern Art is, in a very real sense, that argument. Contemporary art is collected and presented at this Museum as part of modern art—as belonging within, and responding to, and expanding upon the framework of initiatives and challenges established by the earlier history of progressive art since the dawn of the twentieth century.[63]

While these remarks are on one level quite specific to the historical role and immediate interests of one museum, they also represent the currently most developed version of the idea that modernist art is capable of renewing itself from within its own resources. In contrast, Enwezor speaks from the presumption that art emerges, in complex but primary ways, out of each artist's immersion in and engagement with the world's realities.

Few other ideas have had the potential to rival this clash of perspectives. Most have been much smaller in scale, less encompassing in their intended reach—for example, "relational aesthetics" and "postproduction art," proposed by curator Nicolas Bourriaud.[64] He has recently updated his emphasis on this kind of participatory art to include its practitioners who are active outside the centers of Europe and the United States. "Altermodernism" incorporates the modernism of the others (*alter* means "other" in Latin and evokes the ideas of "alternative" and "transform" in English): "instead of aiming at a kind of summation, altermodernism sees itself as a constellation of ideas linked by the emerging and ultimately irresistible will to create a form of modernism for the twenty-first century." Conceiving this spirit as "a leap that would give rise to a synthesis between modernism and post-colonialism," Bourriaud offers this definition:

> Altermodernism can be defined as that moment when it became possible for us to produce something that made sense starting from an assumed heterochrony, that is, from a vision of human history as constituted by multiple temporalities, disdaining nostalgia for the avant-garde and in-

deed for any era—a positive vision of chaos and complexity. It is neither a petrified kind of time advancing in loops (postmodernism) nor a linear vision of history (modernism), but a positive experience of disorientation through an art-form exploring all dimensions of the present, tracing lines in all directions of time and space.[65]

This points to a core aspect of contemporary art—its geopolitical and temporal contemporaneity.[66] It does not, however, amount to a large idea in the sense of the others just discussed: it is constrained by its disavowals. Enwezor has attempted to absorb it into his "postcolonial constellation" by framing it within four categories he identifies "as emblematic of the conditions of modernity today: *Supermodernity, andromodernity, speciousmodernity,* and *aftermodernity*."[67]

REVISING THE NEW ART HISTORY

Whatever one's specific reservations, these examples indicate that a viable theoretical and historical framework for approaching contemporary art—one that captures its actual diversity, but neither prohibitively reduces nor randomly multiplies it—is coming into view. Crucial to this possibility is the work of the generation of art historians who have already begun to undertake close studies of the work of individual artists, small groups, and certain shared tendencies active during what I am calling the shift from modern to contemporary art. They draw on the methodologies of revisionist (or "new") art history, those developed during the past half century to track the birth and the continuing crisis of nineteenth- and twentieth-century modernism and to revisit and recomplicate its modernist history. Their interest in the 1960s and 1970s is not merely retro fashion. The interpretative institutions need to take stock of work by artists either long dead (Warhol, by decades now) or nearing the natural end of long and productive careers. For the current generation of mature art historians, to see the 1960s and 1970s in ways distinct from the interpretations advanced at the time and from the incessant redefinitions promoted by survivors from that moment would be to arrive at an independent view of the great changes in art that occurred then, and to see them in ways useful to present practice and thinking.[68] What seemed to be powerfully coherent, integrated art movements are being minutely examined with an eye to their internal complexities and multiple productivities. Minimalism is being understood as, in some aspects, less of a break with high modernism than it seemed at the time, while, in other respects, more open ended; conceptual art in the United States and Europe now appears as a current within global conceptualism, less subject to the charge that it was "an aesthetic of administration" or a "mourning for modernism," more vital to indirect political critique and subsequent experimentation than it felt at first; previously downgraded groupings such as Fluxus are elevated, as are the innovations of artists working in smaller-scale scenes outside what are still largely considered the major art centers in Europe and the United States; and feminism is being shown to have been much more pervasive, various, and persistent in art than previously acknowledged.[69]

But this revisionist activity remains largely focused on artists who were active in the United States and Europe and trails the presumption that what they did is what counts as real transformation in art as a whole. We are still some way from an accounting that tracks artistic changes as they happened in their specific ways in each of the cultural regions of the world, in actual cities and in the areas associated with them, and in the transnational trafficking between these productive nodes and between them and the major modern art centers. Nevertheless, scholars are beginning record and assess the efforts and achievements of artists from the global South. Some comparative studies are being undertaken. This is where real work needs to be done, urgently, as resources in some settings—Africa, for example—remain fragile.[70]

PERIODIZING CONTEMPORARY ART?

To focus this position, I pose two questions. Are the histories that contemporary art requires best written by continuing to apply the methods, values, and world pictures forged by modern art history, including the revisions that have animated the discipline as a whole since the 1970s? If so, we would expect the characteristics of contemporary art to become clear as these researchers do their work. The danger here is that of being invited to register the present in a state of suspended judgment and only then taking up the task of tracing what would amount to a slow-motion slide of contemporary art back into the advancing maw of a (diluted, falsely modest) modernism. This would also leave us less able to approach the art of the past through the forms in which that art is available to the present. For emerging art historians—those who wish to deal with the art of their time on the terms that it is forging, and those who see past art as part of "history" (a vividly present temporal territory that decades of survey exhibitions, recent virtual reconstructions, and cinematic re-creations have made readily traversable)—this is a frustrating situation, one they have been quick to protest and parody, as in the ironic presentations of the performance group Our Literal Speed.[71]

A more constructive approach has been advanced by Alex Alberro, who argues that the end of the Cold War in 1989, the era of globalization, the spread of integrated electronic culture, and the dominance of economic neoliberalism signal the emergence of a new historical period. He identifies a hegemonic confluence between factors such as global integration and antiglobalization becoming the subject of many artists' works, the proliferation of global exhibitions such as biennials, the rise of a new technological imaginary and high-tech hybrid art forms, a shift in strategy from avant-gardist confrontation toward cooperation and collaboration, and the somewhat surprising reemergence of an aesthetics of affect. He concludes: "These new forms of art and this new spectatorship have come to be discursively constructed as 'the contemporary,'" a new period in the history of art.[72]

This proposition raises a second (and, for the moment, last) question: Does a match between world-historical epoch and universal art-historical period—on the face of it, a quintessentially modern structural pairing—remain viable in contemporary conditions? After all, periodization is a fragile practice in such volatile circumstances. The attacks launched on September 11, 2001, the subsequent incursions into the Middle East, and the "war on terror" conducted inside the United States and abroad—and by various other governments in their home territories and abroad—led many to see 1989 and 2001 as bracketing a post–Cold War moment in which the United States acted as a hyperpower; neoliberal economics prevailed in all economies, while spectacle-led consumption dominated public spheres. By 2008, however, with the administration of US President George W. Bush discredited at home and abroad, the world financial system in a state of collapse, and Barack Obama elected president of the United States in a spirit of all-embracing optimism, some have been prompted to discern a further sea change in world affairs.[73] "The contemporary" is being sliced ever finer.

Immediacy, of course, is natural to it. And this, in turn, puts pressure on the urge to divide into periods—itself natural to historians. Or, to be more accurate, periods have been necessary markers within the narratives of individual and collective agency that constitute the modern approach to writing history.[74] Do they remain necessary in contemporary conditions? If conditions have changed fundamentally, which other kinds of historical markers are called for? Given that art is always subject to larger movements of this kind yet is also, in certain ways, autonomous within them, how might we most accurately map its transformations in these circumstances? These are the questions that prevent us from channeling the self-evident heterogeneity of current practice into a one-to-one match between the contemporary era and contemporary art.

CONTEMPORANEITY AND ART HISTORY

In ordinary language usage—and in much unreflective art-world discourse—the word "contemporary" defaults to whatever is happening, up-to-date, simultaneous, or contemporaneous. But the concept itself, as we have seen, has extraordinary depths of meaning: *con tempus* came into use, and remains in use, because it points to a multiplicity of relations between being and time. It originated in precisely this multiplicity and has served human thought about it ever since. The contemporary also originated, and persists, in contention against other, often more powerful terms—notably, in recent centuries, those associated with the concept of the modern—that have sought to account for similar, often overlapping phenomena with greater precision and according to dominant values. We have sketched its emergence from subservience to the modern. This emergence has brought us to a new place.

Contemporaneity itself has many histories, and histories within the histories of art. While it is, I argue, the grounding condition of contemporary art, and thus the primary object of any history of today's art, contemporaneous qualities may also have been present in art always and everywhere. The art-historical quest unleashed by this idea, I venture to suggest, goes all the way back. It pushes us to ask some unexpected questions. To what extent, and how, was awareness of the disjunctions between being and time registered within the symbolic languages that adorned the caves of Africa, marked the deserts and the rocky plateaus of what became Australia, was painted in the caves of what became Europe, and was created on the plains and islands of Asia and the Pacific? How many ancient bodies did it mark, and what would such a mark look like, compared to those made by the Originary Beings, those given by the ancestors, those that became (in our terms) immanent, traditional, or iconic? And so on, everywhere, up to the present and through it. Nowadays, many more pasts appear—vividly, invitingly—among the multiple territories that constitute our current contemporaneity.

Contemporaneity is, according to standard definitions, "a contemporaneous condition or state." In the expanded sense I describe above, this means a state defined above all by the play of multiple relations between being and time.

Obviously, this has been a vital part of human experience since the beginning of consciousness, from the first cognitive operations (indeed, it is a condition of their operation). Equally self-evident is the fact that other relations—not least structures of religious belief, cultural universalism, systems of thought, and political ideologies—have evolved to mediate the relation between being and time. During the past twenty years, however, the sense has noticeably expanded that the encompassing power of these structures, their force as universalizations, has weakened considerably, not least because of the contestation everywhere evident between them. It is no longer viable to divide the globe into spheres signified by their relative stage of advancement toward the modern utopia that awaits us all. Nowadays, the frictions of multiplicative difference shape all that is around us and within us, everything near and far, every surface and depth. Modernity is aging in Europe and ailing in the United States; having tried Mao's version, China is building on that of Deng Xiaoping and Milton Friedman; in Southeast Asia globalized hubs are continually created; while elsewhere, state after state sacrifices its citizens in the rush to plug itself in as a resource provider to the leading economies. This toxic mix of resignation and aspiration is at odds with the message coming from the planet itself: that pursuit of ever-expanding material well-being for all on the modern model will lead to the extinction of the species. The human compact with the earth is being broken: its repair is urgent; in fact, we may have begun too late. Renewed fundamentalism is just one indicator that almost every kind of past has returned to haunt the present, making its consciousness even stranger to itself.

Do these factors (just some among many others) constitute the outlines of a new era, or does their antinomic mismatching—so evident in the coexistence of multiple incommensurable temporalities but pervasive at every level of human and animal being, and perhaps extending even unto things—indicate that we have passed beyond the cusp of the last historical period that could plausibly be identified as such? This question is, at present (and in principle), unanswerable, but that it can be asked is significant. The forward movement of history, along with the many counterhistories it engendered during the modern period, has been derailed and is in decline. Globalization has recently reached the limits of its hegemonic ambitions, yet it remains powerful in many domains. The decolonized have yet to transform the world in their image (these are, after all, early days in a long struggle, much of it conducted below the radars of publicity). None of these global formations in itself sets the agenda for our times. Their contemporaneity structures our fundamental condition and is manifest in the most distinctive qualities of contemporary life, shaping the interactions between humans and the geosphere, the multeity of cultures, the ideoscape of global politics, and the interiority of individual being.

If the contemporaneity of these forces shapes the situation when periods are past, what are the implications for our understanding of contemporary art? Paradoxically, we might expect close connections between this situation and the art made within it, but they will not, I believe, amount to a structural matching between a historical period and an art-historical one. Atomic heterogeneity might seem more likely, but that may be the other pole of a false dichotomy inherited from modern thinking. A mobile in-between formation is more appropriate to circumstances in which the contemporaneity of differences is the rule. Given the picture of uneven contention between the forces painted above, we might ask whether a similar situation is apparent in art.

My own thoughts on this question are drawn from the lines of inquiry that I have pursued since 2001. I have attempted to discern the lineaments of contemporaneity as a nascent and emergent world condition: an introduction appears in the paragraphs you have just read.[75] I have also traced the emergence of conceptions of the contemporary within modern art discourse, as I summarized above.[76] These explorations have led to certain ideas that may be of interest to those seeking to approach contemporary art from historical perspectives. A schematic summary follows.[77]

The emergence of contemporaneity out of modernity is precipitating (as we write and read) deep changes in contemporary art that are in turn obliging us to revise our understanding of late modern, early modern, and, indeed, much previous art. Of most relevance to this discussion is the recognition that there has been, since the 1950s, a seismic shift from modern to contemporary modes in making, interpreting, and distributing art throughout the world. This has occurred in distinct ways in each region, nation, city, and so on, depending above all on the preexisting local history of art, culture, politics, and so on, and on the positioning of that culture in the world system, itself dynamic. Thus, continuing the "alternative modernities" project into the present, while paying attention to the specifics of the ways in which contemporary art is being generated, embraced, opposed, or tempered, in each place is important.

The main outcome of global warring since the 1950s between the forces of decolonization and those of globalization is that difference has become increasingly contemporaneous, with more of us more aware of what is essentially different, along with what is shared, relative to others. If we were able to step back and look at these diachronic developments synchronically—as if they were moving through the frame of the present from the (always reimagined) past to the (unimaginable) future—we would see, I believe, certain driving flows of energy (or currents) passing across our visual field in three distinct but connected clusters. The first, because most visible, is the continuation of modern practices, beliefs, and aspirations, including their active renewal and their constant but always partial and perhaps decreasingly effective renovation by the leading, most celebrated, and most expensive artists of the day (the efforts I have tagged, with deliberate provocation, remodernism and retro-sensationalism). This current has been threatened and, in many places, overturned by a second: art consequent on the transnational turn in world affairs (their geopolitical contemporaneity), art made mostly outside the Euro-American centers and dedicated to postcolonial critique. Its concerns with identity, nationality, and tradition are shared by artists in exile and in diaspora, as well as by those with critical perspectives working in the centers. Art of this kind fills the main international exhibitions, especially biennials, and is increasingly being collected by museums and others. The third current is that of the ever-growing cohort of (mostly younger) artists who are working at a smaller scale and with more modest, but nonetheless important, ambitions, than those of the other currents. Acting collectively in networked groups, loose associations, or individually, these artists meditate on the changing nature of time, place, media, and mood in the world around them. Among them are artists, architects, and planners who explore sustainable relationships with specific environments, both social and natural, within the framework of ecological values—an obvious response to the planet in crisis. These artists raise questions about the nature of temporality these days, the possibilities of placemaking in the context of dislocation, the meaning of immersion in mediated interactivity, and the fraught exchanges between affect and effect. They share no style, prefer no mode, subscribe to no one outlook: what they share is that their work is the art being called out by the circumstance in which contemporaneity is all.

These remarks are offered as an art-historical hypothesis about current art, descriptive in tone but partial in tendency, and thus also art critical in character. They are, of course, as contentious as those noted above. Yet the discussion here permits, I hope, some more general points in conclusion. Whatever form they take, histories of contemporary art worthy of the name should draw on the efforts to date, but at the same time should be built on a framework that is distinct from those that underlie modern art, the art of modernity. They should recognize the legacies, both positive and problematic, from earlier art—modern, paramodern, premodern, or other. They should show how each underwent, or is still undergoing, its unique yet connected transition to contemporaneity. It is no coincidence that *worldly* art criticism and art-historical scholarship are coming into existence, surpassing modern precedents in European and American art history and criticism because they have—in conflicted, resistant, but nonetheless irresistible manners—been obliged to assimilate perspectives from decolonizing, postcolonial, and Indigenous interpretive practices.[78] In the names of both embedded locality and critical cosmopolitanism, a worldly approach to art defines itself against parochialism, jingoistic nationalism, and universalizing, "globalized" art discourse. We need various kinds of critical practice, each of them alert to the demands, limits, and potentialities of both local and distant worlds, as well as to the actual and possible connections between locality and distance. In practice, translocality amounts to a focus on local artistic manifestations, and on actual, existing connections between them and art and ideas elsewhere, while remaining alert to the possibilities suggested by other, distant arts, ideas, and art-writing practices that could have local or regional relevance. We should not, therefore, subsume these developments under the generalizing distance inherent in the concept of "world art," nor see them as subject to a supposedly hegemonic "global art."

Placemaking, world picturing, and connectivity are the most common concerns of artists these days because they are the substance of contemporary being. Increasingly, they override residual distinctions based on style, mode, medium, and ideology. They are present in all art that is truly contemporary. Distinguishing, precisely, this presence in each artwork is the most important challenge to an art criticism that would be adequate to the demands of contemporaneity. Tracing the currency of each artwork within the larger forces that are shaping this present is the task of contemporary art history.

theorizing the contemporary
and the postcontemporary

Among the more puzzling preoccupations of dialogues around art during the past five years has been "the contemporary," a seemingly self-evident description that, to date, has operated largely in reverse—that has been put forward, in other words, as a meaningful denomination and subject of inquiry in advance of any actual, deductive relationship to the surrounding world. The hope, it would seem, is that the term employed by itself, and evocatively, will help tease out some general understanding of the conditions for art making and its reception today. Yet, unlikely as this might be, the impulse is easy enough to fathom: Artists, art historians, curators, and critics alike wish to find historical trajectories in art today where none immediately announce themselves; a disorienting air of atemporality prevails instead. Indeed, the imperative for historical precedent or distinction becomes only more urgent in light of speculative obsessions with the "new" in a radically expanded art system whose borders have become so porous as to erode the very ideation of art.... If there is a substantive sense of "the contemporary" to be employed here, it is likely to be the "out-of-jointness" that philosopher Giorgio Agamben ascribed to the term: Something is contemporary when it occupies time disjunctively, seeming always at once "too soon" or "too late," or, more accurately in terms of art now, seeming to contain the seeds of its own anachronism.

—TIM GRIFFIN, "OUT OF TIME"

The epigraph for this chapter is a paragraph by Tim Griffin, then-editor of *Artforum*, introducing his review of the 2011 Venice Biennale in that magazine.[1] His remarks are an acute evocation of how "the contemporary" had been, for some years, operating as an ambiguous, but seemingly essential, art-world resonator. As a tentative signifier, it recognizes that many things in art and the world are changing, and are doing so in unfathomable ways, but they also seem to be taking an unconscionable time to configure into a new, identifiable, overall shape to which one name can be attached. When—if?—they do coalesce, the contemporary qualities of both the art and our times are likely to be prominent in what is most distinctive about them. But nothing is certain. In these circumstances, "the contemporary," although a noun phrase, hovers as if it was an adjective, but actually defers that which it usually qualifies. Its core quality, or set of qualities, remains unspoken. Recently, a few other art historians and critics have attempted to plot the sounds within that silence. I review their contributions in the next and final chapter. In this one, I discuss the efforts of the even smaller number of philosophers, theorists, and artists who have recently attempted to do the same.[2]

AGAMBEN'S CONTEMPORARINESS

Seeking something "substantive" within this state of suspension, Griffin refers directly to Giorgio Agamben's essay "What Is the Contemporary?" Translated into English in 2009, but available online since 2007, when Agamben first presented these ideas as a lecture at the European Graduate School, it quickly became the go-to citation for those in the art world who wanted to register, in a gesture, their sense of being caught up in the present moment, but also somehow, at the same time, out of it, and thus able to make some (relatively independent) sense of it.[3] It is worth freezing this frame for a moment, to catch the figure of the gesture and to ask what it might mean for those held by it.

Agamben's opening—his "first and foremost"—question is "What does it mean to be contemporary?" His concern is to articulate "contemporariness" as it is experienced, as an *actualité* found precisely in that experience, in the grasping of its inner registers.[4] He proceeds by posing, mostly via metaphor, one paradox after another to demonstrate the shadow play that arises whenever "the contemporary" is subject to analysis. He finds examples from across the span of modern thinking about such matters, from Nietzsche to contemporary astrophysics. He seeks to explicate a state of being that has special relevance to our present times but does not do so by showing how this state, however preexistent aspects of it may be, has qualities that are characteristic of current conditions—understood, on analogy to David Harvey's identification of "the postmodern condition," as a general or widely shared situation.[5] Instead, Agamben shows how "contemporariness" is experienced—at its most profound, ontological register—by philosophers, poets, and others, that is, by those most capable of understanding its true nature. In much of his text, "the contemporary" means the contemporary thinker who is thinking about what it is to be contemporary.

Yet Agamben also takes "contemporariness" to be a quality of being in time, today and at other times. What is this quality? Agamben uses the word as he reads out his lecture in English. The Italian text prefers *contemporaneità* at these points, for which the standard translation is "contemporaneity" or "contemporaneousness," terms that are usually defined as "a contemporaneous condition or state." Yet clearly Agamben is searching for a term that takes us beyond the mere simultaneity or plain coexistence implied in ordinary and simple usage of the term. "Contemporariness" does appear in Noah Porter's *Webster's Revised Unabridged Dictionary* of 1913, where it means, "Existence at the same time; contemporaneousness." It is absent from most other dictionaries, and from ordinary language usage.[6] But in April 2007, alert editors added it to *Wiktionary*, where it is defined as "The state or quality of being contemporary." This is Agamben's meaning, in the somewhat circular terms of his discussion. Whereas the dictionary definitions envisage the rather straightforward temporally proximate relations between things, events, and people, he wants to show the complexities of their existential necessity as a succession of acts of insight. In this ambition we see the brilliance but also the limits of his account. Let me unpack his argument.

Friedrich Nietzsche's *Untimely Meditations* (1873–76)—above all, the German philosopher's passionate insistence that overweening respect for the determinative power of history had reduced his contemporaries to servile subjects, incapable of making their own lives, let alone future history—is rightly cited as a prime example of the apparently paradoxical proposition that those who are "truly contemporary, truly belong to their time, are those who neither perfectly coincide with it nor adjust themselves to its demands." On the contrary, Agamben insists, "Contemporariness is, then, a singular relationship with one's time, which adheres to it and, at the same time, keeps a distance from it."[7] Total immersion in the present, absolute up-to-dateness, is blindness. Distance within inescapable implication is a necessary condition of truly contemporary being.

But it is not sufficient. We must also ask, What is *critical*, or at least *skeptical* distance? Agamben offers an elegant analysis of Osip Mandelstam's poem "Vek" ("The Century"), in which the linkage between the poet and his era is imagined as that between an empathetic observer and a creature that changes from having the flexibility of youth to having a back broken by age. The contemporary, then, is he "who firmly holds his gaze on his own time so as to perceive not its light, but rather its darkness." A rare observer can see light within this darkness, but only as a "too soon" that is also "too late," an "already" that is also a "not yet."[8] Agamben then ruminates on several examples, in each case evoking others who have speculated on these questions: the logic of fashion (Baudelaire and Barthes), the archaic within the avant-garde's thirst for origins (Poggioli and Baudrillard), the as-yet "unlived" of the present asking us for an archaeological reading of it as a future-filled past (Jameson), and St. Paul's revelation that every present is filled with the potential of the Messiah's return, making us all potential contemporaries of Christ (Kierkegaard). Walter Benjamin brilliantly elaborated this last insight in his concept of the "dialectical image," as did Foucault in his "archaeology of knowledge" project, and Jacques Derrida in his concept of *a-venir*, the truth to come—each a description of what it is to perceive, as a living component of the present, the multitemporal nature of past and future actuality. Insights of this kind have, of course, always been available. Those who had them were the true contemporaries of their eras. St. Augustine, thinking about time in the years 378–79, shares this quality with Benjamin in 1940.

"Contemporariness" is, in this sense, "natural" to insightful speculation on what it is to be in time. Because Agamben is not taking a historical or geopolitical perspective in this text (as distinct from his major contributions in these fields), he does not go on to claim that insights of this kind are especially pertinent to the understanding of contemporary experience now, nor that they are more widely held these days by increasing numbers of intellectuals.[9] I suggest that they are, in fact, eclipsing other kinds of insight into the past, the present, and the future (indeed, that they place the famous triad itself into question). I argue that this is what the times require of us, more so than any other kind of understanding, modern or postmodern, in whatever variant. Almost everything about public culture, economic life, and political processes *invite* us to be contemporary in the obvious sense—that is, to take "our times" on their own terms, in their own words (including "the contemporary"), appearances, and images. But the deeper currents of today's contemporaneity *require* us to be their critical, skeptical contemporaries in the sense that Agamben begins to sketch.

Some crucial aspects of the topic are surprisingly underdeveloped. The sense of being "in" *this* time, *these times*, and "out of" them *at the same time* is, indeed, pervasive. Agamben offers a sequence of metaphors of this state of experience—all intensely poetic and theoretically suggestive—but does little to describe it directly. Each of the authors he cites or alludes to struggles to evoke the experience of feeling that one is in a different kind of time than one that is recalled, a time that currently seems to be common to most of one's contemporaries, a collective time that one also shares. Certain passages indicate that he is sensitive to this state, but less (in this text) to its historicity. "Whoever has seen the skyscrapers of New York for the first time arriving from the ocean at dawn has immediately perceived this archaic *facies* of the present, this contiguousness with the ruins that the atemporal images of September 11th have made evident to us all."[10] This passage evokes a classic experience of modernity displaying itself (as a fascist bundle!) to all comers (as if all such arrivals were immigrants!), and then moves into today's contemporaneity, one definitively inflected with the imagery of 9/11 attacks, along with much else. The reference is so brief that I am uncertain whether I have just read a brilliant encapsulation of the argument of *The Architecture of Aftermath*, or an insouciant gesture toward the capacity of contemporaneity to oblige everything to start again, ab initio, while also shouldering the burden of multiple pasts.

Because he is puzzling over the nature of contemporariness as an, in principle, universal experience, it is of no relevance to him that his instinctive frame of reference is modernity. Mandelstam's poem was written in 1923, and its immediate precedent is the "long" nineteenth century that broke apart during the years of World War I and the Russian Revolution. We can, however, extrapolate its message for our recent millennial transition. It says, the crushing of vertebrae marked the entire twentieth century. For the imagery of spreading darkness, Agamben could have traced a trajectory from Goya's *Black Paintings* to Michelangelo Antonioni's *L'Eclisse*, from Victor Hugo to *Apocalypse Now*, or from Nietzsche's madness through James Joyce's epiphanies and Freud's discontent to the Marxist melancholia of the Frankfurt School of critical theorists. In our contemporaneity, we have become fully aware of the prevalence of dark matter in the universe. We just cannot see it.

But we *can* see the lineaments of other kinds of time within it. To my eye, the most fecund of Agamben's observations points us toward the possibility, and indeed, the necessity, of grasping that certain present relationships between multiple temporalities constitute a new kind of historical phenomena. I pursue this point throughout this chapter, as it is pivotal to the possibility of a truly contemporary way of doing art history. A key passage is this: "Those who have tried to think about contemporariness have been able to do so by splitting it up into several times, by introducing into time an essential dishomogeneity. Those who say 'my time' actually divide time—they inscribe into it a caesura and a discontinuity. But precisely by means of this caesura, this interpolation of the present into the inert homogeneity of linear time, the contemporary puts to work a special relationship between the different times." From which it follows that "the contemporary" thinker is one who, "dividing and interpolating time, is capable of transforming it and putting it in relation to other times. He is able to read history in unforeseen ways, to 'cite it' according to a necessity that does not arise in any way from his will, but from an exigency to which he cannot not respond." His final metaphor follows immediately: "It is as if this invisible light that is the darkness of the present cast its shadow on the past, so that the past, touched by this shadow, acquired the ability to respond to the darkness of the now." If, he concludes, we are able to respond to this exigency and this shadow, we may become contemporaries of "not only our century and the 'now,' but also of its figures in the texts and documents of the past."[11]

That is it, for the contemporary intellectual, in a nutshell.

NANCY'S ORIGINALITY

In 2006, Jean-Luc Nancy began a lecture by explaining why he chose "Art Today" as his title instead of the subject on which he had been invited to speak: "Contemporary Art." He offered the usual reasons, each of them acknowledging one of the meanings of the concept, together amounting to a slippery domain that cannot take one name for itself: contemporary art is an art-historical category still in formation; in ordinary usage, "contemporary" means the past twenty or thirty years; it excludes the art being made in precontemporary modes and thus cannot encompass all current art; and, finally, using it to name kinds of art "violates" not only the traditional categories of the practice-based (plastic) arts but also more recent ones, such as "performance art." In the face of such confusion, "How is it possible that in the history of art we have come to adopt a category that does not designate any particular aesthetic modality the way we would, once, describe hyperrealism, cubism, or even 'body art' or 'land art,' but a category that simply bears the name 'contemporary'?"[12]

He was not tempted to treat this confusion as an indicator of the vacuity of contemporary "thought." Nor did he see it as evidence of the triumph of the witless presentism of those who live only to consume the latest offering, in art as in the general culture. Rather, he went straight to *origins*.[13] At the moment of making, every work of art is ipso facto contemporary with other art being made at the same time. It is also contemporary with its own times in the general sense. Every work of art, therefore, enables us (the artist, the viewer) to feel a "certain formation of the contemporary world, a certain shaping, a certain perception of self in the world." It does so not in the form of an ideological statement ("the meaning of the world is this") but more as a kind of suggestive shaping of possibilities, one that "allows for a circulation of recognitions, identifications, feelings, but without fixing them in a final signification."[14] Thus the contributions of Giotto, Michelangelo, Caravaggio, and others who give us more than the Christian program that occasioned their masterworks, and the secular artists—Picasso, Cézanne, Brâncuşi, and Proust are among his examples—whose art exceeds the factuality of the everyday from which they began. The worlds that they (as artists) are, the worlds that they create, are "there every time to open the world to itself, to its possibility of world." Nancy abhors works of art that "offer a surcharge of significations," conveying messages that seem too obvious and thus effecting a closure for all concerned.[15]

World making in and by works of art is, as Heidegger and, more recently, W. J. T. Mitchell and Caroline A. Jones have shown, as fundamental to the practice of art as is the contemporaneity of every work of art.[16] What, then, is so special about the kind of art that is designated "contemporary"? Or, better, what qualities related to worlding might a work of contemporary art be said to possess? Nancy's first stab at this is that "contemporary art could be defined as the opening of a form that is above all a question, the form of a question." He is not alone in highlighting the interrogatory gesturing of contemporary artists (in contrast to the projective impulses of modernist artists, and the propositional character of late modern transitional art). He quickly realizes, however, that commitment to the interrogatory is not enough: "Perhaps a question does not entirely make a world, or a world in which the circulation of meaning is solely an interrogative and anxious circulation, sometimes anguished; it's a difficult world, a fragile world, an unsettling world."[17]

We might expect that these terms would invite him to attach art practice to the broader condition of being in the world today. He does not take this path, trying out first the (opposite) route of proposing, "Art today is an art that, above all else, asks: 'what is art?'"[18] This is, of course, the central question of one of the two great strands of twentieth-century art, the conceptualist questioning initiated by Duchamp, in contrast to the formal and figural elaborations continued by Picasso and Matisse. Duchamp's lead was taken up by conceptualist artists during the 1970s and acted out in the public provocations of the Young British Artists (yBa) during the 1990s. It was also the question that Andy Warhol's 1963 *Brillo Box* exhibition provoked for Arthur Danto, occasioning the answer: whatever the art world says that it is.[19] Nancy does not pursue this development to its current, most obvious instantiation, where every person adept at any form of social media undertakes art-like practices as a matter of everyday course, and many artists everywhere seek to make art virtually indistinguishable from such practices. Today, the question is, in effect, reversed: "What, nowadays, is not art?"[20] Against this merging and melding, the most ambitious artists take on the challenge of finding new way to make this distinction.

Nancy does, however, offer an unusual inflection on Duchamp's gesture via the readymade, reading it as staging a rendezvous with that which, until that moment of the artist's designation, was not regarded as art: "The question of art is obviously posed as the question of the formation of forms for which no preliminary form is given." By "preliminary form" he means "schema" in Kant's sense, the nonsensible that precedes and makes possible the sensible. He does the same with his suggestion that Picasso's *Guernica* was the last history painting in the grand manner that had prevailed since the later eighteenth century. From this observation, Nancy draws the implication that, subsequently, signification itself went into crisis (one famously identified by Foucault as posthuman and Lyotard as postmodernism): "That whole ensemble of possible schematisms disappeared, even the schematism of man himself, of different figures of man and humanity. . . . [T]his disappearance is what characterizes the present world, which causes us to be in a world that is in a way at a loss for world, at a loss for meaning." This sudden absence of "great schemas, great regulating ideas, whether they be religious, political and hence also aesthetic" removes the "supports" of art, the bases on which artistic form arises. Contemporary art, therefore (and again echoing Danto), begins from "this shapeless state of self."[21] On this shaky ground, contemporary art asks the question "What is art?" necessarily in a new way, one that Duchamp prefigures—perhaps as a lone but increasingly influential precursor, his influence increasing with the accelerating evaporation of the master narratives.

Nancy is here moving toward identifying one of the key elements of what I see as a world-historical shift from modernity through postmodernity to contemporaneity. And he picks out some of the implications for art making in such circumstances. But, having seen a set of connections between epochal changes in world picturing and the interrogatory nature of contemporary art, he retreats toward a set of his core beliefs, above all those concerning art as a fundamental *gesture*, one that "puts us in direct communication with the creation of the world." In favor neither of art for art's sake, nor of art dedicated to religious, political, or ethical purpose, Nancy celebrates art as an act that manifests being, that brings worlds into being. The closest he gets toward identifying what might be contemporary about such art today is this remark: "I would say that a contemporary signal is a signal towards this: there is always, again, as before, there is always the possibility of making a world, it opens up a world to us." He links this with the French preference for the term *mondialisation*—the worldwide creation and circulation of sense by all concerned—over the Euro-America-centric economic and geopolitical schematism underlying the term "globalization."[22]

In the limited framework of a single lecture, we cannot expect more than brief allusions to how contemporary art manifests the spirit of contemporaneity, or how it might be shaped by, or in turn itself shape, broader contemporary conditions. Nancy has, at least, brought his core insights about artistic creativity and metaphysical presence to bear on these questions. To me, the most useful provocation is his recognition that in Duchamp's gesture— and, we might add, that of countless conceptualist artists after him, especially since the 1970s—"the question of art is obviously posed as the question of the formation of forms for which no preliminary form is given."[23] Postmodernist practice, with its reliance on appropriation and pastiche, takes another, more superficial track. What I have called the recursive instinct in remodernist art also relies on preliminary forms, those given by earlier modernist artists' efforts to work ab initio. When we focus on the deeper levels where artistic form originates, can we say that the search for form at these levels is shaped in distinctive ways within contemporary conditions? Today, artists search for the supports that will generate form within a worldscape across which great schematisms—globalization, decolonization, fundamentalism—continue to contend for universal dominance. Yet these schematisms are destined to fail because they presume modern, or antimodern, not contemporary world pictures. Can we speak, nevertheless, about compositional forms that are distinctively contemporary? I believe that we can, and I point to many of them in the earlier chapters in this book.[24] They are, however, discernible only from the close-ups afforded by engaged criticism and from the application of a theory of contemporaneity, not from within the inclination toward generalization about art's eternal recurrence toward its origins that haunts thinkers like Nancy.

RANCIÈRE'S REGIMES

In recent years, the philosophical thinking of Jacques Rancière has, for many art worlders, come to eclipse that of Giorgio Agamben as the standard repository of "all the theory we need." Among active philosophers, except Peter Osborne, Rancière is most familiar with contemporary art, its worlds, and its agents. He believes it to be the current instantiation of an "aesthetic regime of art" that formed during the nineteenth century, originating in Romanticism.

Taking up Foucault's description of discursive formations as "regimes of truth," Rancière defines particular "regimes of the arts" as "a specific type of connection between ways of producing works of art or developing practices, forms of visibility that disclose them, and ways of conceptualizing the former and the latter."[25] In the West, he identifies three as having evolved since ancient Greece. First, the "ethical regime of images," within which the primary concern is the effect of art on the ethos, or way of life, of communities. Plato's polemic against the simulacra offered by paintings, poems, and plays was a call for just such a regime. Second, Aristotle's coupling of poesis and mimesis aimed to establish a "representative regime of art," which accepts art's fictional premise but seeks to contain fiction's potential unruliness by defining the forms proper to it: hierarchies of genre and subject matter; principles such as appropriateness, verisimilitude, and correspondence; distinctions between the arts; and so forth. Third, the "aesthetic regime of the arts" distinguishes "a sensible mode of being specific to artistic products"; it "asserts the absolute singularity of art" and "establishes the autonomy of art," yet it does so, Rancière insists, as a form of modeling the state of being, the kind of emancipation best suited to all—Friedrich Schiller's ideal of mankind aspiring to an "aesthetic state" is, he argues, this regime's "first manifesto."[26] While the two ancient regimes remain with us, the third prevails in modern and contemporary societies.

In his lectures and books, Rancière frequently cites works by contemporary artists to illustrate specific points, and he occasionally discusses a work, such as Jean-Luc Godard's *Histoire(s) du cinéma*, in detail.[27] A 2007 interview in *Artforum* is the most felicitous illumination of the relevance of his general concepts to contemporary art and its theorization. Recalling the moment in France, post-1968, during which he saw the necessity to work against the process of "using defined periods and great historical ruptures to impose interdictions," he characterizes his work on "labor's past" and "art's present" as the same effort "to break down the great divisions—science and ideology, high culture and popular culture, representation and the unrepresentable, the modern and the postmodern, etc.—to contrast historical necessity with a topography of the configuration of possibilities, a perception of the multiple alternations and displacements that make up forms of political subjectivization and artistic invention."[28] He dismisses abstract distinctions between art and politics, along with ideologically branded ones, in favor of paying careful attention to the actual situations in which such distinctions are drawn, and to the inherent indeterminacy of both kinds of distinction. Paralleling his broader conception that making divisions within "the regime of the sensible" is the work of thought and of action in the world (it is "politics" as he sees it, ranging from the "police" actions of the state, industry, commerce, and institutions to the "dissensus" of opposition to the false consensus that such agencies create), he concentrates on what he names "the aesthetic regime of art," describing it as the "paradox wherein art was defined and institutionalized as a sphere of common experience at the very moment when the boundaries between what is and isn't art were being erased." This indeterminable status means that artistic agency is not bound to pursue the "historical mission" of art (which, he believes, it would necessarily fail to fulfill), or to become part of a utopia (which, he believes, would necessarily take a totalitarian form). Art is not, in his view, required to be overtly, publicly "political" in the sense of denouncing "the society of the spectacle" or "consumer society," nor should it aim to activate a spectator who is (falsely) presumed to be passive. Art should renounce "the authority of the imposed message, the target audience, and the univocal mode of explicating the world"; it will become free "when it stops *wanting* to emancipate us." Instead, he insists, "an artistic intervention can be political by modifying the visible, the ways of perceiving it and expressing it, of experiencing it as tolerable or intolerable," while the "aesthetic dimension" of politics is "a common landscape of the given and the possible." Between the two is a "terrain of the sensible on which artistic gestures shake up our modes of perception and on which political gestures redefine our capacity for action." Accordingly, Rancière prefers "dissensus" to "resistance" and similar critical, oppositional approaches. He defines dissensus in disappointingly abstract terms, as "a modification of the co-ordinates of the sensible, a spectacle or a tonality that replaces another."[29]

Rancière's more concrete studies of dissensus within teaching and labor, such as his advocacy of the genuine knowledge possessed by "the ignorant schoolmaster," have been of greater use value.[30] Claire Bishop, for one, drew on them for her descriptions of the goals of participatory art practices, especially the concept of "the emancipated spectator."[31] Yet in the 2007 *Artforum* interview, Rancière was quite specific about the kind of dissenting versus consensual art he had in mind. Gently rejecting the interviewers' condescending dismissal of certain well-known "socially engaged" works as driven by "nostalgia for the counter-culture," he praises Jeremy Deller's *Battle of Orgreave (An Injury to One Is an Injury to All)*—a reenactment in 2001 of a 1984 clash between police and striking miners in a Yorkshire village, in which the artist invited those originally involved to act roles from the other side of that political divide—for breaking up "the dominant imagery of a world where there would otherwise be nothing but high-tech virtuosos or the occasional amused glance at the past, which is complicit with this vision."[32] Similarly, works by Josephine Meckseper on recent protest activity as a kind of youth culture, Sam Durant on sloganeering, Alfredo Jaar on the West's turning a blind eye toward the massacres in Rwanda, the films of Pedro Costa, the installations of Paul Chan, and the blurring of fact, fiction, and fantasy by Walid Raad, Jalal Toufic, and other Lebanese artists—Rancière values each of these for raising awareness of an egregious political division of the sensible, but for doing so in specifically *aesthetic* modes.

Rancière goes on to remark, "A political declaration or manifestation, like an artistic form, is an arrangement of words, a montage of gestures, an occupation of spaces. In both cases what is produced is a modification of the fabric of the sensible, a transformation of the visible given, intensities, names that one can give to things, the landscape of the possible." In contrast, he sees certain works by Jeff Koons, Paul McCarthy, and Jason Rhoades, for example, as pretending to reveal "the omnipotence of market flows, the reign of the spectacle, the pornography of power," when in fact they are entirely "integrated into the space of consensus." He suggests, "If there is a circulation that could be stopped at this point, it's this circulation of stereotypes that critique stereotypes, giant stuffed animals that denounce our infantilization, media images that denounce the media, spectacular installations that denounce the spectacle." Yet if these artists' complicity with consensus is blatant enough, less obvious invitations to indirect complicity are everywhere, even in the most radical-seeming ideas and practices. Thus, "I try to redraw the map of the thinkable in order to bring out the impossibilities and prohibitions that are often lodged at the very heart of thought that imagines itself to be subversive."[33]

These formulations have been welcomed by some and opposed by others. T. J. Demos, for example, notes that "one useful feature" of Rancière's writing is "the reconceptualization of art's autonomy as a potential zone beyond the determinations of governmental policy or activist tactics, one that supersedes as well autonomy's traditional associations with isolationist escapism and artistic essentialism."[34] In contrast, Hal Foster sees Rancière's "redistribution of the sensible" as "a panacea, and, when pitted against the capitalist 'transformation of things into signs,' it is little more than wishful thinking, the new opiate of the art world Left."[35]

To my mind, Rancière's core concept, *le partage du sensible* (the distribution the sensible)—the idea that implicit laws govern our perception of the world and that our perceptions shape explicit laws as well as dissent from these laws, along with our senses of self and our possibilities for creativity—is of such generality that it risks amounting to little more than a simple sociology or, at most, an abstract, apolitical version of Marxist theories of ideology. Prior to any politics, its initiating instinct is to aestheticize experience, totally. And it does so with "politics" as its abhorrent other.

Rancière's regimes are, of course, not intended as art history per se, although he does introduce them by saying, "With regard to what we call *art*, it is in fact possible to distinguish, within the Western tradition, three major regimes of identification."[36] The qualifier regarding the West is essential here, because these regimes are not readily identifiable elsewhere. Regarding the lineages treated in even the most conventional Western art histories, the three regimes leave untouched vast swathes of temporal and geographic territory, including the arts of Indigenous peoples, for example, among many others. What the regimes do cover is usually described as classical art, realism, Romanticism, neoclassicism, or modernism, although Rancière is at pains to avoid these style terms. He explicitly attacks Greenbergian formalism as a reductive modernism (which it was) and regards politically purposed avant-gardism as formalism's twin, the other half of a mistaken belief that modern art is beholden to modernity's unidirectionality. Through a series of convoluted assertions, he dismisses both kinds of modernism as amounting to no more than a self-deluded "modernitarism."[37] As Aleš Erjavec notes, this attack on modernism seems "problematic and risky because it requires a complete reinterpretation of the art of the past two centuries," without giving us a persuasive reason for doing so, or providing an alternative historical hypothesis.[38] In the essays collected in *Aisthesis*, Rancière models a particularistic, immersive approach to instantiations of the aesthetic regime of the arts, exploring in detail works of art, or ideas about art, from Johann Joachim Winkelmann to James Agee.[39] All are modern. Considered as art history, Rancière's approach is highly selective. He dismisses as self-delusion the critiques internal to modernist art, theory, and institutional practice; ignores the strong antimodernist currents that evolved alongside twentieth-century Euromodernism; seems ignorant of the multiple modernities that grew during the same period; and fails to recognize the transformations in art all over the world since the 1960s as a historical paradigm shift. For all his awareness of contemporary works of art and his references to important exhibitions, it never occurs to him that the antinomies of the contemporary condition may be birthing a contemporary regime of the visual image that is not entirely complicit with rampant, globalized capitalism, but that contains within it the seeds of other ways of world-being.[40]

In Néstor García Canclini's 2014 book *Art beyond Itself: Anthropology for a Society without a Story Line*, the Mexican sociologist suggests another way of splitting the impasse between interpretations that tend toward taking art's autonomy as basic and those that see art as of value only when it occurs as an effective cultural, social, or political intervention. He proposes instead that we accept that "art is the place of immanence—the place where we catch sight of things that are just at the point of occurring." This is to make contemporaneity itself the main quality, and subject, of contemporary art, to elevate a quality that much art has had throughout time into one that is specific to the present situation. García Canclini tends in this direction when he elaborates: "Art gains its attraction in part from the fact that it proclaims something that could happen, promising meaning or modifying meaning through insinuations. It makes no unbreakable commitment to hard facts. It leaves what it says hanging."[41] Yet these generalizations are designed to highlight art's current situation, which in his view might be termed "postautonomous." This situation is a direct outcome of having to work within the larger world situation, which, as his title indicates, consists of an assemblage of societies without a shared or even dominant storyline:

> Art became postautonomous in a world that doesn't know what to do with the insignificance or contradictions of narratives. When we talk about this art, disseminated in a globalization that hasn't managed to articulate itself, we can no longer think of a directional history or a transition state of a society unsure of which model for development to choose. We are long past the time when artists argued about what they should do to change life, or at least to represent its transitions by talking about what "the system" was concealing. They can hardly even act, like victims of a catastrophe who try to organize themselves, in the immanence of what might happen next, or in the barely explicable ruins of what globalization has destroyed. Art now works in the footsteps of the ungovernable.[42]

In these circumstances, the most the contemporary artist can do—indeed, should do—is seek "a place for creative transgression, for critical dissent, and for that sense of immanence."[43] My sentiments exactly.

Peter Osborne's *Anywhere or Not at All: Philosophy of Contemporary Art* (2013) is, to date, the most substantial and sustained engagement by a philosopher with contemporary art as it relates to the idea of contemporaneity.[44] For that reason alone, it is worthy of close attention. We do not find this kind of attention in literary theorist Leland del la Durantaye's *Artforum* review of the book, which began from the premise that "the point of a philosophy of contemporary art must be to better illuminate what it is like to experience the art of our time."[45] This is weak: it conjures armchair speculation exercised by an ideal viewer. In contrast, Osborne sets out to articulate something more than a set of reasonable, plausible responses to the art around us. He aims to discern what drives this art and, above all, how it manifests our current contemporaneity. He is concerned not merely with the ideas and practices of those who produce and consume this art, but with what it does as a manifestation of world-being. This is an aim that would flesh out his subtitle and be worthily named "a philosophy of art."

Osborne presents his "main thesis" in these bald terms: "It is the convergence and mutual conditioning of historical transformations in the ontology of the artwork and the social relations of art space . . . that makes contemporary art possible, in the emphatic sense of being an art of contemporaneity." He notes that various "de-bordering" procedures in art and its social settings have occurred. "This has been an extraordinarily complicated and profoundly contradictory historical process, in which artists, art-institutions and markets have negotiated the politics of regionalism, postcolonial nationalism and migration, in order to overwrite the open spatial logic of post-conceptual art with global political-economic dynamics."[46]

Awkwardly put, but a strong hypothesis. It pinpoints two of the three currents that I have outlined in books such as *Contemporary Art: World Currents* and sets these two currents into the same dialectical struggle that I identify and explore in recent writing, including this book. As I try to do, Osborne maps much of the contested terrain within and between these currents, but with a strong presumption in favor of the first. Looked at from outside these debates, one might read his book as registering the influence of these contestations on his philosophical approach. To his credit, his text registers openness to the constant disruption of art-theoretical reflection by the critical, antinomic art practices to which it is so closely wedded. In this sense, it is not a philosophy of art but an art of philosophy that is nascent in Osborne's enterprise. Art, not philosophy, has the agency here. This is an idea with a long lineage in this philosophical tradition, notably for Martin Heidegger and Walter Benjamin, with Alain Badiou prominent among its more recent proponents.[47]

In Ian McLean's careful analysis of *Anywhere or Not at All*, he comments that Osborne does his philosophical work from perspectives entirely within Western thought and is blind to what McLean calls the "post-Western" character of much contemporary life, thought, and art.[48] More precisely, Osborne thinks within a specific line of post-Hegelianism, stemming, as he proudly announces in his introduction, from Theodor W. Adorno in the most immediate instance; but, as his book constantly demonstrates, he is most deeply indebted to the system-subject dynamic in early nineteenth-century German Romantic philosophy, and in style, he owes most to Heidegger's lectures. While fully aware of the existence of other modes of thought, Osborne presumes that this is the only one that counts *as philosophy*, that is, the only one truly capable of arriving at universally valid truth claims.

The result is that, rather than presenting an overall "philosophy of contemporary art," Osborne offers an account of the theoretical grounding of art produced within a significant subcurrent of one of the three main currents I identify in my approach to art made in the conditions of contemporaneity—namely, the tendency within the first current, Euro-American contemporary art, that I have dubbed remodernism. As I outline in previous chapters, remodernism pursues new ways of transforming artistic mediums—especially painting, sculpture, and photography—that were brought to a high level of refinement during the early and mid-twentieth century, so that these mediums can carry content as pertinent as that explored in more contemporary modes, such as installation, video, and performance. Adornian criticality *is* the philosophical approach most appropriate to the artists, theorists, and institutions that drive this subcurrent. Among those who theorize postconceptual art, Osborne has set a new, higher standard, unmatched, certainly, in its philosophical depth.

To add to McLean's argument, I suggest that Osborne is also, paradoxically (and, as he would say, inevitably), trapped by his own most trenchant critical insight. Osborne rightly condemns much discourse about the contemporary, showing, more thoroughly than anyone else has to date, that it is a process of constant, self-serving *fictionalization*. In disassembling the ideational fictions that circulate within much contemporary art discourse, Osborne joins a growing chorus of writers, some of whom have been making these points in similar ways for over a decade now. In England alone, this chorus includes Julian Stallabrass, Gillian Perry, Jonathan Harris, and many others. None is acknowledged in Osborne's book, which from the outset marks itself off from what he regards as the "rushed" and "failed" efforts of contemporary art critics, historians, and "commentators" to theorize their subject.

Osborne is making a core claim that goes beyond the more specific critiques made by the relatively few critical voices in contemporary art discourse. "The concept of the contemporary ... is a productive act of the imagination to the extent to which it performatively projects a non-existent unity onto the disjunctive relations between coeval times. In this respect, in rendering present the absent time of a unity of present times, all constructions of the contemporary are *fictional*, in the sense of fictional as a narrative mode." He is right to go on to say that this is, in fact, "an *operative* fiction: it *regulates the division* between the past and the present within the present." That is, it projects the false sense that our contemporary condition, "albeit internally disjunctive," is "a single historical time." Such a notion, as he says, is "inherently problematic but increasingly inevitable," a kind of necessary evil.[49] Incidentally, this picks up Fredric Jameson's characterization of modernism as a self-defining, historicizing narrative rather than a world-historical reality, an argument outlined in his book *A Singular Modernity*.[50] Osborne applies this idea to contemporary art whole cloth, a repetition that brings contemporaneity, and contemporary art, however disruptively, back within the purview of modernity and modernism.

Osborne is quite clear that "the contemporary" is "primarily a global or planetary fiction," "a fiction of global transnationality" that has "recently displaced the 140-hegemony of an internationalist imaginary, 1848–1989, which came in a variety of political forms," notably modernity, capitalism, and socialism. Today, he goes on to say, "the contemporary (the fictive relational unity of the historical present) is transnational because our modernity is that of a tendentially global capital."[51] He is, of course, fully aware that today, art is made around the world, and that it circulates everywhere. McLean cites Osborne's only allusion to Indigenous artists, in which he rightly condemns their being constructed as "natives" within this transnational discourse (actually Indigenous artists appear only by inference among those artists living in countries that have been or are still subject to colonization). That passage is followed by this paragraph:

This is one of the main functions of the new biennales: they are cultural representatives of the market idea of a global system of societies. They mediate exchange relations with artists via the latest cultural discourse on "globalization," in order to put the latest version of the contemporary on show. Furthermore, by virtue of their power of assembly, international biennales are manifestations of the cultural-economic power of the "center," *wherever* they crop up and *whatever* they show. In short, they are the Research and Development branch of the transnationalization of the culture industry.[52]

To me, this is a half-truth taken as the whole story; it downplays the resistances to globalization, and the challenges to parochialism, that biennials everywhere make possible (in ways always specific to the place and time) but by no means guarantee.[53] It subjects them to the always-already triumph of a presumptively hegemonic global capital. Indeed, Osborne concludes this book by describing the implacable limits imposed by the "horizons of expectation" endlessly woven by dreams of materialist progress, the horizon of a possible third way between socialism and capitalism that was smashed by the rush to money after 1989, and the "counterhorizon" opened up by China's embrace of markets within state management. What hope for art in such a context? "At its best, contemporary art models experimental practices of negation that puncture horizons of expectation."[54]

With this, Osborne ends up in the same place as "the second-generation *October* art historians" whom he pillories in his introduction as incapable of exercising critical judgment about contemporary art.[55] He joins, in fact, the first-generation Octobrists, who continue to exercise such judgment by being unequivocal about their preference for art that, even today, pursues the negation so trenchantly theorized by Adorno over sixty years ago.

We are entitled to ask, *This* is what it is to be contemporary? This is contemporary theory? This is a philosophy adequate to the kinds of contemporary art being made in the world today? Surely, it, too, is an operative fiction, but one that is becoming less operative every day.

Osborne's concept of postconceptual art is definitive for him, and, for him, is definitive of contemporary art per se. He does not mean this "at the level of style, medium, movement, or periodization. . . . Rather, it is a claim made at the level of the historical ontology of the artwork—its mode of being, what it most fundamentally is." As the work of Robert Smithson prefigures, contemporary art is a *transcategorical* practice, which Osborne describes as distinct from "the self-misunderstanding of the main proponents of 'Conceptual Art' (through [whom] the category was, historically, critically, constituted) of art's ideational, ontological, purity."[56]

Who among the 1970s conceptual artists believed *that* about art's purity?[57] While Osborne is a respected chronicler of conceptual art, such a reductive, secondhand, textbook-style summary is disappointing. It is as strange as the long passage that takes Sol LeWitt as the paradigmatic Conceptual Artist (this reads oddly from Art & Language points of view, post-1969).

Perhaps, however, this combination of reductiveness (regarding conceptual art) and expansiveness (regarding the core postconceptual character of contemporary art) indicates something larger and more interesting about Osborne's enterprise. To me, *Anywhere or Not at All* reads as a text written within a philosophical tradition that is, today, profoundly troubled by the antinomies driving contemporary life, thought, and art. A narrowing toward essentialism while claiming to constitute the core of whatever really counts as worthy art today is a rational response in the face of such an onslaught, as is a frank, reflexive accounting of its impact. From Osborne, we get both.

A final point about method, which turns out, somewhat surprisingly, to be about art-historical method. Strangely, despite Osborne's explicit rejection of art-historical approaches, throughout *Anywhere or Not at All*, he constantly recurs to periodization, specifically quite conventional art-historical kinds that chart relationships over time between artworks and their "times." There are many echoes of my account of multiple, localized, yet connected modernities followed by three currents within contemporary conditions, but he insists that the currents he identifies succeed one another in time, rather than manifest a more eccentric, historically contingent cotemporality. On pages 18–22 he identifies three turning points: when the neo-avant-gardes emerged after 1945; contemporary art's appearance around 1960; and, in 1989, the post-avant-garde, the dominance of the culture industry, and transnationalization. This is quite orthodox. On pages 78–86, these developments are further refined to be the last of several charts of the many factors that cluster to constitute periods within the history of modernism more generally. This is bold and original. In his chapter 6, he returns to the developments in his discussion of "art space," his term for art worlds. In each case, these periodizing pictures are offered as heuristics, getting closer each time to an account that might stick, which is his procedure throughout the book. But they remain provisional and do not account for the work of more than a relatively small number of the many contemporary artists working today in active and conscious response to the complex conditions of our contemporaneity.

Subsequent to *Anywhere or Not at All*, Osborne published a brief essay, "The Postconceptual Condition: Or, the Cultural Logic of High Capitalism Today," which offers the most trenchant account of his overall position. It contains his most explicit statement that what "contemporaneity" signifies most deeply is a new form of historical time—that is, "a new, internally disjunctive global historical-temporal form, a totalizing (but not thereby 'total,' since it is open to

no more than distributive unification), radically disjunctive, contemporaneity."
To think of it as a *condition* is, he avers, historically new. As is evident from previous chapters in this book, I am in total accord with this perception and have
been arguing for acknowledgment of it since around 2000. His second major
claim—"Today, 'contemporary art,' critically understood, is a postconceptual
art"—is glossed as follows: "If we try to construct a critical concept of contemporary art from the dual standpoint of a historico-philosophical conception of contemporaneity and a rereading of the history of twentieth century
art—in its established sense as that art that is produced, circulated, exchanged,
consumed, and preserved within the art institutions of the global network of
capitalist societies—the idea of postconceptual art appears as the most intelligible and coherent way of critically unifying this field, historically, within the
present."[58] My caveat here, as noted above, is that contemporary art is scarcely
confined to "the global network of capitalist societies," and further, even within
them, contemporary arts of consequence that take quite other forms have been
present for decades, and continue to emerge.

As in *Anywhere or Not at All*, Osborne urges the term "postconceptual"
as the best descriptor of the *condition* of contemporary art, both its "state of
being" and "the totality of conditions that determine it as 'art.'" He repeats
his points about its "transcategorical" character, which I would support, and
concludes with this statement: "The successful postconceptual work traverses
(crosses, back and forth) the internal temporal disjunctions that constitute the
contemporary, constructing them in such a way as to express them, at the level
of the immanent duality—conceptual and aesthetic—of [their] form. Each a
condensed fragment of the worlding of the globe."[59] I strongly endorse this formulation, provided that the word "condition" appears after "the contemporary"
to mean, as we both do, our contemporaneity, and that the condensation that
is the real *work* of works of art is understood to be a worlding that genuinely
operates throughout the world, on a scale that includes but is not reducible to
or dominated by globalization, and that is shaped by the three currents and the
interactions between them that I have been advocating throughout this book.

THE DUTY OF THE ARTIST

In a recent essay, "The Historicity of the Contemporary Is Now!" visual and
sound artist, critic, and philosopher Jean-Philippe Antoine warned art historians that their relative absence from the scenes of contemporary art making
means, in the words of Mike Kelley, that, "Historical writing becomes a duty

for the artist at this point."[60] Antoine's essay is a fine example. He is refreshingly acute about just what history means to our contemporaries these days, not only to artists wishing to get their work, or that of undervalued colleagues, on the record. He argues that it continues to mean a lot, but in ways quite distinct from the enormous purchase that history had during modern times. Then, its determinative load seemed to grow ever heavier, and its tendency toward recursion accelerated, even as it continued to ruthlessly clear away pasts from its forward march. Antoine answers the narrower question about whether art history as a discipline is capable of writing histories of contemporary art with a vigorous "No!" The form of inquiry he advocates, which I will sketch in a moment, does not

> identify with the existing field of art history, which has a grievous record of stifling the new (as well, just for symmetry, heterogeneous ancientness), while privileging long chains of the same repetitious "influences." Adding "contemporary art" to a long list of centuries in order to bring to a close a universal history of art would be but a short-lived parody of previous historicist endeavors, and a spectacular misunderstanding of the unique methodological and, yes, ethical value of the contemporary for *all* historians.[61]

Leaving aside his use of "the contemporary," Antoine shares with many commentators the recognition that a sense of "uncanny untimeliness," as distinct from being utterly of and with the times as they present themselves, is the first and most striking feature of our current contemporaneity. He traces this awareness back to Friedrich Schiller, to the responsiveness of the poet and some of his contemporaries to Greek and Roman models, a particular past to which they wished to belong, while realizing at the same time that this was impossible, just as it was that they might wholly fit their own times. Antoine then sketches a lineage through the inspirations of subsequent artists, from the Romantic revivalists through the modernist primitivists, then up to Mark Lewis and Tacita Dean's revocations of modernist architecture, and Gerhard Richter's *Abstraktes Bild* series, parodies of modernist abstraction. Antoine argues that each of these appropriations, in different ways, attempts "to define the contemporary through specific connections to historical periods, picked out of a generic, a-historical past."[62] This is the contemporary difference. To put it in my metaphors: the contemporaneity of every past is now available to us, as if each of them was equidistant in space-time from where we are now, just beyond the horizon of the recent past, arranged as if in a galaxy, as stars that we might choose to visit on our improvised, constantly self-repairing, imagining projectile, to understand the temporalities in play in that particular past, and to find out how they might help us understand the temporalities at play our present.

Antoine notes that this sea change in understanding the nature of history's purchase on our present took some time to fully theorize. He usefully reminds us of the various types of temporal valuing plotted in Alois Riegl's landmark essay of 1903, "The Modern Cult of Monuments," and of Marcel Duchamp's expansion of the concept of art through his deployment of readymades. "This widely expanded definition means that art no longer operates as it used to, through the underwriting of the contemporary by supposedly eternal, time-free ideals. It now inhabits a vast, a-historical and boundless warehouse of ancientness, continually revisited and augmented by the present. There all past objects and events have become indifferently available for historical and artistic pick-up."[63] To my mind, these perceptions of the relationship between present and past times are themselves subject to evolutionary historical interpretation, or, at least, they were subject until recently. They count in a distinctive and more widespread way in contemporary conditions than they did before, during modern times. We are now required to hold in our minds simultaneously these two distinct senses of what it is to be in historical time. This leads to the paradox that their availability for historical pickup, to use his terms, has become more pervasive since around 1980, as frameworks such as progress and the inevitability of modernity proved themselves to be fragile constructs and the antinomies of our contemporaneity began to increasingly shape our situation. Antoine is back projecting from an undertheorized present, but this is a salutary exercise. It alerts us to the relatively recent arrival of the sense that modernity is now included in the "generic, a-historical past," and that it might have no more a determinative hold on us than certain earlier moments. More broadly, there is a growing recognition that the choice of which past, or pasts—along with which utopian elements, and which pragmatic fixes—we might use to compose our futures may not already be decided for us, but could be largely a matter of our choosing—provided, of course, that we can mobilize enough people willing to act in the name of that future. Before then, and as a vital part of this mobilization, visual artists can, as I have been arguing for decades, prefigure such possible futures, and many are actively doing so in their collages, installations, videos and films.

Antoine does not call for such an explicitly political project, but he is alert to the ethical dimension of historical inquiry at a time of such seeming ahistoricity. He rightly says that because the historical determinations have fallen away, "precisely because the contemporary work of art and the ancient thing don't already belong to established historical categories, they require—indeed, they *demand*—to become the focus of historical inquiry," otherwise art, thought, and action will be condemned to "reiterate previous constructs and petrified events." But what kind of historical inquiry?

> Such a history will be discontinuous. It will be fragmentary and anach-
> ronistic, as indeed are the relationships between present and past. As
> suggested earlier, one of the signal ways in which a present grows to dif-
> ferentiate itself from what it was, is by appointing, within the bound-
> less storehouse of a generic past, newly targeted moments. This means
> that the contemporary, far from identifying with a "present" reduced to
> a narrow and fugitive slice of chronological time, actually consists in the
> knitting together of a specific variety of times.[64]

These sentiments entirely accord with my emphasis on the contemporaneousness of different kinds of time within our contemporaneity; they echo my emphasis on multeity; and they suggest a mode of contemporary composition, one
available not only to artists, but also to curators, critics, historians, and thinkers
of all kinds—indeed, to all of us. Yet, the "knitting together of a specific variety
of times" is not a calming, regular procedure aimed at securing a habitus. It is
instead the outcome of a past object or event or place insisting on its relevance
to a present that would be ours, as we recover from the shock of its arrival, and
see why it has come to us now. The art to come can arrive as much from one of
our pasts as from the past of another, or it might be waiting for us in the future,
or be already here. I therefore agree with his remark that "acquiring an awareness
of who and what haunts us is a huge part of, if not the main affair in, shaping the
present, as unremarkable a task as it may appear in our present-obsessed times."[65]

CURRENT VERSUS CONTEMPORARY ART

Postconceptual artist Liam Gillick has also taken up Kelley's call. His recent reflections add a certain nuance to those of Antoine, not least because he demonstrates that an essential factor in what makes contemporary art contemporary is
the "industry and intelligence" of a small but growing lineage of artists—"from
Andy Warhol to Andrea Fraser to Hito Steyerl, from Jackson Pollock to Felix
Gonzalez-Torres to R. H. Quaytman"—who consciously work and think at the
edges of the contemporary art world, who are unavoidably immersed in it, but
who operate fundamentally at tangents to its core values, mapping out another
kind of art.[66] Gillick opens his argument describing the relationship between
contemporary conditions and what he prefers to call "current" art: "The term

contemporary art has historically implied a specific accommodation with a loose set of open-minded economic and political values that are mutable, global, and general and therefore have sufficed as an all-encompassing description of *what is being made now—wherever*. But the flexibility of contemporary art as a term is no longer sufficiently capable of encompassing all dynamic current art, if only because an increasing number of artists seek a radical differentiation." He tries out various descriptions of this "specific accommodation" and of various efforts to find a "radical differentiation" from it. Among the accommodations,

"[Artists experience] stress and anxiety about contemporary art's complicity, success, and limits as it attempts to operate as neoliberalism's critical double."

"Art today meanders in direct contradiction or apparently blind to the very significance of the key events that take place around it."

"The inclusiveness of the contemporary is under attack, as this very inclusiveness has helped suppress a critique of what art is and, more importantly, what comes next. We know what comes next as things stand—*more contemporary art*."

"Trying on different personalities is forgiven within this realm. The decision to change is an obligation. Burning paintings is the originating myth. The point is to join the highway via the onramp at full speed. Then choose which lane to occupy. Slowing down or getting on or off again is difficult and undesirable."

"The contemporary comes to terms with accommodation. Fundamental ideas are necessarily evaded, for the idiom of the contemporary still carries the lost late-modernist memory of the democratization of skill and active participation by the viewer. . . . By your nature you are a contemporary artist by taking the decision to announce yourself. . . . The basic assumption of the contemporary is that all we need . . . is a place to show—to be part of and just toward the edge of contemporary art."[67]

Among the radical differentiations,

"Art resides in power relations, speech acts, points of view, and extremely complicated semiotic games. Everything else is luster, hubris, or expressions of pious good taste."

"There has been a proliferation of discussions and parallel practices that appear to operate in a semiautonomous way alongside contemporary art. They ignore it or take [it] as an example of what not to do. A

good example might be the *Unitednationsplaza* and *Nightschool* projects in Berlin, Mexico DF, and New York."
"Current art cannot be left to idle with the contemporary as a question of taste or preferred subjectivity. There are real problems of differentiation that will be reshaped by the new academicization of the contemporary. The contemporary offers the multiplicity of artists we hope will coalesce into a force of implicit resistance, but the contemporary creates anxieties that ensure all operators within it are forever awaiting a specific cue for action."[68]

Yet, as this last quotation indicates, given the mutual implication that Gillick sees as definitive of "the contemporary," each of these trajectories constantly pollutes, or cross-pollinates, the others.

"The contemporary is marked by a displayed self-knowledge, a degree of social awareness, some tolerance, and a little bit of irony, all combined with an acknowledgment of the failure of modernism and postmodernism or at least a respect for trying to come to terms with the memory of something like that failure."
"All the while, students get smarter and recognizably different, ironic in a way that levers the critical tone a little higher and eases the zone a little wider. Within this vague contemporariness people see more and more than they saw before. This is the genius of the regime. Contemporary art is the perfect zone of deferral. No clarity can be overcomplicated when it is reproducing itself endlessly."
"Contemporary art is split and fragmented, and because of this it holds together against attacks both subtle and virulent and from both within and without. It is this simultaneous and constant splitting and fragmentation that gives contemporary art its strange endurance and prevents it from being transcended, at least for the time being."[69]

In his comments on how these developments might be understood as historical phenomena, Gillick sees a distinct difference between "artists, curators, critics, and historians, all of whom are operating within an amoebic system of modular subjectivities (seeing each art act as a moment, cumulative or not), and those who use documentary, research, discourse as a way to attempt to keep alive the social and critical potential of art (seeing borders, boundaries, and paths)." Whether pinpointing the accumulations of amoebas or discerning the links and ruptures in chains, those who think about flows in contemporary art should, he believes, pay attention to recent pasts and near futures, not confine themselves to close or distant versions of either. Feeling that it "is urgent to establish the origins of contemporary art and whether it has an endpoint," he asks, "What period are we in?" and "Are we permanently contemporary?" to which he replies, "It seems unlikely." Finally, he regards both kinds of discourse around contemporary art—the amoebic and the chained—as locked into a "false duality" in which the proponents believe that "the art context is a perfect mirror of rampant neoliberal capitalism containing no resource to counter the complete reach of the marketization of every relationship pitched against an insistence on refusal and resistance via supersubjectivity, reiterated post-formalism, and the superficially political."[70] Put like this, both positions are at once self-subverting and easy prey.

Gillick is obviously an attentive reader of the theorists whose ideas on these subjects I am reviewing in this chapter and in earlier chapters. Indeed, he nominates as a "problem" the ways in which the theoretical writing of recent philosophers is embodied in and constantly reapplied to contemporary art. "They are at the base of most attempts to produce advanced art, even when barely understood by the artist, and crucially are at the base of all attempts to analyze the art once it is produced, even when poorly applied or denied by the critic or curator or artist." These same artworks come to the attention of these same philosophers, and a reciprocal "feedback loop" is generated.[71] His own analysis is, in the end, subject to a similar imbrication, which he acknowledges, yet he doggedly persists (as he must) in teasing out a differentiation. It takes the form of what he names as a "postcontemporary" artistic practice, in which artists, alone yet working within highly connected yet transient groupings, pursue ways of knowing the world that closely parallel those of the knowledge worker within neoliberal capitalism but remain at a distance, mostly because artistic workers have the freedom to *withhold* what they find.[72] Gillick's position resonates within his own language: I have cited it with some frequency and in some density precisely because its tone consciously echoes that of these same knowledge workers, even as he seeks to leaven it with some (hopefully) distancing differentiations.

POSTCONTEMPORARY CONTEMPLATIONS

Does Gillick's use of "postcontemporary" amount to something more than a marker of future possibility, a pro forma acknowledgment that things will inevitably change as artists become more and more like other members of the creative class? Since the 1990s, the term has appeared occasionally, sporadically, in a minor key, and with little effect. Yet that might be changing, as some attempts are now being made to theorize it and make broad claims for its purchase. How do they stand relative to the ideas about contemporary art and contemporaneity I have been advancing in this book?

The one substantial usage prior to the present is the Duke University Press series Post-Contemporary Interventions, launched in 1989, with Fredric Jameson and Stanley Fish as its founding editors, later to be joined by Roberto M. Dainotto and Michael Hardt. Since then, over 120 titles have been published, the most recent in 2013. The original series description, written as a publicity statement, sought "to introduce its readers to the most innovative and ground-breaking work in a number of related disciplines," and claimed that "literary and cultural study has begun to move away from large abstractions and grand methods toward the construction of ad hoc contextual constellations. The trend reflects new conceptions of discourse and language, which encourage provisional constructions rather than systematic formulations. These constructions draw on a variety of movements such as New Historicism, neopragmatism, discourse analysis, a range of feminisms, post-Lacanian psychoanalysis, studies of mass culture and of Third World literatures, and post-modernisms of various kinds."[73]

In 1989, the term "intervention"—a favorite 1970s New Left word for "acts of theory" intended to disrupted prevailing paradigms and lead to action that changed the world in some progressive way—was fast becoming an anachronism. Presumably, the series editors consciously chose to recall that earlier, now endangered, politics. The series aimed to target established approaches to literature and culture, as well as, more generally, the conception of the world as a set of systems. It would do so in the name of a grab bag of recent and current theoretical methodologies that, in the declared absence of an overall approach that would encompass them all, might generate some "provisional constructions." It is hard to imagine a more straightforward declaration of openness to what became known as "contemporary theory." As a rhetorical gesture, however, the "post" in "postcontemporary" now reads like a quasi-parodic attempt at acknowledging and trumping then loud claims for postmodernism, which is rendered as being "of various kinds." Tarrying with the negative, indeed.[74]

The current series rationale, written by Dainotto in 2011, is a brave attempt at updating and, at the same time, restating the deeper impulses of the original intent:

Theory—as a driving impulse in all modern thought—emerged from the realization that the two antithetical temptations of intellectual and cultural work today—system and empiricism—were related symptoms that demanded perpetual critique and rectification. In a wide variety of fields, theory resisted these temptations in equally antithetical ways: wielding the weapon of ideological analysis against system (whether philosophical, aesthetic or more generally disciplinary), and that of totalization against the irrepressible and cyclical revival of empiricism as such—the fear of the universal or the generalizable, the blind faith in the reality of the singular "fact." Theory stands for history by its very post-contemporaneity, identifying what is progressive in present-day intellectual trends by projecting their new directions into the future. In that sense everyone practices theory, but the thing itself is always unseasonable and unwelcome, uncomfortable and unmentionable. It is in this no-man's-land that our series seeks out new kinds of intervention and new kinds of insights.[75]

One might parse the insistence on "theory" in this rationale as pitching Marxist political critique ("ideological analysis") and dialectical materialism ("totalization") against blind insistence on the absolute priority of observable facts about the world ("empiricism"), a narrowness that serves the interests of capitalism ("system"). Thus the sense of the core phrase, "Theory stands for history by its very post-contemporaneity," that is, critical theory is properly historical because it is selective, not accepting, of the present's self-descriptions, and because it projects forward only the "progressive" elements of current "intellectual trends." Although the rationale adopts some of the language of poststructuralist "theory" (thus the claim to be in a "no-man's-land"), it actually wishes to leap over it, into a future, hopefully a postcapitalist future, to come. In this context, "postcontemporaneity" is the name for the mode of theoretical work that uses long-term, historical perspectives to intervene into and against the contemporism fostered by what was seen by many on the Left, not least Jameson himself, as the last phase of capitalism. Back to the postmodern future, anyone?

In this recent rationale, the prefix "post" also echoes the original rhetorical attempt to pick up on the frisson of postmodernist thought, while at the same time claiming to at least partially supersede it, just as postmodernism had claimed in relation to modernism. Although the first book in the series was Stanley Fish's collection of essays on interpretation, *Doing What Comes Naturally: Change, Rhetoric, and the Practice of Theory in Literary and Legal Studies*, since 1991 it has been anchored by Jameson's best-selling *Postmodernism: Or, the Cultural Logic of Late Capitalism*, the collection of essays that elaborate on a revised version of his famous 1984 *New Left Review* essay with that title. Both essay and book worked hard—and, to many of us, with a high degree of success—to wrest postmodernism as a descriptor of current conditions away from its "anything goes" proselytizers. Along with important texts by David Harvey and others, Jameson's analysis turned postmodernity into a critical concept, one that described the operations of culture within what was, even then, turning out to be a resurgent, globalizing capitalism. This battle over nomenclature was won by the early twenty-first century. "Post-contemporary" became collateral damage. Although it persists as the (oddly distracting) title of this strong series of books that range across many fields and kinds of critical theory, I do not believe that any author develops it as a significant concept.

Scattered usages have occurred subsequently. Josephine Meckseper's 2005 installation *The Complete History of Postcontemporary Art*, discussed in chapter 9, is a vivid visualization of the varieties of present anachronism that theorists such as Jameson had in mind. Like him, she does not delude herself that she is actually picturing "the postcontemporary condition." On the contrary, she is showing the shop front of contemporary art, very much embedded in the contemporary conditions that so clearly shape it, yet also already past its time—thus the irony of her title, and the snap of the conceptual trap within it. Few subsequent usages have been as sharply, if passingly, pertinent.

In 2007 two Iranian architects, Abbas Gharib and Bahram Shirdel, began discussion about a synthesis of developments in many fields that they saw as taking on a new configuration. Their catchall conceptualization of PoCo appears in the "Post-contemporary" Wikipedia entry.[76] In 2015, an artists' residency and exhibition space in a deconsecrated church in Troy, New York, renamed itself the Post-Contemporary, or the Post, and declared itself dedicated to the support of "artists thinking and/or working beyond the confines of the established art world, enabling them to influence the development of future concepts, systems, communities."[77] An experimental music group named Post Contemporary Corporation has been active in Milan since 2017. Saatchi Art hosts an online collection curated by Richard T. Scott featuring quasi-surrealist, kitschy figurative paintings such as his own, which he describes as "forward looking paintings that express reconstructive, rather than deconstructive philosophies and emphasize timeless human themes rather than the contemporary and the transient."[78] This desire to present evidently backward-looking practice as art's future (if only we could somehow get beyond the contemporary art behemoth) is common to many websites that claim the art presented on them is "postcontemporary."

To date, the most sustained attempt to theorize the concept of postcontemporary is that of speculative realist theorists Armen Avanessian and Suhail

Malik. In a discussion introducing a special issue of the online journal *Dis Magazine* in 2016—produced in association with the Ninth Berlin Biennale, *The Present in Drag*, which was curated by the magazine's editors—they characterize the postcontemporary as a "time-complex" with the following features, as set out in their synopsis: "Time is changing. Human agency and experience lose their primacy in the complexity and scale of social organization today. The leading actors are instead complex systems, infrastructures and networks in which the future replaces the present as the structuring condition of time. As the political Left and Right struggle to deal with this new situation, we are increasingly wholly pre-empted and post-everything."[79] They gloss these propositions with comments and examples of the growing preponderance of the future over the present: in the perverse logic of the preemptive strike, preventive policing and health provision, futures markets (especially derivatives), and in the algorithms used by Google and Amazon that predict our moods, needs, and desires, loading our communications with information and products to satisfy them, thus shaping a "preemptive personality." Perhaps they should have used "precontemporary" as their key term?

Yet even the prefix "post" is, they argue, "a mark of the deprioritization of the present." This is because "if we are post-contemporary, or post-postmodern, post-internet, or post-whatever—if we are now post-everything—it is because historically-given semantics don't quite work anymore." Historical determinism is manifestly failing to explain many present occurrences, and the explanatory power of the past-present-future triad is diminishing as a fundament of everyday experience and projective imagination, as in the examples just cited. To Avanessian and Malik, "the logic of the contemporary with its fixation on the present" means that the concept of contemporaneity cannot deal with the double whammy being visited on the present: its disconnection from a past that was previously believed to (mostly) determine it and, even more overwhelming, its invasion by all kinds of preemptive futures. They are right about this if the concept of contemporaneity is confined to a simplistic presentism. But the concept advanced in this book—of contemporaneity as a multiplicity of ways of being in time, at the same time as others, within a world condition in which multiple temporalities are in constant complex contingency, while no world picture, no matter how internally various, is able to operate as a totalization or as a last resort—has already anticipated most if not all the elements of the "time-complex" they claim to be freshly defining.[80]

Responses to these new conditions, they say, have taken, primarily, two forms:

a right-wing or reactionary countermanding, looking toward the past as a kind of counter-balance against the negative aspects that everyone observes and feels: the frustrations, disadvantages and mistakes of neoliberal financial neofeudalism. The other standard response to the speculative time structure is the left or critical one, which is also the prevalent one in contemporary art. The focus here is not the past as a place of semantic security but instead on the present as a site or condition of resistance against the change to a speculative time.

To Avanessian and Malik, these responses are variations on the same theme. Being "still vestigially modernist," and thus "still premised on the present as the primary tense," what they call "leftism" remains locked into a contemporaneity that, with the prospect of revolution blocked, can no longer see a future, only "the present as indefinitely extended." Indeed, to the Left, they believe, "the contemporary is a time form that saturates both the past and the future, a metastable condition." This will not be news to readers of this book, nor to, say, the Momentum socialists in England; the postcommunists active throughout Europe; the Resistance, Indivisible, and Black Lives Matter in the United States; Leap in Canada; and other collectives and movements now active throughout the world. The prospect of the current situation continuing, indeed, growing far worse in almost every respect, is precisely what these activists are organizing against and, increasingly, uniting to do so.

For Avanessian and Malik, art is quite simply the worst instantiation of contemporaneity as such. "Contemporary art is both a symptom and surrogate of that futurelessness, with its constant celebration of experience: aesthetic experience, criticality, presentness and so on." To Malik, contemporary art's self-absorption leads to its "becoming the last word in art," and thus "it cancels its own futurity if not the future in general for the sake of its own critical accomplishments, which are of course capture-mechanisms demonstrating contemporary art's salience to everything." Avanessian spells out the depth of this duplicity:

Contemporary art is a good example also because it has not been just a victim of the recent economic and political reordering of neoliberalism, but has really helped build the matrix of that reorganization by implementing its logic on all levels from a left-critical angle. Specifically, it has stressed the dominance of the present or the past as condition for action, and also, as we said before, individuated experience as the main benefit of that reorganization. It takes the lead in a general aestheticization at all

levels: personal/individual creativity, originality etc.; environment and cities as spaces of creativity and "disruptive" entrepreneurialism; the confla-
tion of production and consumption with the prosumer, whose "natural"
habitat is, precisely, the smart city itself turned into a kind-of continual
biennial event. All of this goes back to the fetishization of presentness and
of the aesthetic experience of everyday life at the expense of its reconstruction, which would be the task of poiesis or a poetics.

Given such a comprehensively negative account of contemporary art, no
wonder they see no role for it in this pivotal task. Politically, they aim to create
"a speculative politics capable of accelerating the time-complex in the sense of
introducing a difference into it," while philosophically, they wish they could
"get past contemporaneity and not just Jacques Derrida's criticism of the meta-
physics of presence." Unsurprisingly, given the vague, gestural quality of these
formulations, they do neither. Instead, they concentrate on the need to rethink
the grammatical structures of the speculative time-complex and point to various texts in the issue of the magazine they are editing that posit the need to rethink crucial social infrastructure. Not least among these is Benjamin Bratton's
The Stack, a highly suggestive model of computational infrastructure.[81] On this
showing, the postcontemporary is, today, offering us even less insight into the
important issues of the times than did postmodernism during the 1980s.

A CONTEMPORARY ART HISTORY?

These reflections return us to the issues posed in my introduction, indeed, to my
opening question, which I can now reformulate: Is art history as a discipline—in
response to the demands of our contemporary condition, in response to what art
practices are asking of it, and in light of the conceptual resources made available
by philosophers and theorists such as those discussed in this chapter—showing
any real signs of being able to generate a truly contemporary approach to writing
histories of contemporary art? To me, a really interesting answer would take the
discipline as a whole into consideration, as well as asking, Could art history do
so while facing up to the challenges of interpreting the art of the past (including
modern art) in terms that acknowledge the inherent contemporaneity of every
work of art—that of its originary moment and that which pertains to now? This
second question is a matter for another time.[82] But the first is the core topic of
this book and the focus of its concluding chapter.

writing histories of contemporary art

The Situation Now

In November 2016, the editors of *Dandelion*, an online journal published by graduate students at Birkbeck College, University of London, posted a call for papers for a special issue on "The Contemporary." Inviting submissions from "postgraduate students and early career scholars that address the theme of the contemporary across the spectrum of Arts and Humanities research," they sketched their subject as a set of rhetorical questions.

When will the contemporary end? When did it begin? Contemporary cultural production and questions about the nature of contemporaneity itself have become dominant in recent scholarship but just what is "the contemporary"? What type of creative and scholarly work is being done under its aura? Should we apprehend the contemporary as a noun, offering definition and order to a discrete period in history; or is it rather an adjective, traced with a particular structure of feeling, an interdisciplinary apprehension to what is happening Now and an anxiety towards what comes next? We seek submissions that would address how the social, political, and aesthetic dilemmas that characterize our present are made manifest in the twenty-first century's cultural production. For instance, if the contemporary is the cultural logic of neoliberal capitalism made tangible, then how can its "common sense" be registered, revised, or resisted? Is the contemporary experienced similarly across the globe, or are its pressure points, modes and sites of dissent different depending on their location? How might we pull on the emergency brake?

We are also keen to examine emergent methodologies and debates that offer a barometer of the contemporary in humanities scholarship. For example, how to explicate "the contemporary" is a matter of anxiety for art history: does the term simply denote a period that came after the modern, or were all works of art once contemporary? And what are the conceptual tools and interpretive frameworks we need to study contemporary writing in the present age? As literary scholars have noted, one of the defining features of twenty-first century fiction is the return of the novel about time. How, might we ask, are time and space to be negotiated in an era of transnational literary form and planetary ruination? Finally, we wish also to consider the fate of the humanities, and academic labour itself, inside the contemporary University.[1]

How different is this cluster of questions from those assembled by the editors of *October*, in particular Hal Foster, for that journal's 2009 "Questionnaire on 'The Contemporary'"? I cited the *October* questions earlier, in chapter 2, as the preface to my response, but they are worth repeating as a way of registering how the most reflexive thinking on these questions has developed in the short time, and, it sometimes seems, the ages, since then.

The category of "contemporary art" is not a new one. What is new is the sense that, in its very heterogeneity, much present practice seems to float free of historical determination, conceptual definition, and critical judgment. Such paradigms as "the neo-avant-garde" and "postmodernism," which once oriented some art and theory, have run into the sand, and, arguably, no models of much explanatory reach or intellectual force have risen in their stead. At the same time, perhaps paradoxically, "contemporary art" has become an institutional object in its own right: in the academic world there are professorships and programs, and in the museum world departments and institutions, all devoted to the subject, and most tend to treat it as apart not only from prewar practice but from most postwar practice as well.

Is this floating-free real or imagined? A merely local perception? A simple effect of the end-of-grand-narratives? If it is real, how can we specify some of its principal causes, that is, beyond general reference to "the market" and "globalization"? Or, is it indeed a direct outcome of a neoliberal economy, one that, moreover, is now in crisis? What are some of its salient consequences for artists, critics, curators, and historians— for their formation and their practice alike? Are there collateral effects in other fields of art history? Are there instructive analogies to be drawn from the situation in other arts and disciplines? Finally, are there benefits to this apparent lightness of being?[2]

At first glance, almost nothing has changed. The similarity between the two sets of questions is striking, from their mode of asking to their specifics and sequencing. Dissimilarities are few. Unlike the *October* editors, the Birkbeck students speak of pulling on "the emergency brake," although which aspect of the crisis they wish to halt, and who would do the pulling, is unclear. They also wonder whether certain contemporary novels, especially those that take up time as a topic, might be worth special attention. Of course, they are concerned about who gets to pose these questions and whether, in a shrinking job market, they are likely to be employed to do so. Apart from these not insignificant differences, the second call seems to echo the first, as if in the intervening years, "the contemporary" had succeeded in keeping us all in the same kind of distracted suspension, analysis of it scarcely advanced, with humanities scholarship, including art-historical studies, still asking the same kinds of preparatory questions—indeed, rhetorical ones that evince more disciplinary anxiety than interdisciplinary apprehension, or, with some, smug anticipation of knowing they are unanswerable, and thus no further action in the world will be required.

There is some truth to this profile of a paralyzed if not quite yet palsied profession. But it is not the entire picture. The chapters in this book, and the books they complement—with arguments about the nature of the shifts from modern to contemporary art, and the contention that three currents and their interaction constitute the core dynamic of contemporary art—provide one answer. Other art historians, critics, curators, and theorists, as well as certain artists, have also proposed answers, some of a parallel sort, others with quite different emphases. In 2010, I published a survey of the state of play in an essay in the *Art Bulletin* (chapter 9 in this volume). In chapter 10, I explored the responses of certain philosophers, theorists, and artists to the same and related issues. In this chapter, I review the efforts of a range of art historians and critics who think about contemporary art on its broadest as well as its more specific scales, in ways that go beyond the impotence invited by concepts such as "the contemporary." Only by taking these contributions together can we find ways of going on, productively, within the problematic posed by the contemporary confluence of art practice, history, theory, criticism, curating, and collecting.

Questionnaires, anthologies, and collections of essays are tailor made for testing partial ideas for how to think about contemporary art as it is happening. Most respondents to the *October* questionnaire lamented the disabling repercussions of "the contemporary" impasse on current art practice and theory, yet stayed within the journal's terms, taking them as defining the parameters of contemporary art. In this sense, the authors reflected the larger impotence that pervaded much thinking in the field in the first decade of the twenty-first century, and that, broadly speaking, continues to do so. Those who attempt generalization often take celebrated, successful, and expensive art as representative of all art being made today, and then add to the adulation, pillory it as evidence of profound cultural vacuity and artistic corruption, or waver somewhere in between. In the previous chapter, we saw how this disease can infect philosophers, theorists, and artists as well. Art that is different in kind, intention, form, and affect—in my terms, the critical art made in Euro-America, all the art of transnational transitionality, and much of the art produced within the third current—is regarded as somehow falling short of this gold standard of what counts, like it or not, as contemporary art.

This approach not only confines itself largely to the affirmative artists active in the first of the currents I have identified, it falls into the trap of reductive simplification about the work of even these artists—at least, it does so if we take into account their initial inspirations: for Jeff Koons, the pathologies of commodity fetishism in the United States; for Damien Hirst, those pathologies in religion, science, and the health industries; and for Takashi Murakami, the arrested adolescence pervasive in postwar Japanese culture.[3] Of course, these artists, and many others closely associated with them, soon succumbed to the rewards that follow from serving up to their masters a beguilingly palatable kind of capitalist realism.

Some respondents to the *October* questionnaire sought pathways beyond "the contemporary" impasse. In educator/activist Yates McKee's contribution, he detailed his efforts in his teaching to tackle issues of the actual effectiveness of political art.[4] Curator Okwui Enwezor highlighted the need to display the interplays between modernity and contemporaneity in "off-centered" art-producing regions.[5] His concept of "the postcolonial constellation" within which we all work today is, in my view, an essential component of a model that has the "explanatory reach" and "intellectual force" called for by the *October* editors. Another attempt to see the larger picture, in this case from art-historical perspectives, was that of Alexander Alberro, who argued that a set of factors, emerging around 1989, signaled an epochal change: the end of the Cold War, the globalization of cultural values, the spread of integrated electronic communications, and the dominance of economic neoliberalism. In art, he identified a confluence of global integration and antiglobalization becoming the subject of many artists' works, the proliferation of international exhibitions such as biennials, the rise of a new technological imaginary and high-tech hybrid art forms, a shift in strategy from avant-gardist confrontation toward cooperation and collaboration, and the somewhat surprising reemergence of an aesthetics of affect. Alberro concluded, "These new forms of art [and this new spectatorship] have come to be discursively constructed as 'the contemporary,'" a new period in the history of art.[6] While these are accurate observations, I spelled out in my earlier commentary some reservations about whether this kind of traditional (in fact, modern) mode of art-historical periodization remains appropriate in contemporary conditions.

At the same time *October* launched its questionnaire, the editors of *e-flux journal*—an online storefront and book publishing coalition, which also runs a nonprofit exhibition space in New York, stages discussions, and presents its projects in exhibitionary form, while implying that all this activity is artwork (that of its founder, Anton Vidokle, and of those participating)—decided to establish a simple menu structure to allow users to navigate a wiki archive of contemporary art. They published two issues seeking ideas about how they might develop their "own criteria for browsing and historicizing recent activity in a way that affirms the possibilities of contemporary art's still-incompleteness, of its complex ability to play host to many narratives and trajectories without necessarily having to absorb them into a central logic or determined discourse—at least before it forms a historical narrative and logic of exclusion that we would much rather disavow?" They soon realized, "We are looking at two distinct approaches to contemporaneity: one that has already been fully institutionalized, and another that still evades definition."[7]

This definitive mismatch, the state of being overdetermined and scarcely existent at the same time, is subtly nuanced in Mexican curator Cuauhtémoc Medina's opening essay, "Contemp(t)ory: Eleven Theses."[8] His theses include such succinct formulations as "it is no coincidence that the institutions, media, and cultural structures of the contemporary artworld have become the last refuge of political and social radicalism.... [They] also function as the critical self-consciousness of capitalist hypermodernity." This dangerous double does not lead him to despair. Instead, he dissents from "those theorists who lament the apparent co-opting of radicalism and critique by the official sphere of art," opting instead to suggest that "our task may consist, in large part, of protecting utopia—seen as the necessary collusion of the past with what lies ahead—from its demise at the hands of the ideology of the present time."[9] Thus, he curated Manifesta 9 in 2012, titled *The Deep of the Modern*, an exhibition in a defunct mine in Genk, the center of Limburg, a once thriving coal-mining region in Belgium. In addition to new works by thirty-five artists who were invited to respond to the locality, the exhibition featured a historical display of art from the region as well as an active dialogic framework addressed to "the ecology of industrial capitalism" and the situation facing the region within its European and global contexts.[10]

In Boris Groys's contribution to the *e-flux* anthology, "Comrades of Time," he puns on the German term for "contemporary," *zeitgenössisch*, bemusedly drawing out the sense that we are being asked to nurture a time that, after the abandonment of the communist project in Europe, seems condemned to "repeat its pasts and reproduce itself without leading to any future."[11] To him, the art-like activity of millions throughout the world who are immersed in social media instantiates this state of spectacular pointlessness. In contrast, time-based contemporary art "turns a scarcity of time into an excess of time—and demonstrates itself to be a collaborator, a comrade of time, its true con-temporary."[12] His example was a work by Francis Alÿs, but he could have cited another contributor to the volume, and to Manifesta 9, the Raqs Media Collective, whose work and thought is exemplary of the issues in play. My favorite moment from their essay, "Now and Elsewhere," is their wry observation, "A contemporaneity that is not curious about how it might be surprised is not worth our time."[13]

HIDING FROM THE HISTORICAL PRESENT

Most writing about contemporary art shields itself against the critical, comparative accountability that historical perspectives require by insisting that this art is not, at least for now, subject to such perspectives. A banal yet also hysterical version of this view is to insist that contemporary art is like fashion, always changing, always refreshing itself, so it should be accepted for what it is, in all its brilliant, dazzling instanteity. It can be nothing else; its "history" will never be anything more than whatever residues of this fleeting fashionability happen to survive. It does not need historians, especially not while it is being produced.

A calmer version of this view insists that contemporary art is quintessentially ahistorical, even antihistorical, or at most "posthistorical," as in the postmodern formulation of Arthur Danto.[14] It refuses originality, so it cannot create history if history is understood as a succession of innovations. It instantly forgets its own achievements, and thus has no sense of record. It recognizes no determination, so it creates no traditions and inherits nothing. Instead, contemporary art essentially repeats or rewinds past imagery, or aggregates whatever is out there in the wider visual culture into high-end tchotchkes for those who still believe in "Art." It has no coherent purpose; its goals are short term and unrelated to each other. It is not in any way teleological. This view may be less hysterical than the fashion analogy, but it is also nonsense.

A qualified, quasi-historical position in the face of these refusals of historicity is to acknowledge that a world-historical transformation occurred in the years around 1989, and that history in its modern self-understanding "ended" at that time. For art, the consequence was that it became ahistorical from that moment forward. Since then, contemporary art remains what it became at that moment when history disappeared. It has not evolved in historical ways; it simply diversifies or repeats different versions of itself.

In contrast to these rejections of historicity, a small number of historical approaches have been developed during the past few decades. The apparently most straightforward strategy, adopted in the main by art historians commissioned to write textbooks, is to avoid the deeper problem of whether, and if so, how, contemporary art is subject to orthodox historical inquiry by simply treating it as if it were. That is, choose a selection of current art according to its frequency of display in museums, markets, magazines, biennials, art spaces, and so on; gather basic information about these artists and works; and after uttering some ritual caveats, write them into the canon, with the implication that this amounts to the most recent chapter in the broadly accepted narrative of art history.

To my mind, this list of current strategies adopted by most of those confronted with having to think about contemporary art amounts to a litany of evasion, confusion, and wishful thinking. Yet even within them are glimmers of insight and some brilliant suggestions. Here and there, we find interpretive thinking that matches the art it seeks to elucidate, and we find art being made that requires, and is worthy of, such thought. In sum, there is enough to build on, and to go on with, because this exchange between art and thought—which is at the heart of contemporary art—is unstoppable and will remain so for as long as the thirst for open yet critical accountability prevails against the fear-filled closures that loom around us these days, in every part of the world.

As students continue to demand courses in contemporary art, textbook publishers' assembly lines continue to pump out product, updating chapters in earlier editions and publishing entire books on contemporary art to add to their comprehensive coverage of previous periods in art history. Almost all are based on the assumption that contemporary art, for all of its diversity, is fundamentally an updating of previous art, and that it is best approached as the most recent phase of a continuous history of art. How, then, to identify the major and minor tendencies, choose the representative artists and the key works for description, commentary and illustration? The answer, usually unstated, is that the art-world structures and the professionals working through them are in fact deciding that the work of certain artists is likely to be, or could plausibly be taken to be, the authentic art of our times. Dispute is normal, opinions vary greatly, but a working consensus emerges from the choices of dealers, curators, critics, collectors, advisers, and art lovers. Historians follow, accepting that these choices will do for now. However compromised by mistakes, poor judgment, self-interest, venality, or simply the impossibility of keeping up with everything, everyone involved takes the system to be not only self-perpetuating but also, in time, self-correcting. Books can be revised. Historians have time on their side, although publishers know that when it comes to contemporary art, they must get an up-to-date book out right now. When I surveyed the state of art-historical writing in 2010, I noted that few of the industrial-scale textbooks on modern art acknowledged "contemporary art" as a term, let alone a category or period. Since then, they have all succumbed and been joined by several textbooks explicitly devoted to the topic, as well as surveys and anthologies arranged according to an ever-expanding list of themes. I will comment briefly on some representative publications.

Peter R. Kalb's *Charting the Contemporary: Art since 1980* (2014) is a conscientious attempt to maintain a sense of art-historical flow from the postmodernist questioning of twentieth-century modern art and criticism through the myriad changes in artistic practice and in thinking about art that have come to constitute contemporary art and its discourses.[15]

Kalb opens with an unexamined use of the concept of the contemporary, claiming, anachronistically, that it originated in the "deconstruction" of modernism by the generation of Jasper Johns and Claes Oldenburg, and thus "the main narrative [of *Charting the Contemporary*] starts in the United States, widens its view to include those cities that once constituted satellite art centers, and then considers contemporary art in a global context."[16] The first five chapters—which cover minimalism and feminist art in the 1960s and 1970s; the picture generation appropriators in the 1980s; the return to painting in the same decade; activist art also during the 1980s; and art about and as commodities during that decade and the 1990s—each includes a few European artists whose work parallels that of the mainly New York–based artists who are the backbone of the story. The welcome sixth chapter on activist art begins with the East Village artists, moves on to Group Material, Gran Fury, and ACT UP, and concludes with a long look at the Border Art Workshop/Taller de Arte Fronteriza in San Diego. A central chapter on "Memory and History" starts from Maya Lin's *Vietnam Veterans Memorial*, then moves to the countermemorials of Jochen Gerz, Christian Boltanski, and Rachel Whiteread, followed by a treatment of African American artists concerned with the same issues of memory and history. Next, a section on "Art Histories and Civil Wars" is entirely based *outside* the US, profiling work by Doris Salcedo, William Kentridge, Walid Raad, and Jun Nguyen-Hatsushiba. The widening of view, then, begins halfway through the book and takes a stronger although still implicit form in the next chapter, "Culture, Body, Self," which highlights artists mostly born outside the United States, although many (Tehching Hsieh, Marina Abramović) developed active careers within it. Chapter 8 features minisurveys of art since the 1980s in Russia and China, while the next chapter, "Engaging the Global Present," mixes narrative about developments in the art of a country, Cuba, with attention to diaspora artists from various parts of the world, such as Shirin Neshat (from Iran) and Emily Jacir (from Palestine).

In the final chapters, as Kalb moves into the realm of current practice, his investment in an expansive, additive pluralism suffers a loss of purchase. A chapter titled "New Metaphors and New Narratives" announces a fresh openness to unbridled invention comparable to that of the 1960s and 1970s, yet he begins with a section, "Relearning to Paint," that profiles a selection of artists who have in most cases already receded from critical attention. The artists Kalb covers in his final chapter, "The Art of Contemporary Experience," from Olafur Eliasson, Thomas Hirschhorn, and Harun Farocki, to Omer Fast and Catherine Opie, are all substantial figures, each making significant contributions to understanding our contemporaneity, but the lack of a broader picture leaves it unclear why the work of another list of equally relevant artists was not discussed.

Of course, the textbook framework, shaped by hard-nosed calculations of unit costs, teaching protocols, and student readerships, imposes enormous constraints on how much can be covered, and how one might do so, usually precluding irony, metacommentary, uncertainty, and contradiction—the very elements that drive much art making, theorization, and art-historical reflection. More subtly, the authors of such texts also court the danger of turning these constraints into something like a theory that ends up being quite inadequate to the complexities of its subject. Kalb's concluding sentence, cited below, is a representative instance of the problem:

> The art of the 1970s discussed in Chapter 1 drew attention to the critical lenses through which we might view the confrontation between life and power, focusing particularly on issues of gender, race, and class. As the artworld has extended its networks and become less securely tethered to the local politics of artworld centers, the legacy of the critical analyses refined in the late 1970s and the early 1980s, and inflected in the art and theory of the 1990s, can be felt in the twenty-first century appeal to see and feel with sensitivity, to think openly, and to be active in the studio, museum, and beyond.[17]

In 2014, this was already a dying call. Today, the circumstances cry out for an urgent return to consideration of "the confrontation between life and power, focusing particularly on issues of gender, race, and class."

Another approach, found in a growing number of textbooks and anthologies, is to put aside the challenge of charting a chronological development, and to ignore the dynamics of geographic and geopolitical "spread," in favor of clustering several themes evident in the work of prominent contemporary artists. To begin in the 1980s has the further advantage of glossing over the awkward, and deeply troubled, transitions from modern to contemporary art. By then, and by common (yet unarticulated) consensus, contemporary art had already arrived. Both decisions shape Jean Robertson and Craig McDaniel's *Themes of Contemporary Art: Visual Art after 1980*, now in its fourth edition.[18] Oriented toward studio art students, it illustrates each of the ideas explained in the introduction through discussions of artworks, an approach continued in more detail in the chapters that follow, each devoted to a theme: identity, the body, time, memory, place, language, science, and spirituality. This list follows no logic, in the sense that these themes contain all other possible or imaginable ones. Nor is there any development from one chapter to the other, or a particular chronology evident within them. The implicit claim is that contemporary art simply constellates like this, in the present, in its ahistorical space. The authors do insist that some qualities are important (if not necessarily shared by all contemporary art): an "expanded range of materials" is in use, "content matters," and "meanings are open-ended."[19] Soft pluralism seems endemic to such texts.

As I noted in chapter 9, the editors of *Art since 1900: Modernism, Antimodernism, Postmodernism*, first published in 2004 and now in its third edition, made an ingenious attempt to square the circle between the reductive linearity of historical chronicle and the tedium of repetition that infects the thematic collation, while dismissing the uncertainty about complete coverage that attends all historical retrospect. They opted for an almanac style, mostly year by year, with short essays profiling in some depth, and with acute attention to detail and context, an artwork, exhibition, publication, idea, or event that seemed consequential at its time and has been relevant since.[20] The result is a rich display of the contemporaneity of modern art, of the moments during the twentieth century and since when certain artworks and ideas made their first impressions, followed by instances of their resonance in later art. While chronology is notionally the main organizing principle, no sustained narrative of art-historical development is offered. Readers are left to imagine such histories, as sequences of fragmentary, proximate overlays, as if tracking a set of associations relating to a word in a thesaurus. In its structure, and in the experience it offers to readers, *Art since 1900* is very much a product of its own time, that is, of our contemporary condition.

Within and against which the voices of the contributors—all well-known historians of modernism and critics of contemporary art, as well as editors of the influential journal *October*—suggest strong orientations. Indeed, their differing perspectives, introduced in individual opening essays, imply the existence of three or four parallel (in fact, contemporaneous) histories, or more overtly and rewardingly, several possible viewpoints on the same material. None of these strategies was pursued systematically throughout the book, although possible configurations recur, as a topic of lively disputation, in the roundtable discussions among the editors in the center and at the end of the book. Rosalind Krauss opened the second roundtable with the statement, "We've structured our entries on twentieth century art through the analytical perspective that each one of us tends to favor: Hal's is a psychoanalytic view; Benjamin's, a social-historical view; Yve-Alain's a formalist and structuralist view; and mine, a post-structuralist view." This provokes a lively dispute, beginning with an assertion by Yve-Alain Bois that "none of us is married to a particular method," an assessment not borne out by the discussion that follows.[21]

This roundtable discussion was titled "The Predicament of Contemporary Art." Recorded in 2003, it focused mainly on possible approaches to interpreting postwar art. Toward its end, Hal Foster posed a core question: "Are there plausible ways to narrate the now myriad practices of contemporary art over the past twenty years?"[22] Despair, regret, negativity, or silence was the response, leaving us to wonder whether the fault lay in the art or in its interrogators. In the second edition of 2011 and the third of 2016, this same roundtable is largely repeated, except for the somewhat awkward pasting in of passages, written in 2010, by an additional editor, David Joselit. Author of some well-targeted, subtle studies of television, new media, and painting during the digital age ("Painting 2.0"), Joselit contributes many of the yearly entries covering recent decades, notably on the imagery of sexualities during the 1980s and 1990s, photography from South Africa, relational aesthetics, intermediality in painting, video imagery and war, recent Chinese political and body art, and the artist as digital avatar. These entries, and Joselit's insertions into the roundtable discussions, seem to come from a different time, place, and mindset than those of the other authors, as internally variable as they admittedly are. When, for example, comment is invited on Joselit's suggestion that many contemporary artists view spectacle society as so pervasive that searching for productive alternatives within it, rather than blanket rejection of it, was a sustainable strategy, Buchloh responds, "What place does neo-avant-garde practice have in the present compared to the one it had in the moment of 1968?"[23] Disjunctions like these, along with the small edits that half-heartedly gesture at implying that all discussants were present in the same space at the same time, amount to an amusing instance of the fictive space-time that historical commentary on the present is obliged to inhabit. In this case, however, it might be more accurate to say that the book conjures a fictive time-space, occupied by five (or, perhaps more precisely, four) kinds of discomfort with being where it is.

Joselit's introductory essay, "Globalization, Networks, and the Aggregate as Form," introduces a clear and politically uncompromising account of globalization, something scarcely considered in the first edition. By emphasizing the work of artists from outside the United States and Europe, his essay and entries go some way toward meeting an obvious, and much criticized, shortcoming of the first edition. His discussion of "the aggregate as idea and form" breaks new ground. He notes, "Traditionally, one of the primary purposes of art history has been to discover whether a particular historical epoch, such as the current moment of globalization, generates its own unique aesthetic forms and practices," and, after acknowledging the difficulties of "recentness," proposes "the aggregator" as one such form.[24] Drawing from dictionary definitions the sense that "an aggregate selects and configures relatively autonomous elements," he cites the political concept of the multitude, as theorized by Antonio Negri, Michael Hardt, and Paolo Virno; filters such as Google's search engine algorithm; and more "curated" online content aggregators like *Wikipedia* and, in art contexts, *Contemporary Art Daily* and *e-flux*. His artist aggregators range from Gabriel Orozco's "working tables," Rachel Harrison's uneven, fragile assemblages, and Song Dong's memory-based phantasmal installations to the group Slavs and Tartars, whose installations evoke the multilayered complexities of living, thinking, and imagining the in-between region of Central Asia. He concludes with this pertinent comment: "The central challenge in confronting the contemporary art made under conditions of globalization is to hold together two ostensibly contradictory qualities: first, a shared international language of aesthetic form spoken in common; and second, the texture and nuance of different histories and dialectics that can make the same image or format mean dramatically different things."[25]

From my perspective, the "international language" of contemporary art is that of the interactions and exchanges across cultures, places, and temporalities among artists active within the currents I have identified. The interests and orientations of the current in which they emerged and, usually, continue to work are the primary drivers of their creativity. It is not, of course, confined to such concerns, although they are powerfully insistent. On this model, the qualities Joselit identifies might seem to be contradictory, but they are better understood as being in antinomic relationships to one another. Their internal differentiation requires their doubling with other internally differentiated practices. Their distinctiveness is the other side of their also necessary implication with these others—not one other set of others, in a dialectical relationship, but at least two, in relationships of contingent adjacency. As I have been arguing throughout, this is what makes contemporaneity contemporary in ways that have moved it, albeit messily and with weighty coattails, past the reach of the dialectic double of modern thought, beyond the full grasp of the underlying logic of artistic modernism, and, more broadly, beyond the dynamics of social modernity.

PARTIAL IDEAS, WHICH MAY ACCUMULATE

In Joselit's 2013 book *After Art*, he argues his case for "the aggregator" more fully. He defines "formats," in contrast to "mediums," as "dynamic mechanisms for aggregating content":

> In mediums a material substrate (such as paint on canvas) converges with an aesthetic tradition (such as Painting). Ultimately, mediums lead to objects, and thus reification, but formats are nodal connections and

differential fields; they channel an unpredictable array of ephemeral currents and charges. They are configurations of force rather than discrete objects. In short, formats establish a pattern of links or connections. I use the terms *link* and *connection* advisedly because it is through such modes of association, native to the World Wide Web, that composition occurs under conditions of image population explosion.

Previous notions of composition as a matter of finding coherence within a medium, or of choosing from a given set of conventions the kind of presentational vehicle most suited to what the artist wants to say, no longer apply. Instead, "what now matters most is not the production of new content but its *retrieval* in intelligible patterns through acts of *reframing, capturing, reiterating,* and *documenting.* What counts, in other words, is how widely and easily images connect: not only to messages, but to other social currencies like capital, real estate, politics, and so on. In economies of image overproduction connectivity is key. This is the Epistemology of Search."[26] To me, this is the right place from which to begin a description of the mode of "composition"—in quotation marks to indicate its inherent provisionality—which has come to be natural to artists active in the third current in contemporary art. It picks up their preference for processes rather than objects, working collectively rather than individually, sharing rather than possessing, and networking over staying in place. Nevertheless, the general terms used in the passages cited here could apply equally to the postmodern repeat strategies of artists such as Jeff Koons, and to their unabashed echoing of the ways in which globalizing capital goes about its business. To my mind, a wider range of compositional modes, and a more contentious politics, is abroad today, within each of the currents, and in the interactions between them.[27]

It might seem that Joselit's title, *After Art,* signals his alignment with those who argue that contemporary art is so subject to the practices and values of globalizing capital that it has become incapable of acting as a vehicle of social and political change, and that artists should exit such contexts if they wish to contribute to an effective politics. On the contrary, "after" to him means something more like an afterimage or aftershock of what it is like to act in a world *after* ideologies; even either/or options have had their day yet still reverberate.[28] The contemporary paradox is that, far from becoming powerless, or merely virtual, "the organization of the art world—its format—is as real as it gets when it comes to capital's effects. It's not just the purchase of artworks, but also the self-image of entire nations, the transformation of neighborhoods and cities, and the fashioning of diplomatic identities that art is capable of accomplishing. In fact, [art's] power has probably never been greater."[29]

This is a paraphrase of George Yúdice's argument in *The Expediency of Culture* that the function of art in globalized capital is more than simply to act as an unregulated domain within which the super rich park and whitewash their extraordinary accumulations of wealth, and more than to work as an engine of capital development through tourism and gentrification. Instead, the visual arts world is a vital part of a globalizing cultural economy, an important vector in the constant negotiation between private and corporate enterprise and state power.[30] Joselit concludes that for some exemplary artists, such as Ai Weiwei, what Boris Groys calls "art power" is itself their medium.[31] Even as they compose within globalized capital's penumbra, they make works about the operations of this kind of power, while also boldly demonstrating the workings of other, more local and communal kinds of power. In Ai Weiwei's case, this means the power of individual resistance, mostly his own, but also that of ordinary people, as distinct from that of The People, as determined by The Party in power.

More cautious than Joselit, other authors prefer to announce that it is "too soon" to write the history, or even some histories, of contemporary art, but then proceed to lay down markers for future histories. Some university-based scholars who also act as art critics are fond of this approach. For example, Hal Foster, answering the question he posed in the *Art since 1900* roundtable, opens his 2015 collection of essays, *Bad New Days*, with this remark: "Contemporary art is so vast, so diverse, and, yes, so present as to frustrate any historical overview, and none is offered here." Instead, he goes on immediately to suggest, "A story can be told about some of the art of the past twenty-five years" because "coherent notions do exist for this work, and it remains one task of criticism to articulate such terms as best it can."[32] Notice the narrowing, and its basis: certain kinds of art, certain artworks, have generated or attracted "coherent notions." The critic's job is to parse these in their reviews and essays. Not the art historian's job, at least not yet, because the past twenty-five years is a period that "lies on the threshold of history," so it is "too early to historicize this art." But not, he believes, too early to theorize it. He hastens to warn that he does not mean the application to art of independently developed theories (from philosophy, literary theory, sociology, whatever theory as such). Instead, the goal is "to extract some concepts embedded in some practices."[33] Which he then proceeds to do, exploring in depth, and with his usual acuity, how several European and American artists have evoked and worked through a set of concepts: abjection, the archival, mimetic excess, and precarity. He rightly rejects the idea, widespread in Western art worlds, of the "postcritical." He favors, instead, a critical insistence on "actuality."

A tentative sketch of what actuality might mean appears in the concluding paragraph. He values as "superior" those "artworks that are able to constellate not only different registers of experience (aesthetic, cognitive, and critical) but also different orders of temporality."[34] Right. Long-term readers will have picked up the resonance of Foster's signature insistence on "the real."[35] They will have noted its being updated, made contemporary, by the addition of the imperative to constellate "different orders of temporality." It is interesting that, having denied the valiance of historical perspectives on the present in the main text, in a footnote toward the end of the book, he frames actuality in explicitly art-historiographical terms, as a narrative about the changes in art-historical method I have been tracking in this chapter:

> In a first moment, globalization made some art historians more alert to the spatial extent of art history; then, in a second moment, it sensitized others to its complicated temporality. "Actuality" can be understood as the becoming present of the past, as when we speak of the actuality of an historical figure (artist, author, other), a renewed relevance that often occurs through the medium of a contemporary figure in his or her field. That becoming present of the past is also, of course, a becoming past of the present. In some ways actuality is my attempt to triangulate the claims of both anachronicity and historicity and, in so doing, to resist the indeterminacies of the former and the restrictions of the latter.[36]

THE ZONE OF TRANSLATION: WORLD ART, GLOBAL ART, GLOBALITY

Titles such as *After Art*, *Forgetting the Art World*, and *Bad New Days* signal their authors' recognition (with dismay, delight, or mixed feelings) that the authority structures, evaluative systems, and narrative of art's historical development that had prevailed in the modern era could do so no longer—despite their inner dynamism, the real contradictions that drove them, and the often great art they enabled. Key constituents of modern art worlds have not disappeared—indeed, as we have seen, they constantly struggle to reassert themselves, to update by combining with some of the softer contemporary energies. But larger trajectories arc through the present: Euro-American conceptions of what counts as an art world are being steadily provincialized as art worlds emerge all over the planet, some conjured into existence by central institutions such as museums and auction houses, but most driven by their own expansive needs and energies.

Australian art historian Ian McLean sees this change as the contemporary aspiration for a multiplicitous, dispersed, and networked *world art* overriding the modern concept of a concentrated, centralized *art world*. He points out that "world art" reverses the terms of the "artworld" concept as defined by Arthur Danto in his famous article of 1964, in which the philosopher emphasized that it was defined by an atmosphere of artistic theory, a shared knowledge of the history of art, and an interest in puzzling about what might count as artistic change.[37] McLean charts the prevalence of national art worlds during the twentieth century, the ascendency of New York as a "meta-Artworld" during the Cold War (precisely what Danto was taking as given), and the more recent emergence of the idea of world art, especially as globalization intensified after 1980. After World War II, he suggests, the New York meta–art world could reinforce its claims to universality because of the worldwide economic and political power of the United States. But this was buying time. In fact, the provincialist bind was "not simply an after-effect of a powerful center, but structured the very center of its power," thus making provincialism an "intractable" problem for all concerned.[38] McLean notes that, today, "world art is tolerant of local artworlds, such as indigenous ones, and is predicated on the assumption that it is a zone of translation that can move between artworlds and be in more than one simultaneously."[39] This moves strongly toward the worldliness, or *mondialité*, that, I argue in chapters 7 and 8, is being increasingly embraced by contemporary artists throughout the world, a contested, yet insistent, sense of moving from making an art *of* the world (of the universals, as seen from Euro-America), through being an art generated *from* (the rest of) the world, toward becoming an art *for* the world (as it was, as it is, in its divided, self-consuming state, and as it might become if the coeval commons can be created). We see here, in its most general form, the underlying logic of the relationships between the three contemporaneous currents discussed in earlier chapters, and the layered character of today's *art to come*.

But the seismic shift from modern art to world art, from contemporary art to *art to come*, has been too abrupt and too ragged for most members of most art worlds, local or international. Instead, as we have seen, debate has turned on whether contemporary art has been shaped primarily by the economic, social, and cultural changes introduced by globalizing capitalism, or whether today's art, or at least significant parts of it, is being energized by the thirst of the world's peoples for a viable presence within a complex yet nonetheless in principle shareable world order. "Globalization" or "globality": Which orientation prevails at present, which is likely to persist into our imaginable futures, which *should* do so?[40]

Contemporary artistic practice everywhere was no doubt profoundly shaped by the forces of globalization that, from the 1980s until recently, predominated within international economic exchange, drove much of world politics, and disseminated spectacle as the theater of individual and collective imagination in the lives of people all over the world. Globalized perceptions of contemporary art have been heavily promoted by major museums in search of a competitive edge as centers of attraction within spectacle culture. They continue to be used by the international art market to push up prices in what became, around 2000, its most glamorous, risky, and, in principle, infinitely self-replenishing sector. Every day we see examples of how important contemporary art is to the lifestyle agendas of the recently rich, its prevalence in popular media, and how it is used to anchor massive revitalization efforts or new real estate projects by developers going after high-end markets, and by cities and nations competing for tourist dollars.

Historians of contemporary art want to know the details of how these mediations occurred, why they did so, and how they have changed since their unmistakable confluence in the 1980s. Was the globalization of the art system prefigured in the internationalization of art during the 1960s? If so, was it expressed in aspects of the styles emergent at that time—pop, minimal, conceptual, process, land art, and so forth—or were they mainly manifestations of, and actions against, Cold War configurations? Did globalized art values spread from the modern cultural centers along with the inroads of multinational capital, intergovernmental agencies, and new technologies? Did this lead to homogenization first, followed by the controlled signification of locality as globalizing agents—meeting local resistances and seeking to incorporate them—adopted "glocal" methods of production? What about local agency? Did it not, like the earlier responses to Western modernization, take various forms, ranging from total welcome, through pragmatic accommodation and selective appropriation, to outright rejection? Have these not been as different in each place as were the responses to modernization? Surely, actions and attitudes such as antiglobalist resistance, defiant localism, third world regionalism, critical cosmopolitanism, and evasive tangentiality amount to a diverse set of differences. Should we see such reactions as in dialectical opposition to top-down globalization, as in continuity with previous countercurrents, or as quite distinct emergent modes of living?

First reactions to the effects of the new economic order on the visual arts were swift: rapturous embrace alongside outright condemnation. This was especially evident in the response to the Young British Artists (yBa) phenomenon of the 1990s. The boldness of yBa artists' work, and the extraordinary publicity generated by the artists and their collectors, such as Charles Saatchi, earned them immediate celebrity. Nonetheless, a few English critics—notably, John A. Walker, Julian Stallabrass, and Jonathan Harris—saw them immediately as front men and women for globalization.[41] In the US, by contrast, the contemporary art history academy and much of the art press was, with few exceptions, complicit or quiescent in its response to parallel developments. Against such passivity, the aggressive public campaign against corporate art waged during the 1980s and 1990s by art critic Robert Hughes deserves our praise for its moral vigor if not for the reactionary terms in which it was frequently put.[42]

The Global Art and the Museum project, led by Hans Belting and Andrea Buddensieg between 2006 and 2014, pursued these questions more thoroughly, and on a wider geographic scale, than other art-historical inquiries.[43] Noting that Western museums, scholars, and collectors, as well as many artists and teachers, had hitherto treated "non-Western art" as ahistorical and as ethnic (compared to the historically unfolding, universally relevant art of the West), Belting argued that living artists from these parts of the world feel that their art is "post-historical" and "post-ethnic." That is, they are intent on creating a "global art," contemporary with that being made in Euro-America and as specific, as valuable in itself, as art being made anywhere.[44]

The culmination of the Global Art and the Museum project was the exhibition *The Global Contemporary: Art Worlds after 1989*, presented at the Center for Art and Media, Karlsruhe, in September 2011. Curators Belting, Buddensieg, and Peter Weibel insisted that they wanted to highlight the importance of a "global practice that has changed contemporary art as radically as 'new media' had done previously."[45] Several contemporary artists explicitly state that achieving such a practice is their goal, and many, such as the Raqs Media Collective, are among its most articulate theorists.[46] Some have posed this ambition as a general goal for contemporary art today. For example, Indian cultural theorist and curator Nancy Adajania draws on Okwui Enwezor's identification of a widespread "will to globality" among peoples everywhere to characterize "globalism" as "the foundational premise" of her practice, one that is "not merely a reaction to globalisation, but as the audacious and positive reflection of a desire to release the cultural self towards others in a manner that bypasses dependency and embraces collaboration, thus making for a productive cosmopolitanism."[47] This would amount to a substantial reorientation of the way art is made in the world. It claims that making local issues visible is a value in itself and for itself, and that this is an important way in which both local and global inequities may be renegotiated toward respect for difference. Terms used for these aspirations include a "new internationalism," a "cosmopolitan aesthetic," and a comparative art history based on recognition of the values of each "cultural self" within the exchange.[48]

One of the most compelling articulations of this desire to be deeply, ethically worldly can be found in the Filipino art historian Patrick Flores's account of what he learned during his participation in the Global Art and the Museum project. Reflecting on a drawing by Francisco Goya titled *For Being Born Elsewhere* (1814–23), he says,

> It occurred to me that while in another time, to be born elsewhere meant fate worthy of death, exclusion by virtue of a different genesis, in the ecology of the contemporary, to be birthed elsewhere might be a privilege, in fact an exception by virtue of a genetic, which is natural, difference. For a body to emerge in another place is to affirm a vast worldliness that enables equivalent histories and humanities to reciprocate, to demonstrate the index of belonging and the attendant violence and promise this belonging entails in the process of by turns being conquered and being in the world with others.

He elaborates this core idea as follows:

> "Being born elsewhere" is a condition and at the same time, in light of the word "for," the basis for a decision to claim to have originated locally, to be native and folk not as heritage but as entitlement, and to be self-conscious about this lineage and the modernity of this self-consciousness, just like the feeling of others who have been verisimilarly born elsewhere in their own province and in a world within. It is this locality of origin, this autonomy of emergence eccentrically, that ensures the disposition to move beyond it, to explore the finitude of difference and the infinity of the new. It is this freedom to emerge elsewhere that guarantees the subject of contemporary means to properly participate in the project of emancipation or transcendence—to be free, at last. The "contemporary" is, therefore, radical to the degree that it motivates us to at once internalise the totality of the self and of the universe and to transcend it.

Drawing on the thought of Édouard Glissant, he ties this conception of contemporaneity to contemporary art in a manner that resonates with much of the argument of this book:

It is difficult to grasp this in language, but I think the "global" is nuanced enough a term to probe the "contemporary art" that we so diligently, if not vexingly, contemplate. It insinuates the constraint of the "all"; it prefigures "all" possibility in what a thinker so felicitously conceives as the "sudden vicinity of things." On the one hand, there is the belief that global art or art that is made contemporaneously all over the world in the present is coordinated by some meta-structure of neoliberal persuasion. On the other, there is the always-already resolute desire to resist this totality, an everyday hope that resistance would actually inhere in the truly worldly. In this vein, the "global contemporary" because it lives in the same time but in different places, at discrepant rhythms, through a gamut of vectors, is by nature, to borrow a phrase from the philosopher of the Baroque José Lezama Lima, "errant in form, but firmly rooted in its essences." It is this errant form and essential rootedness that is quite elusive, too nimble to be caught by any instrumentalist impulse. But it is also neither eternally inchoate nor aleatory; it is errant, and therefore conscious of norm, aware of translation, decisively political; it is rooted, and therefore sensitive to origin and the future. It invests in the procedures of communication, dialogue, collaboration, reciprocity; it is determinate at the same time that it is chastened by the "commonality of finitude," and so open to chance and precarity, and the dreams of lastingness. This construction site, this laboratory, this emergent place of making and unmaking, is an effort to create a situation of this play, speculation, critique, bricolage, going out on a limb for art that must outlive certain contexts that oftentimes refuse it, from an earth in near exhaustion to a multitude in unimaginable poverty and persecution.[49]

BIENNIALS AND THE GLOBAL WORK OF ART

In Caroline A. Jones's 2016 book, *The Global Work of Art: World's Fairs, Biennials, and the Aesthetics of Experience*, she boldly theorizes the globality of contemporary art as the outcome of historical developments two centuries in the making.[50] She links large conjectures to in-depth archival research, and philosophical reflection to lively reports of personal experiences, to craft a narrative of how the exhibitionary platforms of the modern era were transformed into those of a globalized world. She argues that the European expositions of industrial manufactures and commercial goods—above all, the 1851 World's Fair in

London—established recurrent, nationally competitive, and thus *international* "festal structures" that were taken up by art biennials, led by Venice in 1895, and that peaked in the art and architectural face-offs at the 1937 Paris World's Fair. At São Paulo in 1951, a second wave of biennials was unleashed. Now numbering over three hundred, and ubiquitous throughout the world, this exhibitionary form is fully global, Jones insists, in the kind of *world-making work* that it requires from "three types of historical actors: organizers/curators, artists, and visitors" (xi). While not claiming to be all-inclusive, this is a strong historical hypothesis that these exhibitionary platforms are the key to how art became contemporary, and about its core characteristics today.

The broad strokes of this argument are commonplace in the collective memories of many institutions and participants, and within the emerging body of historical scholarship about exhibitions and curatorship.[51] Jones remarks in her preface, "While a growing number of publications have examined globalization in contemporary art, none situate 'the contemporary' within the lingering effects and remnant structures of nineteenth-century world's fairs" (xi). It might be more accurate to say that most authors would see such remnants as one among the many modern ruins that resonate in contemporary times, often in spectacularized versions of their former forms. She goes on to suggest, "If one focuses on the emergence of the contemporary biennial, one quickly realizes that the key structures of the current exhibitionary complex, the undisputed foundations of contemporary display, were put in place more than a century ago" (xi). Indeed, Tony Bennett's foundational studies, notably in his *The Birth of the Museum* (1995), have shown that, since the later eighteenth century, an interrelated complex of exhibitionary formats—museums, world's fairs, entertainment zones, and publicity in its multiple forms—developed in the European metropolitan centers and spread throughout their cultural colonies, including the United States.[52]

When we take into account the size, variety, and indeed complexity of this complex—especially its contemporary dimensions, where in the visual arts alone, more than thirty specific, specialized exhibitionary institutions and quasi-institutions have been established, all expanding, interacting, competing, and combining, among which the biennial is but one[53]—we might wonder whether Jones's overall argument does not have the shape of an hourglass, with the enormous energies of nineteenth-century nationalism, mercantile promotion, and individual self-interest flowing down through the rather narrow slot of the few biennials of the first half of the twentieth century, followed by a flood unleashed since the 1990s, leading to a biennialization of almost everything to do with contemporary art, thought, and life, an effect that she dubs "the aesthetics of experience." Museums, private galleries, art criticism, annual exhibitions, as well as some important recurrent exhibitions (the Carnegie International, since 1896; the Whitney Biennial, since 1932), recede into the background, while a dozen (fascinating) pages are devoted to an exhibition, *When Attitudes Become Form*, that was not a biennial (171–83).

We can see the shape of Jones's argument more clearly if we compare it to a parallel response to the same phenomena, also published in 2016: *Biennials, Triennials, and Documentas: The Exhibitions That Created Contemporary Art*, by Charles Green and Anthony Gardner. Their subtitle makes the same general claim and is equally hyperbolic. We can have no such reservation about their more modest contention that "art during the contemporary period has been indelibly marked by the biennials that were held around the globe, and that this situation stretches back to the start of the Cold War." Thus they set out to locate "the cultural geography of biennials during this transition to contemporaneity: in the world at large, not inside one of its zones, looking out."[54] To do so, they pose these questions:

> We replace the usual, reductive, and immobilizing question—do biennials promote or subvert globalization?—with the far more interesting question that others have also raised: are they the artistic playgrounds of neoliberal capitalism or do they enable the forging and testing of alternative, critical, even subtly subversive perspectives? We show that each biennial's success was completely dependent on real and pressing contingencies, but also on understanding that neoliberalism and criticality were not mutually exclusive pathways. And from that, we show that biennials would still face a further question that artists themselves knew was far from trivial and which would remain unresolved: would biennials serve, lead, or be passive spectators to the new "world orders" around them?[55]

They begin with a detailed consideration of Documenta 5, curated in 1972 by Harald Szeemann, reading it, as do most commentators, as "a *statement*, akin to a work of art in itself."[56] More than others, but like Jones, they emphasize the "second wave" of biennials, beginning with São Paulo in 1951, including Sydney from 1973, as exhibitions that "sought to bring the modern North Atlantic to the South," and those, such as Havana from 1984, that promoted "South-South" exchanges between cultures "non-aligned" with the Cold War superpowers. Highlighting Sydney in 1979 and Havana in 1989, they agree with Rafel Niemojewski that these biennials were "early instances of a new type of heterogeneous discursive sphere capable of addressing current art practice while simultaneously exploring some of the most complex predicaments of the time."[57] World's fairs persist as a countermodel, then disappear in the third wave of the 1990s, which saw several biennials inaugurated in eastern Europe, at the edges of Europe (notably Manifesta, the mobile biennial), and in Africa. The wave became a tsunami in Asia, where focusing on the art of the region became a priority (here they draw on the work of John Clark). By the years around 2000, some recurrent mega-exhibitions took on the task of presenting, and also critically interrogating, what had become a global network. Okwui Enwezor's Documenta 11 (2002) was itself globally distributed between five "platforms" in different cities, each of which reviewed an aspect of postcoloniality in conditions of globalization. Enwezor adopted the Havana model of a team of curators mounting various internal exhibitions, as did Francesco Bonami for the 2003 Venice Biennale, a practice that has become common ever since. Noting parallels with the Grand Tours of the eighteenth century, Green and Gardner conclude by highlighting the "globalized biennials" of recent years, which are "coordinated to lure increased international tourism and the global curatorium to visit otherwise scattered networks of exhibitions."[58] Thus they arrive at the questions and answers and further questions cited above.

Jones works in a similarly layered and nuanced fashion, but across a longer historical span. Rather than offering a comprehensive picture of the evolution of the biennial as an exhibitionary form, she homes in on particular times and places. All her in-depth studies are of Western phenomena, a focus that she sets out to trouble even while admitting that her "situation" is "provincial, partial, and located within specific languages and hemispheric histories" (xii). For how long will frank admissions of practical limitations be sufficient when it comes to thinking of globality? Her ambition, on the other hand, is not at all limited: she wants to track the relationships between three universals—world picturing, the work of art, and experience as such—from the mid-nineteenth century to the present. As I discuss regarding world picturing in chapters 7 and 8, none of these are simple and singular in their evolution, nor do the relationships between them unfold steadily. As we would expect during the modern era, dialectic and conflict were the rule, and today, they are all over the place, in every sense.

World's fairs staged world picturing explicitly, linking Enlightenment ideals such as the "ascent of man" and the advancement of knowledge to the dream of material progress for all, meanwhile demonstrating the dynamism of imperialism and colonization as the scarcely hidden subtext. But the lofty aims, Jones rightly insists, were always countered by skeptical others—artists in particular, and many commentators, but also by some festival organizers, then later by biennial curators, artists, and critics, all committed to exposing the dark underbelly of the official world picture, through their practice of what she calls "a blind epistemology," that is, an openness to all the senses, not just the dominant sense of sight.[59] This is a rich idea, which she pursues throughout the book. It grounds, historically, the "critical globalism" that she passionately advocates as "an approach to art-making, a mode of reception for art-viewing, and a hermeneutic for curatorial practice" today [xiii]. Her challenge is "OCCUPY THE GLOBAL!" (xiv). Right on!

Jones's emphasis on the *work* that works of art do, the work that they require from those who make them, exhibit them, and respond to them, is a welcome move from the object-centered obsessions that have become an orthodoxy in recent years. She values "certain kinds of contemporary art that produce us as entangled and enmeshed in worldly being, aware of multiple connections and critical of certain hierarchies implicit within them" (xii). In a stand-out chapter, she works through the archives of a preparatory exhibition—*From Figuration to Abstraction* (1949)—and those of the first São Paulo Bienal to demonstrate that "the brilliance of the Brazilian artists and critics of the 1950s and 1960s" lay in their "incisive comprehension" of an economy in which "artists who would enter large-scale repeating exhibitions' competitions must adopt an international language, in which they are often required to speak of their own difference," but above all in their "thorough going rejection of its terms." This rejection occurred, she argues, in two phases. First, in founder Francisco Matarazzo's shaping of the biennial itself as one in which Brazilian and other Latin American artists would present work understood as being exactly the same kind (of abstraction) as that which was, at the time, celebrated in Europe and the United States. Illuminatingly, she describes this as seeking "import substitution," a challenge to Euro-American internationalization mounted from within (123). Rather than seeing this as an example of provincial dependence, Jones hails this strategy as a self-confident "refusal to speak of difference," that is, of difference determined externally (xiii). Second, the "instrumental revival," by artists such as Lygia Clark and Hélio Oiticica, of "their own theory of *antropofagia*." To Jones, these two maneuvers did more than produce a standard, modernist art-historical rupture that precipitated a progression from concrete to neoconcrete art. Rather, these curators and artists were "metabolizing modernism on a molecular level to hybridize and syncretize a truly contemporary art" (xiii).

Today, few would dispute these characterizations and value judgments, and if they did, they would be wrong. More caution is warranted, however, toward Jones's claims about how quickly these changes occurred and about how widespread their consequence was. The last citation, for example, reminds us that it actually took some decades for the achievement of the Brazilian neoconcretists to fully realize their aims, and even longer for the realization to be acknowledged, in Brazil, in the region, and in the rest of the world (New York museums, for example, have begun to catch up only in the past few years). Similarly, while statements such as "The São Paulo Bienal opened its doors in 1951 and forever changed art-world geography, producing a new, *global* work of art" (113) are exciting, they collapse historical unfolding into an instant, risk mistaking an aim for a result, and exaggerate the effect of one cause among many. The narrative offered by Green and Gardner is more measured in this respect.

What about Jones's third major claim, that the "experience economy" so pervasive today—as if, we might say, all the world were a world's fair, all the time—nevertheless remains open to the "critical globalism" mentioned above, which enables, in turn, an "aesthetics of experience"? That this phrase evokes American pragmatist John Dewey's famous celebration of *Art as Experience*, the title of his book published in 1934, is no accident. Throughout, Jones draws deeply on the thinking of major philosophers, treating their ideas, quite properly, not as distant commentary, but as themselves world making, including in their influence on artists, organizers, and visitors. The Enlightenment project of the world's fairs was of course indebted to the French *philosophes* and to Kant. Heidegger provides her with a crucial insight into why the 1937 Paris World's Fair was such a turning point in the history of such expositions.

When Martin Heidegger began drafting his famous essay "The Age of the World Picture" in 1935, he did so expecting to lead the German delegation to the philosophical congress associated with the world's fair to be held in Paris two years later. The French organizers had decided to devote the Ninth International Congress of Philosophy to a celebration of René Descartes's rationalism. Having just become rector at Freiburg University, long a German nationalist, and recently a Nazi Party sympathizer, Heidegger set out to expand his basic argument against the celebration of technology as definitive of modern life, thought, and aspiration. Lamenting the loss of being as grounded in actual worldly processes, he deplored the fact that "the fundamental event of the modern age is the conquest of the world as picture."[60] As Jones notes, "World's fairs had long functioned to throw 'subjective experience' and art into relief, figured against the 'objective' displays of technoscientific wonders and the industrial sublime," surmising that Heidegger may well have had "the fair mentality" in mind when writing his essay (197). In the event, the German government sent a party hack to the meeting. The real action occurred in the intense symbolic confrontation between the German and Soviet Pavilions at a pivotal point in the fairgrounds, with associated skirmishes happening in smaller pavilions, not least that of the embattled Republic of Spain. Architectural design and works of art—such as Paul Troost's model of the Haus der Kunst at the heart of the German Pavilion, and Picasso's *Guernica* in the Spanish—did ideological battle between opponents already engaged in indirect conflict, soon to consume the continent, and much of the rest of the world, in all-out war.

After which, the world as we know it today became possible. As Jones puts it, "The historical moment of Heidegger's warning regarding an instrumental-ized 'world picture,' the aestheticization of 'the work of art,' and an unreflective 'experience' of both, constitutes a pivot in the fortunes of these concepts" (197). She shows that the critiques of Heideggerian thinking by Adorno, Benjamin, Foucault, Derrida, Lyotard, and Badiou, along with their own critical contribu-tions, have actively aided art and exhibition making to become contemporary.

These are exemplary uses of critical theory to write a richer, more percep-tive history of art's inner workings. Finally, in an unusual but (for an American thinker) quite consistent recursion, John Dewey has the last word. His demo-cratic pragmatism, Jones argues, enables us to see that some important Enlight-enment values still resonate, however faintly. They offer hope for an ethical "aesthetics of experience" to challenge the neoliberal "experience economy," and for a "critical globalism" to challenge globalization in all its forms. While these rather generalizing terms may not convince, Jones *is* convincing (mostly) when she demonstrates how several contemporary artists—from Joan Jonas and Willem Boshoff through Xu Bing, Mariko Mori, and Cai Guo-Qiang to Javier Téllez and Tino Sehgal—are working to challenge globalized cultures and their constraining world pictures, and that they often do so, affectively, and to great effect, from within—that is, in biennials.

MODERNISMS OF THE OTHERS

Chika Okeke-Agulu, historian of Nigerian modernism and, with Okwui En-wezor, of a book on contemporary African art that includes artists of the Af-rican diaspora, expresses concern about "how art history as a field today can effectively accommodate the multiplicity of narratives, methods, and ideologi-cal positions that inform the different manifestations of the discipline in many parts of the world and resist the impulse to homogenize not just the methods, but also the subjects of art historical inquiry."[61] He has in mind the cul-de-sac in which James Elkins found himself when he posed the question "Is art history global?"[62] Given Elkins's presumption that modern Western modes of art-historical inquiry were definitive of the discipline—universally, whatever the context—were the most sophisticated and effective; and were the most powerful anyway, it is no surprise that he found art writing elsewhere to be criticism, biography, national narrative, or mythmaking. Nowhere was it art history, except when taught by Westerners, or when following Western models. Against this, Okeke-Agulu avers: "Haunted as if by the specter of its own self-induced obsolescence, the revitalization of art history will require the rediscovery of the essence of multiculturalism: the recognition of varieties of cultural (and artistic) experiences and histories without the hierarchical assumptions of post-Enlightenment european knowledge systems," from which it follows that "methodologically, this process calls for the development of comparative art history . . . replacing standard units of art historical analysis tied to the enduring notion of fixed borders, nationalities, and regions, with ones that emphasize contact zones and the polycentricity of contemporary artistic production and traffic, and the experience of history."[63]

Okeke-Agulu's call for recognizing the local specificity of cultural values, and for the whole-scale adoption of comparative methods, is first a response to what contemporary art and the conditions of contemporaneity require of its interpreters, including its historians, today. But it is also an appeal with a broader time frame, applying equally to writing the mostly unwritten histories of *modern* art outside the main centers (and, I might add, to the mostly unwritten stories of art making, infrastructure building, and curating the "minor histories" *within* those centers). In practice, for him and many other historians and curators working all over the world, this is a more pressing task, one that has precedence over considering contemporary art. Indeed, many scholars and curators with worldly perspectives sense that the full armory of art-historical research should prioritize making known the detail, depth, and value of the "multiple modernities" created throughout the world during the twentieth century. It may turn out that these modernizations, shaped primarily by local necessities, are still playing out at the present. Perhaps they energize the ever-growing number of biennials, are appearing in new museums, and are slowly entering the world's major museums in the old centers. Perhaps, the argument goes, these other modernisms, the modernisms of the others—along with their contemporaneousness with one another, and their insistence on having a contemporary relevance of a different but equally if not more valuable kind than that of the art being produced in and for the former West—laid the foundations for the "global" or "worldly" contemporary art that we find all around us today. It follows that art historians should focus their gaze on the long histories of these modernisms, from their emergence during the twentieth century through their subsequent development to the present. The contemporary art worth thinking about will occur as the recent and current chapters in this story.

Indeed, it does, and does so in the form of the "transnational transitionality" that I have argued is the major current in world art today. It was not the main artistic transformer in the "becoming contemporary" of much art made in Euro-America from the 1950s to recent years—that was pop, minimalism, and conceptualism in their various forms—although it exists with the first current of contemporary art as an internal critique of the imperialism at a distance conducted from the centers, and it inspired, in part, the return to the real, the misnamed "ethnographic turn," and much of the critical practice in those centers since the 1980s. Respect for the multiplicity of diverse differences is a given within third current art but remains something to be constantly claimed and reclaimed against the reactionary resurgences occurring throughout the world. The struggle for this kind of respect can no longer be corralled under singularizing terms such as "multiculturalism" and is currently battling to maintain the actuality of diversity in officially approved terms such as "diversity."[64]

The comparative study of multiple modernities is a major focus of art-historical research today throughout the world: for example, John Clark's studies of Asian modernisms; Kobena Mercer's "cosmopolitan modernisms" within his Annotating Art's Histories: Cross-Cultural Perspectives in the Visual Arts project; Okeke-Agulu's *Postcolonial Modernism: Art and Decolonization in Twentieth-Century Nigeria*; and the focus on Indigenous modernisms in the Multiple Modernisms: Twentieth Century Artistic Modernism in Global Perspective project, led by a consortium of scholars from Ottawa, Cambridge, Wellington, Johannesburg, and elsewhere.[65] Comparative art history, or what Piotr Piotrowski named "spatial" or "horizontal" art history, rejecting the hierarchies built into modern Western art history, has become a widespread methodology.[66] Mercer puts it this way: "Instead of a narrative sequence of beginnings, middles, and ends that aspires to have the last word, the cultural studies methods I use in my own work are predicated on a provisionality whereby it is accepted that mapping the conjuncture of a closed and total system is impossible, and yet thinking about what joins the parts into an articulated whole is indispensible."[67]

These considerations are becoming widely shared by those interested in plotting the differential emergence of contemporary art in different parts of the world. In 2012, the Hong Kong–based Asia Art Archive, a nonprofit organization that has been documenting the recent history of contemporary art in Asia since 2000, posted its version of the *October* questionnaire. It sent out to its list the following questions:

> What role has the institution played in defining contemporary art? And where does individual practice locate itself in relation to institutional practice? How does the discourse on contemporary art reside within the greater paradigm of visual culture, in the context of the region? Are we trapped in a trope of "the contemporary"? How are temporality and historicity prescribed based on territoriality? Or how is territoriality proscribed by temporality and historicity? How are folk and traditional practices to be understood in relation to contemporary practices? Can the rise of institutions and the growth of the art industry within Asia endanger, rather than benefit, politically engaged art, [which is] an expression of individual agency that has emerged in the region out of necessity?[68]

The forty-one replies came mostly from curators, critics, and art historians, as well as from some artists, most of whom are based in the region. Singapore critic Lee Weng Choy called out *October* for limiting its invitation to potential respondents in the United States and Europe, finding specious its justification that the questions it posed were "specific to these regions." He pointed out that most of the *October* respondents highlighted the global nature of contemporary art, and he guessed that responses from Australia, Asia, and Latin America would be different, but not so different as to be unrecognizable.[69] While this also turned out to be largely true of the Asia Art Archive respondents, concerns specific to the region were flagged in almost all. I pick out just some, that are both specific to the region but also connect to the larger questions of writing histories of contemporary art. Earlier, I cited at length from Patrick Flores's response to the questionnaire: it is a brilliant evocation of the nature of worldly contemporaneity.

Most respondents noted the variation throughout the region in the availability of platforms able to pursue "independent critical thinking" about art and its institutional settings, and to do so relatively free from state control, market values, and private interests. Bangkok-based Australian curator and art historian David Teh profiled distinctive modes of making, exhibiting, marketing, and interpreting art within the region, depending on whether the national cultures were already modern, developed, and en route to becoming postindustrial economies (Japan, South Korea, Taiwan, Hong Kong, and Singapore); were developing, still postcolonial nations (Thailand, the Philippines, and Indonesia); or were "post-socialist laggards" (Laos, Cambodia, and Myanmar). China and India, he believes, are such internally complex societies that elements of all three models may be found unevenly distributed within them, and (I might add) within the same cities. In each place, a particular kind of interplay between what he calls "contemporaneity from above" and "contemporaneity from below" is taking place. He explains this insightful distinction as follows:

> There is something we might call "contemporaneity from below," whereby artists have devised aesthetic strategies for mediating between—and sometimes transcending—their local traditions and modernisms, and what they've seen abroad; and this has brought them into dialogue, and into circulation, with wider international currents. "The contemporary" has been the global, open-source discourse for lassoing many of these positions. There is also something like a contemporaneity from above, whereby institutions (including governments and the market) have picked up on this convergence and put themselves forward as champions and patrons of a local/regional "contemporary art." (In either case, this discourse of the contemporary is inextricable from a certain upswing in transnational flows of bodies and ideas.) In some places, both vectors are visible; but they don't necessarily always meet in the middle.[70]

This takes us beyond the Western versus Asian jingoism that artist Manuel Ocampo deplores in his comments on the welcoming by Manila museums and commercial galleries of art that parrots the "look" of Western contemporary art. In other situations, focusing on international issues can unlock a local blockage: Ahn Soyun, curator at the Man June Paik Art Center in Seoul, argues that in South Korea, the impasse in the 1980s between monochrome painting and *minjung* (peoples') art was broken by work such as that of Yiso Bahc. Teh points out that since 2003, Thailand has had an Office of Contemporary Art and Culture and a closely guarded market infrastructure, around and through which, he remarks, artists have learned to tread carefully "in figuring a contemporaneity that's legible and inoffensive to both local and international audiences.... Negotiating smooth passage between these two barely overlapping spheres distinguishes the most successful contemporary artists. But what qualifies their contemporaneity abroad is often quite differ-ent from what qualifies it at home."[71] These challenges are present for artists, curators, and others throughout the region. Some respondents trace the recent history of how these challenges have been met in various cities, such as curator Iola Lenzi regarding museums in Singapore. The struggle to establish alterna-tive art spaces in indifferent, wary, or hostile social environments is the main concern of Delhi critic and curator Gayatri Sinha, Hong Kong curator Jeff Leung, director of Art Space Project in Seoul Heejin Kim, Beijing critic Carol Lu, and historian of these spaces in Shanghai Karen Smith.

Regarding the necessity of historical perspectives when it comes to under-standing "the contemporary," Hong Kong–based art historian David Clarke, author of *Chinese Art and Its Encounter with the World*, emphasizes that "re-fusal of an artificial distinction between modern and contemporary is particu-larly important in the case of non-Western art, since it has become easy for Western institutions to incorporate art from other parts of the world within decontextualised presentations of the contemporary without any serious threat to Western cultural hegemony."[72] No surprise, then, that many respondents tackled the questions by locating them with short histories of the develop-ment of art worlds in their city, state, or region. Delhi curator Vidya Shivadas sketches the debates in postindependence India as to whether the major na-tional museum of art should be "modern" or "contemporary," with conserva-tives arguing for the latter on the grounds that art in India was not yet ready to be modern. Calcutta historian Tapati Guha Thakurta outlines the cultural role of state institutions in modern India and urges the contemporary value of "disaggregating national modernism" in favor of neglected local and vernacular art histories.[73]

The actualities of uneven development, systemic inequalities, regional dif-ferences, and the chaos sown by what we can now see has been an insurrection-ary globalizing capitalism continue to derail utopic aspirations for art in Asia, as elsewhere. In Ravi Sundaram's comments at an Indian Art Fair forum in 2012 on the topic "Has the Contemporary Come and Gone?" the urbanist and co-founder of the Sari Program at the Center for Study of Developing Societies, Delhi, drew attention to three ways of modeling our contemporaneity that, he believes, have run out of time, mainly because they remain essentially modern. They are, first, Nietzsche's implacable antipathy to "the fever of modernity" and the faith in history that possesses one's contemporaries; second, Agam-ben's identification of an attitude of disidentification with the present, and of openness to multiple temporalities; and, third, "the melodrama of the western decline and the Asian arrival," a world picture that is widespread in his region. He believes that the brutal imposition of nation-state ideologies in Asia, notably in India, since World War II has left the ideal of an "independent cultural public still-born many decades after independence." The recent radical expansion of media infrastructure, however, has created a highly tech-savvy populace. The "productive and fearful" promise of the present, he argues, is that "the old zone of the people has mutated into archivists, activists, archaeologists, media producers, event instigators, producing event scenes, artists, destroyers of the old secrets of power."[74] This takes the third current I identify as occurring, not within art domains, but among the multitudes. Just how it will shape artistic practice is yet to be seen.

FROM MODERN TO CONTEMPORARY ART

In the same spirit as the multiple modernisms/alternative modernities project, increasing numbers of art historians are exploring specific transformations that occurred throughout the world during the 1950s and 1960s, as artists responded to both international tendencies and local situations with a highly developed consciousness of their contemporaneity. Rather than (or as well as) seeing them as moments in the history of modern art, these are (or are also) being reviewed as the origins of tendencies in contemporary art. Attention is focusing on the years immediately following World War II as a time in which some, or many, of the concerns shaping art today first took significant form. Radical revisioning of art-historical narratives of the postwar and Cold War periods are being undertaken in exhibitions throughout the world at the moment, led by curators, who are bringing art historians along with them. This is nowhere more obviously the case than in Germany. *Postwar: Art between the Pacific and the Atlantic, 1945–1965*, at the Haus der Kunst, Munich, from October 14, 2016, to March 26, 2017, curated by Okwui Enwezor, Katy Siegel, and Ulrich Wilmes, showed World War II to be a truly global phenomenon, to which artists everywhere responded in a rich variety of ways. *Art in Europe, 1946–1968: The Continent That Europe Does Not Know*, at ZKM: Center for Art and Media, Karlsruhe, from November 22, 2016, to January 29, 2017, curated by Eckhart J. Gillen and Peter Weibel, focused on artists working in western, central and eastern Europe, including Russia. *Parapolitics: Cultural Freedom and the Cold War*, at the Haus der Kulturen der Welt, Berlin, from November 3, 2017, to January 8, 2018, curated by Anselm Frank, Nida Ghouse, Paz Guvara, and Antonia Majaca, explored the impact of the "freedom offensive" conducted by the CIA through cultural agencies such as the Congress for Cultural Freedom. Although concentrating on the two decades after 1945, these exhibitions clearly reflect elements of the current crises facing Europe today, and Germany in particular.

In such contexts, art historians are showing that contemporaneity itself became an explicit and central point of contention. For example, Reiko Tomii has long been fascinated by the avant-gardist innovations of Japanese artists during the 1960s that paralleled and, in some cases, preceded similar breakthroughs by artists working in art centers in Europe or the United States. At the time, some critics perceived this phenomenon as a kind of "international contemporaneity" (*kokusaiteki dojisei*), suggesting that certain Japanese artists were not only up to date with new tendencies emerging in Euro-American art, but also were producing unique innovations of comparable significance.[75] Tomii's book *Radicalism in the Wilderness: International Contemporaneity and 1960s Art in Japan* demonstrates that certain artists who lived and worked outside Tokyo during this period—Matsuzawa Yutaka and the groups the Play and GUN—were creating with a kind and a degree of experimentalism that, in fact, anteceded similar work made shortly afterward in Tokyo—by Gutai members, for example—and by well-known artists in other countries. Taking off from this set of confluences, she extrapolates contemporaneity as the core methodology for a thoroughly comparativist "world art history" that would be, as she puts it, "truly transnational."

> In constructing world art history, contemporaneity offers an organizing principle, wherein connections and resonances, two markers of contemporaneity, serve to generate contact points with varying degrees of connectedness that can be examined in terms of their similar yet dissimilar nature. These contact points constitute components of multiple narratives. A strategy of world art history, contemporaneity helps us construct and amplify a narrative from bottom up (or "periphery in"), rather than imposing a top-down (or "center-out") abstract framework. Whereas contemporaneity is an overarching macro concept, it becomes a micro concept when deployed in any particular instance. As a foundational tool, comparison of connections and resonances creates contact points that puncture the established Eurocentric narrative. Contact points will open up the existing narrative and paradigm, creating intersecting tangents of perspectives. With each contact point, the rigid linearity of the

familiar narrative is loosened, and new narrative tangents will be drawn in reflection of a local logic and context, with contemporaneity binding them all together.[76]

To date, this is the most concrete application of the concept of contemporaneity (in the multiplicitous sense that I have been advocating) to the everyday tasks of art-historical inquiry: tracking who made which work of art, when, where, how, why, and with which effects, then and since. It lifts this enterprise from the constraints of the empirical because it asks all these questions about each work in relation to those other works with which it is truly contemporary, taking this relationship to be the most important among all those from which the work emerged. It suggests some tools through which contemporal relationships may be plotted, such as "connections" (direct knowledge or exchange) and "resonances" (parallels seen in hindsight). It is alert to the fact that works of art are complex products, with many aspects, some of which may be "similar," others "dissimilar," to aspects of the works of artists active in other places.

As it builds toward a total picture of world art history, this approach begins from inside each national art history and then looks for connections, if they are there, and for comparisons, if they are warranted, to developments within other national histories. It also, as a wider step, tracks developments in the exchanges between these artistic cultures. Tomii comments, "It is not unlike mapping a river with numerous tributaries and branches—but more three dimensionally, factoring undercurrents below its surface at different locations." Having demonstrated how her "micro-expansions with fine-tuned subnarratives and details" can loosen up the Eurocentric master narrative as it applied to 1960s Japan, Tomii suggests, "Any locale where international contemporaneity was at work can likewise be investigated," not least because "the assimilation and internalization of Western ideas and practices was part of the learning process in multiple modernisms," for example, China throughout the twentieth century, and especially since the end of the Cultural Revolution.[77]

Applied to writing histories of contemporary art, Tomii's model is further useful in drawing attention, as she does in her epilogue, to the varying intensities to which "international contemporaneity" prevailed in particular art worlds, especially during the transitional periods in which it originated. Even in 1960s Japan, she admits, its hold was fragile in the face of the "discursive dominance" of the Euro-American centers, which constantly pitched local artists back into belatedness.[78] Contemporaneity in a more general sense, and on a much broader—in fact, worldwide—scale was crucial to the emergence of contemporary art, as she recognizes:

> What is fascinating about the 1960s is that despite all the local differences, contemporaneity more often than not binds together all the practices in widespread places with a resonating overarching challenge—in this case, the challenge to fundamentally call into question the institution of art as codified in modernism. In other words, in the 1960s, modernisms matured in varying degrees, with an increasing number of local times beginning to synchronize and artists of different localities moving in one or more shared directions simultaneously.[79]

Contemporary art was indeed initiated within this questioning and has been pursuing the implications of its answers ever since, along with those that it has found, and is still finding, to the many new challenges that have arisen since those years.

FEMINIST INTERVENTIONS

Feminist art history has scored many victories, and suffered several setbacks, since its early, radical articulations during the transformatory moments of late modernity, while becoming itself one of the key components of our contemporaneity. In the 1970s, a passionate demand arose for due recognition of the historical and current achievements of women artists. It was followed in the 1980s by an excited sense that feminist perspectives could change the discipline as a whole, just as they seemed to be doing in psychoanalysis, in many other disciplines, and in theoretical work of all kinds. Reactionary pushback and institutional passive-aggression have stalled this radicalization, as they have many others. Contemporary conditions are demonstrating, painfully, that the progress of feminism's vision of freedom for all is not inevitable, no more than any other such vision. This war, and its many battles, must be constantly fought, won, won again, and yet again, as the fields of operation keep changing shape. Foundational texts by Linda Nochlin, such as her 1971 essay "Why Have There Been No Great Women Artists?," remain ever relevant, as do the critical writings of Lucy Lippard, bell hooks, and others.[80] Norma Broude and Mary D. Garrard published several anthologies of feminist art history in the 1980s and 1990s that successively highlighted major themes in feminist art historiography.[81] Whitney Chadwick's *Women, Art, and Society*, first published in 1990, reached its fifth edition in 2012.[82] Griselda Pollock's career-long "feminist interventions into art history" includes several powerful art-historiographical reflections, culminating most recently in her frank and searching 2014 essay, "Whither Art History?"[83]

A useful accounting of the fortunes of feminist art practice, history, and theory appears in the introduction to Hilary Robinson's *Feminism Art Theory: An Anthology, 1968–2014*.[84] She poses three questions: "What are the intersections that occur between the politics of feminism, the making of art, and the activities of analysis and critical thinking? How can these intersections be traced from the early encounters between the women's liberation movement and the art world? And how has this movement historicized itself and its own complexity?" Alert to the large-scale changes signaled by events such as the fall of the Berlin Wall in 1989 and the 9/11 attacks, among many others, Robinson notes, "These events required feminists in the West to reconsider not only cultural differences but also the nature of feminist politics, thinking, and histories," with the result that "we cannot assume a narrative that defines progress, or that feminism has become more enlightened and sophisticated, or that it has had increasing success; nor can we presume that feminist thinking started somewhere (usually white, middleclass, America) and then was exported and adopted by other groups and other places." She celebrates the recent resurgence of feminist activism as part of social movements throughout the world, and the prevalence of major exhibitions surveying historical and current work by women artists, but concludes by noting the necessity of "sharp analysis and concerted exposure of the economic realities for women generally and in the artworld in particular."[85] Activist groups composed of artists, critics, historians and others, such as the Guerilla Girls and, more recently, Pussy Galore, have been unstinting in calling out the persistence of gender and race disparities in leading commercial galleries and major museums. Individual artists such as Micol Hebron and curators such as Maura Reilly have done the same.[86] Despite some general improvement, and moments of roughly equal representation, the overall tendency in the major metropolitan art centers remains one of constant recursion to patriarchal norms and racial exclusion. The title of Robinson's introduction, "Feminism Art Theory: Towards a (Political) Historiography," makes it clear that, in contemporary conditions, the feminist project—like that of queer theory—continues to face the challenges of reinventing its forms of struggle. The Women's Marches in cities throughout the world, which led protest against the outcome of the 2016 US presidential election, demonstrate the resilience of this resistance, and its now necessarily global nature.

Ever since the practice of art history took its modern forms in Germany and France in the later nineteenth century, one of its core missions has been to grasp how visual images parse the interactions between multiple temporalities. It has pursued, for example, the strange, or normalizing, afterlife of the classical; the constant updating of settings depicting episodes from the life of Christ; the persistence of pagan motifs in both sacred and secular art; the competitive creation of national art traditions; modernist art's insistence on its own eternal novelty; and the varying lives of "universal" forms in the "art" made at all times and in all places. As Erwin Panofsky insisted on tracking the iconography of images of time to understand the rationality of temporal iconology as represented in works of art, Aby Warburg favored attention to the *Pathosformel* within particular works that suggested the sense of being lost to dominant temporal modes, or that evoked domains adjacent to them.[87]

Such diametrically opposite yet deep drivers alert us to the fact that modern art history has always been an internally contested interdiscipline, rather than an autonomous academic discipline. How is this interdisciplinarity playing out within art history's approach to contemporary art as it searches for methods appropriate to the call of contemporary conditions? In the chapter "Contemporaneity's Heterochronicity" in Keith Moxey's book *Visual Time*, he rightly reminds us, "The phenomenological dimension of art history has always insisted that the visual artifact can create its own history. Arguing that images call for attention and demand interpretation, several recent thinkers have developed the concept of *anachronism* as a means of describing the process of mediation that goes on between artifacts that both solicit an affective response and invite the desire of the contemporary art historian to make meaning."[88] He has in mind the work of Georges Didi-Huberman, Mieke Bal, Hubert Damish, Alexander Nagel, and Christopher Wood, among others.[89] As titles such as *Anachronic Renaissance* and *Medieval Modern* indicate, these scholars are offering accounts of art that was first produced at a past time and place, and they search that art for signs of the temporalities in play at that time and place, and for elements and aspects of the artworks that open them to present concerns, approaches, tastes, and interests. Moxey makes a larger claim: "By emphasizing the contemporaneity of their response to images, by folding the historicity of their own temporal locations within accounts of historical horizons, such scholars effectively disrupt any absolute distinction between past and present." Absolute distinctions, yes, but relative distinctions remain to be made, as Moxey recognizes in remarks such as "the texture of the past is threaded through an account of the work's reception in the present," and "While it seems imperative to distinguish different moments in order to construct the idea of a period, be it in the past or the present, it is also necessary to admit that these distinctions are never permanent and that their difference depends of the interests of the now."[90] While this is a clear admission that approaches to the art of the past have been *contemporized*, it is an oddly nebulous defense of periodization, which is a staple presumption of the linear art history he has just declared redundant.[91]

Moxey concludes by stating, "If the experience of the anachronic power of images insists that we temporarily suspend the systems in which we locate works of art, heterochrony reminds us that such temporal structures are not only desirable but inevitable as we try to understand the images of cultures other than our own."[92] This observation brings him closer to the present, where the transnational transition is so prominent a force. As a scholar of the Renaissance, he does not write about contemporary art, nor do any of the art historians he commends (with the notable exception of Mieke Bal) regularly do so, yet an implication of his book is that judicious forms of "translation" between anachrony and heterochronicity are promising an art-historical methodology that might prove adequate to the art of many, if not all, times and places—including contemporary art. While the "phenomenological dimension" is doubtless crucial to both contemporary art and to our encounters with it, the theorization of this dimension has scarcely begun.

A TEMPORAL TURN?

The same is true for the most obvious topic in the work of contemporary artists: our contemporaneity as the experience of a multiplicity of temporalities. An exception is *The Past Is the Present, It's the Future Too*, in which Christine Ross argues for the significance of a "temporal turn" in contemporary art.[93] She believes that this turn is occurring not only in contemporary societies but also in the disciplines that interpret them. Her first chapter follows a useful summary of some key conceptions of time in the Western philosophical tradition with a close read of Gilles Deleuze's division of the history of cinema into two phases, which he labels "the movement-image" and "the time-image," taking Orson Welles's *Citizen Kane* (1941) as its turning point.[94] This leads to a survey of how "lived time" is at the "forefront of disciplinary research mainly as a predicament, a questionable reality and an unevenness that preclude the institution of any form of universal *a priori* on which to ground the existence of time or to access temporal flow, wholeness, indivisibility, and permanence."[95] Necessarily incomplete, but always suggestive, her survey sketches how disciplines relevant to contemporary art practice are grappling with the issue. These include analytic philosophy; the philosophy of the event; communication, media studies, and the philosophy of technology; psychology; sociology; history; postcolonial studies; and political ecology.[96]

Ross acknowledges the precedent of Pamela M. Lee's *Chronophobia: On Time in the Art of the 1960s*, which profiles the "almost obsessional uneasiness with time and its measure" during a period when accelerated information-based technologies created uncertainty about "the social and technological horizon yet to come."[97] Ross argues, persuasively, that contemporary artists share these modern anxieties but do so with reference to the expanded technological realms that pervade today's societies, paying special attention to the informational flows between disciplines and between artworks and their receivers, as well as to the bridging of "subjective" and "objective" understandings of time, with the result that "recent art has invested in the connections between lived time and history, between the lived passage of time and the historical passage of time ... [such that] artists today have adopted a more historiographical outlook on time and conversely a more temporal outlook on history."[98] These observations are supported by the variety of concerns that many observers have noted are shared by several contemporary artists: deep interest in the operations of allegory, archives, archaeology, history, memory practices, reenactment, trauma, and—if I may add to her list—the possibility of achrony.[99]

Claims about turns—be they linguistic, cultural, pictorial, or planetary (to name only those that have been announced in recent decades)—identify a relatively sudden focus of attention on a previously underexamined aspect of a field, along with a search for a fresh mode of thinking about it, one that may also be interdisciplinary. They also suggest that this interest has been precipitated by a change in the object of study, in the phenomena itself, which requires urgent attention. They do not demand that the discipline drop everything and concentrate on this issue, but they imply that it could be the factor that changes everything. Ross asks, "What are our regimes of historicity? A resilient futurism? Presentism (the present's absorption of the past and the future)?" She answers by stating "the main claim of this book": "Although presentism certainly defines a predominant realignment of the past, present, and future of the contemporary world, it coexists with other regimes of historicity made of less absorbing but still highly significant realignments. Art history has already proposed a notion that highlights this coexistence of historicities: 'contemporaneity.'" Saying that the notion "takes its full resonance in relation to the temporal turn's temporalization of the archival, archaeological, historical and historiographical impulses" in contemporary life ("the interestedness of contemporaneity" is her phrase for what I call its implication in worldliness), she offers a paraphrase that will be familiar to readers of this book. She expresses some concern that my descriptions of the asynchronous temporalities of the globalized world "tend to assume that they connect and that they are perceivable in their connectedness," whereas attention should also be paid to "the persistence of structures that block interconnectedness, as well as the persistence of structures that thin down lived time by isolating it from deep time." Perhaps I did not make these points clearly enough in the early writings that she cites. Nevertheless, she is right to insist, "As we situate the temporal turn within contemporaneity, our main challenge will be to exemplify how coincident worlds are not necessarily connected or easily connectable."[100]

Ross's most useful contribution is the close attention she pays within each chapter to what she calls "experiences of temporal passing," which are emerging as of special interest to many contemporary artists. Works by Tatiana Trouvé, Oscar Muñoz, Francis Alÿs, Guido van der Werve, Mark Lewis, Tacita Dean, Malik Ohanian, Harun Farocki, Nancy Davenport, and Stan Douglas are carefully explored to show how these and other artists are intuitively but also quite systematically probing specific aspects of this passaging, namely, "unproductiveness, fissuration, extendibility, equalization, unframability, and interminability." This is an insightful and original listing.[101] Far from categorizing these as the negative effects of, say, high cultural capitalism, or as evidence of an overall failure of artists to cope with the challenges of our contemporaneity, she pinpoints the constructive work of world making that is occurring in each case. "Unproductiveness" may be a countercapitalist productivity, a search for an alternative, sustainable ecology. Fissuring the narratives inherited from the past thickens the present with potential, as does extending the internal time taken in viewing a work, or in participating in an event. Revaluing now the art of the recent past by inviting its creators to remake it equalizes time. Revisiting the past as if one had all the time in the world dislodges the historical framing that had locked it firmly into temporal distance. It also fills up the present. Ross concludes in an appropriately tentative but also historically oriented way: "The temporal turn, we can now concede, presentifies the modern regime of historicity by keeping the past *as long as possible* in the present in order to influence the future. In the process the present is made interminable.... If contemporaneity in contemporary art is to challenge the modern regime of historicity, it does so by instituting interminability as the most pivotal feature of historical time."[102] Insights such as these offer helpful characterizations of important aspects of the current state of art practice, and of art-critical and historical interpretation of that practice, while both work to thematize the kinds of times in which we now live. As these artists and writers know, temporal experience is generated from within all spheres of life—human, animal, machinic, and what we call natural—and operates across multiple scales, from the personal to the geopolitical, at the same time. Each of these kinds of time is indispensable to thinking about art, historically, today.

Conclusion

concurrence in contemporary world picturing

In the second decade of the twenty-first century, globalization is widely acknowledged to be fading fast as the catchall name of the dominant world current. It now seems to be a matter of visiting history to recall that the events of
1989, above all the collapse of the Soviet empire, led to a widespread perception
that the United States was unchallenged as a geopolitical hyperpower and that
economic globalization—led by companies based in the US and Europe, but
also thriving in parts of Asia—was the latest version of an ever-self-replenishing
capitalism, destined for world domination, yet again. For the West, the 9/11
attacks shook this picture from its false frame. Multitudes living elsewhere
knew this already. Since then, several largely unanticipated, world-scale, geo-
economic changes, notably the marked disjunction between the leading national economies—each with different models of economic organization, each
prioritizing national objectives—and the impending disasters being generated
by global warming have broken the hegemonic grip of neoliberal globalization,
no matter how pervasive it had become as a world picture.[1] In 2008, as financial
markets brought the system to the point of requiring rescue by taxpayer dollars,
it seemed shaky indeed.

Since then, globalization has been increasingly resisted by those who were, from modern perspectives across the political spectrum, viewed as its inevitable, if regrettable, victims: the youth without prospects in the Middle East, resisting authoritarian governments and feeding the civil war between fundamentalisms in that region; the populations of "failed states" in Africa especially, source of desperate migrations, mostly within that continent, but also to Europe and elsewhere; the rural poor throughout the world, flooding into cities unprepared to absorb them; and, finally, the redundant working classes, and the stagnating middle classes, of the United States and Europe, angry at the diminution of their dreams. Each in their different ways, from Tahrir Square, through Islamic extremism and the rise of rightwing parties in Europe, to Brexit and the election of Donald J. Trump as president of the United States, reject neoliberal globalization and government by technocratic elites. By 2016, even the *Economist* was acknowledging the end of the consensus in favor of "open economies" and was asking, somewhat plaintively, "Is globalization no longer a good thing?"[2] Paradoxically, fear of economic collapse has also meant, at least for now, the exercise of unchecked power by representatives of the same elites who brought us shock doctrine globalization. Yet their travesties of good governance and prescient economic management are provoking widespread resistance and are, hopefully, accelerating the coming into being of a world that, whatever forms it may take, will no longer ruled by the priorities of capitalism.[3]

These torrid changes mean that, when looking to identify the major forces that have shaped contemporary art since the 1980s, we need, I believe, an account that locates globalization as one set among others, an account that identifies the nature of each contending force and gauges their strength relative to each other. This is even more the case as we experience the death throes of the postwar "Washington consensus," the evaporation of the post-1989 illusion of the United States as a hyperpower, the fracturing of the European Union, the rise of China in East Asia and its unfolding Belt and Road Initiative, along with many other factors, such that 1945 also looms as a longer historical marker of the prehistory of the present. We return, again, to the need to account for the multiple modernities that shaped life, thought, and art during modern times, and that in turn lead to the multeity that is so pronounced in contemporary life, thought, and art. Complexity reigns in each of these spheres—so, too, does chaos. But repetition and recursion, differentiation and newness, are even more evident, suggesting the operations of a structure. I have argued throughout this book that contemporary life, thought, and art are structured by the operations of three currents and by the antinomic interaction between the currents within and between each of these spheres. A more adequate hypothesis about how the parts join into "an articulated whole" has yet to be proposed. It remains, however, an incomplete explanation—indeed, it is, in principle, impossible to complete. We can, nevertheless, hope to add further precision to it, each time we take up its challenges.

A META–WORLD PICTURE

The visual arts and their discourses are not the only fields today where we find a clustering of similarities and differentiations into three contemporaneous currents. Geopolitics is another such plane and is perhaps the most obvious, not least in the Cold War configurations that continue to recur as if undead. Today, ideology is more multiplicitous in its elements, fluid in its flows, and conflicted in its disjunctures than in the postwar years. It consists of a seemingly limitless number of newly minted futures, an array of partial presents, and the unstoppable reappearance of refreshed pasts. Yet these, too, tend to cluster into three constellations, attracted by a sufficient similarity between some of their elements, and separated by polarities of power, a magnetic tension that shapes their historical unfolding as currents, as it does the interactions between them.

We cannot see these currents directly, but we can identify their existence precisely by how, since World War II, they have clustered our seemingly inchoate efforts to picture the larger world, by how they tend to organize the concepts and terms we use into coherent worldviews. In turn, these clusters configure into a metapicture of world picturing, as the world undertakes it today. The metapicture looks like this.

CONTINUING MODERNITIES: Postwar, Cold War; globalization, post–Cold War hyperpower, clash of civilizations, war on terror, spectacularity, neoconservatism, neoliberal economics; posthistory, invented heritage, remodernisms; anthropocene; reactionary resurgence; postcontemporary.

(Between these, dialectical oppositionality but no prospective resolution.)

TRANSITIONAL TRANSNATIONALITY: Decolonization; indigenization; postcolonial critique, the movement of movements, antiglobalization, globality; postmodern pastiche, new realisms; inverse modernizations (China, Asian "tigers"); revived fundamentalisms; insurrectionary anarchisms; postcommunism; Momentum "socialism."

(Between these, difference, adjacency, antinomic frictions.)

CONTEMPORANEOUS DIFFERENCES: Contemporaneousness of incommensurable master narratives; self-fashioning within immediation; network culture; postcapitalism; cosmopolitanism/planetarity, ranging from world citizenship to as-needed affiliative connectivity (Occupy); ecoactivism; open-form revolutions; the coeval commons.

Each of these concepts is a signpost, a perspectival point that expands to fill out parts of a total world picture. Since 1945, I suggest, they have appeared one after another, and attach to others, forming one of three kinds of current. Think of each current as a major movement of human world picturing, and of the relationships between the currents on analogy to the slow grinding, and the resultant earthquakes and tsunamis, that signal the shifting of the great geological plates that constitute the earth's mobile crust. It will take decades to work through to what will doubtless be a different configuration. But this, I submit, is how we report our contemporaneity to ourselves right now, when we frame it as actual occurrence in the present, when we look for historical patterns passing through our own time. These concepts, in these clusters, are the most evident markers of what I call "the contemporary composition," as we try to imagine it working discursively, on its largest worldwide scales.[4]

Returning here to a theme emphasized in the introduction to this book, I am making a historical argument about the shape of historical forces operating through the present. Underlying it is an intuition about a major shift in the nature of human thinking about thinking, and perhaps in the nature of human thought (if such a thing can still be imagined). These currents, and these shifts in thinking, shape our understandings of today's world into competing clusters. *They are also the basis of the three currents in contemporary art, which are manifestations of their presencing and of their interactions with one another—of, in a word, their concurrence.*

When set out in this way, the reign of incommensurable difference, the lack of coevalness in most of our relationships, is all too obvious. But the desire for coevality is emerging in the third current. Indeed, I believe that it is driving that cluster and turning the whole of world-picturing discourse its way. Everything registered in this chart, I am suggesting, is tending—or to be more realistic, given the reactionary resurgences appearing across the globe today, *should* be tending—toward those last three words: "the coeval commons."

When thinking about how to approach contemporary art from historical perspectives, an interesting instance of the differences between 2009 and 2016 is that, in contrast to the general questions posed by the *October* editors at the earlier date, the *Dandelion* editors, whose call for papers I cite at the beginning of the previous chapter, went beyond their mirror maze of rhetorical questions to list several possible topics:

> Periodisation and the competing temporalities of "the contemporary" across the humanities: Beyond-modernisms, "Post-Post"? Methodological shifts in the humanities: Digital Humanities, Medical Humanities, World Literature, Post-Critical. Tone and the contemporary's affective intensities: Hope and Pessimism, Anxiety and Belonging. The Anthropocene: Environment and Ecocriticism. Mapping the networks and flows of Late Capitalism and Neoliberalism: Towards a contemporary realism? Contemporary Resistances: Digital Commons, the Hacker, Occupy, Black Lives Matter, Indigenous Social Movements. Human, Non-Human, Post-Human: Artificial Intelligence, Prosthetics, and Augmented Reality; Embodiment and Subjectivity. The Future of the Novel: Transnational, Graphic, Documentary, Historical, Science Fiction. The Production, Philosophy, Criticism, and Curating of Contemporary Art. The Relation between Contemporary Art and Art History.[5]

It is a relief to see that "globalization" does not appear in either the questions or the list of topics. Nor does "the market." The implicit dismissal of them in the *October* questionnaire (cited in chapters 2 and 11) as, in their relation, amounting to a sufficient causal explanation of the main features of contemporary art, is now, finally, explicit.

Answers to many of the questions posed by both sets of editors, by those at *e-flux* and at the Asia Art Archive, along with many others, have been offered in the essays in this book. The writers and thinkers I discuss propose their own answers, and deal with many of the above topics. The fact that the *Dandelion* editors could come up with a list of concrete instantiations of "the contemporary" is the clearest signal of an advance from the spirit of ironic skepticism in which the *October* questionnaire was framed. Whatever "the contemporary" is, we can see at a glance that it is a lot less than the sum of these absolutely vital issues. Together, they signal our immersion in the complexities of our contemporaneity as a lived problematic, one that is intensely interested in understanding itself and its relationships to the histories now available to it.

THE POSTCONTEMPORARY DIVERSION

I end chapter 10 by noting that the concept of "the postcontemporary," as theorized by Avanessian and Malik, remains sketchily theorized. A review of the 2016 Montreal Biennale by Canadian art writer Saelan Twerdy offers glimpses of a more suggestive usage, precisely because he adopts an art-historical perspective.[6] The 2014 iteration of the biennial had carried the title *L'avenir* ("That which is to come," or, as an injunction, "Look forward"). Artistic director of the 2016 biennial Phillipe Pirotte, however, deliberately cast his exhibition against the expectation that biennials show current art on a worldwide scale and offer a viewpoint about where contemporary art is right now, as in, for example, Okwui Enwezor's 2015 edition of the Venice Biennale, *All the World's Futures*, which specifically addressed many of the issues I discuss in this book. Pirotte, instead, naming his biennial *La Grand Balcon*, adopted as his guiding trope Jean Genet's play from 1957, *The Balcony*, in which over-the-top metatheatrics are staged in a brothel while insurrection and counterrevolution rage in the streets outside. The exhibition included several performances, some capturing this kind of contradiction in current terms, for example, Anne Imhof's *Angst III* (figure Con.1) from 2016.

Imhof works across a variety of mediums, from painting through drawing, photography, installation, music, and performance, in each of which she shows arresting but transient images of bodies seeking community with others in ambiguous, dislocated spaces. She is best known for her performance installations such as the *Angst* series and *Faust*. The latter was staged in the German Pavilion at the Venice Biennale of 2017, when it won the Golden Lion award for the best pavilion presentation. These multimedia events respond to the given architecture in minimal yet discomforting ways, making it radically transparent or shrouding it in ambiguous mists. A gender fluid, racially diverse group of dancers and musicians from her native Frankfurt, with whom she has worked for several years, are invited to follow and improvise upon a set of prompts. Very few props are used: for *Angst*, a falcon, a drone, fruit randomly distributed on some raised platforms, soda cans and a high wire; for *Faust*, guard dogs, raised glass floors, some wall projections and furniture, running water and a strip of fire, with drawings and a painting at the edges of vision. Separation between performers and audience is not delineated, but has to be constantly

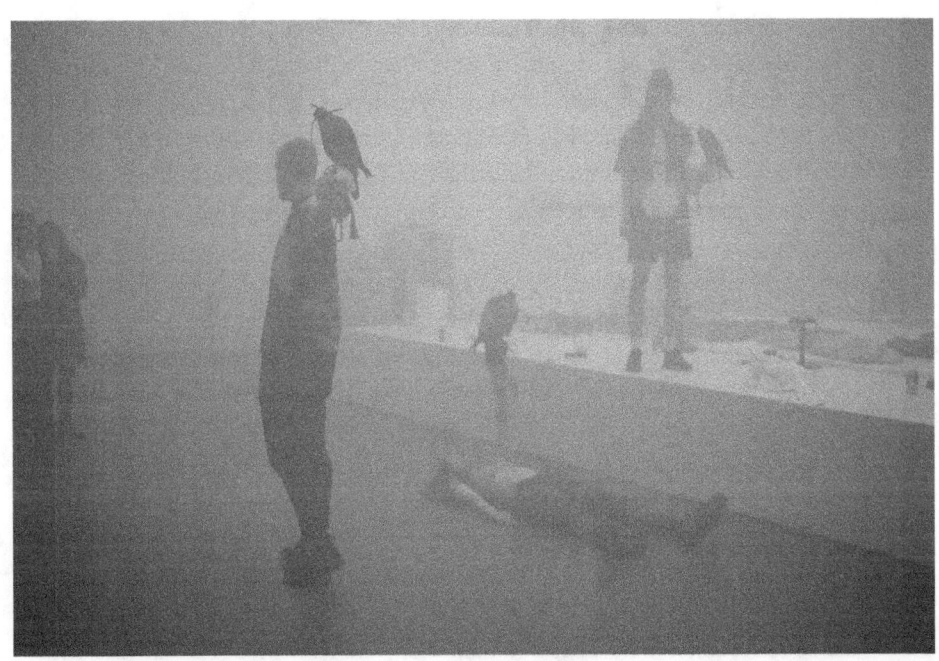

Figure Con.1

Anne Imhof, *Angst III*, 2016. Performers: Billy Bultheel, Frances
Chiaverini, Emma Daniel, Eliza Douglas, Josh Johnson, and
Mickey Mahar, La Biennale de Montréal. Photo by Jonas Lei-
hener. Image courtesy of the artist; Galerie Isabella Bortolozzi,
Berlin; and Galerie Buchholz, Cologne/Berlin/New York.

negotiated, via the mutual movement of bodies and, if the performers wish,
via the images of the event being posted online by viewers' cell phones. Her
aesthetic draws from Francis Bacon, Berlin experimental and political theatre (Der Volksbühne, or People's Theatre, Berlin), punk rock, Goth costum-
ing, rave venues, arcane internet imagery, and predecessors such as Christof
Schlingensief (Venice Biennale 2011). Hers is a late modern/contemporary, not
a postcontemporary practice, drawing unevenly from the interests and anxieties of each of the three currents.

In explicit contrast to Avanessian and Suhail, Twerdy proposes "a simpler historical explanation of what the 'post-contemporary' might mean." He notes, "A number of commentators have argued that the idea of the 'contemporary' as a period came fully into being around 1989, with the fall of the Berlin Wall, the explosion of globalization, and the collapse of any major barriers to the worldwide circulation of neoliberal capital," then remarks, "Since this formation began breaking up after 2008, the most characteristically new forms of art have been the post-internet phenomenon and neo-formalist abstract painting," both of which seem to have peaked. Perhaps, he suggests, they are indicators of a transition between contemporary art and whatever comes next. Recalling the mid-1980s, a moment when "a market-driven painting boom [was] sponsored by an out-of-control financial class," he makes a neat (if rather conventional) art-historical comparison of zombie formalism with neoexpressionism, and post-internet art with simulationist/neogeo art. The 1980s movements, along with "postmodern theory and a climate of entrepreneurial disruption," he rightly says, "formalized the passage (nascent in the '60s and '70s) from modernism to contemporary art." If, he then suggests, we accept that contemporary art has been defined in relation to neoliberal globalization, and take the UK Brexit vote, the election of Donald Trump to the US presidency, along with other factors, to signal the end of that regime, "Can we say that 'contemporary art' is ending, too?"

Perhaps so, if he means institutionalized, market-driven contemporary art, but he then leaps, as so many otherwise acute commentators do, from this one current to a generalization about the "decline" not only of all contemporary art but also the complex, layered conditions that have generated it, and to which it so variously responds: "But will the decline of contemporaneity result in any durable new paradigm? In the era of Trump, will art be able to mount any sufficient resistance, or will its already-exclusive community be conscripted to dress the windows of a fascist regime?"

The three-current contemporaneity outlined in this book is not declining, although, as I have argued, the energies underlying the first current are embattled, on the defensive, and thus prone to unleash their forces of shock and awe—it is, one hopes, their last act of self-defense. Much art is, indeed, likely to be conscripted in the way Twerdy suggests, if such a regime is not successfully resisted. The energies driving the other two currents, in art as in the wider world, are a long way from peaking and are not likely to do so in our lifetimes. Nevertheless, I fully concur with his conclusion: "The post-contemporary aesthetic, as it stands, shows scant resources for withstanding the pressures to come."

To me, the chatter about "the postcontemporary" is yet another symptom of concern within the first current about whether its operative fictions will continue to prevail in both artworld and public perceptions of what counts as contemporary art (although it has to be said that risk economies have always thrived on such anxieties). I warned in chapter 1 that the desire for spectacular impact, the thirst for innervation—that in the years around 2000 animated the most widely celebrated, and expensive, contemporary art—was leading to its enervation. Almost twenty years later, this quality pervades precisely this kind of art, despite every effort to signal the contrary. We can see it hiding in the light, in the place where, at first sight, it seems least evident: the inflated prices achieved at auctions of contemporary art. Far from leading a widespread boom in support for living artists, the market has narrowed its focus to a few, and heaped its resources upon the sale and resale of their work, to the effective exclusion or debilitation of the work of all others. In the first six months of 2017, works by just twenty-five artists (led by the late Jean-Michel Basquiat) sold for US$1.2 billion, that is, 44.6 percent of worldwide auction sales for postwar and contemporary art.[7] It is no coincidence that the work of these artists—and of those who aspire to join them—becomes inflated in character as it moves "up" the market. Their art usually becomes larger, bolder, more attractive, and instantly legible, but thinner in content and meaning—in a word, enervated.

Nor is it a coincidence that the same intense narrowing and accelerating inequality has occurred in the distribution of wealth, both globally and nationally, and that growing amounts of that wealth circulate within the top end of the market for art. By 2017, while the least wealthy half of the global adult population owned less than 1 percent of global assets, the top 1 percent of wealth holders owned nearly half. The latter remain concentrated in the United States and Europe, but their numbers are growing rapidly in Asia, notably China. Art markets follow these distributions closely, as they constitute the traditional collector base and are the main source of new members.[8] As well, art markets have in recent years tended to follow the forms and values of the financial markets, and to shed their previous subscription to aesthetic hierarchies in favor of those based strictly on rapid return on investments. The result: an increasingly vacuous circle.

None of this is news to anyone with eyes open to present realities. It is the persistence and even acceleration of these factors during a period of economic and political crisis that is remarkable. *The Art Market 2017* report, published by the Art Basel fair and the UBS bank, devotes a section to "Wealth Inequality and the Art Market," noting that "broader wealth trends over time show that globalization has brought about a polarization of incomes in emerging and developing economies while, especially since the financial crisis, the middle classes in developing countries have become increasingly squeezed as wealth flows to the top end," and that "the largest art market, the US, has one of the most skewed income distributions of income globally, with levels of inequality in the last ten years reverting to those experienced in the 1920s." These trends have lead some experts to believe that "while the top end of the market has grown fastest in the last ten years, the decline in the market in 2016 was influenced by an increasing thinness and lack of supply at the highest end, particularly in the auction sector." As a result, collectors sought to reduce risk by buying "well-recognized works or those by famous artists," thus creating a self-reinforcing "superstar phenomenon," which becomes, in time, self-defeating for those buyers and "demotivating" for other artists.[9] The market for contemporary art experienced an upsurge in 2017, reflecting a 12 percent rise in the global art market, overall economic growth, and even greater concentration within the 1 percent. To the degree that remodernist art remains subservient to this ever-more-divisive cultural logic, its capacity for regeneration is contaminated from within. Its survival as an authentic practice, therefore, depends on the acuity of critical artists active in the Euro-American centers, those based in these centers, and those who pass through them. All are subject to the forces—destructive, deconstructive, and constructive—that are riving the continuing modernities current in world geopolitics.

So, too, for those artists whose work is shaped by what I have called transnational transitionality, and who are in turn shaping it in different ways. For some decades now they have been pushing an alternative view of their art as of at least equal, if not more, relevance to our contemporary conditions than the art produced within the first current. As is obvious from, say, the list of artists chosen for biennials all over the world, second-current artists have succeeded in occupying much of the space in international art circuits, to grow (despite the vicissitudes) art worlds in their own countries, and to influence (at least somewhat) institutions in the traditional centers. I show in the previous chapter how the evident achievements of second-current artists have inspired art historians throughout the world, in alliance with critical historians from the former West, to research the modern histories of art in their own countries, and to see them as the groundwork of contemporary art's diasporas and diversity. The discipline's ideological borders are being slowly but inevitably breached. *La lutte continue.*

Yet these developments, driven by processes of decolonization that are far from achieving their goals, also face challenges, not least those arising from the interactions between currents, including the spread of neoliberal economics throughout many parts of the world, the struggles of liberated countries to develop economies and find forms of governmentality appropriate to their circumstances, and the defensive nationalisms precipitated by mass immigrations. Just as the sell-offs of public sector institutions in developed countries is shrinking support for experimentality in the visual arts exhibitionary complexes of those countries, rising authoritarianism and civil wars are doing the same to critical arts infrastructure in developing and struggling societies. When it comes to international exchange between the currents, biennials continue to be the preferred platform: 316 as of mid-2018, with only twenty discontinuing since their sudden proliferation in the 1990s. While many commentators lament tendencies toward spectacularization, repetition, and conformism in these recurrent mega-exhibitions—especially as national and state governments and tourist-dependent cities come to play major roles in shaping them, notably in Asia and the peripheries of Europe—all involved acknowledge the singularity of each iteration of each biennial and their importance in stimulating artistic innovation in their host community.[10] Despite these challenges, the main thrust of this current remains the same: to image a world in which differences of race, place, gender, and belief are the basis of human communality rather than the causes of exploitation, exclusion, and war. I have shown many examples of artworks animated by this desire, and have cited critics, curators and historians who articulate it—for example, Patrick Flores, in the previous chapter.

What about the third current? In his speculations about what comes after "the contemporary," Saelan Twerdy, the art writer and PhD student whose response to the Montreal Biennale I cited, is asking how his generation, intent on a third kind of practice—one that is responsible to a vision of a mutually respectful, equitably distributed, and actually sustainable future—might develop that practice in wary adjacency to these powerful yet volatile currents. In March 2018, the Montreal Biennale filed for bankruptcy. It is time for those active in this current to scale up what they do best: invent, then semi-institutionalize, new forms of deinstitutionalization—even when that means, sometimes, reinventing aspects of the good old ones.[11] From inside our contemporary concurrence, the art, curatorial and activist practice of this generation will be the definitive cultural contribution to the contemporaneity to come.

To do so, they must avoid the trap within widespread usages of the concepts of "contemporary" and "postcontemporary" that makes answering the questions that these concepts seem to raise impossible. Both are adjectives missing their nouns. In the opening chapter of this book, I use "the contemporary" in the relatively unreflective way that Tim Griffin characterizes so sharply in his comments cited at the beginning of chapter 10. Instead, we must always ask: "The contemporary . . . *what?*" In most cases, you will find that the speaker is using an abbreviation for a noun phrase such as "the contemporary world," "our contemporary situation," "the contemporary condition," "the contemporary experience," "the desire to demonstrate, in a work of art, something vital about what it is to be contemporary now," or any of the many other actual topics I have been discussing in this book. Uncertainty as to which noun is, in the case in point, most fitting has led art discourse in particular to constantly leave the last word as a blank. In chapter 10, I show some of the greatest philosophers of our time being drawn into the same black hole. "The postcontemporary" strives to survive on its cusp, while at the same time calling for the future to fill the present however it will. Postcontemporists, therefore, join the vast, varied, and mute throngs of those who feel that our times cannot name themselves without fearful consequence. Yet, as I have shown in these essays, answers have been pushing themselves forward for decades. They have generated, driven, and critiqued the currents that course through contemporary art, life, and thought, and they continue to inspire fresh thought.[12]

The real "blank" now is the gaping void in the place that should be filled by a fully shared consciousness of our connected planetarity. We have seen that world picturing, placemaking, and imagining community remain the core preoccupations for artists, thinkers, activists, and policy makers—as they are for all of us, everywhere. The actual contemporary question is, How can we, together, compose our divisive differences into the coeval connectivity that the planet requires of us, to ensure our mutual survival?

Notes

INTRODUCTION

1   Terry Smith, Okwui Enwezor, and Nancy Condee, eds., *Antinomies of Art and Culture: Modernity, Postmodernity, Contemporaneity* (Durham, NC: Duke University Press, 2008), 8–9.

2   For a preliminary outline of contemporaneity in its philosophical and geopolitical dimensions, see my "Defining Contemporaneity: Imagining Planetarity," *Nordic Journal of Aesthetics* 49–50 (2015): 156–74, and "The Contemporary Condition: Composition, Planomena, World Picturing," European Graduate School Video Lectures, August 23, 2016, video, 53:32, January 11, 2017, https://www.youtube.com/watch?v=durNqyZPx-g.

3   In Richard Meyer's book *What Was Contemporary Art?* (Cambridge, MA: MIT Press, 2013), he poses these questions in a vivid way, through anecdotes about his own practice and those of earlier scholars of the art of their times, from Alfred H. Barr Jr. to Rosalind E. Krauss. He argues, as I do, that "contemporary art is not simply a function of the current moment or the immediate past.... [It] is also a relation between an ever-shifting present and the volatile force of history," and he usefully advises us to "slow down" and pay attention to this relation (280–81).

4   For a prefiguration of more extensive consideration of these topics, see Terry Smith, "Rethinking Modernism and Modernity Now," in "Modernism Revisited," ed. Aleš Erjavec and Tyrus Miller, special issue, *Filozofski Vestnik* 35, no. 2 (2014): 271–319.

5   Bernard Smith, "The Role of an Institute of Fine Arts in the University of Sydney," *Arts* 6 (1969): 17.

6   Michel Foucault, "The Discourse on Language," in *The Archaeology of Knowledge*, trans. A. M. Sheridan Smith (New York: Pantheon, 1972), 215–37. See also the translation by Ian McLeod in Robert Young, ed., *Untying the Text: A Post-Structuralist Reader* (Boston: Routledge and Kegan Paul, 1981), 48–78.

7   George Steiner, "What Is Comparative Literature?," in *Comparative Criticism: Spaces: Cities, Gardens, and Wildernesses*, ed. E. S. Shaffer (New York: Cambridge University Press, 1996), 164–65.

8   See "About Us," Power Institute, University of Sydney, last updated May 8, 2009, http://sydney.edu.au/arts/power/about/index.shtml.

9   On Derrida's core concept of "democracy to come," see his *Specters of Marx: The State of the Debt, the Work of Mourning, and the New International*, trans. Peggy Kamuf (New York and London: Routledge, 1994), and *Rogues: Two Essays on Reason*, trans. Pascale-Anne Brault and Michael Naas (Stanford, CA: Stanford University Press, 2005).

10 The classic texts here remain David Harvey, *The Condition of Postmodernity: An Inquiry into Cultural Change* (Oxford: Blackwell, 1990), and Fredric Jameson's essay "Postmodernism: Or, the Cultural Logic of Late Capitalism" (1984), in his book of the same title (Durham, NC: Duke University Press, 1991), 1–54.

11 The papers of the conference appear in Smith, Enwezor, and Condee, *Antinomies of Art and Culture*.

12 Terry Smith, *What Is Contemporary Art?* (Chicago: University of Chicago Press, 2009).

13 Terry Smith, *Contemporary Art: World Currents* (Upper Saddle River, NJ: Prentice Hall, 2011).

14 Hal Foster, "A Questionnaire on 'The Contemporary,'" *October*, no. 130 (Fall 2009): 3.

15 Hal Foster, Rosalind Krauss, Yve-Alain Bois, and Benjamin H. D. Buchloh, eds., *Art since 1900: Modernism, Antimodernism, Postmodernism* (London: Thames and Hudson, 2004).

16 Hal Foster, Rosalind Krauss, Yve-Alain Bois, Benjamin H. D. Buchloh, and David Joselit eds., *Art since 1900: Modernism, Antimodernism, Postmodernism*, vol. 2, *1945 to the present*, 3rd ed. (London: Thames and Hudson, 2016).

17 Guy Debord, *The Society of the Spectacle* (1967; repr., New York: Zone Books, 1994).

18 Terry Smith, *The Architecture of Aftermath* (Chicago: University of Chicago Press, 2006).

19 Francis Fukuyama, *The End of History and the Last Man* (New York: Free Press, 1992), xi. The article "The End of History?" was published in the *National Interest* 16 (Summer 1989): 3–18.

20 Fukuyama, *End of History*, xii.

21 For an exacting, conscientious exploration of the successes and shortcomings of these ambitious projects, see Charles Green and Anthony Gardner, *Biennials, Triennials, and Documenta: The Exhibitions That Created Contemporary Art* (Chichester, UK: Wiley Blackwell, 2016), 155–64, and chap. 6.

22 Ian McLean, *Rattling Spears: A History of Indigenous Australian Art* (London: Reaktion Books, 2016), is the latest, most comprehensive and searching examination of this topic.

23 The College Art Association annually lists US and Canadian dissertations completed and in progress, under headings such as "Eleventh to Fourteenth Century/Medieval," "Twentieth Century Art," and "Twenty First Century Art," the last further broken down into various mediums. See "Dissertations," *CAA Reviews*, accessed December 11, 2017, http://www.collegeart.org/news/2017/12/11/explore-the-2016-dissertation-list/. This usage follows that of the Library of Congress in its subject headings.

24 The *Art Bulletin* essay was intended as a modest echo of a major art historiographic precedent: Paul Frankl's *The Gothic: Literary Sources and Interpretations through Eight Centuries* (Princeton, NJ: Princeton University Press, 1960), which, under Franz Philipp's guidance, I read as a student at the University of Melbourne shortly after its publication. Also relevant as distant inspirations dating back to those student years are Heinrich Wölfflin's dissertation, "Prolegomena to a Psychology of Architecture" (1886), translated by Henry Francis Mallgrave and Elerftherious Ikonomou in Robert Vischer, ed., *Empathy, Form, and Space: Problems in German Aesthetics, 1873–1893* (Santa Monica, CA: Getty, 1994); and Erwin Panofsky's early methodological writings.

25 Elizabeth C. Mansfield, "From the Culture Wars to a Civil War: Institutes of Art Historical Research in the United States," *Perspective* 2 (2015), posted online December 7, 2015, http://perspective.revues.org/5958. Elizabeth C. Mansfield is currently at the J. Paul Getty Museum, Los Angeles. A historian of eighteenth- and nineteenth-century art, she is editor of two anthologies on the history of art history: *Art History and Its Institutions: Founda-*

tions of a Discipline (New York: Routledge, 2002) and *Making Art History: A Changing Discipline and Its Institutions* (New York: Routledge, 2007).

26 Mansfield, "From the Culture Wars to a Civil War," 4.

27 Mansfield, "From the Culture Wars to a Civil War," 12.

28 On the visual art exhibitionary complex and related ideas, see Terry Smith, "Mapping the Contexts of Contemporary Curating: The Visual Arts Exhibitionary Complex," *Journal of Curatorial Studies* 6, no. 2 (2017): 170–80.

1. CONTEMPORARY ART AND ART TO COME

Chapter 1 is based on a lecture given at the University of Sydney on May 1, 2001. This text is a reduced version of one originally published as *What Is Contemporary Art? Contemporary Art, Contemporaneity and Art to Come*, Critical Issues Series 6 (Sydney: Artspace, 2001). Certain passages echo strongly in some of my later publications. They are the first formulations of a kind of contemporary thought that is always, if it remains true to its subject, a thinking to come.

1 I elaborate on this idea in "Enervation, Viscerality: The Fate of the Image in Modernity," my introduction to *Impossible Presence: Surface and Screen in the Photogenic Era*, ed. Terry Smith (Chicago: University of Chicago Press, 2001), 1–38.

2 Adrian Lewis, cited in Rita Hatton and John A. Walker, *Supercollector: A Critique of Charles Saatchi* (London: Ellipsis, 2000), 191.

3 Tate Modern, "Tate Modern, May 2000–May 2001, A Summary of the First Year," press release, May 11, 2001, http://www.tate.org.uk/press/press-releases/tate-modern-may-2000 -may-2001, accessed June 18, 2018.

4 Iwona Blaswick and Simon Wilson, eds., *Tate Modern: The Handbook* (London: Tate Publishing, 2000).

5 Norman Rosenthal and Michael Archer, *Apocalypse: Beauty and Horror in Contemporary Art* (London: Royal Academy of Arts, 2000).

6 For more positive perspectives on the import of Koons's work, see Jeff Koons, *The Jeff Koons Handbook* (London: Thames and Hudson, Anthony d'Offay Gallery, 1992); and Robert Rosenblum, *Jeff Koons: Celebration* (New York: Abrams, 1996).

7 Rosenthal and Archer, *Sensation: Young British Artists from the Saatchi Collection*. For archival material relating to the Brooklyn Museum version and the controversy, see "Sensation: Young British Artists from the Saatchi Collection," Brooklyn Museum, October 2, 1999–January 9, 2000, http://www.brooklynmuseum.org/opencollection/exhibitions /683/.

8 Brian Kennedy, then director of the National Gallery of Australia, emphatically denies that he sought ministerial protection in backing out of the commitment to show *Sensation: Young British Artists from the Saatchi Collection* and argues that the Council of the National Gallery decided to cancel the exhibition in November when its entanglement in commercial gallery support became evident. See his "How Much Do We Care about Museum Ethics?," *Artonview* (the gallery members' magazine), no. 23 (Spring 2000): 3–5. His letter of September 29, 1999, to Senator Richard Alston describing the *Sensation* exhibition

positively yet inquiring whether the senator had any "concerns" about it is on public record (*Australian*, January 25, 2000), as is the senator's antipathy toward work in the exhibition and his frank expression of this view to the Gallery Council on October 12 (see Brian Kennedy, evidence before Senate Estimates Committee, Parliament of Australia, February 10, May 24 and 25, and July 25, 2000, as well as numerous newspaper articles, for example, Valerie Lawson, "The Art of Elimination," *Sydney Morning Herald*, March 4, 2000, Spectrum sec., 1, 4–5). Commercial support for the exhibition undoubtedly increased to an unacceptable degree (apparent, on Kennedy's own evidence, at the end of October 1999) as the Brooklyn Museum sought more private monies in the face of Mayor Giuliani's threat to withdraw public funding from the show. Nevertheless, the intense involvement of advertising guru and art dealer Charles Saatchi in the exhibition, from its conception to every aspect of its presentation, had been a public part of its first showing, two years earlier, at the Royal Academy, London, which attracted three hundred thousand visitors. There is no evidence that Kennedy attempted to negotiate a version of the exhibition on independent terms.

9 There is a long history of important thinking about trauma and modernity, from Walter Benjamin on Baudelaire to Hal Foster on artists such as Warhol, Robert Gober, and Mary Kelly. For Hirst's perspective, see Damien Hirst, *I Want to Spend the Rest of My Life Everywhere, with Everyone, One to One, Always, Forever, Now* (London: Booth-Clibborn, 1997).

10 Bernice Murphy, *Museum of Contemporary Art: Vision and Context* (Sydney: MCA, 1993).

11 See Joseph Kosuth and David Freedberg, *The Play of the Unmentionable: An Installation by Joseph Kosuth at the Brooklyn Museum* (New York: New York University Press, 1992); and Lisa G. Corrin and Fred Wilson, *Mining the Museum: An Installation Confronting History* (Baltimore: Maryland Historical Society, 1994).

12 Charles Baudelaire, "The Painter of Modern Life," *Figaro*, November 26 and 28 and December 3, 1863, trans. J. Mayne, in Charles Baudelaire, *The Painter of Modern Life and Other Essays* (London: Phaidon, 1964), 12.

13 See John McDonald, ed., *Peter Fuller's Modern Painters: Reflections on British Art* (London: Methuen, 1993). Also relevant are Peter Fuller, *Beyond the Crisis in Art* (London: Writers and Readers, 1981), and *Aesthetics after Modernism* (London: Writers and Readers, 1984).

14 Arthur C. Danto, *After the End of Art: Contemporary Art and the Pale of History* (Princeton, NJ: Princeton University Press, 1997), 10. A more subtle and suggestive reading of the "end of art" problematic for contemporary art is Jean-Luc Nancy's "The Vestige of Art," in *The Muses* (Stanford, CA: Stanford University Press, 1996), 81–102.

15 These words are actually Lawrence Rainey's, "In a Dark Mode," *London Review of Books*, January 20, 2000, 15, a review of T. J. Clark, *Farewell to an Idea: Episodes from a History of Modernism* (New Haven, CT: Yale University Press, 1999), referring here to Clark's chapter 4.

16 See the entry "Contemporary Style," in John A. Walker, ed., *Glossary of Art, Architecture and Design since 1945*, 3rd ed. (London: Library Association, 1992), entry 174.

17 While we are considering dictionary entries, mine for "Modernism" and "Modernity" in Jane S. Turner, ed., *Dictionary of Art* (London: Macmillan, 1999), may be worth consulting in this context.

18 Hetti Perkins and Hannah Fink, eds., *Papunya Tula: Genesis and Genius* (Sydney: Art Gallery of New South Wales, 2000). These remarks should not be read as a blanket endorsement of all Aboriginal art as contemporary in the ways I am advocating. While Aboriginal art is clearly implicated, willy-nilly, in all the senses of the contemporary that I have discussed, the movement includes a large amount—indeed, like non-Indigenous art, a majority—of work that is not contemporary in any but the most trivial and banal sense. Amateur, weak, diffident, imitative art is not, in any culture, contemporary in any of the senses to which I am giving significance.

19 Gael Newton and Tracey Moffatt, *Tracey Moffatt: Fever Pitch* (Annandale, NSW: Piper Press, 1995); and Michael Nelson, *Tracey Moffatt* (Brisbane: Institute of Modern Art, 1999).

20 Lyotard's essay first appeared in *Camera Obscura*, no. 12 (1984): 110–25. The quoted passages are from its reprint in *The Lyotard Reader*, ed. Andrew Benjamin (Oxford: Basil Blackwell, 1989), 186, 190. His point about parachrony might usefully be borne in mind by those engaged in contemporary thinking, but I do not endorse Lyotard's "anything goes" looseness on this point. I take the application of present perspectives to the interpretation of past art as both inescapable and welcome, as long as they are leavened with an acute sense of a work's search for meaning in its original conditions, and of its meanings since, and as long as no claim is made in presentist terms about well-formed intentions of artists in the past. Seeing the possibilities for this interplay of interpretations is the starting point for imaginative art history. These points are explored further in chapter 11 below.

21 Lyotard, *Lyotard Reader*, 186, 190.

22 The conversation took place in Paris on June 31, 2001. This paragraph is a broad paraphrase of his remarks. It is interesting that some of the key terms Derrida uses here are the same as those employed by Michael Fried in his famous essay "Art and Objecthood" (1965). Nevertheless, there are major differences, particularly Fried's concern to defend modernist painting against minimalism (which he calls "literalist art") on the grounds that only the former can make available to the spectator a "continuous and entire *presentness*, amounting, as it were, to the perpetual creation of itself, that one experiences as a kind of *instantaneousness*, as though if only one were infinitely more acute, a single infinitely brief instant would be long enough to see everything, to experience the work in all its depth and fullness, to be forever convinced by it." Michael Fried, *Art and Objecthood: Essays and Reviews* (Chicago: University of Chicago Press, 1998), 167. From the perspective of this chapter's current concerns, it is striking to see Fried striving to invest terms from the ordinary language of the contemporary—"presentness," "instantaneousness," "brief"—with the value of the eternal and the immutable. This is to be expected, given his unapologetically high-modernist position. It does raise the prospect, however, that I may be repeating (albeit in reverse) the same strategy, except that my two sets of terms are conformist-with-it-ness and contemporaneity/art to come. I may be advocating this latter basis for truly contemporary (and by implication, socially and art-historically consequential) art and dismissing meditated, spectacularized art according to a value structure that echoes his celebration of high modernism and disdain for minimalism. While acknowledging, gladly, the influence of Fried's criticism on my own over the years, and perhaps particularly the rhetoric of his early

essays, I leave it to you to decide whether what I am saying can be forced into this Hegelian straitjacket. Incidentally, it is a coincidence, I presume, that Fried, on the same page, uses "to come" in connection with what he sees as the time boundedness, the durational drudgery of "literalist art." This is the opposite of my usage, and it is not how the best minimalist sculpture reads now (or did then, to some of us). On the concept "to come," see Jacques Derrida, *Specters of Marx: The State of the Debt, the Work of Mourning, and the New International* (New York: Routledge, 1994).

23 Clement Greenberg, "Avant-Garde Attitudes" (lecture, Power Institute of Fine Arts, Sydney, 1969), reprinted in Bernard Smith, ed., *Concerning Contemporary Art: The Power Lectures, 1968–1973* (Oxford: Clarendon, 1973), 5–15. For my commentary, see Terry Smith, "The 'Style of the Sixties,'" *Quadrant*, no. 58 (March–April 1969): 49–53.

24 These terms are explored in the discussions recorded in Jacques Derrida, *Deconstruction Engaged: The Sydney Seminars*, ed. Paul Patton and Terry Smith (Sydney: Power Publications, 2001).

25 Graham Coulter-Smith, *Mike Parr: The Self-Portrait Project* (Melbourne: Schwarz City, 1994). See also David Bromfield, *Identities: A Critical Study of the Work of Mike Parr, 1970–1990* (Perth: University of Western Australia Press, 1991).

2. ART WITHIN CONTEMPORARY CONDITIONS

Chapter 2 is republished from Terry Smith, "A Questionnaire on 'The Contemporary':
32 Responses," *October* no. 130 (Fall 2009): 46–54, © 2009 by October Magazine, Ltd., and the Massachusetts Institute of Technology, reprinted by permission of the MIT Press.

1 Hal Foster, "A Questionnaire on 'The Contemporary': 32 Responses," *October*, no. 130 (Fall 2009): 3.

2 Franz Kafka, *Aphorisms*, trans. Willa Muir, Edwin Muir, and Michael Hofmann (New York: Schocken, 2015), 118. The passage was written on January 17, 1920.

3 Hannah Arendt, *Between Past and Future* (1961; repr., New York: Penguin, 1993), 7–14.

4 Giorgio Agamben has also drawn attention to the untimely nature of being contemporary. See "What Is the Contemporary?," in *What Is an Apparatus? and Other Essays* (Stanford, CA: Stanford University Press, 2009), 39–54.

5 I suggest a framework in "Writing the History of Contemporary Art: A Distinction, Three Propositions, and Six Lines of Inquiry," in *Crossing Cultures: Conflict, Migration and Convergence*, ed. Jaynie Anderson (Melbourne: Miegunyah, 2009), 918–21. See also Richard Meyer, *What Was Contemporary Art?* (Cambridge, MA: MIT Press, 2013).

6 My contribution is *Contemporary Art: World Currents* (Upper Saddle River, NJ: Prentice Hall, 2011).

7 I discuss contemporaneity in my *The Architecture of Aftermath* (Chicago: University of Chicago Press, 2006), as do several authors in Terry Smith, Okwui Enwezor, and Nancy Condee, eds., *Antinomies of Art and Culture: Modernity, Postmodernity, Contemporaneity* (Durham, NC: Duke University Press, 2008). I first broached the present argument in *What Is Contemporary Art? Contemporary Art, Contemporaneity and Art to Come*, Criti-

cal Issues Series 6 (Sydney: Artspace, 2001), and developed it in, among other places, my "Contemporary Art and Contemporaneity," *Critical Inquiry* 32, no. 4 (Summer 2006): 681–707; in "World Picturing in Contemporary Art: Iconogeographic Turning," *Australian and New Zealand Journal of Art* 7, no. 1 (2006): 24–46; and in detail in *What Is Contemporary Art?* (Chicago: University of Chicago Press, 2009).

8 For example, Eleanor Heartney, *Art and Today* (London: Thames & Hudson, 2008), is organized into chapters according to sixteen themes.

9 Tim Griffin, "A New Novel," *Artforum* 46, no. 10 (Summer 2008): 61.

10 François Jullien, *Vital Nourishment: Departing from Happiness* (New York: Zone Books, 2007), 160.

11 Geraldo Mosquera, "El Tercer Mundo hará la cultura occidental" [The third world makes Western culture], *Revolución y Cultura* (July–September 1986): 39–47.

12 For an assessment of how these currents manifested themselves in the curatorial programs of the Fifty-Second Venice Biennale, Documenta 12, and the Fourth Munster Sculpture Project, see Terry Smith, "The World, from Europe: The Mega-exhibition of Mid-2007," *X-tra Contemporary Art Quarterly* 10, no. 3 (Spring 2008): 4–19.

3. CONTEMPORARY ARCHITECTURE

An earlier version of parts of chapter 3 was originally published in *Architectural Theory Review*, vol. 11, no. 2 (2006): 34–52. Those parts were developed from my inaugural lecture, August 17, 2006, as visiting professor of architecture, Faculty of Architecture, University of Sydney. Thanks to the encouragement of Anna Rubbo, Glenn Hill, and Gevork Hartoonian, these ideas took their first published form in "The Political Economy of Iconotypes and the Architecture of Destination," *Architecture Theory Review* 7, no. 2 (2002): 1–44. They also led to *The Architecture of Aftermath* (Chicago: University of Chicago Press, 2006). I remain deeply grateful for the care devoted to that book by its editor, Susan Bielstein. Further thoughts may be found in "Spectacle Architecture before and after the Aftermath: Situating the Sydney Experience," in *Architecture between Spectacle and Use*, ed. Anthony Vidler (New Haven, CT: Yale University Press for the Clark Institute, 2008). In this chapter, I have considerably developed the ideas expressed in these publications and endeavored to bring them up to date in terms of my understanding of current practice and discourse.

1 Francis D. K. Ching, Mark Jarzombeck, and Vikramaditya Prakash, *A Global History of Architecture*, 3rd ed. (London: Wiley, 2017), xi.

2 Cited in Ching, Jarzombek, and Prakash, *Global History of Architecture*, 793. For robust reflexive commentary on the project of writing "a global history of architecture" as distinct from a Eurocentric "world history," see Mark Jarzombeck, "Architecture: The Global Imaginary in an Antiglobal World," *Grey Room*, no. 61 (Fall 2015): 111–22.

3 Elie G. Haddad and David Rifkind, eds., *A Critical History of Contemporary Architecture, 1960–2010* (Farnham, Surrey: Ashgate, 2014), 46.

4 Charles Jencks, *The Language of Post-Modern Architecture* (New York: Rizzoli, 1977), 9; part 1 is titled "The Death of Modern Architecture."

5 William Curtis, *Architecture since 1900*, 3rd ed. (London: Phaidon, 1996), 16.

6 Aldo van Eyck, "Is Architecture Going to Reconcile Basic Values?," *CIAM '59 in Otterlo* (Stuttgart: Karl Kramer Verlag, 1961), 26.

7 Ernesto Rogers, "Preexisting Conditions and Issues of Contemporary Building Practice," in *Architecture Culture, 1943–1968*, ed. J. Ockman, Columbia Books of Architecture (New York: Rizzoli, 1993), 200–201.

8 See Jean-Luis Cohen, *The Future of Architecture since 1889* (London: Phaidon, 2012).

9 Jean-Luis Cohen, "Crisis as Strategy: Architectural Anxiety since 1950," in *In the End: Architecture—50 Years ARCH+: Project and Utopia*, special issue, *ARCH+*, no. 229, July 25, 2017, http://www.archplus.net/reader/home/ausgabe/229.

10 See Anthony Vidler, *Histories of the Immediate Present: The Invention of Architectural Modernism* (Cambridge, MA: MIT Press, 2008).

11 Haddad and Rifkind, *Critical History of Contemporary Architecture*, 1.

12 Haddad and Rifkind, *Critical History of Contemporary Architecture*, 1.

13 Haddad and Rifkind, *Critical History of Contemporary Architecture*, 4. On this topic, see Peter Herrle and Stephanus Schmitz, eds., *Constructing Identities in Contemporary Architecture: Case Studies from the South* (Berlin: LIT Verlag, 2009).

14 *In the End: Architecture—50 Years ARCH+: Project and Utopia*, special issue, *ARCH+*, no. 229, July 25, 2017, at http://www.archplus.net/reader/home/ausgabe/229.

15 Fredric Jameson, *Postmodernism: Or, the Cultural Logic of Late Capitalism* (London: Verso, 1991), a collection that includes not only the famous 1984 essay but also trenchant examinations of the thinking of Manfredo Tafuri, Frank Gehry's Santa Monica House, and Koolhaas's theorizing. See also Lahiji Nadir, ed., *The Political Unconscious of Architecture: Essays in Honor of Fredric Jameson* (Farnham, Surrey: Ashgate, 2011), including my chapter, "Botanizing the Bonaventura: Base and Superstructure in Jamesonian Architectural Theory," 299–316; Kenneth Frampton, "Critical Regionalism: Six Points for an Architecture of Resistance," in *The Anti-Aesthetic*, ed. Hal Foster (Seattle: Bay Press, 1983), 16–30, and Frampton's *Modern Architecture: A Critical History*, 4th ed. (London: Thames and Hudson, 2007); Robert Venturi, *Complexity and Contradiction in Modern Architecture*, 2nd ed. (New York: Museum of Modern Art, 2002); Charles Jencks, "Post-Modern Architecture," in *Language of Post-Modern Architecture*; Anthony Vidler, *The Architectural Uncanny* (Cambridge, MA: MIT Press, 1992), and his *Warped Space: Art, Architecture, and Anxiety in Modern Culture* (Cambridge, MA: MIT Press, 2000); Peter Eisenman, "Post-Functionalism," *Oppositions* 6 (Fall 1976), reprinted in *Architecture Theory since 1968*, ed. K. Michael Hays (Cambridge, MA: MIT Press, 1998), 236–39; Rem Koolhaas, "Junkspace," in *Harvard Design School Guide to Shopping*, ed. Chuihua Judy Chung and Sze Tsung Leong (Cologne: Taschen, 2001), 408–21, in *October*, no. 100 (Spring 2002): 175–90, and in *Junkspace and Running Room*, ed. Hal Foster (New York: New York Review Books, 2016), 1–37; Teddy Cruz, "Border Postcards: Chronicles from the Edge," James Stirling Memorial Lecture on the City, October 28, 2004, Canadian Centre for Architecture, DVD, 63 min., http://www.cca.qc.ca/en/search/details/library/publication/199497; Mike Davis, *Planet of Slums* (London: Verso, 2006); and Giuliana Bruno, *Atlas of Emotion: Journeys in Art, Architecture, and Film* (London: Verso, 2002).

16 T. Smith, *Architecture of Aftermath*, 1. Kelly Guenther's photograph was published on the front page of the *New York Times*, September 12, 2001.

17 On the imagery of the attack, see David Friend, *Watching the World Change: The Stories behind the Images of 9/11* (New York: Farrar, Straus and Giroux, 2006). On the longer history of such collisions of war and architecture, see Robert Bevan, *The Destruction of Memory: Architecture at War* (London: Reaktion Books, 2006).

18 Osama bin Laden, *Messages to the World: The Statements of Osama bin Laden*, ed. Bruce Lawrence (London: Verso, 2005), 239–40.

19 Cited in Retort, "All Quiet on the Eastern Front," *New Left Review* 41 (September–October 2006), electronic broadsheet, http://newleftreview.org/II/41/retort-all-quiet-on-the-eastern-front.

20 For the Atlas Group archive, see the group's website, accessed June 22, 2018, http://www.theatlasgroup.org. These include the *Sweet Talk: Photographic Documents of Beirut*, an ongoing project initiated in 1973 in which "the foundation recruited dozens of men and women to photograph streets, storefronts, buildings, and other spaces of national, technological, architectural, cultural, political, and economic significance in Beirut," and *My Neck Is Thinner Than a Hair: A History of Car Bombs in the Lebanese Wars (1975–1991)*. See also Chad Elias, *Posthumous Images: Contemporary Art and Memory Politics in Post–Civil War Lebanon* (Durham, NC: Duke University Press, 2018).

21 Retort (Iain Boal, T. J. Clark, Joseph Matthews, Michael Watts), *Afflicted Powers: Capital and Spectacle in a New Age of War*, 2nd ed. (London: Verso, 2006), 198–99.

22 Guy Debord, *The Society of the Spectacle* (1967; New York: Zone Books, 1994).

23 Retort, *Afflicted Powers*, 210.

24 These remarks position this text, and *The Architecture of Aftermath*, as reports from an inquiry that is parallel to, but quite distinct in its ambitions and its politics from, the focus on style, the "enigmatic signifier," and the cosmogenetic in Charles Jencks's *The Iconic Building: The Power of Enigma* (New York: Rizzoli, 2006).

25 Sarah Deyong, "High-Tech: Modernism Redux," in Haddad and Rifkind, *Critical History of Contemporary Architecture*, chap. 3.

26 Discussed in detail in my "Daniel among the Philosophers: The Jewish Museum Berlin and Architecture after Auschwitz," *Architectural Theory Review* 10, no. 1 (2005): 105–25.

27 See Tracy Myers, Lebbeus Woods, and Karsten Harries, *Lebbeus Woods: Experimental Architecture* (Pittsburgh: Carnegie Museum of Art, 2004).

28 In the collection of the Museum of Modern Art, New York. Quotation from Jeremy Kipnis and Ella Zenghelis, *Perfect Acts of Architecture* (New York: Museum of Modern Art, 2005), 33.

29 The projects are illustrated in Suzanne Stephens, Ian Luna, and Ron Broadhurst, *Imagining Ground Zero: Official and Unofficial Proposals for the World Trade Center Site* (New York: Rizzoli, 2004); and in T. Smith, *Architecture of Aftermath*, 172–88.

30 Herbert Muschamp, "Thinking Big: A Plan for Ground Zero and Beyond," *New York Times Magazine*, September 8, 2002, 48–58, https://www.nytimes.com/2002/09/08/magazine/thinking-big.html.

31 Nicolai Ouroussoff, "At Ground Zero, Towers for Forgetting," *New York Times*, September 11, 2006, B1, http://www.nytimes.com/2006/09/11/arts/design/11zero.html?_r=0.

32 For an informative review of recent publications on the rebuilding of the site, see Martin Filler, "World Trade Center: New York's Vast Flop," *New York Review of Books*, March 9, 2017, http://www.nybooks.com/articles/2017/03/09/world-trade-center-new-yorks-vast -flop/.

33 See, for example, Ashok Rapji, *Big and Green: Toward Sustainable Architecture in the 21st Century* (New York: Princeton Architectural Press, 2002).

34 Philip Jodidio, ed., *Architecture Now!*, vol. 4 (Cologne: Taschen, 2006), 496–97. For SITE's rationale, which makes sense in relation to earlier projects but not for this one, see James Wines, *De-architecture* (New York: Rizzoli, 1987).

35 Esra Arcan, "Postcolonial Theories in Architecture," in Haddad and Rifkind, *Critical History of Contemporary Architecture*, 115.

36 Arcan, "Postcolonial Theories in Architecture," 132.

37 For further examples and context, see Felipe Hernández, *Beyond Modernist Masters: Contemporary Architecture from Latin America* (Basel: Birkenhauser, 2009). Exhibitions showing how architects are responding to the needs of underserved communities include *Small Scale, Big Change*, at the Museum of Modern Art, New York, in 2010, and *Design with the Other 90%: CITIES*, a traveling exhibition from Cooper-Hewitt, National Design Museum, Smithsonian Institution, 2011–12.

38 See Terence Riley, ed., *On-Site: New Architecture from Spain* (New York: Museum of Modern Art, 2006), 150–55.

39 Respectively, Philip Jodidio, ed., *Architecture Now!*, vol. 3 (Cologne: Taschen, 2013), 75–79; and Jodidio, *Architecture Now!*, 4:154–57.

40 See "Nomadic Museum, New York, NY," Shigeru Ban Architects, accessed June 23, 2018, http://www.dma-ny.com/site_sba/?page_id=307; Jodidio, *Architecture Now!*, 4:72–79.

41 See the Project Row Houses website, accessed June 23, 2018, https://projectrowhouses.org. For information about its extensive public art programs, see "Public Art," Project Row Houses, accessed June 23, 2018, https://projectrowhouses.org/public-art/.

42 See Theaster Gates, *Twelve Ballads for Huguenot House* (Cologne: Verlag der Buchhandlung Walther König, 2012).

43 See John Colapinto, "The Real-Estate Artist," *New Yorker*, January 20, 2014, http://www .newyorker.com/magazine/2014/01/20/the-real-estate-artist.

44 James Corner Field Operations and Diller Scofidio + Renfro, *The High Line* (New York: Phaidon, 2015).

45 See Christoph Lindner and Brian Rosa, eds., *Deconstructing the High Line: Postindustrial Urbanism and the Rise of the Elevated Park* (New Brunswick, NJ: Rutgers University Press, 2017).

46 On the occasion of Aravenna being awarded the Pritzker Prize for 2016, Elemental released the plans, section, elevations, and details of its Quntia Monroy, Lo Barnechea, Monterrey, and Villa Verde projects as open source ideas for "incremental housing," especially for migrants and the poor. See "ABC of Incremental Housing," Elemental, accessed June 23, 2018, http://www.elementalchile.cl/en/projects/abc-of-incremental-housing/.

47 The details are specified in Peter Myers, "Knockabout Walkabout," *Architecture Australia*, March–April 2000, 72–75.

48 Jodidio, *Architecture Now!*, 3:454–57.

49 Cruz, "Border Postcards."

50 See Camellia Ansari and Katayoun Raeissi, "Sandbag Shelter Prototypes," PowerPoint presentation, Fall 2011–12, OIKODOMOS, http://www.oikodomos.org/workspaces/app /webroot/files/deliveries/camellia21598_204_sandbagb.pdf; Jodidio, *Architecture Now!*, 4:296–301.

51 See Shack/Slumdwellers International website, accessed June 23, 2018, http://www.sdinet.org.

52 See "Global Studio," University of Sydney, Faculty of Architecture, Design and Planning, accessed June 20, 2014, http://peoplebuildingbettercities.org/globalstudio/.

53 See Architects without Frontiers home page, accessed June 23, 2018, http://www .architectswithoutfrontiers.com.au./site/index.php.

54 Paul Memmott, *Gunyah, Goondie and Wurley: The Aboriginal Architecture of Australia* (St. Lucia: University of Queensland Press, 2007), 302. The record of governmental provision has been poor, despite considerable dollar investment in programs such as the Strategic Indigenous Housing and Infrastructure Program, begun in 2009.

55 Jodidio, *Architecture Now!*, 3:390–95.

56 Illustrated and explained in Aldo Aymonio and Valerio Paolo Mosco, *Contemporary Public Space: Un-volumetric Architecture* (Milan: Skira, 2008), 238–51.

57 Jodidio, *Architecture Now!*, 3:446–49.

58 See Dennis Dollens, *Autopoetic Architecture: Can Buildings Think?* (Catalonia: self-published, 2015), posted March 24, 2015, at Issuu, https://issuu.com/exodesic/docs/d-ba3 _autopoietic_architecture; Jodidio, *Architecture Now!*, 4:140–43.

59 Jodidio, *Architecture Now!*, 4:416–21.

60 Jodidio, *Architecture Now!*, 4:268–69, 276–77.

61 Jodidio, *Architecture Now!*, 4:444–49.

62 Hani Rashid, "Learning from the Virtual," *Post-Internet Cities*, e-flux Architecture, July 25, 2017, http://www.e-flux.com/architecture/post-internet-cities/140714/learning-from-the -virtual/. These projects are illustrated and discussed in this essay.

63 See Achim Menges, Bob Sheil, Ruairi Glynn, and Marilena Skavara, eds., *Fabricate 2017: Rethinking Design and Construction* (London: UCL Press, 2017), https://www.ucl.ac .uk/bartlett/architecture/case-studies/2017/apr/fabricate-2017-rethinking-design-and -construction. The pedagogy and the projects produced at the Interactive Architecture Lab at the Bartlett School of Architecture, University College London, launched in 2017, exemplify these changes. See Interactive Architecture Lab website, accessed April 3, 2018, http://www.interactivearchitecture.org.

64 At Post-Internet Cities website, accessed June 23, 2017, https://postinternetcities.weebly .com.

65 Nick Axel, Helena Barranha, Pedro Gadanho, Nikolaus Hirsch, and Anton Vidokle, "Digital Realism," editorial, *Post-Internet Cities*, e-flux Architecture, posted May 2017, http:// www.e-flux.com/architecture/post-internet-cities/147174/editorial-digital-realism/.

66 Marisa Olsen, "On the Internet, No One Knows You're a Doghouse," *Post-Internet Cities*, e-flux Architecture, July 31, 2017, http://www.e-flux.com/architecture/post-internet-cities /140712/on-the-internet-no-one-knows-you-re-a-doghouse/.

67 Forensic Architecture, "About," accessed July 1, 2018, https://www.forensic-architecture .org/project/. See also Eyal Weizman, *Forensic Architecture: Violence on the Threshold of Detectability* (Cambridge, MA: Zone Books, 2017).

68 Eyal Weizman, "Introduction," in Forensic Architecture ed., *Forensis: The Architecture of Public Truth* (Berlin: Sternberg, 2014), 14.

69 See Forensic Architecture, "Drone Strikes," accessed July 1, 2017, https://www.forensic -architecture.org/case/drone-strikes/.

70 See Forensic Architecture, "The Left-To-Die Boat," accessed July 1, 2018, https://www .forensic-architecture.org/case/left-die-boat/.

71 See Forensic Architecture, "The Grenfell Tower Fire," accessed July 1, 2017, https://www .forensic-architecture.org/case/grenfell-tower-fire/.

72 Weizman, "Introduction," *Forensis*, 15.

4. ART, DESIGN, ARCHITECTURE

1 For a stimulating study of this three-way concurrence, see Wouter Davidts, *Triple Bond: Essays on Art, Architecture, and Museums* (Amsterdam: Valiz, 2017).

2 Robert Venturi, Denise Scott-Brown, and Stephen Izenour, *Learning from Las Vegas* (Cambridge, MA: MIT Press, 1972).

3 Paul Goldberger, *Building Art: The Life and Work of Frank Gehry* (New York: Knopf, 2015). Goldberger cites Los Angeles pop artist Billy Al Bengston: "I think that Frank is the foremost artist in the contemporary world," but repeats throughout the book Gehry's demurral, "No, I am an architect." See also Nicholas Fox Weber, "'Building Art: The Life and Work of Frank Gehry,' by Paul Goldberger," *New York Times*, October 3, 2015, https:// www.nytimes.com/2015/10/25/books/review/building-art-the-life-and-work-of-frank gehry by paul goldberger.html.

4 Hal Foster, *Design and Crime, and Other Diatribes* (London: Verso, 2002), 27.

5 Foster, *Design and Crime*, 33.

6 Foster, *Design and Crime*, 37.

7 Cited in Coosje van Bruggen, *Frank O. Gehry: Guggenheim Museum Bilbao* (New York: Guggenheim Foundation, 1997), 66. Gehry regularly evokes metaphors of fish moving through water, and wind catching sails, to convey the same sense.

8 Terry Smith, "The Experience Museum: Bilbao and Beyond," in *What Is Contemporary Art?* (Chicago: University of Chicago Press, 2009), chap. 5, is a detailed exploration of these questions.

9 Giuliana Bruno, *Atlas of Emotion: Journeys in Art, Architecture, and Film* (London: Verso, 2002), and *Public Intimacy: Architecture and the Visual Arts* (Cambridge, MA : MIT Press, 2007).

10 Hal Foster, *The Art-Architecture Complex* (London: Verso, 2011).

11 Sylvia Lavin, *Kissing Architecture* (Princeton, NJ: Princeton University Press, 2011), 4.

12 For a comprehensive picturing of Acconci Studio projects, see the Acconci website, accessed January 18, 2018, http://acconci.com.

13 See Bianca Bosker, "The Veteran Photographer Making Stunning New Buildings," *New York Times Style Magazine*, April 3, 2017, https://www.nytimes.com/2017/04/03/t -magazine/hiroshi-sugimoto-photograph-architect-enoura-observatory.html.

14 Krzysztof Wodiczko, *Critical Vehicles, Writings, Projects, Interviews* (Cambridge, MA: MIT Press, 1999). Wodiczko was trained as an industrial designer in Poland before emigrating in 1977.

15 Gábor Hushegyi, *Ilona Németh* (Bratislava, Slovakia: Kalligram, 2001).

16 For examples, see "ParaSITE," Michael Rakowitz, accessed June 23, 2018, http://www .michaelrakowitz.com/parasite/.

17 See Lucy Orta and Courtenay Smith, eds., *Lucy Orta: Body Architecture* (Paris: Verlag Silkie Schreiber, 2003); and "Refuge Wear," Studio Orta, accessed June 23, 2018, https:// www.studio-orta.com/en/artworks/serie/1/Refuge-Wear.

18 Andrea Zittel, *Critical Space* (New York: New Museum of Contemporary Art, 2006); Richard Julin, *Andrea Zittel: Lay of My Land* (Munich: Prestel Verlag, 2011); and A–Z: An Institute of Investigative Living, accessed June 23, 2018, http://www.zittel.org/work /institute-of-investigative-living-2012-present.

19 See the documentary film *Cities on Speed: Bogata Change*, dir. Andreas Dalsgaard (Copenhagen: Bastard Film, 2010), 58 min., DVD.

20 Philip Jodidio, ed., *Architecture Now!*, vol. 4 (Cologne: Taschen, 2006), 536–43.

21 See Benjamin H. D. Buchloh, Alison M. Gingeras, and Carlos Basualdo, *Thomas Hirschhorn* (London: Phaidon, 2004). See also Benjamin H. D. Buchloh, "An Interview with Thomas Hirschhorn," *October*, no. 113 (Summer 2005): 77–100.

22 Isabelle Loring Wallace and Nora Wendt, eds., *Contemporary Art and Architecture: A Strange Utility* (Farnham, Surrey: Ashgate, 2013), xxii.

23 Wallace and Wendt, *Contemporary Art and Architecture*, 1.

24 Pierre Nora, ed., *Les lieux de mémoire*, 7 vols. (Paris: Gallimard, 1984–94).

25 Wallace and Wendt, *Contemporary Art and Architecture*, 1.

26 See Callum Morton and Stuart Koop, *Callum Morton: More Talk about Buildings and Mood* (Sydney: Museum of Contemporary Art, 2004).

27 On architecture and "the photomodern," see Terry Smith, *Making the Modern: Industry, Art, and Design in America* (Chicago: University of Chicago Press, 1993), 401–4.

28 Mark Lewis, "Is Modernity Our Antiquity?," *Afterall*, no. 14 (Autumn/Winter 2006): 109–17.

29 See Terry Smith, "The Intensity Exhibit: Barneyworld at McGuggenheim," in *What Is Contemporary Art?*, chap. 6.

30 See Thomas Demand, *Thomas Demand: The Complete Papers* (London: MACK Books, 2017).

31 See Deimantas Narkevicius, *Da Capo: Fifteen Films* (Berlin: Archive Books, 2015).

32 Philip Jodidio, ed., *Architecture Now!*, vol. 3 (Cologne: Taschen, 2013), 334–39.

33 For information on Stalker, see Mark Rappolt, "Stalker: Barbed Wire and Windmills," *Contemporary*, no. 35 (2001), http://www.contemporary-magazines.com/architech35 .htm; or Stalker/Osservatorionomade website, accessed June 23, 2018, http://www .osservatorionomade.net.

34 Relevant works by these artists appear in Simon Njami, *Africa Remix: Contemporary Art of a Continent* (London: Hayward Gallery, 2005). On Bruyère, see, "Jean Michel Bruyère," Epidemic, accessed June 23, 2018, http://www.epidemic.net/en/art/bruyere/index.html.

35 Germano Celant, *Art and Architecture* (Milan: Skira, 2004).

36 Iwona Blazwick, ed., *Century City: Art and Culture in the Modern Metropolis* (London: Tate Publications, 2001). Different curators explored the art cultures of these cities in relation to specific periods: Bombay/Mumbai, 1992–2001; Lagos, 1955–70; London, 1990–2001; Moscow, 1916–30; New York, 1969–74; Paris, 1905–15; Rio de Janeiro, 1955–69; Tokyo, 1969–73; and Vienna, 1908–18.

37 Centro de Arte Contemporáneo Wilfredo Lam, *Novena Bienal de la Habana 2006* (Havana: Centro de Arte Contemporáneo Wilfredo Lam, 2006).

38 These exhibitions are well discussed by Wallace and Wendt, *Contemporary Art and Architecture*, 14–16.

39 The Architecture Biennale at Venice often points to this relationship between art and architecture. Other notable initiatives of this kind include those sponsored in recent years by the Sherman Contemporary Art Foundation, Sydney (now the Sherman Center for Culture and Ideas).

40 Steven Holl Architects, Institute for Contemporary Art at Virginia Commonwealth University, Richmond, 2012–15, accessed June 23, 2018, http://www.stevenholl.com/projects/vcu-institute-for-contemporary-art. "Windmueller Artist Lecture Series Presents Steven Holl," Institute for Contemporary Art, accessed June 11, 2013, http://ica.vcu.edu/events/past/video-windmueller-artist-lecture-series-presents-steven-holl/.

41 "New Institute for Contemporary Art at VCU Will Open in October," press release, *VCU News*, February 8, 2017, https://www.news.vcu.edu/article/New_Institute_for_Contemporary_Art_at_VCU_will_open_in_October.

42 For responses from within the architectural profession, see, for example, Rory Olcayto, "Assemble's 2015 Turner Prize," *Architects' Journal*, October 1, 2015, https://www.architectsjournal.co.uk/news/culture/assembles-2015-turner-prize-show/8689825.article.

43 At "About," Assemble website, accessed August 13, 2017, http://assemblestudio.co.uk/?page_id=48. The current description at this address is somewhat more bland. Membership has varied between fifteen and twenty artists. None is a registered architect, and none claims to be an artist.

5. CHINESE CONTEMPORARY ART

I first developed these thoughts for a paper I presented at the first China Contemporary Art Forum, the *Beijing International Conference on Art Theory and Criticism*, May 26–30, 2009, for which I thank James Elkins and Qigu Jiang. My thinking on these questions is indebted to the discussions during that conference, and to gallery and studio visits at the time and during prior and subsequent visits to China. I have also benefited from discussions with my University of Pittsburgh colleague Gao Minglu, my University of Sydney colleague John Clark, and many others, including several of the artists mentioned. I also thank Judith Farquhar of the University of Chicago for drawing my attention to key essays that address the emergence of contemporaneity in China today, although they do not name it so, and for her comments on this text. Material is also drawn from "Chinese Art: Continuity, Modernity, and Contemporaneity," my catalog essay for *What about the Art? Contemporary Art from China*, curated by Cai Guo-Qiang for the Qatar Museums, Dohar, 2016, and published by Guangxi Normal University Press, 2016.

1 "Forum Profile," *First China Contemporary Art Forum—2009 Beijing International Conference on Art Theory and Criticism* (Beijing: China Contemporary Art Forum, 2009), 2. In fairness, it should be noted that comparative organizations everywhere use similar language to describe their policy goals. For example, the International Partnerships section of the US government's National Endowment for the Arts website describes its mission thus: "Through cooperative initiatives with other funders, the National Endowment for the Arts brings the benefit of international exchange to arts organizations, artists, and audiences nationwide. NEA's international activities increase recognition of the excellence of US arts around the world and broaden the scope of experience of American artists, thereby enriching the art they create. Through partnerships with other government agencies and the private sector, the NEA fosters international creative collaboration by strengthening residency programs of foreign artists in communities across the country. Local citizens as well as the arts community benefit from the lasting international ties that result." See "International Partnerships," National Endowment for the Arts, accessed August 30, 2017, http://www.arts.gov/partnerships/international/. The partnerships are mostly small nongovernmental organizations similar to CCAF. The most active prior agency, the United States Information Service, founded in 1953 in a Cold War context, ceased operations in 1999, passing some of its programs to the Office of the Under Secretary for Public Diplomacy and Public Affairs; see "Under Secretary for Public Diplomacy and Public Affairs," US Department of State, accessed August 30, 2017, http://www.state.gov/r/.

2 See, for example, Walter D. Mignolo, *The Darker Side of Western Modernity: Global Futures, Decolonial Options* (Durham, NC: Duke University Press, 2011).

3 Liu Kang, *Globalization and Cultural Trends in China* (Honolulu: University of Hawai'i Press, 2004), 3–4. Immediately above that quotation's text, he writes, "Globalization constitutes a fundamental paradox in the sphere of culture—a tension between the trend toward cultural homogenization through global cultural production and distribution (media, popular culture, and entertainment industry) and the opposite trend toward cultural diversification in terms of local, ethnic and national cultural projects and agendas." Dubbed "glocalization" by Ronald Robertson, an early theorist of the phenomenon mentioned by Kang, this is a broader definition than the more common understanding of globalization, which focuses on the first part of his paradox. See Ronald Robertson, "Glocalization: Time-Space and Homogeneity-Heterogeneity," in *Global Modernities*, ed. Mike Featherstone, Scott Lash, and Ronald Robertson (Thousand Oaks, CA: Sage, 1995), 25–44.

4 Liu, *Globalization and Cultural Trends in China*, 12.

5 Wang Shan, *Di san zhi yanjin kan Zhongguo* [Viewing China through a third eye] (Shanxi: Shanxi Publishing House, 1994).

6 Wang Xiaoming, "A Manifesto for Cultural Studies," in *One China, Many Paths*, ed. Chaohua Wang (London: Verso, 2003), chap. 12, 275–76, 285, 287, 290.

7 Fredric Jameson, foreword to *Politics, Ideology, and Literary Discourse in China: Theoretical Interventions and Cultural Critique*, ed. Liu Kang and Xiaobing Tang (Durham, NC: Duke University Press, 1993), 3.

8 David Harvey, *The Condition of Postmodernity* (London: Wiley-Blackwell, 1991); and Fredric Jameson, *Postmodernism: Or, the Cultural Logic of Late Capitalism* (Durham, NC: Duke University Press, 1991).

9 Liu, *Globalization and Cultural Trends in China*, 26.

10 See, for example, Terry Smith, "Introduction: The Contemporaneity Question," in *Antinomies of Art and Culture: Modernity, Postmodernity, Contemporaneity*, ed. Terry Smith, Okwui Enwezor, and Nancy Condee (Durham, NC: Duke University Press, 2008), 1–19.

11 Jonathan Hay, "Double Modernity, Para-Modernity," in Smith, Enwezor, and Condee, *Antinomies of Art and Culture*, 115. See also Geoff Wade and Laichen Sun, eds., *Southeast Asia in the Fifteenth Century: The China Factor* (Singapore: Singapore University Press, 2010).

12 Pan Gongkai, ed., *Reflections: Chinese Modernities as Self-Conscious Cultural Ventures* (Beijing: Oxford University Press, 2007).

13 Terry Smith, *Contemporary Art: World Currents* (Upper Saddle River, NJ: Prentice Hall, 2011), a chapter on China and East Asia is included within the worldwide survey.

14 See, for example, Gao Minglu, ed., *Inside Out: New Chinese Art* (Berkeley: University of California Press, 1998); Gao Minglu, *The Wall: Reshaping Chinese Contemporary Art* (Buffalo: Albright Knox Gallery of Art, 2005); and Gao Minglu, *Total Modernity and Chinese Avant-Garde Art in the Twentieth Century* (Cambridge, MA: MIT Press, 2011); Wu Hung, ed., *The First Guangzhou Triennial—Reinterpretation: A Decade of Experimental Chinese Art, 1990–2000* (Guangzhou: Guangzhou Museum of Art, 2002), Wu Hung, "A Case of Being 'Contemporary': Conditions, Spheres and Narratives of Contemporary Chinese Art," in Smith, Enwezor, and Condee, *Antinomies of Art and Culture*, 290–306, and *Contemporary Chinese Art* (London: Thames and Hudson, 2014).

15 For example, Lü Peng and Yi Dan, *Zhongguo xiandai yishu shi, 1979–1989* (Changsha: Hunan meishu chubanshe, 1992); Li Xianting, "Major Trends in the Development of Contemporary Chinese Art," in *China's New Art, Post-1989*, ed. Tsong-zung Chang (Hong Kong: Hanart TZ Gallery, 1993), x–xxii; Len Ling, "The China Dream," *Contemporary Art Chinese Type* 1, no. 1 (1997), http://www.chinese-art.com/volume1issue1; and Lü Peng, *Zhongguo dangdai yishu shi, 1990–1999* (Changsha: Hunan meishu chubanshe, 2000).

16 Wu, "A Case of Being 'Contemporary,'" 291–92, 294. See also Aleš Erjavec, ed., *Postmodernism and the Postsocialist Condition: Politicized Art under Late Socialism* (Berkeley: University of California Press, 2003).

17 Wu, "A Case of Being 'Contemporary,'" 294–95.

18 Wu, "A Case of Being 'Contemporary,'" 296–305.

19 Hu Shi quoted in Gao Minglu, "Particular Time, Specific Space, My Truth: Total Modernity in Chinese Contemporary Art," in Smith, Enwezor, and Condee, *Antinomies of Art and Culture*, 137.

20 Gao, "Particular Time, Specific Space," 141.

21 Gao, "Particular Time, Specific Space," 145–62.

22 Gao Minglu, *Chinese Maximalism* (Chongqing: Chongqing Press, 1991).

23 For a description of the visual arts infrastructure in the late 1980s, see Wang Chunchen, "Current State of Chinese Art," 4Art.com, November 10, 2008, http://4art.com/profiles /blogs/current-state-of-chinese-art. This is a topic of constant discussion in the magazines, for example, Danielle Shang, "Orientalism and the Landscape of Contemporary Chinese Art," *Yishu* 8, no. 6 (November–December 2009): 41–50.

24 Artprice.com and Art Market Monitor of Artron (AMMA), *The Art Market in 2012: A Dialogue between East and West* (Paris: Artprice.com, 2013), 5–6, http://imgpublic.artprice .com/pdf/the_art_market2012_online_en.pdf.

25 "Mad about Museums," *Economist*, January 6, 2014, http://www.economist.com/news /special-report/21591710-china-building-thousands-new-museums-how-will-it-fill-them -mad-about-museums. See also Winnie Wong, "Arresting Development: China's Museum Boom," *Artforum* 54, no. 3 (November 2015): 123–26.

26 See "China Crisis Puts Global Art Market on Alert," *Art Newspaper*, no. 272 (October 2015), sec. 2, 4.

27 Rachael A. J. Pownall, *TEFAF Art Market Report 2017* (Helvoirt, The Netherlands: European Fine Art Foundation, 2017).

28 Clare McAndrew, *The Art Market 2017* (Basel: Art Basel and UBS, 2017), https:// d33ipftjqrd91.cloudfront.net/asset/cms/Art_Basel_and_UBS_The_Art_Market_2017.pdf.

29 Relevant general perspectives by Nicholas Jose, Elaine W. Ng, Gene Sherman, Carrillo Gantner, and Britta Erickson are found in Nicholas Jose, ed., *Contemporary Art + Philanthropy, Private Foundations: Asia-Pacific Focus* (Sydney: Power Publications for the Sherman Contemporary Art Foundation, 2009).

30 There is no general study of independent art spaces in China, although each of the spaces just mentioned has a useful website. For an overview of the period through 1993, including some reference to earlier alternative platforms, see Jane DeBevoise, *Between State and Market: Chinese Contemporary Art in the Post-Mao Era* (Leiden: Brill, 2014). For commentary on the recent "hollowing out" of Beijing as an art center and the rise of Shanghai, see Robin Peckham, "The Loss of Centre," *di'van: A Journal of Accounts*, no. 2 (July 2017): 100–107.

31 See Mami Kataoka, Charles Merewether, and Mori Bijutsukan, *Ai Weiwei: According to What?* (Munich: Prestel Verlag, 2012).

32 Xu was inspired to create the first in the series when he learned that Red Army troops had stolen Chinese and Japanese paintings from Berlin museums during World War II. See Robert E. Harrist Jr., "Background Stories: Xu Bing's Art of Transformation," in *Xu Bing*, ed. David Elliot (London: Albion, 2011), 33–43, https://www.britishmuseum.org/pdf /Background-Stories_Xu-Bings-Art-of-Transformation.pdf. For some indications of the interaction between currents in contemporary Chinese art, see, for example, Maxwell K. Hearn and Wu Hung, *Ink Art: Past as Present in Contemporary China* (New York: Metropolitan Museum of Art, 2013).

33 See Cao Fei, "Works: Video," Cao Fei website, accessed August 30, 2017, http://www .caofei.com/works.aspx?wtid=3.

34 See Ellen Larson, "Cao Fei's Nostalgia for the Future" (master's thesis, University of Pittsburgh, Pennsylvania, 2018).

35 See Luise Guest, "I Am Your Agency," *Art Life*, December 5, 2013, http://theartlife.com.au /2013/i-am-your-agency/.

36 *Outsideln: Chinese × American × Contemporary Art* was an exhibition at the Princeton University Art Gallery in 2009. None of the artists exhibited lived in China. One was an American who painted in a Chinese manner (Michael Cherney), another a Vietnamese artist who, the curators argued, made art in a Chinese spirit. See Jerome Silbergeld, "Chinese Art, Made-in-America: An Encounter with Geography, Ethnicity, Contemporaneity, and Cultural Chineseness," in *Outsideln: Chinese × American × Contemporary Art*, ed. Jerome Silbergeld (New Haven, CT: Yale University Press, 2009), 115–39. For commentary, see Sohl Lee, "Outsideln: Chinese × American × Contemporary Art," *Yishu* 8, no. 4 (July– August 2009): 88–97. More generally, see Melissa Chiu, ed., *Breakout: Chinese Art outside China* (New York: Charta, 2006).

37 Ella Liao and Wendt Teo, "China's New Art," *Art Newspaper*, no. 271 (September 2015): 60.

38 See Tu Wei-ming, "Cultural China: The Periphery as the Center," *Daedalus* 120, no. 2 (Spring 1991): 1–32.

39 See, for example, Zhu Qi, "Do Westerners Really Understand Chinese Avant-Garde Art?," in *Chinese Art at the End of the Millennium*, ed. John Clark (Hong Kong: New Art Media, 2000), 55–60. For a review of critical approaches around 2007, see Elizabeth Lee, "Chineseness in Contemporary Chinese Art Criticism," *Journal of Undergraduate Research* 1, no. 3 (2007–8), http://sites.nd.edu/ujournal/2014/07/16/issue-3/.

40 Gao Minglu, *Yi Pai: A Synthetic Theory against Representation* (Guangxi: Normal University Press, 2009). Gao has recently been engaged in an interesting discussion on these matters with Paul Gladston. See the latter's "Writing on *The Wall*—A Critical Response to Recent Chinese Meditations on the 'Chineseness' of Chinese Contemporary Art," *Yishu* 6, no. 1 (March 2007): 26–33; Gao's reply, "Who Is Pounding the Wall?," *Yishu* 6, no. 2 (June 2007): 106–15, followed by Gladston's response, "(More Writing) On *The Wall*," *Yishu* 6, no. 3 (September, 2007): 103–10. See also Paul Gladston, *Contemporary Chinese Art: A Critical History* (London: Reaktion Books, 2014), especially chapter 4, which reviews these issues.

41 Peng Feng, "Paths to the Middle: A Tentative Theory for Chinese Contemporary Art," in *First China Contemporary Art Forum*, 255–64.

42 Jiang Jiehong, "A Monologue on 'The Revolution Continues,'" in *First China Contemporary Art Forum*, 216, 218. Jiang Jiehong curated *The Revolution Continues: New Chinese Art* (London: Jonathan Cape and Saatchi Gallery, 2008).

6. ABORIGINAL AUSTRALIAN ART

Chapter 6 is based on ideas advanced in "What Is Contemporary about Australian Aboriginal Art?," the inaugural John W. and Maria T. Kluge Distinguished Lecture in Arts and Humanities, University of Virginia, February 13, 2008, at the invitation of Margaret Smith; a paper presented at the *Exhibiting Aboriginal Art* symposium, Museum Ludwig, Cologne, February 18–19, 2011, organized by Claus Volkenandt, Kasper König, Emily

Joyce Evans, and Falk Wolf; and discussion of these issues with many people, including many of the artists and curators mentioned and scholars such as Ian McLean, Fred R. Myers, and Henry Skerritt.

1 The Intervention is the colloquial name given to the Northern Territory National Emergency Act promulgated by the conservative government of Prime Minister John Howard in 2007. Inspired by reports of child abuse by Indigenous elders in remote communities, none of which has been brought to prosecution, the package of measures included some increase in community services but also, and primarily, extra policing, reduced recognition of tribal law, compulsory acquisition of townships held under the Native Title Act, and increased restrictions on sales of alcohol. Extended and amended by subsequent Labor Party governments, it remains in force under the weasel-word title Stronger Futures Policy.

2 On the idea that Aboriginal art is an art-historical miracle, see, for example, Japanese museum director Akira Tatehata's characterization of Emily Kame Kngwarreye as an "impossible modernist." Akira Tatehata, "The Impossible Modernist," in *Utopia: The Genius of Emily Kngwarreye*, ed. Margo Neale (Canberra: National Museum of Australia Press, 2008), 85–89. On the claim of Indigenous exceptionality, see, for example, Ashleigh Wilson, "Hetti Perkins Quits NSW State Gallery Position and Calls for National Indigenous Art Space," *Australian*, September 20, 2011, http://www.theaustralian.com.au/arts/hetti -perkins-quits-nsw-state-gallery-position-and-calls-for-national-indigenous-art-space /story-e6frg8n6-1226141285265.

3 David Christian, *This Fleeting World: A Short History of Humanity* (Great Barrington, MA: Berkshire, 2008), 103.

4 While *This Fleeting World* was confined to one hundred pages, David Christian's *Maps of Time: An Introduction to Big History* (Berkeley: University of California Press, 2004) is a substantial treatment of these profound issues. His scholarly reflections on time are also important; see, for example, "History and Time," *Australian Journal of Politics and History* 57, no. 3 (September 2011): 353–65.

5 Okwui Enwezor, "The Postcolonial Constellation," in *Antinomies of Art and Culture: Modernity, Postmodernity, Contemporaneity*, ed. Terry Smith, Okwui Enwezor, and Nancy Condee (Durham, NC: Duke University Press, 2008), 207–34.

6 Richard Bell, "Bells' Theorem: Aboriginal Art—It's a White Thing!," *Kooriweb*, November 2002, at http://www.kooriweb.org/foley/great/art/bell.html.

7 In my view, this is the larger, culturally transformative achievement of the Aboriginal art movement. See Terry Smith, "Creating Value between Cultures: Contemporary Aboriginal Art," in *Beyond Price: Values and Valuing in Art and Culture*, ed. Michael Hütter and David Throsby (Cambridge: Cambridge University Press, 2008), 23–40.

8 The best introductions are Wally Caruana, *Aboriginal Art*, 3rd ed. (London: Thames and Hudson, 2013); Howard Morphy, *Aboriginal Art* (London: Phaidon, 1998); and Ian McLean, *Rattling Spears: A History of Indigenous Australian Art* (London: Routledge, 2016). These texts are astutely compared by Nicolas Rothwell, "Cultural Evolution: Three Pivotal Books Reflect Indigenous Art's Journey from Antiquity to Modernity," *Weekend Australian*, November 26–27, 2016, review 15–17.

9 Anthropologists studying the creative practices of Indigenous peoples in contact situations routinely distinguish between the "ethnic art" made within a community for its own purposes; the "tourist art," or souvenir art, produced for visitors to the area; and works of "fine art" made for sale through art markets, alongside art from other times, places, and peoples, yet within its own subcategory. These distinctions, formalized by Nicholas Graburn in his *Ethnic and Tourist Art: Cultural Expressions from the Fourth World* (Berkeley: University of California Press, 1974), are usefully modified by Howard Morphy in his *Becoming Art: Exploring Cross-Cultural Categories* (Sydney: UNSW Press, 2008), notably, and quite properly, by dropping the word "ethnic" from the first category, thus including the artistic practices of Indigenous peoples within the category "art."

10 These numbers cannot, however, be closely compared, as the questions asked by census takers were changed between those dates to remove direct reference to race and to record Indigenous self-determination more directly. See Kate Ross, "Population Issues, Indigenous Australians, 1996," Occasional Paper no. 4708.0, Australian Bureau of Statistics, February 15, 1999, http://www.abs.gov.au/ausstats/abs@.nsf/525a1b9402141235ca25682000 146abc/5a0ec5f1f21faad6ca256888001daede!OpenDocument; and *Census of Population and Housing; Understanding the Increase in Aboriginal and Torres Strait Islander Counts, 2006–2011*, catalog no. 2077.0, Australian Bureau of Statistics, September 17, 2013, http:// www.abs.gov.au/ausstats/abs@.nsf/Lookup/2077.0main+features22006-2011.

11 These are 2011 figures, as the breakdowns from the 2016 census are yet to be posted. See *Estimates and Projections, Aboriginal and Torres Strait Islanders Australians, 2001 to 2026*, catalog no. 3238.0, Australian Bureau of Statistics, April 30, 2014, http://www.abs.gov.au/ausstats /abs@.nsf/Products/C19A0C6E4794A3FACA257CC900143A3D?opendocument. For a detailed breakdown of Aboriginal and Torres Strait Islander populations into areas ranging from "Major City Areas" to "Very Remote" ones, see "Estimates of Aboriginal and Torres Strait Islander Australians, June 2011," catalog no. 3238.0.55.001, Australian Bureau of Statistics, August 30, 2013, http://www.abs.gov.au/ausstats/abs@.nsf/mf/3238.0.55.001.

12 Statistics from Alice Woodhead and Tim Acker, *The Art Economies Value Chain Report: Artists and Art Centre Production*, CRC-REP Research Report CR007 (Alice Springs: Ninti One, 2014), http://www.crc-rep.com.au/resource/CR007_ArtCentreProduction .pdf. This is the most recent such report.

13 See Adrian Newstead, AIAM100 Index, *Australian Indigenous Art Market Top 100*, November 19, 2015, http://www.cooeeart.com.au/marketplace/market/. Artists, art centers, and funders have responded to this downturn in various ways, including by creating local and regional art fairs oriented between the fine art markets based in the capital cities and the tourist industry of Aboriginal artifacts. See the insightful analysis in Tod Jones, Jessica Booth, and Tim Acker, "The Changing Business of Aboriginal and Torres Strait Islander Art: Markets, Audiences, Artists, and the Large Art Fairs," *Journal of Arts Management, Law, and Society* 46, no. 3 (2016): 107–21.

14 Figures from the two main reports, Rachel A. J. Pownall, *The TEFAF Art Market Report 2017* (Helvoirt, Netherlands: European Fine Art Foundation, 2017); and Clare McAndrew, *The Art Market 2017* (Basel: Art Basel and UBS, 2017). The variation is due to different estimates of private sales within each total.

15 For a comparison between global markets for contemporary art and those for Australian Aboriginal art, see Terry Smith, *What Is Contemporary Art?* (Chicago: University of Chicago Press, 2009), chaps. 7 and 8. For details on markets for Indigenous and non-Indigenous Australian art, see reports of the *Australian Art Sales Digest*. For an analysis, see Meaghan Wilson-Anastasios, "Joining the Dots: The Sustainability of the Aboriginal Art Market," *Art Matters* (blog), July 8, 2010, https://wilsonanastasios.com/2010/07/08 /joining-the-dots-the-sustainability-of-the-aboriginal-art-market/. For statistics on individual artists, see David Throsby, *The Artist in Australia Today*, report of the Committee for the Individual Artists Inquiry, chaired by David Throsby, Australia Council for the Arts (North Sydney: Australia Council, 1983); Gary Prosser, *Visual and Craft Artists: A National Study of the Australian Crafts and Visual Arts Industry* (North Sydney: Australia Council, 1989); David Throsby and Anita Zednik, *Do You Really Expect to Get Paid? An Economic Study of Professional Artists in Australia* (North Sydney: Australia Council, 2010); and "Visual Arts," *Art Facts*, Australia Council for the Arts, accessed June 22, 2018, http://artfacts.australiacouncil.gov.au/visual-arts/.

16 These supporters are profiled in Fred R. Myers, *Painting Culture: The Making of Aboriginal High Art* (Durham, NC: Duke University Press, 2002).

17 Nicolas Rothwell, "Scams in the Desert," *Australian*, March 4–5, 2006, reprinted in his *Another Country* (Melbourne: Black, 2007), 257. Citations to the book edition.

18 Rothwell, "Scams in the Desert," 265–66. For a relatively frank account by one of the in-betweeners, see Adrian Newstead, *The Dealer Is the Devil: An Insider's History of the Aboriginal Art Trade* (Sydney: New South Books, 2014).

19 On the latter and the work of similar groups, see Jennifer Biddle, *Remote Avant-Garde: Aboriginal Art under Occupation* (Durham, NC: Duke University Press, 2016).

20 Ian McLean, "Aboriginal Modernism in Central Australia," in *Exiles, Diasporas, and Strangers*, ed. Kobena Mercer (Cambridge, MA: MIT Press, 2008), 72–93. McLean elaborates this argument into a narrative of Indigenous and white contact since settlement in *Rattling Spears*.

21 Morphy, *Becoming Art*, 194.

22 Morphy, *Becoming Art*, 194–95. See also Howard Morphy, *Ancestral Connections: Art and an Aboriginal System of Knowledge* (Chicago: University of Chicago Press, 1991), for a close study of Yolngu art. Morphy is echoing the argument of George Kubler, *The Shape of Time: Remarks on the History of Things* (New Haven, CT: Yale University Press, 1962).

23 Kobena Mercer, ed., *Cosmopolitan Modernisms* (Cambridge, MA: MIT Press, 2005); see his introduction, 6–24.

24 See McLean, "Aboriginal Modernism in Central Australia," *Rattling Spears*, and "The Authenticity of Australian Aboriginal Art," in *Remembering Forward: Australian Aboriginal Art since 1960*, ed. Kasper König, Emily Joyce Evans, and Falk Wolf (London: Paul Holberton for the Museum Ludwig, Cologne, 2010), 170.

25 See Terry Smith, "Modernism" and "Modernity," in *Dictionary of Art*, ed. Jane Turner (London: Macmillan, 1996), and those entries in *Grove Dictionary of Art* online, last updated April 2018, https://doi.org/10.1093/gao/9781884446054.article.T058785 and https://doi.org/10.1093/gao/9781884446054.article.T058788.

26 See Bernard Smith, "The Myth of Isolation," in *Australian Painting Today: The John Mur-tagh Macrossan Lectures for 1961* (Brisbane: University of Queensland Press, 1962), 3–17, reprinted in Bernard Smith, *The Antipodean Manifesto: Essays in Art and History* (Melbourne: Oxford University Press, 1976), 57–69; and Simon Pierse, *Australian Artists in London, 1950–1965: An Antipodean Summer* (Farnham, Surrey: Ashgate, 2012).

27 See Nadine Amadio, *Albert Namatjira: The Life and Work of an Australian Painter* (Melbourne: Macmillan, 1986); Alison French, *Seeing the Centre: The Art of Albert Namatjira, 1902–1959* (Canberra: National Gallery of Australia, 2002); and Martin Edmond, *Battarbee and Namatjira* (Artarmon, NSW: Giramondo, 2012).

28 Christine Nicholls, "The Art of Emily Kame Kngwarreye: A Utopian Tale," in *Emily Kame Kngwarreye: Body Painting Series* (New York: Robert Steele Gallery with Anima Gallery, Adelaide, 1997), 5.

29 Nicholls, "Art of Emily Kame Kngwarreye," 6. For more considered estimations of the artist's work, see *Utopia: The Genius of Emily Kame Kngwarreye*, National Museum of Australia and National Museum of Art, Osaka, 2008, curated by Margo Neale; and my essay "Kngwarreye Woman Abstract Painter," in *Emily Kngwarreye Paintings*, ed. Jenny Isaacs (Sydney: Craftsman House, 1998), 24–42. For illuminating discussion of the contexts of such work, see, for example, Jennifer Biddle, *Breasts, Bodies, Canvas: Central Desert Art as Experience* (Sydney: University of New South Wales Press, 2007).

30 Djon Mundine, arts adviser at Ramingining for eighteen years, was the curator of this project. See Howard Morphy, "A Memorial for the Dead: John Mundine on a Project to Commemorate 200 Years of Loss," *Artlink* 10, nos. 1–2 (Autumn–Winter 1990): 3–4. See also Terry Smith, "Public Art between Cultures: *The Aboriginal Memorial*," *Critical Inquiry* 27, no. 4 (Summer 2001): 629–61.

31 See "Ngurrara: The Great Sandy Desert Painting," *Aboriginal Art Directory*, June 17, 2008, http://www.aboriginalartdirectory.com/news/feature/ngurrara-the-great-sandy-desert -canvas.php. See also Karen Dayman, "The Ngurrara Artists of the Great Sandy Desert: Painting to Claim Native Title" (PhD diss., University of Sydney, 2017).

32 See Rod Moss, *The Hard Light of Day: An Artist's Story of Friendships in Arrernte Country* (Brisbane: University of Queensland Press, 2011).

33 See Stephen Grant and Bridgit Pirrie, eds., *Two Laws: One Big Spirit* (Sydney: Grant Pirrie, 2004); *The Loaded Ground: Michael Nelson Jagamara and Imants Tillers*, Drill Hall Gallery, Australian National University, Canberra, 2012; and Una Rey, *Black, White and Restive Cross-Cultural Initiatives in Contemporary Australian Art*, Newcastle Art Gallery, Cooks Hill, NSW, 2016. See also Ian McLean, "9 Shots 5 Stories: Imants Tillers and Indigenous Difference," *Art Monthly*, no. 228 (April 2010): 13–16, and no. 229 (May 2010): 12–16.

34 Ian McLean, "How Aborigines Invented the Idea of Contemporary Art," in *How Aborigines Invented the Idea of Contemporary Art*, ed. Ian McLean (Sydney: Power Publications, 2011), 340.

35 Landmark survey exhibitions were staged by Judith Ryan at the National Gallery of Victoria, Wally Caruana at the National Gallery of Australia, and Hetti Perkins at the Art Gallery of New South Wales, among many others. Innovative curatorship in the field

is exemplified by exhibitions such as *Yiwarra Kuju: The Canning Stock Route*, curated by Haley Atkins, Louise Mengil, Terry Murray, John Carty, Monique La Fontaine, and Carly Davenport for the National Museum of Australia, Canberra, 2010, http://www .canningstockrouteproject.com/yiwarra-kuju-exhibition/yiwarra-kuju-the-canning-stock -route/. For ongoing research into Indigenous modernisms, see the *Multiple Modernisms: Twentieth-Century Artistic Modernisms in Global Perspective* project, accessed June 22, 2018, http://multiplemodernisms.org/category/multiple-modernisms-twentieth-century -artistic-modernisms-in-global-perspective/.

36 Prominent public collections in the United States include the Kluge-Ruhe Collection at the University of Virginia; the Kaplan and Levi Collection at the Seattle Art Museum, exhibited there in 2012 under the title *Ancestral Modern: Australian Aboriginal Art*; and the Owen and Wagner Collection at the Hood Museum of Art, Dartmouth College, exhibited there in 2012 under the title *Crossing Cultures*. Private collections include that of John and Barbara Wilkerson, New York, as exhibited in *Icons of the Desert: Early Aboriginal Paintings from Papunya*, curated by Roger Benjamin for the Herbert F. Johnson Museum, Cornell University, and traveling; and the Denis and Debra Scholl Collection, Miami, as exhibited in *No Boundaries: Aboriginal Australian Abstract Painting*, curated by Henry Skerritt and William Fox for the Nevada Museum of Art and touring during 2015–16.

37 Rosalind Krauss usefully distinguishes this as "structural" rather than "morphological" formalism. See her "Formalism and Structuralism," in *Art since 1900*, vol. 2, *1945 to the Present*, ed. Hal Foster, Rosalind Krauss, Yve-Alain Bois, and Benjamin H. D. Buchloh (London: Thames and Hudson, 2004), 32–39.

38 Terry Smith, *The Architecture of Aftermath* (Chicago: University of Chicago Press, 2006), 197–200.

39 See Ian McLean, *The Art of Gordon Bennett* (Sydney: Craftsman House, 1996); and Terry Smith, "Australia's Anxiety Again: Remembering the Art of Gordon Bennett," *Eyeline*, no. 82 (2015): 40–52.

40 Paul Chan, *Paul Chan: The 7 Lights* (New York: Distributed Art Publishers, 2007). Since 2006, Chilean-born artist and designer Sebastian Errazuriz has been making one work a year that reflects on the resonances of the 9/11 attacks. See Sebastian Errazuriz, "Social," accessed July 3, 2018, http://www.meetsebastian.com/social-art/.

41 Nicolas Rothwell, "NATSIAA Shows How Urban Trends Eclipse Aboriginal Art Traditions," *Australian*, August 14, 2014, http://www.theaustralian.com.au/arts/visual-arts /natsiaa-shows-how-urban-trends-eclipse-aboriginal-art-traditions/story-fn9d3avm -1227023421217. For a more deeply reflective response to these events, see Ian McLean, "Double Desire: Becoming Aboriginal," *Contemporary Visual Art + Culture Broadsheet* 43, no. 4 (2014): 65–71.

42 Cited in Terry Smith, "The Governor General and the Post-Colonial: The Australia Day Address 1996," in "Media Imaginaries," ed. Anthony Uhlmann, special issue, *Continuum* (1997): 74. See also Bill Hayden, *Hayden: An Autobiography* (Sydney: Angus and Robertson, 1996).

43 Nicolas Rothwell, "Whose Culture Is It Anyway?," *Weekend Australian*, March 30–31, 1996, 1–2.

44 Emily Kame Kngwarreye, cited in many articles, including Andréa Fernandes, "Desert Monet: Emily Kngwarreye," *Mental Floss*, September 10, 2010, http://mentalfloss.com /article/25734/desert-monet-emily-kngwarreye.

45 Okwui Enwezor, *All the World's Futures: 56th International Art Exhibition* (Venice: Marsilio Editore for La Biennale de Venezia, 2015).

46 See Benjamin Buchloh, "The Whole Earth Show: An Interview with Jean-Hubert Martin by Benjamin Buchloh," *Art in America* 70, no. 5 (May 1989): 150–213.

47 A striking example of these effects is the review of the show by Nicolas Bourriaud, "Magiciens de la Terre," *Flash Art International*, no. 148 (October 1989): 119–21. For a detailed retrospective discussion, see Lucy Steeds, Pablo Lafuente, Jean-Marc Poinsot, and Rasheed Araeen, *Making Art Global (Part 2): Magiciens de la terre 1989* (London: Afterall Books, 2013).

48 For background information, see Bette Clark and Fred R. Myers, *Report on First Contact Group of Pintupi at Kiwirrkura*, to Joint Working Party of Central Land Council and Department of Aboriginal Affairs, 1984 (Alice Springs, NT: Joint Working Party of CLC/ DAA, 1985); and Fred R. Myers, "Locating Ethnographic Practice: Romance, Reality and Politics in the Outback," *American Ethnologist* 15 (1988): 608–24. On the Salon 94 exhibition, see Henry Skerritt's notes at "Maparntjarra," Salon 94, September 9–October 25, 2015, http://www.salon94.com/exhibitions/detail/warlimpirrnga-tjapaltjarri.

49 See "Richard Long, Crescent to Cross," Installations, Sperone Westwater, September 11– October 24, 2015, http://www.speronewestwater.com/exhibitions/richard-long_12/install ations.

50 "Richard Long, Crescent to Cross."

51 "Art: Warlimpirrnga Tjapaltjarri," *New Yorker*, October 5, 2015, 18, most likely written by Peter Schjeldahl, http://www.newyorker.com/goings-on-about-town/art/warlimpirrnga -tjapaltjarri.

52 Roberta Smith, "Art in Review," *New York Times*, October 16, 2015, C24.

53 Cited in Michael Gordon, "Classroom Revolution," *Age*, August 29, 2015, Forum 34.

54 See Maura Reilly, "Vernon Ah Kee Tall Man," *ArtAsiaPacific*, no. 73 (May–June 2011): 136, http://www.milanigallery.com.au/sites/default/files/pdf/Tall_Man_Review.pdf.

55 Pura-lia Meenamatta (Jim Everett) and Jonathan Kimberley, *Meenamatta lena narla puellakanny—Meenamatta Water Country Discussion* (Hobart, TAS: Bett Gallery, 2006), 20, 26.

7. PLACEMAKING, DISPLACEMENT

Parts of chapter 7 are drawn from several lectures and essays, including "Currents of World-Making in Contemporary Art," *World Art* 1, no. 2 (2011): 171–88; "World-Making in Contemporary Art," in "The World and World-Making in Art," ed. Caroline Turner, Michelle Antoinette, and Zara Stanhope, special issue, *Humanities Research Journal* 19, no. 2 (July 2013): 11–25; and my catalog essay for the exhibition *The Sense of Place*, shown at the Wellin Museum, Hamilton College, Clinton, New York, September 28–December 22, 2013, curated by Tracy L. Adler.

1 Martin Heidegger, "Building, Dwelling, Thinking," in *Basic Writings* (San Francisco: Harper and Row, 1977), 336. Useful introductions to place as a subject in contemporary art include Lucy R. Lippard, *The Lure of the Local: Senses of Place in a Multicentered Society* (New York: New Press, 1997); and Tacita Dean and Jeremy Millar, eds., *Place: Art Works* (London: Thames and Hudson, 2005). More generally, see Doreen Massey, *Space, Place, and Gender* (Minneapolis: University of Minnesota Press, 1994); and Edward S. Casey, *The Fate of Place: A Philosophical History* (Berkeley: University of California Press, 1997).

2 W. J. T. Mitchell, *Iconology: Image, Text, Ideology* (Chicago: University of Chicago Press, 1987), 5–6, and *Picture Theory: Essays on Verbal and Visual Representation* (Chicago: University of Chicago Press, 1995), 49.

3 See, for example, Manuel Lima, *Visual Complexity: Mapping Patterns of Information* (New York: Princeton Architectural Press, 2011).

4 Among such maps, see the anonymous one of 1645 in the British Library, "Chinese World Map, 1645," *Learning English Timeline*, British Library, August 30, 2017, http://www.bl.uk /learning/timeline/item103045.html. In 1602 and 1673 respectively, Jesuit priests Mateo Ricci and Ferdinand Verbiest made detailed world maps for the Chinese court that emphasized China. See Natasha Reichle, M. Antoni J. Üçerler, Theodore N. Foss, and Mark Stephen Mir, *China at the Center* (San Francisco: Asian Art Museum, 2016). Maps showing the Ming Empire at their center were common in the early nineteenth century, such as that titled *Cheonhado* (Map of all under heaven), in the Library of Congress, with an estimated date of 1800, accessed August 30, 2017, https://www.loc.gov/item/93684246/. A recently published map, purporting to be a 1763 copy by Mo Yi Tong of a 1418 original that shows knowledge of the American continents, is contested; see "China Beat Columbus to It, Perhaps," *Economist*, January 12, 2006, http://www.economist.com/node/5381851. As we shall see in later discussion of the work of artist Qiu Zhijie, maps are made for various purposes, of which maritime navigation is but one.

5 Samuel P. Huntington, *The Clash of Civilizations and the Remaking of the World Order* (New York: Simon and Schuster, 1996).

6 Martin W. Lewis and Kären E. Wigen, *The Myth of Continents: A Critique of Metageography* (Berkeley: University of California Press, 1997), 187.

7 Ursula K. Heise, *Sense of Place, Sense of Planet: The Environmental Imagination of the Global* (New York: Oxford University Press, 2008), chap. 1.

8 United Nations (UN), *Report of the World Commission on Environment and Development: Our Common Future* (New York: UN, 1987), 1, http://www.un-documents.net/our -common-future.pdf.

9 Heise, *Sense of Place, Sense of Planet*, 63.

10 See, for example, Carlo Rovelli, *Seven Brief Lessons on Physics* (Harmondsworth, UK: Penguin, 2016).

11 See Worldprocessor, accessed June 23, 2018, https://world-processor.com, for four hundred images of the globe as subject to various changes, such as, most recently, acid rain and ocean acidification; agricultural land use; walls, fences, and barriers; and so forth.

12 Donald Goddard, "Newton Harrison, Helen Mayer Harrison: Peninsula Europe," *New York Art World*, 2015, http://www.newyorkartworld.com/reviews/harrison.html.

13　Mark Zuckerberg, "Building Global Community," Facebook, February 17, 2017, https://www.facebook.com/notes/mark-zuckerberg/building-global-community/10154544292806634/. There is a parallel with Hans Rosling's spectacular demonstrations of how mass data can be assembled to support the sense that capitalism has brought about huge increases in world well-being, and that human progress toward greater material well-being is a process as fundamental as evolution or entropy. See "Hans Rosling," TED speaker, TED, accessed March 30, 2007, https://www.ted.com/speakers/hans_rosling.

14　See John Klima, Earth, 2001, accessed November 20, 2002, http://www.cityarts.com/earth/. Klima has since returned to his main activity, punk rock.

15　Seth Price, *Dispersion* (New York: self-published, 2002–), http://sethpriceimages.com/post/42277603863/dispersion-2002-seth-price-download-pdf.

16　Peter Osborne, *Anywhere or Not at All: Philosophy of Contemporary Art* (London: Verso, 2013).

17　See *Art Post-Internet*, Ullens Center for Contemporary Art, March 1–May 11, 2014, http://ucca.org.cn/en/exhibition/art-post-internet/.

18　Quoted in Carolyn Christov-Bakargiev, *William Kentridge* (Brussels: Sociéte des Expositions du Palais des Beaux-Art, 1998), 136.

19　An earlier version of this image appears in the 2007 series of intaglio prints in the collection of the Middlebury College Museum of Art, *L'Inesorabile Avanzata (The Inexorable Advance)*, as *#1: The World*, the first in the series. A variant, *World on Its Hind Legs* (2009), was commissioned by an Italian newspaper seeking to commemorate the Italian invasion of Ethiopia in 1934. It shows the image drawn in ink across an issue of the *Illustrated London News* of 1870. In 2009 Kentridge collaborated with the sculptor Gerhard Marx to create a metal version for the Apartheid Museum, Johannesburg, where it was shown in 2010. In another variant, the figure appears wearing a gas mask. I discuss the artist's touring exhibition *William Kentridge: Five Themes* in "William Kentridge's Activist Uncertainty: Before and After Apartheid," *NKA: Journal of Contemporary African Art*, no. 28 (Spring 2011): 47–55.

20　See Chris Ware, *Building Stories* (New York: Random House, 2012).

21　"Mike Kelley's *Mobile Homestead*, Museum of Contemporary Art Detroit, December 2, 2015, http://mocadetroit.org/wp-content/uploads/2018/04/2015_12_2_MK_MH_BOOKLET.pdf/.

22　Frederick Kiesler, *Inside the Endless House* (New York: Simon and Schuster, 1964), chap. 8. See also Dieter Bogner and Peter Noeve, eds., *Frederick J. Kiesler: Endless Space* (Ostfildern, Germany: Hatje Cantz, 2001).

23　For more on the idea of "iconomy," see Terry Smith, *The Architecture of Aftermath* (Chicago: University of Chicago Press, 2006).

24　UNESCO, *Convention Concerning the Protection of the World Cultural and Natural Heritage* (New York: UN, 1972), preliminary comments, p. 1, http://whc.unesco.org/en/conventiontext/.

25　UNESCO Intergovernmental Committee for the Protection of the World Cultural and Natural Heritage, *Operational Guidelines for the Implementation of the World Heritage Convention* (Paris: World Heritage Committee, 1980). See UNESCO, "The Criteria for Selection," World Heritage Convention, June 30, 2013, http://whc.unesco.org/en/criteria/.

26 In 2008 UNESCO proclaimed a Convention on the Preservation of Intangible Cultural Heritage, including "oral traditions, performing arts, social practices, rituals, festive events, knowledge, and practices concerning nature and the universe and the knowledge and skills to produce traditional crafts." See UNESCO, "What Is Intangible Cultural Heritage?," Intangible Cultural Heritage, UNESCO, accessed June 30, 2013, http://www.unesco.org /culture/ich/?pg=00003.

27 See Alexis Bhagat and Lize Mogel, eds., *An Atlas of Radical Cartography* (Los Angeles: Journal of Aesthetics and Protest Press, 2010).

28 IOM, "Migrants in Times of Crisis: An Emerging Protection Challenge," IOM, October 9, 2012, https://www.iom.int/idmnewyork (click on "background paper"). The IOM's *World Migration Report 2015* concentrates on *Migrants and Cities: New Perspectives to Manage Mobility* (Geneva: IOM, 2015), http://publications.iom.int/system/files/wmr2015_en.pdf.

29 UN, Department of Economic and Social Affairs, Population Division, *International Migration Report 2013* (New York: UN, 2013), http://www.un.org/en/development/desa /population/publications/migration/migration-report-2013.shtml.

30 For a skeptical review of UN and refugee agency reporting, see Guido Mingels, "Global Migration? Actually, the World Is Staying Home," *Spiegel Online*, May 17, 2016, http://www.spiegel .de/international/world/why-global-migration-statistics-do-not-add-up-a-1090736.html.

31 UNHCR, "Figures at a Glance," *Global Trends Report 2017*, accessed July 3, 2018, http:// www.unhcr.org/en-au/figures-at-a-glance.html.

32 See, for example, Sabine Breitwieser, ed., *Allan Sekula: Performance under Working Conditions* (Vienna: Generali Foundation, 2003); and Hilde van Gelder, ed., *Allan Sekula: Ship of Fools/The Docker's Museum* (Leuven, Belgium: Leuven University Press, 2016); on Jaar, see AlfredoJaar.net, accessed June 23, 2018, http://www.alfredojaar.net/index1.html.

33 See Veronica Tello, *Counter-Memorial Aesthetics: Refugee Histories and the Politics of Contemporary Art* (London: Bloomsbury, 2016). I discuss two key works by Charles Green and Lyndell Brown at some length in *The Contemporary Composition* (Berlin: Sternberg, 2016), 38–42.

34 T. J. Demos, *The Migrant Image: The Art and Politics of Documentary during Global Crisis* (Durham, NC: Duke University Press, 2013). See also Terry Smith, "Climate Change: Art and Ecology," in *Contemporary Art: World Currents* (Upper Saddle River, NJ: Prentice Hall, 2011), chap. 11; and Jill Bennett, "Living in the Anthropocene," in *dOCUMENTA (13), Catalog 1/3: The Book of Books*, ed. Carolyn Christov-Bakargiev (Ostfildern, Germany: Hatje Cantz, 2012), 345–47.

35 See Rachel Haidu, "The Imaginary Space of the Wishful Other: Thomas Hirschhorn's Cardboard Utopias," *vector [e-zine]* x, no. 4 (January 2006), http://virose.pt/vector/x_04 /haidu.html#.

36 Grant H. Kester, *Conversation Pieces: Community and Communication in Modern Art* (Berkeley: University of California Press, 2004); Nato Thompson, ed., *Living as Form: Socially Engaged Art from 1991–2011* (Cambridge, MA: MIT Press, 2012); and Claire Bishop, *Artificial Hells: Participatory Art and the Politics of Spectatorship* (London: Verso, 2012).

37 UNHCR, *Displacement: The 21st Century Challenge*, Global Trends Report 2012 (Geneva: UNHCR, 2013), http://unhcr.org/globaltrendsjune2013.

38 Phaptawan Suwannakudt, "Artist Statement," *Locution-(re)-Locations* (Bangkok: 100 Ton-son Gallery, 2011), n.p.

39 Suwannakudt, "Artist Statement."

40 Suwannakudt, "Artist Statement."

41 Simon Njami, "Chaos and Metamorphosis," in *Africa Remix: Contemporary Art of a Continent* (London: Hayward Gallery, 2005), 18.

42 Phaptawan Suwannakudt, statement in *All Our Relations: 18th Biennale of Sydney 2012*, ed. Catherine de Zegher and Gerald McMaster (Sydney: Biennale of Sydney, 2012), 298.

43 See "Site Displacement/Déplacement de Site," Eric Baudelaire website, accessed August 30, 2017, http://baudelaire.net/sitedispl/works/. For illuminating accounts of Baude-laire's earlier works, notably *Sugar Water* (2007) and *The Dreadful Details* (2006), see Pierre Zaoui, "On the Communication of Events," June 2007, and "The Fresco of Icons: On the Dreadful Details by Eric Baudelaire," Autumn 2006, both on the Eric Baudelaire website, http://baudelaire.net/circum/texts/. On Mann, see the Anay Mann website, last updated 2012, http://anaymann.com.

44 Eric Baudelaire website, accessed July 2, 2017, http://baudelaire.net. *The Secessions Sessions* installation at Doha won the 2015 Sharja Biennial Prize. See also Eric Baudelaire, *Letters to Max* (Paris: Poulet-Maassis, 2015).

45 See NSK State Pavilion website, last updated 2017, https://nsk-state-pavilion.net.

8. ARTS OF THE MULTIVERSE

1 See, for example, P. Nilsson, *Primitive Time-Reckoning* (Lund: Gleerup, 1920); Norbert Elias, *An Essay on Time* (1984), vol. 9 of *The Collected Works of Norbert Elias*, ed. Steven Loyal and Stephen Mennell, rev. ed. (Dublin: University College Dublin Press, 2007); Tony Swain, *A Place for Strangers: Towards a History of Australian Aboriginal Being* (Cambridge: Cambridge University Press, 1993); and, more generally, J. R. McNeill and William H. Mc-Neill, *The Human Web: A Bird's Eye View of Human History* (New York: Norton, 2003).

2 See, for example, David W. Penney, *North American Indian Art* (London: Thames and Hudson, 1995); Gerald McMaster and Lee-Ann Martin, eds., *Indigena: Contemporary Native Perspectives* (Vancouver, BC: Douglas and McIntyre, 1992); Allan J. Ryan, *The Trickster Shift: Humour and Irony in Contemporary Native Art* (Victoria: University of British Columbia Press, 1999); and Ruth Phillips and Janet Catherine Berlo, *Native American Art*, rev. ed. (Oxford: Oxford University Press, 2014).

3 Gulumbu Yunupingu, cited in Hetti Perkins, *Art + Soul* (Melbourne: Miegunyah Press, 2010), 262–65.

4 For Fredericks's various photographic and documentary film projects, see Murray Fredericks, Vimeo profile, accessed July 7, 2013, https://vimeo.com/user605877.

5 See James Balog, Extreme Ice Survey website, last updated 2014, http://extremeicesurvey.org.

6 See Robin Kelsey, "An Inversion," *Accumulation*, e-flux Architecture, May 3, 2017, http://www.e-flux.com/architecture/accumulation/96425/an-inversion/.

7 See *Earthworks: Mapping the Anthropocene*, Norton Museum of Art, West Palm Beach, Florida, September 2017 to January 2018. On the general topic, see Guy Abrahams, Bron-

wyn Johnson, and Kelly Gellatly, eds., *Art + Climate = Change* (Melbourne: Melbourne University Press, 2016).

8 Frank White, *The Overview Effect: Space Exploration and Human Evolution*, 2nd ed. (Reston, VA: American Institute of Aeronautics and Astronautics, 1998).

9 At "About," Daily Overview, accessed June 23, 2018, http://www.dailyoverview.com/about/. See also Benjamin Grant, *Overview: A New Perspective of Earth* (New York: Amphoto Books, 2016).

10 See John Grande, "A Conversation with Bill Vazan: Cosmological Shadows," *Sculpture* 21, no. 10 (December 2002), http://www.sculpture.org/documents/scmag02/dec02/Vazan/Vazan.shtml.

11 See Silke Opitz, ed., *William Lamson: On Earth* (Bielefeld, Germany: Kerber, 2011).

12 For images and information, see "How to Entangle the Universe in a Spider Web," Tomás Saraceno website, accessed December 6, 2017, http://tomassaraceno.com/projects/how-to-entangle-the-universe-in-a-spider-web-2/.

13 See the Aerocene website, accessed December 6, 2017, https://aerocene.org.

14 The best framing of these issues is Naomi Klein, *This Changes Everything: Capital versus Climate* (London: Penguin, 2014), and her *No Is Not Enough: Defeating the New Shock Politics* (London: Allen Lane, 2017). On these issues as they relate to the visual arts, see especially T. J. Demos, *Decolonizing Nature: Contemporary Art and the Politics of Ecology* (Berlin: Sternberg, 2016), and the important work of the Center for Creative Ecologies, University of California Santa Cruz, accessed July 3, 2018, https://creativeecologies.ucsc.edu. I thank Lily Brewer for drawing my attention to Anna-Sophie Springer and Etienne Turpin, eds., *The Word for World Is Still Forest* (Berlin: K. Verlag and the Haus der Kulturen der Welt, 2017).

15 Paul Virilio, 2009, cited in "Exit," Diller Scofidio + Renfro, accessed December 6, 2017, https://dsrny.com/project/exit.

16 See *Exit*, Palais de Tokyo, November 24, 2015–September 1, 2016, http://www.palaisdetokyo.com/en/event/exit. For an assessment of these and other works presented during the Paris Climate Change Conference, see Liz Else and Simon Ings, "Paris Climate Talks: Can a Global Cultural Festival Help?," *New Scientist*, December 11, 2015, https://www.newscientist.com/article/dn28661-paris-climate-talks-can-a-global-cultural-festival-help/.

17 Terry Smith, *The Contemporary Composition* (Berlin: Sternberg, 2016), 59–66.

18 See Fundación Jumex, *Cosmogonía doméstica: Damién Ortega,* exhibition at the Museo Jumex, Mexico City, February–May 2014, at https://www.fundacionjumex.org/en/exposiciones/39-cosmogonia-domestica-damian-ortega

19 See Andrew Herod and Melissa W. Wright, eds., *Geographies of Power: Placing Scale* (Oxford: Blackwell, 2002).

9. THE STATE OF ART HISTORY

Chapter 9 was first published in the *Art Bulletin* 92, no. 4 (December 2010): 366–83. This essay is dedicated to the memory of John Hope Franklin, 1915–2009. I thank Richard J. Powell for his editorial guidance and the anonymous readers for the *Art Bulletin*, who provided trenchant and improving comments. My colleagues in the Department of the History of Art and Architecture, University of Pittsburgh, helped me during a seminar on this topic. I also thank those with whom I regularly discuss these questions: their writings are cited throughout. I am grateful to Richard Leeman of the Institut National d'Histoire de l'Art, Paris, for inviting me to pursue these questions there in May 2007, and for publishing an earlier version of parts of my thinking on these matters as "Pour une histoire de l'art contemporain (prolégomènes tardifs et conjectreaux)," *20:21 Siècles*, nos. 5–6 (Autumn 2007): 191–215. Slight modifications have been made to avoid repetitions.

1 These questions were among those identified by the Society of Contemporary Art Historians founders—Suzanne Hudson, Alexander Dumbadze, and Joshua Shannon—and the panelists: Pamela M. Lee, Miwon Kwon, Richard Meyer, and Grant Kester. Resisting the buzz, the College Art Association itself still does not use "contemporary art" as a distinct art-historical category: its list of dissertations by subject follows the Library of Congress in preferring "twenty-first-century art."

2 "A Questionnaire on 'The Contemporary,'" *October*, no. 130 (Fall 2009): 3–124. See also the essays collected in "What Is Contemporary Art?," *e-flux journal*, no. 11 (December 2009), http://www.e-flux.com/journal/11/, and no. 12 (January 2010), http://www.e-flux.com/journal/12/; and "13 Theses on Contemporary Art," *Texte zur Kunst* 19, no. 74 (June 2009): 90–118.

3 Pamela M. Lee, review of *Art since 1900*, by Hal Foster, Rosalind Krauss, Yve-Alain Bois, and Benjamin H. D. Buchloh, *Art Bulletin* 88, no. 2 (2006): 380.

4 Among the approximately sixty essays in the *Art Bulletin* that, since the mid-1980s, comment on a subfield of art history—either as part of the series The State of Art History or A Range of Critical Perspectives, or as studies of a particular impact on the discipline (the "blockbuster" exhibition, the independent scholar)—none discusses contemporary art as a distinct object of inquiry. In Donald Kuspit's "Conflicting Logics: Twentieth-Century Studies at the Crossroads," *Art Bulletin* 68, no. 3 (1986): 536–42, he was concerned above all with the influence of semiotics and poststructuralism on art-historical methodology. This concern is typical: contemporary phenomena are understood, mostly, to affect art history from outside itself, and to disturb its "natural" disposition to retrospection. Contemporary art breaks in occasionally, usually as an example mentioned in passing. An instructive exception is Joseph Kosuth's contribution to the debate in "Writing (and) the History of Art," *Art Bulletin* 78, no. 3 (1996): 398–416. The most prescient prior treatment in this journal is Katy Siegel's review of *Art since 1940: Strategies of Being*, by Jonathan Fineberg; *Abstraction in the Twentieth Century: Total Risk, Freedom, Discipline*, by Mark Rosenthal; and *Theories and Documents of Contemporary Art: A Sourcebook of Artists' Writings*, by Kristine Stiles and Peter Selz, *Art Bulletin* 79, no. 1 (March 1997): 164–69. Siegel's opening paragraph includes this remark: "A discipline without a period, contemporary art history could be defined as the attempt to fill the gap between George Heard Hamilton and *Artforum*." Hamilton is the author of *Painting and Sculpture in Europe, 1880–1940* (Baltimore: Penguin, 1972).

5 An earlier version of these ideas appears in Terry Smith, "Pour une histoire de l'art contemporain (prolégomènes tardifs et conjecturaux)," *20:21 Siècles*, nos. 5–6 (Autumn 2007): 191–215.

6 See, for example, Ian Burn, "Thinking about Tim Clark and Linda Nochlin," *Fox* 1, no. 1 (1975): 136–37; Terry Smith, "Doing Art History," *Fox* 1, no. 2 (1975): 97–104; Michael Baldwin and Mel Ramsden's thinking had a direct influence on the courses at the Open University established under the direction of Charles Harrison, including a course published as *Modern Art and Modernism: Manet to Pollock* (Milton Keynes, UK: Open University Press, 1983). Artists continue to contribute compellingly to this debate. See, for example, Mark Lewis, "Is Modernity Our Antiquity?," in *Documenta 12 Magazine No. 1: Modernity?*, ed. Georg Schöllhammer, Roger M. Buergel, and Ruth Noack (Cologne: Taschen, 2007), reprinted in *Documenta Magazine Nos. 1–3, 2007 Reader*, ed. Georg Schöllhammer (Cologne: Taschen, 2007), 40–65.

7 Michael Fried, *Why Photography Matters as Art as Never Before* (New Haven, CT: Yale University Press, 2008), 66. Wall acknowledges this in an interview by Peter Osborne, "Art after Photography, after Conceptual Art," *Radical Philosophy*, no. 150 (July–August 2008): 47.

8 Fredric Jameson, *A Singular Modernity: Essay on the Ontology of the Present* (London: Verso, 2002). On Meckseper's work, see Marion Ackerman, ed., *Josephine Meckseper* (Ostfildern, Germany: Hatje Cantz for the Kunstmuseum, Stuttgart, 2007).

9 See the projects profiled in Jean-Christophe Royoux, Marina Warner, and Germaine Greer, *Tacita Dean* (London: Phaidon, 2006); and McElheny's discussion of his installation *An End to Modernity* (2005) in Scott Rothkopf, "1000 Words," *Artforum* 44, no. 3 (November 2005): 236–37.

10 I am drawing on the definitions in various versions of the *Oxford English Dictionary* as given in print form in the 1989 revision and subsequently found online at http://www.oed .com.

11 Hans Robert Jauss, "Literarische Tradition und gegenwärtiges Bewußtsein der Modernität," in *Literaturgeschichte als Provokation* (Frankfurt: Suhrkamp, 1970). An English translation, "Modernity and Literary Tradition," is in *Critical Inquiry* 31, no. 2 (Winter 2005): 329–64. An excellent review of the term "modern" with regard to the visual arts appears in chapter 1 of Peter Osborne, *The Politics of Time: Modernity and Avant-Garde* (London: Verso, 1995).

12 Lawrence Rainey, "In a Dark Mode," *London Review of Books*, January 20, 2000, 15. This issue erupted in a debate between Patricia Leighton and Rosalind E. Krauss; see Patricia Leighton, *Reordering the Universe: Picasso and Anarchism 1897–1914* (Princeton, NJ: Princeton University Press, 1989), and Rosalind E. Krauss, *The Picasso Papers* (London: Thames and Hudson, 1998).

13 To arrive at these preliminary observations, I undertook two sample surveys, the first during 2001–2 using the resources of the Getty Research Institute, Los Angeles, the second during 2002–3 at the University of Pittsburgh. In both cases, I supplemented initial searches through WorldCat with searches through a range of worldwide specialist catalogs, guides, and bibliographies, followed by those made available by major US art research institutions, and then by searches through the catalogs of significant American and European libraries. I also searched the holdings of selected South American and Australian libraries and institutions. The search was for the occurrence of the terms "modern" and "contemporary" or their cognates in European languages in the titles of books and

articles, exhibition catalogs, pamphlets, or other publications; and in the naming of visual arts museums, galleries, exhibition spaces, or departments of museums and auction houses. I made two searches through multiple editions of dictionaries of art and glossaries of art terms, noting the incidence of definitions of the words "modern" and "contemporary" and their cognate terms and the content of the entries for modern and contemporary art institutions, movements, associations, and so on. While I do not claim that the survey is complete, the patterns and repetitions in the data suggest the general picture sketched here.

14 Linda Nochlin, *Realism* (Harmondsworth, UK: Penguin, 1971), 25–33.

15 See Nadezda Blazicková-Horová, ed., *19th-Century Art: Guide to the Collections of the National Gallery in Prague* (Prague: National Gallery, 2002), 7.

16 The most thorough study of the mutuality of the institutions dedicated to the display of contemporary art in its broadest sense—their competitiveness, emulation, and interdependence—is J. Pedro Lorente, *Cathedrals of Urban Modernity: The First Museums of Contemporary Art, 1800–1930* (Aldershot, UK: Ashgate, 1998). Bruce Altshuler, *Collecting the New: Museums and Contemporary Art* (Princeton, NJ: Princeton University Press, 2005), has a useful introduction.

17 John R. Lane and John Caldwell, introduction to *Carnegie International 1985* (Pittsburgh: Carnegie Museum of Art, 1985), 11. For a detailed study of the specifics of the early Carnegie Internationals, see Kenneth Neal, *A Wise Extravagance: The Founding of the Carnegie International Exhibitions, 1895–1901* (Pittsburgh: University of Pittsburgh Press, 1996). For another view of this history, and of the subsequent years of the Carnegie International, see Vicky A. Clark, *Carnegie Museum of Art* (Pittsburgh: Carnegie Museum of Art, 1996).

18 See Judith Bumpus, *The Contemporary Art Society, 1910–1985* (London: CAS, 1985); and Alan Bowness, Judith Collins, and Richard Cork, *British Contemporary Art, 1910–1990: Eighty Years of Collecting by the Contemporary Art Society* (London: Herbert Press, 1991).

19 Charter of the Contemporary Art Society, Melbourne, quoted in Bernard Smith with Terry Smith and Christopher Heathcote, *Australian Painting, 1788–2000* (Melbourne: Oxford University Press, 2001), 218.

20 For example, René Huyghe and Germain Bazin's *Histoire de l'art contemporaine: La peinture* (Paris: Éditions Alcan, 1935); and Christian Zervos, *Histoire de l'art contemporaine* (Paris: Cahiers d'Art, 1938).

21 Alfred H. Barr Jr., "An Effort to Secure 3,250,000 for the Museum of Modern Art," official statement, April 1931, Alfred H. Barr Jr. Papers, Museum of Modern Art Archives, the Museum of Modern Art, New York.

22 Angelica Zander Rudenstine, "The Institutionalization of the Modern—Some Historical Observations," in *Post-Modern or Contemporary?*, ed. Jürgen Habermas (Düsseldorf: ICOM, 1981), 48.

23 John Elderfield, *Modern Painting and Sculpture: 1880 to the Present* (New York: Museum of Modern Art, 2004), 12.

24 Institute of Contemporary Art, *Dissent: The Issue of Modern Art in Boston* (Boston: Institute of Contemporary Art, 1985). Its 1948 statement concludes, "In order to disassociate the policy and program of this institution from the widespread and injurious misunder-

standings which surround the term 'modern art,' the Corporation has today changed its name from the Institute of Modern Art to THE INSTITUTE OF CONTEMPORARY ART" (52–53). A reverse situation has recently emerged: the current media and market notoriety of contemporary art has led some of those who are building institutions to house it, seeking the broadest public for it, to return to "modern" as a safer name: thus, the Gallery of Modern Art, Brisbane, which opened in late 2006. See Daniel Thomas, "The Queensland Art Gallery and Its Gallery of Modern Art," *Art Monthly Australia*, no. 197 (March 2007): 23.

25 Wilhelm Pinder, *Das Problem der Generation in der Kunstgeschichte Europas* (Berlin: Frankfurter Verlags-Anstalt, 1926), quoted in and glossed by Arnold Hauser, *The Philosophy of Art History* (Cleveland: Meridian, 1963), 248. The political circumstances of Weimar Germany, and its challenge to Marxist historical materialism, led Ernst Bloch to take contemporaneity and noncontemporaneity as critical analytic concepts. See Bloch, *Heritage of Our Times* (Berkeley: University of California Press, 1991), esp. part 2. This is a direct precedent to my own usage.

26 See, for example, Lesley Jackson, *"Contemporary": Architecture and Interiors of the 1950s* (London: Phaidon, 1994).

27 The best summary of this important art-historical task is the introduction by Kobena Mercer to his book *Cosmopolitan Modernisms* (Cambridge, MA: MIT Press, 2005). Regarding the contemporary in Indian art, see Geeta Kapur, *When Was Modernism: Essays on Contemporary Cultural Practice in India* (New Delhi: Tulika Books, 2000). An important precedent to such studies is the pathbreaking work, since the 1950s, of Australian art historian Bernard Smith. Among his books, most directly relevant to this discussion is *Modernism's History* (Sydney: University of New South Wales Press, 1998).

28 Michael Fried, "Art and Objecthood," *Artforum* (June 1967), reprinted in *Art and Objecthood* (Chicago: University of Chicago Press, 1988), 166.

29 Leo Steinberg, "Contemporary Art and the Plight of Its Public" (lecture, Museum of Modern Art, New York, 1960), published in *Harper's Magazine*, March 1962, and reprinted in Steinberg, *Other Criteria: Confrontations with Twentieth Century Art* (Oxford: Oxford University Press, 1972), 5.

30 Pierre Bourdieu famously argued that this acculturated acceptance of what is essentially an empty experience was, in fact, a full one, which constituted, in bourgeois societies, the "love of art" as such. See Bourdieu and Alain Darbel, *The Love of Art: European Art Museums and Their Public* (London: Polity, 1990).

31 See, for example, Mário Pedrosa, "Environmental Art, Postmodern Art: Hélio Oiticica," *Correio de Manhã*, June 26, 1966, translated and reprinted in Donna de Salvo, *Open Systems: Rethinking Art c. 1970* (London: Tate Publishing, 2005), 82–83.

32 Andrea Giunta, *Avant-Garde, Internationalism, and Politics: Argentine Art in the 1960s* (Durham, NC: Duke University Press, 2007), 9.

33 See Terry Smith, "The Provincialism Problem," *Artforum* 13, no. 1 (September 1974): 54–59.

34 Reiko Tomii, "Historicizing 'Contemporary Art': Some Discursive Practices in Gendai Bijutsu in Japan," *Positions* 12, no. 3 (2004): 611–41. See also Ming Tiampo, "'Create What Has Never Been Done Before!': Historicising Gutai Discourses of Originality," *Third Text* 21, no. 6 (November 2007): 689–706.

35 Olu Oguibe and Okwui Enwezor, *Reading the Contemporary: African Art from Theory to the Market Place* (Cambridge, MA: MIT Press, 1999); Sidney Littlefield Kasfir, *Contemporary African Art* (London: Thames and Hudson, 1999); Simon Njami, "Chaos and Metamorphosis," in *Africa Remix: Contemporary Art of a Continent* (London: Hayward Gallery, 2005), 13–21; and Okwui Enwezor and Chika Okeke-Agulu, *Contemporary African Art since 1980* (Bologna: Damiani, 2009).

36 See, for example, Marina Gržinić, *Situated Contemporary Art Practices: Art, Theory and Activism from (the East of) Europe* (Frankfurt: Revolver, 2004); Group Irwin, *East Art Map: Contemporary Art and Eastern Europe* (Cambridge, MA: MIT Press, 2006); and Boris Groys, *Art and Power* (Cambridge, MA: MIT Press, 2008).

37 See, for example, Li Xianting, "Major Trends in the Development of Contemporary Chinese Art," in *China's New Art, Post-1989*, ed. Chang Tsong-zung (Hong Kong: Hanart TZ Gallery, 1993), x–xxii; John Clark, *Modern Asian Art* (Honolulu: University of Hawai'i Press, 1998), esp. his concluding chapter, "Contemporary Art"; Wu Hung, *Chinese Art at the Crossroads: Between Past and Future, between East and West* (Hong Kong: New Art Media, 2001); chapters by Gao Minglu, Wu Hung, and Jonathan Hay in *Antinomies of Art and Culture: Modernity, Postmodernity, and Contemporaneity*, ed. Terry Smith, Okwui Enwezor, and Nancy Condee (Durham, NC: Duke University Press, 2008); and Qigu Jiang and James Elkins, eds., *First China Contemporary Art Forum—2009 Beijing International Conference on Art Theory and Criticism* (Beijing: China Contemporary Art Forum, 2010).

38 Fredric Jameson, "Postmodernism: Or, the Cultural Logic of Late Capitalism," *New Left Review*, no. 146 (July–August 1984): 59–92, reprinted in his *Postmodernism: Or, the Cultural Logic of Late Capitalism* (Durham, NC: Duke University Press, 1991).

39 Bernice Murphy, *Museum of Contemporary Art: Vision and Context* (Sydney: Museum of Contemporary Art, 1993), 136.

40 Dan Cameron and Anna Palmquist, *Vad är samtida konst? What Is Contemporary Art?* (Mallmö, Sweden: Rooseum, 1989), 7.

41 See Hans Belting, *The End of the History of Art?* (Chicago: University of Chicago Press, 1987), and his *Art History after Modernism* (Chicago: University of Chicago Press, 2003).

42 Arthur C. Danto, *After the End of Art: Contemporary Art and the Pale of History* (Princeton, NJ: Princeton University Press, 1997), 10.

43 Amelia Jones, ed., *A Companion to Contemporary Art since 1945* (Malden, MA: Blackwell, 2006), 15.

44 For example, Edward Lucie-Smith, *The Thames and Hudson Dictionary of Art Terms* (London: Thames and Hudson, 1984), 122; and Erika Langmuir and Norbert Lynton, *The Yale Dictionary of Art and Artists* (New Haven, CT: Yale University Press, 2000), 464–65. My own entry in the *Dictionary of Art* attempted to avoid this dilemma, both in itself and by my insistence on pairing it with an entry on modernity: see Terry Smith, "Modernism" and "Modernity," in *Dictionary of Art*, ed. Jane Turner (London: Macmillan, 1996), 777–78.

45 Reginald G. Haggar, *A Dictionary of Art Terms* (New York: Hawthorne Books, 1962), 92; and N. E. Lathi, *The Language of Art from A to Z: Writ in Plain English* (Terrebonne, OR: York Books, 1997), 39.

46 "Contemporary Art," *Wikipedia*, accessed March 2009, https://en.wikipedia.org/wiki /Contemporary_art.

47 Hugh Honour and John Fleming, *A World History of Art*, 3rd ed. (London: Laurence King, 1991), 695. The authors dropped this heading from their next edition in favor of "Towards the Third Millennium." Honour and Fleming, *A World History of Art*, 4th ed. (London: Laurence King, 1995), 803. A similarly epochal use of the term appeared in the 1991 *Gardner's Art through the Ages*, ed. Helen Gardner, Horst de la Croix, Richard G. Tansey, and Diane Kirkpatrick, 9th ed. (Fort Worth: Harcourt, Brace, Jovanovich, 1991), but had evaporated by 2001. Helen Gardner, Fred S. Kleiner, Christin J. Mamiya, and Richard G. Tansey, eds., *Gardner's Art through the Ages*, 10th ed. (Fort Worth: Harcourt, Brace, Jovanovich, 2001).

48 Marilyn Stokstad, *Art History*, vol. 2, rev. ed. (New York: Abrams, 1999), 1165.

49 Michael Archer, *Art since 1960*, 2nd ed. (London: Thames and Hudson, 2002); and David Hopkins, *After Modern Art: 1945–2000* (Oxford: Oxford University Press, 2000).

50 Burkhard Reimschneider and Uta Grosenick, *Art Now: 137 Artists at the Rise of the New Millennium* (Cologne: Taschen, 2001); and Susan Sollins, *Art 21: Art in the Twenty-First Century* (New York: Abrams, 2001).

51 Mathew Collings, *This Is Modern Art* (New York: Watson-Guptill, 2000).

52 Compilations: Uta Grosenick and Burkhard Reimschneider, eds., *Art at the Turn of the Millennium* (Cologne: Taschen, 1999); Reimschneider and Grosenick, *Art Now*; and Uta Grosenick, ed., *Art Now*, vol. 2, *The New Directory to 136 International Contemporary Artists* (Cologne: Taschen, 2005). Anthology: Zoya Kocur and Simon Leung, eds., *Theory in Contemporary Art since 1985* (Malden, MA: Blackwell, 2005). Thematics: Edward Lucie-Smith, *Art Tomorrow* (Paris: Pierre Terrail, 2002); Linda Weintraub, *In the Making* (New York: Distributed Art Publishers, 2003); Gill Perry and Paul Wood, eds., *Themes in Contemporary Art* (New Haven, CT: Yale University Press, 2004); and Thames and Hudson's excellent series Art Works, including Tacita Dean and Jeremy Millar, *Place* (London: Thames and Hudson, 2005). The list of themes in the text comes from the chapter headings in Jean Robertson and Craig McDaniel, *Themes of Contemporary Art: Visual Art after 1980* (Oxford: Oxford University Press, 2005).

53 Eleanor Heartney, *Art and Today* (London: Thames and Hudson, 2008).

54 Brandon Taylor, *The Art of Today* (London: Weidenfeld and Nicolson, 1995), *Contemporary Art* (London: Penguin, 2004), and *Contemporary Art: Art since 1970* (Upper Saddle River, NJ: Prentice-Hall, 2005).

55 Taylor, *Contemporary Art*, 9. See Julian Stallabrass, *High Art Lite* (London: Verso, 1999), *Art Incorporated: The Story of Contemporary Art* (Oxford: Oxford University Press, 2004), and *Contemporary Art: A Very Short Introduction* (Oxford: Oxford University Press, 2006).

56 Hal Foster, Rosalind E. Krauss, Yve-Alain Bois, Benjamin H. D. Buchloh, and David Joselit, *Art since 1900: Modernism, Antimodernism, Postmodernism* (London: Thames and Hudson, 2005). Foster's interest in psychoanalysis does not lead to a distinct history of modernism, although it certainly issues in distinctive accounts of the works that he, the author of most entries, treats. Among several astute reviews of the book, see Charles Harrison, "After the

Fall," *Art Journal* 65, no. 1 (Spring 2006): 116–19; and various authors in "Interventions Reviews," *Art Bulletin* 88, no. 2 (2006): 373–99.

57 Foster et al., *Art since 1900*, 679.

58 I evoke here the argument of T. J. Clark, *Farewell to an Idea: Episodes from a History of Modernism* (New Haven, CT: Yale University Press, 1999). A less melancholy stance is that historical modernism may have been sidelined by recent developments in art and the world at large, but its core qualities remain capable of serving as the foundation of convincing art, were the right artists to grasp them afresh. As we have seen, this is precisely what Michael Fried argues is occurring in the work of certain contemporary photographers, notably Jeff Wall.

59 Peter Osborne, "Art beyond Aesthetics: Philosophical Criticism, Art History and Contemporary Art," *Art History* 27, no. 4 (September 2004): 666–67.

60 One pertinent paradox is that since the 1970s, criticism of contemporaneous art has been most effectively practiced by writers based in the academies, in contrast to the "out there," implicated situation of the most prominent writers of the previous generation. A further paradox is that these academics have held as models (positive and negative) not only their immediate predecessors but also the engaged reviewers of art since Denis Diderot. See, for example, Terry Smith, "Clement Greenberg at 100: Looking Back to Modern Art," Sackler Museum, Harvard University, April 3–4, 2009, *CAA Reviews*, July 14, 2009, http://www.caareviews.org/reviews/1298.

61 Notably, the exhibitions curated by Okwui Enwezor, including *Trade Routes: History and Geography* (Johannesburg: Greater Johannesburg Metropolitan Council, 1997); and with Chinua Achebe, *The Short Century: Independence and Liberation Movement in Africa, 1945–1994* (Munich: Prestel, 2001); and *Documenta 11, Platform 5: Exhibition* (Ostfildern-Ruit, Germany: Hatje Cantz, 2002).

62 Okwui Enwezor, "The Postcolonial Constellation," in Smith, Enwezor, and Condee, *Antinomies of Art and Culture*, 208–9, 232.

63 Kirk Varnedoe, *Modern Contemporary: Art at MoMA since 1980* (New York: Museum of Modern Art, 2000), 12.

64 Nicolas Bourriaud, *Relational Aesthetics* (Dijon: Les Presses du Réel, 2002), and *Post-Production* (New York: Lucas and Sternberg, 2002). See Claire Bishop, "Antagonism and Relational Aesthetics," *October*, no. 110 (Fall 2004): 51–79.

65 Nicolas Bourriaud, "Altermodern," in *Altermodern: Tate Triennial* (London: Tate Publishing, 2009), 12–13.

66 See Terry Smith, "Contemporary Art and Contemporaneity," *Critical Inquiry* 32, no. 4 (Summer 2006): 681–707, and "Creating Dangerously: Then and Now," in *The Unhomely: Phantom Scenes in Global Society*, ed. Okwui Enwezor (Seville: Bienal Internacional de Arte Contemporáneo de Sevilla, 2006), 114–29.

67 Okwui Enwezor, "Modernity and Postcolonial Ambivalence," in Bourriaud, *Altermodern: Tate Triennial*, 27–40.

68 As argued for by James Meyer, "The Return of the Sixties in Contemporary Art and Criticism," in Smith, Enwezor, and Condee, *Antinomies of Art and Culture*, 323–32.

69 Among exhibitions that have contributed to this direction, see, for example, Ann Gold-
    stein, ed., *Reconsidering the Object of Art: 1965–1975* (Los Angeles: Museum of Con-
    temporary Art, 1995); Paul Schimmel and Russell Ferguson, eds., *Out of Actions: Between
    Performance Art and the Object, 1949–79* (Los Angeles: Museum of Contemporary Art,
    1998); Luiz Camnitzer, Jane Farver, and Rachel Weiss, *Global Conceptualism: Points of
    Origin, 1950s–1980s* (New York: Queens Museum of Art, 1999); Richard Flood and Fran-
    cis Morris, eds., *Zero to Infinity: Arte Povera, 1962–1972* (London: Tate Gallery, 2002);
    Ann Goldstein, ed., *A Minimal Future? Art as Object 1958–1968* (Los Angeles: Museum
    of Contemporary Art, 2004); Helen Molesworth, *Work Ethic* (Baltimore: Baltimore Mu-
    seum of Art, 2003); Carlos Basualdo, ed., *Tropicália: A Revolution in Brazilian Culture,
    1967–1972* (Sao Pãulo: Cosac Naify, 2005); and Mari Carmen Ramírez and Hector Oléa,
    eds., *Inverted Utopias: Avant-Garde Art in Latin America* (New Haven, CT: Yale Univer-
    sity Press for the Museum of Fine Arts, Houston, 2004). Among new scholarship on the
    proto-history of contemporary art, see Pamela M. Lee, *Chronophobia: On Time in the Art
    of the 1960s* (Cambridge, MA: MIT Press, 2004); Martha Buskirk, *The Contingent Object of
    Contemporary Art* (Cambridge, MA: MIT Press, 2003); Anne Reynolds, *Robert Smithson:
    Learning from New Jersey and Elsewhere* (Cambridge, MA: MIT Press, 2003); Alex Al-
    berro, *Conceptual Art and the Politics of Publicity* (Cambridge, MA: MIT Press, 2003); the
    revisions being pursued by the scholars of the art of Asia, South America, Central Europe,
    and elsewhere noted above; and Cornelia Butler, *WACK! Art and the Feminist Revolution*
    (Cambridge, MA: MIT Press, 2007).

70 See, for example, the discussion moderated by Chika Okeke-Agulu, "The Twenty-First
    Century and the Mega Show: A Curator's Roundtable," *NKA: Journal of Contemporary
    African Art*, nos. 22–23 (Spring–Summer 2008): 152–88.

71 See Our Literal Speed, accessed August 29, 2007, http://www.ourliteralspeed.com. A re-
    cent compact disc, *OLSSR: Our Literal Speed Soundtrack Recordings* (San Francisco: Bitter
    Stag Records, 2009), includes tracks such as "Reading Rosalind Krauss" and messages on
    the packaging such as "stuff near art that is not art which is treated as if it were art is now
    the substance of most serious art."

72 Alex Alberro, "Periodising Contemporary Art," in *Crossing Cultures: Conflict, Migration
    and Convergence*, ed. Jaynie Anderson (Melbourne: Miegunyah, 2009), 935–39; also pub-
    lished in *October*, no. 130 (Fall 2009): 55–60.

73 W. J. T. Mitchell, *Cloning Terror: The War of Images, 9/11 to the Present* (Chicago: Univer-
    sity of Chicago Press, 2011).

74 Jameson, *A Singular Modernity*, 94–95.

75 This interpretation is argued more fully in the introduction to Smith, Enwezor, and
    Condee, *Antinomies of Art and Culture*. See also Marc Augé, *The Anthropology of Con-
    temporaneous Worlds* (Stanford, CA: Stanford University Press, 1999); Dipesh Chakrab-
    arty, *Provincializing Europe: Postcolonial Thought and Historical Difference* (Princeton, NJ:
    Princeton University Press, 2000); and Giorgio Agamben, *What Is an Apparatus? and
    Other Essays* (Stanford, CA: Stanford University Press, 2009).

76 See also Richard Meyer, *What Was Contemporary Art?* (Cambridge, MA: MIT Press, 2013).

77 This summary is drawn from Terry Smith, *What Is Contemporary Art?* (Chicago: University of Chicago Press, 2009). Similar but belated shifts from modern to contemporary architecture are explored in my *The Architecture of Aftermath* (Chicago: University of Chicago Press, 2006), and "Currents of Contemporaneity: Architecture in the Aftermath," *Architectural Theory Review* 11, no. 2 (2006): 34–52. The ideas advanced here are positioned in relation to recent debates on world art history in my "World Picturing in Contemporary Art: Iconogeographic Turning," *Journal of the Art Association of Australia and New Zealand* 6, no. 2 (2005), and 7, no. 1 (2006): 24–46. They were first sketched in my *What Is Contemporary Art? Contemporary Art, Contemporaneity and Art to Come*, Critical Issues Series 6 (Sydney: Artspace, 2001), chapter 1 of this volume.

78 See Anderson, *Crossing Cultures*; Rex Butler and Robert Leonard, eds., "21st Century Art History," special issue, *Australian and New Zealand Journal of Art* 9, nos. 1–2 (2008–9); and Hans Belting and Andrea Buddensieg, eds., *The Global Art World: Audiences, Markets, and Museums* (Ostfildern, Germany: Hatje Cantz, 2009).

10. THEORIZING THE CONTEMPORARY AND THE POSTCONTEMPORARY

1 Tim Griffin, "Out of Time," *Artforum* 50, no. 1 (September 2011): 288–89.

2 I discuss in the introduction the first major effort by a philosopher to identify the core elements of the art being made in a situation that understood itself to be *after* modern art, that is, Arthur Danto's argument that, in the 1980s, certain postmodern artistic practices, such as that of painter David Reed, instantiated a "posthistorical" artistic consciousness that was essentially different from that which prevailed for modern artists during modern times. Regrettably, Danto's imagining of the larger world picture converged with the claims, by Francis Fukuyama among others, that the end of the Cold War, and the apparent total triumph of Western market democracies, meant the "end of history." See Arthur C. Danto, *After the End of Art: Contemporary Art and the Pale of History* (Princeton, NJ: Princeton University Press, 1998); and Francis Fukuyama, *The End of History and the Last Man* (London: Penguin, 1992).

3 Giorgio Agamben, "On Contemporaneity," European Graduate School Video Lectures, January 4, 2007, video, 7:28, June 19, 2008, http://www.youtube.com/watch?v=GsS9VPS_gms&feature=related; Agamben, *Che cos'è il contemporaneo?* (Rome: Nottotempo, 2008), and "What Is the Contemporary?," in *What Is an Apparatus? And Other Essays* (Stanford, CA: Stanford University Press, 2009), 39–54.

4 The allusion here is to Michel Foucault's notion of *l'actuel*, a point made by Jon Rajchman in "The Contemporary: A New Idea?," in *Aesthetics and Contemporary Art*, ed. Armen Avanessian and Luke Skrebowski (Berlin: Sternberg, 2011), 126–44. Rajchman's essay is a useful speculation about interplays among contemporary art practice, history, and philosophy that parallels the concerns of these concluding chapters.

5 David Harvey, *The Condition of Postmodernity* (London: Wiley-Blackwell, 1991); Terry Smith, "The Contemporary Question," in *Antinomies of Art and Culture: Modernity, Postmodernity, Contemporaneity*, ed. Terry Smith, Okwui Enwezor, and Nancy Condee (Durham, NC: Duke University Press, 2008), 1–19.

6 Noah Porter, ed., *Webster's Revised Unabridged Dictionary* (Springfield, MA: Merriam, 1913).

7 Agamben, "What Is the Contemporary?," 40–41. Also see Friedrich Nietzsche, *Untimely Meditations* (1873–76; repr., Cambridge: Cambridge University Press, 1997).

8 Agamben, "What Is the Contemporary?," 44, 47.

9 Pivotal works by Agamben of core relevance to grasping the broader conditions of our contemporaneity include his "The State of Exception as a Paradigm of Government," in *State of Exception* (Chicago: University of Chicago Press, 2005), 1–31, and *Homo Sacer: Sovereign Power and Bare Life* (Stanford, CA: Stanford University Press, 1998).

10 Agamben, "What Is the Contemporary?," 50–51.

11 Agamben has made suggestions of importance to art-historical thinking and demonstrated an elegant felicity in the interpretation of visual images. His essay "Aby Warburg and the Nameless Science," in *Potentialities: Collected Essays in Philosophy* (Stanford, CA: Stanford University Press, 1999), 89–103, exemplifies the former; his book *Nymphs* (London: Seagull, 2013) is an engaging example of the latter.

12 Jean-Luc Nancy, "Art Today" (lecture, Accademia di Brera, Milan, 2006); "L'arte, oggi," in *Del contemporaneo*, ed. Federico Ferrari (Milan: Bruno Mondadori, 2007), 1–20, and in *Journal of Visual Culture* 9, no. 1 (April 2010): 91. The following paragraphs are drawn from my essay "'Our' Contemporaneity?," in *Contemporary Art: 1989 to the Present*, ed. Alexander Dumbadze and Suzanne Hudson (Chichester, UK: Wiley-Blackwell, 2013), 17–27.

13 Notably in Jean-Luc Nancy, *The Birth to Presence* (Stanford, CA: Stanford University Press, 1993).

14 Nancy, "Art Today," 92.

15 Nancy, "Art Today," 93, 96.

16 Martin Heidegger, "The Age of the World Picture," in *The Question concerning Technology and Other Essays* (New York: Garland, 1997), 115–54; and W. J. T. Mitchell, "World Pictures: Globalization and Visual Culture," in *Image Science: Iconology, Visual Culture, and Media Aesthetics* (Chicago: University of Chicago Press, 2016), chap. 8. I discuss Caroline A. Jones, *The Global Work of Art: World's Fairs, Biennials, and the Aesthetics of Experience* (Chicago: University of Chicago Press, 2016), in the next chapter.

17 Nancy, "Art Today," 94.

18 Nancy, "Art Today," 94.

19 Arthur C. Danto, "The Art World," *Journal of Philosophy* 61, no. 19 (1964): 571–84.

20 See, for example, Boris Groys, *Going Public* (Berlin: Sternberg, 2010), especially "Comrades of Time," 84–101.

21 Nancy, "Art Today," 94–95.

22 Nancy, "Art Today," 99, 98.

23 Nancy, "Art Today," 94.

24 Terry Smith, *The Contemporary Composition* (Berlin: Sternberg, 2016), is devoted entirely to this question.

25 Jacques Rancière, *The Politics of Aesthetics: The Distribution of the Sensible* (London: Continuum, 2004), 20. On regimes of truth, see Michel Foucault, "The Political Function of the Intellectual," *Radical Philosophy*, no. 17 (Summer 1977): 12–14.

26 Rancière, *Politics of Aesthetics*, 21–24, 91.

27 See Jacques Rancière, "Sentence, Image, History," in *The Future of the Image* (London: Verso, 2007), chap. 2.

28 Fulvia Carnevale and John Kelsey, "Art of the Possible: Fulvia Carnevale and John Kelsey in Conversation with Jacques Rancière," *Artforum* 45, no. 7 (March 2007): 257.

29 Carnevale and Kelsey, "Art of the Possible," 257–59.

30 Jacques Rancière, *The Ignorant Schoolmaster: Five Lessons in Intellectual Emancipation* (Stanford, CA: Stanford University Press, 1991).

31 Jacques Rancière, "The Emancipated Spectator" (2004), *Artforum* 45, no. 7 (March 2007): 270–81. Claire Bishop draws on key aspects of Rancière's work in her *Artificial Hells: Participatory Art and the Politics of Spectatorship* (London: Verso, 2012), notably in chap. 1, and at 266.

32 Carnevale and Kelsey, "Art of the Possible," 259.

33 Carnevale and Kelsey, "Art of the Possible," 264, 266, 269.

34 T. J. Demos, response to "Questionnaire: In What Ways Have Artists, Critics, and Cultural Institutions Responded to the U.S.-Led Invasion of Iraq?," *October*, no. 123 (Winter 2008): 35.

35 See, for example, Hal Foster, "Post-Critical," *Brooklyn Rail*, December 10, 2012, http://www.brooklynrail.org/2012/12/artseen/post-critical. See also the longer version, "Post-Critical," *October*, no. 139 (Winter 2012): 3–8.

36 Rancière, *Politics of Aesthetics*, 20.

37 My term. See Rancière, *Politics of Aesthetics*, 26–30.

38 Aleš Erjavec, "Art and Aesthetics: Three Recent Perspectives," *Society of Aesthetics Journal*, no. 4 (2012): 142–59. Erjavec puts Rancière's rather generalized ideas about the transformative potential of art to interesting use in his anthology *Aesthetic Revolutions and Twentieth-Century Avant-Garde Movements* (Durham, NC: Duke University Press, 2015). In his book *Public Art and the Fragility of Democracy: An Essay in Political Aesthetics* (New York: Columbia University Press, 2018), Fred Evans also compares and contrasts my thinking on these matters with that Rancière.

39 Jacques Rancière, *Aisthesis: Scenes from the Aesthetic Regime of Art* (London: Verso, 2013).

40 For commentary from a visual cultural studies perspective, see Jae Emerling, review of Jacques Rancière, *The Future of the Image*, in *Journal of Visual Culture* 7, no. 3 (December 2008): 376–81; and W. J. T. Mitchell, "Rancière's Route Not Taken," in *Image Science*, chap. 7. For an update on Rancière's perspectives on contemporaneity (within which little has changed), see his "In What Times Do We Live?," in *The State of Things*, ed. Marta Kuzma, Pablo Lafuente, and Jacques Rancière (London: Koenig Books, 2012), 11–37.

41 Néstor García Canclini, *Art beyond Itself: Anthropology for a Society without a Story Line* (Durham, NC: Duke University Press, 2014), xiii.

42 García Canclini, *Art beyond Itself*, xxi–xxii.

43 García Canclini, *Art beyond Itself*, xxiv.

44 Peter Osborne, *Anywhere or Not at All: Philosophy of Contemporary Art* (London: Verso, 2013). The following paragraphs draw on my essay "A Philosophy of Contemporary Art?: Some Comments on Osborne," in *Three Reflections on Contemporary Art History*, ed. Nicholas Croggon and Helen Hughes (Melbourne: Discipline and emaj, 2014), 75–88.

45 Leland del la Durantaye, review, *Artforum* 52, no. 2 (October 2013): 84. See also Leland del la Durantaye, *Giorgio Agamben: A Critical Introduction* (Stanford, CA: Stanford University Press, 2009).

46 Osborne, *Anywhere or Not at All*, 28.

47 See, for example—and for interest rather than illumination—Alain Badiou, "Third Sketch of a Manifesto of Affirmationist Art," in *Polemics* (London: Verso, 2006), 133–48.

48 Ian McLean, "The Necessity of the New: Between the Modern and the Contemporary," in Croggon and Hughes, *Three Reflections*, 15–52. This is a careful comparison of both Osborne's and my positions on these questions.

49 Osborne, *Anywhere or Not at All*, 23, 22.

50 Fredric Jameson, *A Singular Modernity: Essay on the Ontology of the Present* (London: Verso, 2002), 94.

51 Osborne, *Anywhere or Not at All*, 26.

52 Osborne, *Anywhere or Not at All*, 164.

53 Osborne elaborates this reading of biennials in his "Existential Urgency: Contemporaneity, Biennials, and Social Form," *Nordic Journal of Aesthetics*, nos. 49–50 (2015): 175–88. For a more expansive view of this exhibitionary form, see my "Biennials: Four Fundamentals, Many Variations," *Biennial Foundation Magazine*, December 7, 2016, http://www .biennialfoundation.org/2016/12/biennials-four-fundamentals-many-variations/. The most searching and comprehensive study of the subject to date is Charles Green and Anthony Gardner, *Biennials, Triennials, and Documentas: The Exhibitions That Created Contemporary Art* (London: Wiley, 2016).

54 Osborne, *Anywhere or Not at All*, 211.

55 Osborne, *Anywhere or Not at All*, 4.

56 Osborne, *Anywhere or Not at All*, 108–9.

57 For a more specific reading, see Terry Smith, *One and Five Ideas: On Conceptualism as Conceptual Art* (Durham, NC: Duke University Press, 2016), edited and introduced by Robert Bailey.

58 Peter Osborne, "The Postconceptual Condition: Or, the Cultural Logic of High Capitalism Today," *Radical Philosophy*, no. 184 (March–April 2014): 23, 25. This essay appears as the lead chapter in his *The Postconceptual Condition: Critical Essays* (London: Verso, 2018).

59 Osborne, "Postconceptual Condition," 25–26.

60 Jean-Philippe Antoine, "The Historicity of the Contemporary Is Now!," in Dumbadze and Hudson, *Contemporary Art*, 35. Antoine is citing Mike Kelley, "Artist/Critic?," in *Foul Perfection* (Cambridge, MA: MIT Press, 2003), 220–26.

61 Antoine, "Historicity of the Contemporary," 33.

62 Antoine, "Historicity of the Contemporary," 29.

63 Antoine, "Historicity of the Contemporary," 31. Alois Riegl, "The Modern Cult of Monuments: Its Character and Its Origins," *Oppositions*, no. 25 (Fall 1982): 21–51.

64 Antoine, "Historicity of the Contemporary," 32.

65 Antoine, "Historicity of the Contemporary," 34. For suggestive speculations along these lines, see Amelia Birikin, "Zombie History: Contemporary Art in the Jungles of Cosmic Time," in Croggon and Hughes, *Three Reflections*, 55–72.

66 Liam Gillick, *Industry and Intelligence: Contemporary Art since 1820* (New York: Columbia University Press, 2016), x.

67 Gillick, *Industry and Intelligence*, xii, xiii, 5, 8–9.

68 Gillick, *Industry and Intelligence*, xv, 5, 12. Also see Unitednationsplaza Archive, accessed September 2, 2017, http://www.unitednationsplaza.org.

69 Gillick, *Industry and Intelligence*, 7, 11, 17.

70 Gillick, *Industry and Intelligence*, 18–19.

71 Gillick, *Industry and Intelligence*, 19–20.

72 See the concluding chapters of Gillick, *Industry and Intelligence*, especially chapter 15, "Why Work?," which appeared as "The Good of Work," in *e-flux journal*, no. 16 (2010), https://www.e-flux.com/journal/16/61277/the-good-of-work/. See also his "Contemporary Art Does Not Account for That Which Is Taking Place," *e-flux journal*, no. 21 (2010), https://www.e-flux.com/journal/21/67664/contemporary-art-does-not-account-for-that-which-is-taking-place/, for an earlier version of some of the quotations cited above. Gillick finds aspects of his argument confirmed in Dave Beech, *Art and Value: Art's Economic Exceptionalism in Classical, Neoclassical and Marxist Economics* (Chicago: Haymarket Books, 2016). See Gillick's review in *Art Journal* 75, no. 4 (Winter 2016): 62–64.

73 *Duke University Press Catalog: Spring 1989* (Durham, NC: Duke University Press, 1989).

74 To the internal editor at Duke University Press, Reynolds Smith, the series title "was intended to suggest that no matter the subject of any particular series book, or the epoch that book considered, its presence in the series—if not its own argument—openly declared that it emerged in the present and reflected the present, commented on the present—that is, a present that was always-already some moments behind. The name was, for me at least, a rejoinder to the great question that resounded throughout the humanities in the 60s and beyond: Relevance??"—email communication, July 22, 2017.

75 Post Contemporary Interventions series page, Duke University Press, accessed August 13, 2018, https://www.dukeupress.edu/Catalog/ProductList.php?viewby=series&id=52. Dainotto is professor of Italian and Romance studies at Duke University as well as author of *Europe (in Theory)* (Durham, NC: Duke University Press, 2007).

76 See "Post-contemporary," *Wikipedia*, last edited March 29, 2018, https://en.wikipedia.org/wiki/Post-contemporary.

77 See the Post-Contemporary website, last updated September 19, 2015, http://thepost.org.

78 See Richard T. Scott, curator, "Post Contemporary Painting," Saatchi Art, accessed September 20, 2017, https://www.saatchiart.com/art-collection/Painting-Drawing-Photography/Post-Contemporary-Painting/6068/88063/view.

79 At Armen Avanessian and Suhail Malik, "The Time-Complex: Postcontemporary," Discussion, *Dis Magazine*, accessed September 2, 2017, http://dismagazine.com/discussion/81924/the-time-complex-postcontemporary/. The discussion is also available in their edited volume *Der Zeitcomplex: Postcontemporary* (Berlin: Merve Verlag, 2016).

80 They acknowledge Bernard Stiegler's use of this concept in his *Technics and Time*, especially vol. 2, *Disorientation* (Stanford, CA: Stanford University Press, 2008).

81 Benjamin Bratton, *The Stack: On Software and Sovereignty* (Cambridge, MA: MIT Press, 2015).

82 See Terry Smith, "Seeing Art Historically Today: Where We Are and Ways to Go," Power Lecture, Art Gallery of New South Wales, July 20, 2016, video, 1:07, Power Institute, July 26, 2016, https://www.youtube.com/watch?v=w3s1bzEsgHY.

11. WRITING HISTORIES OF CONTEMPORARY ART

1 "CFP: The Contemporary," ArtHist.net, November 9, 2016, http://arthist.net/archive/14158.

2 Hal Foster, "A Questionnaire on 'The Contemporary,'" *October*, no. 130 (Fall 2009): 3.

3 On Koons's early work, see Scott Rothkopf, ed., *Jeff Koons: A Retrospective* (New York: Whitney Museum of American Art, 2014). Sustained and searching assessments of these artists' work have yet to appear.

4 Yates McKee, "A Questionnaire on 'The Contemporary,'" *October*, no. 130 (Fall 2009): 64–73.

5 Okwui Enwezor, "A Questionnaire on 'The Contemporary,'" *October*, no. 130 (Fall 2009): 33–40.

6 Alexander Alberro, "A Questionnaire on 'The Contemporary,'" *October*, no. 130 (Fall 2009): 55–60. Alberro's essay appeared earlier, as "Periodising Contemporary Art," in *Crossing Cultures: Conflict, Migration and Convergence*, ed. Jaynie Anderson (Melbourne: Miegunyah Press, 2009), 935–39. He is working on a book that addresses this theme, which should add considerably to our understanding.

7 "What Is Contemporary Art?," *e-flux journal*, no. 11 (December 2009), http://www.e-flux .com/journal/issue/11, and no. 12 (January 2010), http://www.e-flux.com/journal/issue /12. In book form, Julieta Aranda, Brian Kuan Wood, and Anton Vidokle, eds., *What Is Contemporary Art?* (New York: Sternberg, 2010). On *e-flux* as the artwork of founder Anton Vidokle and others, see Anton Vidokle, *Produce, Distribute, Discuss, Repeat* (New York: Lukas and Sternberg, 2009). Meanwhile in Berlin, the same questions were being asked in "13 Theses on Contemporary Art," *Texte zur Kunst* 19, no. 74 (June 2009): 90–111. These collections were preceded by Jan-Erik Lundström and Johan Sjöström, eds., "Being Here: Mapping the Contemporary, Reader of the Bucharest Biennale 3," 2 vols., special issue, *Pavilion*, no. 12 (2008).

8 Cuauhtémoc Medina, "Contemp(t)ory: Eleven Theses," in Aranda, Wood, and Vidokle, *What Is Contemporary Art?*, 10–21.

9 Medina, "Contemp(t)ory," 19–21.

10 See Manifesta 9, accessed June 27, 2018, http://m9.manifesta.org/en/manifesta-9/. For information on the Arts Mediation program, see "Manifest 9 Art Mediation in Retrospect," Manifesta 9, accessed June 27, 2018, http://m9.manifesta.org/en/news/manifesta-9-art -mediation-in-retrospect/.

11 Boris Groys, "Comrades of Time," in Aranda, Wood, and Vidokle, *What Is Contemporary Art?*, 28.

12 Groys, "Comrades of Time," 39.

13 Raqs Media Collective, "Now and Elsewhere," in Aranda, Wood, and Vidokle, *What Is Contemporary Art?*, 47.

14 Arthur C. Danto, *After the End of Art: Contemporary Art and the Pale of History* (Princeton, NJ: Princeton University Press, 1997).

15 Peter R. Kalb, *Charting the Contemporary: Art since 1980* (London: Laurence King, 2014). Kalb was the updating editor of the fifth edition of H. H. Arnason's *History of Modern Art* (Upper Saddle River, NJ: Prentice Hall, 2003), adding a chapter titled "Resistance and Resolution." *History of Modern Art* is now in its seventh edition, having been updated subsequently by Elizabeth C. Mansfield.

16 Kalb, *Charting the Contemporary*, 14, 17.

17 Kalb, *Charting the Contemporary*, 311.

18 Jean Robertson and Craig McDaniel, *Themes of Contemporary Art: Visual Art after 1980*, 4th ed. (New York: Oxford University Press, 2017).

19 Robertson and McDaniel, *Themes of Contemporary Art*, 7, 38.

20 Hal Foster, Rosalind Krauss, Yve-Alain Bois, Benjamin H. D. Buchloh, eds., *Art since 1900: Modernism, Antimodernism, Postmodernism* (London: Thames and Hudson, 2004).

21 "Roundtable: The Predicament of Contemporary Art," in Foster et al., *Art since 1900*, 677.

22 "Roundtable," 679.

23 "Roundtable," 679.

24 David Joselit, "Globalization, Networks, and the Aggregate as Form," in Hal Foster, Rosalind Krauss, Yve-Alain Bois, Benjamin H. D. Buchloh, and David Joselit, eds., *Art since 1900: Modernism, Antimodernism, Postmodernism*, vol. 2, *1945 to the Present*, 3rd ed. (London: Thames and Hudson, 2016), 57.

25 Joselit, "Globalization, Networks," 60.

26 David Joselit, *After Art* (Princeton, NJ: Princeton University Press, 2013), 55–56.

27 I explore these modes in *The Contemporary Composition* (Berlin: Sternberg, 2016).

28 Joselit, *After Art*, 90–91. Pamela M. Lee's *Forgetting the Art World* (Cambridge, MA: MIT Press, 2012) mounts a parallel argument, locating the potential for critical practice in what she calls "the *work* of art's world" in the real world, not in the duplicitous workings of the global or international art world, which routinizes even "radical" critique. See also her *New Games: Postmodernism after Contemporary Art* (New York: Routledge, 2013).

29 Joselit, *After Art*, 93.

30 George Yúdice, *The Expediency of Culture: The Use of Culture in a Global Age* (Durham, NC: Duke University Press, 2003).

31 Joselit, *After Art*, 93–95; and Boris Groys, *Art Power* (Cambridge, MA: MIT Press, 2008).

32 Hal Foster, *Bad New Days* (London: Verso, 2015), 1.

33 Foster, *Bad New Days*, 3.

34 Foster, *Bad New Days*, 140.

35 See Hal Foster, *The Return of the Real: Art and Theory at the End of the Century* (Cambridge, MA: MIT Press, 1996).

36 Foster, *Bad New Days*, 184. See the review by Mark Kingwell, "Outside the White Box," *Harper's Magazine*, February 2016, 93–97.

37 Ian McLean, "The World Art Artworld," *World Art* 1, no. 2 (September 2011): 161–69; and Arthur Danto, "The Art World," *Journal of Philosophy* 61, no. 19 (October 1964): 571–84.

38 McLean is discussing my "The Provincialism Problem," *Artforum* 13, no. 1 (September 1974): 54–59. "In retrospect," he says, "we can now see that Smith's 1974 article does not so much announce the provincialism problem as write its obituary . . . in a concerted

fashion, it first put the Artworld on notice in the name of world art." McLean, "The World Art Artworld," 166–67.

39 McLean, "The World Art Artworld," 164. Those interested in the broader implications for art-historical method, and for aesthetic theory, in these debates might wish to read Kitty Zijlmans and Wilfred van Damme, eds., *World Art Studies: Exploring Concepts and Approaches* (Amsterdam: Valiz, 2008); my entry "World Art," in the *Encyclopedia of Aesthetics*, vol. 6, ed. Michael Kelly, 2nd ed. (Oxford: Oxford University Press, 2014), 313–17; and the essays in Amy J. Elias and Christian Moraru, eds., *The Planetary Turn: Relationality and Geoaesthetics in the Twenty-First Century* (Evanston, IL: Northwestern University Press, 2013).

40 The following paragraphs are drawn from my essay "Contemporary Art: World Currents in Transition beyond Globalization," in *The Global Contemporary and the Rise of New Art Worlds*, ed. Hans Belting, Andrea Buddensieg, and Peter Weibel (Cambridge, MA: MIT Press for ZKM, Karlsruhe, 2013), 186–92.

41 Key texts by these authors include John A. Walker and Rita Hatton, *Supercollector: A Critique of Charles Saatchi* (London: Ellipses, 2000); Julian Stallabrass, *Art Incorporated: The Story of Contemporary Art* (Oxford: Oxford University Press, 2004); and Jonathan Harris, ed., *Globalization and Contemporary Art* (London: Wiley-Blackwell, 2011).

42 Robert Hughes, *Nothing if Not Critical: Selected Essays on Art and Artists* (London: Harvill, 1990).

43 Peter Weibel and Andrea Buddensieg, eds., *Contemporary Art and the Museum: A Global Perspective* (Ostfildern, Germany: Hatje Cantz, 2007); Hans Belting and Andrea Buddensieg, eds., *The Global Art World: Audiences, Markets, and Museums* (Ostfildern, Germany: Hatje Cantz, 2009); Hans Belting, Andrea Buddensieg, and Peter Weibel, eds., *Global Studies: Mapping Contemporary Art and Culture* (Ostfildern, Germany: Hatje Cantz, 2011); and Belting, Buddensieg, and Weibel, *Global Contemporary*. See also Charlotte Byder, *Global Artworld Inc.: On the Globalization of Contemporary Art* (Uppsala, Sweden: Uppsala University Press, 2004).

44 Hans Belting, "Contemporary Art and the Museum in the Global Age," in Weibel and Buddensieg, *Contemporary Art and the Museum*, 22.

45 Hans Belting and Andrea Buddensieg, introduction to Belting, Buddensieg, and Weibel, *Global Contemporary*, 6. Claire Farago believes that Belting's announcement of the advent of "global art" is premature and not his to make. See her "Cutting and Sharing the 'Global Art' Pie: Why History Matters to Discussions of Contemporary 'Global Art,'" *On Curating*, 35 (December, 2017), accessed July 8, 2018, http://www.on-curating.org /issue-35-reader/cutting-and-sharing-the-global-pie-why-history-matters-to-discussions -of-contemporary-global-art.html#.WoGwMi2B1-U.

46 See, for example, their January 2012 panel discussion at the India Art Fair, Raqs Media Collective, Ravi Sundaram, and Daniela Zyman, "Has the Moment of the Contemporary Come and Gone?," Asia Art Archive, April 1, 2012, http://www.aaa.org.hk/en/ideas/ideas /has-the-moment-of-the-contemporary-come-and-gone.

47 Nancy Adajania, "Time to Restage the World: Theorising a New and Complicated Sense of Solidarity," in *21st Century: Art in the First Decade*, ed. Miranda Wallace (Brisbane: Queensland Art Gallery/Gallery of Modern Art, 2010), 222–29. For the internal quotation,

see Okwui Enwezor, "The Black Box," in *Documenta 11: Platform 5* (Ostfildern-Ruit, Germany: Hatje Cantz, 2002), 42.

48 The Institute for International Visual Arts (Iniva) has pursued the "new internationalism" in its exhibitions and publications since the 1990s; see Jean Fisher, ed., *Global Visions: Towards a New Internationalism in the Visual Arts* (London: Kala, 1994). Marsha Meskimmon, *Contemporary Art and the Cosmopolitan Imagination* (London: Routledge, 2010), and Nikos Papastergiadis, *Cosmopolitanism and Culture* (London: Polity Press, 2012), explore versions of a "cosmopolitan aesthetics."

49 Patrick D. Flores, "Errant in Form," contribution to "An Expanded Questionnaire on the Contemporary: Part I," Asia Art Archive, January 28, 2012, http://www.aaa.org.hk/en/ideas/ideas/an-expanded-questionnaire-on-the-contemporary-part-i/type/essays.

50 Caroline A. Jones, *The Global Work of Art: World's Fairs, Biennials, and the Aesthetics of Experience* (Chicago: University of Chicago Press, 2016). All parenthetical page number citations in this section refer to this text.

51 See, for example, Bruce Altshuler, *Salon to Biennial: Exhibitions That Made Art History, 1863–1959* (London: Phaidon, 2008), and his *Biennials and Beyond: Exhibitions That Made Art History, 1962–2002* (London: Phaidon, 2013). Altshuler and an earlier historian of the Venice Biennale, Lawrence Alloway, both emphasize that this exhibition was a variant on the annual salon exhibitions that, prior to the emergence of private dealers in the mid-nineteenth century, had been the most important connections between artists, collectors, and publics throughout Europe since the seventeenth century. See Lawrence Alloway, *Venice Biennale, 1895–1968: From Salon to Goldfish Bowl* (London: Faber and Faber, 1969). I discuss below the most comprehensive recent study, Charles Green and Anthony Gardner, *Biennials, Triennials, and Documentas: The Exhibitions That Created Contemporary Art* (London: Wiley, 2016).

52 Tony Bennett, *The Birth of the Museum: History, Theory, Politics* (London: Routledge, 1995), especially chap. 6; and his important chapter "The Exhibitionary Complex," in *Thinking about Exhibitions*, ed. Reesa Greenberg, Bruce W. Ferguson, and Sandy Nairne (London: Routledge, 1996), 81–112. Bennett goes unacknowledged except for a brief footnote reference in chapter 2.

53 I develop this idea in "Shifting the Exhibitionary Complex," in *Thinking Contemporary Curating* (New York: Independent Curators International, 2012), chap. 2, and in "Mapping the Contexts of Contemporary Curating: The Visual Arts Exhibitionary Complex," *Journal of Curatorial Studies* 6, no. 2 (2017): 170–80.

54 Green and Gardner, *Biennials, Triennials, and Documentas*, 7, 13.

55 Green and Gardner, *Biennials, Triennials, and Documentas*, 13–14. For an even closer examination of these questions, focusing on the Seventh Berlin Biennale and the Third Athens Biennale, see Panos Kompatsiaris, *The Politics of Contemporary Biennials: Spectacles of Critique, Theory and Art* (London: Routledge, 2017).

56 Green and Gardner, *Biennials, Triennials, and Documentas*, 9.

57 Rafel Niemojewski, "Venice or Havana: A Polemic on the Genesis of the Contemporary Biennale," in *The Biennial Reader*, ed. Elena Filipovic, Marika van Hal, and Solveig Øvstebø (Bergen, Germany: Hatje Cantz, 2010), 98. See Green and Gardner, *Biennials, Triennials, and Documentas*, 9, 10.

58 Green and Gardner, *Biennials, Triennials, and Documentas*, 12.

59 Here, Jones draws on Martin Jay's classic study, *Downcast Eyes: The Denigration of Vision in Twentieth-Century French Thought* (Berkeley: University of California Press, 1993).

60 Martin Heidegger, "The Age of the World Picture" (1938), in *The Question concerning Technology and Other Essays* (New York: Harper Torchbooks, 1977), 134.

61 Chika Okeke-Agulu, "Globalization, Art History, and the Specter of Difference," in *Contemporary Art: 1989 to the Present*, ed. Alexander Dumbadze and Suzanne Hudson (Chichester, UK: Wiley-Blackwell, 2013), 453.

62 James Elkins, *Is Art History Global?* (New York: Routledge, 2006). Elkins is currently pursuing research into the interpretative practices undertaken in various centers outside Europe and the United States with a view to identifying their specificity. See his online project "The Impending Single History of Art: North Atlantic Art History and Its Alternatives," accessed June 27, 2018, http://www.jameselkins.com/index.php/experimental -writing/251-north-atlantic-art-history. A related publication is forthcoming from the University of Singapore Press.

63 Okeke-Agulu, "Globalization, Art History, and the Specter of Difference," 454.

64 "Multiculturalism" takes many forms, doing often quite contrary ideological work, depending on the larger power structures in place. In Great Britain during the 1980s, for example, it disturbed the dominant monoculturalism of the colonizer and opened doors for immigrants from the former colonies. Within a decade, however, it had normalized ethnic identifications in art and culture as an array of close but equidistant differences. These changes are tracked in Kobena Mercer, "Ethnicity and Internationality: New British Art and Diaspora-Based Blackness," *Third Text* 13, no. 49 (Winter 1999–2000): 51–62. Of course, these dates will vary from place to place, according to circumstance. The normalization of the 1990s might start to look good, soon, as officially sanctioned intolerance becomes itself the norm in many societies.

65 See, for example, John Clark, *Asian Modernities: Chinese and Thai Art of the 1980s and 1990s* (Sydney: Power Institute, 2010); Kobena Mercer, ed., *Cosmopolitan Modernisms* (Cambridge, MA: MIT Press for Iniva, London, 2005); Geoffrey Batchen, "Guest Editorial: Local Modernisms," *World Art* 4, no. 1 (May 2014): 7–15; Chika Okeke-Agulu, *Postcolonial Modernism: Art and Decolonization in Twentieth-Century Nigeria* (Durham, NC: Duke University Press, 2015); and *Multiple Modernisms: Twentieth-Century Artistic Modernisms in Global Perspective*, accessed March 20, 2018, http://multiplemodernisms .maa.cam.ac.uk.

66 Piotr Piotrowski, "Towards a Horizontal History of Modern Art," in his *Writing Central European Art History (PATTERNS—Travelling Lecture Set 2008/9)* (Vienna: Erste Foundation Reader no. 1, 2008). For an informal discussion of Piotrowski's exemplary art-historical instincts, see Richard Kosinsky, Jan Elantkowski, and Barbara Dudás, "A Way to Follow: Interview with Piotr Piotrowski," *ARTMargins*, January 29, 2015, http:// artmargins.com/index.php/interviews-sp-837925570/758-a-way-to-follow-interview -with-piotr-piotrowski.

67 Kobena Mercer, "The Cross-Cultural and the Contemporary," in Wallace, *21st Century*, 201. There are echoes here of Louis Althusser's structuralist revision of Marx's base and

superstructure theory, as modified by the major British cultural studies theorist Stuart Hall. See Louis Althusser, "Ideology and Ideological State Apparatuses (Notes Towards an Investigation)," in *Lenin and Philosophy and Other Essays* (1971; repr., New York: Monthly Review Press, 2001), 85–126; and Stuart Hall, "Signification, Representation, Ideology: Althusser and the Post-Structuralist Debates," *Critical Studies in Mass Communications* 2, no. 2 (1985): 91–114. For a succinct summary of Hall's reading of Althusser, see Stuart Hall, *Cultural Studies 1983: A Theoretical History* (Durham, NC: Duke University Press, 2016), chaps. 5 and 6.

68 "An Expanded Questionnaire on the Contemporary: Part I," October 19, 2012. The responses are collected in "The And: An Expanded Questionnaire on the Contemporary: Part I," the inaugural issue of a four-part online publication, *Field Notes*, April 1, 2012.

69 Lee Weng Choy, in "An Expanded Questionnaire on the Contemporary: Part II," Asia Art Archives, January 31, 2012, https://aaa.org.hk/en/ideas/ideas/an-expanded-questionnaire-on-the-contemporary-part-ii/type/essays.

70 David Teh, "An Expanded Questionnaire on the Contemporary: Part II," February 1, 2012.

71 Teh, "Expanded Questionnaire." See also David Teh, *Thai Art* (Cambridge, MA: MIT Press, 2017).

72 David Clarke, "Art Now: Beyond the Contemporary," in "An Expanded Questionnaire on the Contemporary: Part I," January 19, 2012; David Clarke, *Chinese Art and Its Encounter with the World* (Hong Kong: Hong Kong University Press, 2011).

73 Many respondents worry that curatorial studies–type short courses on current theory, rather than art history courses able to model long-term research scholarship, will prevail, to the detriment of critical thought about, and taking historical perspectives toward, the art of the region in its worldly contexts. These included Nora Taylor, David Teh, Caroline Turner, Michelle Antoinette, and Reiko Tomii.

74 See Raqs Media Collective, Sundaram, and Zyman, "Has the Moment of the Contemporary Come and Gone?"

75 See Reiko Tomii, "Historicizing 'Contemporary Art': Some Discursive Practices in *Gendai Bijutsu* in Japan," *Positions* 12, no. 3 (2004): 611–41, and her "'International Contemporaneity' in the 1960s: Discoursing on Art in Japan and Beyond," *Japan Review*, no. 21 (2009): 123–47.

76 Reiko Tomii, *Radicalism in the Wilderness: International Contemporaneity and 1960s Art in Japan* (Cambridge, MA: MIT Press, 2016), 20.

77 Tomii, *Radicalism in the Wilderness*, 25, 217.

78 Tomii, *Radicalism in the Wilderness*, 220. This analysis would benefit from matching with the arguments posed in my "The Provincialism Problem" essay of 1974. There are striking parallels between the situations for artists and critics in Sydney, for example, and Tokyo, during the period; see Terry Smith, "The Provincialism Problem: Now and Then," *ARTMargins* 6, no. 1 (January 2017): 6–32.

79 Tomii, *Radicalism in the Wilderness*, 219.

80 Linda Nochlin, "Why Have There Been No Great Women Artists?," *Art News*, January 1971, reprinted in *Women Artists: The Linda Nochlin Reader*, ed. Maura Reilly (London: Thames and Hudson, 2015), 42–68; and, for example, Arlene Raven, Cassandra L.

Langer, and Joanna Frueh, eds., *Feminist Art Criticism: An Anthology* (New York: Westview, 1991).

81 Norma Broude and Mary D. Garrard, eds., *Feminism and Art History: Questioning the Litany* (New York: Harper and Row, 1982), was followed by their *The Expanding Discourse: Feminism and Art History* (New York: HarperCollins, 1992), and *Reclaiming Female Agency: Feminist Art History after Postmodernism* (Berkeley: University of California Press, 2005).

82 Whitney Chadwick, *Women, Art, and Society*, 5th ed. (London: Thames and Hudson, 2012).

83 Griselda Pollock, "Whither Art History?," *Art Bulletin* 96, no. 1 (2014): 9–23; see also the updated edition of Griselda Pollock and Rozsika Parker, *Old Mistresses: Women, Art and Ideology* (London: I. B. Tauris, 2013).

84 Hilary Robinson, "Feminism Art Theory: Towards a (Political) Historiography," in *Feminism Art Theory: An Anthology, 1968–2014*, ed. Hilary Robinson (Chichester, UK: Wiley-Blackwell, 2015), 1–7. This updates her earlier foundational text *Feminism Art Theory: An Anthology, 1968–2000* (Chichester, UK: Wiley-Blackwell, 2001). Citations are to the 2015 edition.

85 Robinson, *Feminism Art Theory*, 2–3.

86 See Maura Reilly, "Taking the Measure of Sexism: Facts, Figures, and Fixes," *Art News*, May 26, 2015, "Women in the Art World" special feature, http://www.artnews.com/2015 /05/26/taking-the-measure-of-sexism-facts-figures-and-fixes/; and Maura Reilly, *Curatorial Activism: Towards an Ethics of Curating* (London: Thames and Hudson, 2018).

87 On this distinction, see Georges Didi-Huberman, *Confronting Images: Questioning the End of a Certain History of Art* (University Park: Pennsylvania State University Press, 2005), "Preface to the English Edition: The Exorcist" and chap. 1. See also his introduction to Phillipe-Alain Michaud, *Aby Warburg and the Image in Motion* (New York: Zone Books, 2007).

88 Keith Moxey, *Visual Time: The Image in History* (Durham, NC: Duke University Press, 2013), 45.

89 See Georges Didi-Huberman, *Fra Angelico: Dissemblance and Figuration* (Chicago: University of Chicago Press, 1995), and his *Images in Spite of All: Four Photographs from Auschwitz* (Chicago: University of Chicago Press, 2012); Mieke Bal, *Quoting Caravaggio: Contemporary Art, Preposterous History* (Chicago: University of Chicago Press, 1999); Alexander Nagel and Christopher Wood, *Anachronic Renaissance* (New York: Zone Books, 2010); and Alexander Nagel, *Medieval Modern: Art out of Time* (London: Thames and Hudson, 2012).

90 Moxey, *Visual Time*, 45–46.

91 The confusion arises, I believe, because Moxey has taken the account that I give of contemporaneity, and the threat that it poses to modern understandings of periodization, to amount to a claim that contemporary art has entered some kind of "featureless contemporaneity" beyond all conceptions of time, including, and especially, historical time, to which it is no longer subject; Moxey, *Visual Time*, 43–47. Certainly, ideas of this kind do circulate through contemporary art discourse as unreflective mystifications—"the contemporary" principal among them—and I do report them. But readers of my books, with their attacks

on these mystifications and their explicit proposals as to historical hypotheses about contemporary art, will be aware that I do not support such ideas, to put it mildly.

92 Moxey, *Visual Time*, 175.

93 Christine Ross, *The Past Is the Present, It's the Future Too: The Temporal Turn in Contemporary Art* (New York: Bloomsbury, 2014).

94 Gilles Deleuze, *Cinema 1: The Movement-Image* (Minneapolis: University of Minnesota Press, 1986), and *Cinema 2: The Time-Image* (Minneapolis: University of Minnesota Press, 1989).

95 Ross, *The Past Is the Present*, 28.

96 For a similar survey, see Joel Burges and Amy J. Elias, "Introduction: Time Studies Today," in *Time: A Vocabulary of the Present* (New York: NYU Press, 2016), 1–32. See also Russell West-Pavlov, *Temporalities* (London: Routledge, 2013).

97 Pamela M. Lee, *Chronophobia: On Time in the Art of the 1960s* (Cambridge, MA: MIT Press, 2004), xii.

98 Ross, *The Past Is the Present*, 39.

99 See, for example, the essays in Judith Schachter and Stephen Brockmann, eds., *(Im)permanence: Cultures in/out of Time* (Pittsburgh: Center for the Arts in Society, Carnegie Mellon University, 2008). On history as a core concern, see the introductory remarks by Mark Godfrey in his essay "The Artist as Historian," *October*, no. 20 (Spring 2007): 140–72. A more thorough treatment is Jane Blocker, *Becoming Past: History in Contemporary Art* (Minneapolis: University of Minnesota Press, 2016), especially her introduction, "History as Prosthesis." Amelia Barikin, *Parallel Presents: The Art of Pierre Huyghe* (Cambridge, MA: MIT Press, 2012) is a good example of the growing number of profiles of conteporary artists that focus on their treatments of multilpe temporalities.

100 Ross, *The Past Is the Present*, 49, 51. On this issue, Ross cites historian Frederick Cooper's *Colonialism in Question: Theory, Knowledge, History* (Berkeley: University of California Press, 2005), 91–92.

101 Ross, *The Past Is the Present*, 51.

102 Ross, *The Past Is the Present*, 304–5.

CONCLUSION

1 See Wendy Brown, *Undoing the Demos: Neoliberalism's Stealth Revolution* (New York: Zone Books, 2015).

2 John O'Sullivan, ed., "An Open and Shut Case," special report, *Economist*, October 1, 2016, https://www.economist.com/news/special-report/21707833-consensus-favour-open-economies-cracking-says-john-osullivan. For a more insightful analysis, see Adam Tooze, "The Secret History of the Banking Crisis," *Prospect*, August 2017, posted July 14, 2017, https://www.prospectmagazine.co.uk/magazine/the-secret-history-of-the-banking-crisis.

3 See, among other important texts, Paul Mason, *Postcapitalism: A Guide to Our Future* (London: Allen Lane, 2015); and Naomi Klein, *No Is Not Enough: Defeating the New Shock Politics* (London: Allen Lane, 2017).

4 Terry Smith, *The Contemporary Composition* (Berlin: Sternberg, 2016).

5 See "CFP: The Contemporary," ArtHist.net, November 9, 2016, http://arthist.net/archive/14158.

6 Saelan Twerdy, "Morbid Symptoms: In Search of the Post-Contemporary at the 2016 Montreal Biennial," *Momus*, November 22, 2016, http://momus.ca/morbid-symptoms-in-search-of-the-post-contemporary-at-the-2016-montreal-biennial/.

7 Julia Halperin and Eileen Kinsella, "The 'Winner Takes All' Market," *Artnet News*, posted September 20, 2017, https://news.artnet.com/market/25-artists-account-nearly-50-percent-postwar-contemporary-auction-sales-1077026.

8 Clare McAndrew, *The Art Market 2018* (Basel and Zurich: Art Basel and UBS, 2018), 282. See also the section "Global Wealth and Art Buyers," 262–317. Broader studies include Thomas Pikkety, *Capital in the Twenty-First Century*, trans. Arthur Goldhammer (Cambridge, MA: Belknap Press of Harvard University Press, 2014).

9 Clare McAndrew, *The Art Market 2017* (Basel and Zurich: Art Basel and UBS, 2017), 236–37.

10 See Ronald Kolb and Shwetal A. Patel, "Drift: Global Biennial Survey 2018," *On Curating* 39 (June 2018), accessed July 2, 2018, http://www.on-curating.org/issue-39.html#.W0RW1y2B1-U.

11 See Terry Smith, "Is De-Institutionalization Renewable?," in *Were It as If: Beyond an Institution That Is*, ed. Defne Ayes and Bik van der Pol, 86–92 (Rotterdam: Witte de With Center for Contemporary Art, 2017).

12 For example, the Contemporary Condition project, led by Jacob Lund and Geoff Cox, at Aarhus University, Denmark. See Geoff Cox and Jacob Lund, *The Contemporary Condition: Introductory Thoughts in Contemporaneity and Contemporary Art* (Berlin: Sternberg, 2016), and subsequent books in this series.

Index

McLuhan, Marshall, 202
McQueen, Steve, 60, 215
Meckseper, Josephine, 21, 248–51, 265, 290, 307
Medieval Modern (Nagel), 348
Medina, Cuauhtémoc, 315–16
Meenamatta, Pura-lia, 193–97
Meenamatta len narla puellakanny—Meenamatta Water Country Discussion (Kimberley, Mennamatta), 194–95
Meenamatta Water Country Discussion (Kimberley, Meenamatta), 194–95
mega-exhibitions, 72, 269, 334, 363
Mehretu, Julie, 115, 203
Meier, Richard, 15, 77, 80
Meier group, 80
Memmott, Paul, 92
Mendes da Rocha, Paulo, 85
Menges, Achim, 97
Mengil, Louise, 386n35
Menlibayeva, Almagul, 222
Mercator projection, 200–201
Mercer, Kobena, 165–66, 339
Merrima Aboriginal Design Unit, 92
Metro Cable (Urban-Think Tank), 86–87
Metropolitan Museum of Art, 30
Meyer, Hannes, 66
Meyer, Richard, 365n3, 391n1
Michelangelo, 285
Mies van der Rohe, Ludwig, 110, 113
The Migrant Image (Demos), 214–15
Migrants and Cities (IOM), 391n28
migration, 89–90, 149, 168, 181, 212–19, 232, 237–38, 354, 363, 411n64. *See also* displaced peoples; refugees
Migration Report 2015 (IOM), 391n28
Mik, Aernout, 60
Milošević, Slobodan, 117
Milwaukee Art Museum (Calatrava), 77
minimalism, 40, 50, 106, 168, 260, 271, 339, 369n22
Misrach, Richard, 238
Miss, Mary, 234
Mitchell, W. J. T., 200, 285
Mobile Homestead (Kelley), 116, 207–8
Mockus, Antanas, 109

"Modern (or Contemporary) Architecture circa 1959" (Laurence), 66
"The Modern Cult of Monuments" (Riegl), 300
modernism: architecture and, 16, 64–84, 95–97, 101–4, 113–15; art history and, 9–10, 14, 21–23, 245–78, 399n56, 400n58; China and, 18, 128–43, 154–55; contemporary art history and, 312–52; contemporary conditions and, 57–63; contemporary world picturing and, 354–55, 359–62; emergence of contemporary art and, 1–3, 7, 12–13, 29–31, 37–40, 43–44, 50–51, 369n22; Indigenous artists and, 19, 45, 156–60, 163–75, 179, 189–92, 228, 383n2; placemaking and, 209, 228; planetarity and, 232, 242; theories of contemporary art and, 280–88, 291, 295–306, 309, 402n2. *See also* postmodernism; remodernism
modernité, 38, 50, 255
Moffatt, Tracey, 37, 46–47, 60, 158, 170
Molick, Peter, 88
Momentum socialists, 309, 356
Monet, Claude, 31
Monk by the Sea (Friedrich), 41
Montreal Biennale, 358, 363
More, Thomas, 225
Mori, Mariko, 31, 337
Morimura, Yasumasa, 46
Morning Cleaning, Mies van der Rohe Foundation, Barcelona (Wall), 247–48
Morphy, Howard, 164–65, 383–84nn8–9
Morton, Callum, 113–14
Moscow Conceptualists, 142
Mosquera, Geraldo, 61
Moss, Rod, 171
A Mountain Is None the Worse for Being High (Xu), 153
Moxey, Keith, 348–49, 413n91
Mo Yi Tong, 389n4
Multiple Modernisms project, 339
multiverse, 19–20, 228–42. *See also* planetarity
Mundine, Djon, 386n30
Muñoz, Oscar, 351
Murakami, Takashi, 59, 170, 314
Murayama, Naotake, 76
Murcutt, Glen, 65